The Netherlands

Jeremy Gray, Reuben Acciano

Contents

Friesland
p233

Groningen
& Drenthe
p248

Noord Holland
& Flevoland
p137

Overijssel & Gelderland
p261

Utrecht
p172

Zuid Holland
& Zeeland
p184

Noord Brabant
& Limburg
p279

Lonely Planet books
provide independent
advice. Lonely Planet doe
not accept advertising in
guidebooks, nor do we
accept payment in
exchange for listing or
endorsing any place or
business. Lonely Planet
writers do not accept
discounts or payments
in exchange for positive
coverage of any sort.

Lonely Planet boeken
verschaffen onafhankelijk
advies. Lonely Planet
accepteert geen reclame
reisgidsen, noch
accepteren we betaling in
ruil voor vermelding of
aanbeveling van plaatsen
of bedrijven. Lonely Plane
schrijvers accepteren geen
kortingen of betalingen in
ruil voor welke positieve
beschrijving dan ook.

Destination: The Netherlands

There's a popular saying that goes, 'God created the world but the Dutch created the Netherlands'. Take one look at all those dykes, pumping stations and cities below sea level, and it dawns how magnificent this feat was. The Dutch turned a liability into an asset and gained a high profile, so to speak, by lying low.

The Netherlands has spent centuries fine-tuning not just the sea walls but society at large. Its people manage to blend a desire for order with liberal convictions, yet the thirst for novelty is never quenched. In this huge circus the performers can be as radical or rational as they wish without bugging the next guy, and although it's hard to figure out who's what when and to whom, the effect is always captivating.

Amsterdam hogs the limelight but there's so much more. Sure, doing your ABCs – art, buildings and canals (or cafés!) – is great fun in the capital, but gable-spotters won't come up short in Haarlem, Leiden or Delft. The modern edifices of Rotterdam, meanwhile, are enough to alter your centre of gravity.

The north wears a necklace of golden, windswept islands and teems with shimmering lakes for boating. The vestiges of religious empire and Hanseatic wealth are still palpable in places like Utrecht and Deventer, and you even rewind to the Roman era at cosmopolitan Maastricht. An air of genteel wealth pervades Den Haag, home to the queen and parliament but just a stone's throw from the beach party zone. And there's water, water everywhere, although a good bucketful is tamed by fascinating sea defences down in Zeeland.

Everyone's puzzled how it all fits, but that's half the fun of this very big small country.

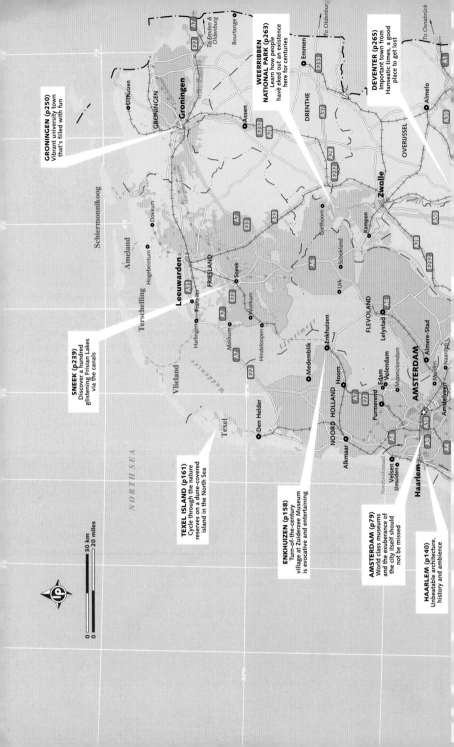

GRONINGEN (p250)
Vibrant university town that's filled with fun

WEERRIBBEN NATIONAL PARK (p263)
Learn how people have eked out an existence here for centuries

DEVENTER (p265)
Important town from Hanseatic times, a good place to get lost

SNEEK (p239)
Discover a hundred glistening Frisian Lakes via the canals

TEXEL ISLAND (p161)
Cycle through the nature reserves on a dune-covered island in the North Sea

ENKHUIZEN (p158)
Turn-of-the-century village at Zuiderzee Museum is evocative and entertaining

AMSTERDAM (p79)
World class museums and the exuberance of the city itself should not be missed

HAARLEM (p140)
Unbeatable architecture, history and ambience

NORTH SEA

0   30 km
0   20 miles

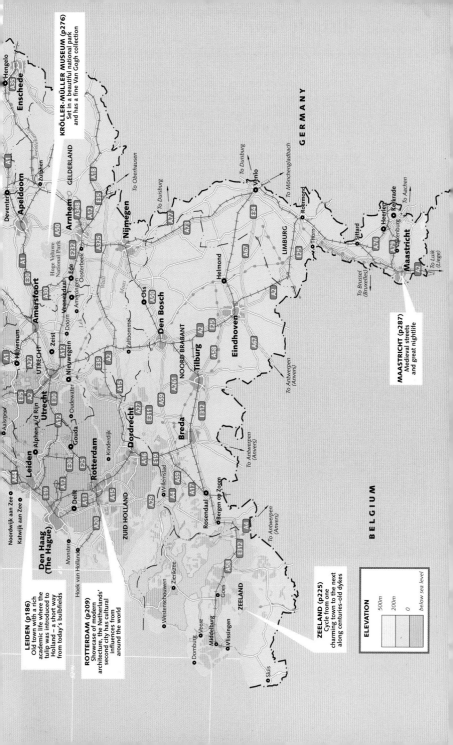

KRÖLLER-MÜLLER MUSEUM (p276)
Set in a beautiful national park and has a fine Van Gogh collection

MAASTRICHT (p287)
Medieval streets and great nightlife

ZEELAND (p225)
Cycle from one charming town to the next along centuries-old dykes

ROTTERDAM (p209)
Showcase of modern architecture, the Netherlands' second city has cultural influences from around the world

LEIDEN (p186)
Old town with a rich academic life where the tulip was introduced to Holland – a short way from today's bulbfields

GERMANY

BELGIUM

GELDERLAND

LIMBURG

NOORD BRABANT

ZUID HOLLAND

UTRECHT

ELEVATION

500m
200m
0
below sea level

Enschede
Hengelo
Deventer
Apeldoorn
Zutphen
Arnhem
Nijmegen
Venlo
Roermond
Sittard
Heerlen
Kerkrade
Maastricht
Valkenburg
To Aachen
To Luik (Liège)
To Brussel (Bruxelles)
To Mönchengladbach
To Duisburg
To Oberhausen
To Duisburg
Helmond
Eindhoven
Oss
Den Bosch
Tilburg
Breda
Dordrecht
Rotterdam
Gouda
Oudewater
Utrecht
Alphen a/d Rijn
Leiden
Delft
Den Haag (The Hague)
Monster
Hoek van Holland
Noordwijk aan Zee
Katwijk aan Zee
Aalsmeer
Hilversum
Amersfoort
Zeist
Nieuwegein
Doorn
Zaltbommel
Ede
Veenendaal
Oosterbeek
Amerongen
Kinderdijk
Willemstad
Bergen op Zoom
Rosendaal
To Antwerpen (Anvers)
To Antwerpen (Anvers)
To Antwerpen (Anvers)
Goes
Middelburg
Veere
Domburg
Vlissingen
Westenschouwen
Zierikzee
Sluis
ZEELAND
Hoge Veluwe National Park
Maas
Waal

To Brussel

The Netherlands' rich heritage is most palpable in its historic towns. The 17th-century ambience of **Haarlem** (p140) comes a close second to Amsterdam's canals and gables. Cosmopolitan **Maastricht** (p287) blends medieval streets with great nightlife. **Leiden** (p186) is a vibrant university town; it was the tulip's launch pad in Holland. **Dordrecht** (p221) was at the convergence of history, but the Hanseatic trading hub was **Deventer** (p265). **Amersfoort** (p180) exudes an aura of wealth from beer and tobacco. The fascinating 18th-century fortress of **Bourtange** (p257) is well off the beaten path.

Be surprised by **Groningen** (p250), a buzzing university town

LEANNE LOGAN

Stroll along **Amsterdam**'s (p79) beautiful canals and gables

JON DAVISON

CHRIS MELLOR

Discover **Delft** (p204), the town behind the blue-and-white gold called delftware

Everywhere you look there's a graceful façade, pointy turret or medieval wall. Tear yourself away from lovely **Amsterdam** (p79) and you'll find the style show continues. **Kasteel de Haar** (p180) and **Muiderslot** (p165) are among the prettiest fortresses in the country. The functionalist lines of the **Rietveld-Schröderhuis** (p177) in Utrecht provide a modern foil. The Gothic finery of the **St Janskathedraal** (p282) in Den Bosch is unparalleled. The cute village of **Zaanse Schans** (p147) uses mills to make dyes and mustard.

Go to **Rotterdam** (p209), a showcase of modern architecture with a go-ahead attitude

CHRIS MELLOR

See all the windmills you want at **Kinderdijk** (p221)

GLENN VAN DER KNIJFF

Marvel at the **Utrecht cathedral** (p176), still oozing ecclesiastic might

GLENN VAN DER KNIJFF

Viewing famous Dutch art is as easy as swinging on a bike. See Van Goghs at the **Kröller-Müller Museum** (p276). For 17th-century portraits visit Haarlem's **Frans Hals Museum** (p142). The **Mauritshuis** (p195) in Den Haag has impressive paintings by Rubens, Vermeer and Rembrandt. The **Groninger Museum** (p251) is a quality venue for modern art, as is Eindhoven's **Stedelijk Van Abbemuseum** (p283). Dutch prosperity relied heavily on shipping, as vividly illustrated in Groningen's **Noordelijk Scheepvaartmuseum** (p251). The recreated village at Enkhuizen's **Zuiderzeemuseum** (p158) is evocative and entertaining. The **Nationaal Oorlogs- en Verzetmuseum** (National War and Resistance Museum; p293) in Limburg covers a dark but determined era.

Learn about Dutch nautical history in the **Scheepvaartmuseum** (p108) in Amsterdam

MARTIN MOOS

See work by tortured genius Van Gogh at the **Van Gogh Museum** (p109) in Amsterdam

Lose yourself in Amsterdam's **Rijksmuseum** (p108), which houses Rembrandt's *Nightwatch* and other Golden Age pieces

MARTIN MOOS

Dutch landscape is more varied than the wetland scenes by Old Masters suggest. **Hoge Veluwe National Park** (p276) has forests, dunes and marshlands, while **Kennemerduinen** (p145) is a pocket of sandy copses next to the sea. Seek out the massive dams of the **Delta Project** (p226) in Zeeland or **Weerribben National Park** (p263) to understand the art of watery survival. Prehistoric burial chambers called **hunebedden** (p259) will pique your curiosity, while the **Hogebeintum** church (p239) is built on the biggest Dutch *terp* (mound of mud). Experience splendid isolation on windswept Frisian islands such as **Vlieland** (p244) and **Ameland** (p246). The diverse lakes called **Loosdrechtse Plassen** (p180) emerged from the flooded digs of peat harvesters.

LIZ BARRY

Silhouette of a windmill against a setting sun

RICHARD NEBESKÝ

Cows under a stormy sky

Tulip field in spring

CHRIS MELLOR

The endless Dutch horizons beckon to be explored by land or by water. Sail through the canals at **Sneek** (p239) to a hundred glistening Frisian lakes, or cycle through dune-filled nature reserves on **Texel Island** (p161). If you can, trade your wheels for skates at the **Elfstedentocht** (p242) or on the frozen ponds and rivers. Bird-watching is easy fun at the marshy **Oostvaardersplassen** (p170). For something more challenging, the 'mountains' of southern **Limburg** (p292) make for great hiking and biking.

Take a cycling tour (p116) through Amsterdam

MARTIN MOOS

RICK GERHARTER

Enjoy some time on the beach

Cycle along the many cycle paths (p70)

CHRIS MELLOR

The Dutch are social creatures. For a course on the subject head to Amsterdam's cosy **brown cafés** (p125), where the locals wet their whistles before converging on **Leidseplein** (p105) for music, performance artists and nightclubs. The capital's open-air **markets** (p132) are great for broccoli, books and bric-a-brac. Busking musicians and lounging lovers set the tone in the **Vondelpark** (p110).

Dress up and drink up at Maastricht's **carnaval** (p290). Plug into the Dutch student buzz in the clubs of **Groningen** (p255).

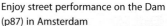

Enjoy street performance on the Dam (p87) in Amsterdam

Let yourself go in **Paradiso** (p127), Amsterdam

Join in the café culture of Amsterdam (p125)

Traditional Dutch condiments are tasty **smoked fish** and ripened Dutch **cheese**, washed down of course by a glass of frothy Dutch **beer** (p64).

CHRIS MELLOR

Find out what cheese should really taste like (p63)

Try salted herring or smoked eel (p62)

MARTIN MOOS

Have a Heineken in its hometown, Amsterdam (p111)

MARTIN MOOS

Getting Started

The Netherlands is an exceedingly user-friendly place to visit. Up-to-date information is plentiful, transport links are swift and there's an abundance of exciting things to do. All this means you can allow a fair amount of spontaneity to your trip.

That said, a bit of foresight is advised to peg some sights at the right time – after all, the bulb fields aren't much to look at before the blossoms open. Amsterdam's best hotels book up months in advance for the Keukenhof and other popular events. Other towns may not have that many sleeping options, so again, reserving ahead makes sense.

The Dutch are especially hospitable about language. English-speakers may recognise Dutch on paper but once spoken, it shoots off into previously uncharted vowel and diphthong realms. Luckily, most Dutch people speak excellent English and are happy to use it.

WHEN TO GO

Any time can be the best time to visit. The high season is June to August, while the shoulder seasons are mid-March to May and September to mid-October. Things are calmest in the off-season, mid-October to mid-March.

Spring is wonderful as the bulbs are in bloom – April for daffodils, May for tulips. Easter is busy in Amsterdam but if you can visit during Koninginnedag (30 April, see p116), it's worth fighting the crowds. In summer, hordes of tourists pulse through the Netherlands but it's the best time to sit on the canals to drink and chat.

See Climate Chart (p298) for more information.

Many Dutch take a summer holiday, and the last July weekend is deadly for traffic. You may be surrounded by other foreigners in August, but the month is crammed with events – see the Directory chapter (p300). Early October with its Indian summers can be an excellent time to come.

In the off-season the weather can be miserable but there are fewer tourists, the museums are quiet and you can mingle with the 'real' Dutch in cosy pubs. Accommodation is relatively cheap (except around New Year) though some hotels might be closed.

The Netherlands has a temperate climate with cool winters and mild summers. The weather is often blustery and changeable, and there are normally only several weeks of sunny days a year – although global warming may be changing that. The summertime (June to September) has hot, sticky spells but it's not quite the Riviera shown in some tourist

---

DON'T LEAVE HOME WITHOUT...

- Travelpacks and daypacks (avoid luggage wheels on cobblestones)
- Passport/EU papers
- Schengen visa if needed – see Directory (p306)
- 220V converter for European plugs
- Travel insurance
- Spare pair of specs or contacts
- Cholesterol meter (*frites!*)

brochures. The winter months (December to February) see periods of slushy snow and temperatures around the freezing point. Precipitation (79cm a year) is spread rather evenly over the calendar, and spring is marked by short, violent showers.

School holidays are staggered according to region but fall around mid-February, early May, July and August, and the end of October (p301).

COSTS

Although some expats will tell you it's possible to scrape by in Amsterdam on a busker's pay, the Netherlands really isn't a budget buy. If you're happy eating chips, sleeping in hostels and walking around, it's possible to hang in the Netherlands for around €30 per day. Those who prefer a couple of solid meals a day, a comfy bed with private facilities and travelling by public transport are looking at €70 per day as a starting point. Things start to feel comfortable, if not pampered, on €100 per day.

There are a lot of free activities to stretch your budget, especially in Amsterdam in summer, and discount passes like the Museumkaart and the Amsterdam Pass (see p299) can save loads on admission. The first Sunday of the month is free at many museums, the Concertgebouw holds lunchtime concerts for free and some restaurants have cheaper kiddie meals.

TRAVEL LITERATURE

Dealing with the Dutch by Jacob Vossestein is a serious but knowledgeable work by an instructor of the Royal Tropical Institute's 'Understanding the Dutch' programme. Subtle aspects of Dutch behaviour are connected in a non-judgmental fashion.

The Low Countries 1780–1940 by EH Kossmann present the Netherlands and Belgium in a compare-and-contrast study. A primer also for natives who wonder why their neighbours are so similar yet so different.

Live & Work in Belgium, the Netherlands and Luxembourg by André de Vries lays out the roadmap to the Benelux, with the ins and outs of bureaucracy for new settlers. A touch Anglocentric but authoritative.

Amsterdam by Geert Mak interweaves tales of ordinary citizens with cultural, social and economic history. Also delves into the psyche, eg why the Dutch eschew nationalism for business reasons.

The UnDutchables by Colin White and Laurie Boucke takes a humorous look at Dutch life, from language and transport to child-rearing and social habits. Sometimes it's spot-on and sometimes so wide of the mark it becomes slapstick.

Read This First: Europe by Lonely Planet covers everything travellers new to the continent will need to know, from what to pack and how to budget to where to visit once they hit the ground.

INTERNET RESOURCES

British Library (www.bl.uk/collections/wider/dutchinternetres2.html) Authoritative lists of links for Dutch and Flemish history, politics and culture.

Lonely Planet's Destination Netherlands (www.lonelyplanet.com/dest/eur/net.htm) News and information about this Low Country from travellers like yourself.

Dutch Ministry of Foreign Affairs (www.minbuza.nl) Wealth of background facts and information, but not officious.

Dutch Tourism Board (www.visitholland.com) Attractions, cultural articles and loads of practical stuff hiding amongst the PR.

Expatica (www.expatica.com/holland) Entertaining all-round guide to life in the Netherlands, with daily news and listings.

Uitlijn (www.uitlijn.nl) Events site for the Netherlands in Dutch, but easy to navigate.

HOW MUCH?

Litre of gas/petrol
€1.15

Litre of bottled water
€0.80

Glass of Heineken
€2.50

Souvenir T-shirt
€10

Patat met (chips/fries with mayonnaise)
€1.75

Local phone call
€0.30

Cinema ticket
€7.50

One hour of parking (Amsterdam)
€3

Bus/tram ticket
€1.60

Bicycle lock
€10

TOP 10S
OUR FAVOURITE FESTIVALS & EVENTS

The Dutch really know how to celebrate, and there's almost always something interesting on around the country. The following list is our Top 10, but for a comprehensive listing of festivals and events throughout the Netherlands, go to p300.

- Carnaval (Limburg, Noord Brabant, Gelderland) February/March (p300)
- Koninginnedag (Queen's Day) 30 April (p300)
- Nationale Molendag (National Mill Day May, p300)
- North Sea Jazz Festival (Den Haag) July (p198)
- Gay Pride Canal Parade (Amsterdam) August (p116)
- Grachtenfestival (Amsterdam) August (p116)
- Holland Festival (Amsterdam) June (p116)
- Uitmarkt (Amsterdam) August (p116)
- Cannabis Cup (Amsterdam) November (p117)
- Sinterklaas 5 December (p301)

MUST-SEE FILMS

Pre-departure planning and dreaming is best done in a comfy lounge with a bowl of popcorn in one hand and a remote in the other. Local video stores just might carry these films but spotty distribution means you may need to order ahead. See p49 for reviews.

- *Abel* (1986) Director: Alex van Warmerdam
- *Amsterdamned* (1987) Director: Dick Maas
- *Amsterdam, Global Village* (1996) Director: Johan van der Keuken
- *Antonia* (Antonia's Line, 1995) Director: Marleen Gorris
- *Diamonds are Forever* (1971) Director: Guy Hamilton
- *Fanfare* (1958) Director: Bert Haanstra
- *Father and Daughter* (2000) Director: Michael Dudok de Wit
- *Karakter* (Character, 1997) Director: Mike van Diem
- *De Vierde Man* (The Fourth Man, 1983) Director: Paul Verhoeven
- *Turks Fruit* (Turkish Delight,1973) Director: Paul Verhoeven

TOP READS

One of the best ways to learn about contemporary issues and culture and grasp a sense of Dutchness is to immerse yourself in a good book about the place. The following page-turners have won critical acclaim (see Literature p48 for reviews).

- *Max Havelaar* Multatuli
- *Dagboek van Anne Frank* (Diary of Anne Frank) Anne Frank
- *Een Handvol Kronkels* (A Dutchman's Slight Adventures) Simon Carmiggelt
- *Het Volgende Verhaal* (The Following Story) Cees Notenboom
- *The Coffee Trader* David Liss
- *De Ontdekking van de Hemel* (The Discovery of Heaven) Harry Mulisch
- *Een Hart van Steen* (A Heart of Stone) Renate Dorrestein
- *Eerst Grijs Dan Wit Dan Blauw* (First Gray, Then White, Then Blue) Margriet de Moor
- *The Happy Hooker* Xaviera Hollander
- *Amsterdam: A Traveler's Literary Companion* Manfred Wolf (editor)

Itineraries
CLASSIC ROUTES

ONE WEEK

What better place to start than the bewitching charms of **Amsterdam** (p79). Visit the **Van Gogh Museum** (p109) or **Rijksmuseum** (p108) and take a **walking tour** through the canal quarter (p113). Club vibes, music and theatre beckon at **Leidseplein** (p105) which also has numerous good restaurants nearby. On the second day board a **canalboat tour** (p115) and check out the **Red Light District** (p98) before hitting a brown café.

Move on to **Haarlem** (p140) for a day, strolling around the compact old quarter and viewing the masterpieces of the **Frans Hals Museum** (p142). Stained glass and an amazing organ are the draws of the **Grote Kerk** (p141). In tulip season (April and May) be sure to witness the unbelievable colours of the **Keukenhof gardens** (p193) south of town.

Spend one day each in **Delft** (p204), for its exquisite porcelain factories and old-world charm, and **Den Haag** (p193), the refined capital of Zuid Holland known for its prestigious art galleries – don't miss the **Mauritshuis** (p195) collection with works from Vermeer to Warhol. Parliamentary tours are on offer at the **Binnenhof** (p195).

This popular route from Amsterdam through the historic Dutch cities of Haarlem, Den Haag and Rotterdam is a mere 103km; the sheer variety of charms will make a week flash by.

On the remaining two days visit **Rotterdam** (p209). Begin with a harbour boat tour and visit either the **Museum Boijmans van Beuningen** (p212) or the **Maritiem Museum Rotterdam** (p213), before poking around the old quarter of **Delfshaven** (p213). The next morning do a **walking tour** of modern architecture (p213) before departing for **Kinderdijk** (p221), a Unesco Heritage site with 19 windmills by a picturesque canal.

TWO WEEKS

Extend your stay in **Amsterdam** (p79) to three days, starting with the **Rijksmuseum** (p108) or **Van Gogh Museum** (p109) and enjoy the buskers on a stroll through leafy **Vondelpark** (p110). Take a meal in the funky **Jordaan** district (p103) and browse the snazzy antique shops and art galleries along **Spiegelstraat** (p104) before taking a load off in a grand café on **Spui** (p101). The next day view the wild kingdom of **Artis Zoo** (p108) and learn about the glories of the Dutch East India Company at the **Scheepvaartmuseum** (p108). Rent a bicycle on the third day and pedal past windmills to the sea along the **Waterland Route** (p72).

Continue as on the one-week tour to Haarlem (Keukenhof in season), Den Haag, Delft and Rotterdam, but add a day for a walk through the old university town of **Leiden** (p186). After seeing the windmills at **Kinderdijk** (p221), spend a day touring the Zeeland deltas around **Middelburg** (p225), either by car or bicycle (see the **Mantelingen Route**, p73). Travel through the rolling hills of Limburg to cosmopolitan **Maastricht** (p287), for great cuisine and a medieval labyrinth of shop-filled streets; two days here will also allow you to take a boat cruise on the Maas. Return north to the Dutch heartland

This grand tour combines the best of Dutch cities and countryside in just two weeks, from royal palaces and Old Masters to sea dykes and lush forest over a total 665km.

to visit **Hoge Veluwe National Park** (p276) whose lush forests and dunes make an enchanting setting for the excellent **Kröller-Müller Museum** (p276). Polish off your trip by exploring the old Hanseatic town of **Deventer** (p265).

ROADS LESS TRAVELLED

ISLANDS ESCAPES
One Week

The necklace of low-lying **Wadden Islands** (p161 & 243) is just the ticket for a week of romantic island-hopping, preferably with a bicycle. Note that some ferry links require advance planning – see Friesland (p243). A full day on **Texel** (p161) is the way to begin, snaking along the western coast from sleepy **Den Hoorn** (p161) through dark copses to the **Ecomare** (p162) seal and bird refuge. Take a catamaran ride near **De Cocksdorp** (p161) before bedding down here for the night. The next day comb the eastern side of the island, admiring pretty thatched houses in **Oosterend** (p161) and visiting the **Maritime & Beachcombers Museum** (p163) in **Oudeschild** (p161).

From De Cocksdorp board the morning ferry to car-free **Vlieland** (p244) to explore the nature and hiking trails before catching the boat to **Harlingen** (p241), a pretty little port on the Frisian coast, to spend the night. From here, head up the coast to Holwerd, where you ferry across for a two-day stay on **Ameland** (p246). Its four towns are pretty for a brief stroll, and the eastern end is ideal to bike away from it all. Return to the former whaling port of **Nes** (p246) for the night. The next day stay put for

This week-long hop along the Wadden Islands covers just 200km, but you will be tempted to spend longer soaking up their wild, enchanting beauty.

a boat tour to the sea lions, and to convene with nature. Your last stop, via the ports of Holwerd and Lauwersoog, is **Schiermonnikoog** (p247), the smallest of the Frisian islands and a wild national park.

TAILORED TRIPS

ART-LOVER'S NETHERLANDS   One Week

Spend a lifetime admiring Dutch art – starting with our one week tour. In your two to three days in Amsterdam, begin with a visit to the **Rijksmuseum** (p108) to admire Rembrandt's masterpiece *Nightwatch* and the definitive Golden Age collection. The next day, go to the **Van Gogh Museum** (p109) for impressive works by the tortured genius. The **Stedelijk Museum** (p109) has one of Europe's best modern art collections. Continue to Hoge Veluwe National Park for the **Kröller-Müller Museum** (p276) and a sprinkling of Renoir, Sysley and Manet besides yet more superb Van Goghs (one day). The **Museum Boijmans van Beuningen** (p212) in Rotterdam has a great collection spanning all eras of Dutch and European art, from Bosch and Breugel to Degas and Dali (one day). Moving on to Den Haag (two days), seek out Vermeer's famous *Girl with a Pearl Earring* among the embarrassment of riches in the **Mauritshuis** (p195), then cross town for a dose of Piet Mondriaan's De Stijl movement at the **Gemeentemuseum** (p197). The drastically restyled **Van Abbemuseum** (p283) in Eindhoven (one day) has an acclaimed selection of 20th-century works from Picasso through Beuys to Van Warmerdam, and the building alone is almost worth the trip.

CASTLE-LOVER'S NETHERLANDS   Five Days

These intriguing old fortresses are knotted around the middle of the country for a convenient five-day circuit (one castle per day). Guided tours are available in English in all, except at Slot Loevestein. **Muiderslot** (p165), a moated fortress at **Muiden**, tells the fascinating story of Count Floris V on his popular medieval tours. The moated **Kasteel de Haar** (p180) near Utrecht is a towering Gothic masterpiece straight out of a stage set, rebuilt in the 19th century with ostentation in mind. The manicured gardens, French and English, are big enough to get lost in. A sturdy 14th-century fortress, **Slot Loevestein** (p287), near Woudrichem, was a toll post and prison for various politicians including Hugo de Groot, who escaped in a bookcase. The diminutive fortified castle in **Amerongen** (p182) had a string of aristocratic owners, and the gardens are ideal for an extended stroll. Nearby, your last stop is **Huis Doorn** (p182), the manor-castle that was also the final port of call for Germany's Kaiser Wilhelm.

The Authors

JEREMY GRAY
Coordinating Author & Amsterdam, Noord Holland & Flevoland, Utrecht

Jeremy co-wrote the first edition of *Netherlands* and returned to co-ordinate this book. Born in the US of English parents, this Europhile worked as a financial journalist in the UK and Germany before moving to the Netherlands, where he cultivates a love of jazz, canalside pubs and *kibbeling*. The Dutch he admires for their open minds, unshakable cheer and ability to do a lot with a little, just about anytime, in any weather. When he's not wandering the globe for Lonely Planet, Jeremy lives in Utrecht and can be spotted on his second-hand bike.

My Favourite Trip

The IJsselmeer towns of Noord Holland take some beating. This is where the diverse charms of Dutch maritime culture come together. **Monnickendam** (p148) is a fine place to start – I never tire of the classic old buildings on Noordeinde. From there, travel 25km north to **Hoorn** (p156). I love the lustrous façades showing the glory days of the Dutch merchant fleet, on the harbour along Veermankade. Drive the 18km northeast along the dyketop road to see the historic sailboats dotting the IJsselmeer, and you reach my absolute favourite, the town of **Enkhuizen** (p158) and its extraordinary Zuiderzeemuseum (p158).

REUBEN ACCIANO
Zuid Holland & Zeeland, Friesland, Groningen & Drenthe, Overijssel & Gelderland, Noord Brabant & Limburg

Born in Australia to Dutch and Italian parents, Reuben's always looked at the world slightly skewwhiff. He played in a loud independent rock band, did a Cultural Studies degree, ran Australia's best student newspaper, worked as a freelance writer/photographer, found time to have a few tempestuous affairs and to visit the Netherlands (among many other places) twice. He loves the Dutch for their punctual trains, the Lowlands festival, endlessly impressive stunt cycling and Total Football, but doesn't like their plateau toilets.

My Favourite Trip

The southern half of the Netherlands is so diverse. **Den Haag**'s (p195) street culture and restaurants were a wonderful surprise. **Leiden** (p186) has history, excellent eating and shopping, all within a beautiful canal belt. Anything goes in **Rotterdam** (p209). I loved **Museum Boijmans van Beuningen** (p212), a sprawling art collection whose adventurousness mimics the city itself. **Maastricht** (p287) is a wonder. Cobbled 16th-century streets, verdant parks, amazing cheeses…plus enviable proximity to a wealth of Trappist breweries! I ate, drank, danced and marvelled at the overall beauty of the town and the friendliness of the locals which is like nowhere else in the Netherlands.

Snapshot

Seen through pink-tulip-coloured glasses, the Netherlands seems a quaint little country of tolerant, clog-wearing bicyclists who seem to insist on consensus in everything. Some outsiders (and quite a few natives) believe that the Dutch have achieved a social nirvana that succeeds in pleasing all the people most of the time, regardless of their colour, creed or ethnic background. But clichés like these are now being challenged.

The hottest topic by far is how to better absorb new immigrants, or how to limit their numbers. Although once taboo, public discussions about quotas, dress codes and language requirements have revealed deep divisions in a country famous for its tolerance towards foreigners. The rise of populist right-wing politician Pim Fortuyn in 2002 struck a nerve across all levels of Dutch society, and his explosive ideas reverberate even after his assassination (see Fortuyn's Legacy, p33).

Bucking tradition, the Dutch royal family has moved recently into the limelight. Queen Beatrix has shed some of her famed aloofness, and the wedding of Crown Prince Willem-Alexander to an Argentinian beauty satisfied the country's appetite for fairy-tale romance. The new princess, Máxima Zorreguieta, is a familiar face on magazine covers and, indeed, tends to outshine the future king. (The populous has forgiven her for being the daughter of a former minister in a disgraced junta government.)

In the 1980s and '90s the Netherlands was widely praised for its consensus-based 'polder' model that relies on cooperation among the government, employers and trade unions to find solutions for labour market problems. Wage moderation, public spending restraint and labour-market reforms were important benefits. But the approach also generated legions of petty rules and regulations, and ministers would debate plans endlessly before taking any action. Some critics have declared the polder model dead since the disintegration of Wim Kok's labour-led coalition in 2002.

The Dutch economy has an enviable track record for such a small country. It's the sixth-largest economy in the world – third-largest in terms of food exports alone – and its GDP per head is now bigger than mighty Germany's. However, the Netherlands' lengthy period of prosperity came to an end with the September 2001 terrorist attacks on the USA, and the subsequent economic slowdown. The Dutch people now face painful austerity measures as the centre-right coalition, led rather shakily by prime minister Jan-Peter Balkenende (p32), cuts deep into the welfare state. Sacred cows such as generous healthcare are going under the knife, and early retirement is no longer a soft option. The country's business reputation, meanwhile, has also been tarnished by scandals in the building sector and at food giant Ahold, owner of Albert Heijn supermarkets.

Congestion on the roads may be relieved by the introduction of electronic tolls, following initiatives in Britain and Germany. This policy, an extension of existing ideas on vehicle limitation, will help pay for maintenance and the classy *fluisterasfalt*, the 'whispering' road surface designed to alleviate noise pollution.

Unseasonably warm weather has put global warming back on the agenda (p55). Once as regular as the tides, cool soggy summers are giving way to a Riviera-like clime, but don't bank on great weather. The higher

FAST FACTS

Population: 16.2 million

Pig population:
10.7 million

Per capita GDP: €27,500

Unemployment rate:
5.5% (2003)

Inflation:
2% (September 2003)

Religion: Catholic 31%,
Protestant 21%, Muslim
5.3%, other 2.7%, not
religious 40%

Number of caravans:
500,000

Height of the average
male: 183cm (6ft)

Number of windmills:
1180

temperatures now mean quite a few peat-based dykes dry out in summer; the threat of collapse is enough to give the Dutch nightmares.

The Netherlands' liberal drugs policy continues to be a reliable source of controversy, in particular rankling France and the USA. The Dutch, in turn, point to relatively low rates of drug-related crime and argue that decriminalisition is the way to go for soft drugs. But the government has stepped up pressure against trafficking in cannabis, hard drugs and designer drugs (the Netherlands is the world's top producer of ecstasy). Police raids have become frequent at nightclubs in Amsterdam, Rotterdam and other cities.

The Dutch have also been trendsetters on other social and moral issues such as abortion, euthanasia and homosexuality. The legalisation of same-sex marriage in 2001 was a landmark decision and other countries have since followed suit. Some gays complain, however, that the entertainment scene isn't as good as it was a few years back.

'Dutch national pride is muted except on the soccer field'

Dutch national pride is muted except on the soccer field. When the Netherlands made it to the semi-finals of the European championships in 2000, more flags fluttered on the streets than on Queen's Day. Otherwise, the Dutch love to downplay their place in the world, and as a nod to sophistication often prefer to speak English with foreign visitors.

Visitors may notice that the country's widespread cigarette smoking seems at odds with the desire to keep the social peace (in this case with nonsmokers). The view prevails that everyone has the right to live their own life provided others aren't offended (much). However, smoking in public is slowly being regulated, and restaurants are now required to have a nonsmoking section.

The Dutch have an acute sense of moral rectitude – some say it's those old Calvinist doctrines. The locals also have a reputation for directness that can be either refreshing or disconcerting, depending on your point of view. It's a misconception, though, that the Dutch have little sense of humour; they do, in fact, have an unusual ability to laugh at themselves.

Last but not least, the Dutch are renowned for their thrift and sharp trading skills. The Netherlands has long had a money culture, with very little aristocratic possession of big landholdings. Trading is still more important today than manufacturing. You won't see bargaining done for retail wares unless big-ticket items are under consideration. Then you'll see the Dutch will bend over backwards to swing a deal.

History

Between the waves of invaders and the invading waves, the Netherlands has a turbulent past that is not immediately apparent to the visitor. One important point to remember is that the Netherlands came into existence only in 1579. Before that, the entire region of the Low Countries – today's Netherlands as well as Belgium and Luxembourg – was intertwined politically and culturally and for the most part, had little say over its own destiny.

FOREIGN DOMINATION

The territory that became the Netherlands struggled long and hard to rid itself of unwanted guests. Among the earliest invaders were the Romans who, under Julius Caesar, conquered a wide region along the Rijn (Rhine) and its tributaries by 59 BC. Fiercely independent by nature, Celtic and Germanic tribes initially bowed to his rule. Over the next three centuries the Romans built advanced towns, farms and the straight roads that still shape the landscape today. However, these heavy troops hardly bothered with soggy regions to the north such as Friesland, where early settlers built homes on mounds of mud (called *terpen*) to escape the frequent floods.

The Romans hung on until the 3rd century. Even during this time, the Franks, an aggressive German tribe to the east, had been sniffing around the region. Between the 7th and 8th centuries, the Franks finished their conquest of the Low Countries and began converting the local populace to Christianity, using force whenever necessary. Charlemagne, the Holy Roman emperor, built a palace at Nijmegen but the empire fell apart after his death in 814.

Next came the Vikings, who sailed up Dutch rivers to loot and pillage. Local rulers developed their own fortified towns and made up their own government and laws, even though strictly speaking they answered to the Pope in Rome.

Conflicts arose between the artists and rich merchants in the towns and the lords who dominated the countryside. The townspeople would back their local lord when he wanted to gain someone else's territory, but in return they would demand various freedoms. Beginning in the 12th century, these relationships were laid down in charters – documents that not only spelt out the lord's power, but also detailed other bureaucratic matters such as taxation.

Dutch towns with sea access like Deventer and Zwolle on the IJssel river joined the Hanseatic League. This mostly German federation of towns and cities grew wealthy through its single-minded development of laws, regulations and other policies that promoted trade. In many ways it was a very early forerunner of the EU.

Meanwhile the many little lords met their match in the dukes of Burgundy, who gradually took over the Low Countries. Duke Philip the Good, who ruled from 1419 to 1467, showed the towns of the Low Countries who was boss by essentially telling them to stuff their charters. Although

www.hunebedden.nl

Pics and history of these megalithic mystery monuments in Drenthe province.

www.let.leidenuniv.nl /history/surf/surf-vg.htm

An extensive listing of Dutch history resources on the Internet, according to Leiden University.

www.inghist.nl

Online catalog of book titles and articles at the Institute for Netherlands History. In Dutch.

1200   **1566**

Founding of Amsterdam | Beginning of 80 Years' War with Spain

The *Dutch Republic: Its Rise, Greatness and Fall 1477–1806*, by Jonathan Israel, provides a thorough account of the emergence of the United Provinces as a great power in the Golden Age and their subsequent decline.

this limited the towns' freedom, it also brought to the region a degree of stability that had been missing during the era of quibbling lords.

The 15th century ushered in great prosperity for the Low Countries. The Dutch became adept at shipbuilding in support of the Hanseatic trade, and merchants thrived by selling luxury items such as tapestries, fashionable clothing and paintings – but also more mundane commodities such as salted herring and beer.

With their wealth tapped through taxes the Low Countries were naturally coveted by a succession of rulers. In 1482 Mary of Burgundy, Philip's granddaughter, passed on the Low Countries to her son, Philip the Fair.

The family intrigues that followed are worthy of a costume drama: Philip married Joanna, the daughter of King Ferdinand and Queen Isabella of Spain; Philip then bequeathed the Low Countries to his son Charles, now a member of the powerful Habsburg dynasty, in 1530. Charles V was crowned Holy Roman Emperor, making him monarch of most of Europe.

Fortunately the rule of Charles V did not stand in the way of the Low Countries' growing wealth. But this all changed in 1555 when Charles handed over Spain and the Low Countries to his son, Philip II.

THE FIGHT FOR INDEPENDENCE

Even Spain's Philip II had no love for the Low Countries. Philip was a staunch Catholic so conflict was inevitable as the protestant reformation spread through his colony. Before the Spanish arrived the religious landscape of the Low Countries was quite diverse: Lutherans wielded great influence but smaller churches had their places too. For instance, the Anabaptists were polygamists and communists, and nudity was promoted as a means of equality among their masses (in the warmer seasons). In the end it was Calvinism that emerged in the Low Countries as the main challenger to the Roman Catholic Church, and to Philip's rule.

www.nationaalarchief.nl

The Dutch National Archive has almost a thousand years of historical documents, maps, drawings and photos. Free access.

A big believer in the Inquisition, Philip went after the Protestants with a vengeance. Matters came to a head in 1566 when the puritanical Calvinists went on a rampage, destroying art and religious icons of Catholic churches in many parts of the Netherlands. Evidence of this is still readily apparent in the barren interiors of Dutch churches today.

www.geheugenvannederland.nl

Contains images and text from Dutch cultural institutions like the Mauritshuis in Den Haag and Amsterdam's Scheepvaartmuseum.

Religion was not the only source of friction between the Dutch and Philip. High taxes – the spark of many a revolution – and trade restrictions stirred dissent among the merchants. Deciding enough was enough, Philip sent one of his cronies, the Duke of Alba, to the Netherlands with an army of 10,000 in 1568. The duke was not one to take prisoners and his forces slaughtered thousands. It was the beginning of the Dutch war of independence, which lasted 80 years.

The Prince van Oranje, Willem the Silent (thus named for his refusal to argue over religious issues) led the Dutch revolt against Spanish rule. He was outlawed by Philip. Willem, who had been Philip's lieutenant in Holland, Zeeland and Utrecht, began to rely on the Dutch Calvinists for his chief support. Willem championed the principle of toleration and this philosophy became part of the foundation of an independent Dutch state. The rebels' cause, however, was hampered by lack of money and patchy support from towns.

1579	late 16th century
United Provinces of the Netherlands	Golden Age begins

In 1572 the war took a turn for the better for the Dutch as for once help, rather than harm, came from the sea. Willem hired a bunch of English pirates to fight for his cause. Known as the Watergeuzen (Sea Beggars) they sailed up the myriad of Dutch rivers and seized town after town from the surprised and land-bound Spanish forces. By the end of the year Willem controlled every city except Amsterdam.

The Spanish responded by sacking the Duke of Alba and sending in a new commander, Alessandro Farnese, who was a more able leader. Much of the 1570s saw a constant shift of power as one side or the other gained temporary supremacy.

THE UNION OF UTRECHT

The Low Countries split for good in 1579 when the more Protestant and rebellious provinces in the north formed the Union of Utrecht. This explicitly anti-Spanish alliance became known as the United Provinces, the basis for the Netherlands as we know it today. The southern regions of the Low Countries had always remained Catholic and were much more open to compromise with Spain. They eventually became Belgium.

Although the United Provinces had declared their independence from Spain, the war dragged on. In 1584, they suffered a major blow when their leader, Willem the Silent, was assassinated in Delft. The English government gave assistance to the Dutch, and the Spanish were weakened further by the English victory over the Armada in 1588. In a series of brilliant military campaigns, the Dutch drove the Spanish out of the United Provinces by the turn of the 17th century. Trouble with Spain was far from over, however, and fighting resumed as part of the larger Thirty Years' War throughout Europe. In 1648 the Treaty of Westphalia, which ended the Thirty Years' War, included the proviso that Spain recognise the independence of the United Provinces, ending the 80-year conflict between the Netherlands and Spain.

THE GOLDEN AGE

In the late 16th century a period of Dutch history began that came to be known as the 'Golden Age' for its great economic prosperity and cultural fruition. Building upon earlier economic success, the United Provinces became the most powerful commercial and maritime country on the Continent, with Amsterdam the financial centre of Europe. Dutch vessels transported most of Europe's cargo. Even at the peak of the rebellion, the Spanish had no alternative but to use Dutch boats for transporting their grain. The Dutch then used this revenue to help fund the revolution.

The arts and sciences flourished in the robust political and economic climate. The Dutch infatuation with tulips began to unfold during the Golden Age, with the tulip market reaching its zenith in the mid-1630s (see Tulipmania, p27).

The merchant fleet known as the Dutch East India Company was formed in 1602. It quickly monopolised key shipping and trade routes east of Africa's Cape of Good Hope and west of the Strait of Magellan, making it the largest trading company of the 17th century. The Dutch East India Company imported precious spices and Asian luxury items

The *Embarrassment of Riches*, by Simon Schama, is a thoughtful look at the tensions generated between vast wealth and Calvinist sobriety in the Golden Age, with implications for modern society.

www.dutch-republic.nl

A resource network for the history of the Dutch republic, with excellent links and lists of source materials.

1602	1637
Dutch East India Company created	Tulipmania fizzles

such as Chinese porcelain. The company was almost as powerful as a sovereign state – it could raise its own armed forces and establish colonies.

Its sister, the Dutch West India Company, traded with Africa and the Americas and was at the very centre of the American slave trade. Seamen working for both companies discovered or conquered lands including Tasmania, New Zealand, Malaysia, Sri Lanka and Mauritius. English explorer Henry Hudson stumbled upon the island of Manhattan in 1609 as he searched for a Northwest Passage, and Dutch settlers named it New Amsterdam.

The Union of Utrecht's promise of religious tolerance led to a surprising amount of religious diversity that was rare in Europe at the time. Calvinism was the official religion of the government, but various other Protestants, Jews and Catholics were allowed to practise their faith. However, in a legacy from the troubles with Spain, Catholics had to worship in private, which led to the creation of clandestine churches. Many of these unusual buildings have survived to the present day.

Culturally the United Provinces flourished in the Golden Age. The wealth of the merchant class supported scores of artists. Among the most renowned were Jan Vermeer, Jan Steen and Frans Hals, with the most illustrious being Rembrandt (see Arts, p43).

The sciences also thrived. Dutch physicist and astronomer Christiaan Huygens discovered Saturn's rings and invented the pendulum clock. Celebrated philosopher Benedict de Spinoza wrote a brilliant thesis saying that the universe was identical with God. Frenchman René Descartes, known for his philosophy, 'I think, therefore I am', found intellectual freedom in the Netherlands and stayed for two decades.

Politically, however, the young Dutch Republic faced internal struggles. The House of Oranje-Nassau fought the republicans for control of the country; while the house wanted to centralise power with the Prince van Oranje as *stadhouder* (chief magistrate), the republicans wanted the cities and provinces to run their own affairs. Prince Willem II won the dispute but died suddenly three months later, one week before his son was born. Dutch regional leaders exploited this power vacuum by abolishing the *stadhouder*, and authority was decentralised.

Perhaps it was inevitable, given their competing interests around the world: England and the United Provinces went to war in 1652. One of the main issues was the English attempt to muscle in on the Dutch merchant fleet. The period was one of drama and political intrigue as the English and Dutch went from allies to enemies again. Both countries entered a hotch-potch of alliances with Spain, France and Sweden in an effort to get the upper hand. The navies fought most of the battles but often had no idea if ships encountered could be considered friends or foe. During one round of treaties, the Dutch agreed to give New Amsterdam to the English (who promptly renamed it New York) in return for Surinam in South America.

In 1672 the French army marched into the Netherlands. Unfortunately for the Dutch, the country had devoted most of its resources to its navy, leaving the country nearly helpless against the land invasion. The country appealed to the House of Oranje, which appointed Willem III as general of the Dutch forces.

The Dutch Seaborne Empire 1600–1800 by CR Boxer, is an academic but readable account about how a small corner of Europe dominated world trade.

Spinoza: A Life by Steven M Nadler is an amazing biography of the 17th-century philosopher, with background on the early Jewish immigrants.

1700	1795
End of Golden Age	French invade Holland

TULIPMANIA

In late 1636 a tulip-trading mania swept the Netherlands. Speculative buying and selling made some individual bulbs more expensive than an Amsterdam house. Even ordinary people sank their life's savings into a few bulbs. Needless to say, the tulip frenzy didn't last.

Tulips originated as wild flowers in Central Asia. They were first cultivated by the Turks, who filled their courts with the stunning blossoms ('tulip' is Turkish for turban). In the mid-1500s some bulbs made their way to Vienna where the imperial botanist, Carolus Clusius, learned how to propagate them. Clusius became director of the Hortus Botanicus in Leiden – Europe's oldest botanical garden – and became an expert in cross-breeding tulips that could thrive in Holland's cool climate and fertile delta soil.

Healthy tulips are solid, smooth and monotone, but in 17th-century Holland the most precious ones had frilly edges and 'flamed' streaks of colour. Ironically these were symptoms of a viral infection carried by a louse that thrived on peaches. (The most striking specimens grew under fruit trees, the Turks had already noticed.) The most beautiful tulips were also the weakest due to heavy cross-breeding and grafting, which made them even more susceptible to the virus. Tulips were notoriously difficult to cultivate and their blossoms unpredictable.

Speculators fell over themselves to out-bid each other in taverns. At the height of Tulipmania in early 1637, a single bulb of the legendary *Semper augustus* fetched more than 10 years' wages of the average worker. One foreign sailor enraged his employer by slicing up what he thought was an onion to eat with his herring. An English botanist bisected one of his host's bulbs and landed in jail until he could raise thousands of florins to compensate.

An Amsterdam doctor, Claes Pietersz, even changed his surname to Tulp (Dutch for tulip) because of his love for the flower. Rembrandt immortalised him in the *Anatomy Lesson of Dr Tulp*, now on display in the Mauritshuis in Den Haag, p195.

The bonanza couldn't last. When some bulbs failed to fetch their expected prices in Haarlem in February 1637, the bottom fell out of the market. Within a matter of weeks a wave of bankruptcies swept the land, hitting wealthy merchants as well as simple folk. Speculators were stuck with unsold bulbs, or bulbs they'd reserved but hadn't yet paid for (the concept of financial options, incidentally, was invented during Tulipmania). The government refused to get involved with a pursuit they regarded as gambling.

The speculative froth is gone but passion for the tulip endures. It remains a relatively expensive flower, and cool-headed growers have perfected their craft. To this day the Dutch are the world leaders in tulip cultivation and supply most of the bulbs exported to Europe and North America. Other bulbs such as daffodils, hyacinths and crocuses are Dutch specialities as well.

So what happened to the flamed, frilly tulips of the past? They've mostly vanished, as the underlying disease that fed the wild colours has been all but eliminated. A few are grown by British bulb collectors while others are healthy replica bulbs created by crossbreeding.

Tulipmania resonates as an early example of human preoccupations, and greed. Search the Internet for the word and you'll find a rash of hits for articles about the South Sea Bubble of 1720, the boom preceding the Great Crash of 1929 and – showing that we are all doomed to relive history – the wild overvaluation of Internet stocks.

In a single stroke, Willem improved relations with the English by marrying his cousin Mary, daughter of the English king James II. Opponents of the king feared that the Roman Catholic Church would be restored in England, so they secretly invited Willem to invade the country in 1688.

Perhaps sensing he was no longer welcome in England, James fled to France, and Willem and Mary were named king and queen of England in

1814	1830
Willem I crowned as king	Belgium declares independence

Tulipomania: The Story of the World's Most Coveted Flower, by Mike Dash, is an engaging look at the bizarre bulb fever that swept the nation in the 17th century.

1689. Using his strong diplomatic skills, Willem created the Grand Alliance that joined England, the United Provinces, Spain, Sweden and several German states to fight the expansionist ambitions of France's Louis XIV.

The Grand Alliance defeated the French several times. In 1697 Louis XIV agreed to give up most of the territory France had conquered. As if to drive the point home, the Dutch again joined the English to fight the French in the War of Spanish Succession, ending with the Treaty of Utrecht in 1713. However, the wars had exhausted the Dutch both politically and economically, and the treaty marked the beginning of the country's decline as an economic and political power.

DUTCH DECLINE & FRENCH RULE

Weakened by the ongoing wars with France, the United Provinces pursued a policy of peace at any cost in the 18th century. The maritime fleet was clapped out after the wars so the French and the British moved in on the trade routes the Dutch had once dominated. Domestically, the population was decreasing and even worse, the dykes were also in a sorry state. There was little money to repair them and widespread floods swept across the country in 1713. Commercially, merchants were more likely to spend their profits on luxuries rather than sensible investments in their businesses. This contributed to the overall economic decline of the Dutch.

A series of political struggles between the House of Oranje and its democratic opponents led to a civil war in 1785, which was settled three years later when the *stadhouders* agreed to limit their own powers. Many Dutch who were eager for constitutional reform welcomed the arrival of French revolutionary forces in the mid-1790s. The United Provinces collapsed and the area was renamed the Batavian Republic. It survived only until 1806 when Napoleon renamed it the Kingdom of Holland, installing his brother Louis Bonaparte as king.

But Louis proved to be not quite the kind of king (or maybe even brother) Napoleon would have liked. He actually seemed to like his subjects and often favoured them over France. His position became untenable after he decided to send less Dutch money back home, and in 1810 Napoleon booted Louis out of office.

With Napoleon's attention diverted elsewhere, the House of Oranje supporters invited Prince Willem VI back. He landed at Scheveningen in 1813 and was named prince sovereign of the Netherlands. The next year he was crowned King Willem I and ruled until 1840.

INDEPENDENT KINGDOM & WWI

The independence of the Netherlands was restored at the Congress of Vienna in 1815; the Netherlands in the north and Belgium in the south were joined into a United Kingdom of the Netherlands, with Willem as king.

The marriage was doomed from the start. The partners had little in common, including their dominant religions (Calvinist and Catholic), languages (Dutch and French) and favoured way of making money (trade and manufacturing). Matters weren't helped by Willem, who generally sided with his fellow northerners.

In 1830 the southern states revolted and nine years later the other European powers forced Willem to let the south go. In a nice historical

1839	1932
First Dutch railway inaugurated	Zuiderzee reclamation begins

twist, Willem abdicated one year later so he could marry – surprise! – a Belgian Catholic. It's not known if he ever spoke French at home.

His son, King Willem II, granted a new and more liberal constitution to the people of the Netherlands in 1848. This included a number of democratic ideals and even made the monarchy the servant of the elected government. This document has remained the foundation of the Dutch government until the present day. Its role on the world stage long over, the Netherlands maintained a policy of strict neutrality from 1815 to 1939 and played only a small part in European affairs.

During WWI, the Netherlands remained neutral although its shipping industry was damaged by both the Allies and the Germans. The Allied forces mounted a blockade that prevented goods from being shipped into the Netherlands for fear the goods would reach Germany, while German submarine warfare claimed many Dutch ships.

Following WWI, the Netherlands embarked on innovative social programmes that targeted poverty, the rights of women and children, and education. Industrially, the coal mines of south Limburg were exploited to great success, Rotterdam became one of Europe's most important ports and the scheme to reclaim the Zuiderzee was launched in 1932.

WWII

The Dutch wished to continue their neutrality during WWII but the Germans had other ideas. The German army flooded over the borders in May 1940 and the tiny Dutch army was powerless to stop it. In an incident that continues to rankle the Dutch, the Germans levelled much of Rotterdam in a raid designed to force the Dutch to surrender. They did.

Queen Wilhelmina issued a proclamation of 'flaming protest' to the nation and escaped with her family to England. The plucky monarch, who had been key in maintaining Dutch neutrality in WWI, now found herself in a much different situation and made encouraging broadcasts to her subjects back home via the BBC and Radio Orange. The Germans put Dutch industry and farms to work for war purposes and there was much deprivation. Thousands of Dutch men were taken to Germany and forced to work in Nazi factories. A far worse fate awaited the country's Jews (p30).

During the five years of German occupation, Dutch resistance was primarily passive. Any open dissent often resulted in execution on the spot, especially later when the war was going badly for the Nazis. However, many Dutch profited from the German occupation and some actively collaborated. Although many Dutch risked all to save Jews, others cheerfully accepted bounties for revealing Jewish hiding places. Some even did it for free, which is what sealed the fate of Anne Frank in Amsterdam.

The worst part of the war for the Dutch was the so-called 'Winter of Hunger' of 1944–45. The British-led Operation Market Garden (p274), through the heart of the Netherlands in the autumn of 1944, had been a huge disaster and the Allies abandoned all efforts to liberate the Dutch. The Germans stripped the country of much of its food and wealth, and mass starvation ensued. Many people were reduced to eating tulip bulbs for their daily subsistence.

The Netherlands was not liberated until just a few days before the end of the war in Europe in May 1945.

http://utchjewry.huji.ac.il

Center for Research on Dutch Jewry has a geneological database and links to Dutch archives and libraries.

The *Diary of Anne Frank*, by Anne Frank, is the world-famous autobiography of a Jewish girl. It movingly describes life in hiding in Nazi-occupied Amsterdam.

A Bridge Too Far: Operation Market Garden by Stephen Badsey provides a blow-by-blow account of the bold and but ultimately disastrous Allied campaign at Arnhem during WWII. Hollywood did its own version in 1977, shooting on location in Arnhem, Deventer and Nijmegen.

1940	1945
Germany invades Netherlands	Netherlands liberated, WWII ends

DUTCH JEWS

The Nazis brought about the almost complete annihilation of the Dutch Jewish community. Before WWII the Netherlands counted 140,000 Jews of whom about two-thirds lived in Amsterdam. Less than 25,000 survived the war.

Jews played a key role in the city's development over the centuries. In medieval times the expulsion of Jews from Spain and Portugal in the 1580s brought a flood of Sephardic refugees to Amsterdam, and more arrived when the Spaniards retook Antwerp a few years later. They settled in Amsterdam's Nieuwmarkt neighbourhood, one of the few places they could afford land.

The guilds kept most trades closed to these newcomers. Some of the Sephardim were diamond cutters, however, for whom there was no guild. Sephardic Jews also introduced printing and tobacco processing, or worked as street retailers, bankers and doctors. The majority eked out a living as labourers and small-time traders on the margins of society. Still, they weren't confined to a ghetto and, with some restrictions, could buy property and exercise their religion – freedoms unheard of elsewhere in Europe.

The 17th century saw another influx of Jewish refugees, this time Ashkenazim fleeing pogroms in Central and Eastern Europe. The two groups didn't always get on well: Sephardim resented the increased competition posed by Ashkenazic newcomers, who soon outnumbered them and were generally much poorer. Separate synagogues were established, helping Amsterdam to become one of Europe's major Jewish centres.

The guilds and all restrictions on Jews were abolished during the French occupation, and the Jewish community thrived in the 19th century. Poverty was still considerable, and the Jewish quarter included some of the worst slums in the city. Still, the economic, social and political emancipation of the Jews helped their middle class who moved into the Plantage area and prosperous suburbs south of the city.

The Holocaust left Amsterdam's Jewish quarter empty, a sinister reminder of a bustling community erased from existence. Many of their homes were looted and stood derelict until their demolition in the 1970s. Throughout the Netherlands there are prewar synagogues with haunting memorials to entire congregations who were taken away.

There are courageous stories of Dutch citizens who risked death by hiding Jews during the war. But there were also Dutch collaborators who turned in Jews to the Nazi authorities. This is how Anne Frank and her family were finally found.

One Dutch deed of sheltering Jews stands out in particular. The tiny village of Nieuwlande in Drenthe decided to take in as many Jews as possible. Led by Arnold Douwes – the son of pastor, Johannes Post, a farmer and town counsellor – the 119 townsfolk protected more than 50 Jews who had been ordered to report to the Westerbork deportation camp (p259). Today the camp serves as a memorial to those who died and as a Holocaust museum. Because the entire town was involved, there was little chance of betrayal.

For many Dutch, their largely passive role in the holocaust remains a deeply disturbing one. The National War and Resistance Museum in Overloon, Limburg (p293) takes an unvarnished look at the Holocaust and the Dutch. Amsterdam's Joods Historisch Museum (p107) also has excellent displays.

Some estimates put the current Jewish population of Amsterdam at 30,000, but many are so integrated into Dutch society that they don't consider themselves distinctly Jewish.

POSTWAR RECONSTRUCTION

The Netherlands faced major concerns in the postwar years both at home and abroad. Domestically, it had to restore its money-making businesses while rebuilding the battered infrastructure. It concentrated

1953	1958
Great floods in Zeeland	Delta Project launched

on its old speciality: trade. The Dutch shipping industry and the Port of Rotterdam expanded their role in transporting goods. The discovery of large natural gas fields in the North Sea off the Dutch coast brought new wealth, while Dutch farmers became among the most productive in Europe. As the economy grew, social programmes were expanded by the liberal governments. Retirement ages were lowered, benefits increased and health care improved.

Overseas, the colonies began to clamour for independence. The Dutch East Indies, occupied by the Japanese during the war, declared itself independent in 1945. After four years of bitter fighting and negotiations, the independence of Indonesia was recognised at the end of 1949. Surinam became independent in 1975, and the Netherlands Antilles decided to remain part of the Kingdom of the Netherlands while retaining autonomous control of its government.

The same social upheavals that swept the world in the 1960s were also felt in the Netherlands. Students, labour groups, hippies and more took to the streets in protest. Among the more colourful were a group that came to be known as the Provos (p32).

The marriage of Princess Beatrix (now Queen) to Claus von Amsberg provoked a huge outcry from some Dutch because he was a German. A huge squatters' movement sprung up in Amsterdam in the 1960s and lasted for more than two decades. Homeless groups took over empty buildings – many of which had once belonged to Jews – and refused to leave.

The Dutch attitudes of tolerance toward drugs and homosexuals emerged in the 1960s and 1970s. The country's drug policy grew out of practical considerations of the time, when a flood of young people populated Amsterdam and made the policing of drug laws impracticable. Official government policy became supportive of homosexuals, who are able to live openly in Dutch cities.

Queen Beatrix ascended the throne in 1980 after her mother Juliana abdicated (as did her mother, Wilhelmina, before her). Beatrix hasn't indicated how long she will remain on the job, but in all likelihood she will pass the reins to her son, Prince Willem-Alexander, within the next decade.

All governments since 1945 have been coalitions, with parties differing mainly over economic policies. However, coalitions shift constantly based on the political climate and in recent years, there has been winds of change (see Fortuyn's Legacy, p33). The most recent election in January 2003 saw the CDA (Christian Democratic Appeal) return as the largest party, with the boyish Jan Peter Balkenende as prime minister in a shaky coalition with the VVD liberals and D66 democrats. Balkenende sees himself as a champion of traditional norms and values, but little action was taken in the first part of his tenure due to coalition squabbles – indeed, it took five months after the 2003 election just to form a cabinet. The biggest task has been to prune the welfare state and despite fierce opposition from unions and interest groups, the government has pushed through massive budget cuts. The fat years are definitely over.

The Dutch are, broadly speaking, enthusiastic supporters of European integration. The launch of the single European currency, the euro, in 2002 went off with hardly a hitch in the Netherlands, although quite a few Dutch still think in good ol' guilders.

The *Collapse of Colonial Society: The Dutch in Indonesia during the Second World War,* by Louis de Jong, is a seminal work based on interviews with Dutch civilians and prisoners of war under the Japanese occupation.

Amsterdam, by Geert Mak, offers revelations, potted dramas, and a perceptive analysis of the cultural revolution that swept the city from the mid-1960s.

A Dutch Miracle by Jelle Visser and Anton Hemerijck, highlights the nitty-gritty behind Dutch economic success into the 1990s, focusing on jobs, the welfare state and corporate governance.

1965	**1980**
Height of Provo happenings in Amsterdam	Queen Beatrix ascends throne

THE PROVOS

The 1960s were famous for a general shake-up of authority, and in the Netherlands this task fell to the Provos. Their core was a small group of anarchic individuals who staged street 'happenings' or creative, playful provocations (hence the name). Exaggerated police reprisals made the general public even more uneasy about the established order.

In 1962 an Amsterdam window cleaner and self-professed sorcerer, Robert Jasper Grootveld, began to deface cigarette billboards with a huge letter 'K' for *kanker* (cancer) to expose the role of advertising in addictive consumerism. He held get-togethers in his garage, dressed as a medicine man and chanted mantras against cigarette smoking (but under the influence of pot).

This attracted even more bizarre characters. Poet 'Johnny the Selfkicker' bombarded his audience with frenzied, stream-of-consciousness recitals. Bart Huges drilled a hole in his forehead – a so-called 'third eye' – to relieve pressure on the brain and expand his consciousness.

In the summer of 1965 crowds gathered at the Lieverdje (Little Darling) on Amsterdam's Spui (p101), the statuette of a street-brat donated to the city by a cigarette company. The police, unsure of how to deal with excited youngsters chanting slogans around 'medicine man' Grootveld, responded with the baton and arbitrary arrests.

Soon it seemed the whole country joined in the heated debate about the Provo movement. Many older people could not understand how the authorities had so completely lost the plot.

In the mid-1960s the Provos unveiled many pro-environment schemes including the famous White Bicycle Plan to ease traffic congestion with a fleet of free white bicycles. Before the movement dissolved in the 1970s it left a lasting legacy: the squatters' movement, which encouraged the poor to occupy uninhabited buildings and in turn, forced the government to adopt measures to help underprivileged tenants.

GOVERNMENT & POLITICS

The Netherlands is a constitutional monarchy headed today by Queen Beatrix. The current prime minister is Jan Peter Balkenende. The constitution of the Netherlands dates from 1814. The document grants the monarch some official powers that, although primarily ceremonial, can exert some genuine influence on government. This has led to some minor friction between Queen Beatrix and successive governments.

www.koninklijkhuis.nl
Official website of the Dutch royal family features mini-biographies and virtual tours of the palaces.

Parliament is officially known as Staten-General (States-General) and consists of two houses: the First Chamber, which has 75 members elected by the province councils, and the more important Second Chamber, which has 150 members who are directly elected by the populace every four years. Like the US Senate or Britain's Upper House of Parliament, the First Chamber may not propose or modify legislation but can approve or reject it. The constitution also provides for a High Council of State.

The main parties are the conservative Christian Democratic Appeal (CDA), the liberal-centrist parties including the Labour Party (PvdA), the People's Party for Freedom and Democracy (VVD) and Democrats 66 (D66), and the socialist-ecologist Green Left Party. There are also couple of dozen tiny parties with few or no seats in parliament, including the Marxist-Leninist party Rode Morgen and the ever-hopeful Bonaparte Party of the Netherlands, which takes its inspirations from the first French republic.

The country consists of 12 provinces. The newest, Flevoland, only came into existence in 1967 after it had been claimed from the sea. The

1988	2001
Netherlands wins the European football championships	First edition of Lonely Planet's *Netherlands*

province of Holland was split into Noord Holland (North Holland) and Zuid Holland (South Holland) during the Napoleonic era. The Catholic population lives mainly in the southeastern provinces of Noord Brabant and Limburg. The province of Zeeland gave New Zealand its name (and Australia used to be known as New Holland).

ECONOMY

The Netherlands has an extraordinarly strong economy for its size. It's a leader in service industries such as banking, electronics (Philips) and multimedia (Polygram), and has a highly developed horticultural industry dealing in bulbs and cut flowers. Agriculture plays an important role, particularly dairy farming and glasshouse fruits and vegetables. Rotterdam harbour handles the largest shipping tonnage in the world, a vital facility in a country that provides more than one-third of Europe's shipping and trucking. Large supplies of natural gas are tapped and refined on the northeast coasts.

The Dutch economic locomotive has come off the rails in recent years, sliding into recession in 2001 and again in 2003. Only a slight rebound is expected in the foreseeable future. Dutch business is largely dependent

---

FORTUYN'S LEGACY

The Netherlands has famously relied on consensus politics to deliver social justice and prosperity. But the status quo came to a crashing halt with the meteoric rise of Pim Fortuyn (pronounced fore-*town*) and his LPF (Lijst Pim Fortuyn) party in 2002.

During his five-month career, the ex-university professor rebuked the traditional parties for being lax on crime; for letting too many immigrants into the country, and for allowing them to stay without learning the language or integrating. Fortuyn declared that the Netherlands was 'full' and that the government should put the needs of mainstream Dutch people first. He rubbished the ruling coalition of the time, led by Wim Kok's labour party PvdA, the liberal VVD and the democrats D66.

Fortuyn's solution? Do away with back-room politics, he said, and elect a government led by business people and visionaries. After years of glacial government (where plans were checked and rechecked incessantly), Fortuyn's dynamism instantly struck a chord in Dutch society.

Thousands of white, low-income earners in Rotterdam and other cities rallied round the gay, dandyish Pim. For a few fleeting months he was fêted as the next prime minister, even though his opponents accused him of pursuing right-wing, racist policies like those of France's Jean-Marie Le Pen.

The charismatic Fortuyn was shot dead by an assassin – a white animal-rights activist – just days before the general election in May 2002. The news sent a seismic jolt through the country. Riots erupted in front of parliament, and for a brief instant the threat of anarchy hung in the air.

The LPF party was included in the next coalition, but a single figure was lacking to unite his followers. Bickering among the LPF's top ministers brought down the coalition in just 87 days. In the January 2003 general election, voters all but deserted the LPF and returned to the traditional parties.

What remains of Fortuyn's legacy? Some Dutch fear he opened a pandora's box of intolerance towards foreigners, and the reverberations are still being felt. But while a social rethink was arguably overdue, it's worth recalling that Dutch open-mindedness towards newcomers goes back for centuries.

2002	**2002**
Euro is adopted	Crown Prince Willem-Alexander weds Argentina's Máxima Zorreguieta

on exports and has been caught in a larger downturn in Europe and the USA.

This is a big change from the heady 1990s, when the Dutch economy was the envy of Europe. Growth averaged over 3% a year during that decade, with unemployment and annual inflation well under the 3% mark. The country's long experience in international trade mean the Dutch will be quick to catch the next global upturn.

One peculiarity of the Dutch economy is its reliance on short-term contracts. These mean the workforce stays flexible and can move from a dying industry to a growing one fairly easily. Social stability is assured by the welfare net for those caught between jobs.

Ajax, The Dutch, The War by Simon Kuper offers an investigation into how Ajax can be considered a Jewish team and Dutch obsessions with football during WWII and in general.

2002	2003
Politician Pim Fortuyn is shot dead	The population of the Netherlands is 16.2 million

The Culture

THE NATIONAL PSYCHE

It may sound like a cliché, but the Dutch are passionately liberal and believe that people should be free to do whatever they want so long it doesn't inconvenience others. The most outrageous conduct in public might go without comment, bringing to mind the Dutch saying 'Act normal, that's crazy enough'. It's hard to appreciate it until you've been there.

Calvinist traditions have had an influence on the Dutch character, even among those people who are Catholic. The Dutch see themselves as sober, hard working, level-headed and to a certain extent unable to enjoy themselves without feeling guilty – all traits that they blame on their Calvinist background. They also have a moralistic streak, and a tendency to wag the finger in disapproval. You'll feel this less in the good-time Catholic south around Maastricht than in the north, and these attitudes are slowly fading anyway in the younger generation. There may be no trace whatsoever in crowded pubs, which can seem downright hedonistic.

The country is crowded and Dutch people tend to be reserved with strangers. On the trains, you'll notice that passengers sit to maintain the greatest distance between each other. The Dutch treasure their privacy because it is such a rare commodity. Still, they're far from antisocial – their inbred *gezelligheid* (convivality) will come out at the drop of a hat. Expect chummy moments at the supermarket.

The Dutch aren't exactly hot-blooded but given the chance, they will speak their minds and expect to be looked in the eye. This manner may seem blunt or even arrogant to foreigners but the impulse comes from the desire to be direct and, wherever possible, honest.

Subjects such as sex are discussed openly, and you might overhear a pub chat where Jan tells of watching a good TV movie and all the details of whoopie made afterwards. Dutch parliament even held a debate on whether to ban a TV show called 'How to Screw' (but decided not to). Prostitution is legal, but promiscuity is the furthest thing from Dutch minds.

Anyone who's worth their weight in bong water knows that you can easily buy marijuana in the Netherlands. This doesn't mean that every Dutch person is a pothead; on the contrary, only about 5% of the population indulge (less than in France where drug policy is much stricter). Many Dutch people think that hanging out in coffeeshops is for slackers and tourists.

People have a love of detail that defies belief. Statistics on the most trivial subjects make the paper (eg the number of applications for dog licenses, incidences of rubbish being put out early), and somewhere down the line it feeds mountains of bureaucracy. That said, when the system breaks down the Dutch aren't rigid about the rules and are happy to improvise. Historically the Dutch had to juggle the interests of religion and trade, which left a strong legacy of pragmatism.

Last but not least, the Dutch are famously thrifty with their money. They often don't know themselves what to think of this – they laugh at their bottle-scraping (see Good to the Last Scrape on p37) and think it irresponsible, gross even, to throw cash around. At the same time, they don't like being called cheap.

LIFESTYLE

Many Dutch live independent, busy lives divided into strict schedules. Almost everyone carries a diary and it's a mark of prestige to have a full

DOS AND DON'TS

Do give a firm handshake or double cheek-kiss.

Do take a number at the post office counter.

Do show up five to 15 minutes late on social occasions.

Do dress casually unless it's an overtly formal affair.

Do say 'goedendag' when you enter a shop.

Don't smoke dope or drink on the streets.

Don't be late for official appointments.

Don't ask about a person's salary.

Don't forget someone's birthday.

Filofax. Advance notice is usually required for everything, including visits to your mother, and it's not done to just 'pop round' anywhere. Socialising is done mainly in the home, through clubs and circles of old friends, which can make it tough for foreigners to 'break in' at first.

Most Dutch families are small, with two or three children. Rents are high so Junior might live with his family well into his 20s or share an apartment; however, Dutch housing policies have made it easier in recent years to get a mortgage, and many more *yups* (yuppies) buy homes than even a decade ago.

The most important festivals for the family are Christmas and Sinterklaas (p301), when small presents are exchanged complete with poems to accompany each item. If you're invited to join a family party you have crossed a major threshold – the Dutch don't invite just *anybody* into their homes, and chances are you've made a friend for life. Birthdays are celebrated in a big way, with oodles of cake and cries of well-wishing loud enough to wake the dead. If you forget the date of someone's birthday (or even the sister of that someone), or if you forget to make a big fuss on the day, then you've dug your own grave.

The 1990s were good times for the Dutch economy and society is noticeably more affluent than a few years ago – although the Dutch don't flaunt the fact that they now earn more per capita than the Germans. Business is no longer booming but spending for luxury items, especially furniture and interior decor, is jogging along nicely. New cars abound and, apart from the individualists, fewer people chug around in old bombs.

The gay community is so well integrated, and the atmosphere so relaxed in the big cities that it rarely makes headlines as a social topic. After all, leading political figures and businessmen are openly gay or lesbian. Relaxed too are attitudes toward gay or lesbian teachers, clergy, doctors and other professions, even among the older Dutch generation.

COFFEESHOPS

Many establishments that call themselves *koffieshop* (as opposed to *koffiehuis*, espresso bar or sandwich shop) are in the cannabis business, though they do serve coffee. There are also a few hash cafés serving alcohol that are barely distinguishable from pubs.

You'll have no trouble finding a coffeeshop; they're noticeably different and emit sweet fumes over a wide radius. In most cases the hemp leaves have been removed to appease the politicians, but it's a safe bet that an establishment showing palm leaves and perhaps Rastafarian colours (red, yellow and green) will have something to do with cannabis – take a look at the clientele and ask at the bar for menu of goods on offer, usually packaged in small bags for around €15. In some places, like Rotterdam, regulations require you to do your buying in a separate place. Fear not, in any town the staff will clue you in on local regulations.

Space cakes and cookies are sold in a rather low-key fashion, mainly because tourists have had problems. If you're unused to their effects, or the time they can take to kick in and run their course, you could indeed be in for a heavy experience. Ask the staff how much you should take and heed their advice, even if nothing happens after an hour. Many coffeeshops sell magic mushrooms which are quite legal as an untreated, natural product (though its status is challenged from time to time by the authorities).

Cannabis products used to be imported but these days the country has top-notch home produce, so-called *nederwiet* (*nay*-der-weet) developed by diligent horticulturists and grown in greenhouses with up to five harvests a year. Even the police admit it's a superior product, especially the potent 'superskunk' with up to 13% of the active substance THC (Nigerian grass has 5% and Colombian 7%). According to a government-sponsored poll of coffeeshop owners, *nederwiet* has captured over half the market and hash is in decline even among tourists.

GOOD TO THE LAST SCRAPE

Arguably no household item represents Dutch thrift better than the *flessenlikker* (bottle-scraper). This miracle tool culminates in a disk on the business end and can tempt the last elusive smears from a mayonnaise jar or salad-dressing bottle. The *flessenlikker* is a hit in the Netherlands but oddly, not in its country of origin – Norway.

Another item you'll find in Dutch supermarkets is the traditional Grolsch beer bottle with the resealable ceramic cap. This design was first introduced in the Calvinist north where the steely-eyed imbibers considered the contents of a bottle far too much to drink in one sitting.

That age-old chestnut, the weather, always makes fodder for conversation. Evening weather reports merit a timeslot of their own, with presenters waxing lyrical about the size of hailstones or the icicles on Limburg fruit orchards. Rain can last virtually for weeks on end so when the sun comes out, people hit the streets and sidewalks – often just outside their own door. Sitting on the front steps with a cup of coffee and a paper is popular on bright summer mornings, or even when it's just warm and not raining.

POPULATION

The need to love thy neighbour is especially strong in the Netherlands, where the population density is the highest in Europe (475 per sq km). Nearly half of the country's 16 million-plus residents live in the western hoop around Amsterdam, Den Haag and Rotterdam, where the Netherlands' slick motorways slow to a crawl at rush hour. At the other end of the scale, the provinces of Drenthe and Overijssel on the German border and Zeeland in the southwest are sparsely settled, in Dutch terms at least.

Nine-tenths of the population are of Dutch stock. The ethnic communities gather in the cities of the Randstad (rim city) – in fact, perhaps half of Rotterdam's 600,000 residents are immigrants or of foreign descent. People from the former colonies of Indonesia, Surinam and the Dutch Antilles, plus more recent arrivals from Turkey and Morocco, account for about 6% of names on the population register.

SPORT

The Netherlands is one sport-happy country. About two-thirds of all Dutch engage in some form of sporty activity, and the average person now spends 20 minutes more a week getting sweaty than in the 1970s. Sport is organised to a fault: about five million people belong to nearly 30,000 clubs and associations in the Netherlands. It's a very social pastime, but the average Dutchie is starting to break away for more solitary exercise, such as a burst of after-work fitness training or a park jog.

Cycling

To say the Dutch are avid cyclists is a bit of an understatement if you've ever been on their bike paths. In sporting terms there's extensive coverage of races in the media, and you'll see uniformed teams whiz by on practice runs in remote quarters. Joop Zoetemelk pedalled to victory in the 1980 Tour de France after finishing second six times. Going's been tougher for Erik Dekker who has won some stages during the great race. The biggest Dutch wheel-off is the Amstel Gold Race around hilly Limburg in late April. The five-day Tour de Nederland speeds through the Netherlands at the end of August.

DID YOU KNOW?

The Dutch invented the VCR (1974), the compact disc (1980), clock pendulums (1656) and donuts (16th century).

DID YOU KNOW?

The Dutch are the tallest people in Europe.

DID YOU KNOW?

Most Dutch wear wedding bands on their right hands.

Brilliant Orange: the Neurotic Genius of Dutch Football, by David Winner, talks with players and their personal experiences, but also a broader enquiry into what it means to be Dutch, from the colonial era to the multi-cultural present.

www.nocnsf.org.
Website of the Netherlands Olympic Committee/Sport Confederation, including an events calendar and general background on Dutch sports.

Football

The Dutch national game is football (soccer), which is no surprise in the land of legendary players such as Johan Cruyff and Ruud Gullit. Passions for football run so high it's almost scary. The national football association counts a million members, and every weekend teams, professional and amateur, hit pitches across the country. Many pro clubs play in modern, high-tech stadiums such as the Amsterdam ArenA (p112), assisted by a modern, high-tech police force to combat hooligans.

The national football team competes in virtually every World Cup, and 'local' teams such as Ajax, Feyenoord and PSV enjoy international renown. Quite a few clubs have hit a rough patch due to expensive new stadiums and falling sponsorship. Still, the unique Dutch approach to the game – known as 'total football' (in which spatial tactics are analysed and carried out with meticulous precision) – fascinates viewers even when the teams aren't at the top of the league.

Coach Guus Hiddink led the South Korean team to the quarter-finals in the 2002 World Cup, and still enjoys a status akin to sainthood in that country.

Skating

Ice skating is as Dutch as *kroketten* (croquettes; p62), and thousands of people hit the ice when the country's lakes and ditches freeze over. When the lakes aren't frozen, the Netherlands has dozens of ice rinks with Olympic-sized tracks with areas for hockey and figure skating. The most famous amateur event is Friesland's 220km-long Elfstedentocht (see A Day at the Races, p242), won in 1997 by a market gardener, Henk Angenent.

Amsterdam's main ice rink was named after Jaap Eden, a legend around 1900. The hero of the hour is Jochem Uytdehaage, celebrated for netting two Olympic gold medals in Salt Lake City in 2002. His native Utrecht was so chuffed that it named a street after 'our Jochie'.

International competitions are held at the Thialf indoor ice stadium in Heerenveen, Friesland.

Swimming

Swimming is the most popular sport when it comes to the raw numbers of practitioners, edging out even football and cycling. One-third of all Dutch swim in the pools, lakes or sea, and fancy aquatic complexes have sprung up in many cities to meet demand. Legions of famous Dutch swimmers have made sporting history since Rie Mastenbroek's splash at the 1936 Berlin Olympics. Today's top amphibian is Sydney-2000 Olympic gold medallist Inge de Bruin, queen of freestyle and butterfly.

Tennis

DID YOU KNOW?
Burgundian duke Philip the Good most likely invented the tennis racket in Holland around 1500.

Tennis has been incredibly popular since Richard Krajicek fell to his knees after clinching the 1996 Wimbledon final. The national tennis club is the country's second largest after football, and many people book time on courts in all-weather sports halls. Krajicek has hung up his racket but there's fresh blood on the circuit like Sjeng Schalken and Martin Verkerk, a finalist at the 2003 French Open.

Other Sports

Golf is the fastest-growing sport with about 170,000 members out on the links every year. The Dutch volleyball team won gold at the Sydney Olympics in 2000. Darts has gained an enthusiastic audience following the victories of Raymond van Barneveld, three times world champion. Also, the Netherlands has long had the world's foremost water polo league.

Over the centuries a number of sporting games have evolved in the Netherlands, some of them quaint and curious. *Kaatsen* is ancient Frisian handball played on a large grass pitch, and taken deadly seriously in northern towns like Franeker. *Polstokspringen* is rural pole vaulting over the canals, a pastime known in Friesland as *fierljeppen*. *Korfbal*, a cross between netball, volleyball and basketball, enjoys a vibrant scene across the country.

Other popular sports include gymnastics, judo, hockey, showjumping and squash.

MULTICULTURALISM

Through much of the 20th century Dutch society was organised along religious or ideological lines. Each group – Catholic or Protestant, socialist or liberal – had its own clubs or associations that pursued essentially the same goals from different angles. This careful allocation of freedoms minimised friction since each group managed to live more or less independently of, but in harmony with, the others.

This social order was called *verzuiling* (pillarisation). Each persuasion had a pillar that supported the status quo in a general 'agreement to disagree'. This practical set-up began to crumble by the 1960s when the old divisions became largely irrelevant. Pillarisation is regarded as old hat now but evidence can still be seen in the media, education and organisations of all kinds. It also left a strong legacy of tolerance that has become a subject of much debate.

Controls on immigration have been tightened in recent years as the Netherlands began to feel distinctly overcrowded. This is a big change from the 1960s and '70s when the government recruited migrant workers from Turkey, Morocco and Surinam to bridge a labour gap. More than 5% of the population still don't have Dutch nationality.

The gates haven't been slammed shut, but admission is now restricted to a few narrow categories – eg people whose presence serves the 'national interest' or those with compelling humanitarian reasons for getting a residence permit. For prospective immigrants from developing countries, the Netherlands is no longer an easy option.

MEDIA

The Dutch value freedom of expression and the media have an independent, pluralistic character. Newspapers, TV and radio are free to decide on the nature and content of their programmes, and the government is supposed to keep its hands off the press. It is, however, responsible for creating the conditions to keep the media ticking over.

Newspapers & Magazines

There are 32 daily newspapers but the biggest by far is the Amsterdam-based *De Telegraaf,* an untidy, right-wing daily with sensationalist news but a good coverage of finance. The populist *Volkskrant* is a one-time Catholic daily with leftish leanings in its political and economic news. The highly regarded *NRC Handelsblad,* a merger of two elitist papers from Rotterdam and Amsterdam, sets the country's journalistic standards. The *Algemeen Dagblad* is down-to-earth but too thin to plumb the depths. Many Amsterdammers swear by *Het Parool* for the lowdown on the capital's culture and politics. *Het Financieele Dagblad* is the country's leading daily for financial and business news. Many commuters pick up copies of the free *Metro* or *Spits* from train-station racks.

DID YOU KNOW?

Wired magazine started life in Amsterdam as the bimonthly Electric World.

English-speakers can easily find European editions of the *Economist, Newsweek* and *Time,* as well as most of the major international newspapers. The main British newspapers are available the same day, while the *International Herald Tribune* has fairly late news. Some English-language magazines catering to expats including *Roundabout,* with mainstream entertainment listings, and *Expats Magazine,* which serves lifestyle, arts and how-to content to the foreign business community.

Practically every Dutch household subscribes to a daily newspaper. There's a striking lack of sensationalist rags like Britain's *Sun;* readers rely more on the pulp society mags to catch up on celebrity gossip and the Dutch royal family.

The main weekly magazines are *Vrij Nederland, HP/De Tijd* and *Elsevier.* Although their readership is fairly small, they're influential in their news commentary. What the popular magazines may lack in influence they make up for in readership: *Libelle* and *Margriet,* both women's titles, have a whopping circulation of 750,000 and 525,000 respectively. Radio and television guides also sell well.

Radio & TV

www.omroep.nl, in Dutch

Official website of Dutch Public Broadcasting offering news and programming of 20 channels.

The Netherlands first set up a public broadcasting system in the 1920s. In an approach that's all Dutch, the airwaves are divided up in an attempt to give everyone a say, and broadcasts are still linked to social or religious groups. The broadcasting associations – AVRO (general), NCRV (Protestant), VARA (social-democratic), KRO (Catholic), TROS (general), VPRO (progressive), EO (Protestant) and BNN (youth programmes) – all have licenses that are renewed like clockwork. These are full-service channels that provide a range of programmes on the arts, education and entertainment. All of the broadcasting associations work together in the Nederlandse Omroep Stichting (Netherlands Broadcasting Service, NOS; www.nos.nl, in Dutch), which has three channels serving up documentary and current affairs programming. Many commercial stations offer a bland diet of movies, talk shows and pseudo-investigative series, but there's also a Dutch-language MTV. The wide availability of foreign channels – BBC, CNN, Germany's ARD and Belgium's Canvas, among others – offers some alternatives. Political parties are entitled to a share of air time, which becomes abundantly clear in campaign season.

RTL 4 is a commercial broadcaster with daily news, while sister RTL5 also has financial news via its unit RTLZ. SBS6 offers the late-night *Hart van Nederland* (Heart of the Netherlands) show with a brief news bulletin and emotional tales of Dutch home life and current events. Foreign programmes are traditionally broadcast in their original version with subtitles. Visitors may be surprised to find that programmes aren't stuffed to the gills with porn.

The best-known commercial radio stations are Noordzee FM (100.7 FM), Radio 538 (102 FM) and Sky Radio (101.2 FM). RTL has its own frequencies as well alongside Radios 1 through 4 from NOS. All broadcast half-hourly news reports (in Dutch), with Europop and chat sandwiched in between.

RELIGION

The number of former churches that house offices and art galleries is the most obvious sign of today's attitude to religion. Nearly 40% of the Dutch over 18 years of age say they have no religious affiliation. Some 31% are Catholic, 21% are Protestant, 5% are Muslim and the remaining 3% are split among other denominations. Only six out of 10 Dutch go to church on a regular basis.

Freedom of religion is guaranteed by the Constitution of 1848. Church and state are separate, which means that the government does not meddle in the affairs of religious or ideological organisations and vice versa. In any case, the influence of the church has been on the decline since the 1950s. Young people are less likely to adopt the religion of their parents, and secularisation is steadily growing among both Protestants and Catholics.

Although the majority of Dutch people no longer belong to a church, the religious communities still have a big say in society – just tune into Sunday morning TV. But traditional religious dogmas play a limited role in everyday life, as witnessed by the Dutch policy of allowing euthanasia.

Vestiges still exist of a religious border between Protestants and Catholics, a product of the Reformation. The area north of a line running roughly from the province of Zeeland in the southwest to the province of Groningen in the northeast was traditionally Protestant, while south of the frontier communities were predominantly Catholic.

The Protestants divided further into the Reformed movement, various orthodox or liberal denominations as well as the Lutheran church. The Dutch Reformed Church is known for its liberal views and is one of the few churches to support same-sex marriage (although it's legal). The term 'Catholic' should be used in preference to 'Roman Catholic' because many Dutch Catholics disagree with the pope on church hierarchy, contraception and abortion.

The Jewish community in the Netherlands dates from the 1600s, when there was an influx of refugees from Spain and Portugal. Many French Huguenots also found refuge in the Netherlands.

Hindus and Muslims began arriving in the mid-20th century from the former Dutch colonies of Indonesia and Surinam and a second wave since the 1960s included immigrants from Morocco and Turkey. The Islamic community has almost doubled in size in the last decade to 920,000, or 5.7% of the population. There are more than 300 mosques.

WOMEN IN THE NETHERLANDS

Dutch women attained the right to vote in 1919, and by the 1970s abortion on demand was paid for by the national health service. Dutch women are a remarkably confident lot; on a social level, equality is taken for granted and women are almost as likely as men to initiate contact with the opposite sex. It's still a different story in the workplace – few women are employed full-time, and fewer still hold positions in senior management.

BOYCOTTING THE EURO-CATHOLICS

All is not well in the coffers of IJsselmuiden, a hamlet in Overijssel not far from Zwolle. Members of the local Reformed Church avoid the euro like the plague, preferring to settle their debts with old-fashioned guilders or by direct debit. The unlikely reason? The church sees European unity as a Catholic conspiracy.

The blue background and the 12 stars of the European flag pay homage to the Catholic Church, says the offended flock. (They point out the Virgin Mary's halo also had 12 stars.) Rather than handle the new currency, the Reformed might ask their greengrocer for a bill and make a bank transfer by phone. On Sundays, church collection bags are filled with guilders horded for that very purpose.

The boycott goes beyond the euro, however. Vehicle plates in the Netherlands bear the tiny EU halo above the letters 'NL', but pious locals in IJsselmuiden cover them with stickers.

The EU explains that the number 12 was 'traditionally the symbol of perfection, completeness and unity', and there are certainly no plans to change the flag. The stars, incidentally, have nothing to do with how many countries belong to the economic bloc.

ARTS

The arts flourished in the Netherlands long before Rembrandt put brush to canvas. The country takes great pride in its world-class museums, the variety of classical and innovative music, and the many theatre productions staged every season. It always seems like there's room for another arts festival, and the variety boggles the mind.

Dance

The Netherlands is a world leader in modern dance. The troupe of the Nederlands Dans Theater in Den Haag, under the artistic direction of Jiri Kylian, leaps and pirouettes to international audiences. There are also many smaller modern dance companies such as Introdans, which can truly be described as poetry in motion.

Originally for youth audiences, Rotterdam's Scapino Ballet has built up a wide repertoire of contemporary dance in recent years. The city's Dansacadamie (the nation's largest dance school) has hired William Forsythe, a high-powered choreographer, to help shape its programme. The National Ballet in Amsterdam performs mainly classical ballets but also presents 20th-century works by Dutch choreographers such as Rudi van Dantzig or Toer van Schayk. The Ballet has helped launch careers of promising dance masters like John Wisman or Ted Brandsen (the latter is now artistic director). The biennial Holland Dance Festival in Den Haag lures some of the world's most sophisticated productions.

The tango has caught on again since Argentinian-born Máxima married into the Dutch royal family. Dance schools are now as likely to offer salsa and tango courses as break or ballroom dancing.

Painting

The Netherlands has spawned a realm of famous painters starting with Hieronymous Bosch whose 15th-century religious works are charged with fear, distorted creatures and agonised people. Rembrandt, with his use of light and shadow, created shimmering religious scenes and led the historic artists of the golden age. Frans Hals and Jan Vermeer were the contemporary masters of portraiture and daily life scenes, two revolutionary themes which became popular due to the decline in the influence of the church as patron of the arts. Although Vincent Van Gogh spent much of his life in Belgium and France, he is very much claimed by the Dutch as one of their own (see Vincent van Gogh, p44). His early works, including the dour *Potato Eaters*, were painted in his homeland, but the later impressionistic works were greatly influenced by French artists.

DE STIJL & BEYOND

An Amersfoort-born painter named Piet Mondriaan changed the direction of 20th century art when he introduced the cubist De Stijl movement in 1917. De Stijl aimed to harmonise all the arts by returning artistic expression to its essence, and the artist – who changed the spelling to 'Mondrian' after moving to Paris – did this by reducing shapes to horizontal and vertical lines. His paintings came to consist of bold rectangular patterns using only a handful of colours, a style known as neoplasticism. The moving ode to the USA entitled *Victory Boogie Woogie* is considered the flagship work of the genre. Amsterdam's Stedelijk Museum has other examples on display such as *Composition with Red, Black, Blue, Yellow & Grey*. The movement influenced a generation of sculptors and designers such as Gerrit Rietveld, who planned the Van Gogh Museum and other buildings along De Stijl lines.

www.ndt.nl.

Performance agenda of the Nederlands Dans Theater as well as details of the troupes, productions and reviews.

The *Golden Age: Dutch Painters of the 17th Century* by Bob Haak. Weighty 500-page tome with beautiful illustrations and inciteful analysis, even for layfolk.

Dutch Painting by Rudolf Fuchs spans the history of Western canvases from the Middle Ages right up to the present. The author casts a critical light on famous works and explains their finer points, down to the use of particular symbols.

REMBRANDT

Painting is the grandchild of nature. It is related to God.

Rembrandt van Rijn

The son of a miller, Rembrandt van Rijn (1606–69) was the greatest and most versatile of all 17th-century artists. In some respects Rembrandt was centuries ahead of his time, as shown by the emotive brushwork of his later works.

Rembrandt grew up in Leiden where he became good at chiaroscuro, the technique of creating depth through light and darkness. In 1631 he moved to Amsterdam to run a painting studio, where he and his staff churned out scores of profitable portraits such as the *Anatomy Lesson of Dr Tulp*. He married the studio owner's niece, Saskia Van Uylenburgh.

After Rembrandt fell out with his boss he bought the house next door, now the Rembrandthuis in Amsterdam. Here he set up his own studio, employing staff in a warehouse in Amsterdam's Jordaan to cope with the demand for 'Rembrandts'. His paintings became all the rage and the studio became the largest in Holland, despite his gruff manners and open agnosticism.

As one of the city's main art collectors Rembrandt often sketched and painted for himself. Amsterdam's Jewish residents acted as models for dramatic biblical scenes.

Business went downhill after Saskia died in 1642. Rembrandt's innovative group portrait, the *Nightwatch*, may have won over the art critics – but his subjects had all paid good money and some were unhappy to appear in the background. The artist's love affairs and lavish lifestyle marred his reputation, and he eventually went bankrupt. His house and art collection were sold and, with the debtors breathing down his neck, Rembrandt took a modest abode on the Jordaan's Rozengracht.

The master continued to paint, draw and etch; on occasion he still got commissions. He painted the monumental *Conspiracy of Claudius Civilis* for the new city hall, but the authorities disliked the political undertones and had it removed. In 1662 he completed the *Staalmeesters* (the Syndics) for the drapers' guild and ensured that everybody remained clearly visible, but it would be his last group portrait.

Works of his later period show that Rembrandt lost none of his touch. No longer constrained by the wishes of wealthy clients, he explored the unconventional while keeping in tune with his subjects – *A Couple: the Jewish Bride* is a good example. His many evocative portraits are milestones in the history of art.

Rembrandt ended life a broken man. An outbreak of the plague claimed his maid-companion Hendrickje, and son Titus died in 1668, just married and aged 27. The painter himself passed a year later, nearly forgotten by the high society he once served.

The last century also saw the perplexing designs of MC Escher, whose impossible images continue to fascinate to this day. A waterfall feeds itself, people go up and down a staircase that ends where it starts, a pair of hands draw each other. He was also a master of organic tile patterns that feed into one another while subtly changing the picture into something else.

After WWII, artists rebelled against artistic conventions and vented their rage in abstract expressionism, the more furious the better. Karel Appel and Constant drew on styles pioneered by other European artists, exploiting bright colours to produce works that leapt off the canvas. In Paris, they met up with Asger Jornand and the Belgian Corneille and together these artists formed the CoBrA group (Copenhagen, Brussels and Amsterdam).

Other schools of the prewar period included the Bergen School, with the expressive realism of Charley Toorop who became one of the exponents of Dutch surrealism.

VINCENT VAN GOGH

I dream of painting and then I paint my dream.

Vincent van Gogh

Without a doubt the greatest 19th-century Dutch painter was Vincent Van Gogh (1853–90), a one-time clerk, schoolteacher and missionary who redrew the artistic map in a short, astonishingly productive career that ended in insanity. His striking use of colour, coarse brushwork and layered contours put him in a league all his own, yet his work was hardly appreciated during his lifetime.

Born in Zundert near the Belgian border, the young Van Gogh started off in his uncle's art dealership in 1869, and was transferred to London. After an unhappy love affair he became unreliable and was fired, but returned to England as an unpaid teacher. The urban squalor he saw awakened a desire to help his fellow men, and Van Gogh trained as a clergyman only to abandon his studies in 1878. Next he became a missionary in a depressed coal-mining district of Belgium, but was dismissed because of his literal interpretations of the Bible.

Around 1880 he decided that art was his true calling and threw himself into it with abandon. Although he often suffered from extreme poverty, his output in his 10 remaining years was staggering: about 800 paintings and a similar number of drawings.

During the first part of his life, Van Gogh lived in locations including Brussels, Den Haag, Antwerp and Drenthe, and scenes from these places reappear in some works. In the Low Countries his paintings were dark and heavy, the most famous example being the *Potato Eaters* (1885). But shortly thereafter he moved to Paris to live with his brother Theo, who worked in a gallery. It was there that Van Gogh met impressionists such as Pissarro, Degas, Gauguin and Toulouse-Lautrec, and the Dutchman's painting was transformed. Out went the gritty social realism; in came blazing flowers, portraits and the wide-open spaces of Paris.

Van Gogh moved to Arles in 1888. During this time he sold no pictures, was skint and suffered nervous attacks with hallucinations and depression. He was enthusiastic about founding an artists' cooperative at Arles, where he was joined by Gauguin. But the two quarreled and the sensitive Van Gogh was plunged into another crisis, cutting off part of his left ear in his despair.

In 1889 he checked into an asylum at St Rémy near Arles. Still he continued to work, producing vibrant pictures such as *Starry Night*. Theo married and in 1890 Vincent moved to Auvers-sur-Oise to be near him, lodging with the physician Dr Paul Gachet. Another burst of activity followed: during the last 70 days of his life he painted on average one canvas a day. But his spiritual anguish and depression became more acute, and on 27 July 1890 he shot himself. The suicide was botched, and the tortured artist hung on for two days before dying in Theo's arms.

Much of his work was left in the care of Theo's son who put it on permanent exhibition in Amsterdam's Stedelijk Museum. When the Van Gogh Foundation was created in 1960, it built the Van Gogh Museum (p109). Although some works hang in galleries from New York to Moscow, a significant number can be viewed in the Dutch capital and at the Kröller-Müller Museum (p276).

During his life Van Gogh sold only one painting, the *Red Vineyard at Arles* (Pushkin Museum, Moscow), and for the most part was penniless and dependent on Theo's handouts. Nowadays a single Van Gogh might sell for US$50 million or more – meaning that his entire body of work is probably worth several billion dollars.

Contemporary Dutch artists are usually well represented at international events such as the Biennale in Venice and the Documenta in Kassel. The ranks of distinguished contemporary artists includes Jan Dibbets, Ger van Elk, Marthe Röling and Marlene Dumas.

Simplicity, clarity and austerity are the hallmarks of Dutch design. From the 1920s onward designers such as Mondriaan, but also Theo van Doesburg and Gerrit Rietveld greatly influenced the art scene. Visitors to the Netherlands can't help but see a designer's hand in a variety of everyday objects, from postage stamps to waste bins, traffic signs and even trains. Form does not always follow function, however – the chic luggage racks on those same trains don't hold much luggage.

Music

The Netherlands has contributed little to the world's music heritage. This can be conveniently blamed on the dour Calvinists of the 17th century, who dismissed music as frivolous. All the Calvinists liked was church organ music because it kept people out of pubs.

Despite this inauspicious start, the music scene in the Netherlands is blisteringly good. Dutch musicians excel in classical music, techno/dance and jazz, and the high level of music appreciation means there's a steady stream of touring talent. The scene in college towns such as Leiden and Groningen is especially electric.

CLASSICAL MUSIC

The Netherlands has many orchestras based in cities throughout the country. Den Haag, Rotterdam and Maastricht have a full calendar of performances by local orchestras and groups, but Amsterdam's Royal Concertgebouw Orchestra towers over them all. It frequently performs abroad, mixing and matching works by famous composers with little-known gems of the modern era. In autumn 2004 its long-serving conductor, Riccardo Chailly, will pass the baton to Mariss Jansons, a stellar talent whose credentials stretch from Riga to Pittsburgh via Munich.

The Orchestra of the 18th Century and the Amsterdam Baroque Orchestra are well-known smaller ensembles for old music. The classics of Bach, Händel and Vivaldi are always in sensitive hands at the Combattimento Consort Amsterdam.

The Dutch have many fine classical musicians. Among pianists, Wibi Soerjadi is one of the most successful and specialises in romantic works. Like many classical instrumentalists Soerjadi studied at Amsterdam's prestigious Sweelinck Conservatory. Halls are always filled for Ronald Brautigam, a grand master and winner of a host of accolades including the Dutch national music prize.

Top violinists include Isabelle van Keulen, who often collaborates with Brautigam. An engaging personality of seemingly endless vitality, van Keulen has founded her own chamber music festival in Delft.

Cellists of note include Quirine Viersen, a powerful, intense soloist who won the International Cello Competition in Paris. The fiery bowing of Pieter Wispelwey from Leiden thrills audiences around the world.

In the voice department there's no diva greater than soprano Charlotte Margiono, who pretty much wrote the book on interpretation in *Le Nozze di Figaro,* the *Magic Flute* and other classics. Mezzo-soprano Jard van Nes has a giant reputation for her solo parts in Mahler's symphonies.

Modern Dutch composers include Louis Andriessen, Theo Loevendie, Klaas de Vries and the late Ton de Leeuw. Many of their works are forays into the uncharted waters of experimental music, and nowhere is the sense of adventure more tangible than in Amsterdam. Look out for The Trio, Asko Ensemble, Nieuw Ensemble and, last but not least, the Schönberg Ensemble conducted by Reinbert de Leeuw. These performers often appear in Amsterdam's IJsbreker music hall.

Opera flourishes in the Netherlands. The Netherlands Opera stages about 10 world-class performances a year at its home, Amsterdam's Muziektheater (p106). Contemporary opera forms an important part of the repertoire, and inevitably stirs up a lot of controversy.

Dear Theo: The Autobiography of Vincent Van Gogh is a fascinating study of the artist's troubled life through his own letters to his brother. Provides general insights into the creative process, if not your own.

www.rijksmuseum.nl.

Exhibition dates, key collection photos and updates of construction work at Amsterdam's Rijksmuseum.

www.concertgebouw.nl.

Schedule and ticket information for the Concertgebouw halls and its resident orchestras in Amsterdam.

The *Essential Guide to Dutch Music: 100 Composers and Their Music*, edited by Jolande van der Klis. Like the label says, a survey of 100 notable Dutch note-writers.

New Dutch Swing, by Kevin Whitehead, explores the 'alternative musical universe' where improvisers and composers band together to create a distinctive sound. With critical evaluations of key recordings and club and concert dates.

www.northseajazz.nl. Concert calendar, news and box office details for the North Sea Jazz Festival held in Den Haag every July.

JAZZ

In the past the Netherlands hasn't bred oodles of jazz talent. However, the phenomenal success of the North Sea Jazz Festival has sown some powerful seeds, and the Dutch jazz scene can now stand on its own two feet. Europe's largest jazzfest, the NSFJ is held in Den Haag every summer. Amsterdam's leading jazz club, Bimhuis (p129), has an concert agenda that's all quality.

The Netherlands has fostered some gifted jazz singers. Familiar to Dutch audiences for decades, the honeyed voice of Denise Jannah finally caught the attention of Blue Note in the 1990s. Her repertoire is American standards with touches of her Surinamese homeland.

Originally a jazz and cabaret vocalist, Astrid Seriese now captures a wider public with a variety of styles, from lyrical Cole Porter to rock and soundtracks for documentaries. Soulful Carmen Gomez is as comfortable singing Aretha Franklin as Ella Fitzgerald tunes. Fleurine is another gifted young chanteuse.

Dutch saxophone romped onto the international stage thanks to Hans and Candy Dulfer, father and daughter of the reeds. On alto sax, Candy is a known commidity thanks to her funky performances with Prince, Van Morrison, Dave Stewart, Pink Floyd and many others. Hans blows jazz standards but also incorporates hip-hop and other genres.

A great soloist on flute is Peter Guidi, who set up the jazz programme at the Muziekschool Amsterdam and leads its Jazzmania big band.

Born in Amsterdam's Jordaan district, trumpeter Saskia Laroo mixes jazz with dance and has been able to 'play for the people while still being innovative', as a critic put it. She leads a number of acts including Smoothgroovy BreakBeats with HotLicks.

For top-rate jazz piano, pick up a CD of Michiel Borstlap, a winner of the Thelonius Monk award who has recorded with Peter Erskine, Toots Thielemans, Ernie Watts and many others. His soul and label mate is bass player Hein van de Geyn.

On guitar, Jesse van Ruller's effortless playing is the stuff of complex refinement, especially on up-tempo pieces. He snagged the Thelonius Monk award in 1996, like Borstlap.

Big band leaders such as Willem Breuker and Willem van Manen (of Contraband) straddle modern classical and improvised music, an acquired taste for some audiences. The XLJazz Orkest, a new big band with strings conducted by composer-arranger Gerrit Jan Brinkhorst, brings together established pros and hungry young blowers.

POP, ROCK & DANCE

Amsterdam is the pop capital of the Netherlands, and bands and DJs are attracted to the city like moths to the flame. If successful they usually jump on a plane to London or Los Angeles, as the Dutch themselves lament.

In the sixties Amsterdam was the hub of counter-culture but the epicentre of pop was in Den Haag. The Scheveningse Boulevard was the place to see bands like Shocking Blue in full view of Veronica, the radio station that broadcast tunes from a harbour ship. In 1969 Golden Earring's *Eight Miles High* album went gold in the USA.

The seventies brought a few more Dutch hits internationally. In 1973 Jan Akkerman's progressive rock band, Focus, conquered the charts with Thijs van Leer as chief yodeller. Herman Brood burst onto the scene with *His Wild Romance* and became a real-life, druggy, self-absorbed rock star.

The squatters' movement spawned a lively punk scene, followed by the manic synthesisers of New Wave. By the mid-1980s Amsterdam became a magnet for guitar-driven rock bands such as Claw Boys Claw, dyed-in-the-wool garage rockers. Most vocalists stuck to lyrics in English but the pop group Doe Maar broke through in Dutch, inspiring scores of bands such as Tröckener Kecks. Around this time Amsterdam also evolved into a capital of club music – house, techno and R&B, with its spiritual base at the überclub Roxy (which later burnt to a crisp).

Dutch bands were power-boosted by the 1991 introduction of commercial radio. In the early 1990s the best known Dutch variant of house was gabber, where the number of beats per minute was lifted beyond belief by groups like Charly Lownoise & Mental Theo. The hip grooves of Candy Dulfer (see Jazz, p46) and the hip-hoppy Urban Dance Squad made America's Top 20 during the decade. Bettie Serveert, a nod to Dutch tennis player Betty Stöve, grew into one of the biggest bands on the club circuit. Amsterdam hip-hop was spearheaded by the Osdorp Posse who rap in their mother tongue.

In 2001 a moody Herman Brood flung himself from the roof of the Amsterdam Hilton, triggering a run on his records and paintings. After his death, the remake *My Way* became Brood's first (and last) No 1 hit in the Netherlands.

The airwaves often seem to be dominated by generic Dutch pop groups, but there's some interesting stuff going on in the clubs – check the reggae of Beef or the Amsterdam Klezmer Band. K-Otic is a preppy vocals-and-guitar outfit created in a star-making stunt organised by several record companies.

Raves are organised at Amsterdam clubs such as Mazzo and Escape. The Dutch have a major presence in the world DJ rankings, most of them big-room clubhouse and trance artists that have appeared in the US and Britain. Tiësto is the undisputed trancemeister, and other top DJs include Armin van Buuren and Ferry Corsten.

Pop festivals come out of the woodwork in the warmer months – Pinkpop in Landgraaf, Parkpop in Den Haag and Dynamo Open Air at Neunen. Dance Valley near Haarlem pulls over 100 bands and even more DJs to the biggest open-air dancefest in the Benelux – some 40,000 visitors rocked there in 2003. Lowlands is a three-day mega alternative-music fest for happy campers held at Six Flags in Flevoland.

DID YOU KNOW?

Guitar whiz Eddie van Halen is originally from Nijmegen.

WORLD MUSIC

Cosmopolitan Amsterdam offers a wealth of world music. Ronald Snijders, a top jazz flautist from Surinam, often participates in world music projects. Another jazz flautist heading towards 'world' is the eternal Chris Hinze with his album *Tibet Impressions*. Most of his repertoire, however, falls in the New Age category. Fra-Fra-Sound plays paramaribop, a unique mixture of traditional Surinamese kaseko and jazz.

But the bulk of world repertoire from Amsterdam is Latin, ranging from Cuban salsa to Dominican merengue and Argentinean tango. The following bands will give you a taste of the Dutch world scene: Nueva Manteca (salsa), Sexteto Canyengue (tango) and Eric Vaarzon Morel (flamenco). A sparkling Dutch–Brazilian band is Zuco 103, which melds bossa nova and samba with DJ rubs on the turntable.

The New Cool Collective is a big band with vocals that serves up a groovy cocktail of Latin, jazz, New Age and sixties go-go. They usually play at Amsterdam's club Panama once a month.

The Amsterdam Roots Music Festival (p116) of world music takes place in Amsterdam's Oosterpark every June.

Literature

The Netherlands has a rich literary heritage, but its gems used to be reserved for Dutch speakers. Most of its best-known contemporary authors were finally translated into English beginning in the mid-1990s.

In the Middle Ages Dutch literature stuck to epic tales of chivalry and allegories. But that changed in the 16th century with Erasmus, a name familiar to school children across the globe. The leading Dutch humanist wrote a satire on the church and society called *His Praise of Folly.*

The literary lights of the Golden Age included Spinoza, an Amsterdam Jew who wrote deep philosophical treatises. Spinoza rejected the concept of free will, contending that humans acted purely out of self-preservation. Mind and body were made of the same stuff he alternately called God and Nature, which got him into all kinds of trouble.

Vondel is regarded as the Dutch Shakespeare. His best tragedy, *Lucifer,* describes the archangel's rebellion against God. Dutch literature flourished in the 17th century under writers such as Bredero, one of the early comic writers, and Hooft, a veritable multitalent who penned poems, plays and history. The Bible was also translated into Dutch in the 17th century, and the publication of *De Statenbijbel* in 1637 was a milestone in the evolution of the Dutch language.

The novel, as we know, emerged as an important literary form in the 19th century. Post-war literature was dominated by three eminent novelists, Willem Frederik Hermans, Harry Mulisch and Gerard Reve, and the war featured prominently in many works. In recent years they were joined by distinguished writers such as Jan Wolkers, Maarten 't Hart and Frederik van der Heijden, but these offerings are still tough to find in English. Many of these authors have been awarded the PC Hooftprijs, the Dutch national literary prize.

The growing interest in Dutch literature has been no accident. The Dutch Literary Production and Translation Fund began propagating the nation's literature abroad in 1991 and the efforts have paid off. Many titles now appearing in English were already bestsellers in German and other languages.

A survey of Netherlands 'lit' since the 19th century might draw on the following titles, with several by non-Dutch writers thrown in for good measure:

www.nlpvf.nl.

The Dutch Literary Production & Translation Fund site carries news and lists of titles translated into English.

Max Havelaar By Multatuli. An indictment of colonial forced-labour policy in the Dutch East Indies (present-day Indonesia). Multatuli – Latin for 'I have suffered greatly' – was the pen name of Eduard Dekker, a colonial bureaucrat.

Diary of Anne Frank *(Het Dagboek van Anne Frank)* By Anne Frank. A moving account of a young Jewish girl's thoughts while hiding from the occupying Germans. In recent years Frank's words have inspired an entire subculture that re-examines and debates her life and work.

A Dutchman's Slight Adventures *(Een Handvol Kronkels)* By Simon Carmiggelt. Comical Amsterdam vignettes by winner of many literary prizes including the PC Hooftprijs. Many items appeared in Amsterdam paper *Het Parool*. Tricky to find in English.

The Happy Hooker By Xaviera Hollander. An unapologetic, yet upbeat look at the world of the sex worker based on a true story. This classic 1972 novel came out when 'damn' still elicited gasps from the audience.

Parents Worry *(Bezorgde Ouders)* By Gerard Reve. Historical novel about one day in the ravaged life of a poet looking for truth and a way out. Out of print but second-hand copies can still be found.

In a Dark Wood Wandering *(Het Woud der Verwachting)* By Hella Haase. Quirky historical novel set during the Hundred Years War, with a cast of believable characters based on great figures from mad Charles VI to Joan of Arc.

The Following Story *(Het Volgende Verhaal)* By Cees Notenboom. One of Holland's top contemporary Dutch writers presents a short fable of a schoolmaster's journey through memory and imagination in the final seconds of his life.

The Discovery of Heaven *(De Ontdekking van de Hemel)* By Harry Mulisch. Two friends find they were conceived on the same day, and share love, hate and women on an extraordinary quest that takes them to St Peter's gate.

A Heart of Stone *(Een Hart van Steen)* By Renate Dorrestein. A terrifying Gothic-style tale of violence, childhood and madness told from inside the minds of three troubled children of a superficially idyllic family.

First Gray, Then White, Then Blue *(Eerst Grijs, Dan Wit, Dan Blauw)* By Margriet de Moor. A literary tale of passion and deception. An woman appears enigmatically after a two-year absence from her husband, with no explanation or remorse.

The Two Hearts of Kwasi Boachi *(De Zwarte met het Witte Hart)* By Arthur Japin. Novel based on the true story of two West African princes sent to study in Holland in the 1830s, where they excel but fail to fit in.

In Babylon By Marcel Moring. The death (by a call girl) of an 80-year-old scholar brings together a Dutch fairy-tale writer and his niece to muse upon the family's tangled history as clockmakers and refugees.

Amsterdam: A Traveler's Literary Companion Edited by Manfred Wolf. Twenty stories by Amsterdam writers, including Harry Mulisch, Cees Nooteboom, Marga Minco and Bas Heijne, that are arranged by neighbourhood. Accessible even for armchair travellers.

Amsterdam By Ian McEwan. Booker-prize-winning novel about two friends who enter a euthanasia pact, and it soon becomes a matter of who kills whom first.

Widow for One Year By John Irving. Complex, classic Irving tale about three crucial periods in the life of a self-contradictory woman, set partly in the Red Light District.

The Acid House By Irvine Welsh. Short story collection about Amsterdam's drugs underworld. From the author of Trainspotting.

The Coffee Trader By David Liss. Dark novel about a Jewish trader who risks all to bring coffee to 17th-century Amsterdam. Provide uncanny parallels to modern financial markets.

Cinema & TV

The Netherlands has a small film industry that produces around 20 feature films a year, often in association with other countries. Private funding is on the increase since government funding was pruned back in the last few years.

From a historical perspective, one of the most important Dutch directors of all time was Joris Ivens (1898–1989), who made lyrical, Russian-influenced documentaries about social and political issues like the Spanish Civil War and impoverished Belgian miners.

Some modern filmmakers have gained an international audience (see p50). The most successful directors still go to Hollywood, such as Paul Verhoeven of *Robocop* and *Basic Instinct* fame. Jan de Bont is known for action thrillers like *Speed* and *Lara Croft II*. Some artsy documentaries have been produced by Johan van der Keuken.

Leading actors Rutger Hauer, Jeroen Krabbé and Famke Janssen are often not recognised as being Dutch – it's those good English skills again.

Several major film festivals are held every year including the Rotterdam International Film Festival in February, Utrecht's Netherlands Film Festival in September and the International Documentary Film Festival, held in Amsterdam in December. The Filmmuseum in Amsterdam plucks interesting films from its huge archive for regular screenings. Movies are rarely ever dubbed but instead merely subtitled in Dutch – as any film purist will tell you they should be.

Dutch television doesn't travel well with the notable exception of the reality series *Big Brother* that was swiftly copied worldwide. Then again,

www.filmfestival.nl.

Nederlands Film Festival programme with list of winners of the 'Gouden Kalf', the Dutch film prize awarded every October.

there's so much foreign fare that watching TV, you might not feel like you're in the Netherlands at all.

Some films and TV series made in (or about) the Netherlands include:

Abel Alex van Warmerdam, 1986. Comedy of sexual revenge: grown-up son is chucked out of the house and falls in love with his father's mistress. The set is like an off-Broadway play.

Amsterdam Global Village Johan van der Keuken, 1996. A four-hour documentary tracing the roots of the city's ethnic inhabitants to the Third World and back again. Nice street scenes with unaffected chat.

Amsterdamned Dick Maas, 1987. A skin-diving serial killer is chased through Amsterdam's canals by a detective who isn't too fond of water. Essentially a B-grade thriller pepped up by the location.

Antonia's Line *(Antonia)* Marleen Gorris, 1995. A strong-willed Dutch woman recalls life in a colourful village where men become increasingly irrelevant. Won an Academy Award for best foreign film.

The Assault *(De Aanslag)* Fons Rademakers, 1986. A physician spends his adult life investigating why his neighbours betrayed his family in WWII. Also picked up an Oscar.

Character *(Karakter)* Mike van Diem, 1997. A dark, complex drama about an intimidating Rotterdam bailiff who is brutally murdered by his own son. Best foreign film in Hollywood that year.

Diamonds are Forever Guy Hamilton, 1971. Agent 007 careens through the canals of Amsterdam to foil a diamond-smuggling ring, but needs help from blond ice maiden.

Fanfare Bert Haanstra, 1958. Two amateur brass bands vie for a single government grant in a film satire of small-town pretentions of Giethoorn, in the boonies of Northern Overijssel (p270).

Father & Daughter Michael Dudok de Wit, 2000. Charming animation short about parting, the changing of the seasons and the desire to return home. Won an Oscar for the genre.

Floris Paul Verhoeven, 1969. One of the funniest TV series about the Middle Ages, about the adventures of Count Floris in medieval Holland. Sword-wielding Rutger Hauer dons Robin Hood tights.

The Fourth Man *(De Vierde Man)* Paul Verhoeven, 1983. Mr *Basic Instinct* brings us a stylish and violent erotic thriller, with Jeroen Krabbé as a struggling bisexual writer and the intended fourth victim of a sexy knife-wielding blond.

Left Luggage Jeroen Krabbé, 1998. A free-spirited student clashes with her parents, both survivors of the concentration camps, in a study of anti-Semitic attitudes in Antwerp. With Isabella Rosselini.

Turkish Delight *(Turks Fruit)* Paul Verhoeven, 1973. A graphic tale with sensitive moments as pretty-boy sculptor Rutger Hauer goes sex-mad to forget an old lover. Internationally released as *Turkish Delight*, and considered by some as the most successful Dutch film ever.

Photography

The Netherlands has a tradition of photography committed to social themes. The first World Press Photo exhibition was held in Amsterdam in 1975, and the exhibition still opens in the city before touring 80 countries around the globe.

Monografieën van Nederlandse Fotografen, by Focus Publishers. Eleven volumes of images by 11 top Dutch photographers past and present, including Nico Jesse, Piet Zwart, Eva Besnyö and Emmy Andriesse.

Documentary photography is a speciality of the younger generation of Dutch photographers, many of whom focus on people, landscapes and cityscapes. The list of famous shooters is lengthy. The late Ed van der Elksen dug up some weird and wonderful characters in cities such as Paris, Hong Kong and Tokyo as well as Africa. Wubbo de Jong was one of the best photojournalists the Netherlands ever had.

The leading lights of today's scene include Rineke Dijkstra and Marie Cecile Thijs, both noted for their thoughtful portraits of children. Henk Braam is a top docu-shooter. Anton Corbijn is famous for his portraits of artists and celebrities including David Bowie, Gerard Depardieu, Kate Moss, Steven Spielberg, Quentin Tarantino and hundreds of others.

www.nfi.nl.

Details of exhibitions and collections at the Netherlands Photography Institute in Rotterdam.

Excellent collections of photographs are in the archives of Amsterdam's Rijksmuseum, though displays will be limited for the next few years due to the renovations. Other top exhibition spaces are at the Stedelijk Museum in Amsterdam and Print Room at Leiden University.

The Netherlands Photography Institute is in Rotterdam, and private galleries in all the major cities hold exhibitions.

Theatre

The Netherlands has a rich theatrical tradition going back to medieval times. In the Golden Age, when Dutch was the language of trade, companies from the Low Countries toured the theatres of Europe. Some highlights of the era – Vondel's tragedies, Bredero's comedies and Hooft's verses – are still performed today, albeit with a modern voice.

By the end of the 19th century, however, theatre had become downright snobbish.

Development stagnated until the 1960s, when disgruntled actors began to throw tomatoes at their older colleagues and engaged the audience in discussion. Avant-garde theatre companies such as Mickery and Shaffy made Amsterdam a centre for experimental theatre, and many smaller companies sprang up in their wake.

There are many professional theatre companies, including traditional repertory companies and smaller companies who are exploring new avenues of theatre, often combining music, mime and new media techniques. The language barrier is, of course, an issue with Dutch productions, though with some it's hardly relevant. English-language companies often visit Amsterdam, especially in summer.

When it's not touring abroad, De Dogtroep stages fancy and unpredictable 'happenings' in quirky venues like an Utrecht archeological dig or Amsterdam's ship passenger terminal. Each show is supported by flashy multimedia effects and technical gadgetry, with every set specially developed by a team of designers and painters. The group started off by performing in squat buildings but it's now gone seriously mainstream. A spin-off of Dogtroep, Warner & Consorten is a variation on the same theme, staging dialogue-free shows that inject humour into everyday situations and objects, while music is generated with weird materials.

Semi-bilingual Amsterdam has lured English-language outfits like Boom Chicago for fast-paced comedy (see Chicago Comedy is Booming, p127). Glitzy large-budget musicals in the *Miss Saigon* mould have won over audiences in recent years. Productions such as *Chicago* and *Mama Mia* play to full houses, with little popularity lost in the tricky Dutch translations.

The Netherlands Theatre Institute helps to promote the performing arts and operates a museum and information centre (see Theatermuseum, p101). Highlights of the Dutch theatre season are performed at the Nederlands Theaterfestival in Amsterdam at the end of August. Other events such as Over Het IJ in Amsterdam keep the contemporary spirit alive, but for a much edgier affair check out Robodock, held at Rotterdam's former ADM shipyards for five days in late September. The shows are driven by feuding robots, ameobic screen projections and choreographed pyrotechnics.

www.tin.nl.

The Theater Instituut Nederland site has a database of all productions since 1945 plus an events listing of the Theater Museum in Amsterdam.

Environment

The Dutch environment has been under strain since humans began tinkering with the landscape almost two millennia ago. Whether it's from pollution, deforestation or flooding, the cumulative dangers to natural and man-made environments are arguably greater than ever. Nearly one-third of the country's surface is devoted to agriculture while much of the rest serves towns and industry.

Lush green pastures and peaceful canals belie the fact that acid, nitrate and phosphate levels in the biosphere here are the highest in Europe. Water in the great European rivers Rijn (Rhine), Maas and Schelde (Scheldt) carry pollutants through the Netherlands and into the North Sea. Sea barriers or no, the coastal situation of low-lying lands means that soil salination is a persistent problem.

In the late 20th century Dutch awareness of the environment grew by leaps and bounds. Citizens now dutifully sort their rubbish, support pro-bicycle schemes, and protest over scores of projects of potential detriment – even the air miles offered at supermarket tills. City-centre congestion has been eased by cutting parking spaces, erecting speed bumps and initiating park-and-ride programs. Country roads tend to favour bike lanes at the cost of motor vehicles.

Water management is taken very seriously. Billions spent on sewage treatment means that Amsterdam's once notorious canals are fairly clean – although you probably wouldn't want to take a sip. Agriculture and industry have been presented with mandatory goals to reduce run-off and pollution.

But progress isn't a given. New EU environmental laws aren't as strict as the Dutch would like, and the economic slowdown has resulted in cutbacks on major clean-up schemes. Still, the Dutch now tend to monitor pollution as they do their dykes – with extreme vigilance.

THE LAND

Flanked by Belgium, Germany and the choppy waters of the North Sea, the land mass of the Netherlands is to a great degree artificial, having been reclaimed from the sea over many centuries. Maps from the Middle Ages are a curious sight today, with large chunks of land 'missing' from Noord Holland and Zeeland. The country now encompasses 41,526 sq km, making it roughly half the size of Scotland or a touch bigger than the USA's state of Maryland.

Most Dutch people shudder at the thought of a leak in the dykes. Half the country lies at or below sea level in the form of polders. If the Netherlands were to lose its 2400km of mighty dykes and dunes – some of which are 25m high – the large cities would be inundated by rivers and well as by sea. Modern pumping stations run around the clock to drain off excess water.

Over the past century alone four vast polders have been created: Wieringermeer in Noord Holland; the Noordoost (Northeast) Polder in Flevoland; and the Noord (North) and Zuid (South) Polders on the province-island of Flevoland. More than 1700 sq km was drained after a barrier dyke closed off the North Sea in 1932 (see Afsluitdijk, p160).

The danger of floods is most acute in the southwest province of Zeeland, a sprawling estuary for the rivers Schelde, Maas, Lek and Waal. The latter two are branches of the Rijn, the final legs of a watery journey that began in the Swiss Alps. The mighty Rijn itself peters out in a pathetic little stream called the Oude Rijn (Old Rhine) at the coast near Katwijk.

The soil in the west and north, of the lower Netherlands, is relatively young and consists of peat and clay formed less than 10,000 years ago. The sandy, gravelly layer throughout the east and south is much older, having been deposited by rivers and then pushed up into ridges during the last ice age. This part of the country is noticeably different in appearance, with patches of forest and heath. The only genuinely hilly area lies in the southeast province of Limburg. Here the highest point in the Netherlands, the Vaalserberg, peeks out over the countryside at a grand elevation of 321m.

WILDLIFE

Human encroachment has meant few wildlife habitats are left intact in the Netherlands. The bird population offers the greatest breadth of species, now heavily protected in sanctuaries and nature reserves. The most popular outdoor activity for animal lovers, naturally, is bird-watching.

Animals

The Netherlands is a paradise for birds and those who love to keep track of our feathered friends. The wetlands are a major migration stop for European birds, particularly in the Wadden Islands, Flevoland and the Delta. Just take the geese: a dozen varieties, from white-fronted to pink-footed, break their V-formations to overwinter here. New wind-energy parks along the routes are controversial because thousands of birds get caught in the big blades.

Along urban canals you'll see plenty of mallards, coots and swans as well as the lovely grebe with its regal head plumage. The graceful blue heron spears frogs and tiny fish in the ditches of the polder lands, but also loiters on canal boats in and out of town. Other frequent guests include the black cormorant, an accomplished diver with a wingspan of nearly 1m. Feral pigeons are rarely in short supply, especially for handouts on town squares.

A variety of fish species dart about the canals and estuaries. One of the most interesting species is the eel, which thrives in both fresh and salt water. These amazing creatures breed in the Sargasso Sea off Bermuda before making the perilous journey to the North Sea (only to land on someone's dinner plate). Freshwater species such as white bream, rudd, pike, perch, stickleback and carp also enjoy the canal environment. You can admire them up close at Amsterdam's Artis Zoo (p108), in an aquarium that simulates a canal environment.

In the coastal waters there are 12 crustacean species including the Chinese mitten crab. This tasty little guy from the Far East has adapted so well in the Dutch estuaries that it's a hazard to river habitats. Further out, the stock of North Sea cod, shrimp and sole has suffered from chronic overfishing, and catches are now limited by EU quotas.

Larger mammals such as the fox, badger and fallow deer have retreated to the national parks and reserves. Some species like boar, mouflon and red deer have been reintroduced to controlled habitats. Herds of seals can be spotted on coastal sandbanks. Muskrats are common in the countryside while their cousins, the water vole and brown rat, find shelter in the canalside nooks and crannies of cities. The cricket-like squeak of dwarf bats can be heard on summer nights – the dune reserves are a good place to see them.

Where to Watch Birds in Holland, Belgium & Northern France (Arnoud van den Berg, Dominque Lafontaine) A regional guide of the best places to see your favourite species with locations of observation hides.

www.dutchbirding.nl. Home to the Dutch Birding Society.

BIRD-WATCHING FOR BEGINNERS

Seen through an amateur birdwatcher's eyes, some of the more interesting sightings might include:

- Avocet – common on the Waddenzee and the Delta, with slender upturned bill, black and white plumage.
- Black woodpecker – drums seldom but loudly. Try woodlands like Hoge Veluwe.
- Bluethroat – song like a free-wheeling bicycle in Biesbosch National Park, Flevoland and the Delta.
- Great white egret – crane-like species common in marshlands. First bred in Flevoland in the early 1990s.
- Marsh harrier – bird of prey, often hovers over reed-beds and arable land.
- Spoonbill – once scarce, this odd-looking fellow has proliferated on coasts in Zeeland and the Wadden Islands.
- White stork – nearly extinct in the 1980s, numbers have since recovered. Enormous nests.

Plants

Mention plant life in the Netherlands and most people think of tulips. Indeed, these cultivated bulbs are in many ways representative of much of country's flora in that they were imported from elsewhere and then commercially exploited. A range of fruits, vegetables and other flowers grown in the Netherlands fits this profile. Tomatoes and sweet peppers, for instance, are among the Netherlands' biggest hothouse products but originated from Central America. Once-exotic mushroom varieties such as shiitake and portabello thrive in the greenhouses of the southeast. There are few varieties of pretty flowers that the Dutch can't grow, from anemones to zinnias.

But there are also thousands of wild varieties on display such as the marsh orchid (pink crown of tiny blooms) or the Zeeland masterwort (bunches of white, compact blooms).

Much of the nondeveloped land is covered by grass, which is widely used for grazing. The wet weather means that the grass remains green and growing for much of the year, on coastal dunes and mudflats, and around brackish lakes and river deltas. Marshes, heaths and peatland are the next most common features. The remnants of oak, beech, ash, and pine forests are carefully managed. Wooded areas such as Hoge Veluwe National Park are mostly products of recent forestation, so trees tend to be young and of a similar age. Even the vegetation on islands such as Ameland is monitored to control erosion.

NATIONAL PARKS

Some 1065 sq km, or nearly 3%, of the Netherlands is protected in the form of national parks. There are 11 such parks in full operation while another seven are in various stages of creation. The concept was adopted late: the first publicly funded national park was established only in 1984. Most average a mere 5000 hectares (12,355 acres) and are not meant to preserve some natural wonder but, rather, open areas of special interest. With so few corners of the Netherlands left untouched, the Dutch tend to cherish every bit of nature that's left.

The better national parks are fascinating places with visitor centres and excellent displays of contemporary flora and fauna. The Hoge Veluwe, established in the 1930s, is one of the largest and oldest parks and was once the country retreat of the wealthy Kröller-Müller family. Forestation is maintained and it is a good place to see the sandy hills that once were prevalent in this part of the Netherlands.

Weerribben in Overijssel preserves a landscape once heavily scarred by the peat harvest. The modern objective is to allow the land to return to nature. Off the coast of Friesland, Schiermonnikoog occupies a good portion of an island once used by a sect of monks. The Biesbosch near Rotterdam was formerly inhabited by reed farmers.

The most interesting national parks (NP) and nature reserves (NR) include:

Name	Features	Activities	Best time to visit	Page
Biesbosch NP	estuarial reed marsh, woodland	canoeing, hiking, bird-watching	Mar-Sep	224
Duinen van Texel NR	dunes, heath, forest	hiking, biking, bird-watching	Mar-Sep	163
Hoge Veluwe NP	marsh, forests, dunes	hiking, biking, wildlife watching	all year	276
Oostvaardersplassen NR	wild reed marsh, grassland	hiking, biking, bird-watching, fishing	all year	170
Schiermonnikoog NP	car-free island, dunes, mud flats	hiking, mud-walking, bird-watching	Mar-Sep	247
Weerribben NP	peat marsh	boating/canoeing, hiking, bird-watching	all year	263
Zuid-Kennemerland NP	dunes, heath, forest	hiking, birding	Mar-Sep	145

ENVIRONMENTAL ISSUES

Beginning in the 1980s a succession of Dutch governments tightened the standards for industrial and farm pollution and made recycling a part of everyday life. Nowadays the Dutch love to debate about how to reconcile the 'triple p's' - planet, people and profit.

The rising tide of motor vehicles on Dutch motorways remains a burning issue. Despite good, reasonably cheap public transportation, private car ownership has risen sharply over the past two decades. Use of vehicles is now about 50% above levels of the late 1980s, which is due also to burgeoning freight transport. Some critics warn that unless action is taken the country's streets and motorways will become gridlocked over the next decade.

Stiff parking fees and outlandish fines have helped curb congestion in the inner cities, thankfully shifting a lot of car drivers onto bicycles, trams and buses. The motorways are trickier to regulate but one solution put forward is that of road tolls to reduce traffic jams, vehicle emissions and probably the nation's blood pressure. Just over the border, Germany has already launched road pricing for trucks, and the Dutch government may well follow suit.

The consequences of global warming are obvious in the Netherlands. Over the past century the winters have become shorter and milder, and three of the warmest years on record occurred in the past decade alone. The long-distance ice skating race known as the Elfstedentocht (see A Day at the Races, p242) may die out because the waterways in the northern province of Friesland rarely freeze hard enough. The Dutch

Jump online and check out these conservation organisations:

www.milieudefensie.nl
Dutch Friends of the Earth

www.snm.nl, in Dutch.
Foundation Nature & Environment

www.greenpeace.org.
Greenpeace

national weather service KNMI predicts that only four to 10 races will be held this century.

But there are bigger worries. If the sea level rises as forecast, the country could theoretically sink beneath the waves, like Atlantis, or at least suffer annual flooding. Extra funds have already been allocated to extend the dykes and storm barriers if necessary.

Water quality in the North Sea appears to be in decline again, with pesticides, unfiltered runoff from farms and industrial waste blamed as the chief culprits. Although Dutch coastal waters are said to meet EU standards, the pollution can be obvious even to the casual observer. The European water-quality watchdog Foundation for Environmental Education (FEE) awarded its coveted 'blue flag' to just 12 Dutch beaches in 2003, most being either in the extreme north or south of the country. However, visitors to popular beaches such as Scheveningen or Bloemendaal (both in Zuid Holland) and Zandvoort (Noord Holland) should probably stick to sunbathing.

A wave of animal diseases has raised questions about intensive farming of cattle, poultry and pigs, a major money-earner for the economy. At one point the Dutch chicken population exceeded 100 million, one of the largest concentrations in the industrialised world. That was before an outbreak of bird flu in 2002 made it necessary to destroy millions of animals to stop the spread of the disease. The swine flu, foot-and-mouth disease, and BSE ('mad cow' disease) have vastly reduced pig and cattle stocks in recent years. Farmers, especially in the provinces of Noord Brabant and Limburg, are still reeling in the aftermath of these epidemics.

Partly to blame for such plagues, critics say, are the great numbers of animals (primarily pigs, cattle and chickens) bred and farmed together in close quarters. Vaccines and stiffer rules on animal transport have been introduced to stem contagion. The crisis has a silver lining, however: fewer farm animals means arable lands have less nitrate-rich manure to absorb (overfertilisation is also chronic in the Netherlands).

More attention is being paid to sustainable development. Bowing to pressure by both the government and green organisations like Greenpeace, Dutch companies are shouldering more responsibility for their impact of their operations on society and the environment. Energy giants such as Shell, Nuon and Gasunie have invested heavily in developing new sources of clean energy such as hydrogen fuel cells for cars. Wind parks in Flevoland and Noord Holland now generate a significant amount of the country's electricity, though at a cost to passing birds and the natural profile of the landscape. Demand has grown for products that are perceived as environmentally friendly, such as free-trade coffee and organic meats and vegetables. So far, however, these products are relegated to a few supermarket shelves or specialist retailers.

DID YOU KNOW?

Dutch car buyers pay an environmental tax upon purchase to cover the vehicle's disposal later.

Architecture

Through the ages, few countries have exerted more influence on architecture than the Netherlands. From sober cathedrals to Golden Age fancies to sleek modern structures, you can time-travel through a thousand years of beautiful buildings. Switch effortlessly from the heart of medieval society into a backdrop of a Rembrandt canvas, and then into a cool functionalist vision.

The Dutch treat these national treasures with a matter of factness that's almost disconcerting. This all goes back to when daily life was awash in the fine arts, and paintings were traded for chickens. Still, people are keenly aware of their duty to keep these architectural wonders open to the public.

You won't find bombastic statements like St Peter's Cathedral or the Louvre – but then again, ostentation was never in keeping with the Dutch character. It's the little surprises that charm most: a subtle joke, a flourish on a 17th-century gable or a clever doorknob recess in De Stijl mode.

ROMANESQUE

Thick walls, small windows and round arches are some of the major characteristics of the Romanesque style which lasted from around 900 to 1250. The Pieterskerk (p176) in Utrecht is the oldest church of this style in the Netherlands. Built in 1048, it's one of five churches that form a cross in the city, with the cathedral at its centre.

Nearly as old, the 16-sided St Nicolaaskapel (p271) in Nijmegen is basically a scaled-down copy of Charlemagne's chapel in Aachen, Germany. The Onze Lieve Vrouwebasiliek (p289) in Maastricht has a fortress-like tower with round turrets, and evokes images of Umberto Eco's novel of monastic intrigue, *The Name of the Rose*.

The windy plains of the north are filled with examples of sturdy brick churches erected in the 12th and 13th centuries. The lonely church perched on a man-made hill in Hogebeintum (p239) in Fryslân shows the simple patterned brick decoration used to enliven church exteriors of the age.

GOTHIC

Pointed arches, ribbed vaulting and dizzying heights were trademarks of the Gothic era (c 1250–1600). Although the Dutch didn't match the size of French Gothic cathedrals, a rich style emerged in Brabant that could compete with anything abroad. The Catholics of Noord Brabant erected stone churches with soaring vaults and buttresses such as Sint Janskathedraal (p282) in Den Bosch and Breda's Grote Kerk (p284). These are good examples of what came to be called the Brabant Gothic style. Note the timber vaulting and the widespread use of brick among the stone.

Although stone was scarce and too heavy for building on marshy ground, there was plenty of clay and sand to produce bricks. Weight limits, especially in the country's west, led architects to build long or wide to compensate for the lack of height. The Sint Janskerk (p202) in Gouda is the longest church in the country, with a nave of 123m, and has a delicate, stately feel of a variant called Flamboyant Gothic. Most of these churches were made of brick, but there are exceptions such as Haarlem's Grote Kerk van St Bavo (p141).

Gothic town halls in Gouda (p202) and Middelburg (p228) are nearly overwhelming in their weightiness and pomp.

www.dutcharchitectu
re.com
What the label says, in
Dutch.

The Story of Western Architecture (Bill Risebero)
Lively, informal overview
of a normally crippling
subject. Has plenty of
Dutch examples, digestible and in context with
informative drawings.

DID YOU KNOW?

The 12-storey Witte
Huis in Rotterdam was
Europe's first 'skyscraper'
(1898).

MANNERISM

The Netherlands excelled in the style known as Mannerism (c 1600–1700), a sort of toned-down baroque. Also known as 'Dutch Renaissance', this unique style retained the bold curving forms and rich ornamentation of baroque but merged them with classical Greek and Roman and also the traditional Dutch styles. The façades made use of pilasters (mock columns), which replaced the simple spout gables with ones of ascending levels. These step gables were richly decorated with sculptures, columns and obelisks. The playful interaction of red brick and horizontal bands of white or yellow sandstone was based on mathematical formulas that pleased the eye.

The largest examples of this are the three churches in Amsterdam designed by Hendrik de Keyser and built in the early 1600s: the Zuiderkerk (p106), the Noorderkerk (p102) and the Westerkerk (p103). All three show a major break from the sober, stolid lines of brick churches located out in the sticks. Their steeples are ornate and built with a variety of contrasting materials, while the windows are framed in white stone set off by the brown brick. Florid details enliven the walls and roof lines.

GOLDEN AGE

After the Netherlands became a world trading power in the 17th century, its rich merchants were able to spend fantastic sums on lavish buildings.

Architecture had to be imposing and emphasize the owner's importance, and the leading lights again turned to ancient Greek and Roman designs for ideas. To make buildings look taller, the step gable was replaced by a neck gable, and pilasters were built to look like imperial columns. Decorative scrolls were added, and the peak wore a triangle or globe to simulate a temple roof. The pilasters began to look more and more grand, complete with pedestals.

A good example of this is the Royal Palace (p88) in Amsterdam, originally built as the town hall in 1648. Its architect, Jacob van Campen, drew on classical designs and dropped many of De Keyser's playful decorations, and the resulting building exuded gravity with its solid lines and shape.

GABLES & HOISTS

Originally, a gable – the vertical triangular or oblong section at the top of a façade – not only hid the roof from public view but also helped to identify the house. (This changed, however, when the occupying French introduced house numbers in 1795.) The more ornate the gable, the easier it was to recognise. Other distinguishing features included façade decorations, signs or cartouches (wall tablets).

There are four main types of Dutch gables. The simple spout gable looks like an upturned funnel with semicircular windows or shutters. A copy of the earliest wooden gables, the spout gable was used mainly for warehouses from the 1580s to the early 1700s. Named for the series of rising ledges on either side, the step gable was a late-Gothic design favoured by Dutch-Renaissance architects from 1580 to 1660. The neck gable, also known as the bottle gable for the stubby protrusion at the top of the façade, was introduced in the 1640s and proved most durable, featuring occasionally in designs of the early 19th century. Some neck gables incorporated a step. The graceful slopes of the bell gable first appeared in the 1660s and became popular in the 18th century.

Many houses built from the 18th century onwards no longer had gables but had straight, horizontal cornices that were richly decorated, often with pseudo-balustrades. Many houses were built with a slight forward lean to allow goods and furniture to be hoisted into the attic without bumping into the house (and windows). A few houses have huge hoist-wheels in the attic with a rope and hook that run through the hoist beam.

Along city canals, businessmen let the world know that they were successful; despite the narrow plots, each building from this time makes a statement at gable level through a myriad of shapes, forms and sculpture. The brothers Philips and Justus Vingboons were specialists in swanky residences. Their most famous works include the Bijbels Museum (p102), the gorgeous Theatermuseum (p101) and houses scattered throughout Amsterdam's Western Canal Belt.

Den Haag has 17th-century showpieces including the Paleis Noordeinde (p197) and the Mauritshuis (p195). There are scores of other examples – you'd be hard pressed to walk the canals of Leiden, Delft, Maastricht or other Dutch towns without finding your own Golden Age favourites.

From the mid-17th century onwards Dutch architecture began to influence France and England, and its colonial styles can still be seen in the Hudson River Valley of New York state.

FRENCH INFLUENCE

During the 18th century Dutch architects began deferring to all things French. Dainty Louis XV furnishings and florid rococo façades became all the rage among the wealthy classes, who by this time had turned their backs on trade for more staid lives in banking or finance. So the time was ripe for new French building trends. Daniel Marot as well as Jean and Anthony Coulon were the first to introduce French interior design with matching exteriors. Good examples of their work can be found along the Lange Voorhout in Den Haag, near the British Embassy. Rooms were bathed in light thanks to stuccoed ceilings and tall sash windows, and everything from staircases to furniture was designed in harmony.

NEOCLASSICISM

Architecture took a back seat during the Napoleanic Wars in the late 18th century. Buildings still needed to be built, of course, and designers dug deep into ancient Greek and Roman blueprints, and eventually came up with neoclassicism (c 1790–1850). Known for its order, symmetry and simplicity, the neoclassical design became popular for houses of worship, courtyards and other official buildings. These included the Groningen Town Hall (p253), which was constructed in dribs and drabs due to money problems. Note the classical pillars, although the use of brick walls is a purely Dutch accent. Many a church was subsidized via the government water ministry, and called itself Waterstaatkerk (State water church) like the one in Schokland (p171).

LATE 19TH CENTURY

Architects again looked to past styles for material, but with more innovation. Many big projects from the 1850s onward were neo-Gothic, harking back to the grand Gothic cathedrals. This followed a boom in church-building after freedom of religion was declared, and Catholics were allowed to build new churches in Protestant areas – Amsterdam's Krijtberg (p101) is one of the most glorious. Another wave of nostalgia, neo-Renaissance, drew heavily on De Keyser's earlier masterpieces. Neo-Renaissance buildings were erected throughout the country, made to look like well-polished veterans from three centuries earlier. For many observers, these stepped gables with alternating stone and brickwork are the epitome of classic Dutch architecture.

One of the leading architects of this period was Pierre Cuypers, who built several neo-Gothic churches but often merged the two styles, as can be seen in Amsterdam's Centraal Station (p87) and Rijksmuseum (p108).

www.bmz.amsterdam.nl /adam/uk/monum.html The capital's treasures and their respective styles.

www.bmz.amsterdam.nl Amsterdam's office of monument protection.

25 Buildings You Should Have Seen In Amsterdam (Cees Nooteboom) Best-selling Dutch novelist takes a tour of the capital's most striking structures, illustrated for those who don't get to all of them.

These are mainly Gothic structures but have Dutch Renaissance brick-work. His St Catherine's Church in Eindhoven was a soaring example of neo-Gothic until it was destroyed by German bombs in WWII.

BERLAGE & THE AMSTERDAM SCHOOL

As the 20th century approached, the neo styles and their reliance on the past were strongly criticised by Hendrik Petrus Berlage, the father of modern Dutch architecture. His spartan, utilitarian designs did away with frivolous ornamentation; the 1902 Beurs van Berlage (Bourse, p88) in Amsterdam displayed these ideals to the full. He cooperated with sculptors, painters and tilers to ensure that ornamentation was integrated into the overall design in a supportive role, rather than being tacked on as an embellishment to hide the structure.

Berlage's residential designs approached a block of buildings as a whole, not as a collection of individual houses. In this he influenced the young architects of what became known as the Amsterdam School, though they rejected his stark rationalism and preferred more creative designs. Leading exponents were Michel de Klerk, Piet Kramer and Johan van der Mey. The latter ushered in the Amsterdam School (c 1916–30) with his Scheepvaarthuis (p105).

These architects built in brick and treated housing blocks as sculptures, with curved corners, oddly placed windows and ornamental, rocket-shaped towers. Their Amsterdam housing estates, such as De Klerk's 'Ship' in the west, have been described as fairy-tale fortresses rendered in a Dutch version of Art Deco. Their preference for form over function meant that their designs were interesting but not always fantastic to live in, with small windows and inefficient use of space.

Many architects of this school worked for the Amsterdam city council and designed the buildings for Oud Zuid (Old South, p108). This was a large-scale expansion of good-quality housing, wide boulevards and cosy squares between the Amstel and what was to become the Olympic Stadium. It was mapped out by Berlage and instigated by the Labour Party, though Berlage didn't get much of a chance to design the buildings, with council architects pushing their own blueprints.

Housing subsidies sparked a frenzy of residential building activity in the 1920s, around Amsterdam, Rotterdam and in other parts of the country.

FUNCTIONALISM

While Amsterdam School-type buildings were being erected all over their namesake city, a new generation of architects began to rebel against the school's impractical (not to mention expensive) structures. Influenced by the Bauhaus School in Germany, Frank Lloyd Wright in the USA and Le Corbusier in France, they formed a group called called 'the 8'. It was the first stirring of Functionalism (1927–70).

Architects such as B Merkelbach and Gerrit Rietveld believed that form should follow function and sang the praises of steel, glass and concrete. Their spacious designs were practical and allowed for plenty of sunlight. The Rietveld-Schröderhuis (p177) is the only house built completely along functionalist De Stijl lines.

However, Amsterdam's planners in the 1930s didn't agree with the new doctrine. The Committee of Aesthetics Control was determined to keep functionalists out of the canal belt, relegating them to housing estates on the outskirts. In other cities, the functionalists made more of an impact on the centre – Utrecht's main post office (p176) is a splendid

Super Dutch (Bart Lootsma) Hang on to your skates for the latest funky buildings by some of the hottest Dutch design firms.

Twentieth-Century Architecture In the Netherlands (Hans van Dijk) Easy-to-read, compact overview of modern Dutch architecture with over 500 illustrations.

De Stijl and Dutch Modernism (Michael White) A critical view of the debates that shaped De Stijl in the 1920s, and the influence of mass culture on the fine arts.

example. The Bijenkorf department store in Rotterdam was a veritable *tour de force* of the style but didn't survive WWII.

After the war, functionalism put its stamp on new suburbs to the west and south of Amsterdam, as well as on blueprints for the rebuilding of Rotterdam and other war-damaged cities. High-rise suburbs were built on a large scale yet weren't sufficient to keep up with the population boom and urbanisation of Dutch life. But functionalism fell out of favour as the smart design aspects were watered down in low-cost housing projects for the masses.

MODERNISM & BEYOND

Construction has been booming in the Netherlands since the 1980s so there has been ample opportunity to flirt with numerous 'isms' such as structuralism, neorationalism, postmodernism and supermodernism. Evidence of these styles can be found in Rotterdam, where city planners have encouraged bold designs that range from Piet Blom's startling cube-shaped Boompjestorens (p213) to Ben van Berkel's graceful Erasmus Bridge (p213). Striking examples in Amsterdam include the NEMO science centre (p108), which recalls a resurfacing submarine, or the new Eastern Docklands housing estate, where 'blue is green' – ie the surrounding water takes the role of lawns and shrubbery.

www.nai.nl

Netherlands Architecture Institute, the top authority on the latest developments.

Food & Drink

Traditionally, the Dutch never paid that much attention to food – there was too much work to be done, and people ate to live rather than vice versa. It is quite revealing that in the Golden Age, spices like pepper were more of a currency than a culinary ingredient.

In recent years, however, these attitudes have been transformed by a culinary revolution sweeping the Netherlands. The Dutch have begun to experiment with their own kitchen, breathing life into centuries-old recipes by giving them a contemporary twist. Smart Dutch chefs now prefer to steam or braise vegetables rather than boil them, and draw on organic ingredients as well as a generous amount of fresh herbs and spices.

Of the many ethnic cuisines in the Netherlands, the refined (and often fiery!) flavours of Indonesia are a special highlight. Throughout the country, more menus feature exotic fare than ever before as influences trickle through from Latin America, Africa and the Pacific Rim.

The Netherlands is not yet a gourmet's dream, but anyone with a serious interest in food can eat extremely well.

DID YOU KNOW?

That Dutch ovens were invented in Pennsylvania?

STAPLES & SPECIALITIES

Until recently, the culinary sweepstakes in the Netherlands were split between traditional Dutch cooking – a hearty, meat-and-potatoes affair – and food from the former colonies of Indonesia and Surinam. After WWII, immigrants from these countries opened restaurants throughout the Netherlands, and the sudden increase in variety was like a breath of fresh air. These 'native' Dutch cuisines are now growing more sophisticated as public awareness of what constitutes a good meal has never been higher.

DID YOU KNOW?

Some Dutch eat *hagelslag* (chocolate sprinkles) on their bread for breakfast.

DUTCH

As indicated by Van Gogh's *Potato Eaters*, the main ingredient in old-fashioned Dutch cooking is potatoes. These are typically boiled and accompanied by meat and boiled vegetables, with gravy. Few restaurants serve exclusively Dutch cuisine but many places have several homeland items on the menu, especially in winter. Some time-honoured favourites include:

- *stamppot* (mashed pot) – potatoes mashed with kale, endive or sauerkraut, and served with smoked sausage or strips of pork.
- *hutspot* (hotchpotch) – similar to *stamppot*, but with potatoes, carrots, onions and braised meat.
- *erwtensoep* (pea soup) – a spoon stuck upright in the pot should fall over slowly; with smoked sausage and bacon. Traditional recipes are passed from mother to daughter, and are closely guarded.
- *asperge* (asparagus) – usually white; very popular in spring; served with ham and butter.
- *kroketten* (croquettes) – dough-ragout with various fillings that are crumbed and deep-fried; often as little spheres called *bitterballen*, a popular pub snack served with mustard.
- *mosselen* (mussels) – cooked with white wine, chopped leeks and onions, and served in a bowl or cooking pot with a side dish of *frites* or *patat* (French fries); it's popular, and best eaten from September to April.

Seafood doesn't feature as prominently as one might expect in a seafaring nation, though there's plenty of it. *Haring* (herring) is a national

---

DISTINCTLY CHEESY

Some Dutch say it makes them tall, others complain it causes nightmares. Whatever the case, the Netherlands is justifiably famous for its cheeses. The Dutch – known as the original cheeseheads – consume 16.5kg of the stuff every year.

Nearly two-thirds of all cheese sold is Gouda. The tastier varieties have strong, complex flavours and are best enjoyed with a bottle of wine of two. Try some *oud* (old) gouda, hard and rich in flavour and a popular bar snack with mustard. *Oud Amsterdammer* is a real delight, deep orange and crumbly with white crystals of ripeness.

Edam is similar to gouda but slightly drier and less creamy. *Leidse* or Leiden cheese is another export hit, laced with cumin or caraway seed and light in flavour.

In the shops you'll also find scores of varieties that are virtually unknown outside the country. Frisian *nagelkaas* might be made with parsley juice, buttermilk, and 'nails' of caraway seed. *Kruidenkaas* has a melange of herbs such as fennel, celery, pepper or onions. *Graskaas* is 'new harvest' Gouda made after cows begin to roam the meadows and munch grass.

Lower-fat cheeses include *Milner*, *Kollumer* and *Maaslander*. One has to start somewhere: the stats show the Dutch are gaining weight despite all that cycling.

---

institution, eaten lightly salted or occasionally pickled but never fried or cooked; *paling* (eel) is usually smoked.

Typical Dutch desserts are fruit pie (apple, cherry or other fruit), *vla* (custard) or ice cream. Many snack bars and pubs serve *appeltaart* (apple pie), which is always good.

Finally, most towns have at least one place serving *pannenkoeken* (pancakes), which come in a huge array of varieties. The mini-version, covered in caster sugar, is *poffertjes*.

INDONESIAN

Indonesian cooking is a rich and complex blend of many cultures: chilli peppers, peanut sauces and stewed curries from Thailand, lemon grass and fish sauces from Vietnam, intricate Indian spice mixes, and Asian cooking methods. Without a doubt this is the tastiest legacy of the Dutch colonial era.

In the Netherlands, Indonesian food is toned down for sensitive Western palates. If you want it hot (*pedis*, pronounced 'p-*dis*'), say so, but be prepared for the ride of a lifetime. You might play it safe by asking for *sambal* (chilli paste) and helping yourself. *Sambal oelek* is red and hot; the dark-brown *sambal badjak* is onion-based, mild and sweet.

The most famous Indonesian dish is rijsttafel (rice table): an array of savoury dishes such as braised beef, pork satay and ribs served with white rice. *Nasi rames* is a plate of boiled rice covered in several condiments, while the same dish with thick noodles is called *bami rames*.

Gado-gado is steamed vegetables and hard-boiled egg, served with peanut sauce and rice. *Sateh* (satay) is marinated, barbecued beef, chicken or pork on small skewers, with peanut sauce. Other stand-bys are *nasi goreng* (fried rice with onions, pork, shrimp and spices, often with a fried egg or shredded omelette) and *bami goreng* (the same thing but with noodles).

SURINAMESE

Dishes from this former colony – known as Dutch Guyana until 1975 – were brought to the Netherlands by waves of immigrants. Specialities from Surinam have Caribbean roots, blending African and Indian flavours with Indonesian from Javanese labourers. Chicken, lamb and beef curries are common menu items. *Roti kip* is a curried chicken served with potatoes, long beans, bean sprouts and a delicious chickpea-flour pancake (roti).

DRINKS
Nonalcoholic
Kraanwater (tap water) is absolutely fine to drink but most Dutch prefer mineral water, which is cheap in supermarkets. You're within your rights to order a glass of *kraanwater* in restaurants, but few Europeans do.

Dairy drinks include chocolate milk, yoghurt drinks, *karnemelk* (buttermilk) and of course milk itself. A wide selection of fruit juices is available, and the better places do their own fresh blends.

TEA & COFFEE
Tea is usually served Continental-style: a cup or pot of hot water with a tea bag on the side. Varieties might be presented in a humidor-like box for you to pick and choose. If you want milk, say *met melk, graag*. Many locals prefer to add a slice of lemon.

More coffee is consumed per capita in the Netherlands than in any other European country bar Denmark. Ordering a *koffie* will get you a sizeable cup of the black stuff and a separate package or jug of *koffiemelk*, a slightly sour-tasting cream akin to condensed milk. *Koffie verkeerd* is similar to latte, served in a big mug with plenty of real milk. If you order espresso or cappuccino you'll be lucky to get a decent Italian version. Don't count on finding decaffeinated coffee, and if you do it may be instant.

Alcoholic
Lager beer is the staple drink, served cool and topped by a head of froth so big it would start a brawl in an Australian bar. Heineken tells us these are 'flavour bubbles', and requests of no head will earn a steely response. *Een bier* or *een pils* will get you a normal glass; *een kleintje pils* is a small glass and *een fluitje* is a tall but thin glass – perfect for multiple refills. Some places serve half-litre mugs to please tourists.

Belgian beers are widely available, with strong and crisp flavours that make Dutch pilsners pale. Some good brands include De Koninck, Palm, Duvel and Westmalle (beware of their doubles and triples). The lighter

---

THE DUTCH AND THE NOBLE BEAN

The coffee plant is believed to have come from Ethiopia, but it was Yemen that first commercialised the product. In 1616 a Dutch visitor to Al-Makha, a Red Sea port in Yemen, noted a caravan of 1000 camels carrying goods including fruit, spices, pottery and coffee – the latest craze in Europe – grown in the Yemeni mountains. Two years later the Dutch built Al-Makha's first coffee factories.

By the 1630s coffee houses were operating in the Netherlands. Prices soared, and the prosperous coffee merchants of Al-Makha built gorgeous villas in the city. The term mocha (*mokka* in Dutch) is still used today for the potent, dark-brown coffee from Arabia, or for a mixture of coffee and chocolate.

Eventually, the coffee plant was smuggled out of Yemen by scheming Dutch traders. By the early 1700s it was cultivated in Ceylon (Sri Lanka) and Java, in the Dutch East Indies. With its monopoly broken, Al-Makha began a slow decline.

Generations have read the famous tale of colonial abuse called *Max Havelaar, or the Coffee Auctions of the Dutch East India Company*. In the 1980s the Max Havelaar Foundation was formed after Mexican coffee-growers said they would forgo Dutch development aid if they could just get a fair price for their coffee.

Products bearing the Max Havelaar logo are bought at a fair price from the producers. The first packet of Max Havelaar coffee was sold in a Dutch shop in 1988, and since then chocolate, tea, honey and bananas have been added. Most Dutch supermarkets now carry the Max Havelaar logo, and the mission has spread to other parts of Europe.

A TASTY BREW

The Dutch have been brewing beer for centuries. By 1870 there were 559 brewers, although only about 50 survive today.

Popular brands of pilsner include Heineken, Amstel, Grolsch and Oranjeboom, brands that generally contain around 5% alcohol. A few of those cute little glasses can pack quite a wallop.

Heineken is considered a 'high-end' beer in the USA but ironically, it has a bit of an image problem at home – 'the beer your cheap father drinks' to quote one wag. Grolsch has tasty seasonal beers such as Lentebok (Spring bock) and Herfstbok (Autumn bock). New ones are trialled every year such as a low-alcohol variety with grapefruit.

The Netherlands also has scores of small brewers including Gulpen, Bavaria, Drie Ringen, Leeuw and Utrecht. La Trappe is the only Dutch trappist beer, brewed close to Tilburg. The potent beers made by Amsterdam's Brouwerij 't IJ (p107) are sold on tap and in some local pubs – try its Columbus brew (9% alcohol).

witbier (blonde beer) is a good choice in balmy weather, and brands such as Hoegaarden are typically served with a slice of lemon and a swizzle stick. (For more on Dutch beers, see A Tasty Brew, above).

Dutch *jenever* or gin is made from juniper berries and drunk chilled from a shot glass filled to the brim. Most people prefer *jonge* (young) jenever, which is smoother; the strong juniper flavour of *oude* (old) jenever can be an acquired taste. The aptly-named *kopstoot* (head butt) is a double-whammy of jenever and a beer chaser. The palette of indigenous liqueurs includes *advocaat* (a kind of eggnog) and the herb-based Beerenburg, a Frisian schnapps.

The Netherlands is a country of beer-drinkers. Still, wine in all varieties is increasingly popular, especially French and Italian (although the New World is catching up). Note that Dutch import duties keep prices on the high side, and that the tab for a restaurant tipple can make one gulp.

CELEBRATIONS

The Dutch sweet tooth really comes out during the annual holidays and festivities. Early December is a good time to sample traditional treats such as spicy *speculaas* biscuits or *pepernoten*, the little crunchy ginger-nuts that are handed out at Sinterklaas (p301). *Oliebollen* are small spherical donuts filled with raisins or other diced fruit, deep-fried and dusted with powdered sugar; you can buy these calorie bombs from street vendors in the run-up to New Year.

Muisjes (little mice) are sugar-coated aniseed sprinkles served on a round *beschuit* (rusk biscuit) to celebrate the birth of a child – blue and white for a boy, pink and white for a girl.

WHERE TO EAT & DRINK

Restaurants abound and cater to a wide variety of tastes and budgets but don't overlook the affordable pub-like eateries called *eetcafés*. They're small and popular but don't always take reservations.

When locals say café they mean a pub, also known as a *kroeg*, and there are over 1000 of them in Amsterdam alone. Coffee is served but as a sideline. (Of course, when people say *coffeeshop* they mean another thing altogether. See Coffeeshops, p36) Many cafés and pubs also serve food, but few open before 9am.

A fixture in many cafés is an outdoor terrace that may be covered and heated in winter. At the first sign of spring, the Dutch flock here to soak up the sun. These are great places to relax and watch passers-by, or read

The Sensible Cook: Dutch Foodways in the Old and the New World, translated by Peter Rose, is a translation of favourite Dutch recipes from the 17th century including fare from the American colonies (ie before the Dutch sold Manhattan).

a paper for a few hours. Once you've ordered a drink you'll be left alone. Some cafés have indoor reading tables with the day's papers and news magazines, often with several in English.

The most famous type is the *bruin café* (brown café). The true specimen has been in business for a while, has a sandy, wooden floor and an atmosphere perfect for deep conversation. Persian rugs on the tables soak up spilled beer. The name comes from the smoky stains on the walls, although recent aspirants just slap on some brown paint.

Grand cafés are more spacious than brown cafés or pubs, and have comfortable furniture. They're all the rage, and any pub that puts in a few solid tables and chairs might call itself a grand café. But some are grand indeed, and from 10am, when they open, they're marvellous for a lazy lunch or brunch with chamber music in the background.

Theatre cafés attract a trendy mix of bohemian and chic – from struggling artists to fashion models and business moguls. There are also a few *proeflokalen* or tasting houses that used to be attached to distilleries. You can sample from dozens of *jenevers* and liqueurs.

Finally, there's no shortage of trendy bars with cool designer interiors. Irish pubs continue to mushroom.

Dutch Kitchen Restaurant Cookbook is written by Mike Stern, the author of *American Gourmet* and *Roadfood*, who dips his fork into the recipe archives of top Dutch restaurants.

Quick Eats

Broodjeszaken (sandwich shops) or snack bars seem to be everywhere. The latter have multicoloured treats in a display case, usually based on some sort of meat and spices, and everything is dumped into a deep-fryer when you order. *Febo* snack bars have long rows of coin-operated windows à la the *Jetsons*.

Vlaamse frites (Flemish fries) are French fries made from whole potatoes rather than the potato pulp you'll get if the sign only says 'frites'. They're supposed to be smothered in mayonnaise (though you can ask for ketchup, curry sauce, garlic sauce or other gloppy toppings). They are a national institution and you can find stands everywhere.

Seafood is good from the street stalls found in every town. One favourite is raw, slightly salted herring cut into bite-sized pieces, served with onion and pickles. *Hollandse nieuwe* is the first catch of the herring season (from late May); locals will toss back their heads and drop it straight into their gullet. Smoked eel also has legions of fans. If you still can't bear the thought, go for *kibbeling* (deep-fried cod parings), always a safe choice.

Lebanese and Turkish snack bars specialise in *shoarma*, a pitta bread filled with sliced lamb from a vertical spit – also known as *gyros* or doner kebab. Such places also do a mean falafel.

Dutch Cooking: The New Kitchen, by Manon Sikkel and Michiel Klonhammer, is a fresh perspective on traditional Dutch cuisine; based on age-old recipes but given a modern kick. Low-fat dishes are covered as well as the legendary apple pie.

VEGETARIANS & VEGANS

The Netherlands is still a meat-and-potatoes kind of place and, sadly, vegetarians aren't terribly well catered for. Many restaurant menus may have one or two veggie dishes, but often you can't be sure whether they're 100% meat or fish-free (meat stock is a common culprit). Vegetarian restaurants often rely on organic ingredients and make everything from bread to cakes in-house.

WHINING & DINING

The Netherlands is a kid-friendly country for eating out. Most restaurants and pubs will have kiddie meals on offer, if not a children's menu, and high chairs are often available. You might feel out of place taking infants into a drop-dead trendy restaurant – ask ahead when you make reservations.

The Dutch sweet tooth will keep the little ones happy; for dessert order them a treacle waffle, pancake or portion of *poffertjes*.

HABITS & CUSTOMS

The main meal of the day is dinner, usually between 6pm and 9.30pm. Popular places fill up by 7pm because the Dutch eat early. If you haven't reserved, arrive early or be prepared to wait at the bar. You could also aim for the 'second sitting' around 8.30pm to 9.30pm when films, concerts and other performances start, bearing in mind that many kitchens tend to close by 10pm. Full-scale restaurants may still serve after midnight.

Many places list a *dagschotel* (special of the day) that will be good value, but don't expect a culinary adventure. The trend in some places is to limit the menu to several options that change regularly; in this case the food can be quite exciting.

Lunch tends to be more of a snack, especially for the working crowd. A half-hour is common for the midday break, just long enough for employees to snag a quick sandwich or empty their lunchbox.

Coffee breaks are frequent during the day, a convenient opening for a little one-on-one chat. Restaurants will serve a single cookie or biscuit with coffee, and in homes you'll be offered one per cup.

The pace of meals can seem a bit rushed to foreigners. The Dutch tend to eat relatively fast, even if they're happy with the quality of the meal. This habit is slowly fading, however, and patrons are increasingly likely to linger over a multicourse dinner for a couple of hours. Social events are in a class of their own, and diners with something to celebrate might camp out in a restaurant for an entire evening.

Service is included in the bill and tipping is at your discretion, though most people round up 5% to 10%; say how much you're paying in total as you settle the bill. In cafés and pubs it's common to put drinks on a tab and to pay when you leave.

Last but not least, beware that many restaurants don't accept credit cards.

EAT YOUR WORDS

Dutch restaurants are skilled in serving foreigners so bilingual or English menus are practically the norm. Refer to the Language chapter (p326) for tips on pronunciation.

Useful Phrases & Words

A beer, please.	*Een pils/bier, alstublieft.*
a bottle of wine	*een fles wijn*
May I see the menu/wine list?	*Mag ik het menu/de wijnkaart zien?*
May I have the bill, please?	*Mag ik de rekening, alstublieft?*
Do you have a menu in English?	*Hebt u een menu in het Engels?*
Bon appétit.	*Eet smakelijk.*
It tastes good/bad.	*Het smaakt lekker/niet lekker.*
Is that dish spicy?	*Is dit gerecht pittig?*
I'm a vegetarian.	*Ik ben vegetariër.*
waiter/waitress	*ober/serveerster*

Menu Decoder

appelmoes	apple sauce
beenham	country ham
belegd broodje	filled roll or sandwich
bitterbal	deep-fried purée meatball covered in breadcrumbs

DOS AND DON'TS

Do round up the bill by 5% to 10%.

Do split the costs.

Do reserve ahead, especially at weekends.

Do take children to pubs and restaurants.

Do bring flowers or wine when invited home.

Don't ask to go 'Dutch'.

Don't ask for a doggie bag.

Don't cut off a tip on the cheese cart (always slice).

Don't make loud complaints about the service (usually counterproductive).

boerenomelet	omelette with vegetables and bacon
dagschotel	dish of the day
drop	sticky liquorice sweet
frikandel	spicy meat patties/balls
hagelslag	chocolate sprinkles
Hollandse nieuwe	filleted herring, first of the season
hoofdgerecht	main course
nagerecht	dessert
pannenkoek	pancake
patat frites	chips/French fries
speculaas	spicy almond biscuit
tosti	toasted cheese sandwich
uitsmijter	fried egg, ham or cheese on bread
vlammetjes	spicy spring rolls
Vlaamse frites	chips/fries made from whole potatoes
voorgerecht	starter

www.dinnersite.nl

For your next meal, search 9000 cafés and restaurants throughout the Netherlands.

www.diningcity.nl

Reviews of Amsterdam restaurants by cuisine, price, location and ambience.

English–Dutch Glossary
COOKING TERMS

boiled	gekookt
braised	gestoofd
fried	gebakken
grilled	geroosterd
medium	half doorbakken
poached	gepocheerd
rare	rood
roasted	gebraden
smoked	gerookt
stuffed	gevuld
well done	gaar

DESSERTS

apple pie	appelgebak
custard	vla
ice cream	ijs
mini pancakes	poffertjes
pie	taart
sweet roll with almond filling	amandelbroodje
whipped cream	slagroom

DRINKS

brandy	brandewijn
fizzy mineral water	spa rood (a brand)
gin	jenever (or genever)
latte	koffie verkeerd
orange juice	jus d'orange/sinaasappelsap
red/white	rood/wit
still mineral water	spa blauw (a brand)
sweet/dry	zoet/droog
tea	thee
with milk/lemon	met melk/citroen

FRUIT & VEG

asparagus	asperge
carrots	wortels

cherries	kersen
garlic	knoflook
lettuce	sla
mushrooms	champignons
peaches	perziken
pears	peren
plums	pruimen
potatoes	aardappelen
spinach	spinazie

INDONESIAN DISHES

banana	pisang
bean sprouts	taugé
beef	daging
casserole of noodles, veggies, pork and shrimp	bami goreng
chicken	ayam
chilli paste	sambal
deep-fried prawn crackers	kroepoek
fried	goreng
fried coconut	seroendeng
fried rice with meat bits and veggies	nasi goreng
peanut sauce	saté
rice	nasi
side dishes of spicy meats, fruits, vegetables and sauces served over rice	rijsttafel
spring rolls	loempia
stewed beef in dry hot sauce	rendang
suckling pig with sweet and sour sauce	babi pangang
vegetables with peanut sauce	gado-gado
very spicy	pedis

www.recepten.nl, in Dutch

Exhaustive archive of Dutch recipes and cooking links. In Dutch but easy to decipher.

MEAT & POULTRY

bacon	spek
beef	rundvlees
chicken	kip
game	wild
lamb	lamsvlees
pork	varkensvlees
rabbit	konijn
smoked sausage	rookworst
turkey	kalkoen
veal	kalfsvlees

SEAFOOD

bass	zeebaars
cod	kabeljauw
eel	paling
mackerel	makreel
plaice	schol
prawns, scampi	garnalen
salmon	zalm
sole	tong
trout	forel
tuna	tonijn

Cycling in the Netherlands

The Netherlands has more bicycles than the country's 16 million citizens. Many Dutch own at least two bikes, a crunchy beast for everyday use and a nicer model for excursions. No mistake, bikes rule and some kids even learn to ride before they can walk.

The largely flat landscape and 20,000km of bike paths makes this an agreeable pastime, and not one exclusively for the fit or sporty. It's a great equalizer: stockbrokers in tailored suits ride alongside pensioners and teenagers, and mutual tolerance prevails.

Dutch cyclists are incredibly skilled. They'll cart anything on the back of a bike while yakking on a mobile phone, applying makeup or rolling a cigarette. Parents might have two or three children strapped on while they're all singing. Fortunately, the abundance of dedicated paths mean that cyclists rarely have to share the road with cars.

INFORMATION

Your first stop is the ANWB, the Dutch motoring association, with offices in cities such as Den Haag (☎ 070-314 71 47; www.anwb.nl; Wassenaarseweg 220) and Amsterdam (Map p006; ☎ 020-673 08 44; Museumplein 5). It has a bewildering selection of route maps as well as camping, recreation and sightseeing guides for cyclists. The ANWB's 1:100,000 series of 20 regional maps includes day trips of 30km to 50km, all well signposted (six-sided signs, green or red print on white background).

Staff will help once you prove membership of your own national motoring association, or you can join the ANWB for €16.50 per year. Many tourist offices also sell ANWB materials and book cycling holidays.

CLOTHING & EQUIPMENT

Wind and rain are an all-too-familiar feature of Dutch weather. A lightweight nylon jacket will provide protection, and a breathing variety (Gore-Tex or the like) stops the sweat from gathering. The same thing applies to cycling trousers or shorts.

As for the vehicle itself, a standard touring bike is ideal for toting a tent and provisions. Gears are useful for riding against the wind, or for tackling a hilly route in Overijssel or Limburg – though the Alps it ain't. Other popular items include a frame bag (for a windcheater and lunch pack), water bottles and a handlebar map-holder so you'll always know where you're going. Few locals wear a helmet although they're sensible protection, especially for children.

Make sure your set of wheels has a bell: paths can get terribly crowded and it becomes a pain if you have to ask to pass every time. Another necessity is a repair kit. Most rental shops will provide one on request.

RENTING

Rental shops are available in abundance. Many day trippers avail themselves of the train-station hire points, called Rijwiel shops, where you can park, rent and buy bicycle parts from early until late. For rentals they all charge about €6 per day or €33 per week. You'll have to show a passport or national ID card, as well as leaving a credit card imprint or paying a deposit (usually €25 to €100). The main drawback is you must return the bike to the same station – a problem if you're not returning to the same place. Private shops charge similar rates but may be more flexible on the form of deposit. In summer, it's advisable to reserve ahead as shops regularly rent out their entire stock. The useful NS (national railway company) excursions book *Er-op-Uit* (€4.50, available from the NS and train station bookshops) lists telephone numbers of Rijwiel shops around the country. Also see Getting Around under individual towns for local rental options.

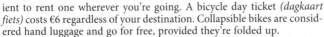

ON THE TRAIN

You can take your bike on the train, but it's often more convenient to rent one wherever you're going. A bicycle day ticket *(dagkaart fiets)* costs €6 regardless of your destination. Collapsible bikes are considered hand luggage and go for free, provided they're folded up.

Dutch trains have special carriages for loading two-wheelers – look for the bicycle logos on the side of the carriage. Remember that you can't take your bike along during rush hour (6.30am to 9am and 4.30pm to 6pm Monday to Friday). The NS publishes a free brochure, *Fiets en Trein* (Bike and Train, in Dutch), which will tell you which stations have bicycle hire and storage facilities – pick one up at the NS ticket counter.

ROAD RULES & SECURITY

Most major roads have separate bike lanes, with their own signs and traffic lights. Generally, the same road rules apply to cyclists as to other vehicles, even if few cyclists seem to observe them (notably in Amsterdam). In theory, you could be fined for running a traffic light or reckless riding, but it rarely happens. Watch out at roundabouts, where right of way may be unclear.

Be sure you have one or two good locks. Hardened chain-link or T-hoop varieties are best for attaching the frame and front wheel to something solid. However, even the toughest lock won't stop a determined thief, so if you have an expensive model it's probably safer to buy or rent a bike locally. Many train-station rental shops also run *fietsenstallingen*, secure storage areas where you can leave your bike for about €1 per day. In some places you'll also encounter rotating bicycle 'lockers' which can be accessed electronically.

Don't ever leave your bike unlocked, even for an instant. Second-hand bikes are a lucrative trade, and hundreds of thousands are stolen in the Netherlands each year. Even if you report the theft to the police, chances of recovery are virtually nil. *C'est la vie.*

CAMPING

Apart from the camping grounds listed in this book, there are plenty of nature camp sites along bike paths, often adjoined to a local farm. They tend to be smaller, simpler and cheaper than the regular camping grounds, and many don't allow cars or caravans. The Stichting Natuur-kampeerterreinen (Nature Campsites Foundation) publishes a map guide to these sites, on sale at the ANWB.

You might also try the *trekkershutten*, basic hikers huts available at many campsites. They sleep up to four people for around €25 per night. See Accommodation section in the Directory chapter for details (p294).

ROUTES

You're spoilt for choice in the Netherlands. Easy day trips can be found in the *Er-op-Uit* book (mentioned under Renting, p72), and we've listed five excursions later in this section.

The Rijwiel shops sell pamphlets of the routes described in *Er-op-Uit* (if you show your train ticket), usually for €1.

If you're seeking more of an odyssey, there are droves of cross-country and international routes to harden your calves. Most have a theme – medieval settlements, say, or some natural feature such as rivers or dunes.

The ANWB sells guides to signposted paths. These include the Noordzeeroute, a coastal trek from Den Helder along dunes and delta to Boulogne-sur-Mer in France (470km), or the Saksenroute from the Waddenzee coast to Twente in eastern Overijssel (230km).

Waterland Route   37km, 3½–5hr

The eastern half of Waterland is culture-shock material: 20 minutes from the centre of Amsterdam you step a few centuries back in time. This is an area of isolated farming communities and flocks of birds amid ditches, dykes and lakes.

It takes a few minutes to get out of town. First, take your bike onto the free Buiksloterwegveer ferry behind Amsterdam's Centraal Station across the IJ river. Then continue 1km along the west bank of the Noordhollands Kanaal. Cross the second bridge, continue along the east bank for a few hundred metres and turn right, under the freeway and along Nieuwendammerdijk past Vliegenbos camping ground. At the end of Nieuwendammerdijk, do a dogleg and continue along Schellingwouderdijk. Follow this under the two major road bridges, when it becomes Durgerdammerdijk and you're on your way.

The pretty town of **Durgerdam** looks out across the water to IJburg, a major land-reclamation project that will eventually house 45,000 people. Further north, the dyke road passes several lakes and former sea inlets – low-lying, drained peat lands that were flooded during storms and now form important bird-breeding areas. Colonies include plovers, godwits, bitterns, golden-eyes, snipes, herons and spoonbills. Climb the dyke at one of the viewing points for uninterrupted views to both sides.

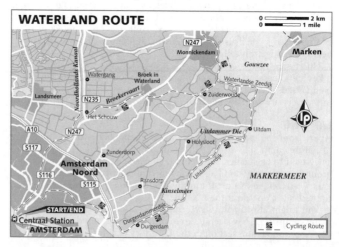

The road – now called Uitdammerdijk – passes the town of Uitdam, after which you turn left (west) towards **Monnickendam** (p148). Alternatively, you could turn right and proceed along the causeway to the former island of **Marken** (p150). After visiting Marken, you could take the summer ferry to **Volendam** (p150) and backtrack along the sea dyke to Monnickendam. Or you could return over the causeway from Marken and pick up our tour again towards Monnickendam. These diversions to Marken and (especially) Volendam would add significantly to the length of your trip (55km, seven to 10 hours).

From Monnickendam, return the way you came, but about 1.5km south of town turn right (southwest) towards Zuiderwoude. From there, continue to **Broek in Waterland** (p148), a pretty town with old, wooden houses. Then cycle along the south bank of the Broekervaart canal towards Het Schouw on the Noordhollands Kanaal. Bird-watchers may want to cross the Noordhollands Kanaal (the bridge is slightly to the north) and head up the west bank towards **Watergang** and its bird-breeding areas. Otherwise, follow the west bank back down to Amsterdam North. From here it's straight cycling all the way to the ferry to Centraal Station.

Mantelingen Route   35km, 3hr

Depart from **Domburg** (p230), a popular beach resort in the southwest coastal province of Zeeland. In the 19th century, Domburg lured the well-to-do to its spa facilities and chic hotels; its most famous resident was the painter Piet Mondriaan, a leading light of the modernist De Stijl movement. The tourist office (☎ 0118-58 13 42, Schuitvlotstraat 32) has a list of bicycle hire shops.

Start at 't Groentje, an eastern suburb of Domburg. If you're up for for the full tour via Westkapelle (making the tour 48km and about 3½hr to 4½hr long), continue west along the coastal path past the golf course. Relish a split view of the earth atop the Westkapelse Zeedijk, a protective sea wall erected following the great flood of 1953. The former fishing village of Westkapelle has an odd church-lighthouse. The occupying French put up the first signal tower here in the early 19th century, and it retained this function even after Napoleon was repelled. Most of the church burnt down in 1831 but the lighthouse was rebuilt on the solitary tower.

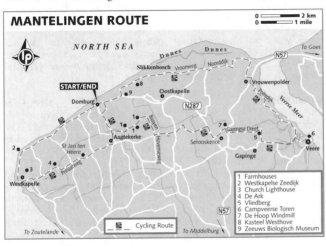

Turning east towards **Aagtekerke**, the way – marked Dorpenroute for this short segment – suddenly enters a green and pleasing pastureland; along Prelaatweg, the tall hawthorn hedges part to reveal the lovely pension De Ark, whose owner has planted a large and breathtaking field of camomile, cornflower and poppy.

For the shorter tour, turn landwards from Domburg along the 'Mantelingenroute' path sheltered on both sides. This region explodes with flowers in season and is rightfully known as 'the garden of Zeeland'. The meadows are typically dotted with *schuren*, tarred farmhouses with green doors. The doorframes are painted white to make them easier to pick out from the rest of the structure – and a blackened sky. Just outside the village of Serooskerke stands a cheerily renovated windmill, **De Hoop**, complete with a farmyard tavern. It's a great spot for an afternoon snack of strawberry waffels.

Further on, as you approach the town of **Veere** (p229), you'll stumble across a **vliedberg**, an artificial rise laid in the 12th century as a defence post and refuge in times of floods. The town itself sits on the south shore of the Veerse Meer, a large lake created by the closing off of an arm of the North Sea. Veere was a wool trading centre in the 16th century, especially for imported Scottish wool. The most striking building in town is the enormous Vrouwekerk, a Gothic-style church that, thanks to multiple attacks, now resembles a fortress; the cistern alongside was once used by Scottish traders to wash their wool for market, in water drained from the church roof.

The route leads beyond the church to the Markt; turn right to glimpse the **Campveerse Toren**, towers which formed part of the old city fortifications. In line with age-old tradition, local youths still dive from the breast wall of the fort into the cold waters of the bay.

Continuing west along the quay in Veere, you'll pass a row of handsome 19th-century houses; at the bridge, turn around for an idyllic scene worthy of a snapshot. West of town, cycle along the Veerse Meer and cross over the N57 road; here begins the chain of dunes that protect the Walcheren Forest from the North Sea. This leafy expanse between the coast and *polders* (drained lands) gives the route its name, Manteling, which roughly translates as mantle or overcoat. There are lots of bicycle storage areas between the dunes if you want to climb up for a sea view. North of Oostkapelle, the path turns dark and leafy in the **Slikkenbosch** forest, a welcome relief after the sun-drenched course up to this point.

Near the end of the journey, as you turn left (south) away from the dunes, you'll pass close by **Kasteel Westhove**, a 16th-century fort that was once the pride of powerful local deacons. Today it houses a youth hostel; in the adjacent orangery there's the **Zeeuws Biologisch Museum** (Zeeland Biology Museum) and a garden of local flora.

Baronie Route
52km, 4–5hr

The province of Noord Brabant in the south of the country has a definite Flemish-Belgian feel to it, in the cuisine and the ornate architecture. The **Baronie** is the area around the town of Breda (p284), which belonged to the princedom of Brabant until the 17th century; the counts of Nassau resided here between 1403 and 1567.

The starting point is Breda train station, which has a bicycle hire shop (☎ 076-521 05 01). The gravel and sand **Baronieroute** (well-signposted) leads along the municipal park to Breda's 16th-century **kasteel** (fort), which houses a military academy. It takes a while to get out of town as you pass through the suburb of Ginneken, but eventually you'll reach a lush forest which girds the town. Between Ulvenhout and Alphen you can

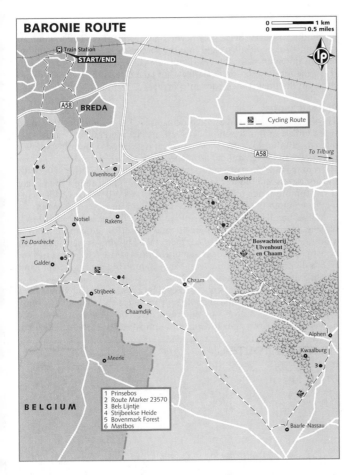

BARONIE ROUTE

0 — 1 km
0 — 0.5 miles

Train Station
START/END

A58 BREDA

Cycling Route

A58   To Tilburg

6
Ulvenhout   Raakeind

1

Notsel   Rakens
Rakens   2
To Dordrecht
Galder   5   Boswachterij
Ulvenhout
en Chaam
Strijbeek   4   Chaam

Chaamdijk

Alphen
Kwaalburg
Meerle   3

BELGIUM
1 Prinsebos
2 Route Marker 23570
3 Bels Lijntje
4 Strijbeekse Heide
5 Bovenmark Forest
6 Mastbos

Baarle-Nassau

pedal about 15km on continuous forest paths. In the **Prinsebos** (Prince's Forest), planted in the early 20th century, you may see sturdy Brabant horses at work hauling timber.

At route marker 23570 you can either turn right to reach Chaam, a Protestant village amid predominantly Catholic Brabant, or follow the Maastrichtse Baan (Maastricht Route) towards Alphen, the birthplace of artist Vincent van Gogh. Shortly before Alphen you'll pass a Gothic chapel from the 16th century – but the tower was built after WWII. From here a number of routes cross over into Belgium, including the Smokkelaarsroute (Smugglers' Route).

The path here is pretty and follows the old Bels Lijntje (Belgium Line), the train line opened in 1867 to link Tilburg with Turnhout. The last passenger train ran in 1934; the route was converted to a cycle path in 1989.

If you have time, stop off for a look around the border town of **Baarle-Nassau**, which has been the object of border disputes since the 12th century. The Belgian and Dutch governments finally settled a 150-year difference in 1995 – and as a result, Belgian territory grew by 2600 sq metres.

Before Baarle-Nassau, veer right and you'll eventually pass a pretty heath, the **Strijbeekse Heide**. Just beyond at the village of Galder, you can cross the bridge and turn right into the **Bovenmark Forest** before doubling back to the main path, the Frieslandroute (LF9). Cross highway A58 to reach the forestry station at **Mastbos**, but take care of the loose sand and rocks on the final stretch back into Breda.

Plateau Route   35 km, 3–4hr

The suggestion is it's flat as a Dutch pancake, but no mistake, this route is the hilliest in our selection. Most ascents are merciful and easily conquered with the aid of gears. Defining features include windmills, sprawling castles and lovely rolling farmland.

From the bike shop at Maastricht train station, head southeast beneath the underpass and follow the bike route marked 'LF6a' and/or 'Bemelen'. It's a 10-minute ride to the city limits. At the ANWB map board Knooppunt 6 you join the Plateauroute; pedal straight on towards **Bemelen**.

At the hamlet St Antoniusbank you leave the paved road behind, passing an abandoned lime kiln on your ascent to the panorama over a limestone quarry. No surprise, then, that Limburg is peppered with structures built from the ochre-coloured mineral. A few kilometres on stands the cheery Van Tienhovenmolen windmill (open every second and fourth Saturday of the month).

At the roundabout that's watched over by a limestone sculpture, take a right into Sibbe. The imposing pile on your left is the Sibbehuis, a 14th-century castle that's now a private residence. The route is a bit unclear in the village; follow signs to Gulpen. From **Scheulder** – where, if desired,

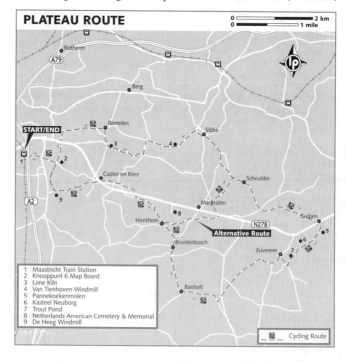

PLATEAU ROUTE

0 ⊏━━━━━━━━━━ 2 km
0 ⊏━━━━━━━━━━ 1 mile

1 Maastricht Train Station
2 Knooppunt 6 Map Board
3 Lime Kiln
4 Van Tienhoven Windmill
5 Pannekoekenmolen
6 Kasteel Neuborg
7 Trout Pond
8 Netherlands American Cemetery & Memorial
9 De Heeg Windmill

Cycling Route

you can halve the journey via a short cut labelled 'Route Afkorting' – you whizz through planted fields and finally downhill into the beer-brewing town of **Gulpen**. Lunchtime is wisely spent at the Pannekoekenmolen, a pancake house in a historic water mill tucked away at Molenweg 2a. To get there, turn left off Rijksweg/N278 at the traffic light onto Molenweg.

Here we suggest a detour to avoid the busy main road. From the pancake house, proceed southeast along cycle path 85, a leafy trail that affords glimpses of the turreted **Kasteel Neubourg**, a medieval castle (closed for renovation). After the trout pond, take the first right towards **Euverum**, where you turn left to rejoin the Plateauroute.

The home stretch to Maastricht is quite countrified, with memorable views of mixed woodlands and livestock wandering the pastures. Pretty half-timbered houses grace the tidy farm villages where fresh potatoes, apples and strawberries are sold to passers-by. In tiny **Banholt** sheep graze peacefully in the town square.

Reminders of a grim era lie in Margraten, about 2km northeast of **Honthem**, at the **Netherlands American Cemetery and Memorial** (p292).

Onward from the hamlet **Cadier en Keer** you can coast downhill towards Maastricht, taking care not to miss the sharp right at the windmill in De Heeg. At the Knooppunt 6 map board, bear left on Bemelerweg towards Maastricht train station.

Paterswoldsemeer Route   40km, 3–4hr
This circuit begins in the lively northern city of Groningen (p250), taking in some attractive green areas to the south. You can rent wheels from the bike shop (☎ 050-312 41 74) at Groningen train station.

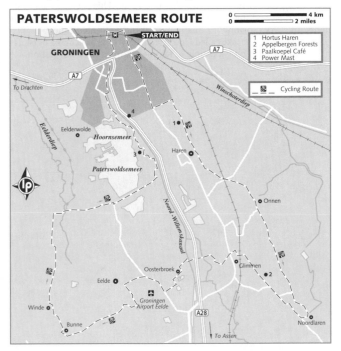

PATERSWOLDSEMEER ROUTE

0 4 km
0 2 miles

GRONINGEN

START/END

A7

A7

To Drachten

Winschoterdiep

1 Hortus Haren
2 Appelbergen Forests
3 Paalkoepel Café
4 Power Mast

Cycling Route

Eelderwolde
Hoornsemeer

Haren

Paterswoldsemeer

Onnen

Noord Willem Kanaal

Oosterbroek
Glimmen

2

Eelde

Winde

Groningen
Airport Eelde

A28

Bunne

Noordlaren

To Assen

With the station entrance at your back, turn right and ride to the Groninger Museum, a yellow-and-green building behind the blue-arched pedestrian bridge. Then turn right again to reach the busy Herenweg. You'll pass rows of shops and then some handsome manor houses as you approach the quiet town of Haren.

Hortus Haren is a delightful garden with tropical greenhouses and a themed outside section including a Chinese walled garden, complete with waterfall and arched wooden bridges. From Haren, continue south to Noordlaren; on your right lie the **Appelbergen** forests, while on your left in the distance you'll see the industrial skyline of Hoogezand, on the fringes of a large natural-gas field.

Just east of the 13th-century church in Noordlaren lies the **Zuidlaarder-meer**, a 560-hectare lake created in the last ice age that's just 1m deep. To get to the lake follow signs to De Bloemert watersports centre.

Returning to the church, ride northwest through the Appelbergen nature reserve, one of the prettiest spots on this route. After the tiny village of Glimmen, you come to **Oosterbroek**, a grouping of large farms in leafy surrounds. To the north you'll see the bright colours of the Gasunie complex, one of Europe's largest natural gas producers.

Emerging from the forest you'll come to Groningen Airport Eelde where you turn north. The landscape really opens up here. After a stretch of well-developed bike path you'll come to the **Paterswoldsemeer**, a lake created from peat harvesting in the 18th and 19th centuries. Stop off at the popular Paalkoepel café, which has a nice spot overlooking the lake on the east side.

Moving north along the busy A28 highway near the canal, you won't miss a large power mast sporting the time 10.40. This is Groningen's official marker, and the number refers to the year of the city's founding. It lights up every morning for one minute at the appointed time.

Once you pass the lake called Hoornse Meer, you're back at the outskirts of Groningen, and only a couple of kilometres from the train station.

Amsterdam

CONTENTS

Personal freedom, liberal drug laws, gay centre of Europe – these images have been synonymous with the Dutch capital since the heady 1960s and '70s, when it was one of Europe's most radical cities.

While the exuberance has dimmed somewhat it has not been extinguished. Tolerance is still a guiding principle that even serious social problems such as a chronic housing shortage have failed to dent.

Just as enduring is the lively mix of the historical and contemporary that you'll savour while exploring the myriad art galleries and museums, relaxing in the canalside cafés or enjoying the open-air entertainment that pulsates throughout the city in summer. Amsterdam buzzes 24 hours a day, and is the kind of place where something is always 'happening'.

Since the Middle Ages the city has lured migrants and nonconformists, making it one of the world's earliest melting pots. Despite (or because of) this transient mix, people accept each other as they are and strive to be *gezellig*, a typically Dutch term that roughly means 'convivial'. This mood is best experienced over a drink in one of its famous brown cafés.

Because Amsterdam is compact, a single day can hold a cross-section of the contrasts – old and new, moralist ethics and sleaze, traditional and alternative – which visitors find at once baffling and delightful.

HIGHLIGHTS

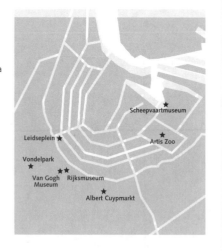

- Viewing Rembrandt's *Nightwatch* at the **Rijksmuseum's** (p108)
- Pondering the canvases in the **Van Gogh Museum** (p109)
- Admiring the Golden Age façades on a **canal-boat tour** (p115)
- Watching the wild and wonderful creatures at **Artis zoo** (p108)
- Listening to free summer concerts in the **Vondelpark** (p110)
- Tasting Dutch conviviality in the **brown cafés** (p125)
- Watching **Leidseplein's** (p105) performance artists
- Browsing the **Albert Cuypmarkt** (p132) for exotic wares
- Meandering in wonder at Dutch architecture on a **walking tour** (p113)
- Exploring the decks of a three-masted rigger at the **Scheepvaartmuseum** (p108)

| TELEPHONE CODE: 020 | POPULATION: 735,000 |

HISTORY

A small fishing town named Aemstelredamme, meaning a dam over the Amstel river, emerged around 1200. The community was freed by the count of Holland from paying tolls on its locks and bridges, a small victory that began a stellar climb. Amsterdam developed into a major sea port and by the late 1400s, nearly two-thirds of ships bound to and from the Baltic Sea were from Holland. Most of their clever owners lived in Amsterdam.

During the Reformation the stern protestant movement known as Calvinism took hold in the Low Countries (which included present-day Belgium). The Calvinists led the region's struggle against the Spanish who had seized these lands for colonisation. Calvinist brigands captured Amsterdam in 1578 and the seven northern provinces, led by Holland and Zeeland, declared themselves a republic.

The stage was set for the power and prosperity of the Golden Age. Merchants and artisans flocked to Amsterdam and a class of monied intellectuals was born. The world's first regular newspaper was printed in Amsterdam (1618). Dutch ships dominated trade between England, France, Spain and the Baltic countries, and had a virtual monopoly on North Sea fishing and Arctic whaling. The East India Company controlled Europe's commercial links to Asia.

By the late 17th century Holland couldn't match the growing might of France and England, and Dutch merchants fell back on money-lending to keep afloat. Amsterdam was fast becoming a backwater until the country's first railway opened in 1839, and the city was revitalised in a stroke. Colonial profits from the Dutch East Indies funded the building of the North Sea Canal (1865–76), so goods and ideas could flow freely from the Industrial Revolution.

Amsterdam was spared major damage during WWII. Postwar growth was rapid, and by the late 20th century, the city had switched from shipping to services like banking, communication and advertising. But its reputation as a cultural and arts centre remains unchallenged.

ORIENTATION

Amsterdam's core lies south of the IJ river, itself an arm of a vast lake called the IJsselmeer. The old town is spread over a network of concentric canals (*grachten*). Think of it as the bottom half of a bicycle wheel, with the main

---

AMSTERDAM IN...

Two Days

Start your day with breakfast in the Negen Straatjes area of the **Western Canal Belt** (p101) – a fine spot to soak up some atmosphere. Visit the **Van Gogh Museum** (p109) and then take a leisurely stroll through the leafy **Vondelpark** (p110). Treat yourself to a candlelit French dinner at **Zuidlande** (p123) followed by a night at one of Amsterdam's boutique hotels, **Seven One Seven** (p120).

On the second day peruse the funky shops and galleries of the **Jordaan** (p103) – and the open-air markets for a change of pace. Take a boat tour of the grand canals before stopping off at **Café de Jaren** (p126) for a terrace lunch on the Amstel river. In the evening sample the varied vibes at **Paradiso** (p127).

Four Days

Follow the above itinerary, then on your third day pay a sobering visit to the **Anne Frankhuis** (p102). Turn over a few antiques and wishful thoughts in **Nieuwe Spiegelstraat** (p104) before dousing your shopper's thirst at **Hoppe** (p126), a brown café on Spui. Order a spicy Indonesian rijsttafel at **Tempo Doeloe** (p123) and round off the evening with a classical concert at the world-renowned **Concertgebouw** (p128).

On the fourth day you could flee the city for a **cycle tour** (see Waterland Route, p72) along lush pastures and windmills. Be sure to get a taste of the Dutch masters at the **Rijksmuseum** (p108) and for contrast, a jaunt through the **Red Light District** (p98). If there's still time on your last day, book a farewell dinner at the enchanting **Blauw Aan de Wal** (p122).

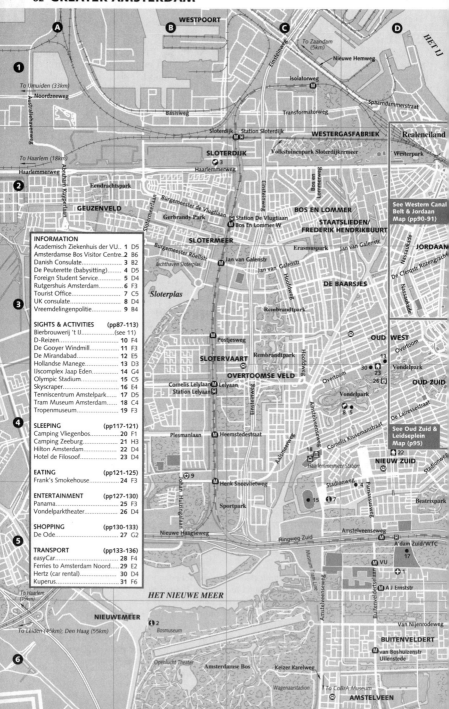

WESTPOORT

To Zaandam (5km)

Nieuwe Hemweg

HET IJ

Isolatorweg

Spaarndammerstraat

Transformatorweg

Basisweg

To IJmuiden (33km)

Noordzeeweg

Australiëhavenweg

WESTERGASFABRIEK

Realeneiland

Sloterdijk Station Sloterdijk

Westerpark

To Haarlem (18km)

Haarlemmermeerpolder

Abraham Kuyperlaan

SLOTERDIJK

Volkstuinenpark Sloterdijkermeer

Haarlemmerweg

See Western Canal
Belt & Jordaan
Map (pp90-91)

Eendrachtspark

GEUZENVELD

Burgemeester de Vlugtlaan

Station De Vlugtlaan
Bos En Lommer W

BOS EN LOMMER

JORDAAN

Gerbrandy Park

STAATSLIEDEN/
FREDERIK HENDRIKBUURT

Nassaukade

De Clerqstr Rozengracht

Sloterdijkmeerlaan

SLOTERMEER

Erasmuspark

Jan van Galenstr.

Nassaukade

Burgemeester Röellstr.

Jan van Galenstr

Jachthaven Sloterplas

Jan van Galenstr

DE BAARSJES

Sloterplas

Hoofdweg

Rembrandtpark

OUD WEST

Overtoom

Postjesweg

Rembrandtpark

Vondelpark

INFORMATION
Academisch Ziekenhuis der VU..	1	D5
Amsterdamse Bos Visitor Centre.	2	B6
Danish Consulate	3	B2
De Peuterette (babysitting)	4	D5
Foreign Student Service	5	D4
Rutgershuis Amsterdam	6	F3
Tourist Office	7	C5
UK consulate	8	D4
Vreemdelingenpolitie	9	B4

SIGHTS & ACTIVITIES   (pp87-113)
Bierbrouwerij 't IJ	(see 11)	
D-Reizen	10	F4
De Gooyer Windmill	11	F3
De Mirandabad	12	E5
Hollandse Manege	13	D3
IJscomplex Jaap Eden	14	G4
Olympic Stadium	15	C5
Skyscraper	16	E4
Tenniscentrum Amstelpark	17	D5
Tram Museum Amsterdam	18	C4
Tropenmuseum	19	F3

SLEEPING   (pp117-121)
Camping Vliegenbos	20	F1
Camping Zeeburg	21	H3
Hilton Amsterdam	22	D4
Hotel de Filosoof	23	D4

EATING   (pp121-125)
Frank's Smokehouse	24	F3

ENTERTAINMENT   (pp127-130)
Panama	25	F3
Vondelparktheater	26	D4

SHOPPING   (pp130-133)
De Ode	27	G2

TRANSPORT   (pp133-136)
easyCar	28	F4
Ferries to Amsterdam Noord	29	E2
Hertz (car rental)	30	D4
Kuperus	31	F6

OUD ZUID

De Lairessestraat

SLOTERVAART

OVERTOOMSE VELD

Cornelis Lelylaan
Station Lelylaan

Lelylaan

See Oud Zuid &
Leidseplein
Map (p95)

Amstelveenseweg

Einsteinweg

Cornelis Krusemanstraat

NIEUW ZUID

Plesmanlaan

Heemstedestraat

Aalsmeerweg

Stadionweg

Haarlemmermeer Station

Beatrixpark

Henk Sneevlietweg

Stadionweg

Sportpark

Parnassusweg

Nieuwe Haagseweg

Amstelveenseweg

Ringweg Zuid

A'dam Zuid/WTC

To Haarlem
(19km)

Museum Tram line

VU

HET NIEUWE MEER

Buitenveldertselaan

A J Ernststr

To Leiden (45km); Den Haag (55km)

NIEUWEMEER

van Nijenrodeweg

Bosmuseum

BUITENVELDERT

van Boshuizenstr
Uilenstede

Openlucht Theater   Amsterdamse Bos

Keizer Karelweg

Wagenaarstadion

To CoBrA Museum

AMSTELVEEN

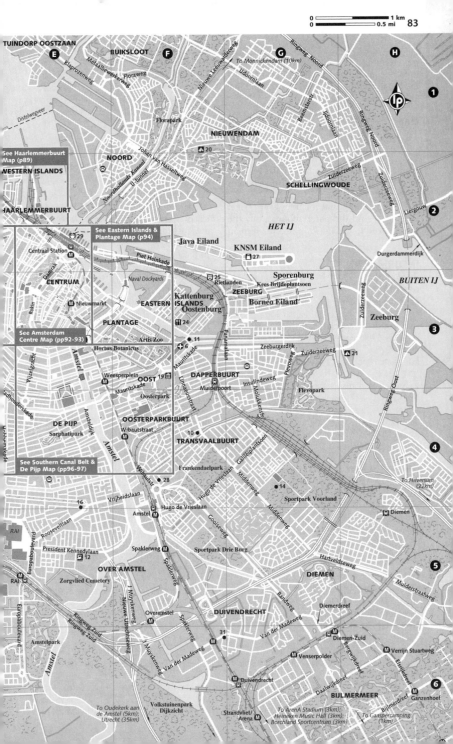

train terminal Centraal Station as the axis and the streets as spokes radiating outward across the canals. Schiphol Airport is on a train line 18km to the southeast.

Maps

The maps in this book will probably be sufficient. Lonely Planet's handy *Amsterdam City Map* has a street index (in rain-proof lamination) that covers most parts of town in detail. The tourist offices also sell maps of the city centre.

For something that includes every street in the city and the outer suburbs, buy the Dutch-produced *Cito Plan* or the German *Falkplan*.

INFORMATION

Bookshops

GENERAL

American Book Center (Map p92; ☎ 625 55 37; Kalverstraat 185) Always jam-packed, this shop has a good travel-guide section and stocks many US newspapers and magazines. It holds interesting sales and offers a 10% student discount.

Athenaeum Bookshop & Newsagency (Map p90; ☎ 622 62 48; Spui 14-16) This enormous multilevel store has a vast assortment of unusual titles. The separate newsagency is piled high with a bewildering choice of newspapers and magazines.

Book Exchange (Map p92; ☎ 626 62 66; Kloveniers-burgwal 58) A rabbit warren of second-hand books, with temptingly priced occult, sci-fi and detective novels. Bring your own and strike a deal with the astute owner.

Scheltema (Map p90; ☎ 523 14 11; Koningsplein 20) The largest bookshop in town is a genuine department store with many foreign titles, New Age and multimedia sections, and a restaurant. Also hosts readings of well-known authors.

Waterstone's (Map p92; ☎ 638 38 21; Kalverstraat 152) Easily mistaken for a library, Waterstone's is the specialist in English-language books with strengths in travel guides, maps and novels. British titles are often marked down.

SPECIALIST

á la Carte (Map p96-97; ☎ 625 06 79; Utrechtsestraat 110) Savvy travellers head here for guidebooks, maps, globes and beautiful photography books.

Architectura & Natura (Map p90; ☎ 623 61 86; Leliegracht 22) This charming canalside shop has architecture, landscape and coffee-table books on the ground floor, antiquarian art and more architecture upstairs.

Au Bout du Monde (Map p90; ☎ 625 13 97; Singel 313) Looking for a new religion or guru? This tranquil shop has Eastern philosophy, alternative medicine and a selection of esoteric gifts.

Joho Company (Map p92; ☎ 471 50 94; Taksteeg 8) Aimed at the independent traveller, this one-stop shop sells a big range of guidebooks, maps, camping and trekking supplies, as well as travel insurance. Staff can also help with information on jobs and study abroad.

Lambiek (Map p95; ☎ 626 75 43; Kerkstraat 78) Serious comic-book buffs linger over titles by Crumb, Avril and Herriman. Doubles as an informal museum with a cartoonists' gallery.

Cultural Centres

British Council (Map p95; ☎ 550 60 60; www .britishcouncil.nl; Weteringschans 85a) Educational and cultural exchanges between UK and the Netherlands, as well as lectures, films, and exhibitions. Visits by appointment only.

De Balie (Map p95; ☎ 553 51 00; Kleine Gartman-plantsoen 10) Covers all the intellectual bases with theatre, seminars, political debates and lectures, as well as a café and restaurant (to think well one must dine well).

Maison Descartes (Map p96-97; ☎ 531 95 00; www.ambafrance-nl.org; Vijzelgracht 2A; ☼ 9.30am-4pm Mon-Fri, library 1-6pm Tue & Thu) This extension of the French consulate offers a wealth of events such as films, lectures and exhibitions.

Emergency

Emergency (☎ 112) Police, ambulance, fire brigade
Police (☎ 0900-8844, ☎ 559 91 11) Theft & other queries.
De Eerste Lijn (The First Line; ☎ 613 02 45) Hotline for victims of sexual violence.

Internet Access

Costs are roughly €1.50 to €2 per hour and most Internet cafés have snappy high-speed lines. You can also surf for free at the **Centrale Bibliotheek** (p85). In addition to the places listed below, many coffeeshops double as Internet cafés – a fine excuse to toke and joke by email (p128).

easyInternetcafé (Map p92; ☎ 320 62 94; www.easy everything.com/map/ams; Reguliersbreestraat 22; ☼ 9am-10pm) Operates an enormous Net café with 275 flat screens and Web cams, Net phone and Microsoft applications. There are smaller outlets at Damrak 33 (Map p92; same hours) and at Leidsestraat 24 (Map p90; ☼ 11am-7pm Mon, 9.30am-7pm Tue-Sat, 11am-6pm Sun).

Internet Café (Map p92; ☎ 627 10 52; Martelaarsgracht 11; ☼ 9am-1am Sun-Thu, 8am-3am Fri-Sat) Has 20-odd PCs a stone's throw from Centraal Station. You can surf for 20 minutes for free with a drink, or just read the papers under the huge cartoon murals.

Internet City (Map p92; ☎ 620 12 92; Nieuwendijk 76; ☼ 10am-midnight) Has over 100 terminals in a bland office not far from the main coffeeshop drag. Draws backpackers and bleary-eyed party animals.

Internet Resources

www.amsterdam.nl The definitive site for visitors and residents alike with sections on tourism, transport, housing, work, education and more.

www.visitamsterdam.nl This official site of the Netherlands Board of Tourism is good for boning up on what's on.

www.amsterdambackdoor.com Quirky site run by students with feature articles.

www.underwateramsterdam.com The site for *Shark*, the monthly underground events 'zine, carries quirky feature stories.

www.amsterdamhotspots.nl Selection of the hippest places to eat, drink, smoke, sleep and party down.

Laundry

Local *wasserettes* or *wassalons* charge about €5 to €6 to wash 5kg; add a few coins for the dryer. Staff will wash, dry and fold your smalls for a few more euros.

Clean Brothers (Map p95; ☎ 622 02 73; Kerkstraat 56) In the gay area near Leidsestraat.

Happy Inn (Map p92; ☎ 624 84 64; Warmoesstraat 30; ☺ closed Sun) A good place to lather up in the Red Light District.

Wasserette Van den Broek (Map p92; ☎ 624 17 00; Oude Doelenstraat 12; ☺ closed Sun) On the eastern extension of Damstraat.

Wasserette Rozengracht (Map p90; ☎ 638 59 75; Rozengracht 59) Soapsuds and cheer in the hip Jordaan district.

Left Luggage

Luggage lockers at Centraal Station can be rented for up to 72 hours, costing €3.50 to €5.50 every 24 hours. For left-luggage facilities at Schiphol Airport, see Air, p133.

Libraries

To borrow books from a public library you'll need to be a resident, but everyone's free to browse or read.

Centrale Bibliotheek (Map p90; ☎ 523 09 00; Prinsengracht 587; ☺ 1-9pm Mon, 10am-9pm Tue-Thu, 10am-5pm Fri & Sat, 1-5pm Sun) The city's main public library. There's a wide range of English-language newspapers and magazines and a coffee bar. Surf the Web for free after registering at the desk.

Media

The free *Uitkrant* is the definitive listings mag for art and entertainment – in Dutch, but you can decipher enough to go on. Pick up a copy at bookshops or newsagents. The tourist office publishes the English-language *What's On in Amsterdam* monthly (€2). *What's Up* is a weekly entertainment freebie that takes a stab at covering the clubs and is available in bars, cafés and clubs.

Anyone wanting to get the lowdown on Amsterdam politics should pick up the left-leaning *Het Parool*. The weekly what's-on listing in its Saturday supplement *PS* is excellent.

For details of national newspapers and magazines, see p39.

Medical Services

For serious problems visit the casualty ward of a *ziekenhuis* (hospital) or ring the **Centrale Doktersdienst** (Central Doctors' Service; ☎ 592 34 34), the 24-hour central medical service that will refer you to a doctor, dentist or pharmacy.

Emergency medical services are excellent by international standards. Hospitals with 24-hour facilities include:

Onze Lieve Vrouwe Gasthuis (Map p96-97; ☎ 599 91 11; Oosterpark 9) Near the Tropenmuseum, this is the closest public hospital to the city centre.

Academisch Ziekenhuis der VU (Map p82-83; ☎ 444 44 44; De Boelelaan 1117) Part of the Free University in the southern suburb of Buitenveldert.

Common medicines like cough syrup or aspirin aren't available in supermarkets. For anything stronger than toothpaste you'll have to find a *drogist* (chemist) or *apotheek* (pharmacy). Only the latter fills prescriptions.

Money

Banks use official exchange rates and charge a fair commission.

Other reliable exchange centres are:

GWK (Map p92; ☎ 627 27 31; Centraal Station; ☺ 7am-10.45pm) First stop for the cash-poor. Converts travellers cheques and books hotel reservations. There's another branch at Schiphol Airport. GWK also books rooms for a €5 commission plus 10% of the hotel fee.

American Express (Map p92; ☎ 504 87 77; Damrak 66; ☺ 9am-5pm Mon-Fri, 9am-noon Sat) No commission on AmEx cheques.

Thomas Cook (Map p92; ☎ 625 09 22; Dam 23-25; ☺ 9am-7pm) Also has branches at Damrak 1-5 (Map p92) opposite Centraal Station and Leidseplein 31A (Map p95). Thomas Cook cheques cashed free.

ATMs are mapped at strategic points on the Amsterdam maps in this book.

Post

Post office Main post office (Map p90; Singel 250; ☺ 9am-7pm Mon-Fri, 9am-noon Sat) Muziektheater (Map p92; Waterlooplein 10; ☺ 9am-6pm Mon-Fri, 10am-1.30pm Sat)

Telephone & Fax

Most local telephones are card-operated. KPN phones and other brands of telephone cards are sold at post offices, train-station counters, tourist and GWK offices, and tobacco shops. The larger post offices have send-only fax machines linked to card-operated pay telephones.

Toilets

There are no public toilets in Amsterdam. Your best bet is to slip into a department store, where you'll pay the toilet attendants €0.25 to €0.50. Public urinals (known here as *pissoirs* or *urinoirs*) are available in the pub-heavy areas.

Tourist Information

The **Amsterdam Tourist Office** (☎ 0900-4004040, from abroad ☎ 020-551 25 25; www.visitamsterdam.nl, www.amsterdamtourist.nl; ☺ 9am-5pm Mon-Fri) runs an information line for hotel reservations and general queries, and it has excellent Web resources.

The VVV, as the Dutch network of tourist offices is called, has four branches in the city and its sister outfit, Holland Tourist Information, runs an information counter at the airport. It's a profit-making outfit so all publications will cost you. Fees for some services are pretty stiff (eg €13 for finding a hotel room). Offices get very busy but it's worth queuing to get an Amsterdam Pass (see Discount Cards, p299).

Tourist Office (Map p92; Stationsplein 10; ☺ 9am-5pm) Main Amsterdam office, in front of Centraal Station; expect queues and variable service.

Tourist Office (Map p92; Centraal Station, platform 2; ☺ 8am-7.45pm Mon-Sat, 9am-5pm Sun) Smaller but tends to be less busy.

Tourist Office (Map p95; Leidseplein 1; ☺ 9am-7pm Mon-Fri, 9am-5pm Sat & Sun) Shares premises with GWK currency exchange.

Tourist Office (Map p82-83; Stadionplein; ☺ 9am-5pm) Next to the old Olympic Stadium. Handy if you're driving from the south (A10, exit S108).

Holland Tourist Information (Schiphol Airport shopping plaza; ☺ 7am-10pm) Less crowded than the tourist offices in Amsterdam.

There's also:

Amsterdam Uitburo (Map p95; ☎ 0900-0191; www.aub.nl; Leidseplein 26; ☺ 10am-6pm Mon-Fri, 10am-9pm Thu, information & ticket line 9am-9pm) For cultural events, it has free magazines and brochures, and sells tickets at a small mark-up.

Travel Agencies

D-Reizen (Map p82-83; ☎ 200 10 12; www.dreizen.nl in Dutch; Linnaeusstraat 112) Friendly service and some good last-minute deals from the majors.

Kilroy Travels (Map p90; ☎ 524 51 00; www.kilroytravels.nl; Singel 413) Specialist in adventure tours, round-the-world and one-way tickets; special deals for under-26s and students under 34.

World Ticket Center (Map p92; ☎ 626 10 11; www.worldticketcenter.nl in Dutch; Nieuwezijds Voorburgwal 159) Decent last-minute offers including long-haul flights.

Universities

Amsterdam has two universities and roughly 38,000 students, although they don't really stand out in this cosmopolitan town. Nearly two-thirds of them attend the **Universiteit van Amsterdam** (UvA; ☎ 525 33 33; www.uva.nl; Binnengasthuisstraat 9), which dates back to back to 1632. There's no campus as such and its buildings are scattered about the city.

The **Foreign Student Service** (Map p82-83; ☎ 671 59 15; Oranje Nassaulaan 5, 1075 AH Amsterdam) provides details of study programmes and language courses, and helps with accommodation, insurance and personal problems.

DANGERS & ANNOYANCES

Amsterdam is utterly safe 99% of the time but big-city street sense remains essential. Although violent crime is unusual, pick-pocketing and outright theft are real problems. Also be mindful of sticky-fingered passengers on the Schiphol Airport–Amsterdam train.

Police stations are mapped in this book. If you have trouble on the train or at the Centraal Station itself, contact the railway police *(spoorwegpolitie)* on platform 2A. You can also report violence or missing/stolen property here.

Touts offering accommodation of varying quality hone in on backpack-toting tourists at Centraal Station. It's a safer bet to book a hotel at the GWK (p85) or tourist-office (p86) counters.

If you're driving note that foreign cars are a popular target for smash-and-grab theft, especially on the canals. Remove valuables, ID papers and, if possible, the radio when you park.

While in the Red Light District you may be approached by shady characters panhandling or selling drugs. A simple *Nee, dank je* (No, thank you) is usually enough. Don't take photos of the prostitutes – they don't like it.

Mosquitoes can be a nuisance in summer as they breed in the canals. Some residents sleep under netting six months of the year.

Non-smoking sections are scarce in pubs and restaurants, although the situation is slowly improving. Watch out for the abundant dog dirt outside – Amsterdam's pavements can be a slippery minefield.

Drugs

With all that sweet smoke on the streets it's hard to believe that cannabis is actually illegal. The trick? Possession of soft drugs for personal use (defined as up to 5g) is 'tolerated' by the authorities. Larger amounts qualify you as a dealer.

Hard drugs are another matter: police regularly raid clubs known to be dealing in ecstasy and heroin. Registered addicts, meanwhile, are treated as medical cases. Welcome to the Netherlands.

For more about soft drugs, see Coffeeshops, p36.

Lost & Found

Items left on buses, trams or metro might turn up at the **GVB Information Office** (Map p92; ☎ 551 58 58; Stationsplein) opposite Centraal Station. If something goes missing on a train, contact **Gevonden Voorwerpen** (Lost & Found; ☎ 557 85 31) near the luggage lockers.

Scams

Beware of thieves masquerading as police in plain clothes. Usually these fraudsters address tourists in English, flash a false ID and demand to see money and credit cards for 'verification' or some other nonsense. They might also go through the victim's pockets and pretend to look for drugs. Dutch police rarely conduct this kind of search. To foil the crooks, ask to see their police identity card (note that Dutch police don't have badges as ID). Then call the real cops at ☎ 0900-8844.

SIGHTS

Amsterdam's major sights are found in or near the **city centre.** The old town is so compact that you can usually get from A to B within 20 minutes without taking a tram or bus.

The **canal belt** is the place to encounter Amsterdam at its most seductive – Golden Age façades, tinkling carillons, brown cafés and hidden courtyards. The heart of the city is at the **Dam** (see below). Other centres of activity include **Leidseplein** (p105), the mini Times Square of Amsterdam; **Rembrandtplein** (p104), a brash, neon-lit clubber's mecca; and **Nieuwmarkt** (p99), a vast cobblestone square with open-air markets and a clutch of well-visited pubs. The seamy **Red Light District** (p98) is fairly self-contained.

The fanciest 17th-century homes occupy the western canals **Prinsengracht** (pp102 & 105), **Keizersgracht** (pp102 & 104) and **Herengracht** (p101 & p103) – heaven for those smitten with beautiful gables. The **Jordaan** (p103), the cosiest quarter, was working class but is now filled with quirky shops, bohemian bars and art galleries. The world-class **Van Gogh Museum** (p109) and **Rijksmuseum** (p108) are close to the old centre.

Outside the canal belt, you can dip your toes in the ethnic melting-pot of **De Pijp** (p111) district. **Oud Zuid** (p98) is quietly posh and residential, while **Nieuw Zuid** (p111) is about 20th-century housing projects, many of them attractive in their own right. The **Eastern Docklands** (see Modernism & Beyond, p61) has emerged as a showcase of modern Dutch architecture.

Damrak, Dam & Rokin   Map p92

Most visitors arriving at **Centraal Station** step outside, then look back, gasp and reach for their cameras. This gleaming, turreted marvel from 1889 was designed by the master architects of the Rijksmuseum and Concertgebouw, AL Ghent and Pierre Cuypers. You can easily see its resemblance to the Rijksmuseum: a central section with Gothic towers and wings on either side.

St Nicolaaskerk (☎ 624 87 49; Prins Hendrikkade 73; ⊙ 11am-4pm Mon-Sat, 10.30am service Sun) is the city's main Catholic church built in 1887. The interior definitely has gravitas with black marble pillars, and an ethereal bluish aura in the soaring dome. The high altar is unusual for its depiction of Maximilian's bulging yellow crown.

DAMRAK

Once part of the old harbour, **Damrak** today is an agonising stretch of souvenir shops, exchange bureaux and cramped hotels. Most visitors walk down here at least once before finding an alternate route.

The **Seksmuseum Amsterdam** (☎ 622 83 76; Damrak 18; admission €2.50; ⊙ 10am-11.30pm) lurks behind a Greek-temple façade reminiscent of a Hollywood film. This erratic collection of pornography, from ancient sex toys and naughty Delft tiles to sketches by John Lennon, is scattered over a labyrinth of rooms. It's more funny than tantalising.

The **Beurs van Berlage** (☎ 530 41 41; Damrak 243; adult/child €5/3.50; ⊙ 11am-5pm Tue-Sun) is the old stock and commodities exchange designed by renowned architect HP Berlage. The functional lines and chunky square clock tower are considered a landmark of Dutch urban architecture. Today the one-time bourse is a cultural centre and home to the Netherlands Philharmonic Orchestra.

Visitors can roam the premises. The large central hall with its steel and glass roof was the Victorian-style trading floor for commodities and colonial merchandise. The rich decorations here include three Art Deco **tile mosaics** by Jan Toorop; stockbrokers distrusted these works because of their anti-capitalist flavour. Be sure to check out the **basement vaults** where discreet patrons used to store their stock certificates, money and jewellery. The **clock tower** affords a view of the old town, and there are more Art Deco features in the **café** on the Beursplein side.

Trading quickly grew out of the Beurs van Berlage and moved a few metres to the neoclassical **Effectenbeurs** (Stock Exchange; Beursplein 5), built in 1913.

DAM

Damrak ends at the **Dam**, the very spot where a barrier giving the city its name was built across the Amstel river. It seems a bit empty now, besieged by thousands of pigeons and the occasional fun fair.

The **Nationaal Monument** on the eastern side of the Dam commemorates those who died during WWII; the fallen are honoured in a Remembrance Day ceremony here every 4 May. The statues around the phallic white obelisk stand for war, peace and resistance. In the 1960s hippies used to camp out here before being shooed away by police.

Opposite, **Koninklijk Paleis** (Royal Palace; ☎ 624 86 98; adult/child €4.50/3.60; ⊙ 12.30-5pm Sep-Jun, 11am-5pm Jul & Aug) is the official residence of Queen Beatrix, although she actually lives in Den Haag. Built as a grand city hall in 1665, it later became the palace of Napoleon's fairly incompetent brother, Louis. The interior (particularly the chandeliered Civic Hall) is more lavish than the sober façade suggests. Tours in Dutch and English are given at 2pm.

The **Nieuwe Kerk** (New Church; ☎ 638 69 09; Dam) is the coronation church of Dutch royalty – Crown Prince Willem Alexander and Máxima took their vows here in 2002. This Gothic basilica from the 15th century is only 'new' in relation to the Oude Kerk (Old Church). A few monumental items dominate the otherwise spartan interior – a magnificent carved oak chancel, a bronze choir screen, a massive organ and enormous stained-glass windows. Exhibitions and organ concerts are held but church services are no more. Opening times and admission fees vary, depending on the exhibition.

Want to see the queen? Visit **Madame Tussaud's** (☎ 522 10 10; Dam 20; adult/child €18.50/10; ⊙ 10am-6.30pm Sep-Jun, 9.30am-8.30pm Jul & Aug) where the royal family and all manner of celebrities are given the wax treatment over three floors of displays.

ROKIN

South of the Dam, the **Rokin** begins to show the business side of Amsterdam with office buildings, snazzy shops and art dealers. At Grimburgwal stands a **statue of Queen Wilhelmina** on horseback, a reminder of the monarch's trots through Amsterdam during official processions.

The rather undervisited **Allard Pierson Museum** (☎ 525 25 56; www.uba.uva.nl/apm; Oude Turfmarkt 127; adult/child €4.30/1.40; ⊙ 10am-5pm Tue-Fri, 1-5pm Sat & Sun) has a rich collection of archaeological

(Continued on page 98)

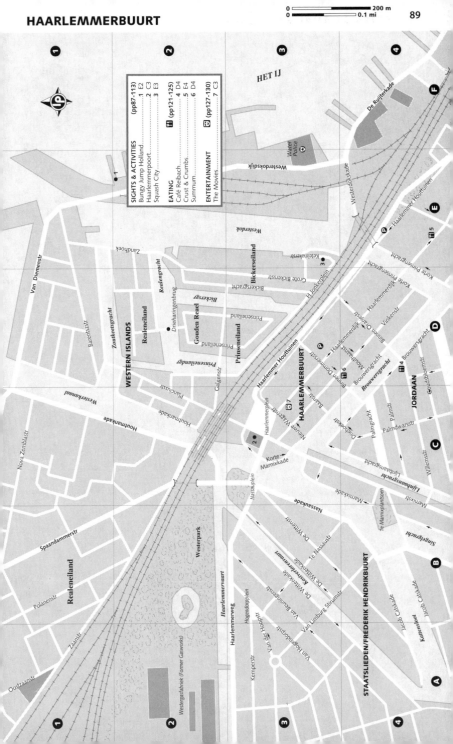

| | 0 | 200 m |
| 0 | | 0.1 mi |

SIGHTS & ACTIVITIES (pp87–113)
Bungy Jump Holland.................1 E2
Haarlemmerpoort.....................2 C3
Squash City...............................3 B3

EATING (pp121–125)
Café Reibach..............................4 D4
Crust & Crumbs.........................5 E4
Summum....................................6 D4

ENTERTAINMENT (pp127–130)
The Movies..................................7 C3

INFORMATION
Athenaeum Bookshop & Newsagency......**1** D5
Au Bout du Monde................................**2** D5
Centrale Bibliotheek............................**3** C6
COC Amsterdam...................................**4** C4
easyInternetcafé..................................**5** D6
Kilroy Travels......................................**6** D5
Scheltema..**7** D6
Wasserette Rozengracht......................**8** C3

SIGHTS & ACTIVITIES   (pp87-113)
Anne Frankhuis....................................**9** C3
Art Multiples......................................**10** D6
Bartolotti House..................................**11** D3
Bijbels Museum...................................**12** D5
Greenland Warehouses........................**13** D1
Greenpeace Building...........................**14** D3
Homomonument..................................**15** C3
House with the Heads..........................**16** D2
Krijtberg...**17** D6
Let's Go...**18** D3
Lutheran Church..................................**19** D5
Noorderkerk.......................................**20** D1
PC Hooft Store....................................**21** D6
Pianola Museum..................................**22** C2
Theatermuseum...................................**23** D3
Thermos Day Sauna.............................**24** C6
Vrankrijk..**25** D4
Westerkerk...**26** C3

SLEEPING   (pp117-121)
't Hotel..**27** D3
Ambassade Hotel................................**28** D5

Blake's...**29** C5
Canal House Hotel..............................**30** D2
Hotel Clemens....................................**31** D3
Hotel Pax...**32** D3
Hotel Pulitzer.....................................**33** C4
The Shelter Jordan..............................**34** B4

EATING   (pp121-125)
Albatros...**35** B2
Albert Heijn Supermarket....................**36** D6
Bordewijk...**37** D1
Burger's Patio....................................**38** C2
Casa di David.....................................**39** D5
Casa Juan...**40** D1
Christophe..**41** D3
De Bolhoed..**42** D2
Dimitri's...**43** D2
Duende..**44** D1
d'Vijff Vlieghen Restaurant.................**45** D5
Foodism...**46** D3
Grekas...**47** D5
Koh-I-Noor...**48** C3
Nielsen...**49** C5
Nomads..**50** B4
Pancake Bakery..................................**51** D2
Rakang Thai..**52** C5
Stoop...**53** C2
Turquoise...**54** D5

DRINKING   (pp125-127)
Café 't Smalle.....................................**55** C2
Café Dante...**56** D5
Café de Vergulde Gaper.....................**57** D2

Café Nol...**58** C2
De 2 Zwaantjes...................................**59** C2
De Pieper...**60** C6
Gollem...**61** D5
Het Papeneiland.................................**62** D1
Hoppe..**63** D5
Luxembourg.......................................**64** D5
Van Puffelen.......................................**65** C4

ENTERTAINMENT   (pp127-130)
Felix Meritis..**66** C5
Grey Area...**67** D3
Korsakoff..**68** B5
La Tertulia..**69** C5
Maloe Melo...**70** B5
Mazzo...**71** B4
Odeon..**72** D6

SHOPPING   (pp130-133)
Analik...**73** D4
Architectura & Natura Bookshop..........**74** D3
De Looier..**75** B5
Galleria d'Arte Rinascimento...............**76** C3
Gallery Donkersloot............................**77** C6
Metz & Co...**78** D6
Razzmatazz..**79** D5
Santa Jet..**80** D2
Van Ravenstein...................................**81** C5

TRANSPORT   (pp133-136)
Avis Autoverhuur................................**82** B6
Bike City...**83** C3
Marnixstr bus station...........................**84** B5

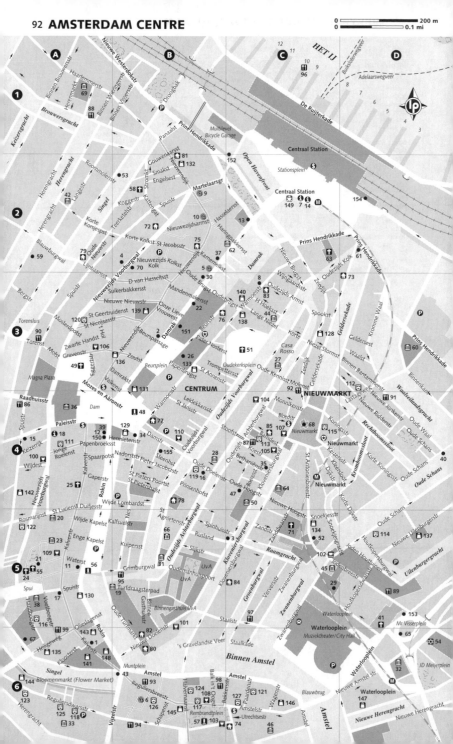

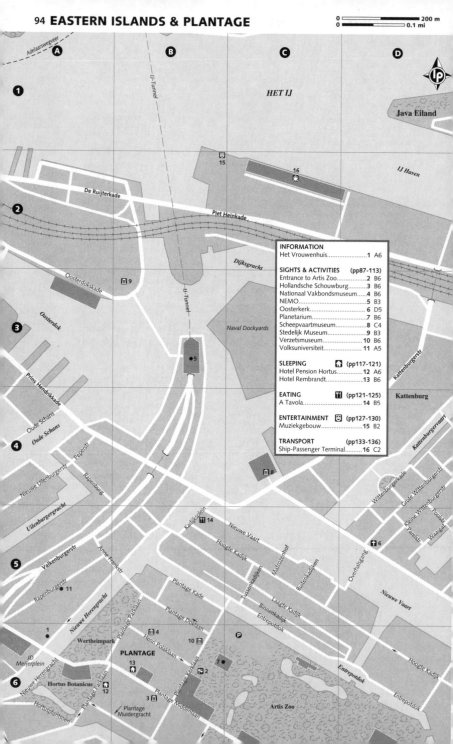

0   200 m
0   0.1 mi

HET IJ

Java Eiland

IJ Haven

De Ruijterkade

Piet Heinkade

Dijksgracht

Oosterdokskade

Oosterdok

Naval Dockyards

Prins Hendrikkade

Oude Schans

Nieuwe Uilenburgerstr

Uilenburgergracht

Valkenburgerstr

Rapenburgerstr

Nieuwe Herengracht

Wertheimpark

JD Meijerplein

Hortus Botanicus

Hortusplantsoen

Plantage Muidergracht

PLANTAGE

Nieuwe Vaart

Hoogte Kadijk

Plantage Kade

Plantage Doklaan

Anne Frankstr

Kadijksplein

Henri Polaklaan

Plantage Kerklaan

Plantage Middenlaan

Artis Zoo

Tussenkadijken

Laagte Kadijk

Binnenkadijk

Entrepotdok

Overhaalsgang

Nieuwe Vaart

Buitenkadijken

Entrepotdok

Hoogte Kadijk

Kattenburg

Kattenburgerstr

Kattenburgervaart

Wittenburgerkade

Wittenburgerstr

Grote Wittenburgerstr

Kleine Wittenburgerstr

Paststr

Waalstr

INFORMATION	
Het Vrouwenhuis.....................**1** A6	

SIGHTS & ACTIVITIES	(pp87-113)
Entrance to Artis Zoo.................**2** B6	
Hollandsche Schouwburg...........**3** B6	
Nationaal Vakbondsmuseum.....**4** B6	
NEMO.....................................**5** B3	
Oosterkerk..............................**6** D5	
Planetarium.............................**7** B6	
Scheepvaartmuseum.................**8** C4	
Stedelijk Museum.....................**9** B3	
Verzetsmuseum........................**10** B6	
Volksuniversiteit.......................**11** A5	

SLEEPING	🏠 (pp117-121)
Hotel Pension Hortus...............**12** A6	
Hotel Rembrandt......................**13** B6	

EATING	🍽 (pp121-125)
A Tavola.................................**14** B5	

ENTERTAINMENT	🎭 (pp127-130)
Muziekgebouw........................**15** B2	

TRANSPORT	(pp133-136)
Ship-Passenger Terminal..........**16** C2	

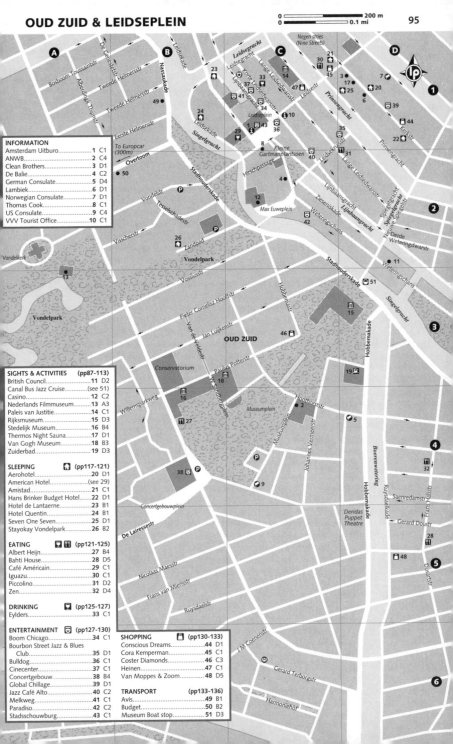

INFORMATION
Amsterdam Uitburo	1 C1
ANWB	2 C4
Clean Brothers	3 D1
De Balie	4 C2
German Consulate	5 D4
Lambiek	6 D1
Norwegian Consulate	7 D1
Thomas Cook	8 C1
US Consulate	9 C4
VVV Tourist Office	10 C1

SIGHTS & ACTIVITIES (pp87–113)
British Council	11 D2
Canal Bus Jazz Cruise	(see 51)
Casino	12 C2
Nederlands Filmmuseum	13 A3
Paleis van Justitie	14 C1
Rijksmuseum	15 D3
Stedelijk Museum	16 B4
Thermos Night Sauna	17 D1
Van Gogh Museum	18 B3
Zuiderbad	19 D3

SLEEPING (pp117–121)
Aerohotel	20 D1
American Hotel	(see 29)
Amistad	21 C1
Hans Brinker Budget Hotel	22 D1
Hotel de Lantaerne	23 B1
Hotel Quentin	24 B1
Seven One Seven	25 D1
Stayokay Vondelpark	26 B2

EATING (pp121–125)
Albert Heijn	27 B4
Bahti House	28 D5
Café Américain	29 C1
Iguazu	30 C1
Piccolino	31 D2
Zen	32 D4

DRINKING (pp125–127)
Eylders	33 C1

ENTERTAINMENT (pp127–130)
Boom Chicago	34 C1
Bourbon Street Jazz & Blues Club	35 D1
Bulldog	36 C1
Cinecenter	37 C1
Concertgebouw	38 B4
Global Chillage	39 D1
Jazz Café Alto	40 C2
Melkweg	41 C1
Paradiso	42 C2
Stadsschouwburg	43 C1

SHOPPING (pp130–133)
Conscious Dreams	44 D1
Cora Kemperman	45 C1
Coster Diamonds	46 C3
Heinen	47 C1
Van Moppes & Zoom	48 D5

TRANSPORT (pp133–136)
Avis	49 B1
Budget	50 B2
Museum Boat stop	51 D3

A B C D

1

2

3

4

5

6

Golden Bend
Herengracht
Keizersgracht
27
39
11
40
41
Nieuwe Spiegelstr
2
9
6
Keizersgracht
12
Kerkstr
Rembrandtplein
Thorbeckeplein
15
Herengracht
Utrechtstr
Reguliergracht
21
29
31
Keizersgracht
32
30
Kerkstraat
18
Nieuwe Keizersgracht
Nieuwe Kerkstr
Magere Brug
Amstel

Eerste Weteringdwarsstr
Tweede Weteringdwarsstr
Derde Weteringdwarsstr
Vijzelgracht
Prinsengracht
Noorderstr
Nieuwe Looiersstr
Fokke Simonszstr
Lijnbaansgracht
Weteringschans
Den Texstr
7 Amstelveld
19
5
28
Falckstr
Frederiksplein
4
Weteringschans
Westeinde
Prinsengracht
35
16
Achtergracht
Achtergracht
maarten Kosterstr
Sarphatistr
Achter Oosteinde
Sarphatikade
Amstelsluizen
36
Amstel
Utrechtsedwarsstr

Weteringcircuit
Weteringcircuit
33
17
Nicolaas Witsenkade
Nicolaas Witsenstr
Singelgracht
10
Stadhouderskade

34
Frans Halsstr
Marie Heinekenplein
24
26
Eerste van der Helststr
Tweede Jacob van Campenstr
Quellijnstr
Stadhouderskade
Nic Beuchenstr
Hemonylaan
Govert Flinckstr
Hemonystr
Tweede Jan Steenstr
Tweede Jan van der Heijdenstr
DE PIJP
Amsteldijk

Saenredamstr
Gerard Doustr
22
23
Albert Cuypstr
Govert Flinckstr
Daniëlstr
Albert Cuypmarkt
25
Eerste van der Helststr
Sarphatipark
Eerste Sweelinckstr

Tweede van der Helststr
Van Ostadestr
Rustenburgerstr
Van der Helstplein
Karel du Jardinstr

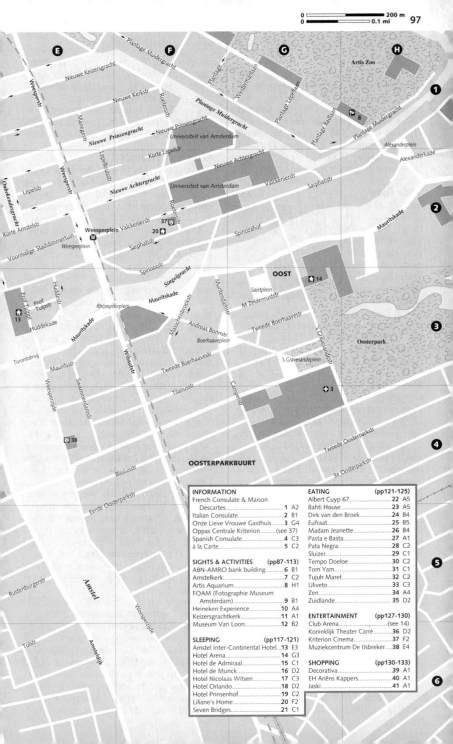

AMSTERDAM

(Continued from page 88)
material going back to the Iron and Bronze Ages. Mummy fans won't be disappointed.

The Rokin ends at Muntplein, a busy intersection dominated by the **Munttoren** (Mint Tower). When the French occupied Holland in the 19th century the national mint was transferred here from Dordrecht for safe-keeping. The French got the mint later anyway when they took Amsterdam.

Oude Zijde   Map p92

East of the Damrak-Rokin axis is the **Oude Zijde** (Old Side) of the medieval city. It's a misnomer: the Nieuwe Zijde (New Side) to the west is actually older, though the Oude Zijde got the dubious honour of absorbing the Red Light District in the 14th century. Originally the city didn't extend further south than Grimburgwal, where the filled-in parts of the Rokin ends today.

WARMOESSTRAAT

One of the original dykes on the Amstel river ran along **Warmoesstraat**, where the city's wealthiest merchants used to live (it up). Today it's an outgrowth of the Red Light District with rough-edged bars, hotels and sex shops luridly rubbing shoulders with some great old architecture. **Geels & Co** (☎ 624 06 83; Warmoesstraat 67; ☷ museum 2-4pm Tue, Fri & Sat) is a tea-and-coffee shop with a fun little museum about tea and coffee upstairs.

OUDE KERK

Just east off Warmoesstraat stands the mighty **Oude Kerk** (Old Church; ☎ 625 82 84; Oudekerksplein 23; adult/child €4/3; ☷ 11am-5pm Mon-Sat, 1-5pm Sun), built to honour the city's patron saint, St Nicholas (the inspiration for red-suited Saint Nick). The location of the city's oldest surviving building (1306) is one of Amsterdam's great moral contradictions: it's in full view of the Red Light District, with passers-by getting chatted up a stone's throw from the church walls.

Inside there's a stunning Müller organ, gilded oak vaults and fantastic stained-glass windows from 1555. Some of the 15th-century carvings on the choir stalls are downright

naughty. As in the Nieuwekerk, many famous Amsterdammers are buried under worn tombstones, including Rembrandt's first wife, Saskia van Uylenburgh.

The church's **tower** (tour bookings ☷ 689 25 65; €40) is arguably the most beautiful in Amsterdam and affords a magnificent view.

RED LIGHT DISTRICT

Amsterdam's (in)famous **Red Light District** is bordered by Warmoesstraat in the west, Zeedijk and Kloveniersburgwal in the east, and Damstraat, Oude Doelenstraat and Oude Hoogstraat in the south, and is known locally as De Wallen, the canals that run down the middle. For centuries its houses of ill repute and distilleries were the undoing of countless sailors. The clientele has changed but the basic storyline is unchanged: of the world's oldest profession plying its trade for a song with all the ancillary services close by. Business never stops: day or night, prostitutes give their come-hither looks from big neon-lit windows that line the canal. Some sections are in stereo with windows on two floors.

It's seamy for sure, but the ambience is far less threatening than in sex districts elsewhere. Crowds of middle-class sightseers gape wide-eyed at the displays, mingling with pimps, drunks, weirdos and Salvation Army volunteers; police chat with the working girls. Some places even appear to parody themselves, like the nightclub **Casa Rosso** (☎ 627 89 54; Oudezijds Achterburgwal 106-108), which has a marble penis fountain with rotating balls at the entrance.

Several museums that might have withered elsewhere flourish in this neighbourhood. The **Hash Marihuana & Hemp Museum** (☎ 623 59 61; admission €5.70; Oudezijds Achterburgwal 148; ☷ 11am-10pm) gives the lowdown on the wicked weed. The **Erotic Museum** (☎ 624 73 03; Oudezijds Achterburgwal 54; admission €3; ☷ noon-midnight) is far less entertaining than the Seksmuseum (p88) on Damrak.

Though a bit unexpected in these surrounds, the **Museum Amstelkring** (☎ 624 66 04; Oudezijds Voorburgwal 40; adult/child €6/1; ☷ 10am-7pm Mon-Sat, 1-7pm Sun) is worth a visit for its 'secret' church called Ons' Lieve Heer op Solder (Our Dear Lord in the Attic). This Catholic chapel was set up after the Calvinists seized power and remained in use through the 1880s. Curious horizontal steel poles at balcony level provide extra support, unwittingly emphasizing the claustrophobic air of the place. The chaplain's amazingly cramped quarters only confirm this impression.

ZEEDIJK

Once the first stop for wine, women and song, the street called **Zeedijk** is now more harmless than the Red Light District to the southeast. The southern end is a little Chinatown with rows of cheap eateries, and the street turns to entertainment with a mixed bag of gay and straight bars further north. Stop briefly for the house at No 1, one of just two half-timbered façades in the city (the other is in the Begijnhof).

East of the Zeedijk is the wide, forlorn and rather stinky Geldersekade. The small brick tower at the tip of this canal is the **Schreierstoren**, where English captain Henry Hudson set sail to find a northern passage to the East Indies (and ended up buying Manhattan instead).

NIEUWMARKT

Golden Age ships used to load and unload produce at **Nieuwmarkt** (New Market). The imposing **Waag** (Weigh House) originally formed part of the city fortifications but served a variety of functions later, including a spot for public executions. Today it's a so-so café-restaurant with beautifully restored interiors that have a distinctly medieval feel – candles on round chandeliers are the only source of light.

SOUTH OF NIEUWMARKT

On the east side of Kloveniersburgwal at No 29 is the **Trippenhuis**, built for the brothers Trip, who made their fortune in artillery and ammunition; note the mortar-shaped chimneys. A ridiculously narrow house stands across the canal at No 26 (see In a Tight Spot, above).

To the southeast stands the **Oostindisch Huis**, the former head office of the mighty VOC (the United East India Company). The structure now belongs to the University of Amsterdam. Enter the courtyard through the small gate at Oude Hoogstraat 24 to spot the door-top emblem across the courtyard – the only trace of VOC history here.

OUDE ZIJDE, SOUTHERN SECTION

The Oude Zijde south of Damstraat, Oude Doelenstraat and Oude Hoogstraat, is

---

> ### IN A TIGHT SPOT
>
> Amsterdam is chock-full of slender homes because property used to be taxed on frontage – the narrower your façade, the less you paid.
>
> Witness the house at Oude Hoogstraat 22 (Map p92), east of the Dam. It's 2.02m wide, 6m deep and several storeys tall, occupying a mere 12 sq m per storey. This could well be the tiniest (self-contained) house in Europe.
>
> The **Kleine Trippenhuis** (Map p92) at Kloveniersburgwal 26 is 2.44m wide. It stands opposite the mansion once owned by the wealthy Trip brothers, and as the story goes their coachman exclaimed: 'If only I could have a house as wide as my masters' door!'

---

distinctly residential – making the Red Light District seem miles away. The University of Amsterdam has a stronghold at the southern end of Oudezijds Voorburgwal, marked by a jumble of parked bicycles.

The **Universiteitsmuseum De Agnietenkapel** (☎ 525 33 39; Oudezijds Voorburgwal 231; free; ⏰ 9am-5pm Mon-Fri) has portraits of humanist giants like Erasmus, a collection of amusing old public-health posters and some fantastic stained glass in the Gothic chapel.

Just south of the Agnietenkapel is the **Huis aan de Drie Grachten** (House on the Three Canals), a gorgeous building that passed through generations of prominent Amsterdam families. It's now a linguistics and literature bookshop.

Across Oudezijds Achterburgwal, just before Grimburgwal, is a small arched gateway called **Oudemanhuispoort** (Old Man's House Gate). The spectacles above the gateway recall how an almshouse for senior citizens was sponsored by a public lottery in 1601. A venerable used-books market operates from cases lining the passage.

A few steps south of here, another gateway leads to the former inner-city hospital, the **Binnengasthuis**. It's now a mini-campus of the University of Amsterdam.

Nieuwe Zijde

West of the Damrak-Rokin axis is the **Nieuwe Zijde** (New Side) of the medieval

AMSTERDAM

city, which oddly enough was settled earlier than the Oude Zijde (p98) – the district name comes from the Nieuwe Kerk (New Church). Amsterdam's first houses were built in this neighbourhood.

NIEUWENDIJK

The oldest dyke in the city, **Nieuwendijk** (Map p92) used to link up with the road to Haarlem, and its businesses served (read: fleeced) travellers on their way to market. This pedestrian shopping street is fairly commercial but a few side alleys still have charming vendors like rubber-stamp makers or pipe manufacturers.

SINGEL, NORTHERN SECTION   Map p92

On the east side of the Singel stands the domed **Ronde Lutherse Kerk** (Round Lutheran Church). It has the distinction of being the only round Protestant church in the country. Now a conference centre, it still holds free chamber-music performances on Sunday mornings.

Across the canal, tied up at No 40, is the **Poezenboot** (Cat Boat; ☎ 625 87 94; ♥ 1-3pm), which is owned by an eccentric woman who looks after several hundred stray moggies. Visitors are welcome, in return for a donation towards cat food.

Further along the Singel is **Torensluis**, one of the widest bridges in the city. The big moustachioed bust is of **Multatuli**, the pen name of the brilliant 19th-century author Eduard Douwes Dekker, who exposed colonial narrow-mindedness in a novel about a coffee merchant. The nearby **Multatuli Museum** (☎ 638 19 38; Korsjespoortsteeg 20; free; ♥ 10am-5pm Tue, noon-5pm Sat-Sun; closed Sat Jul & Aug) tells the story.

MAGNA PLAZA   Map p92

Behind the Royal Palace stands the magnificent grand orange-and-white facade of **Magna Plaza**. Built in the late 19th century as the main post office, the complex on Nieuwezijds Voorburgwal has been converted into a multi-level shopping centre, with columned galleries and dozens of upmarket clothing shops.

KALVERSTRAAT   Map p92

South of the Dam is **Kalverstraat**, the shopping heart of town where consumers work themselves into a fever pitch over the latest sales. Solace is offered in the 19th-century Catholic church, **De Papagaai** (The Parrot; Kalverstraat 58; ♥ 10am-6pm Mon-Sat), so named for the feathered friend carved on the archway.

Housed in the former civic orphanage, the **Amsterdams Historisch Museum** (☎ 523 18 22; www.ahm.nl; Kalverstraat 92; adult/child €6/3; ♥ 10am-5pm Mon-Fri, 11am-5pm Sat & Sun) provides an engaging overview of the city's history in chronological order. Pick up a free English-language booklet.

There are interactive displays, including the ground-floor map which shows Amsterdam's growth, as well as models and paintings with push-button music. The collection of wonderfully simple navigational instruments makes you wonder how Dutch explorers discovered anything, and there's a room of paintings recalling the Amsterdam Miracle (in 1345, when a regurgitated Host was thrown into the fire but would not burn). Recordings of the city's various carillons tinkle at the touch of a button.

From the orphanage's courtyard – note the cupboards where the orphans used to store their possessions – walk through to the **Civic Guard Gallery**. The static group portraits are in stark contrast to the more dynamic treatment in Rembrandt's *Nightwatch*.

BEGIJNHOF   Map p92

Hidden behind the walls north of Spui is the **Begijnhof** (☎ 623 35 65; ♥ 8-11am), a former convent from the early 14th century. Rows of tiny houses and postage-stamp gardens overlook a well-preened courtyard. The house at No 34 dates from around 1465, giving it claim to being the oldest maintained wooden house in the country.

The Beguines were a Catholic order of unmarried or widowed women who cared for the elderly. After their Gothic church was seized by the Calvinists, the Beguines worshipped in the clandestine church opposite. The paintings and stained-glass windows here commemorate the Miracle of Amsterdam, and some of the pulpit panels were designed by De Stijl artist Piet Mondriaan. The Gothic church today serves as a Presbyterian church, and is booked months in advance for weddings.

SPUI

The square called **Spui** (Map p92) used to be water until 1882. (The name means 'sluice' and is pronounced 'spou', a bit like 'spouse'.) The statuette of an Amsterdam street-brat, *Het Lieverdje* (Little Darling), was the favoured venue for Provo protests in the 1960s.

Spui is now a meeting spot for members of the intelligentsia, who congregate in the pubs and bookshops nearby. A book market is held Fridays, followed by an art market on Sunday.

The classicist building between Voetboogstraat and Handboogstraat is the **Maagdenhuis** (Virgins' House; Map p92), built as a Catholic girls' orphanage. The handsome **Lutheran Church** (Map p90) next door still holds services.

SINGEL, SOUTHERN SECTION

The citizen's arrow militia (one of the city's civil defence forces in the 16th and 17th centuries) used to meet at the **University Library** (Map p92; ☎ 523 09 00; Singel 421–425; ☺ 9.30am-5pm Mon, Wed & Fri; 9.30am-8pm Tue & Thu, 9.30am-1pm Sat), and one building in this ensemble became the city arsenal in the early 1600s.

On the opposite canalside are the soaring turrets of the **Krijtberg** (Chalk Mountain; Map p90; ☺ 1.30-5pm Tue-Thu & Sun). It's one of the city's most beautiful Gothic churches (1883) thanks largely to its colourful interior – a stark contrast to the rather spartan Calvinist churches. You can visit during Mass at noon or 5pm, or Sunday morning services. A house here belonged to a chalk merchant, hence the name.

Back along the Singel, the southern side of the canal between Koningsplein and Vijzelstraat is occupied by the **Bloemenmarkt** (Flower Market; Map p92; ☺ 9am-5pm Mon-Sat) – see p132. Amsterdam has specialised in flower markets since the 17th century (see Tulipmania, p27).

Western Canal Belt

From the late 16th century, new canals (**Herengracht**, **Keizersgracht** and **Prinsengracht**) were added, each telling their own stories of the city's progress.

Just west of Prinsengracht lies the **Jordaan**, the old working-class quarter that's widely regarded as the hippest place to live in central Amsterdam.

WESTERN ISLANDS Map p89

The **Western Islands** were raised from the riverbed to accommodate warehouses for Dutch colonial goods. **Prinseneiland** and **Realeneiland** are the prettiest of this tiny archipelago. A narrow bridge linking the two, the **Drieharingenbrug** (Three Herrings Bridge), replaced a pontoon bridge that used to be pulled aside to let ships through.

HAARLEMMERBUURT

Over the past decade the **Haarlemmerbuurt** (Haarlem Quarter; Map p89) has evolved into one of Amsterdam's quirkiest districts. New Age shops, wacky boutiques and ethnic gift emporiums line the main **Haarlemmerstraat** (Map p89).

The landmark **Westindisch Huis** (Map p92) on Herenmarkt is the former head office of the West India Company. When Admiral Piet Heyn captured the Spanish silver fleet off Cuba in 1628, the booty was stored here.

The busy road to Haarlem led through the **Haarlemmerpoort** (Haarlem Gate; Map p89) on Haarlemmerplein, where travellers heading into town had to leave their horses and carts. The gateway was built for King Willem II to pass through on the way to his coronation.

BROUWERSGRACHT Map p89

With its humpback bridges, shiny shutters and tree-lined towpaths, the **Brouwersgracht** (Brewers' Canal) acts like a love potion on whoever gazes upon it. The dozens of breweries and warehouses that used to operate here have been converted to apartments; houseboats lining the quays add to the lazy residential character.

HERENGRACHT Map p90

The **Herengracht** (Gentlemen's Canal) was named after the '17 Gentlemen' of the United East India Company. The first section south from Brouwersgracht shows that these bigwigs sunk some of their profits into showpiece residences.

The **Theatermuseum** (☎ 623 51 04; www.tin.nl; Herengracht 170; adult/child €4.50/2.25; ☺ 11am-5pm Tue-Fri, 1-5pm Sat & Sun), run by the Netherlands

Theatre Institute, has rotating exhibits of costumes, set designs, posters and props. Its stunning interior has lots of intricate plasterwork, extensive paintings by Jacob de Wit and a magnificent spiral staircase.

The institute spills over into the **Bartolottihuis** at No 172, one of the most captivating façades in the city – a red-brick, Renaissance job that follows the bend of the canal. It was built in 1615 for a brewer.

Just beyond, Herengracht is crossed by Raadhuisstraat, which links the Jordaan with the Dam. Note the **shopping arcade** on the far side (west); designed for an insurance company, the façade bears sculptures of vicious animals to stress the dangers of life without insurance.

Much more diverse than the name suggests, the **Bijbels Museum** (Biblical Museum; ☎ 624 24 36; Herengracht 364-370; adult/child €5/2.50; ☑ 10am-5pm Mon-Sat, 11am-5pm Sun) has a large number of model temples, freshly restored 18th-century ceiling frescos by Jacob de Wit, and several centuries of the good book including the *Delft Bible*, printed in 1477. There's even a 'scent cabinet', where visitors can smell biblical odours. The pretty back garden focuses on a wistful sculpture called *Apocalypse*.

KEIZERSGRACHT Map p90
The 'emperor's canal' was named in honour of Maximilian I, ruler of Habsburg and later the Holy Roman Empire.

The three **Greenland warehouses** (Keizersgracht 40-44), with their step gables, belonged to the Greenland (or Nordic) Company, which dominated Arctic whaling from the early 17th century. Many houses along here used to belong to whaling executives and still bear decorations of their trade.

Further south on the opposite side is the goofy **Huis met de Hoofden** (House with the Heads) at No 123. The beautiful step gable has six heads at door level, representing the classical muses. Popular lore has it that these were burglars decapitated by an axe-wielding maid as they tried to break in.

The tall **Greenpeace Building** (No 174-176), which houses the body's international headquarters, is a rare example of Art Nouveau style in Amsterdam. It was built in 1905 for an insurance company – note the tiled scene of a guardian angel, who is surely peddling a life policy.

On the same side of the canal, you'll see the pink granite triangles of the unique **Homomonument** at Westermarkt. It commemorates gays and lesbians who were persecuted by the Nazis, and flowers are laid out on Liberation Day (4 May). A mobile kiosk nearby, **Pink Point of Presence** (PPP; ☑ noon-6pm Mar-Aug, limited hours Sep-Feb), distributes brochures and souvenirs.

Further along Keizersgracht stands the **Felix Meritis building** at No 324. The society promoted the ideals of the Enlightenment through the study of science, arts and commerce, and composers such as Brahms, Grieg and Saint Saëns performed in its oval concert hall. Today the Felix Meritis Foundation stages European performing-arts events (p130) and the building itself (1787) is worth a gander.

PRINSENGRACHT Map p90
Prinsengracht, named after Prince Willem van Oranje, is the least showy of the main canals. It's peppered with cafés and shops rather than stately offices and banks, and the houses are smaller and narrower than along the other canals. Houseboats line the quays.

The **Noorderkerk** at Noordermarkt, near the northern end of the canal, was a Calvinist church for the 'common' people in the Jordaan. It's shaped like a Greek cross – four arms of equal length – around a central pulpit. A sculpture near the entrance commemorates the bloody Jordaan riots of July 1934, when five people died in protests over government austerity measures. The **Noordermarkt** on the edge of the Jordaan hosts a flea market on Monday morning and a *boerenmarkt* (farmers market) on Saturday morning.

Anne Frankhuis
Although few of its original furnishings remain, the **Anne Frankhuis** (☎ 556 71 00; www .annefrank.nl; Prinsengracht 263; adult/child €6.50/3; ☑ 9am-7pm Sep-Mar, 9am-9pm Apr-Aug) is a powerful attraction of global renown. Over 900,000 visitors pass through its display rooms every year.

The Jewish Frank family hid here to escape deportation during WWII. As the German occupiers tightened the noose around the city's Jewish inhabitants, Otto Frank – together with his wife, two daughters and several friends – moved into the rear annex in July 1942, and the entrance was concealed behind a revolving bookcase.

The Franks were betrayed to the Gestapo in August 1944 and deported; Anne died in Bergen-Belsen concentration camp in March 1945, just weeks before it was liberated. Her father Otto was the only one of their group to survive. After the war Anne's diary was found among the litter in the annex, and her father published it. The diary, which gives a moving account of wartime horrors through a young girl's eyes, has sold 25 million copies and been translated into 60 languages – the original is on permanent display. The modern extension of the museum is for contemporary exhibitions.

Queues into the museum can be brutally long, so consider going in the early evening when the crowds are lightest.

Westerkerk

The tallest steeple in the city (85m) belongs to the **Westerkerk** (☎ 624 77 66; Prinsengracht 281; admission €3; ☑ 11am-3pm Mon-Fri, Easter–mid-Sep; tower 10am-5pm Mon-Sat Apr-Sep). It's topped by a fat rendition of the imperial crown of Habsburg emperor Maximilian I. The tower is the tourist logo of Amsterdam and bears the trademark XXX of St Andrew's crosses.

The church is the main gathering place for Amsterdam's Dutch Reformed community. Rembrandt, who died bankrupt in 1669 at nearby Rozengracht, is buried somewhere in the church – perhaps near the grave of his son Titus, where there's a commemorative plaque.

Tours of the tower leave on the hour. Ascend the 465 steps through several levels including a cute little museum, and you'll be rewarded with a splendid view of the old town.

JORDAAN

Originally a stronghold of the working class, the **Jordaan** (Maps pp89 & 90) is now probably the hippest neighbourhood in Amsterdam. It's a pastiche of modest old residences and a few modern carbuncles, all squashed into a skewed grid of tiny lanes and peppered with bite-sized cafés and shops. Its intimacy is contagious, and nowadays the average Jordan-dweller is more likely to be a fashion model or gallery owner than a blue-collar labourer.

The name Jordaan may be a corruption of the French *jardin* (garden), as many French Huguenots settled here in what used to be the market gardens. But some historians point to *joden*, the Dutch word for Jews, or even a biblical connection to the river Jordan.

Jordaan-dwellers have a rebellious streak. Dozens died in the Eel Riot of 1886 – after a policeman interfered with a curious pastime known as 'eel-pulling' – and 1934 saw unrest over a cut in unemployment benefits.

Many of the Jordaan's narrow canals have been filled in, though the old labels remain: **Lindengracht** (Linden Canal), **Rozengracht** (Rose Canal) and **Palmgracht** (Palm Canal). Pretty **Bloemgracht** (Flower Canal) was spared a similar fate, thanks to lobbying by artisans who owned smart canalside homes.

The Jordaan also has many *hofjes* – private courtyards surrounded by old almshouses. Some have beautiful restored houses and stunning gardens; if the entrance is unlocked, you can usually take a discreet peek.

At the **Pianola Museum** (Map p90; ☎ 627 96 24; Westerstraat 106; adult/child €3.75/2.50; ☑ 11.30am-5.30pm Sun) you can hear concerts of player pianos from the early 1900s, with rare classical or jazz tunes composed especially for the instrument. The curator gives demonstrations with great zest.

Southern Canal Belt

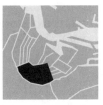

This wealthy residential area was the soul of discretion, and you'll see that the 17th- and 18th-century façades are less ostentatious than those to the north. The corner of Herengracht and Leidsegracht is a particularly tranquil spot, despite its proximity to the heady action at Leidseplein.

HERENGRACHT

By the mid-17th century many Amsterdam merchants had amassed stupendous fortunes, and they saw to it that restrictions on the size of canalside plots were relaxed. So the southern stretch of **Herengracht** (Maps pp92 & 96–97) has buildings noticeably larger than in the western section.

The Herengracht between Leidsestraat and Vijzelstraat, known as the **Golden Bend** (Map p96-97), had some of the largest private mansions in the city. Most of them now belong to bankers, lawyers and financial advisors. French culture was all the rage among the city's wealthy class, so most styles are Gallic with a Dutch twist. A prime example is the interior of the **Goethe Institut** at No 470 (Map p96-97).

Back on the even side of Herengracht, the corner with Vijzelstraat is dominated by the colossal **ABN-AMRO bank building** (Map p96-97) that continues all the way to Keizersgracht. It was completed in 1923 as head office for the Netherlands Trading Society, a Dutch overseas bank. Its successor teamed up with a competitor to form ABN-AMRO, the largest bank in the country.

At **Reguliersgracht** (Map p96-97), canal tour boats halt for photos at the beautiful 'canal of the seven bridges', cut in 1664. The arches are illuminated at night and reflect dreamily on the rippling water.

North of here, across Herengracht towards the centre of town, is **Thorbeckeplein** (Map p96-97), with a statue of Jan Rudolf Thorbecke, the Liberal politician who created the Dutch parliamentary system in 1848. A modern art market is held here Sundays in spring and summer.

Beyond Thorbeckeplein is the raucous **Rembrandtplein** (Map p92), focused around the statue of the *Nightwatch* artist. The grassy square is lined with pubs, grand cafés and restaurants, and is usually buzzing with suburbanites looking for high times and potent toxins.

The street running west from Rembrandt-plein to Muntplein is **Reguliersbreestraat** (Map p92), home to strange bedfellows such as an art gallery, fast-food joints and a glorious Art Deco cinema, the **Tuschinski Theater** (Map p92; ☎ 626 26 33; Reguliersbreestraat 26-28). Built in the roaring '20s and fully renovated in 2001, this cinema is a riot of flamboyant design inside and out – the lobby alone is an eyeful.

A night out on Rembrandtplein is best preceded by a meander down **Utrechtsestraat** (Maps pp92 & 96-97). It's relaxed as shopping streets go, with the occasional tram going past cosy restaurants like Sluizer (p124) and unique stores like the travel map-and-book specialist á la Carte (p84).

Further east along Herengracht is **Museum Willet-Holthuysen** (Map p92; ☎ 523 18 22; Herengracht 605; adult/child €4/2; ⊙ 10am-5pm Mon-Fri, 11am-5pm Sat & Sun), a beautiful house with a sumptuous interior bequeathed to the city a century ago. There aren't many chances to see lavish residences like this one from the inside.

KEIZERSGRACHT

Department store **Metz & Co** (Map p90; ☎ 520 70 36; Keizersgracht 455) was built in 1891 for a life insurance company. The functionalist architect Gerrit Rietveld added the top-floor gallery, where you can have lunch with a panoramic view over the canals.

Across the canal at No 508 is the former **PC Hooft store** (Map p90), built for a cigar manufacturer in 1881. It's a nod to poet, playwright and national icon Pieter Cornelisz Hooft, whose 300th birthday (1948) was commemorated with this Dutch-Renaissance gem that has a curious Germanic tower.

Further along on this side of the canal, beyond Leidsestraat, is the solid yet elegant **Keizersgrachtkerk** (Map p96-97) at No 566. It was built in 1888 to house the orthodox-Calvinist reformed community, which had left the Dutch Reformed Church.

The next side street is **Nieuwe Spiegelstraat** (Map p96-97), lined with swish antique shops and art galleries. The extension of this street, the pretty **Spiegelgracht**, leads past more antiques and paintings to the Rijksmuseum.

SIGHTS ON REGULIERSGRACHT

A stroll down Reguliersgracht (Map p96-97) offers many little gems and surprises, including:

- No 34 with its massive eagle gable commemorating the original owner, Arent ('Eagle') van den Bergh

- Superb panorama towards Herengracht from the bridge at Keizersgracht, with artful leaning houses

- Dutch/German woodwork at No 57-59 reminiscent of the city's medieval wooden houses, built in 1879 for a carpenter

- Amstelveld with the white, wooden Amstelkerk at Prinsengracht

- Stork statuette at the corner house No 92

Further along Keizersgracht from Nieuwe Spiegelstraat, across windswept Vijzelstraat, is **Museum Van Loon** (Map p96-97; ☎ 624 52 55; Keizersgracht 672; adult/child €4.50/free; 🕑 11am-5pm Fri-Mon), built in 1672 for a wealthy arms dealer. The house recalls canalside living in Amsterdam when money was no object for the wealthy. The rococo rose garden is particularly fetching.

FOAM (Map p96-97; ☎ 551 65 00; Keizersgracht 609; adult/child €5/free; 🕑 10am-5pm Sat-Wed, 10am-9pm Thu & Fri) has simple, functionalist and large galleries, some with skylights or grand windows for natural light. They are the setting for this impressive new museum of photography – accessible and inspiring, yet always critical. Cross the inner footbridge to witness the world as seen through lenses of renown.

PRINSENGRACHT

Near the corner with Leidsegracht is the **Paleis van Justitie** (Court of Appeal; Map p95) at No 436, a huge, neoclassical edifice that served as an orphanage during the 19th century.

A hundred metres down Leidsestraat is **Leidseplein** (Map p95), one of the liveliest squares in the city. This was once the gateway for travellers heading south towards Leiden; the oil-lamps have given way to screaming neon signs, but street musicians and artists are still drawn to the cobblestone square. There's something for everyone here: cinemas, cafés, pubs and nightclubs as well as a smorgasbord of restaurants. The casino nearby is shaped like a roulette table.

Like so many public buildings, the **Stadsschouwburg** (City Theatre; Map p95; Leidseplein 25) had a difficult birth. Public criticism of the 1894 edifice stopped funding for the striking façade-cum-arcade, and the architect, Jan Springer, promptly retired. A new theatre hall will incorporate the neighbouring Melkweg venue in a single performing-arts complex by 2006, an attempt to win back performances that moved to the Muziektheater and other newer venues.

South across Marnixstraat, the **American Hotel** (Map p95) is an Art Nouveau landmark from 1902. No visit to Amsterdam would be complete without a coffee in its stylish Café Américain.

Much further southeast, beyond the intersection of Prinsengracht and Reguliersgracht, stands the wooden **Amstelkerk** (Map p96–97). The city planners had envisaged four new Protestant churches in the southern canal belt, but the only one that materialised was the **Oosterkerk** (Map p94). The Amstelkerk (1670) was meant to be a temporary house of worship, but when funds were lacking for a grander structure it became permanent.

Continue to the river Amstel and you'll see the **Amstelsluizen** (Map p96–97). These mighty sluices allowed the canals to be flushed with fresh river water, and were still operated by hand until a few years ago. Across the river stands **Carré** (p130), originally built as a circus but now the city's largest theatre.

To your left is the **Magere Brug** (Map p96–97), the most photographed drawbridge in the city. Often mistranslated as the 'Skinny Bridge', it was actually named after the Mager sisters, who lived on opposite sides of the canal. As the sweet tale goes, the sisters had a footbridge built so they could visit each other more easily.

Nieuwmarkt Quarter   Map p92

This used to be the heart of Jewish Amsterdam, an industrious community that traded in diamonds, tobacco and clothes. In the 1970s the Nieuwmarkt area was embroiled in a squatters' dispute; hairy activists and long-time residents united in waves of protest against the construction of modern housing estates and a new metro line. The city prevailed and much of the area was razed and rebuilt, with dubious results.

East of Nieuwmarkt square there are panoramic views over the **Oude Schans** canal towards the striking **Montelbaanstoren**, a proud old defensive tower. To the northwest, at Binnenkant and Prins Hendrikkade, stands the **Scheepvaarthuis** (Shipping House), a remarkable structure that resembles a ship's bow. This was the first building of the Amsterdam School and it still turns heads today.

NIEUWMARKT ISLANDS   MAP P92

In the late 1500s more land was created to accommodate an influx of Jewish immigrants from Spain and Portugal. Several rectangular blobs emerged east of Oude Schans, one of which, Uilenburg, is still recognisable as an island today.

On Uilenburg, the vast factory of **Gassan Diamonds** (☎ 622 53 33; Nieuwe Uilenburgerstraat 173-175; admission free; ☾ 9am-5pm) was the first to use steam power in the 1880s (see Payments are Forever, p131).

SOUTHERN NIEUWMARKT QUARTER
Map p92

Land from the Amstel was reclaimed in the 16th century, creating the island of Vlooienburg. *Vlooien* means 'to flow' or 'fleas', an apt label for the present-day wares hawked at Waterlooplein market.

The **Pintohuis** at St Antoniesbreestraat 69 used to belong to a wealthy Sephardi, Isaac de Pinto, who had it remodelled with Italianate pilasters in the 1680s. Locals, in fact, used to mutter how someone was 'as rich as Pinto'. It's now a library, so you can peek inside at the beautiful ceilings.

A passageway in the modern housing estate across St Anthoniebreestraat leads to the **Zuiderkerk** (Southern Church; ☎ 622 29 62; ☾ noon-5pm Mon-Fri, noon-8pm Thu). Built in the early 1600s, this was the first custom-built Protestant church in Amsterdam (based on a Catholic design). At the end of WWII it served as a morgue. It now houses the city's planning centre for public housing, where you'll find Amsterdam's urban blueprints.

South of here, across the beautiful **Raamgracht**, is the narrow **Verversstraat** (Painters' Street) with a melange of old and new architecture typical of this area. The name refers to the paint factories that lined this avenue beyond the city walls. At the end of Verversstraat, turn right to the steel drawbridge over the pretty **Groenburgwal**.

Jodenbuurt   Map p92

The heart of the **Jodenbuurt** (Jewish Quarter) lies in and around the wide Jodenbreestraat, a remnant of a controversial freeway that was never

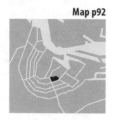

completed. At one time the squares and cramped alleys around here used to echo with the sounds of morning prayer on the Sabbath.

Museum Het Rembrandthuis (☎ 520 04 00; www.rembrandthuis.nl; Jodenbreestraat 4-6; adult/child €7.50/1.50; ☾ 10am-5pm Mon-Sat, 1-5pm Sun) depicts the life of the master painter at the height of his fame. Rembrandt ran the largest painting studio in Holland from this plush residence but ruined it all by making enemies and squandering his earnings. Chronic debt forced him to spend his final years in more humble digs in the Jordaan. The museum has nearly every etching Rembrandt is known to have made.

Next door is the **Holland Experience 3D** (☎ 422 22 33; Waterlooplein 17; adult/child €8/6.85; ☾ 10am-6pm). This hype-fest lurches from tulips to windmills to threatened dykes. Perfume is puffed in when tulips appear, and the audience is sprinkled with water as the dykes crumble.

WATERLOOPLEIN

Once lined with homes of Jewish traders, **Waterlooplein** today hosts a daily flea market – the best spot to pick up bicycle parts, imitation Calvin Kleins and some very imaginative junk.

Formally known as the Muziektheater, the **Stopera** opened in 1986 after nearly two decades of controversy; the nickname comes from 'Stop the Opera' protests. One critic remarked that the building 'has all the charm of an Ikea chair' and the theatre has been plagued by logistical problems; the acoustics aren't great, and the ballet practice room has low ceilings. Still, many productions, such as *The Nutcracker* (a highlight for its monumental stage sets), have earned accolades here. The Stopera is in the same complex as the **city hall**.

The neoclassical **Mozes en Aäronkerk**, a Catholic church, was built on the northeastern corner of Waterlooplein, just as many Jews began to move to the suburbs. Note the plaque of Moses on the corner of Jodenbreestraat and Waterlooplein. It's still a functioning church and a centre for social and cultural organisations.

MR VISSERPLEIN & AROUND

On the east side of Mr Visserplein traffic circle stands the majestic **Portuguese-Israelite**

Synagogue (☎ 624 53 51; adult/child €4.50/3.50; ☺ 10am-4pm Sun-Fri). Built for the Sephardic community in the 17th century, the synagogue was Europe's largest at the time and was based on the Temple of Solomon. The large Jewish wedding canopy *(chuppah)* is made from jacaranda wood, and services are still held beneath large lit candelabra. The Ets Haim seminary contains one of the most important Jewish libraries in Europe.

Under the traffic circle, **Tun Fun** (☎ 689 43 00; Mr Visserplein; adult/child under 12 free/€7.50; ☺ 10am-7pm) is a kiddie playground built in an old underpass. It has neat-o slides, ball pools, trampolines, a mini-cinema, a soccer field and a snack bar. Children must be accompanied by an adult.

South of the synagogue is the **Joods Historisch Museum** (Jewish Historical Museum; ☎ 626 99 45; www.jhm.nl; Jonas Daniël Meijerplein 2-4; adult/child €6.50/3; ☺ 11am-5pm). This beautifully restored complex of four Ashkenazic synagogues is linked by glass-covered walkways. These synagogues include the Grote Sjoel (Great Synagogue, 1671), the first public synagogue in Western Europe; the Obbene Sjoel (Upstairs Synagogue, 1686); the Dritt Sjoel (Third Synagogue, 1700 with a 19th-century façade); and the Neie Sjoel (New Synagogue, 1752), the largest in the complex.

The Great Synagogue contains religious objects as well as displays showing the rise of Jewish enterprise and its role in the Dutch economy; displays tend to be on the academic side. The New Synagogue focuses on aspects of Jewish identity and the history of Jews in the Netherlands. A kosher coffeeshop serves Jewish specialities.

Plantage

In the 19th century the Jewish elite began to move from the city's centre into the area called **Plantage** (Plantation) where they built imposing villas. Until then Plantage had been a district of parks and gardens.

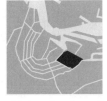

The **Hortus Botanicus** (Botanical Garden; Map p94; ☎ 625 84 11; Plantage Middenlaan 2A; adult/child €6/3; ☺ 9am-5pm Mon-Fri, 11am-5pm Sat & Sun) was founded in 1638 as a herb garden for the city's doctors. It quickly became a repository for tropical seeds and plants brought by Dutch ships from the East and West Indies, and coffee, pineapple, cinnamon and oil palm were distributed from here throughout the world. Guided tours are given on Sunday at 2pm.

The wonderful mixture of colonial and modern structures includes a restored, octagonal seed house; a modern, three-climate glasshouse with subtropical, tropical and desert plants; and a monumental palm house. The 400-year-old cycad here is the world's oldest potted plant. The Hortus Medicus is a medicinal herb garden that attracts students from around the globe.

Several buildings in the area serve as poignant reminders of its Jewish past. The **Nationaal Vakbondsmuseum** (National Trade Union Museum; Map p94; ☎ 624 11 66; Henri Polaklaan 9; adult/child €2.30/1.15; ☺ 11am-5pm Tue-Fri, 1-5pm Sun) used to house a powerful diamond workers' union. Visiting union members will be in their element but most people come just to see the fanciful design – it's an Art Deco showcase, designed by HP Berlage.

Around the corner, the **Verzetsmuseum** (Resistance Museum; Map p94; ☎ 620 25 35; Plantage Kerklaan 61A; adult/child €4.50/free; ☺ 10am-5pm Tue-Fri, noon-5pm Sat & Sun) describes the daily realities of resisting the Germans in WWII. Fascinating tales of active and passive resistance are told through photos, documents and sound fragments. There's also a library here in the Plancius building, built in 1876 as the social club for a Jewish choir.

The **Hollandsche Schouwburg** (Holland Theatre; Map p94; ☎ 626 99 45; Plantage Middenlaan 24; free; ☺ 11am-4pm) played a tragic role during WWII. After 1942 the theatre became a detention centre for Jews awaiting deportation. Little more than the façade is left standing today, and there's a memorial room and an exhibition room with videos and documents on the building's history.

East of Artis zoo stands an 18th-century grain mill known as **De Gooyer** (Map p82–83), the sole survivor of five windmills from this corner of the city. The former public baths alongside now house the **Bierbrouwerij 't IJ** (Map p82-83; ☎ 622 83 25; Funenkade 7; ☺ 3-7.45pm Wed-Sun), a small brewery producing potent but tasty beers under the distinctive ostrich label. There's a tour of the brewery on Friday at 4pm.

ARTIS
MAP P94 & 96-97

The oldest zoo on the European continent, **Artis** (Map p94 & p96-97; ☎ 523 34 00; www.artis.nl; Plantage Kerklaan 38-40; adult/child €14/10.50; ⊙ 9am-5pm Oct-May, 9am-6pm Jun-Sep) has an alphabet's soup of wildlife – alligators, birds, chimps and so on up to zebras. The layout is full of delightful ponds, statues and leafy winding pathways, and themed habitats like African savannah or the tropical rainforest are pretty convincing. For many, the aquarium complex is *the* highlight with its coral reefs, shark tanks and an Amsterdam canal displayed from a fish's point of view. There's also a planetarium and a kiddie petting zoo. Admission is about 25% cheaper in September – an old Artis tradition.

Eastern Islands
Map p94

This area is about modern housing, but some splendid façades of old gabled homes remain along Wittenburgergracht. The ex-islands of Oostenburg, Wit-

tenburg and Kattenburg are now seamlessly linked to central Amsterdam. **Kattenburg** used to be the seat of the Dutch admiralty, and its dockyards here once fitted men o' war for the royal navy.

SCHEEPVAARTMUSEUM

Once the headquarters of Holland's navy, this imposing pile on Amsterdam harbour is now home to the **Scheepvaartmuseum** (Shipping Museum; ☎ 523 22 22; www.generali.nl /scheepvaartmuseum; Kattenburgerplein 1; adult/child €7/4; ⊙ 10am-5pm Tue-Sun year-round, 10am-5pm Mon Jun-Aug). You won't find better displays on the topic although most labels are in Dutch only. The heyday of Dutch seafaring comes alive with scores of magnificent paintings – horizons crowded with three-masted merchant schooners, or naval ships engaged in fiery cannon battles. Model ships abound but there are also a few full-sized vessels, such as the swanky sloop built for King Willem I in the early 1800s. The cinema shows a vivid re-enactment of a voyage to the East Indies.

The *pièce de resistance* is the replica of the *Amsterdam*, a beautiful historic square

rigger moored alongside the museum. The stern bears the three crosses of Amsterdam's emblem, as well as the brightly painted statues of Mercurius (god of trade) and Neptune (god of the sea). Apparently the gods weren't watching over the *Amsterdam* on its maiden voyage in 1749: it became stranded off the English coast and was stripped of all valuables including its iron nails. Climb on board, peruse the captain's quarters and watch actors recreate life at sea.

NEMO

The green shiplike building on the eastern harbour is **NEMO** (☎ 531 32 33; www.e-nemo.nl; Oosterdok; admission €10; ⊙ 10am-5pm Tue-Sun), an interactive science museum with hands-on displays aimed at children and school groups. Normally free, in summer the rooftop plaza is transformed into a faux 'beach' and charges admission.

Oud Zuid

The posh neighbourhood of Oud Zuid (Old South) has many fine examples of the Amsterdam School of architecture, with porthole windows, mock prows and

other maritime motifs gracing the façades of weighty a partment complexes. The area is subdivided into Museum Quarter, Concertgebouw area and Vondelpark, names that also appear on street signs.

Behind the Rijksmuseum, the sprawling square known as Museumplein hosted the World Exhibition of 1883. It has only recently been transformed into a huge park, with an underground Albert Heijn supermarket under the slanting 'donkey's ear' near the Concertgebouw.

RIJKSMUSEUM

The *non plus ultra* of Dutch classical art with a collection valued in the billions, the **Rijksmuseum** (Map p95; ☎ 674 70 47; www.rijksmuseum.nl; Stadhouderskade 42; adult/under 19 €9/free; ⊙ 10am-5pm) is the jewel in the Netherlands' cultural crown, attracting 1.2 million visitors every year. Before renovation some 5000 paintings and other artworks were displayed in several hundred exhibition galleries. Until 2008,

---

UNDER CONSTRUCTION: RIJKSMUSEUM & STEDELIJK MUSEUM

Hearts stopped at Amsterdam tourist offices as it became clear that the Rijksmuseum and Stedeljik Museum, two of the world's greatest vaults of art treasure, would have to close for renovations lasting years – and heaven forbid – at the same time. Structural wear, shrinking space and even fire regulations were blamed as city elders wrung their hands in horror. But take heart, art lovers: a game plan emerged to prevent aesthetic withdrawal.

---

however, visitors will have to make do with 200 masterpieces chosen from five major collections. This mega project (price tag: around €300 million) will hopefully create more accessible exhibition halls as well as the underground gallery that PJ Cuypers, its talented 19th-century architect, laid down in his blueprints. If all goes well, the entire building will be returned to its original 1885 glory.

Never mind the building dust, the much-loved Dutch and Flemish paintings from the Golden Age will remain on display. The museum's crowning glory is here too: Rembrandt's mesmerizing *Nightwatch* (1650), the artist's breathtaking group portrait of an Amsterdam civil militia led by Frans Banningh Cocq, a future mayor and apparently not the brightest of lights. The painting only acquired its name in later years after grime darkened the oils, long after Rembrandt painted the scene in a hotel near Muntplein. Other household names still on display include Johannes Vermeer *(The Kitchen Maid* and *Woman in Blue Reading a Letter)*, Frans Hals *(The Merry Drinker)* and Jan Steen *(The Merry Family)*. Other must-sees are in Sculpture & Applied Art (Delftware, beautiful doll houses, porcelain, furniture) and Asiatic Art (including the famous 12th-century *Dancing Shiva*), as well as highlights from the museum's store of 800,000 prints and drawings.

Rather than being returned to storage, many old gems will be put on display in grateful venues around the country. Check the schedules for Amsterdam's Nieuwe Kerk (p88), Maastricht's Bonnefantenmuseum (p289), and the Dordrechts Museum (p222), among other exhibition locations.

The exterior of the Rijksmuseum remains a feast for the eye, with tiled murals, faux-Gothic towers and glints of gold harking back to Golden Age fortune. It wasn't popular with everyone: as the finishing touches were being laid on, King Willem III dubbed the Rijksmuseum 'the archbishop's palace' because of the Catholic influence on Cuypers' designs. The magnificent underpass with its dreamy acoustics will be closed for the face-lift, to the chagrin of local buskers (we do hope that great Mongolian string band moves no further than the Vondelpark).

STEDELIJK MUSEUM

From April 2004 the modernist statements of Amsterdam's **Stedelijk Museum** (Map p95; ☎ 573 27 37; www.stedelijk.nl; Paulus Potterstraat 13; adult/child €7/3.50; 🕑 11am-5pm) will appear in an unlikely location: a former post-office high-rise (Map p94, Oosterdoksdijk 5) on Oosterdok Island near Centraal Station. While the venue doesn't exactly sparkle, the catalogue still reads like a *Who's Who* of modern classics: blazing impressionists such as Monet, Cézanne, Matisse, Picasso and Chagall; larger-than-life sculptures by Rodin, Renoir and Moore; De Stijl landmarks by Piet Mondriaan; and postwar, abstract works by Appel and the CoBrA movement. The late 20th century finds expression in the glowing pastels of Andy Warhol and iconic cartoons of Roy Liechtenstein.

The 2nd, 3rd and 11th floors will be occupied for permanent and temporary exhibitions until 2007. In the meantime the Stedelijk's former home on Museumplein (next to the Van Gogh Museum) is undergoing a vigorous face-lift. The responsibility rests heavy on the guardians of Amsterdam's art heritage: 600,000 visitors per year are expected after a spanking new museum is unveiled. Like the Rijksmuseum, the Stedelijk is presenting some of its works around the country for the duration.

VAN GOGH MUSEUM

A repository of works by the world's greatest dead artist, the **Van Gogh Museum** (Map p95; ☎ 570 52 00; www.vangoghmuseum.nl; Paulus Potterstraat 7; adult/child €9/2.50; 🕑 10am-6pm) is also one of the greatest impressionist galleries on earth. The museum opened in 1973 to house the collection of Vincent's younger brother Theo. It consists of about 200 paintings and 500 drawings by Vincent and his friends or contemporaries, such as Gauguin, Toulouse-Lautrec, Monet and Bernard.

Van Gogh's paintings are shown in chronological order on the 1st floor, from his moody Brabant canvases *(The Potato Eaters)* to the famous works from his French period *(The Yellow House in Arles, The Bedroom at Arles* and several self-portraits). Sunflowers and other blossoms display his knack for using Mediterranean light and colour. One of his last paintings, *Wheatfield with Crows,* is an ominous work that he painted shortly before committing suicide. Other floors display his drawings and Japanese prints, as well as works by friends and contemporaries.

Designed by Gerrit Rietveld, the exhibition spaces are generous enough to accommodate insane crowds without obscuring the paintings. The sleek rear annex hosts changing exhibitions and is an attraction in its own right, looking very much like an enormous clam – it's nicknamed 'the mussel'. The library opens weekdays only.

CONCERTGEBOUW

The neo-Renaissance gem that is the **Concertgebouw** (Concert Building; Map p95; ☎ 671 83 45 for tickets 10am-5pm; www.concertgebouw.nl; Concertgebouwplein 2-6) attracts 840,000 visitors a year, making it the busiest concert hall in the world.

Under the 50-year guidance of composer and conductor Willem Mengelberg (1871–1951), the Koninklijk Concertgebouw Orkest (Royal Concert Building Orchestra) developed into one of the world's finest. Dozens of landmark performances have been recorded here; the lure of playing here is so strong that local musicians accept pay that's lower than in many other countries.

The Grote Zaal (Great Hall) has near-perfect acoustics. The layout is surprisingly free of divisions, with a simple flat viewing area and a balcony around the perimeter. Weighty inscriptions show who the world's leading composers were in 1888, its year of construction. Recitals take place in the Kleine Zaal (Small Hall), a replica of the hall in the Felix Meritis building (p102).

Tickets are available at the door until 7pm, or through the tourist office and Amsterdam

Uitburo (see Tourist Information, p86). Free lunch-time concerts are held on Wednesday at noon.

VONDELPARK & AROUND

This English-style park (Maps pp82–83 & 95) with ponds, lawns, thickets and winding footpaths was laid out in the 1860s and '70s for the bourgeoisie. It was named after the poet and playwright Joost van den Vondel, whom the Dutch celebrate as their Shakespeare.

The park is popular with joggers, in-line skaters, street musicians, couples in love, families – in short, everybody. Free concerts are held in summer at its **open-air theatre** (☎ 673 14 99), and musicians are always performing throughout the park. The round blue teahouse is a wonderful little multilevel structure that serves coffee and cake. A stand at the Vondeltuin Cafetaria, near the Amstelveenseweg entrance, rents in-line skates and gear.

The **Nederlands Filmmuseum** (Map p95; ☎ 589 14 00; www.filmmuseum.nl; Vondelpark 3; adult/child €6.25/5; ☒ screenings 7-10pm Mon-Sat, 1-10pm Sun) isn't a museum per se but presides over a priceless archive of films screened in its two theatres, sometimes with live music. One theatre contains the Art Deco interior of Cinema Parisien, an early Amsterdam cinema. The museum's charming **Café Vertigo** (☎ 612 30 21) is a popular meeting place, and an ideal spot to people-watch; on summer evenings films are shown on the outdoor terrace. Adjoining the museum is an impressive **library** (☎ 589 14 35; ☒ 10am-5pm Tue-Fri, 11am-5pm Sat) and study centre.

Built in 1882, the neoclassical **Hollandse Manege** (Map p82-83; ☎ 618 09 42; Vondelstraat 140) is an indoor riding school inspired by the famous Spanish Riding School in Vienna. Through the passage to the rear door and up the stairs is a café where you can sip a beer or coffee while watching the instructor put the horses through their paces. Opening times vary so ring ahead.

The **Tram Museum Amsterdam** (Map p82-83; ☎ 673 75 38; Amstelveenseweg 264; adult/child return €3/1.50; ☒ 11am-5pm Sun mid-Apr–Oct, 1.45pm & 3.15pm Wed Jul & Aug) isn't really a museum, but a starting point for historic trams that clang from here to the Amsterdamse Bos recreation area – a great 1¼-hour outing. The museum is just southwest of

Vondelpark in the former Haarlemmermeer train station.

De Pijp   Map p96-97

This district, lying south of the broad Stadhouderskade, probably got its name from its straight and narrow streets that are said to resemble the stems of old clay pipes. This was the city's first 19th-century slum but it's now undergoing a determined yuppification. De Pijp is still often called the 'Quartier Latin' thanks to its lively mix of people – labourers, intellectuals, new immigrants, prostitutes and, more recently, yuppies.

The locals are best viewed at the **Albert Cuypmarkt** (Albert Cuypstraat; 9am-5pm Mon-Sat), Amsterdam's largest and busiest market. Here you'll find food, clothes and other general goods of every description and origin, often cheaper than anywhere else, as well as quite a bit of plain junk. This is Amsterdam at its multicultural best.

The area's other draw is the **Heineken Experience** (523 94 36; Stadhouderskade 78; admission €7.50; 10am-6pm Tue-Sat), commonly known as the Heineken Brewery. The brewery itself has relocated but you can still peer inside the malt silos and look at memorabilia from the Heineken clan. Mornings are less crowded and perfect for a hair of the dog – tickets include three glasses of the good stuff.

South of Albert Cuypstraat is the **Sarphatipark**, an English-style park named after the shrewd 19th-century Jewish doctor, chemist and businessman Samuel Sarphati. With its ponds, fountains and abundant bird life, it's a great spot for a picnic lunch.

A TALL COOL ONE

Apart from his duties as international beer magnate, Freddy Heineken (1924–2002) had a reputation as a ladies' man. As the story goes, an attractive young lady approached the bar and uttered the familiar phrase: 'I'd like a Heineken, please'. Freddy (stationed nearby) replied: 'I'm right here.'

Oosterpark District

This southeastern district (Map p96-97), named after the lush park at its core, was built in the 1880s for diamond-industry workers. Many of them were Jewish families who'd done good and had the means to leave the cramped centre.

A visit to the cultural anthropological **Tropenmuseum** (Tropics Museum; Map pp82-83; 568 82 15; www.tropenmuseum.nl; Linnaeusstraat 2; adult/child €6.80/3.40; 10am-5pm) is a pleasant and easy way to dip your toes into exotic cultures. You can stroll through an African market or a Mexican-style cantina, or listen to recordings of exotic musical instruments. The **children's section** (568 82 23) offers guides in Dutch for six- to 12-year-olds if you book ahead. There's an extensive library, a shop selling books, gifts and CDs, and the Ekeko café serving exotic snacks and meals. The Tropeninstituut Theater screens films and hosts music, dance and plays by visiting international artists. It's a grand place to spend a lazy Monday, when most other museums are closed.

Nieuw Zuid   Map p82–83

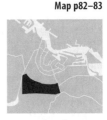

In Nieuw Zuid (New South), the area between Amstel river and the Olympic Stadium, urban planners, architects and municipal authorities joined forces in the early 20th century to produce housing, wide boulevards and cosy squares.

Some of the first residents were Jewish refugees from Germany and Austria, including writers and artists who settled around Beethovenstraat. The Frank family lived at Merwedeplein further to the east, where Churchilllaan and Rooseveltlaan merge around the **Skyscraper** (1930), a 12-storey building with spacious luxury apartments designed by JF Staal.

The **RAI** (549 12 12; www.rai.nl; Europaplein 22), an exhibition and conference centre, is the largest complex of its kind in the country.

From boats and caravans to fashion shows, few events are beyond its reach.

Amstelveen   Map p82–83

This quiet dormitory town is next to the **Amsterdamse Bos** (Amsterdam Woods). The result of a 1930s job-creation scheme, this vast tract of lakes, woods and 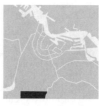 meadows draws many Amsterdammers looking for a leafy time-out from the city. Its only drawback is the background noise from nearby Schiphol Airport.

The **visitors centre** (☎ 643 14 14; Nieuwe Kalfjeslaan 4; 🕑 10am-5pm) has leaflets on walking and cycling paths. You'll also find an animal enclosure with bison, a goat farm, and a rowing course with watercraft for hire. The **Bosmuseum** (Forestry Museum; ☎ 676 21 52; Koenenkade 56; free; 🕑 10am-5pm Mon-Sat, 1-5pm Sun) has displays about flora and fauna. There's a **bike rental** (☎ 644 54 73; 10am-6pm Jun-Sep) at the main entrance at Van Nijenrodeweg. Take the historic tram from Haarlemmermeer Station (see Tram Museum Amsterdam, p110) or bus Nos 170, 171 or 172 from Centraal Station.

Nearby is the **CoBrA Museum** (☎ 547 50 50; www.cobra-museum.nl; Sandbergplein 1-3; adult/child €6/2.50; 🕑 11am-5pm Tue-Sun). Formed by artists from Copenhagen, Brussels and Amsterdam after WWII, the CoBrA movement vented the fury of abstract expressionism. The modern paintings, ceramics and statues on display here still polarise audiences today. It's opposite the Amstelveen bus terminal (bus Nos 170, 171 or 172 from Centraal Station in Amsterdam).

Amsterdam Noord   Map p82–83

Several hundred years ago, **Amsterdam Noord** (North) was a place for social outcasts and an area where the bodies of executed criminals were dumped. Since the 19th century this residential area north of the IJ river has been upgraded to  working class. It's a world away from the rest of Amsterdam, and worth half a day to explore on foot or by bicycle. See the Waterland Route (p72).

To get there, take the free pedestrian ferry marked 'Buiksloterwegveer' (between Piers 8 and 9) from behind Centraal Station.

Zuidoost   Map p82–83

Few Amsterdammers hurry to **Zuidoost** (Southeast) unless they're going to work at one of the many banks and office complexes, or to visit the **Amsterdam ArenA & Ajax Museum** (☎ 311 13 36; www.amsterdamarena.nl; Arena Boulevard 1; adult/child €8.20/7.20; 🕑 10am-5pm Mon-Sat Oct-Mar, 10am-6pm daily Apr-Sep). Ajax (*eye*-axe) is one of Europe's most successful football clubs. The displays include oodles of trophies and video highlights of key games. Visits begin with a one-hour walking tour around the high-tech Amsterdam ArenA stadium – a flying saucer with an enormous sliding roof.

ACTIVITIES
Swimming Pools

Amsterdam has a good selection of pools and we've listed those closest to the city centre. Ring ahead to find out the times of the restricted sessions (nude, children, women, seniors and so on). This might be just what you're after, of course, but remember that the schedules change frequently.

De Mirandabad (Map p82-83; ☎ 642 80 80; De Mirandalaan 9; admission €3.15; 🕑 7am-9pm), a tropical 'aquatic centre', comes complete with indoor and outdoor pools, twisting slides, a beach and a wave machine. It also has squash courts and a fitness room.

Zuiderbad (Map p95; ☎ 678 13 90; Hobbemastraat 26; adult/child €2.80/2.50; 🕑 7am-6pm Mon & Thu, 7am-10pm Tue, Wed & Fri, 8am-3.30pm Sat, 10am-3.30pm Sun) is a venerable indoor pool (1912) that has been restored to its original Art Deco splendour. A stone's throw from the Rijksmuseum, it's perfect for chilling after a culture fix.

Skating (Ice and In-line)

After a hard freeze Amsterdam's ponds resemble an old Dutch painting as the ice skaters appear, their colourful scarves trailing in the headwind.

IJscomplex Jaap Eden (Map p82-83; ☎ 694 96 52; Radioweg 64; skate rentals per day €5 ; 🕑 7am-midnight) has indoor and outdoor rinks in the eastern suburb of Watergraafsmeer. Before you go check the schedule for periods of *vrij schaatsen* (open skating). In winter you can also skate on the pond at **Museumplein** (Map p95) for a modest fee.

In-line skating has a big following in Amsterdam, and the freewheeling daredevils are always sussing out new spots to strut their stuff. Rows of cups become practice pylons near the Filmmuseum in the Vondelpark (Map p95), and the half-pipe at Museumplein (Map p95) is popular with skaters and skateboarders alike.

In fine weather hundreds of enthusiasts gather for a **Friday Night Skate** – a 15km whiz through town – at the gates of the Vondelpark. You needn't be a pro but braking skills and protective gear are essential. The chaperoned tour starts between 8pm and 8.30pm and lasts about two hours. For skates and gear, try **Rent-a-Skate** (☎ 664 50 91; Vondelpark 7; adult/child per hr €5/3.90; ☾ Mar-Oct) near the Amstelveenseweg entrance.

Saunas

Saunas are mixed and most guests go nude, so check your modesty at the front desk – or rent a towel.

Sauna Deco (Map p92; ☎ 623 82 15; Herengracht 115; adult/child €14.50/7.25; ☾ noon-11pm Mon-Sat, 1-6pm Sun) is the most elegant sauna in town, with Art Deco furnishings that once graced a Parisian department store. When you're not being stewed, massaged or packed in mud, it's a pleasure to pad round and gasp at the wrought iron, fanciful murals and ethereal lighting. Admission is cheaper till 2pm.

Tennis & Squash

Borchland Sportcentrum (Map p82-83; ☎ 563 33 33; Borchlandweg 8-12; ☾ 8am-midnight) is a sprawling complex with tennis, squash and badminton courts, bowling alleys and after-sweat facilities including a restaurant. It's next to the Amsterdam ArenA stadium in Bijlmer suburb (metro: Duivendrecht or Strandvliet).

Tenniscentrum Amstelpark (Map p82-83; ☎ 301 07 00; Karel Lotsylaan 8; court hire per hr €20; ☾ 8am-11pm Mon-Fri, 8am-9pm Sat & Sun) has 42 open and covered courts – no wonder the country's biggest tennis school is run here. There are also 12 squash courts, a sauna and a swimming pool.

Squash City (Map p89; ☎ 626 78 83; Ketelmakerstraat 6; court hire €13.60/18 per day/evening; ☾ 8.45am-

midnight) is the closest squash option to the city centre. It also offers fitness rooms and aerobics sessions, either separately or in combination with squash time.

Bungy Jumping

At **Bungy Jump Holland** (Map p89; ☎ 419 60 05; Westerdoksdijk 44; 1/2/10 jumps €50/90/250; ☾ noon-8pm Wed-Sun) you can relish a few seconds of absolute terror from a 75m crane at the edge of Amsterdam harbour. Couples can scream their lungs out while jumping together.

WALKING TOUR: THE MERCHANT'S DISTRICT

duration 1 to 1½ hours
start The Dam
end Magna Plaza

Start on the Dam, at the **Koninklijk Paleis (1)**, flanked by the towering **Nieuwe Kerk (2)**. Cross the broad Nieuwezijds Voorburgwal towards the Singel to arrive in the heart of the old merchants' district. Atop the Torensteeg bridge stands the clay-like statue of writer **Multatuli (3)**. Zig-zagging north takes you past richly ornamented façades to Herenmarkt, with its 17th-century **Westindisch**

LIST OF SIGHTS

- Koninklijk Paleis (p88)
- Nieuwe Kerk (p88)
- Multatuli statue (p100)
- Westindisch Huis (p101)
- Noorderkerk (p102)
- Huis met de Hoofden (p102)
- Greenpeace Building (p102)
- Anne Frankhuis (p102)
- Westerkerk (p103)
- Felix Meritis building (p102)
- Bijbels Museum (p102)
- Spui (p101)
- Begijnhof (p100)
- Amsterdams Historisch Museum (p100)
- Magna Plaza (p100)

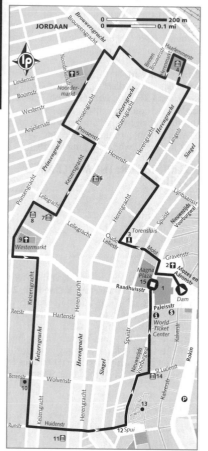

the gate on the northern side opens into the **Begijnhof (13)**. The **Amsterdams Historisch Museum (14)** is just up the street. Continue north to **Magna Plaza (15)**, a stunning former post office that now houses a chic shopping mall behind the Dam.

COURSES
Language
To avoid double Dutch you'll need to learn the proper lingo. Mainstream courses and intensive courses run for a couple of weeks or several months.

The **Volksuniversiteit Amsterdam** (Map p94; ☎ 626 16 26; www.volksuniversiteitamsterdam.nl; Rapenburgerstraat 73; courses €202-353) offers a range of day and evening courses that are well regarded.

The **British Language Training Centre** (Map p92; ☎ 622 36 34; Nieuwezijds Voorburgwal 328; www.bltc.nl; courses €290-575) gives courses in Dutch and English, and qualifications are recognized in both the UK and the Netherlands.

AMSTERDAM FOR CHILDREN
If you're feeling nervous about travelling with kids, Amsterdam is a good place to put your mind at ease.

You won't need a car to get around, and bicycles with **baby seats** are available at many railway stations and bike shops. Book a mid-price hotel or better, as budget guesthouses and hostels can be a bit druggy and often don't take reservations.

For babysitters in Amsterdam, try **Oppas Centrale Kriterion** (Map p96-97; ☎ 624 58 48; Roetersstraat 170; office ☺ 5-8pm), which seems to be consistently reliable, or **De Peuterette** (Map p82-83; ☎ 679 67 93; Hectorstraat 20). Expect to pay €5 to €6 per hour, and a bit more on weekends.

Kid's Stuff
For address and admission details of the sights listed below, see the Sights & Activities section in this chapter.

Artis (p108) has a great aquarium and you can come face-to-face with bison at the children's farm in **Amsterdamse Bos** (p112), in the south of the city. But start with a canal cruise. Then climb the steeple of the **Westerkerk** (p103), with the crazy imperial crown on top. And visit the **Anne Frankhuis** (p102) where she wrote her famous diary while hiding from the Nazis.

Huis (4), the one-time seat of Dutch shipping merchants. After a brief stroll down romantic Brouwersgracht, turn south on Prinsengracht and take in the imposing **Noorderkerk (5)**, where bustling markets are held on the square. Make a dogleg into Keizersgracht, with the curious **Huis met de Hoofden (6)** opposite. At peaceful Leliegracht by the **Greenpeace Building (7)**, return to Prinsengracht to pass the **Anne Frankhuis (8)** and the soaring tower of the **Westerkerk (9)**, whose bells Anne heard while writing her diary.

On Keizersgracht you won't miss seeing the quirky **Felix Meritis building (10)**, a one-time deep-thinkers' club turned cultural centre. Then pass the **Bijbels Museum (11)** into **Spui (12)**, home to weekend book and art markets;

The **Holland Experience 3D** (p106) is a bit tacky but the film is interactive: kids like being sprinkled with water when the dam breaks.

NEMO (p108) is hands-on and a hit with the little ones. At the **Scheepvaartmuseum** (Shipping Museum, p108) they can clamber on a replica of the *Amsterdam*, the ship that wrecked off the coast of England. Round the day off riding a historic tram at the **Tram Museum Amsterdam** (p110).

For pure entertainment, kids love **Madame Tussaud's** (p88) on the Dam and don't care if they can't recognise all the waxworks. The **Amsterdam Marionette Theatre** (Map p92; ☎ 620 80 27; Nieuwe Jonkerstraat 8; adult/child €12/4.50; shows ☺ 8pm Fri, check for other dates) near Nieuwmarkt gives captivating shows like Mozart's *The Magic Flute*, and over Christmas there's usually a circus in **Carré** (p130).

If they're still not exhausted, try the swimming pools at **De Mirandabad** (p112) in the south of the city where there's a beach and wave machine. The place to chill out is the **IJscomplex Jaap Eden** (p112) in the eastern suburbs, with both indoor and outdoor ice-skating rinks.

Oud Zuid (p108) is a good neighbourhood for cycling with the kids in tow – wide streets, parks and fine old residential areas. The best place for picnics is the **Vondelpark** (p110) where there are plenty of ducks and kiddie swings. Finally, if all else fails the underground **Tun Fun** (p107) playground is good for soaking up excess energy.

QUIRKY AMSTERDAM

After about 10 minutes in Amsterdam you'll notice that the 'alternative' tends to be fairly mainstream. So something has to be pretty offbeat to qualify as genuinely quirky. Here are a few items that took our fancy:

The **Kattenkabinet** (Cats' Cabinet; Map p92; ☎ 626 53 78; Herengracht 497; adult/child €4.50/2.25; ☺ 10am-2pm Mon-Fri, 1-7pm Sat & Sun) was founded by a wealthy financier, in memory of his tomcat. The displays (by Picasso, Rembrandt and many others) are devoted to the feline presence in art.

Who says you can't take it with you? **De Ode** (Map p82-83; ☎ 419 08 82; Levantkade 51, KNSM Island) will build a bookcase that converts to a coffin, or a coffin on wheels with a bicycle towbar – perfect for taking a friend on a last cycle tour.

St Nicolaas Boat Tours (☎ 423 01 01; Korte Leidsedwarsstraat 12; €10 donation; Mar-Oct) runs hour-long 'smoking' tours on small canal boats through the Red Light District. You're encouraged to bring your own snacks and smokes (wink wink). Book at the Boom Chicago comedy club (p127).

There's little left of the squatters' movement, but one holdout is **Vrankrijk** (Map p90; Spuistraat 216). Behind the 18th-century façade (defaced with bold political graffiti, of course) lies a gritty bar for 'squatters, anarchists and activists who support any supra-parliamentary movement'. Subversive? You bet. In the 1980s police suspected that riots were organised here. Since then the revolutionary flames have died down and the bar has obtained a proper license.

TOURS

Quite a few tour operators take a spin round the sights in spring and summer, and competition is fierce.

Bus Tours

Holland International (Map p92; ☎ 625 30 35; adult/child €18/9; Damrak 34; ☺ 10am & 2.30pm) This 2½-hour bus tour includes the Rijksmuseum, a whirl through the Jordaan and a diamond factory visit. For €4 extra you get a 3½-hour bus-and-boat tour. Also offers tours to Volendam and Marken, Delft and the Keukenhof tulip fields.

Keytours (Map p92; ☎ 520 00 80; adult/child €28/14; Dam 19) Offers four-hour city sightseeing tours in summer covering a canal cruise, the Anne Frankhuis (including admission), a diamond-cutter's and a windmill.

Lindbergh Tours (Map p92; ☎ 622 27 66; www.lindbergh.nl; Damrak 26; adult/child €18/9; ☺ 10am & 2.30pm) Does 2½-hour city bus sightseeing tours; add €4 for a one-hour canal-boat tour.

Canal Tours

Sure, the windows may fog up and the commentary can be a bit stale, but the big glassed-in canal boats do offer a unique view of Amsterdam's fantastic buildings. Several operators depart from moorings at Centraal Station, Damrak, Rokin and opposite the Rijksmuseum – just hop on board.

Lovers (Map p92; ☎ 622 21 81; adult/child €8/5.75) Conducts cruises along three different routes. There are also evening cruises by candlelight, or with wine and cheese.

Canal Bus Jazz Cruise (Map p95; ☎ 623 98 86; adult/child €39/20; ☻ 8pm Sat Apr-Oct) Sends out its live jazz vibes over a large radius. It's hard to resist an offer that includes 'unlimited' wine, beer, soft drinks, cheese and nuts. Departure is from the mooring opposite Rijksmuseum.

Bicycle Tours

Several tour operators lead cyclists through Amsterdam in the summertime, which is a good thing given the volume of two-wheel traffic.

Let's Go (Map p90; ☎ 0365-45 00 80; www.letsgo -amsterdam.com; Keizersgracht 181) Does 4½-hour bike tours to Edam and Volendam, or a 'Castle & Windmills' tour east of the city, for €22 – including bike hire – plus train tickets. Also does a tour of the dazzling tulip fields in season. Starting point is the tourist office in front of Centraal Station.

Yellow Bike Tours (Map p92; ☎ 620 69 40; www.yellowbike.nl; Nieuwezijds Kolk 29) Join two- and three-hour bicycle tours for €15 and €17, respectively, through the canal belt, the Red Light District and the Jordaan. It also offers a six-hour bucolic trek to Broek in Waterland, north of Amsterdam (€22.50), with a stop for lunch in a Dutch pancake house.

For details of a day's bicycle tour from Amsterdam, see the Waterland Route (p72).

FESTIVALS & EVENTS

Amsterdam's cultural calendar is filled to the max but there always seems to be room for another event. Summer is the busiest time.

February
Carnaval A Catholic tradition best known in the south of the country, but Amsterdammers also don silly costumes and party.

Commemoration of the February Strike
(25 February) In memory of the anti-Nazi general strike in 1941.

April
Koninginnedag (Queen's Day, 30 April) A huge flea market blankets the city, with street parties, dense crowds and beer galore – in short, collective madness.

May
Remembrance Day (4 May) For the fallen of WWII. Queen Beatrix lays a wreath on the Dam (p87), and the city observes two minutes' silence at 8pm.

GAY & LESBIAN AMSTERDAM

Amsterdam's gay and lesbian community just goes from strength to strength. For many it's Europe's gay capital despite stiff competition from the likes of Berlin and Barcelona, and no-one raises an eyebrow if two men (or women) hold hands or kiss in public. Amsterdam's **Homomonument** (p102), dedicated to persecuted gays and lesbians in WWII, is the first of its kind in the world. The crowning glory came in 2001 when the Netherlands became the first country in the world to legalise same-sex marriages.

Information

The best information source is the **Gay & Lesbian Switchboard** (☎ 623 65 65). The **COC** (Map p90; ☎ 626 30 87; Rozenstraat 14) is Amsterdam's gay and lesbian social centre, with a café and a nightclub.

Gay News Amsterdam (www.gaynews.nl) is the Netherlands' top-selling gay publication; a good lifestyle site is www.gay amsterdam .com. **Vrolijk** (Map p92; ☎ 623 51 42; Paleisstraat 135) has a huge selection of worldwide and local magazines as well as novels, guidebooks and postcards.

Close to 100 gay bars, clubs, hotels and restaurants are dotted all over town. Many popular gay places are along **Reguliers- dwarsstraat** (Map p92), while **Rembrandt- plein** (p104) is real queen territory. Kinky Amsterdam congregates over on **Warmoes- straat** (p98) in the Red Light District.

The biggest single party is the **Roze Wester** thrown at the Homomunument on Queen's Day on 30 April, with bands and street dancing. **Amsterdam Pride** is the only water-borne gay pride parade in the world, held the first weekend of August.

Saunas

Thermos Day (Map p90; ☎ 623 91 58; Raamstraat 33; ☻ noon-11pm Mon-Fri, noon- 10pm Sat & Sun) This large, leisurely sauna is cruising terrain with a small porn cinema and private (or not so private) darkrooms, a bar and a restaurant. Its nocturnal mate, **Thermos Night** (Map p95; ☎ 623 49 36; Kerkstraat 58-60; ☻ 11pm-8am Sun-Fri, 11pm- 10am Sat) is similar to the day sauna except there's no restaurant.

June
Holland Festival (Virtually all month) The country's biggest extravaganza for theatre, dance, film and pop music, with a justified claim to cutting-edge innovation (www.hollandfestival.nl).

Vondelpark Open-Air Theatre (Until late August) Free events held 'for the people' under the intimate shell of the Vondelpark open-air theatre (p110). There's high drama and concerts across the genres from pop and world to classical and jazz (www.openluchttheater.nl).

Roots Music Festival (Last week of June) A refreshing blast of world music and culture with performances, parades, workshops and a market, all in the Oosterpark (p111; www.amsterdamroots.nl).

July
Robeco Zomerconcerten (Until late August) A quality line-up of 80-odd classical, jazz, and world music concerts at Amsterdam's top concert venue, the Concertgebouw (p110; www.robecozomerconcerten.nl).

August
Gay Pride Canal Parade (First Saturday) The only water-borne gay parade in the world, with lots of pride showing on the outlandish floats.

Grachtenfestival (Canal Festival, late August) Five days of free classical concerts in courtyards and private canalside homes, as well as on the canals themselves (www.grachtenfestival.nl).

Uitmarkt (Late August) The re-opening of Amsterdam's cultural season with three days of free concerts and information booths around the big museums and Leidseplein (www.uitmarkt.nl).

September
Bloemencorso (Flower Parade, first Saturday) Spectacular procession of blossomy floats from Aalsmeer to the Dam, and back again.

November
Cannabis Cup (Third week) Marijuana festival hosted by *High Times* magazine, with trophies for the best grass.

SLEEPING

Amsterdam can get crazy with visitors any time of year so book well ahead. It's worth paying a bit extra for something central so you can enjoy the nightlife without resorting to night buses or taxis. Many visitors sadly overlook the Museum Quarter and the Vondelpark area, which both offer quality digs only a short walk from the action at Leidseplein.

Be very sure to ask about parking if you're driving. In Amsterdam probably the best you'll do is pay-and-display or find a security-guarded garage, unless you're staying at a top-end hotel.

Amsterdam has no shortage of luxury accommodation, from intimate boutique hotels to towering modern complexes. Historic hotels in the old centre have been upgraded but you'll still come across places without air-con or a lift (elevator). This is often compensated for by their ritzy antiques, such as Louis XIV suites, grandfather clocks and original art by Dutch masters.

The top-end rates do not include breakfast, which costs another €13 to € 25.

Bookings
The tourist offices or the GWK exchange office at Centraal Station have hotel-booking services that are your emergency chute during busy periods – see Tourist Information (p86) for details.

Budget hotels are popular with backpackers but often won't take telephone bookings, so start door-knocking from 10am.

As summer hits Amsterdam the official HI hostels fill up, so bookings are strongly advised. Other hostels won't always take telephone reservations so you'll have to risk turning up.

The price categories for double rooms with private facilities are as follows: budget (under €70), mid-range (€70 to €150) and top end (from €150).

Inside the Canal Belt
BUDGET
Hotel de Lantaerne (Map p95; ☎ 623 22 21; www.hoteld elantaerne.com; Leidsegracht 111; s €50-75, d €60-90, tr €90-120, incl breakfast) The perfect place to tumble into after a night on Leidseplein, just 100m away. The hotel is fairly quiet at the junction of two canals, with some nice views. The smart linen compensate for cubicle bathrooms and some carpets with Rorschach test stains.

Hotel Pax (Map p90; ☎ 624 97 35; Raadhuisstraat 37; d without bathroom €35-70, with bathroom €55-95) Our favourite budget choice in hotel-lined Raadhuisstraat – run by two friendly, funky brothers – has a real artsy-student vibe. All eight rooms have a TV and each is individually decorated. The larger rooms face the busy street with noisy trams, so bring some earplugs.

Anna Youth Hostel (Map p92; ☎ 620 11 55; Spuistraat 6; dm €20, d/tr €80/100 with bathroom; 🖳)

Funky Anna's has an inviting feel and caring proprietor. Unlike most hostels there's a quiet respectful vibe and a wonderful, cheery Middle Eastern–style interior – our fave in this category. Rates (10% lower on weekdays) include linen, towels and a safe.

Hotel Groenendael (Map p92; ☎ 624 48 22; Nieuwendijk 15; s/d without bathroom €25/50, incl breakfast) In coffeeshop land this hotel is a surprise – rooms clean as a whistle and a breakfast big enough to fuel a day of sightseeing. The Dutch-American owners are full of cheer, the clientele's not too wild and you can chill in the lounge with a stereo and a TV. As always in this part of town, the quietest rooms are at the back.

Frisco Inn (Map p92; ☎ 620 16 10; www .friscoinn.com; Beursstraat 5; s/d €50/70, incl breakfast; 🖳) Cheerful Irish-run outfit that's been recently renovated; its 10 rooms all have private amenities. Some rooms have a clear view over Damrak and Centraal Station. The bar's a friendly place to hang out, with music for all moods.

Hotel Pension Hortus (Map p94; ☎ 625 99 96; www.hotelhortus.com; Plantage Parklaan 8; d €50 incl breakfast) Facing the Botanical Garden, this comfy, 20-room hotel has small doubles with or without bathroom (luck of the draw). Its relaxed clientele includes young and happy tokers.

Hans Brinker Budget Hotel (Map p95; ☎ 622 06 87; www.hans-brinker.com; Kerkstraat 136; dm €20-25, d without bathroom €60-75, incl breakfast) A lobby that's always in a state of mayhem, spartan rooms that have all the ambience of a public hospital – and 538 beds almost always filled to capacity. The bustling corridors have a crazy, frat-house feel and the barn-like bar is usually filled with bouncy backpackers.

Flying Pig Downtown Hostel (Map p92; ☎ 420 68 22; www.flyingpig.nl; Nieuwendijk 100; dm €14.50-31.50; 🖳) This insanely popular joint has a lobby filled with unhurried dope smokers lounging around on cushions to rock music. The rooms could be cleaner but no-one seems to mind, especially when the bar is abuzz.

The Shelter Jordan (Map p90; ☎ 624 47 17; www.shelter.nl; Bloemstraat 179; dm €16.50 Sep-Jun, €18.50 Jul-Aug, incl breakfast; ✖) Despite the no-smokin', -drinkin' and -spliffin' policy and 2am curfew, this Christian youth hostel is a gem. Single-sex dorms are quiet and clean, and the breakfasts – especially the fluffy pancakes – are a beaut on the garden patio.

The Shelter City (Map p92; ☎ 625 32 30; www.shelter.nl; Barndesteeg 21; dm €16.50 Sep-Jun, €18.50 Jul-Aug, incl breakfast; ✖) The Shelter Jordan's sister hostel, near the Red Light District, has more missionary zeal and a midnight curfew.

Stadsdoelen Youth Hostel (Map p92; ☎ 624 68 32; Kloveniersburgwal 97; dm €21.65, d €53.30, incl breakfast; ✖) The eight nonsmoking, ultra-clean dorms, each with 20 beds and free lockers, offer a modicum of privacy. There's a mix of single-sex and co-ed dorms and bathrooms, a big TV room, a bar with pool table, laundry, Internet facilities and a 2am curfew.

MID-RANGE

Hotel Prinsenhof (Map p96-97; ☎ 623 17 72; www.hotelprinsenhof.com; Prinsengracht 810; s with/ without bathroom €75/40, d with/without bathroom €80/ 60, incl breakfast) This beautiful 18th-century house has canal views to sigh over. Staff are affable and the rooms spacious with natty antique furnishings. The attic quarters with diagonal beams are most popular. Note the electric luggage hoist, 'Captain Hook', in the central stairwell.

Hotel Orlando (Map p96-97; ☎ 638 69 15; hotelorlando@zonnet.nl; Prinsengracht 1099; s €70-110, d €80-130, incl breakfast) The plain entrance hall belies the joys that lie beyond: big canalside rooms, big views, low rates. Impeccably chic, boutique style, though the bathrooms need a little work. The hospitable, gay-friendly host serves breakfast on the tranquil mezzanine.

't Hotel (Map p90; ☎ 422 27 41; Leliegracht 18; r €134, incl breakfast) Quiet, familiar and understated, 't Hotel is a genuine find. It's a 17th-century canal house with only eight rooms, all with comfortable, Art Deco–inspired furnishings. Be sure to book Room 7, a sun-filled space with a gabled roof and large windows overlooking the canal.

Hotel Quentin (Map p95; ☎ 626 21 87; www .quentinhotels.com; Leidsekade 89; s/d without bathroom €40/75, with bathroom from €65/90, incl breakfast) Popular with lesbians and international actors from the nearby theatres, the Quentin is decorated with colourful murals and handmade furniture. Rooms are quite varied; some have balconies, canal views and TVs.

Hotel Résidence Le Coin (Map p92; ☎ 524 68 00; www.lecoin.nl; Nieuwe Doelenstraat 5; s/d/q €110/130/218) This shiny new hotel, run by the University of Amsterdam, offers high-class apartments spread over seven historical buildings, all equipped with designer furniture and kitchenettes – and all reachable by lift. Breakfast (€8) is served in a nearby café.

Hotel Brouwer (Map p92; ☎ 624 63 58; Singel 83; s/d €50/85, incl breakfast; ✗) A former sea-captain's home, this renovated canal house oozes 17th-century charm at near-budget prices. All eight rooms are immaculately furnished with high-quality duvets and linen, buffed floors, private bathrooms and great views of the Singel. A real gem.

Hotel De Munck (Map p96-97; ☎ 623 62 83; demunck@wxs.nl; Achtergracht 3; d/tr €95/150, incl breakfast) De Munck's brilliant breakfast room looks like a replica of a 1950s diner with its working jukebox. The 14 spacious, renovated rooms will also make you smile – comfy contemporary furnishings, TVs and telephones. The flower-filled courtyard is as welcoming as the English host.

Amistad (Map p95; ☎ 624 80 74; www.amistad.nl; Kerkstraat 42; s/d from €63/77, incl breakfast) Rooms at this gay bijou hotel are dotted with hip designer flourishes like Philippe Starck chairs, CD players, chic soft furnishings (and TV, phone, safe and fridge). After breakfasting in the kitchen/dining room with ruby red walls, have a surf in the cool Internet lounge.

Hotel Clemens (Map p90; ☎ 624 60 89; www.clemenshotel.com; Raadhuisstraat 39; s without bathroom €55, d with/without bathroom €110/70; ☐) Tidy, renovated, steep-staired Clemens gears itself to all budgets. Take your pick of the chic themed rooms (one with a sexy red-gold interior, another with delicate French antiques), all with phone, safe and fridge. Your hostess lends PCs for in-house wireless Internet use. Breakfast is €8 extra.

City Hotel (Map p92; ☎ 627 23 23; www.city-hotel.nl; Utrechtsestraat 2; d/q without bathroom €60/100, d/tr/q with bathroom €80/105/120; ☐) Above the Old Bell pub, this is an unexpectedly fab choice. It's clean, neat, well run and good value. All rooms are decorated with crisp blue and white linen. We enjoyed the six-bed room (€45 per person) with skylights and curved girders overlooking Utrechtsestraat.

Hotel de Admiraal (Map p96-97; ☎ 626 21 50; fax 623 46 25; Herengracht 563; d €70-115, q €120-190) For sound sleepers in the thick of the action near Rembrandtplein, with beautiful canal views. Room 12 in the old attic store is the most popular double. Breakfast costs €5.

Hotel Nicolaas Witsen (Map p96-97; ☎ 626 65 46; www.hotelnicolaaswitsen.nl; Nicolaas Witsenstraat 4-8; s/d

€65/89, incl breakfast; ☐) Style aficionados may squirm at the bland pastel décor but there's no quibbling over the amenities. All 29 rooms are neat and come with phone, safe and in some cases even baths. In summer ask for the basement room that's as cool as air-con. There's a lift too.

Aerohotel (Map p95; ☎ 622 77 28; www.aerohotel .nl; Kerkstraat 49; d without bathroom €75, with bathroom €85, incl breakfast; ☐) In the middle of the gay action, this popular gay hotel has preened rooms with flowered sheets, video players and a well-guarded feeling of privacy.

Black Tulip Hotel (Map p92; ☎ 427 09 33; www.blacktulip.nl; Geldersekade 16; s €110, d €140-185, incl breakfast) Bondage boys will feel right at home in nine rooms that have a mind-boggling array of toys – cages, bondage chairs, stocks, racks, hoists and more. Most of its freedom-seeking guests are from abroad.

Liliane's Home (Map p96-97; ☎ 627 40 06; Sarphatistraat 119; s/d €55/90) This women-only hotel is more like a private home, with nine rooms, balconies and loads of personality.

Stablemaster Hotel (Map p92; ☎ 625 01 48; www.stablemaster.nl; Warmoesstraat 23; s/d/tr €70/105/125, incl breakfast) Worn rooms with lots of extras for the leather crowd; JO parties in the bar for a fun-loving gay clientele.

TOP END

Blakes (Map p90; ☎ 530 20 10; www.blakesamsterdam .com; Keizersgracht 384; d €367-472, ste from €682; ✗ P) London hotelier Anouska Hempel's newest creation is a true temple of style with drop-dead gorgeous staff, rooms and restaurant. Slink through the courtyard of this 17th-century canal house and ensconce yourself in the themed rooms: a sophisticated, two-tone colour palette, fluffy towels and silk pillows piled high.

Hotel Pulitzer (Map p90; ☎ 523 52 35; www .pulitzer.nl; Prinsengracht 315-331; d €190-470; ✗ ✗ P) Occupying a row of 17th-century canal houses, Pulitzer packs a mighty punch. It manages to combine big-hotel efficiency with boutique-hotel charm. Beautifully restored rooms with mod cons galore, a cigar bar, art gallery, garden courtyards and a wonderful restaurant are high on elegance but not pompous.

Ambassade Hotel (Map p90; ☎ 555 02 22; www.ambassade-hotel.nl; Herengracht 341; s/d €158/0188; ✗) Flick through Ambassade's spiffy little library and you'll find signed copies by Salman Rushdie and Umberto Eco. The antique furniture and fixtures are traditional without being cloying, but prepare for steep winding stairwells.

Grand Hotel Krasnapolsky (Map p92; ☎ 554 91 11; www.krasnapolsky.nl; Dam 9; d €370-420, ste from €474; ✸ ✗ P) This elegant, historic hotel on Amsterdam's prime patch of real estate make up for any size issues you have. The 19th-century 'winter garden' breakfast room, the tented Shibli Bedouin Restaurant with hookah pipes, Persian carpets and comfy cushions are absolutely gob-smacking.

Grand Sofitel Demeure (Map p92; ☎ 555 31 11; www.thegrand.nl; Oudezijds Voorburgwal 197; d €380-465; ste €560-1495; ✸ ✗ P) The Demeure – Amsterdam's former city hall (1808–1987) – was the scene of Queen Beatrix's civil wedding in 1966. You may feel like a royal yourself as you wander the cavernous lobby, spacious inner courtyard or mull dinner in one of eight banquet chambers.

Amstel Inter-Continental Hotel (Map p96-97; ☎ 622 60 60; www.interconti.com; Professor Tulpplein 1; d €371-495, ste from €950; ✗ ✸ ▣ P) Everything about this five-star edifice is spectacular, from its imposing location overlooking the Amstel to its magnificent colonnaded lobby and heart-stopping prices. Lavishly decorated rooms, reverential service and deluxe amenities such as a Michelin-starred restaurant, chauffeured limos and heated indoor pool delight even the fussiest transatlantic celebrities and Euro-royals.

Hotel de l'Europe (Map p92; ☎ 531 17 77; www.leurope.nl; Nieuwe Doelenstraat 2-8; s/d €295/350, ste from €445; ▣ ✸ P ☎) Oozing Victorian elegance, l'Europe has welcomed the likes of Arnold Schwarzenegger with its glam chandelier and cavernous lobby. The rooms are gloriously large and have marble bathrooms, and the attached Excelsior Restaurant, chi-chi gym and swimming pool are equally impressive. You can arrive by private boat at its dining terrace on the Amstel.

Outside the Canal Belt
BUDGET

Stayokay Vondelpark (Map p95; ☎ 589 89 96; www.stayokay.com/vondelpark; Zandpad 5; dm €21-23, d €65-77, incl breakfast; ✗) This has the leafiest location of Amsterdam's hostels – a modern, attractive 536-bed facility, with one section

---

THE AUTHOR'S CHOICE

Seven One Seven (Map p95; ☎ 427 07 17; www.717hotel.nl; Prinsengracht 717; d €390-640; ✸) Without doubt the most wonderful hotel in Amsterdam. Hyper-plush, deliciously appointed rooms with that rare luxury in Amsterdam: space. Check into the splashy Picasso suite – with its soaring ceiling, commodious furniture, gorgeous contemporary and antique décor, and a bathroom as big as some European principalities.

Canal House Hotel (Map p90; ☎ 622 51 82; www.canalhouse.nl; Keizersgracht 148; d €140-190, incl breakfast) It's hard to know where to spend your time in this splendid boutique hotel. The 17th-century dining room with chandeliers, grand piano and garden views? Or perhaps the plush, burgundy-hued bar? The small but inviting guest rooms are filled with antiques, all equipped with phones but no TVs.

Hotel Rembrandt (Map p94; ☎ 627 27 14; fax 638 02 93; Plantage Middenlaan 17; d €65-100, incl breakfast; ▣) You'll pour another coffee just to spend more time in the stunning, wood-panelled breakfast room with chandeliers and 17th-century paintings. Rooms are spic and span and have phones. To get the most bang for your buck ask for Room 2 (a large double with a balcony overlooking a small garden) or 21 (quad, split-level, sunny and modern).

Seven Bridges (Map p96-97; ☎ 623 13 29; Reguliersgracht 31; d €100-175, ste €200, incl breakfast; ✗) Private and sophisticated, Seven Bridges is one of the city's loveliest little hotels on one of its loveliest canals, with nine spacious, well-appointed rooms (lush Oriental rugs and elegant antiques). The rear suite has a separate full kitchen and private terrace for breakfast, which is served on fine china.

Hotel De Filosoof (Map p82-83; ☎ 683 30 13; www.hotelfilosoof.nl; Anna van den Vondelstraat 6; d €111-135) This stately hotel near leafy Vondelpark has rooms decorated after famous philosophers or writers including Aristotle, Wittgenstein and Spinoza. The furniture can be lush or Zen minimalist, depending. Ask to see the simpler (and less expensive) rooms in the house across the street.

occupying a tall, half-timbered 19th-century school building with views into the park.

Gaaspercamping (Map p82-83; ☎ 696 73 26; www.gaaspercamping.nl; Loosdrechtdreef 7, Gaasperdam; camp sites €5-6, plus person €4.25, car €3.75, caravan €5-6; ◷ mid-Mar–Dec) This large park-cum-recreation area has a café, a restaurant, a bar, barbecues, a supermarket and – wait for it – a lake with a swimming beach. From Centraal Station, take Metro No 53 to Gaasperplas in the southeastern suburbs.

Camping Vliegenbos (Map p82-83; ☎ 636 88 55; www.vliegenbos.com; Meeuwenlaan 138; camp site per person €7.60, car/caravan €7.20/20.70; ◷ Apr-Sep) This well-equipped camping ground in Amsterdam North is just a few minutes' bus ride from the city centre. There's a shop, laundry, hot showers, cabins and 25 hectares of woodland to explore by bike. From Centraal Station take bus No 32 or 36 to Zamenhofstraat/Merelstraat stop.

Camping Zeeburg (Map p82-83; ☎ 694 4430; info@campingzeeburg.nl; Zuider IJdijk 20; person/tent/car/caravan €4.50/3.50/4/5) Bed down 2m below sea level at this sprawling camping ground that feels more like a summer camp. There's a swimming pool, a restaurant, a supermarket, bike rental and even a small animal farm, all on the shores of the IJssel river. Pre-fab cabins for two to six people cost €35 to €105. Take bus No 22 from Centraal Station to Kramatweg and cross the bridge.

MID-RANGE

Hotel Arena (Map p96-97; ☎ 694 74 44; www.hotelarena.nl; 's-Gravesandestraat 51; d €100-175, incl breakfast; 💻) After changing from chapel into orphanage, then becoming a backpackers hostel, Arena is now a super-mod 121-room hotel with a fashionable restaurant, a café and an energized nightclub. The split-level doubles with separate lounge are a sunny delight. Rooms are phoneless.

TOP END

Hilton Amsterdam (Map p82-83; ☎ 710 60 00; www.hilton.com; Apollolaan 138-140; d €275-353, ste from €400; 🍴 🅿 💻) Pop stars love this luxury hotel: John Lennon and Yoko Ono staged their 'bed-in' for world peace here, and Dutch rocker Herman Brood was a regular guest at the bar. The hotel boasts a rooftop club room with city views, and is situated in a stately area with a private marina.

EATING

Amsterdam has a dynamic culinary scene with hundreds of restaurants and *eetcafés* (pubs serving meals) catering to all tastes.

Meal prices have risen sharply in recent years – a development widely blamed on the switch to the euro, Europe's single currency. On a global scale the price/quality ratio in Amsterdam may be roughly on par with similar establishments in London and New York. In a mid-range restaurant you can easily spend €45 to €70 for a three-course meal for two including drinks.

The streets around Leidseplein (Lange Leidsedwarsstraat and Korte Leidsedwarsstraat) are packed with restaurants – a veritable culinary melting pot. These places don't see a lot of return business so quality can be mediocre; a short walk to another quarter will increase the chances of a memorable meal.

You're likely to score a hit on Utrechtsestraat (the honey-pot of casual eateries in the Jordaan or Western Canal Belt), which runs the gamut from congenial cafés to starched-linen establishments. Cheap ethnic eats are easily found at the Chinese hole-in-the-walls on Zeedijk near Nieuwmarkt Square, or in the Indian, Turkish and Surinamese places along Albert Cuypstraat.

Assyrian

Eufraat (Map p96-97; ☎ 672 05 79; Eerste van der Helststraat 72; mains €9-15; ◷ dinner) This no-frills, friendly *eetcafé* is hailed from far and wide for its excellent Assyrian–Middle Eastern food. A good-value portion of Assyrian pancakes filled with chicken and cheese is sure to hit the spot, along with a fuel-injected cup of Arabic coffee.

Cafés

You may have trouble finding places that serve breakfast before 9am or 10am. But in the right places you'll discover plenty of small cafés serving hearty breakfasts and good quality sandwiches, soups and cakes for lunch. The more interesting ones are in the side streets of the canal belt, the Jordaan and around Nieuwmarkt.

Dimitri's (Map p90; ☎ 627 93 93; Prinsenstraat 3; mains €3.50-11) A carbon-copy of a Parisian brasserie, sophisticated Dimitri's serves an international menu of gargantuan salads, pastas and burgers. Mornings see media types nibbling on croissants or, if they're feeling perky, ordering the champagne breakfast.

Foodism (Map p90; ☎ 427 51 03; Oude Leliestraat 8; mains €6-8) A hip little lounge bathed in colours so garish they're gorgeous. All-day breakfasts, filled sandwiches and salads made up the day menu; night-time sees patrons tuck into big platefuls of pasta. Try the 'Pinky' – tagliatelle with salmon pesto and almonds (€9).

Nielsen (Map p90; ☎ 330 60 06; Berenstraat 19; mains €3.50-8.50) Spread over two levels filled with vases of fresh flowers, this sunny café does a tasty set breakfast: eggs, toast, fruit, juice and coffee (€8), which is hard to beat. For lunch, the tasty salads or club sandwiches (gigantic turkey or chicken) are fantastic.

Puccini (Map p92; ☎ 626 54 74; Staalstraat 21; mains €3-11; ☾ lunch & dinner, closed Mon) Refuel on Italian panini rolls and salads with sun-dried ingredients, or slurp a fresh blend at this small, chic sandwich bar. It also runs its own chocolate and cake shop next door, one of Amsterdam's heavenly best.

Café Reibach (Map p89; ☎ 626 77 08; Brouwersgracht 139; mains €2.50-11) Look no further for a magnificent breakfast: a platter laden with Dutch cheese, pâté, smoked salmon, eggs, coffee and fresh juice. It's also pleasant for afternoon cake and coffee (try the creamy cheesecake).

Stoop (Map p90; ☎ 639 24 80; Eerste Anjeliersdwarsstraat 4; mains €18-21; ☾ dinner) Great bistro-style food such as grilled Marlin over lemon linguini.

Chinese

For genuine Chinese at affordable prices, visit the strip of ethnic restaurants along the Zeedijk near Nieuwmarkt.

Hoi Tin (Map p92; ☎ 625 64 51; Zeedijk 122; mains €7-18; ☾ lunch & dinner) Cheap, cheerful and perpetually packed with people tucking into unpretentious Cantonese fare. The huge menu – as long as the Great Wall – features all your old faves like sweet-and-sour chicken and beef in black-bean sauce.

Dutch

Pannenkoekenhuis Upstairs (Map p92; ☎ 626 56 03; Grimburgwal 2; mains €4-7; ☾ lunch & dinner) Climb some of Amsterdam's steepest stairs to reach this cubbyhole. The reward is flavoursome, filling pancakes (chicken

ragout!) and kooky décor (vintage teapots hanging from the ceiling).

d'Vijff Vlieghen Restaurant (Map p90; ☎ 624 83 69; Spuistraat 294-302; mains €22-28; ☾ dinner) The second you set foot in this dining complex of five 17th-century canal houses, you know you're in for a treat. Ask to be seated in the Rembrandt Room (with four original etchings) and join splurging business groups being treated to silver service and Dutch 'New Kitchen' dishes.

Pancake Bakery (Map p90; ☎ 625 13 33; Prinsengracht 191; mains €5-10; ☾ lunch & dinner) One of the best places to try delicious, filling Dutch pancakes (savoury or sweet) is at this restored old warehouse. It has dozens of varieties as well as omelettes, soups and desserts.

Blauw aan de Wal (Map p92; ☎ 330 22 57; Oudezijds Achterburgwal 99; mains €24-26; ☾ dinner Mon-Sat; ☒) You've got to know where to look for this gem, tucked away in a little alley in the Red Light District. Carefully prepared modern Dutch dishes like suckling pig or wild bass are served in this charming 17th-century herb warehouse, complete with old steel weights and measures. The leafy courtyard backs onto a monastery.

French

Christophe (Map p90; ☎ 625 08 07; Leliegracht 46; mains €30-52; ☾ dinner) Jean Christophe's subtly swanky restaurant lives up to its two Michelin stars with dishes like roasted filet of red mullet with orange and cardamom, saffron pasta (€32) or the stewed lobster with pumpkin mousseline (€52).

De Belhamel (Map p92; ☎ 622 10 95; Brouwersgracht 60; mains €18-20; ☾ dinner) Belhamel's gorgeous Art Nouveau interior is a fitting backdrop of excellent French-inspired dishes like beef with poached shallots and a chanterelle-Armagnac sauce. This is a quality spot for a romantic evening.

Fusion

Summum (Map p89; ☎ 770 04 07; Binnen Dommersstraat 13; mains €17-22; ☾ dinner) The melt-in-your-mouth *ceviche* of scallops is one of Amsterdam's taste sensations. Punchy Italian or Thai culinary creations, spunky waiters and the sophisticated décor means bookings are essential.

Szmulewicz (Map p92; ☎ 620 28 22; Bakkersstraat 12; mains €10-18) Szmulewicz's menu darts around the globe: expect big serves of

Indian curries, Mexican burritos and Indonesian satays. The ambience is fitting, especially in summer when enthusiastic buskers play music on the terrace.

Greek

Grekas (Map p90; ☎ 620 35 90; Singel 311; mains €9-12; ☽ dinner) Ignore the catering-shop ambience and sit down for generous portions of the best Greek home cooking. The chicken, spinach and rice stew is a hearty delight.

Indian

Koh-I-Noor (Map p90; ☎ 623 31 33; Westermarkt 29; mains €10-18; ☽ dinner) Yep, the interior is about as gaudy as it gets but the food is consistently good, running the gamut from soothingly mild to palate-searing for curries, tandoori and biryani dishes. The tandoori mix of chicken, lamb, kebabs and prawns is big enough for two.

Memories of India (Map p92; ☎ 623 57 10; Reguliersdwarsstraat 88; mains €13-26; ☽ dinner). This chichi yet ineffably relaxed restaurant produces great, greaseless samosas and

deftly spiced subcontinental standards like tandoori lamb chops and Bengal prawns in lime, chilli and ginger. The vegetarian set meal is good too.

Indonesian

Tempo Doeloe (Map p96-97; ☎ 625 67 18; Utrechtsestraat 75; mains €18-22; ☽ dinner) You'll have to buzz your way into this top-notch Indonesian restaurant. Dishes come quite spicy yet you can still taste all the subtle flavours – giant shrimp in coconut-curry sauce is a perfect example. The wine list is laden with well-chosen New World vintages. No reservation means no table and no arguments.

Tujuh Maret (Map p96-97; ☎ 427 98 65; Utrechtsestraat 73; mains €13-19; ☽ dinner) Excellent veggie rijsttafel and Sulawesi-style treats.

Italian

A Tavola (Map p94; ☽ 625 49 94; Kadijksplein 9; mains €12-21; ☽ dinner) Overlooked by most tourists, this authentic Italian restaurant near the Scheepvaartmuseum (p108) serves mouth-wateringly tender meats and superb pastas

THE AUTHOR'S CHOICE

Pier 10 (Map p92; ☎ 624 82 76; De Ruyterkade Steigers 10; mains €18-19; ☽ dinner) Perched at the end of a pier behind Centraal Station, this old toll station offers harbour views worthy of a Monet painting. Book a table in the waterside rotunda, order red mullet with apple capers and watch the sun set over the North Sea Canal. The entire building was moved across the IJ river during harbour renovations – ask your kind host about the meticulous planning.

Hemelse Modder (Heavenly Mud; Map p92; ☎ 624 32 03; Oude Waal 9; mains €16, set meals €26; ☽ dinner) This beautifully decorated, gay-run restaurant has floor-to-ceiling mauve velvet curtains and displays of tropical flowers. The speciality is chocolate mousse (hence the restaurant's name). Extraordinary care goes into dishes, without a hint of the blandness that plagues Dutch cuisine. The changing repertoire might include pot-au-feu with a succulent young chicken or polenta soufflé served with baby artichokes.

Bahti House (Map p96-97; ☎ 470 89 17; Albert Cuypstraat 41; mains €10-18; ☽ dinner) One of the best-kept secrets in De Pijp is this exceedingly friendly, quick-serving, always-tasty Indian restaurant. The butter chicken masala (€12.50) is consistently smooth and tender but the fiery tandooris and biryanis won't disappoint either. Start with a rich mango lassi and a chapati amuse-bouche on the shady terrace.

Zuidlande (Map p96-97; ☎ 620 73 93; Utrechtsedwarsstraat 141; mains €12-24; ☽ dinner) The restaurant's chef-owner Arend Nieboer trained under French cooking guru Paul Bocuse. Creative and flavoursome French-Med dishes such as duck breast with caramelised apple syrup are served in this romantic restaurant lit by oil lamps. The four-course meal (€40) is always memorable, and the waiters are happy to advise on the excellent wines.

Nomads (Map p90; ☎ 344 64 01; Rozengracht 131-133; set menu €42.50; ☽ dinner) The ultimate in Amsterdam's themed dinner clubs, Nomads lets you wine, dine and recline on stuffed cushions in a hall festooned with Moroccan curtains under UFO-sized chandeliers. Graze on platters of mod Middle Eastern snacks and drink in the decadence. As the evening progresses, the belly dancers and DJs come out to complete a sexy dining experience.

AMSTERDAM

that cry out for a selection from its excellent wine list. Reservations are a must.

Casa di David (Map p90; ☎ 624 50 93; Singel 426; mains €8-25; ⏰ lunch & dinner) This is a saucy Italian place with a cool dark interior, ceiling beams and hunky waiters. The menu is simple but the ingredients in its crispy pizzas, mixed salads and scaloppini are incredibly fresh. The single upstairs table overlooking the Singel offers a lovely dining experience, so book ahead.

Burger's Patio (Map p90; ☎ 623 68 54; Tweede Tuindwarsstraat 12; 3-course menu €23; ⏰ dinner) Despite the name, burgers aren't the speciality here and there's no patio, but a small garden courtyard. What you will find is a sensibly priced Italian set meal with a French accent.

Piccolino (Map p95; ☎ 623 14 95; Lange Leidsedwarsstraat 63; mains €6-19; ⏰ lunch & dinner) This busy Italian place in the Leidseplein area is affordable and always packed. No surprises on the menu, just a whole lot of pastas and pizzas with all your favourite toppings. The pizza calzone is great.

Pasta e Basta (Map p96-97; ☎ 422 22 26; Nieuwe Spiegelstraat 8; set meals €35; ⏰ dinner) Live opera serenades over antipasto and pasta.

Madam Jeanette (Map p96-97; ☎ 673 33 32; Eerste van der Helststraat 42; mains €14-20; ⏰ dinner) Ultra-foxy models have made this trendy café their spiritual home. While they're getting air-kissy at the 1970s-style bar, grab a table and treat yourself to fab European dishes such as guinea fowl filled with ricotta or sweet-potato tortellini.

Japanese

Zen (Map p96-97; ☎ 627 06 07; Frans Halsstraat 38; mains €9-12; ⏰ lunch & dinner Tue-Sat) Hidden in a little street in De Pijp, this Japanese place is a real find. There are only two tables that seat up to six people each in the simple interior, but the food is delicious. Choose from sushi or *donburi* (beef, chicken and salmon on rice) or do takeaway rolls from €4.

Quick Eats

Crust & Crumbs (Map p89; ☎ 528 64 30; Haarlemmerstraat 108; ⏰ 11am-7pm Mon, 8am-7pm Tue-Fri, 9am-5pm Sat) This designer bakery serves flaky quiches, fruity tarts, and filled baguettes from top-notch ingredients. Try a crusty brown chicken sandwich with rucola, pepper and olive mayonnaise (€5).

Gary's Muffins (Map p82-83; ☎ 421 59 30; Jodenbreestraat 15; ⏰ 9am-5.30pm) Tasty fresh bagels, warm chocolate brownies and sweet and savoury muffins go down well after a morning nosing round the treasures of Waterlooplein market.

Hema (Map p92; ☎ 623 41 76; Nieuwendijk 174) The designer cafeteria upstairs in this department store has good sandwiches, coffee and ice cream. Rarely discovered by tourists.

MAOZ Falafel (Map p92; ☎ 427 97 20; Regulierbreestraat 35) Its flagship falafel sandwich (€3.50) is always crispy and hot, with endless toppings from the self-service salad bar. The half-dozen branches around town include one at Leidsestraat 85.

Vlaams Friteshuis (Map p92; Voetboogstraat 31) The top fries joint in town has a battery of sauces near Spui.

Tom Yam (Map p96-97; ☎ 623 15 64; Utrechtsestraat 55; set meals €9; ⏰ dinner) This bright Thai takeaway offers tasty dishes such as chicken curry stewed in banana peel, meat balls with chili and coriander, and spicy duck with celery.

Uliveto (Map p96-97; ☎ 423 00 99; Weteringschans 118; mains €5-8; ⏰ 11am-6pm) It's impossible not to stop and gape at the mouth-watering displays of fresh pastas, salads and creamy desserts. Buy a takeaway or dine at the large marble table under the designer milk urns.

Seafood

Sluizer (Map p96-97; ☎ 622 63 76; Utrechtsestraat 43-45; mains €13-22; ⏰ dinner) This lively Amsterdam institution with a super-romantic, enclosed terrace actually comprises two restaurants: a renowned fish restaurant at No 45 and a Parisian-style 'meat' restaurant at No 43, although both menus are offered in either. Spare ribs and bouillabaisse are the house specialities.

Albatros (Map p90; ☎ 627 99 32; Westerstraat 264; mains €16-23; ⏰ dinner, closed Wed) Garish decorations like plastic lobsters in hanging fishnets can't detract from the lovingly cooked seafood dishes – like freshly grilled brill or gurnard, or the oven-baked lobster. There's a smoke-free section.

Self-Catering

Frank's Smokehouse (Map p82-83; ☎ 670 07 74; Wittenburgergracht 303; set meals €6-10; ⏰ 10am-5pm Tue-Fri, 10am-4.30pm Sat) The place to assemble a swish picnic of lobster soup, wild boar

Reguliersgracht (p104) at night, Amsterdam

Flower delivery, Amsterdam (p79)

Amsterdam (p79)

Houses reflected in a canal, Amsterdam (p115)

The Cannabis University, Amsterdam (p79)

JULIET COOMBE

Leidseplein (p105), Amsterdam

IZZET KERIBAR

Water pipes on display at Conscious Dreams (p132), Amsterdam

MARTIN MOOS

Coffeeshop sign, Amsterdam (p128)

ELLIOT GERARD DAN

Wooden tulips, Amsterdam (p79)

Souvenirs at Waterlooplein flea
market (p132), Amsterdam

Souvenirs for sale on the Dam (p87),
Amsterdam

Tour boats (p115), Amsterdam

Centraal Station, Amsterdam (p87)

Colourful bike (p134), Amsterdam

Tram (p136), Amsterdam

stew or hearty veggie pies – not to mention a peerless selection of tasty smoked fish and meats. The Alaska salmon is an absolute hit with the restaurant chefs.

Albert Heijn (Map p92; Nieuwezijds Voorburgwal 226) This upmarket supermarket chain sells takeaway meals and has branches at Koningsplein 6 (Map p90) and Museumplein (Map p95).

Dirk van den Broek (Map p96-97; Eerste van der Helststraat 25) The best choice for a wide range of cut-rate groceries.

Spanish

Casa Juan (Map p90; ☎ 623 78 38; Lindengracht 59; tapas €3-8, mains €12-17; dinner) Fantastic Spanish food – some say the best in Amsterdam – is served here at reasonable prices. Juan's wife runs the floor while Juan whips up his signature paella. Be sure to book.

Pata Negra (Map p96-97; ☎ 422 62 50; Utrechtsestraat 142; tapas €3-15; dinner) An eyeful of fun, with its alluringly tiled exterior and an equally exuberant crowd inside. Weekends are quite a scene with boisterous groups sharing sangria and tapas plates (try the garlic-fried shrimps and grilled sardines).

Duende (Map p90; ☎ 420 66 92; Lindengracht 62; tapas €2-11; dinner) Reasonably priced tapas and flamenco on Saturdays.

Steakhouses

Iguazu (Map p95; ☎ 420 39 10; Prinsengracht 703; mains €11-32; lunch & dinner) This Brazilian-Argentinian steakhouse serves cuts so tender they practically dissolve in your mouth, and everything tastes great with *chimichurri* (a spicy sauce), which sits in a small jar on every table. Relax on the canal terrace over Bahia chicken with shrimp, palm oil and coconut milk (€16), or over a stove-top mix of three delectable meats (€20).

Surinamese

Surinamese restaurants tend to be small and simple, and specialise in takeaway food. The streets near the Albert Cuypmarkt are lined with 'em. Most close by 10pm.

Albert Cuyp 67 (Map p96-97; ☎ 671 13 96; Albert Cuypstraat 67; mains €4-7; lunch & dinner) A colossal portion of *roti kip* (chicken curry, flaky roti bread, potatoes, egg and cabbage) refills any tank after a couple of hours at the Albert Cuypmarkt.

Thai

Rakang Thai (Map p90; ☎ 627 50 12; Elandsgracht 29; mains €15-21; dinner) Goofy decorations, such as chairs wrapped in hospital bandages, don't obscure the delicious cooking. Go for the duck salad – a crunchy, spicy delight.

Turkish

Turquoise (Map p90; ☎ 624 20 26; Wolvenstraat 22; mains €10-21; lunch & dinner) Turquoise's four dining rooms are a stylish dark blue with gold trim, the perfect setting for live Turkish music on Sunday nights. Dishes like chicken fillet stuffed with mushrooms and walnuts hint that fusion is creeping into the menu, but they still tickles the tastebuds.

Vegetarian

De Bolhoed (Map p90; ☎ 626 18 03; Prinsengracht 60-62; mains €6-12; lunch & dinner) This popular vegetarian eatery prides itself on the freshness of its organic food. Pancakes, salads, burritos, homemade breads and amazing cakes are prepared with gusto in artsy surroundings, and it's usually packed to the gills.

Green Planet (Map p92; ☎ 625 82 80; Spuistraat 122; mains €6-16; lunch & dinner) This modern veggie eatery cares – about your health, biodegradable packaging, peace, love and reasonably low prices. Come for a quick burger, crostini, wrap, fresh pastry, biscuits or homemade cake.

DRINKING

Anytime of day or night it's hard to go dry in Amsterdam. The selection of drinking establishments simply boggles the mind.

Brown Cafés

The medieval centre is teeming with atmospheric brown cafés. This is what old-style drinking was all about: gritty locals, sandy floors, potent beer and no feeling for the passing hours.

Café 't Smalle (Map p90; ☎ 623 96 17; Egelantiersgracht 12) This charming café has a pretty and convivial terrace that's just above water level and always packed. It was opened in 1786 as a *jenever* (Dutch gin) distillery and tasting house. The interior has been restored with antique porcelain beer pumps and lead-frame windows.

Café de Sluyswacht (Map p82-83; ☎ 625 76 11; Jodenbreestraat 1) Possibly the prettiest drinking spot in the city, this lock-keeper's house is listing like a waterlogged ship but has secluded tables overlooking a broad canal. The picture-book view paints a thousand words.

Hoppe (Map p90; ☎ 420 44 20; Spui 18) One of the city's best, this gritty brown café has been enticing drinkers behind its thick curtain for more than 300 years, and its beer sales are among the highest in Amsterdam. In summer the boisterous business crowd spills over onto Spui.

Het Papeneiland (Papists' Island; Map p90; ☎ 624 19 89; Prinsengracht 2) This 17th-century gem is awash in Delft-blue tiles. The name harks back to the Reformation when a tunnel linked the café to a clandestine Catholic church across the canal. Or so they say.

Lokaal 't Loosje (Map p92; ☎ 627 26 35; Nieuwmarkt 32-34) With its beautiful etched-glass windows and tile tableaux, this venerable locale is one of the prettiest in the Nieuwmarkt area, drawing a vibrant mix of students, locals and tourists.

Pilsener Club (Map p92; ☎ 623 17 77; Begijnensteeg 4) Also known as *Engelse Reet* (English Arse), this narrow, ramshackle place from 1893 is typical of the hole-in-the-walls around Spui. Beer comes straight from the vat behind the draughting alcove and connoisseurs say they can taste the difference.

De 2 Zwaantjes (The Two Swans; Map p90; ☎ 625 27 29; Prinsengracht 114) A dyed-in-the-wood Jordaan café and a refuge of card-playing locals. At weekends tourists get swept up in raucous, sing-along Dutch folk tunes. Check the amazing awning over the bar.

Café Nol (Map p90; ☎ 624 53 80; Westerstraat 109) This is the epitome of the lively Jordaan café, a place where the original Jordaanese still sing oompah ballads with drunken abandon. The kitsch interior is a must-see.

Other recommendations:

Van Puffelen (Map p90; ☎ 624 62 70; Prinsengracht 377) Popular among cashed-up professionals and intellectuals.

Eylders (Map p95; ☎ 624 27 04; Korte Leidsedwars-straat 47) Meeting place for dissident artists during WWII. Exhibits art.

De Pieper (Map p90; ☎ 626 47 75; Prinsengracht 424) Venerable café from 1664, with stained-glass windows and antique Delft beer mugs.

Grand Cafés

Café de Jaren (Map p92; ☎ 625 57 71; Nieuwe Doelenstraat 20) Watch the Amstel float by from the waterside terrace and balcony of this huge, bright grand café. The great reading table has loads of foreign publications for whiling away an hour over a beer or light lunch of smoked salmon rolls.

Café Dante (Map p90; ☎ 638 88 39; Spuistraat 320) This large, Art Deco–style space has an art gallery upstairs, where Dutch artist-rocker Herman Brood kept a studio. Peaceful during the day, in the evening hours it morphs into a boisterous bar for suits and glamour girls.

Luxembourg (Map p90; ☎ 620 62 64; Spui 22-24) This café occupies the prime people-watching spot on Spui. Our advice: grab a newspaper from the reading table, procure a terrace seat in the sun and order the 'Royale' snack platter (bread, cured meats, Dutch cheese and deep-fried croquettes).

Café Américain (Map p95; ☎ 556 32 32; Leidsekade 97) Arguably Amsterdam's most stylish grand café, located in the American Hotel. This Art Deco monument attracts rafts of celebrities to its forecourt tables just off Leidseplein or for a tête-á-tête in the fashionable Nightwatch bar.

Café De Kroon (Map p92; ☎ 625 20 11; Rembrandtplein 17-1) The pearl of the grand cafés, this neocolonial gem overlooks Rembrandtplein from a covered terrace. The armchairs are sumptuous, while the chandeliers and ornaments have a biological twist (ancient microscopes and cabinets with pinned butterflies and animal skeletons).

Café de Vergulde Gaper (Map p90; ☎ 624 89 75; Prinsenstraat 30) Decorated with old chemist bottles and vintage posters, this ex-pharmacy has a pleasant terrace that fills with media types for afternoon drinks.

Tap Houses

De Drie Fleschjes (Map p92; ☎ 624 84 43; Gravenstraat 18; ⌚ noon-8.30pm Mon-Sat, 3-7pm Sun) This place has 52 vats full of liqueurs and *jenever* rented out to members to help themselves. Try something exotic, like a macaroon liqueur, and take a peek at the collection of *kalkoentjes* (bottles with hand-painted portraits of mayors).

Proeflokaal Wijnand Fockinck (Map p92; ☎ 639 26 95; Pijlsteeg 31) This small tasting house behind the Grand Hotel Krasnapolsky serves scores of *jenevers* and liqueurs, and has a pretty courtyard serving lunch and snacks.

Also recommended:

Café Schiller (Map p92; ☎ 624 98 46; Rembrandtplein 26) Has a stylish, Art Deco interior with portraits of Dutch actors and cabaret artists.

Gollem (Map p90; ☎ 626 66 45; Raamsteeg 4) The pioneer of Amsterdam 'beer cafés' with a small interior choc-a-bloc with coasters, bottles and beer posters.

De Bekeerde Suster (Map p92; ☎ 423 01 12; Kloveniersburgwal 6-8) A rambling brew-pub with copper kettles and steam-brewed beer on tap.

Bar Bep (Map p92; ☎ 626 56 49; Nieuwezijds Voorburgwal 260) A touch of sleaze, like a 1950s Eastern European cabaret lounge.

ENTERTAINMENT
Cinemas

Amsterdam's cinemas always have a good choice, including plenty of 'art' movies for discriminating cinephiles. Film listings are pinned up at cinemas and in many pubs, or you can check Thursday's paper. Film classification 'AL' means *alle leeftijden* (all ages); while for some films, 12 or 16 are the minimum ages for admission.

The Movies (Map p89; ☎ 638 60 16; Haarlemmerdijk 161) Art-house films mixed with independent American and Brit pics at a beautiful Art Deco cinema. Its restaurant offers meal-and-movie specials for a full night out.

Kriterion (Map p96-97; ☎ 623 17 08; Roetersstraat 170) This Amsterdam School–Art Deco building screens cult movies, kids' flicks and 'sneak previews' of upcoming films. It has a lively and popular café (and even its own petrol station on the outskirts of town).

Tuschinskitheater (Map p92; ☎ 626 26 33; Reguliersbreestraat 26) The country's most beautiful cinema – screening mainstream block-busters – is a monument worth visiting for its sumptuous Art Deco interior, especially in its main auditorium No 1.

Nederlands Filmmuseum (Map p95; ☎ 589 14 00; Vondelpark 3) The esteemed Filmmuseum's program appeals to a broad audience. There are cult schlock-horror, cutting-edge foreign films and specials devoted to screen legends, and genres such as Bollywood musicals.

Three halls of 1960s mod cinema screen regular offerings of fare at the **Filmmuseum Cinerama** (Map p95; ☎ 623 78 14; Marnixstraat 400).

Cinecenter (Map p95; ☎ 623 66 15; Lijnbaansgracht 236) Euro and American art-house fare is the flavour of the day at this modern cinema complex. The last Monday of the month is devoted to queer films.

CHICAGO COMEDY IS BOOMING

Chicago-style comedy in Amsterdam? At one time the idea of doing rapid-fire stand-up here in English was about as sexy as a cold croquette. Yet three Yanks had the vision to set up **Boom Chicago** (Map p95; ☎ 423 01 01; Leidseplein 12), a comedy nightclub that has evolved into the best (English-language) improvisational and comedy club in the Netherlands. What's more, it feeds talent to the likes of Second City TV (a production company) which spawned the careers of comedy stars like John Belushi, Bill Murray, Mike Myers and Dan Aykroyd. Boom's shows are super-fast, musical, political and very funny, so be sure to book ahead.

Clubs

Amsterdam's clubbers live in a time zone of their own: not much happens before 10pm and some places don't open till well after midnight. Many clubs are *alleen voor leden* (only for members), but you can 'join' at the door if the bouncer likes the look of you. Dress standards are generally casual, with admission anywhere between €3 and €20. Most clubs churn till 4am or 5am, with Thursday to Sunday the busiest nights.

Paradiso (Map p95; ☎ 626 45 21; Weteringschans 6) This 19th-century church venue holds regular student-indie nights on Wednesdays and Thursdays with live bands. Saturday's 'Paradisco' draws smart dressers for a sharp line-up of international DJs, and the monthly 'Kindred Spirits' is a hip-hop show-stopper.

Panama (Map p82-83; ☎ 311 86 86; Oostelijke Handelskade 4) This brilliant venue combines a nightclub, theatre and restaurant for stylish 20- to 40-somethings. There's a salsa-tango dance salon as well as Latin-jazz big bands, Brazilian circus acts and a selection of soulful DJs.

Club Arena (Map p96-97; ☎ 694 74 44; 's-Gravesandestraat 51) A makeover has given this former hostel dance floor a second lease on life. Two floors of crowd-pleasing tunes, from 1960s rock to house and techno, lure loads of merry students and guests from the attached hotel every weekend.

Escape (Map p92; ☎ 622 11 11; Rembrandtplein 11) Resident DJs host weekly sessions of thumping house and techno at this massively popular club, Amsterdam's largest.

A dressed-up crowd of serious dancers takes Saturday's 'Chemistry' night by storm.

Exit (Map p92; ☎ 625 87 88; Reguliersdwarsstraat 42) This multistorey nightclub in the thick of the gay quarter plays underground house and has a selection of theme bars, dance floors and a busy darkroom. Erupts into a street party at weekends.

Soho (Map p92; ☎ 626 15 73; Reguliersdwarsstraat 36) Decorated like an old Victorian library, this enormous two-storey bar hums with a young, ridiculously cute gay clientele and an increasing number of straights, who flirt on the upstairs Chesterfield sofas.

Montmartre (Map p92; ☎ 620 76 22; Halvemaansteeg 17) This place is quite an experience: bar staff, queens and toy boys belting out Dutch ballads and pop songs (think Abba) at the top of their lungs. It's kind of like a camp Eurovision song contest.

Vive la Vie (Map p92; ☎ 624 01 14; Amstelstraat 7) This popular 'lipstick lesbian' café has loud music, large windows and flirty grrlz, though men are also welcome. In summer patrons exchange the mini bar for the outdoor terrace.

Also recommended:

Mazzo (Map p90; ☎ 626 75 00; Rozengracht 114) Small club with first-rate DJs; everything from deep house to Latin.

Ministry (Map p92; ☎ 623 39 81; Reguliersdwarsstraat 12) Small, well-designed temple of speed garage and R & B.

K2 (Map p92; ☎ 627 27 10; Paardenstraat 13) 'Aprés-ski lounge' for campy 30-somethings, with vodkas on ice in the Yeti Bar.

Dansen bij Jansen (Map p92; ☎ 620 17 79; Handboogstraat 11) Student-union grooves, cheap drinks and theme nights.

Odeon (Map p90; ☎ 624 97 11; Singel 460) Three beautiful floors of easily digestible music for students and office types.

Coffeeshops

Amsterdam has more than 250 coffeeshops. Price and quality are reasonable. Most are open 10am to 1am Sunday to Thursday, and till 3am Friday and Saturday.

Grey Area (Map p90; ☎ 420 43 01; Oude Leliestraat 2) Owned by a couple of laid-back American guys, this tiny shop introduced the extrasticky, flavourful 'Double Bubble Gum' weed to the city. The extra-relaxed staff advise on the lengthy menu and welcome visiting TV camera crews.

Greenhouse (Map p92; ☎ 627 17 39; Oudezijds Voorburgwal 191) Winner of many awards at the annual High Times festival, this Indonesian-inspired coffeeshop charms the tokers with its undersea mosaics, psychedelic stained-glass windows and high-quality weed and hash. The alcohol licence doesn't hurt either.

Homegrown Fantasy (Map p92; ☎ 627 56 83; Nieuwezijds Voorburgwal 87A) Quality Dutch-grown product, pleasant staff and good tunes make this popular with backpackers from nearby hostels. Patrons can latch on to the three-foot glass bongs to suck hydroponic weed such as 'Blue Haze'.

Bulldog (Map p95; ☎ 627 19 08; Leidseplein 13-17) Amsterdam's most famous coffeeshop chain has five branches around town. This is the largest one with Internet facilities, two bars, pool tables and fabulous fluorescent décor. There's also a café serving decent grub.

Also recommended:

La Tertulia (Map p90; Prinsengracht 312) Mother-and-daughter-run shop with mini-fish pond and Van Gogh murals.

Abraxas (Map p92; ☎ 626 57 63; Jonge Roelensteeg 12) Three floors of Middle Eastern–style décor, games and live DJs.

Kandinsky (Map p92; ☎ 624 70 23; Rosmarijnsteeg 9) Hidden delight with good hash and flying-saucer choco cookies.

Global Chillage (Map p95; ☎ 777 97 77; Kerkstraat 51) A little forest of trippy murals and chilled music.

Music
CLASSICAL & CONTEMPORARY

A number of venues offer free lunch-time concerts (except June to August). Some churches also hold concerts and can have wonderful acoustics.

Concertgebouw (Map p95; ☎ 671 83 45, recording in Dutch; Concertgebouwplein 4-6; ticket office ☺ 10am-7pm) World-famous concert hall (p110) with near-perfect acoustics. Free lunchtime chamber-music or classical concerts on Wednesday, sometimes also jazz.

Beurs van Berlage (Map p92; ☎ 627 04 66; Damrak 243; ticket office ☺ 2-5pm Tue-Fri) Two small concert halls housed in the former commodities exchange (p88).

Muziekcentrum De IJsbreker (Map p96-97; ☎ 693 90 93; Weesperzijde 23; ticket office ☺ 9.30am-5.30pm) Centre for contemporary music; moving to the Muziekgebouw complex (Map p94) in the Eastern Docklands in late 2004.

Bethaniënklooster (Map p92; ☎ 625 00 78; Barndesteeg 6B) Small former monastery near Nieuwmarkt. Free lunchtime concerts on

Fridays at 12.30pm, anything from medieval to contemporary.

Muziektheater (Map p92; ☎ 625 54 55; Waterlooplein 22; ticket office 10am-6pm Mon-Sat, 11.30am-6pm Sun) Large-scale ballet and opera. Free lunchtime concerts of 20th-century music on Tuesday.

JAZZ & BLUES

Apart from a couple of grand venues, Amsterdam's jazz scene is café-based. Indigenous talent can be thin on the ground but big names turn up for regular concerts at the Concertgebouw (p128) and Bimhuis. Genuine heart-on-your-sleeve blues can be harder to find.

Bimhuis (Map p92; ☎ 623 33 73; Oude Schans 73-77; 8pm-2am Thu-Sat, closed Jul & Aug) Amsterdam's main jazz venue for nearly 30 years has intimate stage-side seating and a spiffy bar. Top talents like Brandford Marsalis, Mike Manieri, Dave Holland and Nicholas Payton appear regularly. Come early for the 9pm concerts, even if you've reserved a ticket, because seats aren't numbered. In late 2004 it's due to move to the new Muziekgebouw complex (Map p92) next to the ship passenger terminal in the Eastern Docklands.

Jazz Café Alto (Map p95; ☎ 626 32 49; Korte Leidsedwarsstraat 115) A slightly older crowd toptaps to serious jazz and blues at this small brown café, although offerings may be a touch on the conventional side. Saxophonist Hans Dulfer is a regular performer.

Also recommended:

Maloe Melo (Map p90; ☎ 420 45 92; Lijnbaansgracht 163; 9pm-3am) Small, smoky and home to the city's blues scene.

Cotton Club (Map p92; ☎ 626 61 92; Nieuwmarkt 5) Dark, bustling brown café with live jazz every Saturday (from 4pm).

Bourbon Street Jazz & Blues Club (Map p95; ☎ 623 34 40; Leidsekruisstraat 6-8; 10pm-4am) Blues, soul and rock and roll, with performances that wax poetic.

ROCK & POP VENUES

Amsterdam rocks with a vengeance. Tickets for pop, dance and rock events are available from Amsterdam Uitburo or at the venues, but for large concerts ring **Ticketlijn** (☎ 0900-3001250).

Paradiso (Map p95; ☎ 626 45 21; Weteringschans 6) This converted church has long been a premier rock venue. Big names like Sonic Youth, David Bowie and even the Rolling Stones strut their stuff here.

Melkweg (Milky Way; Map p95; ☎ 624 17 77; Lijnbaansgracht 234A) This former milk factory off Leidseplein has been a top cultural venue since the 1970s. It is an all-in-one entertainment complex with an art gallery, a café, a multimedia centre and killer rock and pop. There's live music almost every night. On Saturdays there are two dance floors with a huge variety of beats (reggae to ragga, and dancehall to dub).

Heineken Music Hall (Map p82-83; ☎ 409 79 79; Arena Blvd, Bijlmermeer) A mid-sized hall that draws a steady stream of international acts. High-class acoustics and light shows.

Amsterdam ArenA (Map p82-83; ☎ 311 13 33; Arena Blvd 11, Bijlmermeer) The ultimate stadium venue, seating 52,000 for mega-shows like Eminem, Robbie Williams and Bon Jovi.

Korsakoff (Map p90; ☎ 625 78 54; Lijnbaansgracht 161) Still grungy after all these years, drawing crunchy crowds for lashings of punk, metal and Goth.

Sport

The few spectator sports worth seeking out are soccer, field hockey and the country's own unique sport, *korfbal*. For general information on sporting events, ring the **Amsterdam Sports Council** (☎ 552 24 90).

SOCCER

Local club **Ajax** is usually at or near the top of the European league. The red-and-white stormers play in the **Amsterdam ArenA** (Map p82-83; ☎ 311 13 33; Arena Blvd 11, Bijlmermeer). Matches usually take place Saturday evening and Sunday afternoon during season (August to May).

HOCKEY

Dutch field-hockey teams compete at world-championship level. In contrast to soccer, hockey is still a rather elitist sport played by either sex on expensive club fields. For general and match information, contact **Hockey Club Hurley** (☎ 645 44 68; Nieuwe Kalfjeslaan 21, Amsterdamse Bos). Mixed, informal games are played Monday and Tuesday evening and children's games are on Saturday morning.

KORFBAL

A cross between netball, volleyball and basketball, this sport elicits giggles from foreigners but it has a lively local club scene. For information contact the **Amsterdam Sport Council** (☎ 552 24 90) or try **SVK Groen-Wit** (☎ 646 15 15; Kinderdijkstraat 29).

Theatre

Amsterdam's theatre scene never lacks for variety at its 50-odd performing-arts venues. Performances are usually in Dutch but you can sometimes catch them in English, especially in summer.

Koninklijk Theater Carré (Map p96-97; ☎ 622 52 25; Amstel 115-125; ticket office ☿ 10am-7pm Mon-Sat, 1-7pm Sun) The largest theatre in town with mainstream international shows, musicals, cabaret, opera, operetta, ballet and circuses. Backstage tours are at 3pm on Saturday and Wednesday. Closed for renovations in 2004.

Felix Meritis (Map p90; ☎ 623 13 11; Keizersgracht 324) A hub of experimental theatre, music and dance, with a bevy of coproductions between Eastern and Western European artists.

Stadsschouwburg (Map p95; ☎ 624 23 11; Leidseplein 26; ticket office ☿ 10am-performance, Mon-Sat) The municipal theatre offers a diet of light and experimental operettas, musicals and plays, some in English.

Vondelpark Theatre (Map p82-83; ☎ 673 14 99; Vondelpark) This open-air amphitheatre gives a wide range of free performances in summer, with a folk festival atmosphere.

SHOPPING

The Dutch empire has crumbled but its knack for trading remains. Amsterdam's shops fill all the niches, whether it be glowing Mexican shrines, banana-flavoured condoms, clogs, wheels of cheese, funny smoking gear and *jenever*.

The most popular shopping streets are lowbrow Nieuwendijk and manic Kalverstraat, with a selection of department stores, clothing boutiques and speciality shops. Well-heeled buyers head for the boutiques along PC Hooftstraat, while antique and art buffs should check out Nieuwe Spiegelstraat and Spiegelgracht. The Negen Straatjes (Nine Streets) area of the Western Canal Belt, north of Leidsestraat, is a hot spot for quirky shops and galleries. It is bordered by Raadhuisstraat in the north.

Books

Amsterdam is a major European printing centre so bibliophiles have ample chances to indulge themselves. For a list of bookshops, see p84. For gay and lesbian bookshop Vrolijk, see Gay & Lesbian Amsterdam (p116). Book markets are covered in the Markets section (p132).

Art & Antiques

Amsterdam teems with art galleries, from hole-in-the-wall operations to huge museum-like complexes. Their opening hours are normally noon to 6pm Tuesday to Sunday. Most of the city's best antique stores are found in Nieuwe Spiegelstraat and the nearby side streets.

Arti et Amicitiae (Map p92; ☎ 626 08 39; Rokin 112) This well-established artists' club exhibits contemporary art, hitting everything from computer graphics to cutting-edge work by grad students.

Decorativa (Map p96-97; ☎ 420 50 66; Nieuwe Spiegelstraat 7) An amazing and massive jumble of European antiques, collectables and weird vintage gifts.

EH Ariëns Kappers (Map p96-97; ☎ 623 53 56; Nieuwe Spiegelstraat 32) This pretty gallery stocks original prints, etchings, engravings, lithographs and maps from the 17th to 19th centuries, as well as Japanese woodblock prints.

Jaski (Map p96-97; ☎ 620 39 39; Nieuwe Spiegelstraat 27-29) A large commercial gallery selling paintings, prints, ceramics and sculptures by the most famous members of the CoBrA movement.

Prestige Art Gallery (Map p92; ☎ 624 01 04; Reguliersbreestraat 46) This gallery near Rembrandtplein is stuffed to the gills with 17th- to 20th-century oil paintings and bronzes, and has a display of art on loan from Joods Historisch Museum (p107).

Gallery Donkersloot (Map p90; ☎ 572 27 22; Leidsegracht 76; ☿ noon-8pm Tue-Sat) This studio art dealer bridges an important gap in the serious art scene by combining sophistication with accessibility, and you'll see works from Donkersloot in hotels and restaurants around town. Painting sessions with professional artists are held some Fridays.

Clothing

Extravagant designer garments are the domain of Amsterdam's small boutiques. The Calvinist ethos frowns on conspicuous consumption so clothing elsewhere tends to be low-key.

Analik (Map p90; ☎ 422 05 61; Hartenstraat 36) Amsterdam's pre-eminent fashion designer creates stylish, very feminine pieces. Check out the swish handbags and accessories by Dutch artists and innovative designers in her next-door extension.

Cora Kemperman (Map p95; ☎ 625 12 84; Leidsestraat 72) This successful Dutch designer specialises in floaty, layered separates and dresses in raw silk, cotton and wool. Not exclusive but stylish enough to turn heads.

Fun Fashion (Map p92; ☎ 420 50 96; Nieuwendijk 200) This busy shop has street, surf and skate wear for guys and gals. Brands include Carhartt, Stussy, Oakley and Birkenstock. Good place to revamp ahead of the Friday Night Skate (p113) at the Vondelpark.

Razzmatazz (Map p90; ☎ 420 04 83; Wolvenstraat 19) Flamboyant and expensive designer outfits and avant-garde club clothes for women and men include labels like Westwood, Frankie Morello and Andrew Mackenzie. The Negen Straatjes (p130) area of the Jordaan is full of places like this.

Van Ravenstein (Map p90; ☎ 639 00 67; Keizersgracht 359) Sleek men and women with good credit shop here for upmarket Belgian designers like Dries Van Noten, Ann Demeulemeester and Dirk Bikkembergs. Free prizes for pronouncing the designers' names backwards.

Department Stores

Amsterdam's few department stores tend to stick to safe, mainstream products. You can also find upmarket fashion, gift and jewellery shops in the **Kalvertoren shopping centre** (Map p92; Singel 457) and the grand **Magna Plaza** (Map p92; Nieuwezijds Voorburgwal 182).

Bijenkorf (Map p92; ☎ 621 80 80; Dam 1) The city's most fashionable department store (with the beehive logo) has quality clothing, toys, household accessories and books. Designer items are tasteful but not outlandish; check out the 'Chill Out' section for club and street wear.

Hema (Map p92; ☎ 638 99 63; Nieuwendijk 174) This Woolworth's clone has undergone a face-lift and now attracts as many design nuts as bargain-hunters. Reasonable prices and a wide-ranging stock from paint to wine and deli foods.

Maison de Bonneterie (Map p92; ☎ 531 34 00; Rokin 140) Carries exclusive and classic lines of garments for the whole family. Men are

PAYMENTS ARE FOREVER

Amsterdam has been a major diamond centre since the 16th century, and about a dozen diamond-cutters still operate in the city today. Of the five offering free guided tours, Gassan Diamonds is probably the best. Caution is advised, for that glint in your eye could lead to a lengthy series of monthly instalments.

Amsterdam Diamond Center (Map p92; ☎ 624 57 87; Rokin 1; ☺ 10.30am-6pm Mon-Wed & Fri-Sun, 10.30am-8.30pm Thu)
Coster Diamonds (Map p95; ☎ 305 55 55; Paulus Potterstraat 2-6; ☺ 9am-5pm)
Gassan Diamonds (Map p92; ☎ 622 53 33; Nieuwe Uilenburgerstraat 173-175; ☺ 9am-5pm)
Stoeltie Diamonds (Map p92; ☎ 623 76 01; Wagenstraat 13-17; ☺ 8.30am-5pm)
Van Moppes & Zoon (Map p95; ☎ 676 12 42; Albert Cuypstraat 2-6; ☺ 9am-5pm)

catered to with labels like Ralph Lauren, Tommy Hilfiger and Armani, best snapped up during the 50%-off sales.

Metz & Co (Map p90; ☎ 520 70 36; Keizersgracht 455) This boutique store does a fine line in luxury furnishings and homewares, upmarket designer clothes and gifts. The top-floor restaurant affords a stunning panorama over the old town.

Vroom & Dreesmann (Map p92; ☎ 622 01 71; Kalverstraat 201) Slightly more discerning than Hema, the national 'V & D' chain is popular for its clothing and cosmetics, but don't expect great flights of fantasy.

Ethnic Culture & New Age

This is a great city to get in touch with the developing, nature and the inner you, often all at once.

African Heritage (Map p92; ☎ 627 27 65; Zeedijk 59) Breathtakingly cramped, this fascinating shop in the Red Light District has African curios, clothing, masks, wooden toys and musical instruments.

Fair Trade Shop (Map p92; ☎ 625 22 45; Heiligeweg 45) This charitable shop features quality developing-world products including clothes, gifts, CDs and intriguing ceramics. This company works directly with producers and provides ongoing business training, so you know you're purchasing wisely.

Himalaya (Map p92; ☎ 626 08 99; Warmoesstraat 56) A peaceful New Age oasis in the middle of the Red Light District, this is the place to stock up on crystals, ambient CDs and books on the healing arts. More good karma is available in the tea room.

Markets

No visit to Amsterdam is complete if you don't experience its lively markets. The following is merely a selection.

Albert Cuypmarkt (Map p96-97; Albert Cuypstraat; ☺ 9am-5pm, closed Sun) This general market has food, clothing, hardware and household goods at killer cheap prices. A wide ethnic mix of wares, vendors and clientele.

Antiques market (Map p92; Nieuwmarkt; ☺ 9am-5pm Sun May-Sep) Many genuine articles here for the eagle-eyed bargain-hunter, along with books and bric-a-brac.

De Looier (Map p90; Elandsgracht 109; ☺ 11am-5pm Sat-Thu) In the Jordaan. Indoor stalls sell jewellery, furniture, art and collectibles from all over the world.

Bloemenmarkt (Map p92; Singel; ☺ 9am-5pm, closed Sun in winter) Near Muntplein and colourful in the extreme. The 'floating' flower market is actually on pilings; touristy but with a wide selection. Traders should be able to tell you if you can take flower bulbs back home. Take care in the crowds – the place is notorious for pickpockets.

Boerenmarkt (Farmers' Market; Maps pp90 & 92; Noordermarkt & Nieuwmarkt; ☺ 10am-3pm Sat) Pick up home-grown produce, organic foods and picnic provisions from these delightful markets. It's a little trip to the country.

There's a book market on **Spui** (Map p92; Spui; 10am-6pm Fri), a venerable market that isn't cheap but has a good selection, and one on **Oudemanhuispoort** (Map p92; 11am-4pm Mon-Fri), a small laneway near the university. The latter is a goldmine of obscure stuff like a semantic analysis of Icelandic sagas.

Waterlooplein flea market (Map p92; Waterlooplein; ☺ 9am-5pm Mon-Fri, 8.30am-5.30pm Sat) Amsterdam's most famous flea market is stacked with curios, second-hand clothing, music, used Doc Martens, ageing electronic gear and New Age gifts. Not to mention cheap bicycle parts and locks.

Smart Drugs

'Get smart' with organic hallucinogens like magic mushrooms, herbal joints, seeds,

mood enhancers and aphrodisiacs. Before you gift-wrap for friends back home, remember those friendly sniffer dogs belong to the customs department.

The Pollinator (Map p92; ☎ 470 88 89; Nieuwe Herengracht 25; ☺ 11am-7pm Mon-Sat) Highly recommended for its potent psychoactive plants and huge range of hemp products. This resourceful shop has also developed a machine that extracts the goods from the waste-leaf material of marijuana and transforms them into high-quality hash.

Chills & Thrills (Map p92; ☎ 638 00 15; Nieuwendijk 17; ☺ noon-8pm Mon-Wed, 11am-9pm Thu, 11am-10pm Fri-Sun) The most commercial smart shop in the city, selling herbal trips, mushrooms, psychoactive cacti, novelty bongs and life-sized alien sculptures. It's always packed with tourists trying to hear each other over the techno music.

Conscious Dreams (Map p95; ☎ 626 69 07; Kerkstraat 117; ☺ 11am-7pm Mon-Wed, 11am-8pm Thu-Sat, 2-6pm Sun) Amsterdam's original smart shop sells magic mushrooms and other natural products that enhance whatever needs enhancing. There are books on psychedelia and esoteria and club flyers on upcoming trance/ambient events.

Magic Mushroom Gallery (Map p92; ☎ 427 57 65; Spuistraat 249; ☺ 11am-10pm Sun-Thu, 10am-10pm Fri-Sat) The top 'shroom joint in town with fresh and dried varieties on sale alongside growing kits, herbal ecstasy and smart drinks. Ask for tips on smooth fungal trips.

Speciality Shops

At a loss for souvenirs or gifts? Try some of the following:

Art Multiples (Map p90; ☎ 624 84 19; Keizersgracht 510) You could spend hours here flipping through thousands of postcards on unusual topics; the raunchy 3D ones are popular. It also sells beautiful art posters and museum-shop gifts.

Condomerie Het Gulden Vlies (Map p92; ☎ 627 41 74; www.condomerie.nl; Warmoesstraat 141) Perfectly situated in the Red Light District, this shop stocks hundreds of kooky condoms plus lubricants and saucy gifts. Check out its amazing website for an overview.

Maranón Hangmatten (Map p92; ☎ 420 71 21; Singel 488) Those who love hanging around should explore Europe's largest selection of hammocks, just off the Bloemenmarkt.

Santa Jet (Map p90; ☎ 427 20 70; Prinsenstraat 7) For your information the interior's vivid colours are very real, not some residual high from the coffeeshop yesterday. There are dazzling Mexican shrines, religious icons, lanterns, Day of the Dead paraphernalia, candles and love potions.

Traditional Souvenirs

Need a memento of your visit to Amsterdam? Best pick up a pair of clogs, some tulip bulbs or a Delft vase. Mother will love it.

For flower bulbs, visit the **Bloemenmarkt** (p132).

Galleria d'Arte Rinascimento (Map p90; ☎ 622 75 09; Prinsengracht 170) This pretty shop sells Royal Delftware, all manner of vases, platters, brooches and Christmas ornaments, as well as 19th-century wall tiles and plaques. Items range from the traditional to ultra-modern, with creative window displays.

Heinen (Map p95; ☎ 627 82 99; Prinsengracht 440) With four floors of Delftware, all the major factories are represented and all budgets are catered for – from €5 spoons to 17th-century tulip vases costing thousands. Careful shipping is offered.

De Klompenboer (Map p92; ☎ 623 06 32; Sint Antoniesbreestraat 51) Bruno, the eccentric owner of this basement shop, gets his mum to hand-paint all the wooden shoes. Brush up on the history of clogs at the tiny museum (behind the stuffed-toy shop), which has specimens such as a 700-year-old pair.

GETTING THERE & AWAY

Amsterdam is well connected to the rest of the world. If you're looking for cheap deals, advice, or shared rides, this is the best spot in the country.

Air

Most major airlines fly directly to **Schiphol airport**, 18km southwest of the city centre. Renowned for its tax-free shopping, Schiphol is a smooth-running, ever-expanding, very international airport. For flight information call ☎ 0900-0141 or go to www .schiphol.nl.

Luggage may be deposited at the **left luggage office** (☎ 601 24 43) in the basement between arrival areas 1 and 2. Costs are

€4.65 for the first 24 hours, €3.30 for each subsequent 24 hours (days two to five), and €2.80 per day thereafter.

For information about getting to and from the Netherlands, including airline offices in Amsterdam, see the Transport chapter (p308).

Boat

Fast Flying Ferries (☎ 639 22 47; adult/child €7.45/4.35 return) runs a hydrofoil from Pier 7 behind Amsterdam Centraal Station to Velsen (hourly on the hour, half-hourly during peak times). The 25-minute trip drops you in Velsen, 3km short of IJmuiden, where you can catch Connexxion bus No 82 or 83 into IJmuiden. For travellers to the UK and beyond, Scandinavian Seaways sails from IJmuiden to Newcastle (see Sea in the Transport chapter, p314).

Bus

For details of regional buses in the Netherlands, call the **transport information service** (☎ 0900-9292, €0.50 a minute). Fares and travel durations are covered under towns in the regional chapters.

Amsterdam has good long-distance bus links with the rest of Europe and North Africa.

Eurolines (Map p92; ☎ 560 87 87; www.eurolines.nl; Rokin 10) tickets can be bought at their office near the Dam, and at most travel agencies and NS Reisburo (Netherlands Railways Travel Bureau) in Centraal Station. Fares are consistently lower than the train, and departures are from the **bus station** (☎ 694 56 31) next to Amstelstation.

Busabout tickets can bought through its London office (in UK ☎ 020-7950 1661; www.bus about.com) or on the coaches themselves. Coaches stop at Hotel Hans Brinker (p118) on Kerkstraat, smack in the middle of the city.

For further details on Eurolines, Busabout and other coach services, see the Transport chapter (p312).

Car & Motorcycle

Motorways link Amsterdam to Den Haag and Rotterdam in the south, and to Utrecht and Amersfoort in the southeast. The A10/E22 ring road encircles the city. Amsterdam is about 480km (six hours' drive) from Paris, 840km from Munich, 680km from Berlin and 730km from Copenhagen.

The ferry port at Hoek van Holland is about 80km away; the one at IJmuiden is just up the road along the Noordzeekanaal – see the Transport chapter (p314) for ferry details.

The Dutch automobile association, **ANWB** (Map p95; ☎ 673 08 44; Museumplein 5) provides a welter of information and services if you can prove membership of your own association.

Hitching

Looking for a ride out of Amsterdam? The **Bugride** website (http://europe.bugride.com) lists fares, destinations and contact details of drivers migrating across Europe. Also try the notice boards at the main public library at Prinsengracht 587 (p85), the Tropenmuseum (p111) or youth hostels.

Train

Amsterdam's main train station is Centraal Station (CS). See the Transport chapter (pp313 & 314) for general information about international trains. For international train information and reservations, visit the **NS international office** (Centraal Station; www.ns.nl; ⏰ 6.30am-10.30pm). The purchase area of the website is in Dutch only.

Destination	Price (€)	Duration (min)	Frequency (per hr)
Den Haag	8.50	50	4
Groningen	24.50	129	2
Haarlem	3.10	15	5
Maastricht	24.50	156	2
Rotterdam	11.20	62	4
Schiphol Airport	6.10	15	6
Utrecht	5.60	35	5

GETTING AROUND
To/From the Airport

A taxi into Amsterdam from Schiphol airport takes 20 to 45 minutes (maybe longer in rush hour) and costs about €30. Trains to Centraal Station leave every 15 minutes, take 15 to 20 minutes and cost €3.10/5.50 per single/return. Train-ticket counters are in the central court of Schiphol Plaza; buy your ticket before taking the escalator down to the platforms. Buy a *strippenkaart* here while you're at it (see Transport, p317). Public bus services such as **Connexxion** No 197 or **Interliner** No 370 also run regular services to/from central Amsterdam.

Another way to the airport is by **Schiphol Travel Taxi** (☎ 0900-8876; www.schiphol.nl). This minivan service takes up to eight people from anywhere in the country to the departure terminal, provided you book a day ahead. From central Amsterdam the fare is fixed at €22 per person, one way.

By car, take the A4 freeway to/from the A10 ring road around Amsterdam. A short stretch of A9 connects to the A4 close to Schiphol. Car-rental offices at the airport are in the right corner, near the central exits of Schiphol Plaza.

PARKING

The airport's short-term parking garages charge €1.70 per half-hour for the first three hours, then €2.50 per hour. The charge is €22.50 a day for the first three days, €11.50 a day thereafter. The long-term parking area charges a minimum €45 for up to three days and €5 for each day thereafter – a reasonable alternative to parking in the city (see also Car & Motorcycle, p133).

Bicycle

Amsterdam is an urban cyclist's dream – flat, beautiful, and crammed full with dedicated bike paths. Local cyclists have a liberal interpretation of traffic rules but almost everyone catches on quick. About 80,000 bicycles are stolen each year in Amsterdam alone – no surprise that many bikes carry locks worth more than the thing itself.

You could buy a used bike if you're spending a month or more in town. Bicycle shops sell solid second-hand models from about €75, but you'll need to add another €20 or so for a decent lock. Drug addicts routinely steal bikes and re-offer them for as little as €15 – sometimes to the erstwhile owner.

The Dutch automobile association, **ANWB** (Map p95; ☎ 673 08 44; Museumplein 5), provides cycling maps and information. For details on bicycling laws, tours and more, see the special section Cycling in the Netherlands (p70).

BICYCLE RENTAL

Prices listed below are for standard coaster-brake bikes; models with gears cost a bit more. There's also the *bakfiets* (a carrier tricycle that looks like an ice cream vendor's), which is perfect for carting around kids (or drinking buddies). All companies listed here require a passport or ID and a credit-card imprint or cash deposit; all open no later than 9am and close around 6pm.

Bike City (Map p90; ☎ 626 37 21; Bloemgracht 68-70) Conveniently located near the Anne Frankhuis in the Jordaan, charging €6.75/38.50 a day/week. Bikes bear no advertising so you blend in better with the locals.
Holland Rent-a-Bike (Map p92; ☎ 622 32 07; Damrak 247) Charges €6.25 per day, €32.50 for a week.
MacBike (Map p92; ☎ 620 09 85; Mr Visserplein 2) Charges €6.50/29.75 a day/week for bikes with the enormous MacBike logo. Other outlets include Stationsplein 12 (Map p92; ☎ 624 83 91) at east end of the Centraal Station, near the city bus stops.
Rent-a-Bike Damstraat (Map p92; ☎ 625 50 29; Damstraat 20) Discreet bikes sans logo for €7/31 a day/week.

Boat
FERRIES
Two free ferries to Amsterdam North leave from the piers directly behind Centraal Station (Map p92). The ferry called *Buiksloterwegveer* runs every six to 10 minutes around the clock, while the *Adelaarswegveer* stops running at 9pm and takes Sunday off. Cars and motorbikes aren't allowed and the crossing takes only a couple of minutes.

CANAL BOAT, BUS & BIKE
The **Lovers Museum Boat** (Map p92; ☎ 622 21 81; day pass adult/child €14.25/9.50) leaves every 30 or 45 minutes from the Lovers terminal in front of Centraal Station. It does a circuit through the canal belt with stops at the Scheepvaartmuseum, Rembrandthuis, Bloemenmarkt, Leidseplein, Rijksmuseum and Anne Frankhuis.

The **Canal Bus** (Map p92; ☎ 623 98 86; day pass adult/child €15/10.50) does several circuits between Centraal Station and the Rijksmuseum between 9.50am and 8pm. The day pass is valid until noon the next day.

The quaintly-named **canal bikes** – paddleboats, in fact – can be hired from kiosks at Leidseplein, the corner of Keizersgracht and Leidsestraat, the Anne Frankhuis and the Rijksmuseum; two-/four-seaters cost €8/7 per person per hour.

Car & Motorcycle
Parking hits you where it hurts in Amsterdam. Pay-and-display applies in the central zone from 9am to midnight Monday to Saturday, and noon to midnight on Sunday, and costs €3 per hour, €18 per day (9am to 7pm) or €12 per evening (7pm to midnight). Prices ease as you move away from the centre. In the next zone it costs 40% less and Sunday parking is free. Day passes are available from the ticket machines, provided you have enough coins.

They might look mild-mannered but the parking police are merciless. Non-payers in the Centrum district will find a bright yellow *wielklem* (wheel clamp) attached to their car and will have to pay €69 to get it removed. If not, the vehicle will be towed within 24 hours and the fine skyrockets to €245.

To avoid any hassle try the **Transferium parking garage** (Map p82-83; ☎ 400 17 21) under the Amsterdam ArenA stadium in the southeastern suburb of Bijlmer. It charges €5.50 per day including two free return tickets for public transport to Centraal Station – now that's a deal. Another park-and-ride is available at Stadionplein in the southwestern outskirts. If none of this appeals, park in Amsterdam North for free and take the ferry across.

Parking garages in the city centre include ones at Damrak, near Leidseplein and under the Stopera, but they're often full and cost more than a parking permit.

CAR RENTAL
Local companies are usually cheaper than the big multinationals like Avis, Budget, Hertz and Europcar, but don't offer as much backup or flexibility (eg one-way rentals). Rates change almost weekly, so it pays to call around. Rentals at Schiphol airport incur an extra €40 surcharge.

Bargain-basement deals can be had from **easyCar** (Map p82-83; www.easycar.nl; Stephensonstraat 16), an earth-bound cousin of easyJet. Its Amsterdam base is near Amstelstation, but you can only book on line – in fact it's the only way to contact the office. The sooner you book the cheaper it gets, and you might get a Ford Focus or similar for as little as €6 a day. There's a €5.50 start fee and a €0.12 per km surcharge after the first 100km.
Avis Autoverhuur (Map p95; ☎ 0800-2352847; ☎ 683 60 61; www.avis.nl; Nassaukade 380; ⏱ 7am-8pm Mon-Fri, 8am-4pm Sat, 9am-5pm Sun) International reservations weekdays only.

Budget Rent a Car (Map p95; ☎ 0900-1576; www.budget.nl in Dutch; Overtoom 121; 7.30am-6pm Mon-Thu, 7.30am-7pm Fri, 8am-4pm Sat, 9am-1pm Sun)

Europcar Autoverhuur (Map p82-83; international reservations ☎ 070-381 18 91 Mon-Fri, ☎ 683 21 23; www.europcar.nl in Dutch; Overtoom 197; ☺ 7am-6pm Mon-Thu, 7am-7pm Fri, 8am-6pm Sat, 9am-noon & 5-8pm Sun)

Hertz (Map p82-83; ☎ 0900-235543789, ☎ 612 24 41; www.hertz.nl; Overtoom 333; 8am-8pm)

Kuperus Autoverhuur (Map p82-83; ☎ 668 33 11; www.autoverhuur-kuperus.nl in Dutch; Van der Madeweg 1; 8am-6pm Mon-Fri, 8am-5pm Sat)

Public Transport

When the masses need to move, Amsterdam's public transport – tram, *sneltram* (fast tram), bus and metro – gets them there with startling efficiently. Most tram and bus lines, as well as the metro converge at Centraal Station. Apart from the regular city buses you'll see the tiny Opstapper, an eight-seat short bus that runs up and down the Prinsengracht between Centraal Station and the Muziektheater (Stopera). It operates from 7.30am to 6.30pm, Monday to Saturday. You can flag it down and ride with a normal ticket (see Tickets & Passes below).

The **GVB** (Amsterdam Transport Authority; Map p92; ☎ 460 59 59; www.gvb.nl; Stationsplein; ☺ 7am-9pm Mon-Fri, 8am-9pm Sat & Sun) has an information office in front of Centraal Station. Tickets and passes are sold here. Grab a copy of its free *Tourist Guide to Public Transport Amsterdam* that has several transport maps. For transport information, call the national transport line on ☎ 0900-9292 (€0.50 a minute); Dutch readers can consult www.ov9292.nl.

TICKETS & PASSES

The best deal is the *strippenkaart*: a multi-fare 'strip ticket' that's valid on all buses, trams and metros (p317). The GVB office (Map p92) in front of Centraal Station also sells a one-week pass valid in all zones for

€16. Should you have to board without a ticket, the driver sells 1-/2-/3-zone tickets for €1.60/2.40/3.20. Ticketing is based on zones (see Stripp Tease in the Transport chapter, p318).

Night buses take over shortly after midnight when the trams and regular buses stop running. Drivers sell single tickets for €2.50, or you can stamp three strips off your strip card and pay a €1.50 surcharge (which is marginally more expensive). Day passes are valid on night buses but the surcharge still applies.

TRAIN

You're most likely to use the train in Amsterdam when travelling to and from Schiphol airport. You can use strip tickets for trains in the Amsterdam region: to Centraal Station; Lelylaan, De Vlugtlaan and Sloterdijk in the western suburbs; Zuid WTC and RAI in the southern suburbs; or Duivendrecht and Diemen-Zuid in the southeastern suburbs. Strip tickets are no good on trips to or from Schiphol Airport, which requires a regular train ticket.

Taxi

You're not supposed to hail taxis on the street but many will stop if you do. Know that Amsterdam taxis are expensive, and that even the price of short journeys can come as a bit of a shock.

The most reliable bet is probably **Taxicentrale Amsterdam** (☎ 677 77 77). Taxis cost the same day or night – flag fall is €2.90 and €1.80 per kilometre, plus a 5% to 10% tip at the end. Before the meter starts running, always ask the cabbie for an estimate.

The pedal-powered **WielerTaxi** (☎ 06-28247550) is a more relaxed way to get around. The covered three-wheelers charge a flat €2.50 plus €1 per kilometre per person, or €15 for a half-hour tour with two passengers. Tots go free and kids from two to 12 years ride half-price.

Noord Holland & Flevoland

CONTENTS

After the nonstop buzz of Amsterdam the province of Noord (North) Holland is bucolic sedation. Many visitors are lured for gentle hiking and cycling tours on well-marked trails. The comely villages, windmills and lush pastures are just what the doctor ordered.

Among the highlights to the west, stylish Haarlem has an aura of 17th-century grandeur, outstanding museums and some very cosy pubs. Seaside resorts such as Zandvoort pepper the North Sea coast, and although there's no shortage of wide beaches the superior treasures lie in natural reserves such as Kennemerduinen, a strangely varied and evocative dunescape.

Moving north, the Gouwzee Bay towns of Edam, Volendam and Marken in the north hold special places in Dutch culture for cheese, traditional customs and defiance of the sea, but you'll have to share their charms with the tour buses. Monnickendam is less frequented but has a treasury of 17th-century architecture. The Golden Age ports of Hoorn and Enkhuizen have engaging old centres and the latter an excellent open-air museum. The traditional cheese auction at Alkmaar is kitschy but unforgettable. Generous sandhills built generations ago can be explored on sheep-covered Texel, a gem of an island with fine beaches and outdoor recreation.

To the east of Amsterdam, the leafy forests of Het Gooi are a refuge for urbanites and the towns of Muiden and Naarden have remarkable old fortresses worth a visit. Water sports and tender nature reserves are defining features of young Flevoland, pumped dry less than a half-century ago.

HIGHLIGHTS

- Wander the historic settlements at Enkhuizen's **Zuiderzeemuseum** (p158).

- Cycle through grassy dunes and dark forests on **Texel Island** (p161).

- Marvel over masterpieces at Haarlem's **Frans Hals Museum** (p142).

- Get lost on purpose in the **Kennemerduinen Nature Reserve** (p145).

- Clamber about the decks of the 17th-century frigate **Batavia** (p169).

- Peruse the medieval armour at **Muiden Castle** (p165) and ponder the count's demise.

- Clamber round the creaking wooden works of windmills at **Zaanse Schans** (p147).

- Spy white-tailed eagles and other camera-shy species in the **Oostvaardersplassen Nature Reserve** (p170).

NOORD HOLLAND

History

The peninsula now known as North Holland was part of Friesland until the 12th century, when storm floods created the Zuiderzee and isolated West Friesland. By this time the mercantile Counts of Holland ruled the area – or thought they did. One of the early counts, Willem II became king of the Holy Roman Empire in 1247 but perished in a raid against the West Frisians (his horse fell through the ice). His son, Count Floris V, succeeded in taming his defiant subjects 40 years later (see Kasteel Radboud, p160).

West Friesland was now owned by the county of Holland, a founding member of the Republic of Seven United Netherlands (1579). Northern Holland played a key role in the long struggle against Spanish domination and the town of Alkmaar was the first to throw off the yoke. The era of prosperity known as the Golden Age ensued and North Holland has its fair share of richly ornamented buildings from this period. The fishing and trading ports of Enkhuizen, Medemblik and Edam were at the centre of this boom.

Napoleon invaded Holland in 1795 and split it in two to break its economic power. Even after Holland came under the House of Orange in 1813, a divide remained and the provinces of North and South Holland were established in 1840.

Today North Holland's main business is agriculture.

Transport

Noord Holland is well served by the national rail service and where the train ends, the bus networks take over. Motorways run north–south from Haarlem to Alkmaar (the A9), and from Amsterdam to Den Oever (the A7), which continues on to Friesland via the 30km-long Afsluitdijk. From Enkhuizen there's another fast dyke road, the N302, running across the IJsselmeer to Lelystad in Flevoland. Bike trails lace the province in almost every direction, and you can cover the flat stretch from Amsterdam to Den Helder in two days at a leisurely pace.

See the Getting There & Away sections under individual towns for full details of train and bus schedules.

HAARLEM

☎ 023 / pop 148,000

It's hard to find anyone who isn't enthusiastic about Haarlem, which has retained more of its 17th-century layout than any other Randstad city. The wealth of historic buildings, courtyards and posh antique shops lends an air of refined elegance to a town that's the curator of a truly great archive of Golden Age paintings – the Frans Hals Museum. With its moderately priced hotels and a vibrant culinary scene, the capital of Noord Holland also makes a fine base for seeing Amsterdam or the tulip fields at Keukenhof.

History

The name Haarlem derives from *Haarloheim*, meaning a wooded place on high, sandy soil. Its origins date back to the 10th century when the counts of Holland set up a toll post on the Spaarne River. Haarlem quickly became the most important inland port after Amsterdam, but suffered a major setback when the Spanish invaded in 1572. The city surrendered after a seven-month siege but worse was yet to come: upon capitulation virtually the entire population was slaughtered. After the Spanish were finally repelled by Willem van Oranje, Haarlem soared into the prosperity of the Golden Age, attracting painters and artists from throughout Europe.

Orientation

Grote Markt is the main square. The centre has a large pedestrianised section, with lots of pubs and restaurants along Zijlstraat, Grote Houtstraat and especially Lange Veerstraat. From Grote Markt, a 500m walk to the north, the train station is an Art Deco masterpiece in its own right.

Information

My Beautiful Laundrette (Botermarkt 20; ☽ 8.30am-8.30pm) Takes last loads at 7pm.

Library (☎ 515 76 00; Doelenplein 1; ☽ 10am-6pm Mon-Fri, noon-5pm Sat) Has five Internet terminals that can be tapped for free.

GWK exchange office In the train station. There's also an ATM.

Main post office (Gedempte Oude Gracht 2)

Tourist office (☎ 0900-616 16 00; www.vvvzk.nl; Stationsplein 1; ☽ 9.30am-5.30pm Mon-Fri, 10am-2pm Sat) To the right as you exit the train station. Staff will reserve local accommodation for a small fee.

levels. Elsewhere you'll find fossils, ancient relics and mineral crystals.

On Grote Markt, the **Vleeshal** holds contemporary art exhibitions; the **Verweyhal** next door, in a fancy Renaissance building designed by Lieven de Key, houses the Frans Hals Museum's collection of modern art, including works by Dutch impressionists and the CoBrA movement. The museums are known collectively as **De Hallen** (adult/child €7/3.50; 11am-5pm Mon-Sat, noon-5pm Sun).

Tours
Woltheus Cruises (☎ 535 77 23; adult/senior/child €7/5/3.50 10.30am-4.30pm) Canal boat tours in English. Tours run every 1½ hours, five times a day, from April to October. Departure is from opposite the Teylers Museum.

Sleeping
The tourist office has a list of B&Bs from €20 per person.

Joops Hotel (☎ 532 20 08; joops@easynet.nl; Oude Groenmarkt 20; s without bathroom €28, d with/without bathroom €75/55) The friendly Joops Hotel has 100-plus very individual rooms spread over an entire block near the Grote Kerk. Space isn't an issue and the studios have a kitchenette. Breakfast costs €9.50. Reception is on the ground floor in the Belly & Bolly antique shop run by a pair of amiable gents.

Hotel Amadeus (☎ 532 45 30; www.amadeus-hotel.com; Grote Markt 10; s/d €53/74, incl breakfast; 🖳) Enjoying a brilliant spot, Amadeus is nestled in a row of old gabled houses on the main square. Rooms are comfy with mod cons, and guests can surf the Internet at the bar.

Hotel Carillon (☎ 531 05 91; fax 531 49 09; Grote Markt 27; s with/without bathroom €53/28, d with bathroom €68, incl breakfast) Run by a friendly young crew, this small hotel has ageing but completely OK rooms in the shadow of the Grote Kerk. Breakfast can be taken in wicker chairs on the sidewalk café.

Haarlem Stayokay Hostel (☎ 537 37 93; www.stayokay.com; Jan Gijzenpad 3; dm/d €15/25, incl breakfast; Apr-Dec; 🖳) This lakeside youth hostel has a 10pm silence rule but there's no curfew. Laundry and cooking facilities are available. Take bus No 2 (direction Haarlem Noord) from the train station (10 minutes).

Campsite De Liede (☎ 533 23 60; fax 535 86 66; Lieoever 68; per caravan/tent/person/car €2.85) This leafy site 2.5km east of the old centre enjoys a lakeside location and rents canoes and paddle boats. Take bus No 2 from the train station (direction Zuidpolder) and alight at Zoete Inval.

Eating
The streets around the Dom and Lange Veerstraat offer a treasure-trove of enticing restaurants. It's a good idea to reserve ahead, although the huge selection means you'll find a table somewhere.

Ma van Rossum (☎ 551 06 80; Lange Veerstraat 14; mains €12-23; dinner Tue-Sun) has some wonderfully lacy chandeliers and side booths perfect for a romantic tête-à-tête. The red snapper's good, or you can go all the way on the châteaubriand (€30).

Pieck Jacobus (☎ 532 61 44; Warmoesstraat 18; mains €12-17; lunch & dinner, Mon-Sat) This little *eetcafé* with the big front windows has delightful specials that might include a salad, kebab sausages, Turkish bread and yoghurt, all for €9. Or try the 'Casablanca', a spicy lamb fillet with tabbuleh.

Specktakel (☎ 532 38 41; Spekstraat 4; mains €17; dinner, lunch Sat) This Dutch diner is vying for United Nations membership judging by its worldly menu of Australian smoked kangaroo to Thai pork fillet. Here too there's terrace dining just off the Grote Markt.

Eko Eetkafé (☎ 532 65 66; Ziljstraat 19; mains €7-16; lunch & dinner) An offshoot of the Eko organic foods association, this obliging little eatery offers fish and vegetarian dishes with a clear conscience. It's a short walk from town centre but definitely worth the effort.

Café Applause (☎ 531 14 25; Grote Markt 3; mains €6-20; lunch & dinner) An elegant, *fin de siècle* mood is anyone's game inside while the biz kids munch on the busy terrace just off the main square. At lunchtime it serves pastas, salads and tasty filled sandwiches but goes seriously upmarket later on (set dinners from €25).

De Haerlemsche Vlaamse (☎ 532 59 91; Spekstraat 3) Practically on the doorstep of the Grote Kerk, this *frites* joint not much bigger than a telephone box is a local institution. A regular portion with one of a dozen sauces such as peanut or lemon mayo costs €1.70.

Also recommended:

Flamboyant (☎ 542 15 03; Kleine Houtstraat 3; mains €13-20; 6-9.30pm, closed Tue) Probably Haarlem's finest Indonesian restaurant.

Maharadja of India (☎ 31 66 49; Kleine Houtstraat 31; dinner) Good subcontinental specials with all the trimmings.

A la Turka (☎ 534 11 62; Zijlstraat 95; mains €13-19; ☺ lunch & dinner Tue-Sun) As the package says, Turkish cuisine.

Drinking

Haarlem has a slew of atmospheric places to down a few. See the Entertainment below for more options.

Café Het Melkwoud (☎ 531 35 35; Zijlstraat 63) A great place to nurse a beer with crunchy locals behind those ceiling-high windows. You can't miss the sign – a tree shaped like a woman.

Café Studio (☎ 531 00 33; Grote Markt 25; ☺ 5pm-2am) Next to Café Applause, its cool see-and-be-seen terrace belies the welcoming interior of warm oak panelling. Other cafés line the north side of Grote Markt.

Entertainment

To find out what's on, grab a copy of the free local paper *De Haarlemmer* or the listings handout *Luna* at the tourist office or pubs. *Uitloper* is the cinema programme guide.

CINEMA

Call ☎ 076-587 75 67 for programme details or 0900-93 63 to reserve tickets.

Brinkmann (Brinkmannpassage 11) English-language films with Dutch subtitles.

Cinema Palace (Grote Houtstraat 111) English-language films with Dutch subtitles.

CLUBS

Café Stiels (☎ 531 69 40; Smedestraat 21) For jazz and rhythm & blues, bands play on the back stage of almost every night of the week from 9pm.

Proeflokaal In den Uiver (☎ 532 53 99; Rivierfischmarkt 13; ☺ 5pm-2am) This quirky old place has shipping knick-knacks and a schooner sailing right over the bar. There's jazz on Thursday and Sunday evenings.

Café van Stoffelen (☎ 532 59 40; Kruisstraat 23) Live pop, soul, Latin and jazz emanates from this intimate stage on Sunday evenings from 5pm.

Patronaat (☎ 532 41 03; Zijlsingel 2) Haarlem's top music and dance club attracts bands from all thumps of life. Events in this cavernous venue usually start around 7pm or 9pm unless it's a midnight rave.

THEATRE

Toneelschuur (☎ 517 39 10; Lange Begijnestraat 9) This far-out multilevel stage complex (designed by

a Dutch cartoonist, Joost Swarte) has a daring agenda of experimental dance, theatre and art house cinema, and acts as a production house for up-and-coming directors.

Concertgebouw (☎ 512 12 12; Klokhuisplein 2) Haarlem's venerable concert hall.

Stadsschouwburg (☎ 512 12 12; Wilsonsplein 23) The municipal theatre. Together Concertgebouw and Stadsschouwburg present a range of large-scale productions – everything from the Chippendales to Tchaikovsky. Haarlem is home to the Holland Symfonia, the Dutch ballet and symphony orchestra whose season runs from September to June. Both buildings are undergoing a huge face-lift and will remain closed until early 2005.

Shopping

Markets are held at Botermarkt and Grote Markt all day Monday, and again on Saturday with a flower market at Grote Markt.

Getting There & Away

Haarlem is served by frequent trains on the Amsterdam–Rotterdam line.

Destination	Price (€)	Duration (min)	Frequency (per hr)
Alkmaar	5.10	30-40	3
Amsterdam	3.10	15	4-5
Den Haag	6.40	35	4
Rotterdam	9.00	55	4

The red Zuidtangent bus line links Haarlem train station and Schiphol airport (30 minutes, six times hourly). Connexxion bus No 80 stops at Houtplein south of the centre and goes to/from Amsterdam Marnixstraat (40 minutes, two to four times hourly). Bus No 81 goes to Zandvoort bus station via Overveen (15 minutes, twice hourly). IJmuiden's Dennekoplaan, close to the locks and the beach, can be reached via bus No 70 (40 minutes, four times hourly).

During the tulip season from late March to late May, Connexxion also runs buses from Haarlem to the Keukenhof bulb fields via Lisse (45 minutes, two to four times hourly). Return tickets cost €15.50/13/8.50 per adult/senior/child four to 11 years.

Getting Around

The bus information kiosk opposite the train station is open till at least 6pm, and there's a large schedule board at the departure bays. Bus Nos 2, 7, 50 and plenty of others stop at Ziljstraat, just east of Grote Markt (5 minutes).

Regular **taxis** (☎ 515 15 15) are everywhere in Haarlem.

There's also a large **bicycle shop** (☎ 531 70 66) for rentals in the train station.

AROUND HAARLEM
Zandvoort

Just 5km west of Haarlem's plush outskirts lies **Zandvoort**, a popular seaside resort. It's no great shakes as beach towns go and drab apartment blocks line the main drag, but its proximity to Amsterdam ensures a steady flow of pleasure-seekers.

That background hum to the north is the **Circuit Park Zandvoort** (☎ 023-574 07 40). The legendary Holland Grand Prix Formula One race was held here until 1985, and it's where racing greats such as Stirling Moss and Jackie Stewart sped to their victories. Local limits on noise mean the track has been demoted to smaller sportscar events.

The Hogeweg in Zandvoort is littered with hotels like **Pension Schier** (☎ 571 95 41; www.pensionschier.com; Hogeweg 45, Zandvoort; s/d €35/50, incl breakfast) This hospitable guesthouse pulls folk from all over Europe for the bang-up beach parties nearby. Some rooms have kitchenettes and you can have breakfast on the patio.

Trains link Zandvoort to Amsterdam Centraal Station twice hourly (€4.10, 35 minutes) via Haarlem (€1.50, 10 minutes).

Cruquius Museum (☎ 528 57 04; Cruquiusdijk 27; adult/child €4/2; ☼ 10am-5pm Mon-Fri, 11am-5pm Sat & Sun) This steam-driven pump station with tarantula-like rocker arms helped to drain the Haarlemmermeer in the 19th century. The chief display is a sophisticated model that cheerfully shows which regions would flood if the dykes broke. From Haarlem, take bus No 140 or 170 to the Cruquius stop (20 minutes).

Kennemerduinen Nature Reserve

Between Haarlem and the beach lies Kennemerduinen, an appealing tract of coastal dunes and forest. At 1250 hectares it's the largest and most diverse area in the Nationaal Park Zuid-Kennemerland that extends north to IJmuiden. Its wild, windswept beauty belies the problems caused by excessive drainage, water collection and the construction of the North Sea canal, all of which are turning the ground to desert.

At the entrances Koevlak or Parnassia you can park and pay the paltry entry fee (adult/child €1/0.30). The paths snake through hilltop copses of Corsican firs and valleys of low-lying thickets; at the western edge you reach a massive barrier of golden sand that's 1000 years old.

The dunes sprout an extra layer of colour in spring including desert orchids, the bright rosettes of the century weed and the white-blooming grass of Parnassus. Red foxes, fallow deer and many species of birds are native to the area; bats slumber in the park's abandoned bunkers before appearing at dusk.

Among main features, the **Vogelmeer** lake has a bird observation hut above the south shore. The man-made lake **'t Wed** teems with bathers in summer. Lookout points are scattered throughout with evocative names like Hazenberg (hare mountain). At 50m, the **Kopje van Bloemendaal** is the highest dune in the country, just outside the eastern border of the park with views of the sea and Amsterdam.

On a sombre note, the WWII cemetery **Erebegraafplaats Bloemendaal** (☎ 020-660 1945; ☼ 9am-5pm) is the resting place of 372 members of the Dutch resistance. Its walled compound in the dunes is isolated from the rest of the park and accessible only via the main road.

The tourist offices in Zandvoort or Haarlem can provide walking maps, but there's also a visitors centre called **De Zandwaaier** (☎ 023-541 11 23; www.npzk.nl; Zeeweg, Overveen; ☼ 10am-5pm Tue-Sun). Bicycles are forbidden except on a few dedicated paths. Rough camping is also a no-no but the park-run site **De Lakens** (☎ 0900-3846226; www.kennemerduinencampings.nl; camp site & car €26) enjoys a sandy, grassy and certainly breezy spot just a few metres from the beach. Ticks in the dunes are known to carry Lyme Disease so insect repellent is a good idea.

To reach the park, visitors centre and campground, take bus No 71 from Haarlem train station or drive the N200 towards Bloemendaal aan Zee.

KENNEMERDUINEN NATURE RESERVE

0 — 1 km
0 — 0.5 mi

NORTH HOLLAND & FLEVOLAND

IJMUIDEN

☎ 0255 / pop 7000

Just five kilometres up the coast from beautiful Haarlem is the rather dreary town of IJmuiden, whose huge **North Sea locks** are, however, the main attraction at the mouth of the Noordzeekanaal (North Sea Canal). The largest is the Zuidersluis (south lock), some 400m long and 45m wide. Few people realise that IJmuiden is also the largest fishing port in Western Europe, home to the factory trawlers that plough the North Atlantic for weeks at a time. The huge beach is a kite-flyer's delight at low tide, but unfortunately the view is marred by the steel mills north of the locks.

Getting There & Around

It's a blast taking the **hydrofoil** (☎ 020-639 22 47 or ☎ 0900-2666399; adult/child return €7.45/4.35; 🕑 7am-7pm Mon-Fri, 10am-5.30pm Sat & Sun) from Pier 7 behind Amsterdam Centraal Station (hourly on the hour, half-hourly during peak times). It skims along the North Sea Canal jn 25 minutes and deposits you in Velsen, 3km short of IJmuiden, where you catch Connexxion bus No 82 or 83 into town. It's a good idea to take a bicycle (an extra €3.60 return) because things are spread out. Cycle from Velsen along the dyke towards the locks and go across the 'small' and 'middle' locks to the big lock on the far side; along the way you'll find an information centre, **Noordzeekanaal in Zicht**

(North Sea Canal in Pictures; ☎ 51 91 12; Noordersluisweg 120; 🕑 1-5pm Mon, Wed & Sun).

If you travel by road along the North Sea Canal, you'll have the surreal experience of passing huge, ocean-going ships that float well above road level.

AALSMEER
☎ 0297

A few kilometres southwest of Amsterdam, the town of Aalsmeer hosts the world's biggest **flower auction** (☎ 39 21 85; Legmeerdijk 313; adult/child €4/2; 🕑 Mon-Fri 7.30-11am), not far from the world's largest tulip garden (p193). The action takes place in Europe's largest commercial complex – one million square metres – and the experience will blow you away. About 90 million flowers and plants worth €6 million change hands here every single day. Bidding starts early so arrive by 9am to catch the spectacle from the viewing gallery. Selling is conducted – surprise! – by Dutch auction, with a huge clock showing the starting price, dropping until someone takes up the offer. There's a self-guided tour of the site with audio boxes at strategic points. Pick your days carefully: Mondays are quiet and Thursdays very, very busy.

Take Connexxion bus No 171 or 172 from Amsterdam Centraal Station to the Aalsmeer VBA stop (50 minutes, five times hourly).

ZAANSE SCHANS
☎ 075

Just 10km from Amsterdam, Zaanse Schansan open-air, museum-piece village – is a good stab at re-creating a local village from the 17th and 18th centuries. What's so special about an open-air museum? Its residents are genuine, rather than actors who go home at the end of the day, and its historic structures were brought from around the country. The workshops, shops and raised wooden homes sit on a sweet little tract complete with canals and tulip gardens. On a sunny day it's a grand day out despite the inevitable crowds. The **visitors centre** (☎ 616 82 18; Schansend 1; 🕑 10am-5pm Tue-Sun Mar-Oct, Sat & Sun only Nov-Feb) hands out the free maps you'll need.

The most striking structures are the six working windmills that stand along the riverbanks. One mill sells fat jars of its freshly ground mustard, while the others turn out pigments, oils, meal and sawed wood. All are open for inspection, and it's a treat to clamber about the creaking works while the mills shake in the North Sea breeze.

The cutest shops include an Albert Heijn colonial supermarket, a cheesemaker and a popular **clog factory** with exhibits of pointy old footwear. The clogmaker will demonstrate a device that grounds out wooden shoes in tandem, like keys. The engaging **pewtersmith** will explain in several languages the story behind dozens of tiny figures while the soft metal sets in the moulds.

When you're finished poking round the village, a **tour boat** (adult/child €5/2.50, 🕑 Tue-Sun Apr-Sep) does 50-minute spins on the river Zaan several times a day.

On the adjacent lot, the shiny new **Zaans Museum** (☎ 616 28 62; adult/child €4.50/2.70; 🕑 10am-5pm Tue-Sat, noon-5pm Sun) runs temporary exhibitions of historical objects of the Zaan river communities, often with a dramatic or artsy twist such as audiovisual light shows.

Getting There & Away

Trains from Amsterdam take about 20 minutes (€2.50, four times hourly). From Centraal Station, take the stop train towards Alkmaar and get off at Koog Zaandijk – it's a well-signposted 400m walk to Zaanse Schans.

ZAANDAM
☎ 075 / pop 25,800

A stone's throw from Zaanse Schans, Zaandam has had two famous residents: Russia's Peter the Great and impressionist master Claude Monet. Claude stayed in a nice hotel while Peter preferred a rickety wooden shack, now a shrine and the main reason for visiting this commuter town.

The **Czaar Peterhuisje** (☎ 616 13 90; Krimp 23; adult/child €2/1; 🕑 1-5pm Tue-Sun Apr-Oct) is the gritty abode where Peter spent a week of his life in 1697. The Russian ruler arrived incognito as sailor Peter Mikhailov to garner support for Western forces against the Turks. Despite the hush-hush, news spread and hordes of fans practically beseiged the cabin to get a glimpse of his czarness. Peter eventually slipped away to the wharves to learn shipbuilding and swearing in Dutch and became adept at both.

Many Russians came here on a pilgrimage in the 19th century to scrawl their graffiti. So great was the PR value that Grand Duchess Anna Paulowna (wife of Dutch King Willem II) commissioned a brick shelter over the house, which finally emerged in Russian orthodox style by the late 1800s. There's a small exhibit about the czar, his links to the Netherlands and marble tablets engraved with the monikers of royal visitors. Napoleon stopped by and was apparently delighted.

Getting There & Away
To get to the Czaar Perhuisje from Zaanse Schans, board bus No 88 and ask the driver to let you out at Gedempte Gracht in the pedestrian shopping mall; Krimp is a side street at the eastern end of the mall. To get there from Amsterdam Centraal, take the train toward Enkhuizen and get off at Zaandam (€2, 10 minutes, twice hourly).

WATERLAND REGION
☎ 075
Time seems to move more slowly in this rural area about 9km north of Amsterdam, where some farmers still carry scythes, the meadows turn a succulent shade of green and herons stand motionless alongside watery furrows. Despite a large shipping canal nearby it remains an important bird sanctuary, and picturesque for the mindful visitor.

Broek in Waterland is a precious little burg where some 17th and 18th century houses are painted a particular shade of grey that came to be known as *Broeker grijs* after the landscapes painted here by Monet and other masters. The village church was burned by the Spanish in 1573 but restored with a pretty stained-glass window recalling the tragic event. On the lake's edge stands the so-called **Napoleonhuisje**, a white pagoda where the French emperor and the mayor met in 1811.

There's not much to see but if you want to stay over, seek out **De Bedstede** (☎ 020-403 32 89; www.bedstede.nl; Laan 38; s €30-55, d €40-65, incl breakfast) This hotel occupies a romantic Dutch manor house that's ideal for those bent on a rural holiday. Lunch becomes unnecessary after the generous breakfast platter of meats, cheese, breads and fresh fruit.

Near the town of Landsmeer, 9km north of Amsterdam, lies the nature reserve and

recreational area **Het Twiske**. This is where urbanites go for a calculated dose of nature: well-marked walking trails, playgrounds and artificial but quite decent beaches, especially for families. A full one-third of the area is water and there are several hides for bird-watchers on the lakeshores. You can also wander around **De Marsen**, a farm with bleating sheep and goats that affords close contact with these friendly furry critters. Picnic spots are marked throughout for barbecuing. The **visitors centre** (☎ 684 43 38; Noorderlaak 1; 8am-5pm Mon-Fri, 10am-6pm Sun) is next to the canoe rental shop.

BEVERWIJK
☎ 0251
Every weekend up to 80,000 visitors flock to the town of Beverwijk to visit the covered **Beverwijkse Bazaar** (☎ 26 26 26; Montageweg 35; ⏰ 8.30am-4.30pm Sat, 8.30am-5.30pm Sun), one of Europe's largest ethnic markets. Piled high are Arabian foods and spices, Turkish rugs, garments and hand-crafted ornaments.

The liveliest of the three biggest halls is the **Zwarte Markt** (adult €2.80-3.20, child free). This 'black market' is really an enormous flea market with a carnival attitude. You can haggle with one of the 3000-plus vendors or just bask in the market chatter, live music and exotic aromas. Entry is free to the other warehouses including the **Oosterse Markt** and the **Grand Bazaar**, where the booths are larger and more professional. There's even a giant playground called **Darteldorp** (child €5.70; ⏰ 10am-6pm) where you can safely leave the little ones while you shop.

Getting There & Away
Parking is free but come by 9.30am in an attempt to beat the crowds. From Amsterdam drive the A9 or A10 towards Alkmaar, exit at Beverwijk and follow signs to the bazaar; or take the train to Beverwijk (€4.50, 30 minutes, four times hourly) and then Bus No 94 (six minutes).

MONNICKENDAM
☎ 0299 / pop 10,105
Founded in 1356 for the Benedictines who built a dam here, Monnickendam (monks + dam, get it?) became a prosperous port for goods moving inland towards Alkmaar. After the fishing industry died,

Monnickendam reinvented itself as a yachting resort, and today the beautiful old trawlers catch mainly pleasure-seekers. History still pervades the narrow lanes around the shipyards and fish smokehouses that have been operating for hundreds of years. Smoked eel remains a local delicacy. Eel is one of the few species still caught in bulk in the IJsselmeer.

Sights

The town's trademark building is the 15th-century **Speeltoren**, the elegant, Italianate clock tower and former town hall. The tower's carillon (glockenspiel) performs only at 11am and noon on Saturday, when the four mechanical knights prance in the open wooden window twice before retiring. If the tone rings true it's because the bells were cast by master bellmaker, Peter van de Ghein, over 400 years ago.

Next door, the **Historisch Museum** (☎ 65 22 03; Noordeinde 4; adult/child €1.25/0.50; ✹ 10am-4pm Tue-Sat, 1-4pm Sun-Mon) takes a look at the 1920s building of the Afsluitdijk (Barrier Dyke; see boxed text, p160) from a local perspective, with archaeological finds, ceramics and model ships. These are offerings for the true aficionado.

The Gothic **Grote Kerk** (De Zarken; ✹ 10am-4pm Tue-Sat, 2-4pm Sun-Mon Jun-Aug) is notable for its triple nave, tower galleries and a dazzling oak choir screen dating from the 16th century. It's impossible not to focus on the enormous organ in the nave, a statement of higher glory and a striking contrast with the spartan interior.

Other stars in the architecture department include the **Waag** (Weigh house) on the central canal. Built in 1669, this focal point of local economic life was equipped in 1905 with grand Tuscan columns, a common trick of the day to make it look much older and more impressive. **In de Bonten Os** (The Coloured Ox; Noordeinde 26) is the only house that's left in its original 17th century state. In the days before proper glass, the curious vertical shutters at street level were made to let in air and light.

The old harbour along Haringburgwal is famous for its **fish smokehouses**, and you can poke your head inside for a glimpse of the process. A bronze statue of a fisherman curing eels on a spit stands where the central canal meets the harbour.

Activities

As elsewhere on the IJsselmeer large pleasure boats are the thing in Monnickendam. In July and August you can feel the spray in your face on day trips on an antique clipper. Reserve at **Holland Zeilcharters** (☎ 65 23 51; www.sailing.nl; Het Prooyen 4a; per person from €43).

The harbour bristles with splendid old *tjalken*, *botters* and *klippers*, historic boats available for group hire and a skipper if need be. The *botters* can be hired out from around €385 per day for up to 14 passengers. The sky's the limit at the top end, eg three-masted clippers for as long as you (and your wallet) see fit.

Smaller craft can be found at **Bootvloot** (☎ 65 34 84; Hemmeland beach; ✹ 10am-5.30pm Apr-Oct) where two- to four-person sailboats cost €35/50 per half-day/day, with a €50 deposit. It's a 500m walk through the leafy Hemmeland recreation area northeast of Monnickendam marina – just follow the sign 'Zeilbootverhuur'.

Sleeping & Eating

Monnickendam has only one hotel, so you might consider staying in nearby Edam where's there's a better selection of accommodation.

Hotel Lake Land (☎ 65 37 51; fax 65 45 87; Jachthaven 1; s/d €46/67) Situated on the marina this is the town's sole hotel, fairly anonymous but convenient and comfortable, with harbour views and a restaurant.

Camping-Jachthaven Uitdam (☎ 020-403 14 33; www.campinguitdam.nl; Zeedijk 2, Uitdam; camp site with car/hiker hut/caravan €17/35/21; ✹ Mar-Oct) Tucked away behind a dyke on the IJsselmeer, this well-equipped site has mooring facilities, beach, laundry, snack bar and bicycle rental. Take the dyke road 5km southeast of Monnickendam or bus No 111.

De Roef (☎ 65 18 60; Noordeinde 40; mains €15-25; ✹ dinner) The meat cuts like butter at this Western-style steakhouse where Argentine tenderloin or sea bass is prepared over charcoal flames. Half the fun is watching dinner approach your table sizzling atop a red-hot grill.

't Markerveerhuis (☎ 65 16 75; Brugstraat 6; mains €5-13; ✹ lunch & dinner) The best place for a light lunch of *kibbeling* (deep-fried cod parings) or a cold beer on its pretty harbour terrace. Dutch folk music emanates from the stage at weekends.

Stands selling smoked eel and other fruits of the sea are clustered around the old harbour – just follow your nose.

Getting There & Around

Connexxion bus No 111 links the centre of Monnickendam to Amsterdam Centraal Station, harbour side (30 minutes, three to four times an hour); bus No 115 makes the trip hourly. Bus No 111 continues on to Marken (12 minutes, hourly). Bus Nos 114 and 117 go north to Edam (10 minutes) and Hoorn (30 to 45 minutes) twice an hour.

Ber Koning (☎ 65 12 67; Noordeinde 12) and **Van Driel** (☎ 65 32 64; Dirksznlaan 109) both rent touring bicycles.

> **YE OLDE CHEESE FARMS**
>
> Edam and the surrounding regions have centuries-old reputations as producers of toothsome cheese. About 8km south of Edam, there are several cheese farms that can be visited daily: Irene Hoeve, Jacobs Hoeve (both on Hoogedijk) and Simone Hoeve (on Wagenweg). Cheesemaking is a fascinating art but prepare for a pretty cheesy experience as presenters in traditional duds run through their well-oiled routine before referring you to the shop. Irene Hoeve also runs a clog-making outfit.

VOLENDAM & MARKEN

☎ **0299 / pop 20,700**

Some 22km northeast of Amsterdam lies Volendam, a former fishing port turned tourist trap. It's quaint all right, with its rows of wooden houses and locals who don traditional dress for church and festive events. Best escape the hordes of camera-toting visitors and explore some of the pretty streets behind the harbour for a glimpse of what the old Volendam was really like.

Across Gouwzee Bay lies scenic Marken with a small and determined population. It was an isolated island in the Zuiderzee until 1957 when a causeway linked up with the mainland, effectively turning it into a museum-piece village. Expect to spend half a day poking around both places.

Information

Tourist office (☎ 36 37 47; www.vvv-volendam.nl; Zeestraat 39, Volendam; 🕓 10am-5pm) Has tonnes of information for its hordes of visitors, including a brochure with a walking tour of Volendam. The old harbour district is about 400m to the southeast.

Sights & Activities

The **Volendams Museum** (☎ 36 92 58; Zeestraat 37, Volendam; adult/child €2/1; 🕓 10am-5pm) is a must for cigar aficionados. Local culture is covered with traditional costumes, prints and paintings of harbour scenes, but this place is really devoted to lovers of cheap cigars: some 11 million bands are plastered on its walls.

In Marken, the colourful Kerkbuurt is the most authentic area, with tarred or painted houses raised on pilings to escape the Zuiderzee floods. A row of eel-smoking houses here has been converted to the **Marker Museum** (☎ 60 19 04; Kerkbuurt 44, Marken; admission free; 🕓 10am-5pm Mon-Sat, noon-4pm Sun Apr-Oct). Enjoy an overview of the island's history and the re-created interior of a fisherman's home, with a wealth of personal odds and ends.

Sleeping

Hotel Spaander (☎ 36 35 95; spaander@bestwestern.nl; Haven 15-19, Volendam; s/d €91, incl breakfast; P) The town's best hotel has retained much of its atmosphere from the olden days, with traditional carved balconies and cushy rooms that have welcomed the likes of Picasso and Monet. There's an indoor swimming pool too.

Hotel Lutine (☎ 36 32 34; www.lutinevolendam.nl; Haven 80, Volendam; s/d €52/77, incl breakfast) With just eight rooms the mood is intimate, the owners perenially charming and the harbour view as nice as anywhere, provided you ask for a room at the front.

Eating

Seafood is the undisputed king in Volendam, and the main street is lined with vendors offering smoked cod, eel and herring.

Hotel Spaander (☎ 36 35 95; spaander@bestwestern.nl; Haven 15-19; mains €15-33) This grand place does a splendid job with all things fishy, be it salmon, stewed eel or bouillabaisse. The waiters fillet your fish right at your table and the dining area is fantastically quaint, with paintings by renowned artists covering every inch of available wall space.

Old Dutch Restaurant Le Pompadour (☎ 39 98 88; Haven 142; mains €13-28) Even the name can't take away the olde-worlde flair of a place where faded yellow light falls from Art Deco lamps. Try the North Sea *tong* (sole) in a changing symphony of sauces.

Getting There & Around

There's no train service to Volendam. Connexxion bus No 110 runs between Volendam and Amsterdam (30 minutes) and Edam (12 minutes) every hour until about midnight. Bus No 111 goes from Amsterdam via Monnickendam to Marken (30 minutes, half-hourly). Connexxion buses stop at Zeestraat.

The **Marken Express ferry** (adult/child return €6.25/3.50; ✆ 10.30am-6pm) runs from March to September, making the 30-minute crossing from Volendam to Marken every half

hour. In Volendam, the ferry leaves from the docks at Havendijkje.

EDAM

☎ 0299 / pop 7400

Once a renowned whaling port, this scenic little town is a surprisingly calm place after the tourist rabble of Volendam. In its 17th-century heyday it had 33 shipyards that built the fleet of legendary admiral Michiel de Ruijter. Its dreamy canals, hand-operated drawbridges and old shipping warehouses make Edam an intriguing place to wander through, and for some reason it attracts relatively few visitors – except during its famous cheese market in summer, that is.

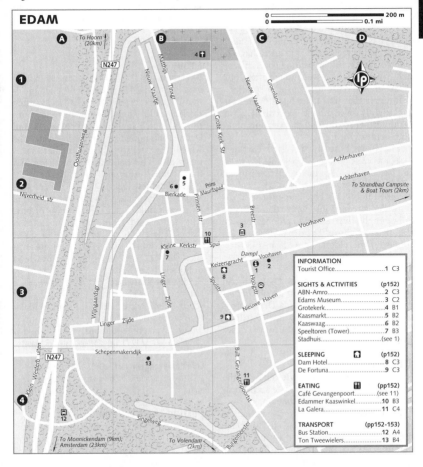

EDAM

0   200 m
0   0.1 mi

INFORMATION	
Tourist Office	1 C3

SIGHTS & ACTIVITIES	(p152)
ABN-Amro	2 C3
Edams Museum	3 C2
Grotekerk	4 B1
Kaasmarkt	5 B2
Kaaswaag	6 B2
Speeltoren (Tower)	7 B3
Stadhuis	(see 1)

SLEEPING	(p152)
Dam Hotel	8 C3
De Fortuna	9 C3

EATING	(pp152)
Café Gevangenpoort	(see 11)
Edammer Kaaswinkel	10 B3
La Galera	11 C4

TRANSPORT	(pp152-153)
Bus Station	12 A4
Ton Tweewielers	13 B4

Information

Tourist office (☎ 31 51 25; www.vvv-edam.nl; Damplein; ☯ 10am-5pm Mon-Sat Apr-Oct, 10am-5pm Mon-Sat & 1-4pm Sun Jul & Aug) Housed in the splendid 18th-century town hall. Pick up the good English-language booklet for self-guided tours, *A Stroll Through Edam*.

Sights & Activities

In the 16th century, Willem van Oranje bestowed on Edam the right to hold a **Kaasmarkt** (Cheese Market; ☯ 10am-noon Wed Jul & Aug), the town's economic anchor right through the 1920s. At its peak 250,000 rounds of cheese were sold here every year. On the western side of Kaasmarkt stands the old Kaaswaag, the cheese weigh house with a free display on the town's chief product. The cheese market is smaller than the one in Alkmaar but about as touristy.

The 15th-century **Grote Kerk** (free; ☯ 2-4.30pm Apr-Oct) has has an unfortunate past that stands witness to the vagaries of Dutch weather. The stained-glass windows bearing coats of arms and historical scenes were added after 1602, when the church burned to a crisp after a lightning strike. The taller Speeltoren, leaning slightly over Kleine Kerkstraat about 100m further south, is all that remains of the 15th-century Kleine Kerk.

The **Edams Museum** (☎ 37 24 31; Damplein 8; adult/child €5/2.50; ☯ 10am-4.30pm Mon-Sat, 1.30-4.30pm Sun) has a so-so collection of old furnishings, porcelain and silverware, spread over three cramped floors. It's best know for its floating cellar, a remarkable pantry that rises and falls with the river's swell to reduce stress on the structure above. The ornate brick structure is Edam's oldest, dating from 1530.

Tours

The tourist office organises 1½-hour **boat tours** (from €25; 11am-7pm Wed-Sat) on old *botters* in summer, weather permitting. Departure is from the Strandbad Edam camp site (p152). You can also rent a boat via the tourist office from about €225 for an afternoon.

Sleeping

In addition to the places reviewed here, the tourist office has a list of private accommodation from about €15 per person.

De Fortuna (☎ 37 16 71; www.fortuna-edam.nl; Spuistraat 7; s/d from €63/85, incl breakfast) This place might have stood model for an old Dutch painting. Its six picturesque 17th-century

cottages have not only a garden but a stretch of private canal. The rooms are stuffed with quilts and little perks like coffee and tea facilities, though the bathrooms are tiny.

Dam Hotel (☎ 37 17 66; www.damhotel.nl; Keizersgracht 1; s/d €55/90, incl breakfast) The next best bet after De Fortuna, and superbly situated on Edam's main square. The comfy rooms have a 1960s air to be relished by the retro-minded, and patrons can waltz in an old-fashioned ballroom which is lined with heavy velvet curtains.

Strandbad Edam (☎ 37 19 94; www.campingstrandbad .nl; Zeevangszeedijk 7a; per person/tent/caravan €2.75/ 4.10/4.10) This sprawling seaside campsite has a swimming beach, laundry and restaurant. It's usually overrun but remains a convenient base for boat trips into the IJsselmeer – the docks are right outside the campsite (see Tours above).

Eating

De Fortuna (☎ 37 16 71; www.fortuna-edam.nl; Spuistraat 7; mains €15-22) Elaborate set French meals that change every six to eight weeks, often starring wild game. The owner cultivates the Old Dutch angle with oil paintings, and leather seats buffed shiny over the years. The wine list is extensive and the menu features many dishes beyond the common formulas that may pass as French in Holland.

Dam Hotel Restaurant (☎ 37 17 66; www.damhotel .nl; Keizersgracht 1; mains €14-20) Decent game (such as smoked quail with bacon in port wine sauce) and a generous choice of fish dishes. The dining hall is pink to the point of painful but the waiters compensate with slick service. Forecourt diners enjoy views of the old town hall.

Edammer Kaaswinkel (☎ 37 16 83; cnr Spui & Prinsenstraat) For cheese try this place, which sends its red waxed balls of Edam to lucky recipients around the globe.

Other recommendations:
La Galera (☎ 37 19 71; Gevangenpoortsteeg 3; mains €7-16) Pizzas & pastas.
Café de Gevangenpoort (☎ 37 42 52; Gevangenpoortsteeg 1; mains €4-8) Earthy sandwich pub with live music.

Getting There & Around

Edam doesn't have a train station. Connexxion bus No 110 stops twice an hour at the bus station and continues to Monnickendam

(25 minutes) and Amsterdam (40 minutes). Bus No 114 travels to Hoorn (25 minutes, twice hourly), and No 113 makes jaunts to Volendam (10 minutes, once or twice an hour). Bicycles can be rented at **Ton Tweewielers** (☎ 37 19 22; Schepenmakersdijk 6).

ALKMAAR

☎ 072 / pop 93,000

One hour's train journey north of Amsterdam lies the picturesque ringed town of Alkmaar. It holds a special place in Dutch hearts as the first town, in 1573, to repel occupying Spanish troops; locals opened the locks and flooded the area with sea water, forcing the perplexed invaders to retreat. The victory also won the town weighing rights, which laid the foundation for its fame today – the traditional cheese market.

Orientation & Information

The town centre is focused on Waagplein, the main square where the famous cheese market is held (see boxed text, p154). Langestraat is a pedestrianised shopping street with charming restaurants and bars around the Waag and the quay named Bierkade. The pretty, canal-bound centre is 500m southeast of the train station.

Library (☎ 51 5 66 44; Gasthuisstraat 2; 🕙 11am-9pm Tue-Fri, 11am-3pm Sat) Rows of Internet terminals where you can surf for €0.25 per 10 minutes.

Tourist office (☎ 511 42 84; www.vvvalkmaar.nl; Waagplein 2; 🕙 10am-5.30pm) In the Waaggebouw, the towering old weigh house. Staff will book accommodation for a small fee.

Sights

Built as a chapel in the 14th century, the **Waaggebouw** (🕙 6.30pm & 7.30pm Thu, noon & 1pm Sat, 11am & noon Fri, mid-Apr to mid-Sep) was pressed into service as a weigh house two centuries later. The mechanical tower carillon with jousting knights still springs to life. This handsome building houses the tourist office and upstairs, the **Hollands Kaasmuseum** (Dutch Cheese Museum; ☎ 511 42 84; adult/child €3/2; 🕙 10am-4pm, Mon-Sat), a reverential display of cheese-making utensils, photos and a curious stock of paintings by 16th-century female artists.

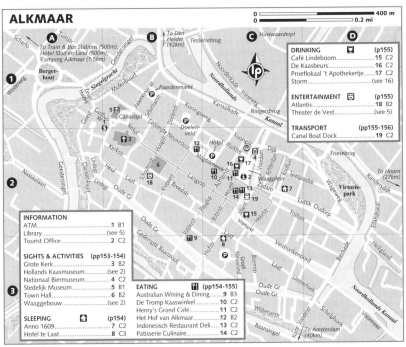

THE CHEESE MARKET

Alkmaar's traditional **cheese market** (Waagplein; ☷ 10am-noon Fri, Apr-Sep) goes back to the 17th century. Every Friday morning the waxed rounds of Gouda, Edam, and Leiden *kaas* (cheese) are ceremoniously stacked on Waagplein, and soon the porters appear in their colourful hats, ready to spring into action. The dealers (looking official in white smocks) insert a hollow rod to extract a cheese sample and go into taste-test mode, sniffing and crumbling to check fat and moisture content. This is one of the few Dutch towns where the old cheese guilds still operate, and the porters' bright green, red and yellow hats denote which company they belong to. Once deals are struck the porters whisk the cheeses on wooden sledges to the old cheese scale, accompanied by a zillion camera clicks. It's primarily for show: nowadays the modern dairy combines have a lock on the cheese trade. Still, as living relics go it's a spectacle not to be missed.

The **Stedelijk Museum** (Municipal Museum; ☎ 511 07 37; Doelenstraat 3; adult/child €3/2; ☷ 10am-5pm Tue-Fri, 1-5pm Sat & Sun) is overlooked by many visitors who don't get past the cheese market. This is a shame because its collection includes oil paintings by Dutch masters, including impressive life-sized portraits of Alkmaar nobles. A splendid panorama shows the Spanish siege of the city in 1573, its citizens holding off the intruders with spears and boiling oil. Works of later periods show Alkmaar in post–Golden Age decline; sombre scenes of almswomen caring for the poor recall how the church's role grew as trade declined. The few modern works on display include Charley Toorop's odd oil painting of the Alkmaar cheese market. Her cheese-bearers with grotesque features remain controversial – maybe that's why it's tucked away in a small upstairs gallery.

Housed in the attractive old De Boom brewery, the **Nationaal Biermuseum** (☎ 511 38 01; Houttil 1; adult/child €3/1.50; ☷ 10am-4pm Tue-Fri, 1-4pm Sat & Sun) has a decent collection of beer-making equipment and wax dummies showing how the suds were made. The rare video of Dutch beer commercials since the 1950s is a real howler. Cool off in the friendly bar with a freshly tapped beer of the month.

The most interesting historic buildings include the **town hall** on Langestraat. It's a mishmash of ostentatious 16th- and 17th-century styles with Renaissance interiors that you can peek at on weekdays.

The **Grote Kerk** (adult/child €2.50; ☷ 10am-5pm Tue-Sun) will remind visitors that Noord Holland has a particularly high concentration of church organs. The most famous one here is the small 'Swallow Organ' in the north ambulatory, one of the country's oldest (1511). The huge beast in the nave was designed by Jacob van Campen, a leading organ-maker in the 16th century. Summer recitals take place on Friday – check with the tourist office for times. The church itself is a Gothic showpiece restored to its original glory in 1996.

Tours

Tours (☎ 511 77 50; adult/child €4/2.50; ☷ 11am-5pm Mon-Sat May-Aug) The 45-minute tours, with multilingual commentary, depart from Mient near the Waag. During cheese-market season, boats go every 20 minutes starting at 9.30am.

Sleeping

The tourist office has a list of private rooms from about €20 per person.

Hotel Stad en Land (☎ 561 39 11; info@stadenland .com; Stationsweg 92, s/d €50/70, incl breakfast) It's hard to quibble with a safe choice that's opposite the train station, and it has a decent restaurant to boot. Of the four rooms those at the rear are the quietest and overlook a little pond.

Hotel te Laat (☎ 512 55 06; www.hoteltelaat.com; Laat 17; d €55-80; 🖥 ℗) This attractive inn has seven smartly designed rooms above a pub-eatery in Art Deco style. Some have balconies with views of the weigh house and old town. The owner happens to be a sledge-bearer on the cheese market, just 150m down the street.

Camping Alkmaar (☎ 511 69 24; Bergerweg 201; per adult/tent/car €4/3.50/2; ☷ Apr–mid-Sep) This site lies in a pleasant copse convenient to the ring road, 1km west of the train station. There are cabins too. Take bus No 160 or 162 to Sportpark (10 minutes).

Eating

Alkmaar has a fine variety of restaurants and cafés.

Indonesisch Restaurant Deli (☎ 515 40 82; Mient 8; mains €13-27; ☷ dinner, closed Mon & Tue) Offers

A NIGHT IN THE GRANARY

Anno 1609 (☎ 511 61 11; www.anno1609.nl; Luttik Oudorp 110; d €225) Have something to celebrate? Book a night or two in the lap of luxury at Anno 1609. The sole suite extends over an entire floor of this beautiful 17th-century granary, and the furnishings ooze exclusivity – a freestanding French bath, designer chandeliers, and polished parquet illuminated by sunlight pouring through the lead-light windows. Two nights cost €290 including a four-course dinner with champagne. It's the soul of discretion – outside there's no hint that this listed monument is even a hotel.

good-value dishes such as maduras beef as well as elaborate rijsttafels. It's been around for ages, comes highly recommended and has aircon.

Patisserie Culinaire (☎ 511 29 27; Houttil 11; mains €5-13; 🕙 11am-7pm Mon-Sat) Artsy and offers freshly made filled baguettes and croissants, quiche and big salads that spill off your plate. Or just sip a coffee at the sidewalk tables and watch the world go by.

About a dozen restaurants and cafés are tightly packed together on Waagplein, all offering much the same thing.

Henry's Grand Café (☎ 511 32 83; Houttil 34; mains €12-18; 🕙 lunch & dinner) A convivial place serving soups, salads, sandwiches and set meals including pork or chicken satay, backed up by a good range of beers.

Het Hof van Alkmaar (☎ 512 12 12; Hof van Sonoy 1; mains €15-20; 🕙 lunch & dinner Tue-Sun) Occupies a former 15th-century nunnery with a rustic dining room overlooking the former nuns' *hofje* (courtyard). The menu is full of inventions like Victoria bass in chili-coconut sauce, but should your palate desire something simpler at lunch, there are chicken saté's and sandwiches.

Australian Wining & Dining (☎ 512 1144; Fridsen 101; mains €17-27; 🕙 dinner Wed-Sun) Homesick Aussies will be tickled pink. Pull out your *Crocodile Dundee* knife for shark steak, fillet of kangaroo or yabbies (crayfish), all cooked on the barbie.

De Tromp Kaaswinkel (☎ 511 34 22; Magdalenenstraat 11) An excellent and pungent selection of Dutch and French cheeses, stacked high in shelves on all sides of the shop.

Drinking

Bars and brown cafés hug the north side of Waagplein.

Proeflokaal 't Apothekertje (☎ 512 41 07; Waagplein 16) An old-style drinking hole done up like a chemist's shop.

Café Lindeboom (☎ 512 17 43; Verdronkenoord 114) Over by the old fish market is this cosy bar where talkative locals live it up on the canal terrace.

De Kaasbeurs (☎ 511 31 67; Houttil 26) Regular jazz till the wee hours.

Storm (☎ 511 47 53; Houttil 32) Trendy Storm offers a diet of DJ-spun lounge and club music, with the occasional live act.

Entertainment

Alkmaar has a lively arts scene – pick up a copy of the *Alkmaar Agenda* to see what's on.

Theater De Vest (☎ 519 18 19; www.theaterdevest.nl; Canadaplein 2) Runs the gamut from traditional plays and puppet shows to avant-garde dance. In summer Canadaplein turns into a stage for the performing arts festival *Zomer op het plein*.

Atlantis (☎ 511 83 90; www.atlantispodium.nl; Breedstraat 33) *The* downtown music club, always fresh and unpredictable. It's a Black Sabbath tribute one night, a choir rehearsal the next, so it pays to check the schedule. The Creatif Centrum upstairs offers arts courses and the café runs exhibitions.

Getting There & Away

Direct trains to/from Alkmaar include:

Destination	Price (€)	Duration (min)	Frequency (per hr)
Amsterdam	5.60	40	4
Hoorn	3.70	25	2
Den Helder	6.20	60	2
Enkhuizen	6.20	60	2

Alkmaar is served by many regional bus lines but key destinations involve changes. From Amsterdam Centraal Station, take bus 94 via Zaandam (10 minutes, half-hourly) to Beverwijk and change to bus No 167 or 168 to Alkmaar.

Getting Around

The old town lies about 500m southeast of the train station. You can also take

Connexxion bus Nos 10, 22 and 127 to Kanaalkade (5 minutes).

There's a **bicycle shop** (☎ 511 79 07) at the train station that rents all sorts of two-wheelers.

BROEK OP LANGEDIJK
☎ 0226

In the town Broek op Langedijk, about 8km northeast of Alkmaar, the **Museum Broeker Veiling** (Museum Broeker Auction; ☎ 31 38 07; Broek op Langedijk; adult/child €5.65/3.25; ☺ 10am-5pm Mon-Fri, 11am-5pm Sat & Sun) bills itself as the 'oldest sail-through vegetable auction'. Only when you've entered the auction hall – a stunning Art Deco building on the water – does it become clear how this works.

The show begins as barges laden with baskets of produce float in beneath the feet of the auctioneer, who encourages visitors to bid on the old auction clock. It's entertaining, instructive and above all easy to get carried away, so remember how many tomatoes or bunches of broccoli you can realistically consume.

The museum also runs 45-minute boat tours around the dozens of tiny island plots nearby that once supplied the auction with regular greens. Combination tickets for museum and boat cost adult child €8.95/4.95.

From Amsterdam, take the A9 to Alkmaar and N25 to Heerhugowaard, exiting for Broek op Langedijk. By train, go to Alkmaar (€6.40, 45 minutes, four times hourly) and change to bus No 155 (20 minutes, twice hourly).

HOORN
☎ 0229 / pop 65,500

This lively little port was once capital of West Friesland and, thanks to the presence of the Dutch merchant fleet, a mighty trading city. As a member of the league of Seven Cities, it helped free the country from the Spanish who occupied the town in 1569. It also earned its keep from catching herring until the late 17th century, when the Zuiderzee began to silt up, reducing catches and making navigation tricky.

Its most famous son was explorer Willem Schoutens, who named South America's storm-lashed tip – Cape Horn – after his home town in 1616.

An air of old money pervades the central square and harbour, the latter now a playground for weekend skippers.

Orientation & Information

The old quarter begins about 1km southwest of the train station. From the station, walk south along broad Veemarkt to Gedempte Turfhaven, turn right and take the first left into Grote Noord, the pedestrianised shopping street. At the end is the scenic main square, Rode Steen, and the harbour area is a stone's throw further south, down Grote Havensteeg.

Library (Wisselstraat 8; ☺ 1-8.30pm Mon, Wed & Thu, 1-5pm Tue, 11am-5.30pm Fri, 10am-1pm Sat) You can check your email for €0.70 per 15 minutes.

Tourist office (☎ 511 4284; www.vvvlnternet.nl; Veemarkt 4; ☺ 1-6pm Mon, 9.30am-6pm Tue-Fri, 9.30am-5pm Sat) About 250m south of the train station.

Sights & Activities

Hoorn's heyday as a shipping centre is long gone but the imposing **statue of Jan Peterszoon Coen**, founder of the Dutch East India Company, still watches over the Rode Steen (red stone or fortress), the square named for the blood that once flowed from the gallows. On the northeastern side of the square it's impossible to overlook the **Waag**, the 17th-century weigh house that houses a café-restaurant.

On the square also stands the former seat of the **Staten-College** (states' council), the body that once governed seven towns in North Holland (Alkmaar, Hoorn, Enkhuizen, Medemblik, Edam, Monnickendam and Purmerend). Its wedding-cake façade bears the coat of arms of Oranje-Nassau, the Dutch-German royal dynasty that the Dutch named as rulers when Napoleon left Holland. It now houses the Westfries Museum.

The scenic harbour is lined by stately gabled houses. Overshadowing them all is the massive **Hoofdtoren** (1532), a defensive gate that now hosts a bar and restaurant. The tiny belfry was an afterthought.

The **Museum Stoomtram** (☎ 21 92 31; adult/child one way €9.20/7, return €15/12; ☺ 11.05am Tue-Sat Apr-Oct, Mon Jul-Aug) isn't a museum in the traditional sense but rather a historic locomotive that puffs an hour between Hoorn station and Medemblik. You can combine the train and boat for a route called the 'Historic Triangle': first from Hoorn to Medemblik by train and

Edam (p151)

Enkhuizen (p158)

Enkhuizen (p158)

Haarlem (p140)

Cheese market in Alkmaar (p154)

Tiled entrance to a house, Haarlem (p140)

then back by boat *and* train via Enkhuizen. Add a visit to the Zuiderzeemuseum in Enkhuizen (see p158 for museum details) and the whole package costs €25/19.

The **Westfries Museum** (☎ 21 48 62; Rode Steen; adult/child €2.50/1.25; ☻ 11am-5pm Mon-Fri, 2-5pm Sat & Sun) now resides in this remarkable building recalling Hoorn's history. Particularly worthwhile are its historical paintings – highlights here include four large group portraits of prominent *schutters* or civic guards by Jan A Rotius (1624–66), wearing ruff collars and smug expressions. Rotius himself can be seen at the far right in one scene. The rear courtyard has a number of curious stone tablets from local façades.

The **Affiche Museum** (Dutch Poster Museum; ☎ 29 98 46; Grote Oost 2-4; adult/child €4.50/2.25; ☻ 11-5pm Tue-Sat, noon-5pm Sun) has an extensive collection including every single poster made for the annual Holland Festival since 1948. You'll also find contemporary artwork from big-name designers like Anthon Beeke and Gert Dumbar (of Studio Dumbar fame). It's virtually opposite the old weigh house.

Housed in two old cheese warehouses, the **Museum of the 20th Century** (☎ 21 40 01; Bierkade 4; adult/child €3.50/2 ☻ 10am-5pm Tue-Sun) is devoted mainly to household goods and modern inventions. Of the few eye-openers there are a 1964 Philips mainframe computer – a clunky bookcase-sized unit with a whole 1KB of memory – and a 30-sq-metre scale *maquette* (model) of Hoorn in 1650, with taped commentary in several languages.

Sleeping
The tourist office also has a list of B&Bs from around €20 per person.

Hotel de Keizerskroon (☎ 21 27 17; keizerskroon @tiscali.nl; Breed 31; s/d €50/70, incl breakfast) Very much in the middle of things, this 25-room hotel-restaurant has rooms that are spacious, modern, and above all brown. Its insulated windows afford a view of the bustling market streets below.

Hotel de Magneet (☎ 21 50 21; fax 23 70 44; Kleine Oost 5D; s with/without bathroom €36/27, d €54/41, incl breakfast; **P**) This family-run guesthouse lies in a quiet street just east of the old centre, with a bar and restaurant. Rooms are large for Dutch standards, comfy too but not long on atmosphere. The proximity to the coastal paths makes the hotel popular with cyclists' clubs.

Eating
Brasserie Bontekoe (☎ 21 73 24; Nieuwendam 1; mains €12-18; ☻ Wed-Sat) This cosy, terraced brown café enjoys a strategic view of canals and marina. There's an extensive sandwich menu alongside lamb, pork and chicken dishes, and a veggie curry to die for.

De Waag Café-Restaurant (☎ 21 51 95; Rode Steen 8; mains €5-15) This imposing pile couldn't be much more central, serving hot ciabatta sandwiches and salads on the terrace outside the old weigh house on the main square.

Vishandel Leen Parlevliet (rolls from €2, meals from €5) Next to the Hoofdtoren at the harbour this small glass pod sells wonderful seafood rolls and bigger seafood meals. Munch and admire the graceful movements of the *bruine vloot* (brown fleet) sailing on the horizon.

Delikaas (☎ 21 03 52; Breed 38) This specialist vendor in an ornate colonial-style building sells cheese, freshly roasted nuts, dried meats and wine.

Open-air markets are held Wednesday and Saturday along Breed.

Other recommendations:

Hendrickje Stoffels (☎ 21 04 17; Oude Doelenkade 3-5; mains €24; ☻ dinner, closed Wed-Thu) Progressive French & fish.

Nusa Java (☎ 29 60 39; cnr Vismarkt & Wijdesteeg; mains €8-12; ☻ dinner) Indonesian dishes and bamboo-esque decor.

Getting There & Around
Regular train services to/from Hoorn include the following:

Destination	Price (€)	Duration (min)	Frequency (per hr)
Amsterdam	6.20	40	2
Enkhuizen	3.00	75	2
Alkmaar	3.70	25	2

The bus station is right outside Hoorn train station. Connexxion bus No 133 goes twice hourly to Den Helder (a one-hour ride) and Leeuwarden (two hours, change buses at Den Oever). Connexxion bus No 114 serves Edam (30 minutes, twice hourly).

Hire your two-wheelers at the **bicycle shop** (☎ 21 70 96) at Hoorn train station.

ENKHUIZEN

☎ 0228 / pop 17,000

In the Golden Age the strategic harbour of Enkhuizen sheltered the Dutch merchant fleet. Like other Zuiderzee ports, the town slipped into relative obscurity in the late 17th century. Today it still possesses one of the largest fleets on the IJsselmeer – of recreational vessels. Boating aside, its main draw is the superb Zuiderzeemuseum, which shows how locals lived before the completion of the Afsluitdijk (Barrier Dyke). With its venerable harbour, canals and rows of handsome gabled houses, it is one of the most engaging towns in Noord Holland.

Orientation

The train station is a terminus on the line to Amsterdam and stands on the southern edge of town. The yacht-filled Buitenhaven (outer harbour) and the narrower Oude Haven (Old Harbour) bisect the town roughly east to west; canals encircle the old centre. Dijk is the main café-and-restaurant strip, on the northern bank of Oude Haven. About 200m further north, the long, pedestrianised Westerstraat runs parallel and is lined with impressive historic buildings.

Information

Library (☎ 22 83 89; Kwakespad 3; 1.30-9pm Mon & Fri, 1.30-5.30pm Tue-Wed, 10am-noon Thur) About 500m west along Westerstraat – turn right into the canalside road Kwakespad. Surfing the Internet costs €0.70 per 15 minutes.

Tourist office (☎ 31 31 64; www.vvv-enkhuizen.nl; Tussen Twee Havens 1; 9am-5pm) Just east of the train station sells ferry tickets and a self-guided tour booklet in English.

Sights & Activities

Moving east along Westerstraat you'll spy the remarkable **Westerkerk**, a 15th-century Gothic church with a removable wooden belfry. The ornate choir screen and imposing pulpit are worth a look. Opposite the church is the **Weeshuis**, a 17th-century orphanage with a sugary, curlicued portal.

At the other end of Westerstraat stands the 16th-century **Waag** (weigh house) on the old cheese market, and nearby the classical **town hall**, modelled after the Amsterdam town hall that once stood on the Dam. You can peek through the windows at the lavish Gobelins and tapestries (closed to the public).

Between the Buitenhaven and the Oude Haven, the **Drommedaris** was built as a defence tower as part of the 16th-century town walls. Once a formidable prison, it now serves as a an elevated meeting hall. Its clock-tower carillon still tinkles a playful tune on the hour.

The old harbour is choc-a-bloc with historic pleasure boats, the polished schooners, smacks and *tjalks* of a slower era. They're available for rent in many cases (see p296 for addresses of yacht hire companies). More modest skippers can hire kayaks, canoes and electric boats at **De Waterspiegel** (☎ 31 74 56; Olifantsteiger 3; kayaks/canoes/ electric boats per hour €5/7/15), mainly for use on the inner canals.

ZUIDERZEEMUSEUM

The impressive **Zuiderzeemuseum** (☎ 35 11 11; www.zuiderzeemuseum.nl; adult/child €9.50/7.50; parking €5; 10am-5pm) consists of two parts: the open-air or Buitenmuseum with 130-odd rebuilt dwellings and workshops, and an indoor Binnenmuseum devoted to farming, fishing and shipping. The two parts lie about 300m from each other, but to relieve congestion visitors are encouraged to leave their vehicles at a car park at the edge of town. A ferry (fare included in your ticket) then takes you across the bay to the outdoor displays. Plan a half-day for an unhurried visit to both sections.

The Buitenmuseum is captivating. Opened in 1983 it was carefully assembled from houses, farms and sheds trucked in from around the region to show Zuiderzee life as it was from 1880 to 1932. Every conceivable detail has been thought of, from the fencetop decorations and choice of shrubbery to the entire layout of villages. You have to hand it to the planners because the place feels authentic. It pays to pick up the illustrated guide (in English) because without you can easily miss some buildings.

Inhabitants wear traditional dress, and there are real shops such as a bakery, chemist and sweet shop. Workshops run demonstrations throughout the day. Though varying in character the displays join seamlessly: lime kilns from Akersloot stand but a few metres from Zuidende and its row of Monnickendam houses, originally built outside the dykes. Don't miss the **Urk quarter** raised to simulate the island town before the Noordoostpolder was drained. For a special postmark drop your letters at the old post office from Den Oever. The **Marker Haven** is a copy of the harbour built in 1830 on what was then the island of Marken.

Exit at the rear and walk 300m to reach the Binnenmuseum, which occupies a museum complex adjoining the **Peperhuis**, the former home and warehouse of a Dutch shipping merchant. The displays include a fine shipping hall: paintings, prints and other materials relating the rise and fall of the fishing industry, and the construction of the dykes. Here too are cultural artefacts such as regional costumes, porcelain, silver, and jewellery that indicate the extent of Holland's riches at the time.

Sleeping

The tourist office has a list of private rooms from about €18, including breakfast.

Hotel Garni Recuerdos (☎ 56 24 69; www .recuerdos.nl; Westerstraat 217; s/d €55/80, incl breakfast) Owned by a music society patron this stately manor house is the picture of calm, with three immaculate rooms overlooking a manicured garden. Spanish guitar concerts are held in the lounge area downstairs.

Hotel Centrum (☎ 31 28 27; info@hetcentrum.com; Westerstraat 153; d €60, incl breakfast) The clean, modern rooms are up the steep stairs above an atmospheric brown café, a favourite with local bands and pool players. There are more bars within staggering distance.

Appartement Hotel Driebanen (☎ 31 61 81; info@hoteldriebanen.com; Driebanen 59; s with/without bathroom €55/42, d €79/57, incl breakfast) This tranquil canalside guesthouse has cheerful rooms that are ideal for longer-term stays, and the host is a goldmine of local information.

Camping Enkhuizer Zand (☎ 31 72 89; fax 31 22 11; Kooizandweg 4; per adult/tent/camper €5.50/4.50/4.50; Apr-Sep) Next to the Zuiderzeemuseum, this popular site is a model of self-sufficiency, with an indoor pool, sandy beaches, tennis courts and grocery.

Eating & Drinking

De Kapel (☎ 32 32 72; Westerstraat 128a; mains €11-16; lunch & dinner Tue-Sat) Tucked away in a renovated 17th-century chapel opposite the Oude Weeshuis, here you'll find exotic *panga* fillet (African fish) alongside

traditional Dutch *stoofpotje* (meat and vegetable stew) and veggie lasagne.

Restaurant De Boei (☎ 31 42 80; Havenweg 5; mains €20; lunch & dinner Mar-Oct only) If you want to get packed to the gills, try the all-you-can-eat skate with fries (€20) or the delectable 'market menu', a four-part *tour de force*.

Restaurant de Drie Haringhe (☎ 31 86 10; Dijk 28; mains €21; lunch & dinner, closed Tue) This upmarket locale excels in Dutch and French-inspired cuisine such as seawolf fillet wrapped in green mustard sauce. Though next to a main street the walled garden is an oasis of calm at mealtimes.

Schipperscafé 't Ankertje (☎ 31 35 00; Dijk 80; mains €6-15) This canalside café is a prime spot for the classic Dutch formula of coffee, apple pie and chit-chat till the cows come home. You may be treated to a spectacle of youths diving from the drawbridge on the open terrace.

Dikke Mik (☎ 31 64 04; HJ Schimmelstraat 10; mains €7-15) In warm weather the quay fills with aromas of spare ribs, Mexican chicken and a fish stew that'll stick to your ribs; in winter the clientele holes up in the cosy *eetcafé*.

Getting There & Away

Regular train services to/from Enkhuizen include the following:

Destination	Price (€)	Duration (min)	Frequency (per hr)
Amsterdam	8.20	60	2
Hoorn	3.00	25	2
Alkmaar	6.20	60	2
Den Helder	9.20	90	2

Connections to Den Helder involve a change of train at both Hoorn and Heerhugowaard – inconvenient but the fastest option for public transport. The bus station behind Enkhuizen train station serves mainly local destinations. Of the few useful bus links, No 150 goes five times daily to Lelystad (40 minutes).

There are ferries three times daily from Enkhuizen-Spoorhaven to Urk (1¾ hours), Stavoren (1¼ hours) and Medemblik (1¼ hours). All single/return tickets cost €7.50/10.

Free parking is behind the train station, it's 200m to the old centre along the pretty, mast-filled outer harbour.

DYKE ROAD

The N302 between Enkhuizen and Lelystad deserves a special mention because it runs along a 32km-long dyke, completed in 1976 as the first step of the reclamation of the Markerwaard (see the boxed text below). As you get underway you'll pass beneath a high-tech causeway that connects Enkhuizen harbour with the IJsselmeer, with ships floating surreally over the motorway.

Sights are few along the route, apart from the boats bobbing on the IJsselmeer and a stone monument at the halfway mark in the form of a chain link symbolising the joining of West Friesland with Flevoland.

MEDEMBLIK

☎ 0227 / pop 7900

About 12km northwest of Enkhuizen lies Medemblik, the oldest port on the IJsselmeer dating back to the 12th century. It was here that Count Floris V built a medieval fortress to keep the feisty natives under his thumb.

Orientation & Information

The castle stands on the eastern side and is signposted from the harbour. The richly decorated façades on Kaasmarkt, Torenstraat, Nieuwstraat and along the Achterom canal are impressive. The old town is only 1km across and thus quickly absorbed.

Tourist office (☎ 54 28 52; www.vvv-medemblik.nl; Kaasmarkt 1; ☺ 9am-5pm) A folksy all-in-one place, with a good stock of maps behind the supermarket and post office.

Sights & Activities

Among the sites, the 13th-century **Kasteel Radboud** (☎ 54 19 60; adult/child €3/2; ☺ 10am-5pm Tue-Fri, 2-5pm Sat) deserves most of your attention. Looking at this rather puny fortress today it's hard to imagine that its master, Count Floris V, thought it an effective deterrent to rebellion among the feisty West Frisians. Ironically the plot that killed the count was hatched not at home but in London, after Floris switched his allegiance to the French.

The structure served as a prison before a 19th-century restoration by Pierre Cuypers, the designer of Amsterdam's Rijksmuseum. The original floor plan has been preserved, and the imposing **Ridderzaal** (Knights' Hall) still looks much as it did in the Middle Ages. The self-guided tour gives details of the castle's long history and the count's undoing.

Stoommachine Museum (Steam Engine Museum; ☎ 54 47 32; Oosterdijk 4; adult/child €4.20/2.10; ☺ 10am-5pm Tue-Sat, noon-5pm Sun) Ever wondered what drove the industrial revolution? Part of the answer lies here, in the old pump station outside Medemblik. Thirty handsome old steam engines from Holland, England and Germany are fired up for demonstrations in summer months, and kids can stoke small coal-fired models on Wednesdays and weekends.

The **Museum Stoomtram** (see Hoorn, p156) departs from the old train station where there's a small display of railway artefacts (free).

THE AFSLUITDIJK

For three centuries the Dutch dreamed of draining the Zuiderzee (literally South Sea) to create a huge tract of valuable farmland. Opening into the North Sea this bay was lined with villages dependent on saltwater fishing and Golden Age ports that kept the goods flowing to and from the colonies. Unfortunately the shallow Zuiderzee washed over the coast during big storms. The only way to tame the waves, it seems, was to block them off.

By the late 19th century new techniques allowed engineer Cornelis Lely to sketch out a retaining barrier. A major flood in 1916 finally set the plan in motion, and construction began in 1927 amid worries from fishermen about their livelihood, as well as fears that the Wadden Islands would vanish in the rising seas.

In 1932 the Zuiderzee was ceremoniously sealed off by the Afsluitdijk (Barrier Dyke). The water level remained steady but the fishing industry was effectively killed as the basin gradually filled with fresh water from the river IJssel. The IJsselmeer was born.

This impressive dam (30km long and 90m wide) links the provinces of Noord Holland and Friesland. A second barrier between Enkhuizen and Lelystad was to usher in the next phase of land reclamation, but the plan was shelved to protect the environment.

Sleeping & Eating

The tourist office has a list of **private rooms** from €18 per person.

Hotel B&B de Waeg (☎ /fax 54 12 03; Oostersingel 5; s/d €25/50, incl breakfast) This friendly family-run pension is excellent value in a prim suburb a short walk from the harbour. The only drawback, if there is one, is the 1km walk from the bus station if you're without a car.

Camping Opperdoes (☎ 54 23 45; campingkleingie thoorn@hi.nl; Oosteinde 12; site €14; ☻ Apr-Sep) Camp sites don't get much quieter than this one: 50 tent sites and hook-ups at the back of the leafy caravan park, reachable over a canal bridge. Take bus No 39 to Opperdoes, 2km west of Medemblik.

De Driemaster (☎ 54 30 20; Pekelharinghaven 49; mains €12-24; ☻ lunch & dinner) Ahh – lovely views of the harbour and IJsselmeer as you relish a braised turbot or launch into a filled croissant. The best spots are canalside for watching the big pleasure boats drift under the drawbridge.

Café Restaurant de Tijd (☎ 54 13 86; Westerhaven 1; mains €16-21; ☻ lunch & dinner Wed-Sun) Occupying another prime spot on the west harbour, with an extensive menu of seafood and pancake specialities.

Getting There & Around

The nearest real train station is in Hoorn, where you'll have to change to a Connexxion bus for many destinations. From Amsterdam, take the train or bus No 114 to Hoorn (one hour, twice hourly) and change to bus No 39 (another hour, twice hourly). From Enkhuizen, take the train to Hoorn and change to No 39 (one hour).

A ferry runs three times daily from Medemblik to Enkhuizen-Spoorhaven. Single/return tickets cost €7.50/10 (1¼ hours one way).

Smit (☎ 54 12 00; Vooreiland 1) on the eastern side of town has a huge selection of bicycles for hire.

TEXEL ISLAND

☎ 0222 / pop 13,450

About 3km north of the coast of Noord Holland lies Texel (pronounced *tes*-sel), the largest of the Wadden Islands. It's a remarkably diverse place with broad white beaches, lush nature reserves, forests and picture-book villages. Now 25km long and 9km

wide, it actually consisted of two islands until 1835 when a spit of land to Eyerland Island was pumped dry.

Before the Noordzeekanaal (North Sea Canal) opened in the 19th century, Texel was a main stop for ships en route to Asia, Africa and North America: the first trade mission to the East Indies began and ended here. It was also the scene of a spectacular maritime disaster: on Christmas Day 1593, hurricane-force winds battered a merchant fleet moored off the coast and 44 vessels sank, drowning about a thousand seamen.

Texel relies chiefly on tourism, with the majority of visitors being either Dutch or German. Spectators line the beaches in mid-June for the largest catamaran race in the world, the Cisco Trophy. The local wool is highly prized and there are sheep everywhere, lazing, grazing or tippy-toeing along the dykes.

Orientation

The first thing you'll see is the ferry jetty at 't Horntje on the south side of the isle. All buses pass through the modest capital of Den Burg, located 6km north.

Oudeschild is home to a beachcombers' museum and a pretty little harbour for fishing-boat excursions.

Oosterend is a quiet hamlet with distinctive architecture and Texel's oldest church (12th century).

De Cocksdorp is a launch pad into the nature reserves, or for a hop to the island of Vlieland.

De Koog is a tacky tourist mecca; whereas Den Hoorn is close to tulip fields in the southwest and is the best town to stay and dine in relative seclusion.

Information

Library (Drijverstraat 7, Den Burg; ☻ 2-5pm Tue-Fri, 10.30am-12.30pm Sat & Mon) Lets you surf the Internet for €0.50 per 15 minutes.

ABN-Amro (cnr Binnenburg & Kantoorstraat) In Den Burg, about 50m east of the imposing Hervormde Kerk (Dutch Reform Church). Other banks are in De Koog and De Cocksdorp.

Tourist office (☎ 31 47 41; www.vvv-texel.nl; Emmalaan 66, Den Burg; ☻ 9am-6pm Mon-Fri, 9am-5pm Sat, 10.30am-1.30pm Sun) It lies on the southern fringe of town and is signposted from the ferry terminal. Staff book accommodation for a small fee.

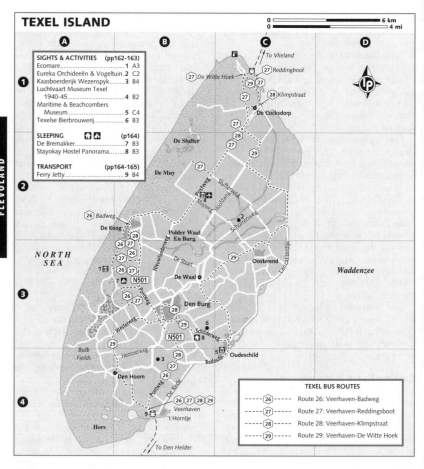

TEXEL ISLAND

0 — 6 km
0 — 4 mi

SIGHTS & ACTIVITIES (pp162-163)
Ecomare......................................1 A3
Eureka Orchideeën & Vogeltuin.2 C2
Kaasboerderijk Wezenspyk........3 B4
Luchtvaart Museum Texel
1940-45.................................4 B2
Maritime & Beachcombers
Museum.................................5 C4
Texelse Bierbrouwerij...............6 B3

SLEEPING (p164)
De Bremakker..........................7 B3
Stayokay Hostel Panorama.......8 B3

TRANSPORT (pp164-165)
Ferry Jetty..............................9 B4

To Vlieland
Reddingsboot 27
De Witte Hoek 27
29 27
Klimpstraat 28
27
De Cocksdorp
27
De Sluffer 28
27
29
De Muy 27

North Sea

Badweg 26
De Koog
28
Polder Waal 26 27
En Burg 27 26
26 27 Oosterend
1 26 27 De Staart 29
7 N501
26 Den Burg
27
28
6
29 Schilderweg
N501 8
Bulb
Fields 28
Den Hoorn 3 5 Oudeschild
27
Redout
29
26 27 28 29
Veerhaven
Hors 9
't Horntje

Waddenzee

To Den Helder

TEXEL BUS ROUTES
- - - - 26 - - - - Route 26: Veerhaven-Badweg
- - - - 27 - - - - Route 27: Veerhaven-Reddingsboot
- - - - 28 - - - - Route 28: Veerhaven-Klimpstraat
- - - - 29 - - - - Route 29: Veerhaven-De Witte Hoek

Sights

Texel's wonderful beaches are pristinely white and clean. Lining the western North Sea shore only, each has a numbered *paal* (piling) as an address marker. Lifeguards are on duty from No 9 southeast of Den Hoorn to No 21 near De Koog in summer. There are two nudist beaches, at No 9 and at No 27 in the north. Swimming is prohibited between Nos 31 and 33 near the lighthouse at De Cocksdorp due to the treacherous riptides between Texel and Vlieland.

Ecomare (☎ 31 77 41; Ruyslaan 92, De Koog; adult/child €7/3.50; ☼ 9am-5pm) is chiefly a refuge for sick seals retrieved from the Waddenzee. Their playful water ballet lacking in any apparent effort will delight all but the most jaded

visitor. Rescued birds are the other main tenants and there are exhibits about Texel's bewildering range of feathered friends. At the aquariums you can sidle up to sharks and even pat a seaskate. The hot favourites remain the seal feedings at 11am and 3pm.

Dress lightly for the steamy **Eureka Orchideeën & Vogeltuin** (Eureka Orchid & Bird Garden; ☎ 31 83 64; Schorrenweg 20, Oosterend; adult/child €3.50/2.50; ☼ 8.30am-6pm Mon-Fri, 8.30am-5pm Sat). Exotic specimens such as blue kittas and torakoos flash through this tropical greenhouse where the ponds are filled with goldfish and carp. A number of native orchid species can be viewed in all their tender, quivering glory, and the mix of bird and plant colours can be breathtaking.

The isle's only brewery, the **Texelse Bierbrouwerij** (☎ 31 32 29; Schilderweg 214b, Oudeschild; adult/child €5/2.50; 🕑 2-6pm Wed & Sat) divulges the secrets of its suds including its tasty *Speciaalbier* on afternoon tours. The former dairy on the property has a terrace ideal for downing a few.

The small **cheese farm** (☎ 31 50 90; Hoondernweg 29), the Kaasboerderijk Wezenspyk, between Den Hoorn and Den Burg is the place to scoop up tasty rounds produced from the local cows, sheep and goats.

DUINEN VAN TEXEL NATIONAL PARK
For many nature lovers this patchwork of varied dunescape running along the entire western coast of the island is the prime reason for visiting Texel. Salt fens and heath alternate with velvety, grass-covered dunes, and you'll find plants endemic to this habitat like the dainty marsh orchid or sea buckthorn, a ragged shrub with bright orange berries. Much of the area is bird sanctuary and accessible only on foot.

De Slufter became a brackish wetland after an attempt at land reclamation failed; when a storm breached the dykes in the early 1900s the area was allowed to flood and a unique ecosystem developed. To the south, **De Muy** is renowned for its colony of spoonbills that are monitored with great zeal by local naturalists.

Only a stone's throw from the windswept beach lies the dark, leafy forest of **De Dennen** between Den Hoorn and De Koog. Originally planted as a source of lumber, today it has an enchanting network of walking and biking paths. In springtime the forest floor is carpeted with snowdrops that were first planted here in the 1930s.

MUSEUMS
The **Maritime and Beachcombers Museum** (☎ 31 49 56; Barentszstraat 21, Oudeschild; adult/child €4.10/2.05; 🕑 10am-5pm Tue-Sat) has an extraordinary variety of junk recovered from sunken ships –it's a bit like perusing flotsam from the *Titanic*. In the outdoor section there are demonstrations by rope-makers, fish-smokers and blacksmiths, while the indoor displays cover everything from underwater archaeology to windmill technology.

Next to the airfield, the **Luchtvaart Museum Texel 1940–1945** (Texel Aviation Museum; ☎ 31 16 89; adult/child €3/1.85; 🕑 Tue-Sun 11am-5pm) revisits the glory days of the island's pint-sized squadron. Artefacts include old aircraft or bits thereof, such as the cockpit of a 1913 Fokker.

Activities
The tourist office sells a useful booklet of cycle routes and can advise on the hiking trails that crisscross the island. The well-marked 80km-long 'Texel Path' takes you through the dunes and over the mud flats before veering inland through the island's villages; the circular local routes along the way make for nice one- to three-hour hikes or bike trips.

Boat trips (leaving from Oudeschild) are conducted by shrimp trawlers such as the **Emmie TX 10** (☎ 31 36 39; Oudeschild; adult/child €6/5; 🕑 10.30am & 2pm Mon-Sat). The two-hour trip around the island sails close to an endangered seal colony on the sandbanks. Some shrimp caught on the journey are prepared fresh for passengers. Try your luck or book at the tourist office or directly by phone. Other boats such as **Rival** (☎ 31 34 10; anglers/observers €15/7.50) do outings for sports fishermen, complete with fishing equipment. If there's a late tide some boats also go out at around 4.30pm.

Catamarans can be hired from **De Eilander** (☎ 06-20634413; www.deeilander.com; Paal 33, De Cocksdorp; catamarans per hr €36; 🕑 May-Oct) near the Vlieland boat dock. You can board as a passenger for €25 per hour – recommended for novices when the North Sea is rough (ie most of the time). Five-hour sailing courses cost €130.

To gather your own beach treasure, board a horse-drawn wagon run by **Jutters Plezier** (☎ 39 01 11; De Cocksdorp; adult/child €7/3.50). The 1½-hour trips are more for the journey than the treasure really, and end at the owner's private lair for a round of herbal schnapps. Tours (minimum 15 persons) depart from the lighthouse – check with the tourist office for times.

Tessel Air (☎ 31 14 36; www.paracentrumtexel.nl; Texel Airport) offers pleasure flights over Texel from €25 per person, and for bit more cash they'll explore the other Wadden Islands. To really feel the wind in your face, try paragliding (€180 per jump) from 3000m after a whirlwind course by qualified instructors. You can even get a video of your jump for an extra €95. Expect a surcharge in high season, and book before you drop in.

Sleeping

There are 3000 hotel beds on the island but it pays to book ahead, especially in July and August. The tourist office also has a list of B&Bs from around €20 per person per night. Touristy De Koog has by far the most options, but hamlets such as Den Hoorn or De Cocksdorp are much more agreeable. All hotel prices listed here include a private bathroom and breakfast. Prices drop in the off-season when island life slips into a lower gear.

Hotel De 14 Sterren (☎ 32 26 81; www.14sterren.nl; Smitsweg 4, Den Burg; d €59-66; ✗) You couldn't wish for a nicer spot on the edge of De Dennen forest and next to the barn house restaurant De Worselteltent (see Eating below). Each of its 14 rooms is decorated in warm Mediterranean hues, and most have a terrace or balcony with garden views, and all are great value for money on Texel.

Loodman's Welvaren (☎ 31 92 28; www.welvaart texel.nl; Herenstraat 12, Den Hoorn; s/d/ste €66/83/105) Rooms in this splendidly renovated skipper's inn are cheery and spacious with mod cons like minibar, phone and TV. The plush top-floor suite affords a wonderful feeling of privacy.

't Anker (☎ /fax 31 62 74; Kikkertstraat 24, De Cocksdorp; d €41) The spacious interior belies its spot in an ordinary row of terraced homes. Enjoy the hunting-lodge atmosphere, the lush garden and your host's easy charm.

Hotel De Merel (☎ 31 31 32; www.hoteldemerel.nl; Warmoesstraat 22, Den Burg; s/d €41/73; 🖳) This family-run hotel in a quiet street off the marketplace has a grand piano, extras like a solarium and a bar that's truly *gezellig* (cosy). The rear opens onto a lawnside patio where guests take their breakfast in peace.

Stayokay Hostel Panorama (☎ 31 54 41; www .stayokay.com; Schansweg 7; dm €22, d €60, incl breakfast; ✗) About 2km east of Den Burg, this sprawling, relaxed youth hostel occupies a pretty thatched house near the nature reserve *Hoge Berg* (at 15m, the island's 'Big Mountain'). Singles and rooms for up to six persons are also available. Take bus No 29 to the de Keet stop.

Texel's many camp sites teem in summer; the tourist office in Den Burg can tell you which ones have vacancies. Many farms also offer rooms and camp sites.

De Bremakker (☎ 31 28 63; www.bremakker.nl; Templierweg 40; camp site for 2 people €25; ☽ Apr-Oct)

This leafy campground is situated between Den Burg and De Koog at the forest's edge, about 1km from the beach. There is a laundry and snack bar, plus sports facilities and almost always an abundance of calm. Take bus No 26 to Templierweg.

Eating

With thousands of sheep roaming the island, lamb naturally gets top billing and seafood comes a close second.

Bij Jef (☎ 31 96 23; www.bijjef.nl; Herenstraat 34, Den Hoorn; mains €19-23, 4-course menu €45; ☽ lunch & dinner) Great care goes into the seasonal creations of Jef, a rising star on Texel's culinary heaven. Like the restaurant's stylish interior, the French-influenced cuisine is economical but tastefully blended. The four-course Hedonist's menu featuring seasonal and always fresh ingredients is a real showstopper.

De Worstelteltent (☎ 31 02 88; Smitsweg 6, Den Burg; mains €14-18; ☽ lunch & dinner) Enjoy refined dishes with a dash of the Italian in this converted 300-year-old barn. The wine list is copious, the steaks tender and vegetarians won't come up short either – start with the baked goat's cheese in filo pastry. It's 2km west of Den Burg.

Rôtisserie Kerckeplein (☎ 31 89 50; Oesterstraat 6, Oosterend; mains €22-35; ☽ dinner Wed-Sun) This cosy Texel–French restaurant has definitely got lamb down to a fine art, with seven choices in this category alone. You can sit in the cosy loft and wash it all down with a dark *Texels Speciaalbier*. In high season it also opens at lunchtime.

Het Schoutenhuys (☎ 31 20 41; Groeneplaats 14, Den Burg; mains €14-17; ☽ dinner Wed-Sun) Atmospheric brown café with a range of standard dishes like rib eye, beef fillet, lamb stew and red snapper. The panelled interior is graced with old advertising plaques and pics of rock stars; the owner is obviously a Doors fan.

Vispaleis-Rokerij De Ster (☎ 31 24 41; Heemskerck-straat 13, Oudeschild; snacks €3-6, mains €5-8) There are plenty of fish takeaway joints but this is arguably the island's top pick – it cures its own catch behind the harbour dam. Plonk down at a plastic table for an eel or herring sandwich, or its trademark fish soup.

Getting There & Away

Trains from Amsterdam to Den Helder (€10.90, 1¼ hours, twice hourly) are met by a bus that whisks you to the awaiting car ferry.

The **ferry** (☎ 36 96 00; adult/child/car return €4/2/38; ☉ 6.35am-9.35pm) from Den Helder makes the crossing in 20 minutes, leaving at 35 minutes past the hour. Returning boats leave hourly from 't Horntje between 6.05am to 9.05pm. On some summer days there's a service every half-hour – check the timetable to be sure. If you're driving in high season, show up at the docks 15 to 30 minutes before departure as there'll be a queue. Fares are 30% cheaper from Tuesday to Thursday in summer.

The ferry **De Vriendschap** (☎ 31 64 51; De Cocksdorp; adult/child return €14/8) makes the half-hour crossing from De Cocksdorp to car-free Vlieland, the nearest of the Wadden Islands. In July and August it departs at 10.30am and returns from Vlieland at 5pm; service is irregular the rest of the summer, so check times with the tourist office. For more details, see the Friesland chapter (p233).

Getting Around

Connexxion/AOT (☎ 0900-9292; 7am-10pm) operates four circular bus routes on the island; a day pass is great value for €3.90. Bus No 26 links incoming ferries in 't Horntje with Den Burg (seven minutes), De Koog (another 15 minutes) and Oudeschild (eight minutes from Den Burg). Bus No 28 goes to Den Burg and De Koog before returning via the Ecomare museum. Bus No 29 links 't Horntje to Den Hoorn and Den Burg and snakes along the eastern shore to Oudeschild, Oosterend and De Cocksdorp. Bus No 27 is an evening service between 't Horntje with De Koog.

The welter of bicycle shops include **Zegel** (☎ 31 25 30; 14 Parkstraat, Den Burg) charging €4/16 for touring bikes per day/week and €6/22.50 for three-speeds. Near the ferry terminal, **Verhuur Heijne** (☎ 31 95 88; Pontweg 2, 't Horntje) charges similar rates.

The **Telekom Taxi** (☎ 32 22 11) takes you between any two destinations on the island for €4 per person. Book at least an hour in advance, or buy a ticket at the Teso counter in the Den Helder ferry terminal; taxis wait by the ferry jetty in 't Horntje.

DEN HELDER
☎ 0223

Before you reach Texel the only attraction in the unspectacular naval town of Den Helder is the **Maritime Museum** (☎ 65 75 34; Hoofdgracht 3; adult/child €4.50/2.30; ☉ 10am-5pm Mon-Fri, noon-5pm Sat & Sun). It's housed in a suitable town in a suitable spot, the former armoury of the Dutch Royal Navy. The display covers naval history mainly after 1815, the year the Netherlands became a kingdom. You can board several vessels moored on the docks outside, including an ironclad ram ship and a submarine (not for the claustrophobic).

MUIDEN
☎ 0294 / pop 3400

Southeast of Amsterdam, this historic town at the mouth of the Vecht river is renowned for its red-brick castle, the Muiderslot. Life otherwise focuses on the central lock that funnels scores of pleasure boats out into the vast IJsselmeer.

Information

Tourist office (☎ 26 13 89; Kazernestraat 10; ☉ 1-5pm Mon, 10am-5pm Tue-Fri, 10am-2pm Sat, Apr–mid-Oct) Housed in the old barracks.

Sights

The prime reason to visit is the excellent **Muiderslot** (Muiden Castle; ☎ 26 13 25; Herengracht 1; adult/child €6/4; ☉ 10am-5pm Mon-Fri). The fortress was built in 1280 by the ambitious count Floris V, son of Willem II. The castle was one of the first in Holland to be equipped with round towers, a French innovation. The popular Floris was also a champion of the poor and French sympathiser, which was bound to spell trouble; the count was imprisoned in 1296 and murdered while trying to flee.

In the 17th century historian PC Hooft entertained some of the century's greatest writers, artists and scientists here, a group famously known as the Muiderkring (Muiden Circle). Today it's the most visited castle in the country, with precious furnishings, weapons, and Gobelin hangings designed to re-create Hooft's era. The interior can be seen only on guided tours; tours may be partly improvised in English. Reserve ahead if you want an English-only tour.

Off the coast lies a derelict fort on the island of **Pampus** (adult/child ferry & guided tour €11/7; ☉ Apr-Oct). This massive 19th-century bunker was a key member of a ring of 42 fortresses built to defend Amsterdam.

Rescued from disrepair by Unesco, the facility now receives preservation funds as a part of our world's heritage. Ferries to Pampus depart from Muiderslot port at 11am, 1pm and 2pm.

Activities

You won't find a better area on the IJsselmeer for boating and windsurfing. Boat firms at Muiden harbour rent large, often luxurious motor and sailing boats from about €300 to €1300 per week. For smaller craft, the **Watersportcentrum Muiderberg** (☎ 26 25 79; www.wscmuiderberg.com; ☺ Apr–mid-Oct) rents small sailboats for two to four persons (€17 per day) as well as windsurf boards and canoes (€7.50 per hour) in Muiderberg, 3½km from Muiden. The shop isn't signposted but seek out the green beach hut and ask for Jeroen.

Eating & Drinking

Graaf Floris V van Muiden (☎ 26 12 96; Herengracht 72; mains €8-17; ☺ lunch & dinner) This sprawling pub-restaurant dominates the local scene with its wonderful salads, ribs and steaks. Grab a table on the terrace next to the lock that swings open for the pleasure boats, and dig in.

Café Ome Ko (☎ 0294-261 330; ☺ 8am-2am) In warm weather the clientele of this little bar turns the street outside into one big party. Sometimes there's live music – look out for Johnny & the Gangsters of Love who belt out Chuck Berry tunes atop a classic Pontiac convertible.

Getting There & Away

Connexxion bus No 136 links Muiden with Amsterdam's Amstelstation (20 minutes, twice hourly). From Muiden, the same line goes on to Muiderberg (five minutes), Naarden (15 minutes) and Hilversum (25 minutes). Muiden is a leisurely hour's bicycle ride from Amsterdam.

HET GOOI

Along the slow-moving Vecht River southeast of Amsterdam lies Het Gooi, a shady woodland speckled with lakes and heath. In the 17th century, this 'Garden of Amsterdam' was a popular retreat for wealthy merchants, and nature-hungry urbanites still flock to its leafy trails to hike and cycle today. The area's main centre is Hilversum,

a one-time commuter town given a fresh start by the Dutch broadcasting industry, which has its headquarters here. The area is roughly bordered by Laren, a well-heeled town a few kilometres to the northeast with a good art museum, Huizen on the Gooimeer to the north, and Loosdrecht, on the artificial lakes known as the Loosdrechtse Plassen to the east. Huizen and Loosdrecht are popular water-sports centres, while Naarden, on the Gooimeer to the north, has an intriguing fortress.

Naarden

☎ 035 / pop 17,000

Naarden's **fortress** is best seen from the air: a 12-pointed star, with arrowheads at each tip. This defence system, one of the best preserved in the country, was unfortunately built only after the Spanish massacred the inhabitants in the 16th century. The bastions were still staffed by the Dutch army throughout the 1920s, although its strategic importance had already paled before WWI.

INFORMATION

Tourist office (☎ 694 28 36; www.vvvnaarden.nl; Adriaan Dortsmanplein 1B; ☺ 10am-5pm Mon-Fri, 10am-3pm Sat, noon-3pm Sun) In the old barracks has an English-language leaflet with a self-guided walking tour of the town.

SIGHTS & ACTIVITIES

Most of Naarden's quaint little houses date from 1572, the year the Spaniards razed the place during their colonisation of North Holland. The bloodbath led by Don Frederick of Toledo is commemorated by a stone tablet on the building at Turfpoortstraat 7.

The **Vestingmuseum** (Fortress Museum; ☎ 694 54 59; Westwalstraat 6; adult/child €5/4.50; ☺ 10.30am-5pm Tue-Fri, noon-5pm Sat & Sun) is a star-shaped fortress thought to be the only one in Europe featuring a buffer of two walls and two moats. You can stroll around on the rolling battlements before descending into the casements for glimpses of a cramped soldier's life.

Marvel in the **Grote Kerk** (adult/child €2/1.25; ☺ 2pm & 3pm summer), a Gothic basilica with stunning 16th-century vault paintings of biblical scenes. You can climb the tower (265 steps) for a good view of the leafy Gooi and the Vecht River. St Matthew Passion performances are held over Easter.

The 17th-century Czech educational reformer, Jan Amos Komensky (Comenius), is buried here in the Waalse Kapel. His life and work are related next door at the **Comenius Museum** (☎ 694 30 45; Kloosterstraat 33; adult/child €2.50/1.50; ☒ noon-5pm Wed-Sun).

The tourist office also organises one-hour **boat tours** (€2) around the moat.

SLEEPING & EATING

Poorters (☎ /fax 694 48 68; Marktstraat 66; s/d without bathroom €55/65) The sole hotel within the old town walls is splendidly renovated with four simple but atmospheric rooms (only one has private shower and toilet). There's a cosy bar, a restaurant (mains €8 to €18) with canalside dining and regular art exhibitions.

Jachthaven (☎ 694 21 06; Onderwal 4; hut €30) There's no camp site or hostel close to Naarden, but you can book one of the basic *trekkershutten* (hikers' huts) for up to four people at this yacht harbour. They're in a corner of the marina near a leafy recreation area, with hundreds of boats to view and a restaurant on-site. Take bus No 136 to Jachthaven (five minutes).

Eetcafé 't Hert (☎ 694 80 55; Cattenhagestraat 12; mains €10-17; ☒ lunch & dinner) Tucked away in one of Naarden's backstreets, this pleasant pub-café cum garden serves up sandwiches, salads and regional specialities such as Texel lamb or smoked salmon.

Het Arsenaal (☎ 695 11 49; Kooltjesbuurt 1; mains from €26; ☒ lunch & dinner) This is one of the region's strongholds of swank, with French three-course meals for €45. The separate brasserie offers more pedestrian fare at lunchtime. You can also judge Dutch design here in the furniture showrooms of Jan de Bouvrie, one of the Netherlands' fashionable interior designers.

GETTING THERE & AWAY

There are direct trains between Amsterdam Centraal Station and Naarden-Bussum (€3.60, 20 minutes, twice hourly). There are more trains if you change at Weesp. Bus No 136 also runs to/from Amsterdam (35 minutes, four times an hour).

Hilversum
☎ 035 / pop 83,100
Hilversum is best known to the Dutch as the national broadcasting center. Commentary from abroad is beamed back here rather than to Den Haag, the seat of Dutch parliament, or to the nation's capital in Amsterdam – a quirk of Dutch history as the first radio station was founded in Hilversum

The city serves as a good launch point for excursions into the leafy region Het Gooi. It also has decent museums of architecture and broadcasting.

ORIENTATION & INFORMATION

The few attractions are in or near the pedestrianised centre, which is immediately west of the train station. Ringed by a street network defined by the old city walls, the centre of Hilversum measures about 1.5km across and is easy to navigate.

Library (☎ 621 29 42; 's Gravelandse Weg 55; ☒ 1-8pm Mon-Fri, 11am-4pm Sat) A dozen Internet terminals that you can use for free.

Tourist office (☎ 624 17 51; www.vvvhilversum.nl; Noordse Bosje 1; ☒ 9.30am-6pm Mon-Fri, 9.30am-5pm Sat) It's signposted up Spoorstraat and then Kerkstraat. A smaller office at Schapenkamp 25 near the train station keeps similar hours.

SIGHTS & ACTIVITIES

With all the plush old villas on the outskirts, you'd expect the city to have an interesting core. Alas, modern planning has marred the legacy of Willem Dudok, the architect who shaped the city in the early 20th century. The tourist office sells a walking guide to Dudok's buildings in the town.

Nearly 100 buildings in Hilversum bear Dudok's stamp, including the beautiful, modernist **Raadhuis** (Town Hall; Dudokpark 1), 700m west of the train station. Marvel at the fabulous interior, with simple, elegant lines that recall Frank Lloyd Wright or the Bauhaus movement. The tower restored in 1996 is stunning in its symmetry and inventive arrangement of horizontal and vertical brick. Inside is the **Dudok Centrum** (☎ 629 2262; ☒ noon-4.30pm Wed, Fri & Sun), which holds regular architecture exhibitions.

The Raadhuis also houses the **Goois Museum** (☎ 629 28 26; Dudokpark 1; adult/child €1.50/0.75; ☒ 1-5pm Tue-Sun), which is worth checking out if you plan to explore Het Gooi – 'Amsterdam's Back Garden'. Displays include archaeological finds from early Gooi-dwellers and the history of the region. It's due to reopen in summer 2004 as Museum Hilversum after a lengthy renovation that will incorporate the Dudok Centrum.

The **Nederlands Omroepmuseum** (Dutch Broadcast Museum; ☎ 688 58 88; Oude Amersfoortseweg 121; adult/child €5/4; ☻ 10am-5pm Tue-Fri, noon-5pm Sat & Sun) tells the history of Dutch television and radio going back to 1919. The first broadcasting license was granted to a Hilversum station and the Dutch broadcasting industry grew up around it. An interesting aspect is the background about the various political and religious groups now represented on the media landscape, a product of the social 'pillarisation' that moulded 20th-century Dutch life. In late 2005 the displays will move to Hilversum's Media Park and reopen as the Museum voor Beeld & Geluid in a spectacular new building inspired by the audiovisual media.

The tourist office sells a huge range of cycling and hiking maps to the area, including the *Wandelroutes* and *Fietsroutes in 't Gooi en Omstreeken* (Hiking Routes and Biking Routes in 't Gooi and Surrounds). If you don't read Dutch, it's no problem as the routes are clearly marked. The cycling series cover 12 paths in the vicinity, all of which are well signposted, with distances of 35km to 70km. Our favourite, the *Last Days of Florian V*, named after the murdered count (see Muiden, p165), starts at Muiden and leads via Hilversum to the popular Vriens pancake restaurant in Loenen near Utrecht (67km).

SLEEPING & EATING

Hotel de Waag (☎ 624 65 17; fax 621 84 60; Groest 17; s/d €80, incl breakfast) You probably won't spend the night in Hilversum but if you do this is your best bet. It's a jolly place with an unusually good location in the centre and a nice cosy café. The sidewalk café hums with activity.

De Kaarseboom (☎ 621 21 61; Groest 53; mains €8-12; ☻ lunch & dinner) In a nice spot on the pedestrian zone, De Kaarseboom has a leafy front terrace and hearty set meals for reasonable prices. It also does soups and sandwiches.

Three nice restaurants share a pretty old weaver's barn on the eastern side of town. Forecourt dining here is a cut above most eateries in the centre.

De Buren (☎ 628 14 93; Laanstraat 35; mains €15-22) French–Dutch and prides itself on three-course menus with a big choice of combinations.

De Jonge Graef van Buuren (☎ 624 54 02; Laanstraat 35; mains €5-12) A pub-eatery that serves more straightforward fare like deep-fried plaice with chips.

Proeverij de Open Keuken (☎ 623 07 72; Laanstraat 35; mains €8-15, tapas €4-8) Best visited for its generous choice of tapas.

GETTING THERE & AROUND

Direct train services to/from Hilversum include the following:

Destination	Price (€)	Duration (min)	Frequency (per hr)
Amsterdam	4.50	25	2
Lelystad	7.30	60	2
Utrecht	3.00	20	4
Naarden–Bussum	1.50	5	3

The rather slow Connexxion bus No 136 goes to/from Hilversum train station to Laren (30 minutes). City bus No 2 or 135 go from the train station to the Goois Museum in the centre (five minutes).

Around Hilversum

In Laren, which is 5km northeast of Hilversum, the **Singer Museum** (☎ 539 39 39; Oude Drift 1; adult/child €7.50/free; ☻ 11am-5pm Tue-Sat, noon-5pm Sun) houses a splendid collection of Dutch and foreign paintings, mostly modernist and impressionist works from 1880 to 1950. Not all works are displayed at once, with exhibitions such as 'Painters of the Village' changing several times a year. Take bus Nos 136 or 137 from Hilversum train station to Laren Kermisterrein (15 minutes).

FLEVOLAND

The Netherland's 12th and youngest province, Flevoland, is a masterpiece of Dutch hydro-engineering. In the early 1920s, an ambitious scheme went ahead to reclaim more than 1400 sq km of land – an idea mooted as far back as the 17th century. The completion of the Afsluitdijk (Barrier Dyke; see The Afsluitdijk, p160) at the opening of the Zuiderzee in 1932 paved the way for the creation of Flevoland. Ringed dykes were erected, allowing water to be pumped out at a snail-like pace. Once part of Overijssel province, the Noordoostpolder was inaugurated in 1942, followed by the Eastern Flevoland (1957) and Southern Flevoland (1968). First residential rights were granted to workers who'd helped in reclamation and to farmers, especially from Zeeland, who lost everything in the great flood of 1953.

The cities that sprang up bring to mind anything but the Golden Age. The main hubs of Almere, Lelystad and Emmeloord across the narrow Ketelmeer to the north are grindingly dull places, laid out in grid patterns for affordable housing. The star attractions in Flevoland are the Bataviawerf museum at Lelystad, old fishing villages such as Urk and Schokland and the bird-filled nature reserve of Oostvaardersplassen.

LELYSTAD

☎ 0320 / pop 67,000

The capital of Flevoland Province, Lelystad is a good example of urban planning gone awry. The town was named for pioneer engineer Cornelius Lely, whose blueprints were adopted in the Zuiderzee Reclamation Act of 1918. The main reason for visiting this expanse of steel and concrete lies west of town – the fascinating Bataviawerf Museum on the IJsselmeer shore.

Orientation & Information

Most shops and restaurants are in the pedestrianised knot of streets opposite the station; the key museums are a short bus ride west on the IJsselmeer shore.

Tourist office (☎ 24 34 44; www.vvvflevoland.nl; Stationsplein 186; 9am-5pm Mon-Fri, 9am-3pm Sat) Just southeast across the road from the combined train and bus station. Staff will reserve accommodation free of charge. Sells cycling and hiking maps.

Sights

Signs in Lelystad refer to a mock fort containing an outlet shopping centre, Bataviastad, 3km west of the train station. Three museums nearby on Oostvaardersdijk and Museumweg can be reached by bus No 150 from the train station (five minutes, twice hourly).

Behind Bataviastad lies **Bataviawerf Museum** (☎ 26 07 99; Oostvaardersdijk 1-9; adult/child €8/7; 10am-5pm) and its star attraction: a replica of a 17th-century Dutch merchant frigate, the *Batavia*, which took 10 years to reconstruct until its reinauguration in 1985. The original was a 17th-century *Titanic* – big, expensive and supposedly unsinkable. True to comparison, the *Batavia*, filled to the brim

with cannon and goods for the colonies, went down in 1629 on its maiden voyage off the west coast of Australia. There's ample evidence of the era's wealth on the upper decks where you'll see carved wooden likenesses of merchant seamen and a gold-leaf lantern above the captain's quarters. Little imagination is required, however, to grasp how punishing a sailor's life could be, especially for those who broke the rules: stealing a loaf of bread might merit a month's confinement in a cramped hole so constructed that it was impossible to either sit or stand upright.

The wooden skeleton alongside belongs to the *Seven Provinces*, a replica of Admiral Michiel de Ruijter's massive flagship that's scheduled for completion in 2005. In a separate building on the northern perimeter, the Netherlands Institute for Maritime Archaeology has a 16th-century marketboat on display as well as garments, vases and tools dating from Roman times.

Nearly half of the Netherlands was created by massive land reclamation and **Nieuwland Poldermuseum** (☎ 26 07 99; Oostvaardersdijk 1-13; adult/child €4.30/2; 10am-5pm Mon-Fri, 11.30am-5pm Sat & Sun) is the definitive museum on the topic. It's a surefire winner with kids who can build model bridges or dams, and navigate ships through their locks.

Nederlands Sportmuseum Olympion (☎ 26 10 10; Museumweg 10; adult/child €4.50/3.50) is worth a giggle, but not much more, for the glories of every discipline the Dutch have ever engaged in. It takes a hard look at cycling, ice skating, and swimming, but the best section covers the origins of golf with collections of old *colfstokken* (golf clubs) and stitched leather golf balls.

No expense has been spared for **Luchtvaart Themapark Aviodrome** (☎ 289 98 40; www.aviodrome.nl; Dakotaweg 11a; adult/child €12.80/10.80; 10am-5pm). This is a huge, spanking new museum. Its 70 historic aircraft includes a replica of the Wright Brother's 1902 Flyer, Baron von Richthofen's WWI triplane, a Spitfire and a Dakota. You can also play air-traffic controller in a re-created flight tower or watch aviation films in the mega-cinema. It's at Lelystad Airport 4km east of town (bus No 148 from the train station).

Activities

Surfschool Paradiso (☎ 25 68 93; Uilenweg 8; canoe/windsurf board/catamaran per hr €8/8/15; Apr-Oct) rents small catamarans (up to four persons), windsurf boards and two-seat canoes. You can take a day's windsurfing lessons for €62. To get there, see directions to Campground Het Oppertje (see below).

Other rental services at Lelystad harbour include **Flevo Sailing** (☎ 26 03 24; www.flevosailing.nl; Oostvaardersdijk 59c; yachts per day from €205), which rents four-passenger sailing yachts.

Sleeping

Few visitors spend the night in Lelystad – or in Flevoland, for that matter – so options are limited.

Hotel de Lange Jammer (☎ 26 04 15; fax 26 20 19; Oostvaardersdijk 31; s/d €30/60, incl breakfast) This ageing family-run motel on Lelystad harbour is high on nostalgia value – think Clarke Gable and Claudette Colbert in *It Happened One Night*. The ground-floor units are spacious, quiet and discreetly veiled in shrubbery.

Campground Het Oppertje (☎ 036-538 44 16; Uilenweg; per adult/child/tent/caravan €3.50/1.50/4/4; ☼ Apr-Oct) Visitors to the nature reserve camp here, a calm, green waterside site blessed with a constant sea breeze. You can shuffle in beach thongs to the café or take windsurfing lessons next door (see Activities above). Take bus No 1 or a taxi from Lelystad train station.

Eating

Cantina Estrellas VIPs (☎ 23 41 68; Agoraweg 11; mains €7-14; ☼ dinner) In the shopping area just east of the train station, this funky Mexican–Argentinian eatery has tasty tortillas, salads and filled Argentine pastries. The owner lets down her hair and plays guitar most evenings.

Sailors Grand Café Restaurant (☎ 26 43 04; Bataviaplein 52; mains €6-11; ☼ lunch & dinner) The best bet in the Bataviastad shopping mall, this place is convenient to the museums and has a varied menu including rich butterfish and 'polder burgers' (ie with whiskey sauce).

Getting There & Around

Lelystad station is a terminus so there are no trains due north. Direct services include:

Destination	Price (€)	Duration (min)	Frequency (per hr)
Amsterdam	7.30	45	2
Utrecht	9.50	75	4

Flevoland has poor regional bus services. From Amsterdam and other points south, buses go no further north than Almere, so take the train if you can. Bus No 150 goes from Lelystad station to Enkhuizen via the IJsselmeer dyke road N302 (35 minutes, every two hours). Bus No 143 goes east to Kampen in Overijssel (one hour, every half-hour). The Qliner bus No 315 goes to Groningen (2¼ hours, every two hours).

A taxi is a good way to get to the museums on Sundays when buses are scarce.

Meerens (☎ 0320-228389; Waagpassage 17) rents out bicycles from the shopping centre opposite the train station.

OOSTVAARDERSPLASSEN NATURE RESERVE

Between Lelystad and Almere lies the mushy realm of Oostvaardersplassen, a 6000 hectare reserve of mostly swampy lake that developed virtually by accident. When Flevoland province opened in 1968 this area was earmarked for an industrial estate, but the planners dawdled and nature stepped in. A virgin landscape of reeds, willows and rough grasslands emerged, a bit like the Camargue in southern France.

Today it's a bird sanctuary of international repute with a formidable variety of species. Great white egrets, cormorants and spoonbills can be seen nesting, and lucky visitors may also catch a glimpse of endangered species such as the white-tailed eagle. Illustrated boards around the park help to identify what appears in your sights.

You'll also see quirky mammals such as the conic (a docile pony), the horned heck cattle as well as red deer, all of which serve as lawn mowers on the meadows around the perimeter.

Entry into the marsh itself isn't allowed, but the next best thing is a visit to the De Kluut observation hut on the northeastern edge of the reserve. The various hiking and bicycle paths begin here, including a 35km route around the entire lake. The Schollevaar observation post near a cormorant colony can only be visited with a park ranger.

The **visitors centre** (☎ 25 45 85; Kitsweg 1; ☼ 10am-5pm Tue-Sun) has good wildlife exhibits, free hiking maps and vending machines for coffee and cold drinks. To get there by car from Amsterdam, drive the A6 north and take exit No 10 towards Lelystad on the N302 and take a left after 5km onto Buizardweg (also signposted 'Oostvaardersplassen'). Or rent a bicycle (see Lelystad, Getting There & Around, p170).

SIX FLAGS HOLLAND

This American-style amusement park lies 21km southeast of Lelystad. **Six Flags** (☎ 0321-33 21 78; Biddinghuizen; adult/child €23/19; ☼ Apr-Oct) really packs the families in with a variety of prepackaged thrills. The crowd-pleasers here include rollercoasters such as 'Goliath' (a 46m drop), cartoon characters in Bugs Bunny World and explosive motorcycle chases with Batman.

Connexxion buses offer a good deal covering return fare from Lelystad train station and entrance to the park, for €22.

URK

☎ 0527 / pop 16,500

This pious village was once a proud little island, home to a sizeable fishing fleet and an important signal post for ships passing into the North Sea. In the 1940s Urk reluctantly joined the mainland when the surrounding Noordoostpolder was pumped dry, and even today some locals pine for the isolation of island life, as tough as it obviously was.

Although now cut off from the North Sea the town is still a centre of the seafood industry, a holdover from the days when its fleet sailed into the open Zuiderzee. That sweet smell on the air comes from the several fish factories located here.

You'll see dozens of historic fishing boats moored around the harbour including the brown-sailed *botters* with gleaming wooden hulls and oversized leeboards. At the western end of town, take the coastal walk around the lighthouse for a pinch of local folklore. Just 70m off the shore lies the **Ommelebommelestien**, a slippery rock said to be the birthplace of all native Urkers. Legend also has it that unlike the stork, dad had to take a rowboat to pick up his newborn.

The supports of the village church, **Kerkje aan de Zee**, are made entirely out of masts of VOC (Dutch East India Company) ships that brought back exotic goods from the East Indies. Nearby you'll find the **Fishermen's Monument**, a moving statue of a woman in a billowing dress gazing seaward where her loved ones were lost. Marble tablets around the perimeter list the Urk

seafarers who never returned – name, age and ship's ID number – and room has been left for further casualties.

Restaurant De Kaap (☎ 68 15 09; www .restaurant dekaap.nl; Wijk 5; mains €10-22; s/d with bath & breakfast €35/56) This is simply *the* place to sample Urk specialities, such as smoked gurnard, while taking in gorgeous views of harbour and IJsselmeer. The interior is richly decorated with maritime ornaments; the hotel rooms (in a separate house) are comfy and quiet.

Bus No 141 runs between Urk and Zwolle several times an hour (1¼ hours). On Sunday there's only a handful of buses starting in the late afternoon.

SCHOKLAND

☎ 0527

A bleak variation on the island theme, the community of Schokland eked out an existence for hundreds of years on a long, narrow strip of land in the Zuiderzee. By the mid-19th century the clock had run out: fish prices plummeted and vicious storms were literally eroding the island away. The plucky locals hung on, despite the appalling living conditions, prompting Willem III to order their removal in 1859. Schokland was eventually swallowed up by the Noordoostpolder in the 20th century, just like Urk.

Now a Unesco World Heritage Site, the **Schokland Museum** (☎ 25 13 96; www.schokland.nl; Middelbuurt 3; adult/child €2.50/1.80; ☼ 11am-5pm Tue-Sun, Fri-Sun only Nov-Mar) affords glimpses into this tortured past. The island's heritage is described in detail with a good historical slide presentation in English. Views from the lower path hint just how big the waves were here, at the prow-shaped barrier constructed from tall wooden pilings. Ironically since the area was drained the foundations have begun to dry out. Schokland is sinking but luckily, no longer into the sea.

Be sure to stop by the church, the **Waterstaatkerk**, built to replace the one virtually washed away in the storm of 1825. Here as in so many Dutch fishing towns, a model ship hangs high above the congregation – the symbol of a union between sea and religious belief.

There's no easy public transportation to the museum; you can ride a bike 14km south from Kampen. Turn west off the N50 on the road at Ens and go another 2.5km.

Utrecht

UTRECHT

The petite province of Utrecht is virtually a city-state. Many visitors overlook the charms of the region as a whole, focusing instead on the capital's landmark cathedral and major university. Destinations here make for pleasant outings from Amsterdam but certainly hold enough interest for a few days' stay in Utrecht city itself.

The splendid Kasteel de Haar on the city's doorstep is one of the Netherlands' most beautiful castles. The many shallow lakes such as Loosdrechtse Plassen near Utrecht city are a magnet for boaters and swimmers alike, and the countryside is laced with easy bike paths such as those along the lazy bends of the Vecht river, particularly towards the small town of Breukelen.

Amersfoort is a pretty walled town in the northeast corner that made its mark in beer and wool trades. Pleasant Oudewater in the southwest is synonymous with witchcraft. There are palatial mansions to the southeast in Doorn, where a defeated German Kaiser went into exile, and in Amerongen, seat of well-to-do aristocrats since the 13th century.

The rest of Utrecht is mostly farmland with some creeping suburbanisation from Amsterdam in the northwest. Tracks converge on the city like a spiderweb so train travellers usually alight at Utrecht city at some point – an excellent chance to explore its tree-lined canals and medieval quarter.

UTRECHT

HIGHLIGHTS

- Strolling along Utrecht's **canals** near the cathedral (p176)
- Pondering De Stijl in Utrecht's **Rietveld-Schröderhuis** (p177)
- Discovering Gothic romance at **Kasteel de Haar** (p180)
- Reliving the last days of Kaiser Wilhelm II at **Huis Doorn** (p182)
- Weighing witches in **Oudewater** (p182)
- Cycling round the flooded peat digs of the **Loosdrechtse Plassen** (p180)

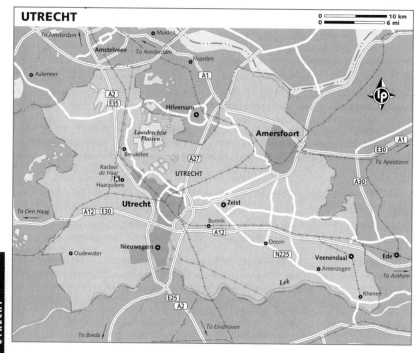

UTRECHT

| 0 | 10 km |
| 0 | 6 mi |

To Amsterdam • Muiden
Amstelveen To Amsterdam • Naarden
• Aalsmeer
A1
A2
E35
Hilversum
Loosdrechtse
Plassen
Amersfoort A1
• Breukelen E30
A27 To Apeldoorn
Kasteel UTRECHT A30
de Haar
Haarzuilens
Utrecht • Zeist
To Den Haag A12 E30 Bunnik
A12
Doorn
Nieuwegein • N225
• Oudewater Veenendaal • Ede •
• Amerongen
To Arnhem
Lek Rhenen
E25 • To Eindhoven
A2
To Breda

History

The city of Utrecht arose as a main outpost of the Roman Empire along the river Rhine. It was visited by emperors and the elaborate churches here were built to promote Christianity. By the early Middle Ages, Utrecht became the ecclesiastical centre of the Low Countries at a time when Amsterdam was but a modest trading post.

Over the centuries Utrecht was also a centre of war and peace. Napoleon based himself in the area when waging campaigns. The Treaties of Utrecht had far-reaching implications, which, among other things, ended the war of Spanish Succession in 1713.

But Utrecht's fortunes waned as Amsterdam's grew and as the gradual secularisation of Dutch society led to a decline in the church's influence. These days industries such as software development and advertising are among the region's chief money makers, and the faculties of the city's university enjoy international renown.

Getting There & Away

Utrecht city and Amersfoort are both major rail junctions. The rest of the sights are accessible by bus or bike.

UTRECHT CITY

☎ 030 / pop 256,000

Utrecht's antique frame contains an increasingly modern interior, lorded over by the tower of the storm-ravaged Dom, or cathedral, with the country's tallest church spire. Its mechanical carillon has a huge repertoire of tunes that echo cheerily through the centre's streets, much to the delight (or consternation) of local residents.

The striking **canal wharves**, built in the 13th century, are well below street level, a feature that's unique to Utrecht. The streets along the canals now brim with chic shops, restaurants and cafés, and the city's student community of 40,000 is the largest in the country.

Orientation

Utrecht is bisected by two canals, the **Oudegracht** and **Nieuwegracht**, the old and new canals (from the 11th and 14th centuries). A third canal called the **Singel** surrounds the old core. Most of the interesting bits lie within 500m of the Domtoren, or cathedral tower, although the Museum Quarter is a pleasant 500m stroll south.

The historic quarters are to the east from the centre of the city, but reaching the streets from the train station means traversing Hoog Catharijne, a modern, claustrophic shopping mall that will leave you gasping for air when you finally get outside.

Information

Broese Wristers (☎ 223 52 00; Stadhuisbrug 5) A roomy, modern store that provides most of the academic

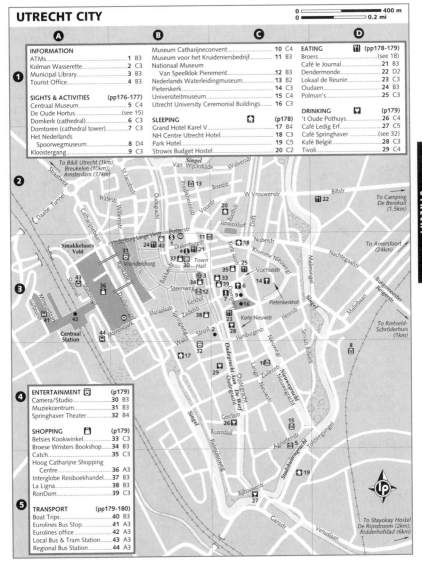

UTRECHT CITY

0 ━━━━━━ 400 m
0 ━━━━━━ 0.2 mi

INFORMATION	
ATMs	1 B3
Kolman Wasserette	2 C3
Municipal Library	3 B3
Tourist Office	4 B3

SIGHTS & ACTIVITIES	(pp176-177)
Centraal Museum	5 C4
De Oude Hortus	(see 15)
Domkerk (cathedral)	6 C3
Domtoren (cathedral tower)	7 C3
Het Nederlands Spoorwegmuseum	8 D4
Kloostergang	9 C3
Museum Catharijneconvent	10 C4
Museum voor het Kruideniersbedrijf	11 B3
Nationaal Museum Van Speelklok Pierement	12 B3
Nederlands Waterleidingmuseum	13 B2
Pieterskerk	14 C3
Universiteitmuseum	15 C4
Utrecht University Ceremonial Buildings	16 C3

SLEEPING	(p178)
Grand Hotel Karel V	17 B4
NH Centre Utrecht Hotel	18 C3
Park Hotel	19 C5
Strowis Budget Hostel	20 C2

EATING	(pp178-179)
Broers	(see 18)
Café le Journal	21 B3
Dendermonde	22 D2
Lokaal de Reunie	23 C3
Oudaen	24 B3
Polman's	25 C3

DRINKING	(p179)
't Oude Pothuys	26 C4
Café Ledig Erf	27 C5
Café Springhaver	(see 32)
Kafé België	28 C3
Tivoli	29 C4

ENTERTAINMENT	(p179)
Camera/Studio	30 B3
Muziekcentrum	31 B3
Springhaver Theater	32 B4

SHOPPING	(p179)
Betsies Kookwinkel	33 C3
Broese Wristers Bookshop	34 B3
Catch	35 C3
Hoog Catharijne Shopping Centre	36 A3
Interglobe Reisboekhandel	37 B3
La Ligna	38 B3
RonDom	39 C3

TRANSPORT	(pp179-180)
Boat Trips	40 B3
Eurolines Bus Stop	41 A3
Eurolines office	42 A3
Local Bus & Tram Station	43 A3
Regional Bus Station	44 A3

UTRECHT

books in the region, with a good selection of travel, general interest and English-language books.

Interglobe Reisboekhandel (☎ 234 04 01; Vinkenburgstraat 7) Packed to the hilt with travel books and maps bundled in drawers and plastic bins.

Kolman Wasserette (☎ 231 82 62; Oudegracht 177; 7am-9pm) Charges €5 for a load.

Municipal library (☎ 286 18 00; Oudegracht 167; 10am-9pm Mon, 11am-6pm Tue-Fri, 10am-5pm Sat) Offers Internet access for €0.20 per six minutes.

GWK currency exchange At Centraal Station (CS) near platform No 12. There are numerous ATMs in town, especially around the post office at .

Post office (Neude 11) Even if you don't need stamps, go inside the cathedral-like main hall and marvel at the artful brick patterns. An early gem of the functionalist style.

Tourist office (☎ 234 73 70; www.utrechtstad.com; Vinkenburgstraat 19; 9.30am-5.30pm Mon-Wed & Fri, 9.30am-9pm Thu, 9.30am-5pm Sat) Extremely well stocked, staff are friendly and the good free map has a full street index.

Sights

Almost all sights within Utrecht's old town are within 10 minutes' walking distance of each other. In two to three hours you can easily cover the cathedral area and the main canals and have time left over for a museum visit.

AROUND CATHEDRAL TOWER

There are 465 steps leading up to excellent views from the **Domtoren** (cathedral tower; ☎ 233 30 36; Domplein; adult/child €6/3.60; 10am-5pm Mon-Sat, noon-5pm Sun). As well as views of the city from 112m up, you can ponder the former size of the cathedral. Built in the 14th century, the cathedral and its tower were medieval landmarks. In 1674 the North Sea winds became a mite stronger than usual; in fact, they reached hurricane force and blew down the cathedral's nave, leaving the tower and transept behind.

Once back on the ground, you can find a row of paving stones marking the extents of the nave. Across this extent is the **Dom** (cathedral; ☎ 231 04 03; 10am-5pm Mon-Fri May-Sept, 11am-4pm Mon-Fri Oct-Apr, 11am-3.30pm Sat, 2-4pm Sun), the surviving chancel of the cathedral. It has a few tombs within.

Behind the church is the most charming component of this ecclesiastical troika. The **Kloostergang** is a monastic garden that's a peaceful refuge, as the many pigeons and pot smokers will attest.

The 19th-century buildings on the western side of Domplein are the **ceremonial buildings** of Utrecht University. They surround the old church chapter house where the Treaty of Utrecht was signed in 1579, forming a military alliance of the northern provinces.

Walking down Voetiusstraat from behind the cathedral leads you to **Pieterskerk**. Built in 1048, it is the oldest Romanesque church in the Netherlands. Much damage was caused during a storm in 1674 and more during a dubious 1965 restoration. Opening hours are sporadic but try on Friday or Saturday.

CANALS

Scene of many a wedding photo, the photogenic bend in the Oudegracht is illuminated by lamplight in the evening, and hundreds sit outside cafés here by day. However, it's south of this point where the canal is at its most evocative. The streets are quieter and stretch 1km to the southern tip of the old town.

A section of the Singel called the Stadsbuitengracht has its own turn as a lovely canal on the eastern side of the old quarter where it follows many parks built on the site of the old fortifications. You can stroll down beside this canal and back north through Nieuwegracht, a peaceful stretch of plush canal houses that are towered over by grand old elms.

MUSEUM QUARTER

There are 14 museums, many of them bizarre hideaways for odd pursuits – a sewer museum is but one example. However, those around the Museum Quarter, about 1km south of the cathedral tower, are reasonably serious.

The pick of the litter by far is the **Museum Catharijneconvent** (☎ 231 72 96; Nieuwegracht 63; adult/child €6/3; 10am-5pm Tue-Fri, 11am-5pm Sat & Sun), which has the finest collection of medieval religious art in the Netherlands. It's housed in a Gothic former convent and an 18th-century canalside house. The history of Christianity in the country is presented here. It's an excellent museum and all but the most jaded will marvel at the many beautiful illuminated manuscripts. Allow about 1½ hours here to take it all in. Bus No 2 from Centraal Station (CS) passes the front entrance.

The **Centraal Museum** (☎ 236 23 62; Agnietenstraat 1; adult/child €6/3; 10am-5pm Tue-Sat, noon-

5pm Sun) has a wide-ranging collection that always seems to be getting rearranged. There's applied arts dating back to the 17th century as well as paintings by some of the Utrecht School artists. There's even a 12th-century boat that was dug out of the local mud. Take bus No 6 from CS.

The **Universiteitsmuseum** (☎ 253 80 08; Lange Nieuwstraat 106; adult/child €4/2; ⏱ 11am-5pm Tue-Sun) is a mixed bag. There's a re-created late-19th-century classroom, historic dentistry tools (ouch!) and just way too many models of medical maladies. You can find refuge out back in **De Oude Hortus**, the old botanical garden with venerable trees and plants collected by the Dutch during their world exploits. The garden is an oasis of calm, sheltering numerous rare flowers and plants such as an ancient *Gingko biloba* tree.

The **Nederlands Spoorwegmuseum** (Dutch Railway Museum; ☎ 230 62 06; Maliebaanstation; adult/child €8/6; ⏱ 10am-5pm Tue-Fri, 11.30am-5pm Sat-Sun) has a good collection of historic locomotives in an old train station building. A miniature high-speed train takes kids on a spin around the grounds. Note that the museum will be closed for renovations until spring 2005. Take bus No 3 from CS to Maliebaan and walk east for five minutes.

SMALL MUSEUMS

The following museums are all within a 10-minute walk from the cathedral tower.

The **Nationaal Museum Van Speelklok tot Pierement** (National Museum From Musical Clock to Street Organ; ☎ 231 27 89; Buurkerkhof 10; adult/child €6/4; ⏱ 10am-5pm Tue-Sat, noon-5pm Sun) has a colourful collection of musical machines from the 18th century onwards, demonstrated with gusto on hourly tours. Most impressive are the street and fairground organs from around Europe including some gargantuan burping models by the Belgian master organ-builder, Mortier.

The **Museum voor het Kruideniersbedrijf** (Grocery Museum; ☎ 231 66 28; Hoogt 6; free; ⏱ 12.30-4.30pm Tue-Sat) has original cans and packages of yesteryear in a replica of an old grocery. Ladies in old-fashioned aprons sell sweets and tea in decorative containers that make nice souvenirs. Pick up a block of white licorice candy to add to hot milk – an old Dutch tradition.

In the base of an old water tower, the **Nederlands Waterleidingmuseum** (Sewer Museum; ☎ 248 72 11; Lauwerhof 29; adult/child €2/1; ⏱ 1.30-5pm

Tue-Fri & Sun, 11am-4pm Sat) takes a hard look at what happens to water before and after humans use it. Just so that no-one will think it doesn't have something for everyone, the museum also has displays of historic irons and ironing boards.

RIETVELD-SCHRÖDERHUIS

Located just out of the city, the **Rietveld-Schröderhuis** (☎ 236 23 10; Prins Hendriklaan 50; adult/child €16/8; ⏱ 11am-5pm Wed-Sat, noon-5pm Sun) is a Unesco-protected landmark built in 1924 by Utrecht architect Gerrit Rietveld. Inside and out, the entire structure conforms to principles of De Stijl architecture (see p60), and it's the only house that can make this claim. Only six colours are used: red, blue, yellow, white, grey and black. The 'form follows function' concept has been followed faithfully, as even the interior walls can be moved to alter the floor plan.

A second building, a **model apartment** (Erasmuslaan 9) from 1931, is now open to the public behind the main house. It is included in the admission to Rietveld-Schröderhuis – perhaps a reason for the hefty fee? Tours of both properties take 90 minutes and are given on the hour. The house is about 1.5km east of the Nederlands Spoorwegmuseum; take bus No 4 from CS to the De Hoogstraat stop.

Activities

There are one-hour **canal boat trips** (☎ 272 01 11; adult/child €6.25/4.70; ⏱ 11am-6pm) that trace a circular route through the old town. The landing is on Oudegracht just south of Lange Viestraat. You can also rent **canal bikes** (paddleboats; per person per hr €6) from in front of the municipal library.

Canoes and kayaks are available for hire on an old arm of the Rhine. Try **De Rijnstroom** (☎ 252 13 11; Weg naar Rhijnauwen 2; 2-person model per hr €6.50) – it's about 2km southeast of centre between Utrecht and Bunnik.

Festivals & Events

Holland Festival Oude Muziek (Holland Festival of Ancient Music; ☎ 236 22 36; www.oudemuziek.nl) Just what the name says. The event is held in late August and brings in musicians who specialise in music from long ago.
Nederlands Film Festival (☎ 232 26 84; www.filmfestival.nl) The Dutch may only produce about 20 films annually, but each year in late September all are shown throughout Utrecht, culminating in the awarding of the coveted Golden Calf.

Sleeping

CAMPING

Camping De Berekuil (☎ 271 38 70; Ariënslaan 50; per person €4.40, per tent €4.40) This self-contained site sits on a virtual island surrounded by canals 1.5km from the centre. There's a shop, bar, laundry, swimming pool and pleasant walking paths through the woods. Take bus No 57 from CS to Biltse Rading.

HOSTELS

Strowis Budget Hostel (☎ 238 02 80; Boothstraat 8; www.strowis.nl; dm €12, d €45; 🖳) Run by a clever group of ex-squatters, this 17th-century building near the centre has been lovingly restored and converted into a hostel. It's open 24 hours a day and has a cosy bar. Walk 1km from CS or take bus Nos 3, 4, 8 or 11 to the Janskerkhof stop.

B&B Utrecht (☎ 06-50434884; www.hotelinfo.nl; Egelantierstraat 25; amitie@xs4all.nl; dm €12, s/d €45/50; 🖳) Comprising several buildings in a quiet neighbourhood northwest of the centre, this friendly place has rooms in all flavours and sizes. It's popular with students, some of whom work here for their rent. Someone even may pick you up from the station – try calling. Otherwise it's a 15-minute ride on frequent bus No 3 from CS to Watertoren, then walk two blocks west.

Stayokay Hostel Ridderhofstad (☎ 656 12 77; www.stayokay.nl; Rhijnauwenselaan 14; dm €22-24) This charming old mansion overlooks a canal on the fringes of a nature reserve, 6km east of the city centre in Bunnik. Rooms are newly renovated and upgraded. It's easily reachable from the centre by bike or from CS by bus Nos 40, 41 or 43.

HOTELS

Park Hotel (☎ 251 67 12; fax 254 04 01; Tolsteegsingel 34; s/d €50/63; P) You'll sleep tight in this comfy eight-room guesthouse occupying a canal house. It's not far from Utrecht's buzzing nightlife, and breakfast can be taken in the pretty garden out the back.

NH Centre Utrecht Hotel (☎ 231 31 69; www.nh-hotels.com; Janskerkhof 10; s/d €120; P ✕) Forget the unglamourous name and instead focus on the atmospheric old building (1870) and views of the old church square. The rooms have all the conveniences a business traveller would expect as well as the nice Broers restaurant downstairs (see below).

Grand Hotel Karel V (☎ 233 75 55; Geertebolwerk 1; www.karelv.nl; s/d from €210/235; P 🔀 🖳) The best accommodation in Utrecht can be found in this former knights' gathering hall from the 14th century. The service and décor are understated but flawless, and the restaurant is excellent. Note that room prices plummet on the weekend.

Eating

Do as the discerning locals do: avoid the cluster of wharf-side restaurants on the Oudegracht in the dead centre of the old town near the town hall. It's a pretty spot better known for its views than culinary delights. Utrecht's best restaurants lie elsewhere.

Dendermonde (☎ 231 46 99; Biltstraat 29; mains €15; 🕓 dinner) Delectable three-course Belgian meals (€25) are served here in a chichi interior with buffed parquet or in the bright rear hall with a sliding roof. Traditional Belgian dishes like *waterzooi* (chicken casserole) are usually given a modern twist and the quality is consistently good.

Lokaal de Reunie (☎ 231 01 00; 't Wed 3A; mains €8-15; 🕓 lunch & dinner) This is one of many atmospheric cafés on this street near the cathedral tower. There's sawdust on the floors to soak up spilled beer, and it has an attractive airy interior – even the candles are a cut above the norm. The menu has salads, sandwiches and more.

Oudaen (☎ 231 18 64; Oudegracht 99; mains €8-19; 🕓 lunch & dinner) The best choice on this popular stretch of the canal. Set in a restored 14th-century banquet hall, it has a varied menu of salads and steaks. Best of all, it brews its own beer, guaranteeing high times under the high ceilings.

Café le Journal (☎ 236 48 39; Neude 32-34; mains from €5; 🕓 lunch & dinner) This classy grand café sits on a busy square that's a hive of activity in summer. The salads are inventive and the brown bread has many fans. In the evening the atmosphere is more of a pub-eatery.

Broers (☎ 234 34 06; Janskerkhof 9; mains €16-25; 🕓 lunch & dinner) This stylish, modern version of a brown café sprawls over several rooms and there are good views out onto the streets and square. On some nights there's live music and dancing. Its elegant dining area is a lovely spot for three-course meals of pasta, steak and the like.

Polman's (☎ 231 33 68; cnr Jansdam & Keistraat; mains €18-25; 🕓 lunch & dinner Mon-Sat) Diners are welcomed in an elegant former ballroom with ceiling frescos, a hangover from its days as an elite gentlemen's club. The French and Italian menus are honed for the discriminating palate.

Drinking

Kafé België (☎ 231 26 66; Oudegracht 196) This lively bar keeps a large inflatable shark to watch over its alternative patrons. The beer menu has about 200 varieties and the friendly staff will be happy to advise on your choice.

Café Ledig Erf (☎ 231 75 77; Tolsteegbrug 3) This classy pub overlooks a confluence of canals at the southern tip of town. Patrons gather on tables around the oversized chessboards on the terrace, and it's always packed in warm weather.

Café Springhaver (☎ 231 37 89; Springweg 50-52) This incredibly cosy bar next door the Springhaver Theater is a perfect spot to order a drink before the feature picture, or just to pore over the daily news.

Entertainment

't Oude Pothuys (☎ 231 89 70; Oudegracht 279) Small and dark, this basement pub has nightly music – jam sessions with locals trying their hand at rock and jazz, but also touring pro bands. The sound system's tops.

Springhaver Theater (☎ 231 37 89; Springweg 50-52) This Art Deco complex has two intimate cinemas showing arthouse and independent films.

Tivoli (☎ 231 14 91; www.tivoli.nl; Oudegracht 245) This former monastery remains a fixture on Utrecht's student-oriented music scene. Whether it's for old rockers from REM, a video jockey or big-band jazz, events at this cavernous dance hall with medieval chandeliers are often sold out.

Utrecht has quite a few theatres and a fairly lively agenda for contemporary drama.

Camera/Studio (☎ 231 77 08; Oudegracht 156) One of the more professional, known for its productions by modern Dutch playwrights.

Muziekcentrum (☎ 231 45 44; Vredenburgpassage 77) The main performing arts complex, with superb acoustics. A quick flip through its diverse monthly calendar might reveal flamenco, marionette theatre, Ellington or Weber – in short, something for everyone.

Shopping

Hoog Catharijne, the largest shopping mall in the country, is nothing to write home about. Instead, you might look out for interesting boutiques and special interest stores on the less frenetic stretch of **Oudegracht** south of the cathedral tower, **Springweg** and the streets around **Janskerkhof**.

Catch (☎ 231 12 77; Domstraat 5-19) One of several good art galleries on Domstraat and Oudkerkhof, just north of the cathedral tower. Prints, paintings, greeting cards and designer picture frames are just some of the items they'll be happy to gift wrap for you.

Betsies Kookwinkel (☎ 232 19 33; Vismarkt 6) Here you'll find a large variety of semi-professional cooking gear, top end in quality and price. The place for that silver-plated milk agitator, designer bottle stopper or classy Visser pots and pans.

La Ligna (☎ 234 09 68; Lijnmarkt 19) Prices are often slashed on mix-and-match casuals in this pleasant fashion boutique, one of several in this part of town.

RonDom (☎ 233 3036; Domplein 9-10) The cathedral's information office offers unique souvenirs like CDs of the city's tinkling carillons.

Vredenburg is the site of a large **outdoor market** on Wednesday (organic produce) and Saturday (general food and clothing).

Getting There & Away

Utrecht is a travel hub: train lines and motorways converge on the city from all directions.

BUS

Eurolines (☎ 296 90 90; Jaarbeurstraverse 6) buses stop at Jaarbeursplein at the back of the train station. Tickets can be bought from its office on the covered walkway that joins Centraal Station to Jaarbeursplein. For information on their services, see Transport, p312.

TRAIN

You'll be overwhelmed by Utrecht's vast Centraal Station (CS) even before you're swallowed up by the adjoining shopping mall. Lockers are by platform No 4 on the main concourse. Utrecht is the national hub for Dutch rail services so you'll probably change trains here at some point.

UTRECHT

Some of the main services include:

Destination	Price (€)	Duration (min)	Frequency (per hr)
Amsterdam	5.60	35	4
Den Helder	15.00	110	2
Groningen	22.30	120	2
Maastricht	21.00	120	2
Rotterdam	7.50	35	2

Getting Around
Local buses and trams leave from underneath the passage linking Centraal Station to Hoog Catharijne. Regional buses leave from the southerly adjoining area.

For a **taxi**, dial ☎ 230 04 00.

In Centraal Station, the **bicycle rental shop** (☎ 231 11 59) is down by the local buses.

AROUND UTRECHT
About 10km northwest of Utrecht is the town of Breukelen, the inspiration for the New York district of Brooklyn (that's right). While unremarkable in itself, the town is the gateway to the **Loosdrechtse Plassen**, a large series of lakes formed from the flooded digs of peat harvesters.

There are all manner of bike paths around the waters and quite a bit of interesting scenery. Parts of the lakes are desolate, while others are surrounded by lovely homes on small islands joined to the road by cute little bridges.

The best way to visit is by bike from Utrecht. Follow the signs to Breukelen. Otherwise, it's just a short run by train to Breukelen from Utrecht CS (€2, 11 minutes, twice per hour).

Kasteel de Haar
One of the most imposing castles in the country, **Kasteel de Haar** (☎ 030-677 85 15; www.kasteeldehaar.nl; Kasteellaan 1; adult/child €7.50/5; ☼ 10am-5pm; P €2.50) evokes images of medieval feasts and knights. In fact, the castle was restored in a fit of nostalgia little more than a century ago, long after its Gothic turrets ceased to have any defensive purpose. But architect PJ Cuypers (of Rijksmuseum fame) misjudged the weight on the centuries-old foundations; big cracks can be seen above moat level with the naked eye.

What you see now is a spiffed-up version of the fortress as it was believed to look around 1500, but (understandably) equipped with all the creature comforts available in the late 19th century, such as electric lighting and running water. The project was so extensive that the church and the nearby hamlet of **Haarzuilens** got involved. The castle owner, Baron Etienne van Zuylen, spared little expense and had the entire village moved so there'd be adequate space for the park and hunting grounds.

The castle is surrounded by a large English landscaped garden with broad paths, canal-like stretches of pond and statues throughout. The French baroque garden near the entrance bears the stamp of Hélène de Rothschild, the Baron's wife and heir of the renowned Rothschild banking family – it was her fortune that paid for the 19th-century restoration.

Bear in mind that some rooms will be closed for renovations over the next few years. The park and castle exteriors can always be viewed on their own for a reduced fee (adult/child €3/2).

To get here from Utrecht, take the A2 north to exit 6 (Maarssen) and drive 2km east to Haarzuilens. By bus, take No 127 from Utrecht train station towards Breukelen and get off at Brink, from where it's a 15-minute walk.

AMERSFOORT
☎ 033 / pop 128,000
Beer, wool and later tobacco made Amersfoort an exceedingly rich town from the 16th century onwards. Well-heeled with a touch of the provincial, the town has many striking merchants' homes that have been charmingly restored. Largely ignored by foreign visitors, the egg-shaped old town offers quiet strolls along canals and narrow alleys that still ooze medieval atmosphere.

Information
GWK currency exchange In the train station
Post office (Utrechtseweg 8). The main post office.
Tourist office (☎ 0900-1122364; Stationsplein 9-11; www.vvvamersfoort.nl, in Dutch; ☼ 9.30am-5.30pm Mon-Fri, 10am-2pm Sat) Well-stocked, and to the left as you exit the train station.

Sights & Activities
Much of Amersfoort's appeal comes from wandering the old centre, which has a couple of attractive little canals and over

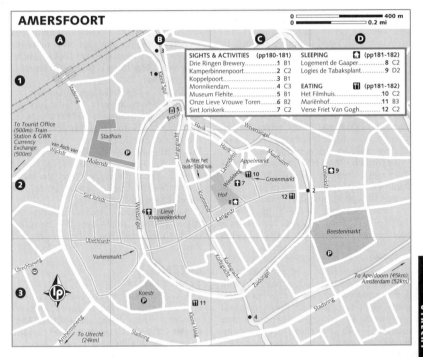

300 buildings from before the 18th century. **Zuidsingel** is a fine place to start; the inner ring on the north side of town along **Muurhuizen** is quaint and good for walks. **Langestraat** is the main shopping drag.

Onze Lieve Vrouwe Toren (adult/child €4/3; ☼ 10am-5pm Tue-Sat Jul & Aug) is the surviving 15th-century Gothic tower of the church that used to stand on this spot. Like so many Dutch churches it was destroyed by tragedy – in this case a gunpowder explosion in 1787. The square out front, **Lieve Vrouwekerkhof**, is the most charming place in town. A flower market is held here on Friday morning.

Amersfoort's surviving old church is the **Sint Joriskerk** (Hof 1; admission €0.50; ☼ 2-4.30pm Mon-Fri Jul & Aug). It was rebuilt in a sort of Gothic-cum-aircraft-hangar style in the 16th century after the original Romanesque church burnt down (obviously insuring Dutch churches has never been a lucrative proposition).

Museum Flehite (☎ 461 99 87; Westsingel 50; adult/child €4/2.50; ☼ 11am-6pm Tue-Fri, 11am-5pm Sat & Sun) looks better from the outside than within. The buildings are attractively set at a junction of canals and you enter the museum courtyard over a bridge. The collections cover local geology, history and decorative arts.

The town has three surviving gateways, either to the city roads or over the canals. The **Koppelpoort** guards the north and was built in the 15th century, the **Kamperbinnenpoort** is at the eastern end and dates from the 13th century, while the picturesque **Monnikendam** to the southeast was built in 1430.

Possibly the most fun you'll have in Amersfoort is touring **Drie Ringen Bierbrouwerij** (☎ 465 65 75; Kleine Spui 18; ☼ 1-7pm Thu-Sat). You can wander around this much-heralded micro-brewery and then try one of the five beers on tap.

Sleeping & Eating

Amersfoort is a day trip from Utrecht for most visitors, but if you wish to linger there are nice hotels in the old town.

Logies de Tabaksplant (☎ 472 97 97; www.tabaksplant.nl; Coninckstraat 15; s with/without bathroom €52/34, d €75/54) Just beyond the old town gate of Kamperbinnenpoort, this small hotel is run by a lovely host and the rooms are smart and cheery. Prices include shower and breakfast. This listed building was built by the owner of a tabacco plantation.

Logement de Gaaper (☎ 453 17 95; www.degaaper .nl; Hof 39; s/d €45/70) Home to a pharmacy in the 19th century, this smartly renovated hotel occupies a prime spot on the main square, and all 11 front rooms have great views of Sint Joriskerk. Some of the original structure is visible inside but the emphasis is on modern comfort. Prices include breakfast.

Het Filmhuis (☎ 465 55 50; Groenmarkt 8; mains €6-19; ☽ lunch & dinner) Several cafés lurk in the shadow of Sint Joriskerk, but this bright, airy grand café with Spanish-Mediterranean flair is a choice bet. Stars of the 'script' (menu) include grilled tuna steak and shiitake mushrooms, and its tapas and sandwiches are well suited to the sunny terrace.

Mariënhof (☎ 463 29 79; Kleine Haag 2; mains €18-35; ☽ lunch & dinner Tue-Sat) Chef Jon Sistermans combines *haute cuisine* (eg venison filet with figs and couscous in baked chestnut sauce) with classy service in one of the region's best restaurants. The dining hall is in a former monastery with lavish interiors, courtyard gardens and even a little culinary museum.

Verse Friet Van Gogh (Langestraat 143; ☽ noon-7pm) This venerable joint is really the artist of *frites* (potato chips). All the potatoes are freshly hand-cut and cost €2 for a bulging portion that'll feed two.

Getting There & Around

Some train fares and schedules include:

Destination	Price (€)	Duration (min)	Frequency (per hr)
Amsterdam	6.40	40	4
Apeldoorn	6.30	25	2
Utrecht	3.50	15	4

The **bicycle shop** (☎ 461 49 85) rents out two-wheelers at the train station.

DOORN

☎ 0343 / pop 10,200

Some 20km southeast of Utrecht lies Doorn, a wealthy little burg that holds a quirky bit of 20th-century Dutch history. The town's sole draw is **Huis Doorn** (☎ 42 10 20; adult/child €5.50/1; ☽ 10am-5pm Tue-Sat, 1-5pm Sun mid-Mar–mid-Oct; 1-5pm Tues-Sun mid-Oct–mid-Mar), a 14th-century

castle that was turned into a sort of indefensible mansion in the 1700s. It had numerous owners during its time, but none more infamous than Kaiser Wilhelm II of Germany who lived there in exile from 1920 until his death in 1941.

There is a fine collection of German art that the Kaiser appears to have brought with him from various German palaces. You can stroll the grounds and ponder the fate of the Kaiser, who had been allowed into exile by the Dutch as long as he remained under 'house arrest' (some house!). Events throughout the year recall his highness: at Christmas you can drop by for gluhwein and lebkuchen.

Bus No 50 from Utrecht CS makes the 20km journey to Doorn (50 minutes) every 30 minutes. The castle is right near the bus stop.

AMERONGEN

☎ 0343 / pop 7200

The countryside around this small town on the Nederrijn river is dotted with old wooden tobacco-drying sheds. **Kasteel Amerongen** (☎ 45 42 12; Drostestraat 20; ☽ 10am-5pm Tue-Fri, 1-5pm Sat & Sun Apr-Oct) was a fortified castle in the 13th century, taking on its present twee appearance in the late 1600s. It was originally owned by Europe's old aristocracy. The interior is closed for a lengthy renovation but you can stroll through the lovely gardens before taking coffee and cake in the orangery.

OUDEWATER

☎ 0348 / pop 9800

There's only one real reason to visit the sweet little town of Oudewater in the province's southwest: witchcraft.

Until the 17th century the **Heksenwaag** (Witches' Weigh House; ☎ 56 34 00; Leeuweringerstraat 2; adult/child €1.50/0.75; ☽ 10am-5pm Tue-Sat, noon-5pm Sun) in the town centre was thought to have the most accurate scales in the land. Women came from far and wide to be weighed, as popular belief held that any woman who was too light for the size of her frame was obviously a witch. A woman who weighed the 'proper' amount was too heavy to ride a broom and thus was not a witch. We're not making any of this up!

Women who passed the weight test were given a certificate good for life proclaiming them to be a nonwitch. Those who failed the test, which was entirely subjective, were advised to start eating a lot, although many subjects were put to painful death. Fans of the movie *Monty Python and the Holy Grail* will be familiar with the procedure.

The house has a modest display of witchcraft history in the loft upstairs, and at the end of your visit you'll be invited to step onto the old scale. If you feel light on your feet it's because your *'certificaet van weginghe'* (weight certificate) makes your weight shrink – an old Dutch pound is 10% heavier than today's unit.

Oudewater is on the route of bus No 180, which runs in either direction between Gouda (22 minutes) and Utrecht CS (40 minutes) every 30 minutes.

UTRECHT

Zuid Holland & Zeeland

Once visitors leave Amsterdam to explore the Netherlands, Zuid (South) Holland and Zeeland will probably be the first areas they visit. The major cities are worthy of a day or more: Leiden for its university culture and old town, not to mention proximity to the bulb fields; Den Haag (The Hague) for its museums and stately air amidst the more obvious hedonism of neighbouring cities; Delft for its simple charms and beauty; and Rotterdam for its irrepressible energy, cultural diversity, and challenging modern architecture. The area has several smaller places that are also worth time. Gouda is a perfect little old canal town and Dordrecht surprises many who don't overlook it.

Besides dykes and the most concentrated profusion of real windmills, that other Dutch icon, the tulip, is much in evidence here. The Keukenhof gardens are a place of pilgrimage for lovers of the plant. The land around the gardens and along the border with Noord Holland is the centre of the Dutch tulip industry and every April it comes alive with colour.

The area is great for biking and hiking, and trails and paths are everywhere, especially along the dykes. The built-up beaches of Noordwijk aan Zee and south to Scheveningen are popular with locals, and can be surprisingly comforting for those who are used to a more authentic or familiar sun-drenched beach experience.

Further South, Zeeland is the dyke-protected province that people often associate with the Netherlands when they think of its huge areas below sea level. Middelburg is the centre, with a serenity belying its proximity to the tragedies that necessitated the Delta works.

HIGHLIGHTS

- Gaze at the rainbow colours of the tulips in the **Keukenhof Gardens** (p193)
- Check out Rotterdam's **architecture** (p213)
- Take notice of some incredible art at Den Haag's **Mauritshuis** (p195)
- Get drunk on charm in old-world **Delft** (p204)
- Visit Rotterdam's **Boijmans van Beuningen Museum** (p212), one of Europe's best
- Spin around the windmills of **Kinderdijk** (p221)
- Bike the **Delta Project** (p226) in Zeeland
- Admire St Janskerk's beautiful windows in **Gouda** (p202) and taste the fab cheese
- Dine at the Netherlands' finest restaurant, **Parkheuvel** (p217) in Rotterdam
- Play with *your* tonal centre at Den Haag's **North Sea Jazz Festival** (p198)

ZUID HOLLAND & ZEELAND

ZUID HOLLAND & ZEELAND

0 —————— 20 km
0 —————— 12 mi

Haarlem
AMSTERDAM
Almere-Stad
Amstelveen
Aalsmeer
Keukenhof
Noordwijk aan Zee
Katwijk aan Zee
Hilversum
Leiden
Alphen
a/d Rijn
UTRECHT
Den Haag
(The Hague)
Utrecht
NORTH SEA
Oudewater
Nieuwegein
Monster
Delft
Gouda
Hoek van Holland
Rotterdam
Kinderdijk
ZUID HOLLAND
Zaltbommel
Dordrecht
Biesbosch
National Park
Den
Bosch
Willemstad
Schouwen-
Duiveland
Westerschouwen
NOORD BRABANT
Delta Expo
Zierikzee
Domburg
Noord-
Beveland
Veere
Breda
Tilburg
Walcheren
Roosendaal
Middelburg
Goes
Vlissingen
Zuid-Beveland
Bergen op Zoom
Zeeuws-Vlaanderen
ZEELAND
To Antwerpen
(Anvers)
To Antwerpen
(Anvers)
BELGIUM
To Antwerpen
(Anvers)
Oosterschelde
Westerschelde

ZUID HOLLAND

Along with Noord Holland and Utrecht, Zuid Holland is part of the Randstad, the population and economic centre of the Netherlands.

Two of the nation's most important cities are here – Den Haag (The Hague), the royal family's and government's seat, and Rotterdam. The latter is Europe's busiest port, an exciting town with all Amsterdam's energy, but a totally different feel. Just southeast, Kinderdijk is a must-see for windmill lovers.

Within easy reach of these bigger cities are Leiden, a great old university town, and Gouda and Delft, which are just plain enjoyable. Just east of lovely Dordrecht is Biesbosch National Park, a sprawling natural area along the border with Noord Brabant. The website www.zuid-hollandinfo.nl has plenty of information on the region.

LEIDEN

☎ 071 / pop 117,700

Home to the country's oldest university, Leiden's effervescent, intellectual aura is partly generated by the 20,000 students, one-sixth of the population. The university was a gift from Willem the Silent for withstanding two Spanish sieges in 1574. It was a terrible time, ending when the Sea Beggars arrived and repelled the invaders.

According to lore, the retreating Spanish left so quickly, they abandoned a kettle of *hutspot* (hotchpotch). *Hutspot* is still a staple of Dutch menus today, both at home and in restaurants.

Decades later, Protestants fleeing persecution elsewhere in the Low Countries, France and England, arrived in Leiden to a somewhat warmer welcome. Most notable was the group led by John Robinson, who would sail to America and into history as the pilgrims aboard the *Mayflower*, even though that momentous journey was not without a false start. See the boxed text 'Pilgrims' Progress' (p189) for details.

Wealth from the linen industry buttressed Leiden's growing prosperity, and during the 17th century the town produced several brilliant artists, most famously Rembrandt van Rijn – better known by his first name alone. Rembrandt was born here in 1606 and remained in Leiden for 26 years before achieving greater fame in Amsterdam.

The town's other sadly notable event happened in 1807 when a canal barge carrying gunpowder blew up, wiping out a large area around Steenschuur.

Today Leiden is a typical old Dutch town with a refreshing overlay of vibrancy from the students. Look for the literary quotes painted on many walls in their original languages – everything from Russian to Hebrew to Spanish.

Orientation

Old Leiden is a compact town. Arriving at the station (Centraal) you may be tempted to stay on the train or bus as the area in front of the station has been grimly redeveloped in a rather Eastern-bloc style. A five-minute walk brings you to Beestenmarkt, where the views improve.

Haarlemmerstraat and Breestraat are the town's pedestrian arteries and most sights are within five minutes of either. The town is bisected by many waterways, the most notable being the Oude Rijn and also the Nieuwe Rijn which meet at Hoogstraat to form a canal called simply the Rijn.

Information
BOOKSHOPS
The Joho Company (☎ 514 50 07; Stille Rijn 8-9) An oasis for the traveller, and not just because it stocks nearly every LP title published. It has tons of other books, maps, travel gear and supplies and Internet access. It's open the usual shopping hours.

Reisboekhandel Zandvliet (☎ 512 70 09; Stille Rijn 13) Stocks nothing but travel books and maps.

EMERGENCY
For all emergencies call ☎ 112. For non-immediate matters call the Leiden **police** (☎ 525 88 88). If you need a doctor after hours or on public holidays, call ☎ 0900-7763337.

INTERNET ACCESS
Centrale Bibliotheek (Central Library; ☎ 514 99 43; Nieuwstraat; web access per hr €2; ☉ 11am-5pm Oct-Apr, closed Sun Jun-Sep)

LAUNDRY
Zelf Was (☎ 512 03 38; Morsstraat 50; ☉ 8am-8pm)
MONEY
GWK money exchange (☉ 7am-9pm) In the train station.

ATMs Outside the station and many more along Stationsweg.

POST
Post office (☎ 514 17 88; Breestraat 46; ☉ 9am-6pm Mon-Fri, 10am-1.30pm Sat) The most convenient post office on one of Leiden's biggest shopping streets.

TOURIST INFORMATION
Tourist office (☎ 0900-2222333; www.leiden.nl; Stationsweg 2D; ☉ 10am-6.30pm Mon-Fri, 10am-2pm Sat) Five minutes' walk from the station. It has a good number of printed guides for walks. Worth special mention are 'In the Young Rembrandt's Footsteps' (€2) and the lavish 'A Walk Around Locations Related to the 17th-Century Painters' (€3). It also rents 'Talking Walls' audio walking tours of the city (€5). These excellent CDs present events and history keyed to specific sites.

Sights
Most of the sights are concentrated within Leiden's pretty canal belt and are best experienced on foot.

RIJKSMUSEUM VAN OUDHEDEN
Learn to walk like an Egyptian in the **Rijksmuseum van Oudheden** (National Museum of Antiquities; ☎ 516 31 63; www.rmo.nl; Rapenburg 28; adult/child under 18 €6/5.50; ☉ 10am-5pm Tue-Fri, noon-5pm Sat & Sun) – you'll get lots of clues from the hieroglyphs on display here, with a world-class collection, including 32 human and 62 animal mummies.

LEIDEN

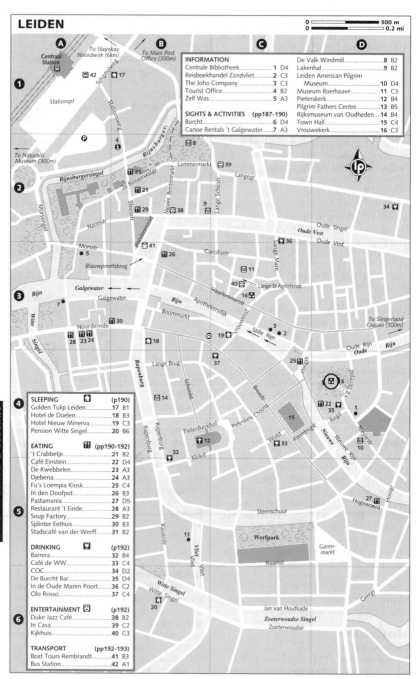

0 ———————— 300 m
0 ———————— 0.2 mi

Oudegracht (p176), Utrecht

Cathedral (Dom) tower,
Utrecht (p176)

View over Utrecht from the cathedral tower (p176)

LEANNE LOC

Old-style Dutch restaurant, Leiden (p191)

Hortus Botanicus, Leiden (p186)

JEREMY GE

JEREMY GRAY

Sign in Leiden (p186)

Keukenhof Gardens (p193)

LIZ BAR

The entrance hall contains the *actual* Temple of Taffeh, a gift from Egypt in 1969 for the Netherlands' help in saving ancient monuments from inundation when the Aswan High Dam was built.

OTHER ATTRACTIONS

The 17th-century **Lakenhal** (Cloth Hall; ☎ 516 53 60; www.lakenhal.nl; Oude Singel 28-32; adult/child €2/1; 🕙 10am-5pm Tue-Fri, noon-5pm Sat & Sun) houses the Municipal Museum, with an assortment of works by old masters, as well as period rooms and temporary exhibits. The 1st floor has been restored to the way it would have looked when Leiden was at the peak of its prosperity from the cloth trade.

Leiden's landmark windmill, **De Valk** (The Falcon; ☎ 516 53 53; 2e Binnenvestgracht 1; adult/child €2.50/1.50; 🕙 10am-5pm Tue-Sat, is a museum that will blow away notions that windmills were a Dutch invention. It's been carefully restored and once inside you'll see how, in both construction and operation, Dutch windmills were much like the sailing ships of their day.

Leiden University was an early centre for Dutch medical research and you can see the often grisly results at the **Museum Boerhaave** (☎ 521 42 24; www.musueumboerhaave.nl; Lange St Agnie-tenstraat 10; €2/1; 🕙 10am-5pm Tue-Sat, noon-5pm Sun). There are five centuries of pickled organs, surgical tools and skeletons in the Anatomy

---

PILGRIMS' PROGRESS

In 1608 a group of Calvinist Protestants who had split with the Anglican Church, left persecution in Nottinghamshire, England, for a journey that would span decades and thousands of miles. Travelling first to Amsterdam under the leadership of John Robinson, they encountered theological clashes with local Dutch Protestants.

In Leiden they found a more liberal atmosphere thanks to the university and some like-minded Calvinists who already lived there. They also found company with other refugees from persecution elsewhere.

However, their past was to catch up with them. In 1618 King James I of England announced he would assume control over the Calvinists living in Leiden. In addition, the local Dutch were becoming less tolerant of religious splinter groups.

The first group of English left Leiden in 1620 for Delfshaven in what is today Rotterdam, where they bought the *Speedwell* with the intention of sailing to the New World in hopes of finally putting their problems behind them. Unfortunately, the *Speedwell* didn't live up to its name; after several attempts at sailing the Atlantic, the group gave up and, against their better judgement, put into Southampton in England. Here they swapped the leaky *Speedwell* for the much more seaworthy *Mayflower* and sailed, as it were, into history as the Pilgrims.

This legendary voyage was actually just one of many involving the Leiden group. It wasn't until 1630 that most had made their way to the American colonies founded in what is today New England. Some 1000 people made the voyages, including a number of Dutch, considered oddballs for their unusual beliefs.

Traces of the Pilgrims today in Leiden are elusive. The best place to start is the **Leiden American Pilgrim Museum** (☎ 512 24 13, Beschuitsteeg 9; admission €2; 🕙 1-5pm Wed-Sat), an absolutely fascinating restoration of a house occupied around 1610 by the soon-to-be Pilgrims. The house itself dates from 1375, but the furnishings are contemporary to the Pilgrims' period. Note the tiles on the floor, which are the originals from the 14th century. Pick up a walking-tour brochure (€1) which helps you explore the surviving parts of 17th-century Leiden.

One of the few other sites with direct links to the Pilgrims is the surviving wall of the **Vrouwekerk**, the church where the Pilgrims worshipped. Although it's not much to look at, its significance is unquestioned and it's been the cause of controversy of late. Developers who want to build a disco on the site are at loggerheads with preservationists.

Around the **Pieterskerk** are the other significant sites with a Pilgrim connection. It's here that John Robinson is buried, having never made it to America.

The **Pilgrim Fathers Center** (☎ 512 01 91; Vliet 45; 🕙 9.30am-5.30pm Mon-Fri, 9.30am-noon Sat) has displays and is the place to check out whether your ancestors came from Nottinghamshire by way of Leiden.

Theatre. The museum is housed in the hospital where the chronically (and ironically?) ill Herman Boerhaave taught medicine from his sick bed until his death in 1738.

A stuffed elephant greets you at **Naturalis – Nationaal Natuurhistorisch Museum** (National Museum of Natural History; ☎ 568 76 00; www.naturalis.nl; Darwinweg 2; adult/child €8/4.50; ✆ 10am-6pm Tue-Sun). This is a large and well-funded collection of all the usual dead critters and the 1,000,000 year-old Java Man, discovered by Dutch anthropologist Eugene Dubois in 1891. This striking building is 300m west of the train station.

Activities

You can paddle your way around the canals on a rented canoe or kayak year-round from **Botenverhuur 't Galgewater** (☎ 514 97 90; per hr €3.50; ✆ 11am-6pm Oct-May, 11am-10pm Jun-Sep).

Tours

Rederij Rembrandt (☎ 513 49 38; Beestenmarkt; adult/child €4/2.25) gives one-hour boat tours of Leiden at various times throughout the year. Check the schedules at the dock.

There are longer, three-hour cruises of the waterways and lakes around Leiden, operated by **Rederij Slingerland** (☎ 521 98 75; adult/child €10/5.50; ✆ 1pm departure Sun-Wed Jun-Sep), cruises depart from a dock at Haven, 700m east of the Burcht.

Festivals & Events

Leiden grinds to a halt for **Leidens Ontzet** (3 October) to commemorate the day the starvation caused by the Spanish ended in 1574. The revelry is undiminished even four centuries later and there is much eating of the ceremonial *hutspot*, herring and white bread. But more than anything, consumption focuses on liquid bread (beer) and a drunken time is had by all, especially the night before.

Sleeping

Leiden has less accommodation than you'd expect since many visitors choose to stay in Amsterdam.

CAMPING

The closest seaside grounds are in Katwijk aan Zee, 8km to the west.

De Zuidduinen (☎ 401 47 50; info-zuidduinen@ tours.nl; Zuidduinseweg 1; site €14; ✆ Apr-Oct) and **De Noordduinen** (☎ 402 52 95; info-noordduinen@tours.nl;

Campingweg 1; site €14; ✆ Apr-Oct) Both can be reached from Leiden on bus No 31 or 41.

HOSTELS

The nearest hostel, **Stayokay Noordwijk** (☎ 0252-37 29 20; www.stayokay.com/noordwijk; Langeveldlaan 45; dm from €20), is 45 minutes away. Predictable Stayokay ambience, augmented by proximity to a pretty tacky, yet popular beach. Take bus No 57 or 90 (last bus at 11pm) to Sancta Maria hospital and walk for 10 minutes.

HOTELS & PENSIONS

Pension Witte Singel (☎ 512 45 92; fax 514 28 90; Witte Singel 80; s/d €42/63.50) On a peaceful canal south of the town centre, prices include breakfast, rooms have shower, and it's run by a lovely lady. It's a 15-minute walk from the station and is one of the best-value places in town.

Hotel de Doelen (☎ 512 05 27; www.dedoelen.com; Rapenburg 2; s/d/extra bed €70/90/15) A stately and classic place, though not so stately that breakfast is included (€8 extra). Some of the canalside rooms are bordering on palatial opulence – remarkable at this price – and even the more basic rooms have bath, phone and TV.

Hotel Nieuwe Minerva (☎ 512 63 58; www .nieuwminerva.nl; Boommarkt 23; s/d/tr/q €75/100/125/ 150) The Minerva – and really, you gotta respect any place named after a goddess – has a traditional look and a quiet canalside location. The rooms are comfy and well equipped. There's an optional champagne breakfast served in your room for €23 extra.

Golden Tulip Leiden (☎ 522 11 21; Schipholweg 3; s/d €144/168; ▨ ▢ ✕ P) Large and modern. The rooms are aimed at business travellers who will often trade architectural charm for amenities. You'll get all the charm you can handle out on the town's pretty canalside streets.

Eating

Eating out in Leiden is surprisingly diverse and often cheap. There's also a cluster of excellent, slightly pricier and quite inventive places on Noordeinde.

CAFÉS

Splinter Eethuis (☎ 514 95 19; Noordeinde 30; 2-course menu €9.50; ✆ Thu-Sun) A popular student haunt, Splinter looks austere but has generous two-course meals, featuring a

ZUID HOLLAND & ZEELAND

different ethnic cuisine every week plus decent vegetarian options. There's nothing on the menu over €12.25 and it features heady stuff such as Peruvian beef steak with onion and tomato, garnished with egg and parsley. Brilliant.

Pastamania (☎ 512 33 11; Hogewoerd 18; daily special €5.80, ☺ dinner) Another student hit, mostly for its delicious, filling pasta and meat dishes (all under €9) and big pitchers of red wine for €12. The *pasta alla spinaci* with pecans, spinach, mixed basil and blue cheese is a gut-busting vegetarian stunner for €6.40.

Stadscafé van der Werff (☎ 512 61 20; Stationsweg 7-9; light meals €3-5, lunch €8-13) In a leafy stretch on the site of the old fortifications. It's bright, with large windows and the usual café menu (*broodjes* – filled breadrolls – coffees, beers, Dutch bar snacks). A great spot to discretely people-watch, as it's much easier to see out than in.

Café Einstein (☎ 512 53 70; Nieuwe Rijn 19; snacks €3-6; ☺ lunch & dinner) This charming place bustles with locals popping in for a drink, a snack and a chat from early to late. There is a sky-lit room in the rear and chairs next to the canal. A lovely place to while away a few hours with something to read.

QUICK EATS
Soup Factory (☺ noon-10pm) Difficult to miss at the corner of Steenstraat and Narmstraat. It's in bright, fast-food-garish colours but is actually quite a healthy option. It does cheap but excellent soups (small/large €3/3.90) which are tasty, and can be augmented with breads, drinks and other sides to make a cheap meal-on-the-run.

Fu's Loempia Kiosk on Hoogstraat is an especially good example of this Dutch-colonial fast-food staple; a loempia is basically a spring roll with elephantiasis and costs €1.50. There are also various noodle and rice dishes.

RESTAURANTS
In den Doofpot (☎ 512 24 34; www.indendoofpot.nl; Turfmarkt 9; mains €18-38; ☺ dinner) There's little chance you're going to walk away from this elegant place not full. Twists on Dutch home-style cooking with elaborate French brushes and other less bulky options.

Djebena (☎ 513 68 33; Noordeinde 21; mains around €11; ☺ dinner) This Eritrean/Ethiopian restaurant is an eclectic and very appealing alternative to the more obvious European options surrounding it. Try *injera*, a kind of pancake made with grist, water, wheat

---

TULIPS – THE BELOVED BULB

Tulips have captured the fancy of the Dutch, and humans in general, for centuries. In fact, at times this love has become an absolute mania (see Tulipmania, p27).

The first stop on any tulip tour is, naturally, the Keukenhof, the world's largest flower garden, located between the towns of Hillegom and Lisse, south of Haarlem. The 32-hectare park attracts a staggering 800,000 people for a mere eight weeks every year. Nature's talents are combined with artificial precision to create a garden where millions of tulips and daffodils bloom every year, perfectly in place and exactly on time.

The broad stripes of colour stretching as far as one can see are a spectacular feast for the eye. Postcards just don't do justice to the vast fields of colour. The bulbs are left to bloom fully so that they will gain full strength during the growing season, after which over €500 million worth of bulbs are exported worldwide.

To appreciate the blooms you have several options. By train, opt for one of the frequent local (meaning slow) trains between Haarlem and Leiden. These pass through the heart of the fields. By car, cover the same area on the N206 and N208, branching off down tiny side roads as you wish. But like so much of the Netherlands, perhaps the best way to see the bulb fields is by bicycle. You can set your course along the smallest roads and get lost in a sea of colour.

In Lisse, the **tourist office** (☎ 0252-41 42 62; Grachtweg 53A; ☺ 9am-5pm Tue-Fri, noon-5pm Mon, 9am-4pm Sat) can give you many options for bulb field touring by whatever means of transport you prefer. Also in Lisse, the small **Museum de Zwarte Tulp** (Museum of the Black Tulip; ☎ 0252-41 79 00; Grachtweg 2A; admission €2; ☺ 1-5pm Tue-Sun) displays everything you want to know about bulbs, including why there's no such thing as a black tulip.

For details on the Aalsmeer Flower Auction, the world's largest, see p147.

ZUID HOLLAND & ZEELAND

and cornmeal, piled up with vegetables and pulses augmented by some amazing aromatic spices.

De Kwebbelen (☎ 512 6190; Noordeinde 19; 3-course menu €17.50; ☾ dinner) The most fun restaurant in Leiden, right down to the kitschy Renoir place-mats and menu featuring cunning punning. The kid steak is 'Entregoat', 'Joe Formaggio' is their wicked grin-inducing fondue and our personal fave, the tragic 'Jack the Spare Ribber' is... you get it. The only thing to take seriously here is the fantastic cooking.

't Crabbetje (☎ 512 88 46; St Aagtenstraat 5; mains €15-25; ☾ dinner, 5pm-late) 'The Little Crab' is, unsurprisingly, a (great) seafood place. It's a little beige at first glance, but sampling their wonderful sea-sourced treats will erase any impressions of blandness. Here, you'll eat something that will swim no more, except in your happy belly, delivered with panache by restaurateurs Margot Reurink and Andre Brak.

Restaurant 't Einde (☎ 512 21 15; Rembrandtstraat 2; mains from €15; ☾ dinner Tue-Sun) A small, classy place with an excellent menu featuring informed wine and beer suggestions to complement each of the exquisite meat, fish, poultry and seafood variations on offer. Not too traditional, not too nouvelle cuisine, it's mildly progressive and always delicious food, carefully but unpretentiously presented. Sophisticated, with excellent service.

Drinking

Evenings revolve around the town's lively cafés.

De Burcht (☎ 514 23 89; Burgsteeg 14) A literary bar next to the Burcht that's popular with professorial types.

Olo Rosso (☎ 514 34 44; Breestraat 49; tapas €5-7) Popular with students, despite a name change and style overhaul. Olo Rosso's super-cool Latina cantina/wine-bar vibe suggests there's an officious DJ lurking around a corner somewhere, but the people about are more approachable.

Barrera (☎ 514 66 31; Rapenburg 56) A classic brown café with a good corner location for people-watching. There's plenty to recommend this excellent bar which draws a decent crowd of its own, namely good beer and a friendly, welcoming atmosphere.

In de Oude Maren Poort (☎ 514 32 15; Lange Mare 36) Overlooks Oude Vest canal and has

very pleasant outside seating. A great bar is often so because of its clientele, and it is so in this case; pull up a chair, order a beer, start a conversation. It doesn't get any more complicated than that.

COC (☎ 522 06 40; Langegracht 65) Bar run by the national gay and lesbian organisation, and its acronymic name is a subtle wordplay.

Entertainment
MUSIC

In Casa (☎ 512 49 38; Lammermarkt 100) This place is huge and looks like it has no atmosphere from the outside, but appearances can be deceiving. It has live music, a dance floor, comedy and a variety of other events. Opening hours and admission depend on the programme.

Café de WW (☎ 512 59 00; Wolsteeg 6) Live rock is played to a young crowd in the over-loud, hormonally charged atmosphere. The possibility of falling in love with a real-live drummer is restricted mostly to Fridays. Other nights there's a DJ.

Duke Jazz Café (☎ 566 15 85; Oude Singel 2) Features jazz in the usual dark and contemplative atmosphere. Opening hours are less dependable than closing times; it depends how big a party they had the night before, doesn't it?

CINEMAS

The **Kijkhuis** (☎ 566 15 85; Vrouwenkerksteeg 10) has an alternative film programme.

Getting There & Away

Centraal Station (CS) is bright and modern. It has all the usual conveniences and the lockers are near platform No 5. Service is frequent in all directions and includes:

Destination	Price (€)	Duration (min)	Frequency (per hr)
Amsterdam	5.80	34	6
Schiphol Airport	4.50	18	4
Den Haag	2.80	10	6

Regional and local buses leave from the bus station directly in front of Centraal Station.

Getting Around

Leiden is compact and you'll have a hard time walking for more than 20 minutes in any one direction.

If you are in need of a **taxi**, call ☎ 521 21 44.

The **bicycle shop** (☎ 512 00 68) in Centraal Station is around the back.

AROUND LEIDEN
Keukenhof Gardens

The eye-poppingly gorgeous **Keukenhof gardens** (www.keukenhof.nl; adult/child under 11 €11.50/5.50; ☑ 8am-7.30pm, cashier to 6pm) in Lisse stretch on and on and there are greenhouses full of more delicate varieties of flowers besides the ephemeral tulips (see the boxed text p191). You'll forgive the presence of thousands of other tourists – little can detract from the rainbow of natural beauty. Wandering about can easily take half a day. From the edges of the gardens, you can see the stark beauty of the commercial bulb fields stretching in all directions.

The Keukenhof is open from late March to May but dates vary yearly, so check with any tourist office, or with the Keukenhof itself.

If you're unsure of anything, it's best to contact the garden's management directly via their excellent multilingual website.

There are several options for reaching the park, which is off the N208. By car, you will have to pay a parking fee (around €3) but you'll have the freedom of exploring the surrounding bulb fields at leisure.

By train, Netherlands Railways sells a special Keukenhof ticket (€15.50) that combines entrance to the gardens and travel by express bus from Leiden CS, which takes about 20 minutes. It can be combined with any rail ticket to Leiden CS. The buses leave Leiden throughout the day until 5pm and return to Leiden CS until the park closes. The last bus (7.36pm) leaves the gardens just a few minutes after they close, so don't linger.

On regular buses, bus No 54 travels from Leiden through Lisse to Keukenhof. You can also take bus No 50 from Haarlem to Lisse and then change to the No 54 bus for the final leg. Both of these buses run every 30 minutes.

DEN HAAG (THE HAGUE)
☎ 070 / pop 463,900

Trivial Pursuit boffins take note: prior to 1806, the capital *was* Den Haag (The Hague). However, that year, Louis Bonaparte installed his government in Amsterdam. Eight years later when the French had been ousted, the government returned to Den Haag, but the title of capital and the king, remained in Amsterdam.

Officially known as 's-Gravenhage ('the Count's Domain') because a count built a castle here in the 13th century, Den Haag is the country's seat of government and residence of the royal family, though the capital is Amsterdam. It has a refined air, thanks to the stately mansions and palatial embassies lining its green boulevards. It's known for its prestigious art galleries and one of the world's best jazz festivals, the North Sea Jazz Festival (p198), held annually near the seaside suburb of Scheveningen.

In the 20th century, Den Haag became the home of several international legal entities including the UN's International Court of Justice and the Academy of International Law. These genteel organisations and the legions of diplomats give the town its rather sedate and urbane air today. If you're looking for ribaldry head to Amsterdam, for old Dutch charm to nearby Delft.

Den Haag is worth a stop mainly for its arts organs and surprisingly good restaurants. The beach resort of Scheveningen, about 4km northwest of the centre, is for real beach or postmodern-kitsch fanatics only.

Orientation

Den Haag sprawls over a fairly large area; hey, all those 19th-century mansions require space. Centraal Station (CS) is near the heart of town. Hollands Spoor Station (HS), which is on the main line from Amsterdam to Rotterdam and further south, is 1km south of the centre in a less pretty part of town. Most streets heading west reach Scheveningen, 4km away, but it's more pleasantly approached as the end of a 15- to 20-minute bike ride that will take you past the lush homes of some of Den Haag's most well-heeled residents. Delft is close enough to be reached within 30 minutes on the No 11 tram or 8 minutes by train.

Den Haag has no true centre; rather, there are several areas of concentration, including the Binnenhof and the nearby Kerkplein.

Information
BOOKSHOPS

Van Stockum (Map p196; ☎ 365 68 08; Venestraat 11) A large bookshop with a good selection of travel books and magazines.

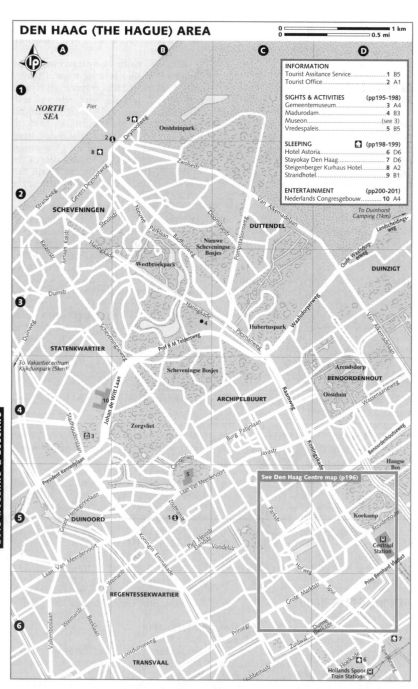

DEN HAAG (THE HAGUE) AREA

0 _____ 1 km
0 _____ 0.5 mi

INFORMATION
Tourist Assitance Service...............1 B5
Tourist Office...............................2 A1

SIGHTS & ACTIVITIES (pp195-198)
Gemeentemuseum.........................3 A4
Madurodam..................................4 B3
Museon....................................(see 3)
Vredespaleis................................5 B5

SLEEPING (pp198-199)
Hotel Astoria................................6 D6
Stayokay Den Haag........................7 D6
Steigenberger Kurhaus Hotel............8 A2
Strandhotel..................................9 B1

ENTERTAINMENT (pp200-201)
Nederlands Congresgebouw............10 A4

EMERGENCY

For all emergencies call ☎ 112. To contact the police for other reasons call ☎ 310 49 11.

Tourist Assistance Service (TAS; Map p194; ☎ 310 32 74; Zoutmanstraat 44) It helps visitors who've been the victim of a crime or an accident. For general medical information call ☎ 0900-8600 (after hours ☎ 346 96 69).

LAUNDRY

De Wassalon (Map p196; ☎ 385 84 03; Theresiastraat 250) This coin laundry is 1km east of CS. Take bus No 4 three stops to Laan van NOI in the direction of Leidschendam 't Lien.

LIBRARY

Koninklijke Bibliotheek (Royal Library; Map p196; ☎ 314 09 11; www.kb.nl; Spui 168; web access per hr €3; ☺ 9am-5pm Mon-Fri, 9am-8pm Tue, 9am-1pm Sat) Housed in a huge, new, sparkling white building, it has collections of newspapers, magazines, books and more from around the world. It also has all the latest on-line connections and databases.

MONEY

GWK money exchange (☺ 7am-9pm Mon-Sat, 8am-9pm Sun) In CS. ATMs abound, both in the station and around town.

POST

Post office (Map p196; ☎ 365 38 43; Kerkplein 6; ☺ 9am-6pm Mon-Wed & Fri, 9am-8pm Thu, 9am-4pm Sat) Next to the Grote Kerk.

TOURIST INFORMATION

The main **tourist office** (Map p196; ☎ 0900-3403505; info@vvvdenhaag.nl; Koningin Julianaplein 30; ☺ 8.30am-5.30pm Mon-Sat year-round, 10am-2pm Sun Jul & Aug) is next to CS. The one in Scheveningen (Map p194; ☎ 0900-3403505; vvvscheveningen@spdh.net; Gevers Deynootweg 1134; ☺ 9am-5.30pm Mon-Fri, 9am-7pm Sat year-round, 10am-2pm Sun Jul & Aug) is in the Palace Promenade shopping centre. Both book accommodation (€3.50), sell transport and entertainment tickets and have numerous English-language publications. Among the better ones are two with themed walks of art/antique stores and architecture.

Dangers & Annoyances

There is a poorer side to all the finery, and the area south of the centre (the Schilderswijk) near HS can seem far removed from its urbane counterpart to the north, with an ominousness and iniquity in the air that suggests that even the mostly valid Dutch

reputation for tolerance, openness and social justice actually has its limits in practice.

Sights & Activities

Den Haag has no true core, rather a scattering of districts, some heavier on the carousing options, some thicker with diplomatic and cultural insititutions. All, however, are easily reachable with public transport or by bike. You could traverse Den Haag fairly easily on foot, but only its tree-lined outskirts are particularly picturesque.

MAURITSHUIS

The **Mauritshuis** (Map p196; ☎ 302 34 56; www .mauritshuis.nl; Korte Vijverberg 8; adult/child €7/3.50; ☺ 10am-5pm Tue-Sat, 11am-5pm Sun) is a small but grand museum. It houses Dutch and Flemish masterpieces, including several of the most famous Vermeers, and a touch of the contemporary with Andy Warhol's Queen Beatrix.

The building was constructed as a mansion in 1640 in classical style; all its dimensions are roughly the same (25m) and the detailing shows exquisite care. In 1822 it was made the home of the royal collection.

The small assortment is displayed in 16 rooms on two floors, but what a collection it is! All killer, no filler – almost every piece is a masterpiece. Rather than slogging along looking for the best stuff, at the Mauritshuis you can see spectacular works in about an hour and then get going. Even if you're just passing Den Haag on the train, it's worth hopping off to visit.

Highlights include *Girl with a Pearl Earring* by Johannes Vermeer and Rembrandt self-portraits at age 20 and 63. Note that some paintings are loaned occasionally.

There are excellent English guides, and if you want even more detail there are audio guides for €2.50. The gift shop is refreshingly low-key; you won't find any Vermeer toilet seats here.

BINNENHOF   Map p196

The parliamentary buildings around the adjoining Binnenhof (Inner Court) have long been the heart of Dutch politics, though parliament now meets in a modern building (1992) on the south side.

The central courtyard looks sterile now but was once used for executions. A highlight of

ZUID HOLLAND & ZEELAND

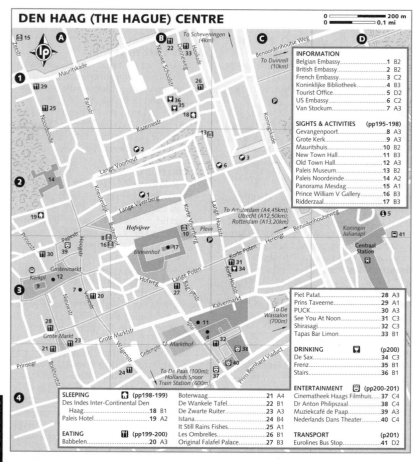

DEN HAAG (THE HAGUE) CENTRE

INFORMATION
Belgian Embassy	1	B2
British Embassy	2	B2
French Embassy	3	C2
Koninklijke Bibliotheek	4	B3
Tourist Office	5	D2
US Embassy	6	C2
Van Stockum	7	A3

SIGHTS & ACTIVITIES (pp195-198)
Gevangenpoort	8	A3
Grote Kerk	9	A3
Mauritshuis	10	B2
New Town Hall	11	B3
Old Town Hall	12	A3
Paleis Museum	13	B2
Paleis Noordeinde	14	A2
Panorama Mesdag	15	A1
Prince William V Gallery	16	B3
Ridderzaal	17	B3

Piet Patat	28	A3
Prins Taveerne	29	A1
PUCK	30	A3
See You At Noon	31	C3
Shirasagi	32	C3
Tapas Bar Limon	33	B1

DRINKING (p200)
De Sax	34	C3
Frenz	35	B1
Stairs	36	B1

ENTERTAINMENT (pp200-201)
Cinematheek Haags Filmhuis	37	C4
Dr Anton Philipszaal	38	C4
Muziekcafé de Paap	39	A3
Nederlands Dans Theater	40	C4

TRANSPORT (p201)
Eurolines Bus Stop	41	D2

SLEEPING (pp198-199)
Des Indes Inter-Continental Den Haag	18	B1
Paleis Hotel	19	A2

EATING (pp199-200)
Babbelen	20	A3
Boterwaag	21	A4
De Wankele Tafel	22	B1
De Zwarte Ruiter	23	A3
Istana	24	B4
It Still Rains Fishes	25	A1
Les Ombrelles	26	B1
Original Falafel Palace	27	B3

the complex is the 13th-century **Ridderzaal** (Knights' Hall). The Gothic dining hall has been carefully restored and you may find yourself wanting to yell, 'More mead!'

The North Wing is still home to the Upper Chamber of the Dutch Parliament, who meet in 17th-century splendour. The Lower Chamber used to meet in the ballroom, in the 19th-century wing. It all looks a bit twee and you can see why the politicians were anxious to decamp to the sleek new extension nearby.

The best way to see the Binnenhof's buildings is by a one-hour tour which leaves from the **visitors centre** (☎ 364 61 44; adult/child €3.50/1.50; ☼ 10am-3.45 Mon-Sat). Here you can see a model showing the hotch-

potch of buildings that comprise the Binnenhof and learn about the turbulent past of the Low Countries, where invaders have flooded in more often than the waters.

After your walk, stroll around the Hofvijver, where the reflections of the Binnenhof and the Mauritshuis have inspired countless snapshots.

DEN HAAG: OLD AND NEW   Map p196
Across the Hofvijver, the **Gevangenpoort** (Prison Gate; ☎ 346 08 61; Buitenhof 33; tour adult/child €3/2; ☼ 11am-4pm Tue-Fri, noon-4pm Sat & Sun) is a surviving remnant of the 13th-century city fortifications. It has hourly tours showing how justice was dispensed back then – needless to say, it hurt. But not for long.

ZUID HOLLAND & ZEELAND

Next door, the **Galerij Prins Willem V** (☎ 362 44 44; Buitenhof 35; adult/child €1.50/1; ❧ 11am-4pm Tue-Sun) was the first public museum in the Netherlands when it opened in 1773. It's been restored to its original appearance and the paintings are hung in the manner popular in the 18th century; not a skerrick of wall is left bare.

The **Grote Kerk** (☎ 302 86 30; Rond de Grote Kerk 12), dating from 1450, has a fine pulpit constructed 100 years later. The neighbouring 1565 **old town hall** is a splendid example of Dutch Renaissance architecture.

The huge **new town hall** (Spui 170) is the hotly debated work by US architect Richard Meier. The 'official' nickname of the building is the 'white swan', but locals prefer the 'ice palace'. Even better are the local nicknames for two government buildings nearby; if allowed, take the elevator to the town hall's 11th floor and look at the complex which has two pointed towers at one end and a dome-topped round tower at the other. The local moniker is 'the tits and penis'.

Names are more polite for the king and queen's official quarters at **Paleis Noordeinde**. The Renaissance formality of the structure bespeaks regal digs. It's not open to the public and the strong gates ensure security should the populace revolt for having their taxes spent on anatomically suggestive buildings.

The **Paleis Museum** (☎ 338 11 20; Lange Voorhout; admission €5; ❧ 11am-5pm Tue-Sun) is on a beautiful avenue. The 18th-century shack was the home of Queen Emma, great-grandmother of Queen Beatrix. Now its elegant interior is used for art exhibitions. Opening times and admission prices vary depending on the exhibition that's on.

GEMEENTEMUSEUM

Admirers of De Stijl, and in particular of Piet Mondriaan, mustn't miss the Berlage-designed **Gemeentemuseum** (Municipal Museum; Map p194; ☎ 338 11 20; Stadhouderslaan 41; adult/concession/child under 18 €7.50/5/free; ❧ 11am-5pm Tue-Sat). It houses a large collection of works by neoplasticist artists and others from the late 19th century, as well as extensive exhibits of applied arts, costumes and musical instruments.

Mondriaan's unfinished *Victory Boogie Woogie* takes pride of place (it should; the museum paid €30 million for it) and

there are also a few Picassos and other works by some of the better-known names of the 20th century. A great repository on par with many others of similar size in the country, it's also home to a fabulous **Photography Museum**.

The adjoining **Museon** (Map p194; ☎ 338 13 38; adult/concession/child under 18 €7.50/5/free; ❧ 11am-5pm Tue-Sat) explores the world and its people for school kids.

PANORAMA MESDAG

Just past the north end of Noordeinde is another art exhibit, the **Panorama Mesdag** (Map p196; ☎ 364 45 44; www.panorama-mesdag.nl; Zeestraat 65; adult/child €4/2; ❧ Mon-Sat 10am-5pm, Sun/holidays noon-5pm). The impressive *Panorama* (1881) is a gigantic, 360-degree painting of Scheveningen viewed from a dune, painted by Hendrik Willem Mesdag (1831–1915).

VREDESPALEIS

The **Vredespaleis** (Peace Palace; Map p194; ☎ 302 41 37; Carnegieplein 2; ❧ 10am-4pm Mon-Fri; tour adult/child €2.50/1.50) houses the UN's International Court of Justice. The grand building was donated by American steel maker Andrew Carnegie for use by the International Court of Arbitration, an early international body whose goal was the prevention of war. Sadly, big buildings and grand names can't accomplish what humans won't and WWI broke out one year after it opened in 1913.

There are hourly guided tours, but if the courts are in session these may be cancelled – check with the tourist office. You need to book ahead (security is strict). Take tram No 7 from CS or tram No 8 from HS.

MADURODAM

Towards Scheveningen, **Madurodam** (Map p194; ☎ 355 39 00; www.madurodam.nl; George Maduroplein 1; adult/child under 11 €11/8; ❧ 9am-8pm) is a miniaturised world containing everything that's quintessentially Netherlands. There are lots of little buildings, people, airplanes and more. But given that much of the real thing lies within an hour of Den Haag, it seems a little odd to seek out this shrunken, sanitised version. Not surprisingly, it's big with children. Look away from the glitz for the memorial by the entrance to learn about the history of Madurodam. It was started by JML Maduro as a memorial to his son who fought the Nazi invasion and later died at Dachau.

Always a little overpriced and slightly tacky, but also, curiously, one of those very Dutch reference points: even most of the locals who decry it as touristy will admit to having been. *Everyone* knows Madurodam.

Take tram No 1 from CS, or tram No 1 or 9 from HS.

SCHEVENINGEN

Scheveningen is an overdeveloped seaside resort north of town making much of its status as 'the most popular beach' in the Netherlands. 'Most popular' translates as 'obscenely crowded' when the temperature manages to crack about 22°C. That said, the Dutch must be praised for the verve and enthusiasm with which they approach their rarefied beaching; the limited window of benign conditions seems inversely proportionate to the pleasure taken. No whining about the heat here, just games of beach volleyball, a smattering of casual nudity and a general good-time vibe fuels that other universal beach activity: ogling.

There's lots of the usual seashore schlock, and a long pier which, in deference to the dubious North Sea weather, was recently glassed over.

You can hurl yourself 60m from the top of a crane at the recently opened **Bungy Jumping Scheveningen** (☎ 345 36 62; www.bungy.nl; Scheveningen Piert; packages from €80; ◷ noon-8pm Thu-Sun May, Jun, Sep & Oct; noon-9pm daily Jul & Aug).

You can escape the mobs by heading north along the beach past the end of the tram line. Here the dunes are more pristine and the further you walk/ride, the greater the rewards. See Getting Around (p201) for transport details between Den Haag and Scheveningen.

DID YOU KNOW?

An oft-repeated story concerns how Dutch resistance fighters during WWII used 'Scheveningen' as a password. It seems that while the Germans could easily learn Dutch, the accent required to properly pronounce 'Scheveningen' was impossible to learn. To this day, in fact, if you claim to be able to speak any Dutch, some native will test you by predictably piping up with a joyfully dubious 'Go on, say "Scheveningen!"' (practice: s'CHay-fuh-ninger).

Tours

The tourist office offers a good bus tour. The two-hour **Royal Tour** (☎ 335 58 15; €26.50; ◷ 1pm Den Haag, 1.20pm Scheveningen, Thu-Sat Apr-Sep) is an overview of the area's highlights, including many listed above. There's also an 'Architecture Tour' using a specialist guide. It departs from the tourist office at CS. Inquire for times, as they flux with demand.

There's a great range of boat tours. Ask at the tourist office or contact **De Ooievaart** (www.ooievaart.nl; €8.50/4.50; ◷ departures 11am-4.45pm), who have four different 1½ routes taking in Den Haag's most interesting sights at canal level.

Festivals & Events

One of the world's most-respected jazz events, the **North Sea Jazz Festival** (☎ 214 89 00; Churchillplein 10) draws some of the best musicians on the planet. It's held the second weekend of July at the vast Nederlands Congresgebouw. Rooms throughout the region are at a premium as thousands of fans descend on the city from all around. You're best off staying elsewhere and commuting, or booking far in advance. A lot of the acts organise smokin' unofficial jams outside the festival dates, a kind of pre-festival mini-festival.

Sleeping

Diplomats and royalty call Den Haag home and you can too, for a price; or Scheveningen has oodles of cheap joints catering to holiday-makers.

CAMPING

There are camp sites in the dunes either side of Scheveningen.

Duinhorst (Map p194; ☎ 324 22 70; www.duinhorst.nl; Buurtweg 135; person/tent €3.75/2.75; ◷ Apr-Sep) The best campground is to the east. Ride bus No 28 from HS or No 29 from CS to the end of the line at Oude Waalsdorperweg and then walk about 1km west, or take a taxi.

HOSTELS

Stayokay Den Haag (☎ 315 78 88; www.stayokay.com /denhaag; Scheepmakerstraat 27; dm from €20) This well-equipped hostel is in a grand, restored building northeast of HS. You'll know the hostel at night from its decorative lights. It's no more than 15 safe-ish minutes on foot (or 5 to 10 on a bike) from all the action the city has to offer.

HOTELS

Hotel Astoria (☎ /fax 384 04 01; Stationsweg 139; s/d €40/50) The hotel has rooms with TV and WC. It's 20m from HS, and looks like it's in a pretty dodgy area. OK, it *is* in a pretty dodgy area. But the staff are knowledgeable and vigilant and you shouldn't lose too much sleep here.

Strandhotel (☎ 354 01 93; www.strandhotel.demon .nl; Zeekant 111 & Gevers Deynootweg 1344 Scheveningen; s/d €37.50/62.50; ⊠ ✕ P) On the beach and right above several bars, the rooms have an unreconstructed 1950s motif which is fun/kitschy if you're into that. Book ahead and watch the weather; prices skyrocket in summer, so get in early if it's a hot spring.

Paleis Hotel (☎ 362 46 21; www.paleishotel.nl; Molenstraat 26; s/d €97.50/110; ✕ P) It has an austere style and great location near Noordeinde. If the sun doesn't shine you can get a tan in the solarium. The well-equipped rooms are on the pricey side for what they are, but very comfortable.

Des Indes Inter-Continental Den Haag (☎ 363 29 32; Lange Voorhout 54-56; r from €145; ⌨ ✕ P) Visiting heads-of-state, fire your PA if you're not booked into this sumptuous hotel. Originally built for the Baron Van Brienen in 1858, mincers on the Internet suggest some of its glory has faded in recent years. We think its rooms are still positively sybaritic.

Steigenberger Kurhaus Hotel (☎ 416 26 36; www.kurhaus.nl; Gevers Deynootplein 30; r €215-660; ⊠ ⌨ ✕ P) At the top end of things and right on the beach. First built in 1885, this elegant building has been extended and restored several times. The noted thermal baths are there still, amongst a plethora of luxuries including a casino.

Eating

Den Haag's gastronomic scene is fairly central and very good, with quality matched by variety. The cobbled streets off Denneweg are one of the livelier areas. Plan on dining before 9pm or you'll find closed kitchens and slumbering waiters.

There's no shortage of fast-food places in Scheveningen with little to differentiate them – these tend to stay open until people stop spending money, so a lot depends on the weather.

CAFÉS

De Zwarte Ruiter (The Black Rider; Map p196; ☎ 364 95 49; www.september.nl, in Dutch; Grote Markt 27; ☺ lunch & dinner Mon-Sat) The Rider's dark 'postmodern– Art Deco' design encompasses a mezzanine and enviable terrace. The beer list is great without being specialist, and the lunch specials are fine (tasty *paninis* for under €5). A classic café, hip bar and casual meeting point simultaneously, the crowd is eclectic. Music approaches the ambient DJ end of things, but certainly won't alienate those who can remember when drummers had arms.

Boterwaag (Map p196; ☎ 365 96 86; www.september .nl, in Dutch ; Grote Markt 8a; ☺ lunch & dinner Mon-Sat) A restored 17th-century building where butter was once weighed, Boterwaag has high ceilings and large windows, making for an untypically airy and classy café atmosphere. With a superior list of beers and cheap lunches (from €4), it's chilled, and a great place to linger over drinks. Though it's huge, the private nooks and corners of the mostly original brickwork make it a great choice for a slightly more intimate setting.

Prins Taveerne (Map p196; ☎ 364 38 75; Noordeinde 165; lunch €3-5; ☺ lunch & dinner) It straddles the line between café and bar, but it does have good lunch salads and sandwiches. It's a classic place with leaded-glass windows and a prime corner location. A laid-back foil to the toff-y air this side of town.

See You At Noon (Map p196; ☎ 413 790 26; Korte Houtstraat 14; paninis €4-7; ☺ lunch Mon-Sat) A simple new place that does great value, healthy *panini* sandwiches (toasted or not) and good coffee. A pleasant place for a quick bite, it's spotlessly clean, with minimalist red, white and black decor. Amanda and Leon (who run the place) are lovely folk who'll spare time for a chat if it isn't busy.

QUICK EATS

Original Falafel Palace (Map p196; ☎ 427 72 20; Lange Poten 7; falafel sandwich €3) Sparkling and friendly. Buy the namesake sandwich and peruse the self-serve bar of fillings.

Piet Patat (☎ 364 80 19; Grote Markt 3) Some of the best frites in town (less than €2).

RESTAURANTS
Budget

Istana (Map p196; ☎ 360 09 97; Wagenstraat 71-73; lunch under €5; ☺ lunch) For super cheap, authentic and delicious Indonesian food, look no further than this bargain winner with a lunch deal that's not advertised anywhere except on the signs out front. Unmatched value for delicious food.

De Wankele Tafel (The Wobbly Table; Map p196; ☎ 364 32 67; Mauritskade 79; 3-course menu €8-10; ✍ dinner Mon-Sat) A homey little vegetarian haunt with filling three-course meals that clean out the fruit and veg section of the market – and at great prices, too.

Tapas Bar Limon (Map p196; ☎ 356 14 65; Denneweg 59A; tapas €4-6, mains €10-15; ✍ dinner) This place has tiled floors, wooden tables and pitchers of sangria. Delicious, authentic Spanish tapas make a wonderful meal/break from browsing the interesting shops nearby.

Babbelen (Map p196; ☎ 362 24 31; fax 392 53 53; Kettingstraat 1B; mains €11; ✍ lunch & dinner) Usually brimming with satisfied locals, Babbelen's food is delicious, service warm, portions enormous, and its cosy dining rooms spread over two compact floors are cheerily inviting. 'Devil's Chicken' – a fiery Malay curry – is one of several brilliant mains. A real treat, with no scrimping on quality.

Mid-Range

Les Ombrelles (The Umbrellas; Map p196; ☎ 365 87 89; Hooistraat 4A; mains €20-30; ✍ dinner) This is as elegant as the fish is fresh. The service is very professional, there's an extensive wine list and the specials are brill and monkfish. It's a great seafood choice, especially if you're after a refined ambience to dine in.

It Still Rains Fishes (Map p196; ☎ 365 25 98; Noordeinde 123; mains €20-27; ✍ dinner) This is another top seafood place, with a delightfully bizarre name. And your taste buds will rain joy after sampling their catch: grilled, fried, poached, mussels, scallops, fish – they're all sensational options. Oozing quality on every level – but never feeling exclusive – this multi-award-winning restaurant is a perfect place to land yourself a memorable meal.

Top End

Dunne Bierkade (Map p194) has been signposted by the *gemeente* (municipality) as Den Haag's *avenue culinaire* and with good reason: there are excellent restaurants and bars on it, too many to list. It's 'established' and 'top end' and almost any place you choose will be a good dining experience. You'll be looking at more than €20 per person.

PUCK (Pure Unique Californian Kitchen; Map p196; ☎ 427 76 49; www.puckfoodandwines.nl; Prinsestraat 33; mains from €20; ✍ lunch & dinner Tue-Sat) A brash eatery for lovers of innovation, with the coolest, most outrageous menu in the Netherlands. Traditionalists who can't imagine lamb without mint sauce, look away… 'Spicy cilantro bouillabaise over giant saffron couscous' is typical of the fusion boldness on display. PUCK also does 'bites' – sample-sized portions (€2.50 to €8), matched to one of its more than 50 wines. Daring dining for fearless foodies.

Shirasagi (Map p196; ☎ 346 47 00; www.shirasagi.nl; Spui 170; noodle soups/lunch special €12/23; ✍ lunch & dinner Tue-Fri, dinner Sat-Mon) An amazing Japanese restaurant worthy of any stately high-flyer, but with a few options accessible to us rank and file folk. Traditional menus are stunning, beautifully presented arrangements of the finest ingredients (starting from €29.50) with many favourites you'll recognise – and plenty of elite items you won't – on the extensive list. The *yakimono* (grills) are delicious.

Drinking

De Paas (Map p194; ☎ 392 00 02; Dunne Bierkade 16A) The best beer café in town. It's brown and moody with candles on the tables and over 150 beers available, on the 'officially designated' dining street in Den Haag. A friendly yet quiet place with imbibers pondering their brews.

De Sax (Map p196; ☎ 346 67 55; Korte Houtstraat 14A) This little jazz bar feels like cold beer tastes on a sizzling hot day (chiiiiiilllled) and is just off the Plein. It has a good vibe, not the least of which is due to the cool music oozing from the sound system. Very dark, very cosy, very friendly.

Frenz (Map p196; ☎ 363 66 57; Kazernestraat 106) Look for the big rainbow flag flying out the front at this friendly gay bar that's open until late.

Stairs (Map p196; ☎ 364 81 91; Nieuwe Schoolstraat 39) Near a tiny canal, this is another gathering place for Den Haag's gays and lesbians.

Entertainment

Diplomats go to bed early and so does the rest of the town. Amsterdam isn't far away though, and those looking for late-night action can catch one of the trains that run all night.

MUSIC
Muziekcafé de Paap (Map p196; ☎ 365 20 02; www.depaap.nl; Papestraat 32) Den Haag's best place for live music, and just a great, versatile nightspot. It's atmospheric, has a fab restaurant and bar where you can kick off early, and the carryings-on once you pop next door into the Muziekcafé continue well into the wee hours. A young-ish, cool crowd, but really geared to anyone who's into music. Like, everyone. Admission and opening hours vary with programme.

DANCE
Nederlands Dans Theater (Map p196; ☎ 360 49 30, reservations ☎ 360 38 73; www.ndt.nl; box office 10am-6pm) This dance company has gained worldwide fame since its formation in 1959 by a group of dancers frustrated by the ossified creativity of the old Ballet of the Netherlands company. Today the Nederlands Dans Theater comprises three companies: NDT1, the main troupe of 32 dancers; NDT2, a small group of 12 dancers under 21; and NDT3, a group of dancers over age 40 who perform more dramatic works. Performances are at the **Lucent Dance Theatre** (Spui 152) which has a 1000-seat main hall under a rippling roof and several smaller venues. It's widely thought to be the largest dance-only venue in the world. With three companies, tickets aren't impossible to come by.

OTHER ENTERTAINMENT
Dr Anton Philipszaal (Map p196; ☎ 360 98 10; Spui 150) Near the Lucent Dance Theatre, this is home to the Residentie Orkest, Den Haag's very own local classical symphony orchestra.

Cinematheek Haags Filmhuis (Map p196; ☎ 345 99 00; Spui 191) Screens foreign and art movies.

Shopping
There are several good streets for galleries, antiques and interesting boutiques; try Denneweg, Noordeinde – which also has some great restaurants and bars – and Molenstraat.

Getting There & Away
TRAIN
Den Haag has two main train stations, causing endless confusion. CS, a terminus, is close to the centre. It has the usual services and is a hub for local trams and buses.

HS is about 1km south of the centre and is on the main railway line between Amsterdam and Rotterdam and the south. Thalys high-speed trains to/from Paris stop here as do many other through-services. HS also has all the usual services.

Don't worry too much which station your train will stop at – only pokey locals serve both – as both stations have numerous tram and bus links.

Some sample train services, good for both CS and HS, are:

Destination	Price (€)	Duration (min)	Frequency (per hr)
Amsterdam	8.50	50	4
Leiden	2.50	13	4
Rotterdam	3.50	22	4
Utrecht	8.50	40	4

BUS
Eurolines long-distance buses stop on the east side of CS. Regional buses depart from the bus station above the tracks at CS.

Getting Around
For anything out of the centre you may want to use the web of tram and bus services provided by HTM (☎ 384 86 66). Most routes converge on CS, the tram and bus station above the tracks. A number of routes also serve HS, including the jack-of-all-trades tram No 1, which starts in Scheveningen and runs all the way to Delft, passing the centre of Den Haag and CS along the way. A transit map (€1) sold at tourist offices and at the train stations covers the region south to Rotterdam.

Tram Nos 1, 8 and 9 link Scheveningen with Den Haag; the fare is three strips. The last tram runs in either direction at about 1.30am. There is a multiday pass for the region which is a good deal if you plan on using public transport a lot. It costs €5/7.50/10 for one/two/three days. A version which includes all the services south to Delft costs €6/9/12. The passes are available from tourist offices, hotels and HTM kiosks.

Call **ATC Taxi** (☎ 317 88 77) for a cab. You can hail any free taxi, if you can find one.

The **bicycle shop** (☎ 385 32 35) in CS is under the terminal. The **HS counterpart** (☎ 389 08 30) is at the south end of the station. Both rent bikes.

GOUDA

☎ 0182 / pop 71,700

If you think of Gouda and you think of mild cheese, you're not far off the mark. This town's namesake cheese is among the Netherlands' most well-known exports. However, if you think that Gouda cheese is only the gentle stuff on your local supermarket's shelf, you're in for a surprise.

Gouda enjoyed economic success and decline in the same manner as the rest of Holland from the 16th century onwards. Its cheese has brought recent wealth, as has the country's largest candle factory, which stays busy supplying all those Dutch brown cafés. The acclaimed 16th-century stained-glass windows in its church are a highlight.

On any day, Gouda is a quick day trip from any city in Zuid Holland. The compact centre is entirely ringed by canals and is less than five minutes' walk from the station. The large central square, the Markt, is the focus of the town.

Information

Tourist office (☎ 0900-46832888; www.vvvgouda.nl; Markt 27; ⏰ 9am-5pm Mon-Sat year-round, 9am-5pm Sat Apr-Oct, 9am-4pm Sat Nov-Mar, noon-3pm Sun Jun-Aug)

GWK money exchange (⏰ 8am-7.30pm) In the train station.

Post office (☎ 52 21 00; Westhaven 37; ⏰ 7am-5pm Mon-Fri, 7am-1.30pm Sat) South of the Markt.

Sights

Gouda is small, and cute as a button. Most of the notable sights are within 10 minutes walk of the strangely enormous Markt.

THE MARKT

The central Markt is one of the largest such squares in the Netherlands. Right in the middle is the gorgeous mid-15th-century **town hall**. Constructed from shimmering sandstone, this regal Gothic structure bespeaks the wealth that Gouda enjoyed from the cloth trade when it was built. The red-and-white shutters provide a fine counterpoint to the carefully maintained stonework.

On the north side of the Markt, you can't miss the **Waag**, a former cheese-weighing house built in 1668. If you have any doubt about its use, check out the reliefs carved into the side showing the cheese being weighed. It houses the **Kaaswaag** (☎ 52 99 96;

adult/child €2.50/1; ⏰ 1-5pm Tue-Sun Apr-Oct), a museum that follows the history of cheese trade in the Netherlands and especially Gouda.

SINT JANSKERK AND AROUND

Just to the south of the Markt is **Sint Janskerk** (☎ 51 26 84; Achter de Kerk; adult/child €2/1; ⏰ 9am-5pm Mar-Nov, 10am-4pm Dec-Feb, closed Sun). The church

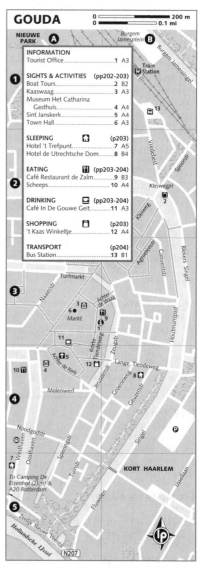

GOUDA   0 —— 200 m / 0 —— 0.1 mi

| INFORMATION | |
| Tourist Office | 1 A3 |

SIGHTS & ACTIVITIES	(pp202-203)
Boat Tours	2 B2
Kaaswaag	3 A3
Museum Het Catharina Gasthuis	4 A4
Sint Janskerk	5 A4
Town Hall	6 A3

SLEEPING 🛏	(p203)
Hotel 't Trefpunt	7 A5
Hotel de Utrechtsche Dom	8 B4

EATING 🍴	(pp203-204)
Café Restaurant de Zalm	9 B3
Scheeps	10 A4

| DRINKING 🍷 | (pp203-204) |
| Café In De Gouwe Geit | 11 A3 |

| SHOPPING 🛍 | (p203) |
| 't Kaas Winkeltje | 12 A4 |

| TRANSPORT | (p204) |
| Bus Station | 13 B1 |

itself had a chequered start: it burned down with ungodly regularity every 100 years or so from 1361 until the mid-16th century when what you see today was finished. As a building, Sint Janskerk is an attractive late-Gothic church in need of a better steeple. But it's in its huge windows that the church is set apart. The greatest of these were created by Dirck Crabeth, his brother Wouter and Lambert van Noort from around 1550 to 1570. Their works, which are numbered, include highlights such as window No 6 (John the Baptist; the folks on either side paid for the window) and No 22 (Jesus purifies the temple; note the look on the face of the money-changer).

To the immediate south of the church, near a small canal, the **Museum Het Catharina Gasthuis** (☎ 58 84 40; Oosthaven 10; adult/child €2.50/1; ✆ 10am-5pm Mon-Sat, noon-5pm Sun) covers Gouda's history and has a few artworks. It is housed in an old hospital.

OTHER ATTRACTIONS

Wandering the streets away from the Markt is rewarding, especially Lange Tiendeweg and Zeugstraat with its tiny canal and even tinier bridges. To prove that Gouda cheese really isn't bland, visit **'t Kaaswinkeltje** (☎ 51 42 69; Lange Tiendeweg 30). This cheese shop is filled with fabulous smells and it's here that you can sample some of the aged Goudas that the Dutch wisely keep for themselves. The older the cheese, the sharper the flavour, and some of the very old Goudas have an almost Parmesan texture and a rich, smoky taste. With a little mustard smeared on, a hunk of this is great with beer.

Tours

In July and August, there are **boat trips** (2 per day, 3hrs, €5.50) through the canals around Gouda to the nearby Reeuwijk lake district. Contact the tourist office.

Festivals & Events

Once upon a time the Gouda **cheese market** was the real thing, as the Waag will attest. But the days when more than 1000 dairymen and cheesemakers would assemble in the Markt for a raucous day of buying, selling and trading are long past. Now it's just hundreds of tour buses that assemble every Thursday morning from June to August for an orgy of buying, selling and very little trading.

A few men dress up in traditional costume and go through the motions for the mobs of tourists, but the event is really more of an excuse for a huge market to be set up offering not just cheese, but wooden shoes, fake Delft pottery etc. Unless you're into this sort of spectacle, you might want to avoid Gouda at these times.

Sleeping

Given that Gouda is such a natural day trip, you might not think of staying here, but you may appreciate its somnolent charms after dark. The tourist office has a list of a few private rooms it will book for a small fee. These rooms usually cost €18 to €25 per person.

Camping De Elzenhof (☎ 52 44 56; Broekweg 6; site from €10) This camp site wouldn't be far from town if you were a crow. Because you have to detour around canals and waterways and because there is no bus, it's a 45-minute haul. Go south from the centre of Gouda, cross the Julianasluis bridge and follow the signs.

Hotel 't Trefpunt (☎ 51 28 79; Westhaven 46; s/d with shared bathroom €40/50) A decent and simple place. Sharing a bathroom isn't the worst thing in the world, and the rooms are quite nice.

Hotel de Utrechtsche Dom (☎ 52 88 33; www.rsnet.nl/hotel; Geuzenstraat 6; r from €59) Neat, clean and on a quiet street. Okay, they're all pretty quiet in Gouda, but you get what we mean. It's a lovely, low-key place to stay with good amenities. There's parking no more than 100m away.

Eating & Drinking

Café In de Gouwe Geit (☎ 5288 85; Achter de Kerk 7a; snacks/light meals €3-5) For Gouda, it positively heaves, but in an inviting 'come one, come all' way. In the shadow (literally) of Sint Janskerk, it's a great place for a swift beer after an hour of craning your neck to appreciate the stained-glass windows. It even has its own little biannual Boules tournament in July, a community favourite, with a first prize of €50.

Café Restaurant de Zalm (☎ 52 53 45; Markt 34; mains up to €16; ✆ lunch & dinner) 'The Salmon' is in an old hotel with big windows looking out onto the enormous Markt. The excellent salads and omelettes are filling, healthy and good-value lunch options (around €6).

At dinner they have Dutch and vegetarian (note the distinction…) main courses.

Scheeps (☎ 51 75 72; www.restaurantscheeps .nl; Westhaven 4; 3-course menu €27, ☺ lunch & dinner) Still considered to be Gouda's best restaurant, Scheeps' popularity prompted a move to larger premises in 2002. You'll find a good choice of fish and local specialties, and vegetarians have not been forgotten. In summer you can dine outside in the lovely garden.

Getting There & Around

Gouda's train station is close to the centre and all you'll need are your feet for local transport. The lockers are in the tunnel under the tracks. Sample fares and schedules are:

Destination	Price (€)	Duration (min)	Frequency (per hr)
Den Haag	4	19	4
Rotterdam	3.50	19	4
Utrecht	4	22	4

For Amsterdam (€8.40) you can take a direct train (one hour), or change in either Utrecht or Den Haag.

The bus station is immediately to the left as you exit the train station on the *Centrum* side. The one bus of interest here is No 180 to Oudewater. See p182 for details.

There are large parking lots for your car or motorcycle on the town's periphery. Gouda is near the A12 motorway between Den Haag and Utrecht and the A20 to Rotterdam.

The **bicycle shop** (☎ 51 97 51) is in the train station.

DELFT

☎ 015 / pop 96,100

Had the potters who lived in Delft long ago not been so accomplished, today's townsfolk would probably live in relative peace. But the distinctive blue-and-white pottery which the 17th-century artisans duplicated from Chinese porcelain became famous worldwide as 'delftware'.

If you're here in summer, the number of day-tripping tourists will probably make you wish you weren't; in winter its old-world charm and narrow, canal-lined streets make a pleasant day trip from Rotterdam or Den Haag.

Delft was founded around 1100 and grew rich from weaving and trade in the 13th and 14th centuries. In the 15th century a canal was dug to the Maas River and the small port there, Delfshaven, was eventually absorbed by Rotterdam.

Beyond china, Delft has a strong association with the Dutch royal family and was the home of Vermeer.

Orientation

The train and neighbouring bus station are a 10-minute stroll south of the central Markt.

Information

Boekhandel Huyser (☎ 212 38 20; Choorstraat 12-14) Good travel section and lots of English-language books.

Rein-Tex Wasserette (☎ 214 54 39; Nieuwe Langendijk 4A; ☺ 10am-7pm Mon-Fri, 10am-6 pm Sat)

Library (☎ 212 34 50; Kruisstraat 71; web access per hr €2; ☺ 10am-7pm Mon-Fri, 10am-3pm Sat) At the corner with Molslaan.

GWK money exchange (☺ 8am-7pm Mon-Fri, 8am-6pm Sat & Sun) At the station. The number of ATMs in Delft is infinitesimal. It's best to use the two ATMs just outside the train station to the left as you exit.

Post office (☎ 212 45 11; Hippolytusbuurt 14; ☺ 9am-5pm Mon-Fri, 10am-1.30pm Sat) A five-minute walk from the train station, and two minutes from the Markt.

Sights & Activities

Best seen on foot, Delft is a beautiful little town, with the only real eyesore being the fake Delftware in every second shop window – ironic in a town where you can actually find the real thing. Almost all the interesting sights lie within a 1km radius of the Markt.

DELFTWARE

Think Delft and you think delftware, the ubiquitous blue-and-white china that is almost a cliché. Given that the process was first developed in China, it's ironic that the mass of fake delftware sold in tourist shops also comes from China. The real stuff is produced in fairly small quantities at four factories in and around Delft. There are three places where you can see the artists working.

The most central and modest outfit is the **Aardewerkatelier de Candelaer** (☎ 213 18 48; Kerkstraat 14; ☺ 9am-5pm Mon-Sat Nov-Feb; 9am-6pm Mon-Sat, 9am-5pm Sun Mar-Oct) just off the Markt. It has five artists, a few of whom work most

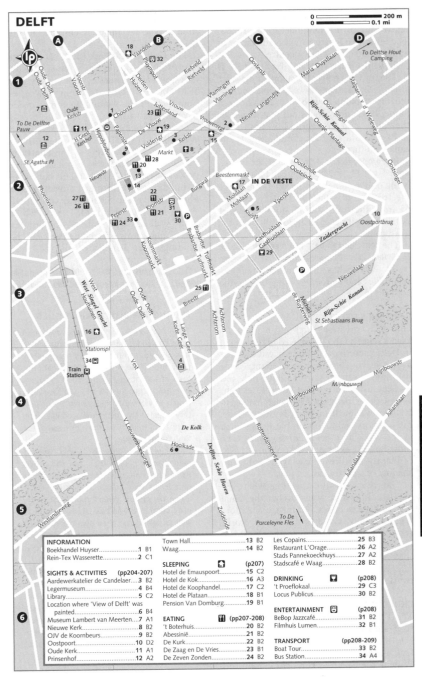

DELFT

0 — 200 m
0 — 0.1 mi

To Delftse Hout Camping

To De Delftse Pauw

St Agatha Pl

IN DE VESTE

Oostpoortbrug

St Sebastiaans Brug

Stationspl

Train Station

De Kolk

Hooikade

To De Porceleyne Fles

ZUID HOLLAND & ZEELAND

days. When it's quiet they'll give you a detailed tour of the manufacturing process. The other two locations are really factories and are outside the town centre.

De Delftse Pauw (The Delft Peacock; ☎ 212 49 20; Delftweg 133; ☉ 9am-4.30pm Mon-Fri year-round, 11am-1pm Sat & Sun Nov-Mar) is the smaller, employing 35 painters who work mainly from home. It has daily tours but you won't see the painters on weekends. Take tram No 1 to Pasgeld, walk up Broekmolenweg to the canal and turn left.

De Porceleyne Fles (☎ 251 20 30; Rotterdamseweg 196; tour €3; ☉ 9.30am-5pm, closed Sun Nov-Mar) is the only original factory operating since the 1650s, and is slick and pricey. Bus No 63 from the train station stops nearby at Jaffalaan, or it's a 25-minute walk from the town centre.

The **Museum Lambert van Meerten** (☎ 260 23 58; Oude Delft 199; adult/child €2/1; ☉ 10am-5pm Tue-Sat, 1-5pm Sun) has a fine collection of porcelain tiles and delftware dating back to the 16th century.

VERMEER'S DELFT

One of the greatest Dutch old masters, **Johannes Vermeer** (1632–75) lived his entire life in Delft, fathering 11 children and dying at age 43, leaving behind a mere 35 incredible paintings. Vermeer's works have rich and meticulous colouring and he captures light as few other painters have ever managed. His scenes come from everyday life in Delft, his interiors capturing simple things such as the *Girl with a Pearl Earring*. Vermeer's most famous exterior work, *View of Delft*, brilliantly captures the play of light and shadow of a partly cloudy day.

You can visit the location where he painted this work – it's across the canal at Hooikade, southeast of the train station. Unfortunately, none of Vermeer's works remain in Delft. The two works above can be seen at the Mauritshuis in Den Haag (p195), while his most famous painting, *The Milkmaid*, spends most of its time in Amsterdam's Rijksmuseum (p108).

CHURCHES

The 14th-century **Nieuwe Kerk** (☎ 212 30 25; Markt; admission €2.50; ☉ 9am-6pm Apr-Oct, 11am-4pm Nov-Mar, closed Sun) houses the crypt of the Dutch royal family and the mausoleum of Willem the Silent. There are exhibitions about the House of Orange and the church. The fee includes entrance to the Oude Kerk.

The Gothic **Oude Kerk** (☎ 212 30 15; Heilige Geestkerkhof; admission €2.50; ☉ 9am-6pm Apr-Oct, 11am-4pm Nov-Mar, closed Sun) looks every one of its 800 years, with its leaning tower 2m from the vertical. Among the tombs inside is Vermeer's.

MUSEUMS

Opposite the Oude Kerk is the **Prinsenhof** (☎ 260 23 58; St Agathaplein 1; adult/child €2.20/1; ☉ 10am-5pm Tue-Sat, 1-5pm Sun). This collection of buildings is a former convent and is where Willem the Silent held court until he was assassinated in 1584. The bullet hole in the wall has been enlarged by visitors' fingers and is now covered by Perspex. The buildings host displays of historical and contemporary art.

The **Legermuseum** (☎ 215 05 00; Korte Geer 1; adult/child €3/2; ☉ 10am-5pm Mon-Fri, noon-5pm Sat & Sun) has

---

MAKING THE BLUE & WHITE GOLD

The alabaster clay used for delftware comes from England. After it is mixed with water, it is poured into moulds and then quickly poured out. The remaining thin coating is fired at a relatively gentle 600°C. Artisans wanted to produce works with corners, which obviously is impossible using pottery wheels – the technique used in Europe until that time – so they borrowed the Chinese technique.

The resulting piece is cleaned up and made smooth; only then can the artists paint their designs. Most people think blue is the only colour used, but there is a rich palette of colours. Individual artists use time-tested – and saleable – designs as well as developing their own designs each year. Once painted and glazed, the piece makes another trip into the oven and is then ready for sale.

Although complex pieces can be costly, simple bowls that still exhibit the qualities of delftware sell for about €10. When in doubt about a piece's authenticity, check the bottom. There should be a number designating which mould was used, the initials of the artist and a two-letter code for the year of manufacture (eg 'AY' designates 2000).

a collection of old Dutch military hardware displayed in a restored 17th-century arsenal. There are also displays on the modern Dutch army, including the controversial and disastrous role played as part of the Bosnian peacekeeping force during the 1990s.

OLD DELFT

Much of the town dates from the 17th century and is remarkably well preserved, and there are some spots where it is possible to get away from the crowds and contemplate this past. Before you flee the crowded Markt, check out the **town hall** with its unusual combination of Renaissance construction surrounding a 13th-century tower and, behind it, the **Waag**, a 1644 weigh house.

East of here, **Beestenmarkt** is a large open space surrounded by fine buildings. Further east, **Oostpoort** is the sole surviving piece of the town's walls. **Koornmarkt**, leading south from the Waag, is a quiet and tree-lined canal.

Tours

One of the best ways to see Delft is by a **boat tour** (☎ 212 63 85; adult/child €4.50/2.50; ⏱ 9.30am-6pm mid-Mar–Oct) on the canals. Boats depart from Koornmarkt 113.

Sleeping
CAMPING

Delftse Hout (☎ 213 00 40; Korftlaan 5; tent site €20; ⏱ year-round) The camping ground is just to the northeast of town. Take bus No 64 from the station.

HOSTELS

There's no real budget/backpacker-type accommodation in Delft, but then Den Haag is only 10 minutes away, and there's a **Stayokay** there (see p198 for details).

HOTELS

Delft has a few decent hotels, some in lovely locations, but in summer they are heavily booked.

Hotel De Emauspoort (☎ 219 02 19; www .emauspoort.nl; Vrouwenregt 9-11; caravan/apt €82.50/92.50) Here you get the added indulgence of waking to the smell of the neighbouring bakery's fresh bread every morning. All 16 rooms in the hotel are lovely and feature typical conveniences. Or you can stay in the restored 'gypsy' caravans (charming 'Pipo de Clown' or 'Mammaloe') parked in the

courtyard. Wonderfully private, these two are as cosy as it gets.

Pension Van Domburg (☎ 212 30 29; Voldersgracht 24; s/d without bathroom €35/40) No-frills but very centrally located. Look for the entrance next to a cigar shop. The basic rooms without bathroom are fairly agreeable.

Hotel de Kok (☎ 212 21 25; www.hoteldekok.nl; Houttuinen 15; s/d/extra bed from €61/71/14; ℗) A simple but very conveniently located place with plenty of parking and very near the train station. Run by lovely affable folk, it has a sweet garden terrace. The diverse breakfast buffet (included) is a great start to the day.

Hotel de Koophandel (☎ 214 23 02; www.hotel dekoophandel.nl; Beestenmarkt 30; s/d/extra bed from €75/90/25; ⏱ reception until 11pm) De Koophandel is a little bland, but spotlessly clean, efficiently run and in a wonderful location on the former livestock-trading marketplace. Readers of Tracy Chevalier's novel *Girl With a Pearl Earring* will, if luckily placed, be able to look out their window and see where passages in the book are set.

Hotel de Plataan (☎ 212 60 46; www.hotelde plataan.nl; Doelenplein 10; s/d/extra bed €82.50/92.50/35) Delft's nicest accommodation is on a delightful square and has a cool café on the ground floor. The breakfast room is downright dignified. Rooms are small but all have bathroom, fridge and cable TV. The friendly staff do their utmost to match Delft's aesthetic charms with appropriate hospitality.

Eating

Horeca, the hospitality industry regulating body in the Netherlands, publishes a brochure called *Hotels, Restaurants, Cafés en Zalen in Delft*, which lists tons of great places to eat. It also lists a few websites (such as www.delftrestaurants.nl) worth checking out. It is available from the tourist office and most retailers in Delft.

CAFÉS

Stadscafé de Waag (☎ 213 03 93; Markt 11; dinner €14.50; ⏱ lunch & dinner Tue-Sat) Centrally located in the old weigh house, right on the Markt square. There's a huge array of light lunches, including *broodjes* and generous-sized snack portions of great aged cheese from nearby Gouda (and further afield). Dinners are super-filling low-countries affairs, and fair value, too. Dark, moody, and in an evocative and obviously very old building.

De Kurk (☎ 214 14 74; Kromstraat 20; daily special €8-10) This classic café has fab local cuisine. This is why they call Delft 'typically Dutch'. *Broodjes*, lots of meaty treats and the ubiquitous potato variations all rear their lovely heads. Get stuffed – and we mean that in the nicest possible way – for great prices and in a setting that will make you feel like you've stepped into a Golden Age painting.

Boterhuis (The Butterhouse; ☎ 213 49 96; Markt 15-17a; snacks €3-5, main meals €14-16) A delightful place with a gorgeous floating terrace out the back, so if the weather's nice, you can enjoy a view of the canal rather than the airy, often garishly commercial Markt.

RESTAURANTS

Stads Pannekoeckhuys (☎ 213 01 93; Oude Delft 113; €3-10; ☺ lunch & dinner) This typical pancake kitchen has 90 kinds of pancakes at good prices. The pea soup, a classic Dutch dish, is also pretty good.

Abessinië (☎ 213 52 60; Kromstraat 21; dish/combo of 4 specials €13/29; ☺ dinner) This Ethiopian place has comfy straw chairs and delicious fare. West African cuisine is very very tasty, with combinations of starchy tubers, meats and pulses combined with spices, sauces and herbs you'll find familiar but may have been unlikely to try in these particular combinations before.

De Zeven Zonden (The Seven Sins; ☎ 215 86 89; Oude Delft 78; mains €15; ☺ dinner) This unique, off-beat restaurant is a cosy place with unexpectedly exotic items – there's a great kangaroo dish, for example, cooked in a provincial French style.

De Zaag en De Vries (☎ 213 70 15; Vrouw Juttenland 17; mains €17; ☺ dinner, closed Mon) Great food in a cheery orange place with a long vegetarian menu. It serves beer and wine, too, and is an excellent herbivorous option. Inventive salads and lovely breads also make appearances. A great place to park your karma.

Les Copains (☎ 214 40 83; Breestraat 8; seafood mains €20-25; ☺ dinner) A delightful little seafood restaurant. The clean, quiet, dining room belies the exciting dishes on the extensive menu. There's a hint of Gallic flamboyance maximising the potential of the great local produce. Try something classically French and fishy like *sole meunière*.

Restaurant L'Orage (☎ 212 36 29; Oude Delft 111B; mains €24; ☺ dinner Tue-Sun) A fine French restaurant with a salubrious interior. All the usual suspects are here: *coq au vin, boeuf bourguignon* and more extravagant and filling mains. The ratatouille is sublime.

Drinking

Locus Publicus (☎ 213 46 32; Brabantse Turfmarkt 67; snacks €3-4) Its more than 200 beers make this one of the best beer cafés in the region, if not the country. It's a friendly place with good music and warm vibes. It's also dark enough to induce eye-strain, so if you can't read the menu, ask the friendly and knowledgeable staff for help. Delft's best watering hole.

Café 't Proeflokaal (☎ 212 49 22; Gashuislaan 36-40; snacks €3-5) Hypothetical astrological situation: you're with a picky Virgo or change-fearing Taurus who just *can't* choose a beer at Locus Publicus. What do you do? Head here, where they have about 100 more beers; that's over 300 to choose from!

Entertainment

The 13,000 students at Delft's technical university ensure that there's no shortage of places to grab a cheap beer and hear some music.

Bebop Jazzcafé (☎ 213 52 10; Kromstraat 33; snacks €4-6) This jazz café is the Platonic ideal. Dark, small, open late with a great selection of beers, moody music and laid-back, unpretentious staff. It's popular with the locals, but not big enough to pack many of them in!

OJV de Koornbeurs (☎ 212 47 42; Voldersgracht 1; admission €3-4; ☺ midnight-4am) An underground dance floor with alternative tunes. Black-clad misanthropes who want to compare piercings and nihilist ideologies will feel comfortable, but anyone's welcome really.

Filmhuis Lumen (☎ 214 02 26; Doelenplein 5; screenings around €5) This cinema screens alternative films.

Getting There & Around

Delft is well served by trains. They include:

Destination	Price (€)	Duration (min)	Frequency (per hr)
Den Haag	2	8	4
Rotterdam	2.80	13	4
Amsterdam	8.50	50	2

Lockers are in the main concourse and there are all the usual amenities.

Alternatively, bus No 129 makes the run to/from Rotterdam every hour along a pretty canal. The ride lasts 30 minutes and takes five strips. Buses depart from the front of the station.

Den Haag is linked to Delft not just by trains but by tram No 1. The not-especially-scenic ride takes 30 minutes and takes five strips.

The **bicycle shop** (☎ 214 30 33) is in the train station.

ROTTERDAM

☎ 010 / pop 600,000

Nearly destroyed during WWII, the Netherlands' second-largest city spent most of the 20th century rebuilding its centre. Although early efforts were in the typically dire style of the 1950s and '60s, more recent projects have given Rotterdam a look that's unique in Europe; by turns vibrant, ugly, impressive, astonishing. Forget the iconic simplicity of the phallic Euromast – a walk along the Nieuwe Maas River is an exploration of modern architecture's variations. Even some of the metro/train stations can make you double-take: Blaak station looks like a miniature Golden Gate Bridge making sweet, sweet love to a flying saucer.

West of the city is Europe's busiest port. Rotterdam's history as a shipping nexus dates back to the 16th century. In 1572, Spaniards being pursued by the rebel Sea Beggars were given shelter in the harbour. They rewarded this generosity by pillaging the town. Needless to say, Rotterdam soon joined the revolution, becoming a major port during the conflict.

Almost 400 years later, Rotterdam found itself, literally, in the wars again. On 14 May 1940 the invading Germans issued an ultimatum to the Dutch: surrender, or Rotterdam (among other cities) would be destroyed. The government capitulated, but the raid was carried out anyway. The historic centre was razed.

Today Rotterdam has a crackling energy that seems to feed off the 'anything goes' attitude for reconstruction. The nightlife is fantastic, a large immigrant community feeds the diversity and there's a cluster of excellent museums – including one of the nation's best (the Museum Boijmans van Beuningen).

Rotterdam is a must on any itinerary for the Netherlands; it's arguably a more

interesting cultural centre than even Amsterdam in some ways, and certainly a more realistic sample of Dutch society than the insidiously charming capital. It's certainly no gentle beauty, but has a dynamic, Berlin-like postmodern-metropolis aesthetic of its own that's not entirely disagreeable.

If you've already seen and loved Amsterdam, it's time to walk on the even wilder side.

Orientation

Rotterdam is split by the Nieuwe Maas, a vast shipping channel. It is crossed by a series of tunnels and bridges, most photogenic of which is the Erasmusbrug (opened in 1996) nicknamed 'The Swan'.

The mostly reconstructed centre is on the north side of the water. Huge new neighbourhoods are rising to the south. From Centraal Station (CS), a 15-minute walk along the canal-like ponds (they don't 'flow') leads to the waterfront. The commercial centre is to the east, and most of the museums to the west. The historic neighbourhood of Delfshaven is a further 3km west.

It's difficult to get lost in Rotterdam, mostly because so many of the buildings are such distinctive, memorable landmarks. Give the loony edifices weird nicknames as you pass them for the first time, then revel in how easy it is to find your way home.

Information
BOOKSHOPS
Donner (☎ 413 20 70; Lijnbaan 150) A large, multistorey bookseller.

EMERGENCY
For all emergencies, dial ☎ 112. To report crimes to the police after the event, call ☎ 247 991.

INTERNET ACCESS
EasyInternetcafé (www.easyeverything.com/map/rot; Stadhuisplein 16-18; per hr €1-2; ☻ 11am-8pm Mon, 9.30am-8pm Tue-Thu & Sat, 9.30am-9pm Fri, noon-8pm Sun) Around the corner from the main tourist office.

LAUNDRY
Self Service West (☎ 425 93 74; Nieuwe Binnenweg 251; around €4-6; ☻ 9am-9pm)

LIBRARY
Library (☎ 281 62 62; Hoogstraat 110; web access per hr €2; ☻ 10am-9pm Mon-Fri, 10am-5pm Sat, 1-5pm Sun) A

ROTTERDAM

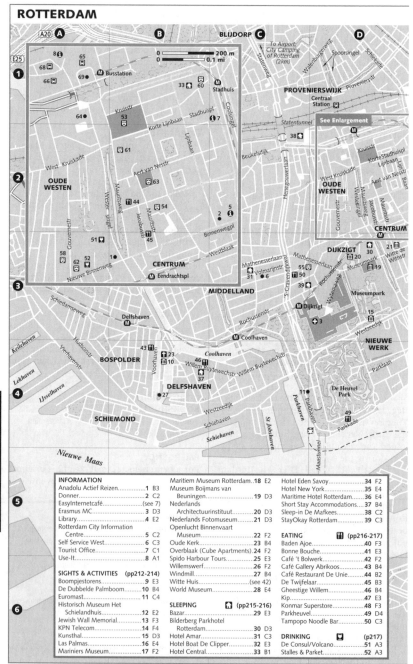

0 ——— 500 m
0 ——— 0.3 mi

RUBROEK
Goudse Rijweg
Admiraal de Ruyterweg
Bozzemweg
Hofplein
Goudse Singel
Oostpl
34
Hoogstr
Gelderse kade
Blaak
24
Haringvliet
Beurs
22
Boompjes
Maasboulevard
17 42
Blaak
12
Churchillpl
18
Oude
Haven
Willemsspoortunnel
26
To Locus
Publicus
(500m)
Wittenbrug
WATERSTAD
32
Schiedamsedijk
Leuvehaven
Boompjes
Scheepmakershaven
29
Leuvehaven
Maaskade
9
Nieuwe Maas
NOORDER
EILAND
Prins Hendrikkade
Koninginnehoofd
Handelspl
56
25
48 40
13
Vasteland
Stieltjesstr
41
47
Erasmusbrug
Levie Vorststr
36
28
Willemskade
Wilhelminapl
14
59
Posthumalaan
Veerhaven
67
Laan op Zuid
Wilhelminakade
35
16
Rijn Haven
Rijnhaven
KATENDRECHT
Maashaven N Z
Hillelaan
Dordtse-Laan

ENTERTAINMENT 🎭 (pp217-218)
De Doelen.......................53 B1
De Regenboog..................54 B2
Desire.............................55 C3
Gay Palace.......................56 E3
Jazz Café Dizzy's...............57 C3
Lantaren/Venster...............58 A3
Luxor Theater....................59 F4
Off Corso.........................60 B1
Pathé Cinemas...................61 B2
Rotown............................62 A3
Schouwburg......................63 B2

TRANSPORT (pp219-220)
Avis.................................64 A1
Bus Station........................65 A1
Eurolines Office..................66 A1
Fast Ferry to Dordrecht........67 E4
Long-Distance Bus Stops.......68 A1
RET Information Office...........69 A1
Tram Station.....................(see 65)

destination in itself, with a café, an indoor life-sized chess board and Internet access.

MEDICAL SERVICES
Erasmus MC (☎ 463 92 22; Dr Molenwaterplein 40) Formerly known as Dijkzigt, this is a major teaching hospital. It's also a big, very visible white landmark by which to orient yourself, especially for the Museumplein and sites nearby. The hospital's reception/lobby is also home to the few public phones in the city that don't have a block on the 0800 toll-free numbers of many international phonecards. Heh, heh.

MONEY
GWK money exchange (⏰ 7am-9pm) In CS. There are ATMs everywhere, including right outside the station.

POST
Post office (☎ 233 02 55; Coolsingel 42; ⏰ 9am-6pm Mon-Wed & Fri, 9am-8.30 Thu, 9.30-3pm Sat) Housed in a glorious building that survived the war.

TOURIST INFORMATION
Tourist office (☎ 0900-4034065; vvvrotterdam@anwb .nl; Coolsingel 67; ⏰ 9am-6pm Mon-Fri, 9am-5pm Sat & Sun) Five minutes from CS and sharing a large facility with the ANWB (p306). It sells theatre and concert tickets and organises city tours (see Tours, p214). The city also has its own website (www.rotterdam.nl). There is a branch, focusing more closely on the city's architecture, at the **Netherlands Architecture Institute** (☎ 440 12 00; Museumpark 25; ⏰ 10am-5pm Tue-Sat, 11am-5pm Sun & holidays).

Use-It (☎ 240 91 58; www.use-it.nl; Conradstraat 2; ⏰ 9am-6pm Tue-Sun mid-May–mid-Sep, 9am-5pm Tue-Sat mid-Sep–mid-May) This excellent tourist information alternative – also city-financed – is aimed at young travellers, but the enthusiastic staff will help anyone 'young at heart'. It's a great place to stop (they know *everyone* who works in the hospitality or tourism industry in town) and if you book your accommodation through them, you'll probably score a discount. Use-It publish a free annual pocket-sized guide to Rotterdam sights and attractions, the brilliant *Simply The Best*. It's riddled with advertising, but it's very portable. Because it's written by style- and trend-conscious Rotterdammers, it's most useful for its nightlife and eating listings.

TRAVEL AGENCIES
Anadolu Actief Reizen (☎ 436 26 00; Nieuwe Binnenweg 1) For cheap tickets worldwide.

Dangers & Annoyances

Note that the area about 1km west of CS is the scene of many hard drug deals and accompanying dubious behaviour. In general, try not to be alone and scared-looking around CS late at night.

Bike theft, as in any Dutch city with a significant junkie population, is rampant.

Sights & Activities

Rotterdam is easy to navigate, with so many memorable, if not downright weird-looking, buildings to landmark yourself by. The centre is also a lot smaller than it seems for such a bustling metropolis – you might never need to use the efficient public transport. The best way to see it is by bike, though be alert – both bike theft and car use are higher in Rotterdam than in cities of similar size. As you might expect, many galleries are concentrated around Museumpark.

MUSEUM BOIJMANS VAN BEUNINGEN

Recently expanded, the **Museum Boijmans van Beuningen** (☎ 441 94 00; www.boijmans.rotterdam.nl; Museumpark 18-20; adult/child under 18 €7/free; ☺ 10am-5pm Tue-Sat, 11am-5pm Sun & holidays) is Rotterdam's wonderful art museum, and one of the best in the Netherlands, if not Europe. If you're an art buff at all, it's reason enough to visit Rotterdam. The sheer breadth of the museum's collection plus it's ambitious roster of temporary exhibits make it a must-see.

The collection spans all eras of Dutch and European art and includes superb Old Masters. Among the highlights: *The Marriage at Cana* by Hieronymus Bosch, the *Three Maries at the Open Sepulchre* by Van Eyck, the minutely detailed *Tower of Babel* by Pieter Bruegel the Elder, and *Portrait of Titus* and *Man in a Red Cap* by Rembrandt. Renaissance Italy is well represented; look for *The Wise and Foolish Virgins* by Tintoretto and *Satyr and Nymph* by Titian.

Paintings and sculpture since the mid-19th century are another strength. There are many Monets and other French impressionists, Van Gogh and his pal Gauguin are given space, and there are statues by Degas. The museum rightly prides itself on its collection by a group it calls 'the other surrealists'; creators like the original multimedia weirdo Marcel Duchamp, visual pun master René Magritte, and the first truly experimental photographer, Man Ray. Salvador Dali

gained a special room in the recent expansion and the collection is one of the largest of his work outside Spain and France.

Even the traditional 'museum floor plan' is abetted by an innovation the curators call 'The Data Cloud', a 3D interactive multimedia map on the entrance floor that is a brilliant work of design in itself, allowing visitors to find the location of and information about any item in the museum's 120,000 piece collection 'instantly' via a 'holographic projection portal'.

There's even a good café for resting between masterpieces, a pleasant sculpture garden (featuring Claes Oldenburg's famous *Bent Screw* among others), a library with more than 125,000 reference books and wheelchair access/assistance throughout. On one of Rotterdam's numerous grey days, the Museum Boijmans van Beuningen can easily fill many hours.

You can get there with the No 5 tram, the metro (station: Eendrachtsplein) or in 15 minutes on foot from Rotterdam CS.

KUNSTHAL

At the south end of Museum Park, the **Kunsthal** (☎ 440 03 00; www.kunsthal.nl; Westzeedijk 341; adult/child under 18/under 12/under 6 €7.50/4.50/1/free; ☺ 10am-5pm Tue-Sat, 11am-5pm Sun & holidays) hosts temporary exhibitions. The building is a sight itself, angling up the hill between the park and the dyke. The staff can be a little artsy-surly, but it's worth putting up with them to see one of the 20 or so exhibitions that visit this fab exhibition space each year.

EUROMAST

Sticking 185m into the Rotterdam sky, the **Euromast** (☎ 436 48 11; www.euromast.com; Parkhaven 20; adult/child €7/4.50; ☺ 10am-10.30pm Jul & Aug, 10am-7pm Apr-Jun & Sep, 10am-5pm Oct-Mar) is one of the less successful – yet most recognisable – examples of modern architecture in the city. But if the sky is clear, you can go to the top and see great views of the city that *don't* include it.

To help attract visitors a few years back, the operators opted for a *faux* space-flight scenario to get you to the very top; originally 100 metres high, the 'space ride' tacked on the extra 85m. The tower is in Heuvel Park, immediately southwest of Museum Park.

Closed for renovations during the 2003/2004 winter, the wonder-pole is due to re-open to the public in April 2004, re-vitalised by its transition into the hands of new owners (the Hotel New York). They've gone all out; the Euromast's already famous Panorama Restaurant has now been gussied up by hot-shot architect/designer Jan des Bouvrie, co-designer of the Maaskant.

MARITIME ROTTERDAM
Maritiem Museum Rotterdam (☎ 413 26 80; www.maritiemmuseum.nl; Leuvehaven 1; adult/child 4-16 €5/3; ☼ 10am-5pm Tue-Sat, 11am-5pm Sun & holidays year-round; 10am-5pm Mon Jul & Aug) is a comprehensive museum that looks at the Netherlands' rich maritime traditions. There's the usual array of models that any youngster would love to take into the tub, plus more interesting and explanatory displays.

The **Oude Haven** area, near the Blaak train, metro and tram station, preserves bits of the oldest part of the harbour, some of which

date from the 14th century. It's a decent place for a stroll, especially if you take time to look at the large collection of historic boats.

The **Openlucht Binnenvaart Museum** (☎ 411 88 67; Koningsdam 1; admission free; ☼ 8am-8pm) has a collection of historic inland waterway boats that fills much of the basin. You can see the ongoing restoration and stroll around looking at the boats even outside the official opening hours.

Just around the corner, the small **Mariniers Museum** (☎ 412 96 00; Wijnhaven 7-9; adult/child €3/1.50) has a collection on the lives of those who served in the Dutch navy.

DELFSHAVEN
One of the oldest surviving districts, Delfshaven was once the official seaport for the city of Delft. A reconstructed 18th-century **windmill** overlooks the water at Voorhaven 210. One of the area's claims to fame is that

---

ROTTERDAM ARCHITECTURE

Architects and architecture buffs will thrill not just to the many stunning buildings lining Rotterdam's streets, but also to the many local educational resources.

A brief tour can begin at the north end of the **Erasmusbrug** (1996), near the Leuvehaven metro station. Ben van Berkel designed the 800m-long Erasmus bridge with its graceful supports. Walk part of the way across and you'll see the **KPN Telecom** building (2000). It's hard to miss given that it looks like it's about to fall over but for a long pole giving it support. It's the work of Renzo Piano who also did the Pompidou Centre in Paris. Retrace your steps and walk northeast alongside the water on Boompjes. You'll see the three **Boompjestorens** (1988), which are apartment blocks. Continue along the water until you see the striking **Willemswerf** (1988), the headquarters of the huge Nedlloyd shipping company. Note the dramatic lines casting shadows on its sleek, white surface.

Another 100m will bring you to Rotterdam's other signature bridge, the **Willemsbrug** (1981), which makes a bold statement with its red pylons. Turn north at Oude Haven on Geldersekade. The regal 12-storey building on the corner is the **Witte Huis** (White House; 1897), a rare survivor of the pre-war period, giving an idea of the wealth Rotterdam achieved thanks to the shipping industry.

Walk north for about three minutes to Blaak and the metro station of the same name. Here the last stop is the surprising **Overblaak** (1978–84), to your right, marked by the cube-shaped apartments and pencil-shaped tower. Designed by Piet Blom, the project has graced a thousand postcards. One unit, No 70, is open for **tours** (☎ 414 22 85; adult/child under 12 €1.75/1.25; ☼ 11am-5pm, closed Mon-Thu Jan & Feb).

The **Nederlands Architectuur Instituut** (☎ 440 12 00; Museumpark 25; adult/child under 16 €5/3; ☼ 10am-5pm Tue-Sat, 11am-5pm Sun & holidays) is fittingly in an architecturally stunning building. One side is surrounded by a reflecting moat, while another comprises a sweeping flow of brick along Rochussenstraat. The institute stages a series of ambitious special exhibitions through the year in its cavernous public spaces. There is a good café with seats outside, and a large library.

The tourist office in association with the Nederlands Architectuur Instituut offers **architecture tours** of the city. For information, call the NAI or visit one of the tourist offices, including the one in the institute. The schedules vary by season and the costs depend on the tour.

Rotterdam City Information Centre (☎ 489 77 77; Coolsingel 197; ☼ 1-5.30pm Mon, 9am-5.30pm Tue-Fri, 11am-6pm Sat) has vast amounts of information – much in English – about the city's architecture and its urban planning.

it was where the Pilgrims left Holland for America aboard the *Speedwell*. They could barely keep the leaky boat afloat and eventually transferred to the *Mayflower*, and the rest is history (see boxed text, p189). The **Oude Kerk** on Voorhaven is where the Pilgrims prayed for the last time before leaving on 22 July 1620.

Just south, **De Dubbele Palmboom** (☎ 476 15 33; Voorhaven 12; adult/child €3/1.50; ✆ 10am-5pm Tue-Sat, 11am-5pm Sun & holidays) is a history museum housing an excellent collection of items relating to Rotterdam's history as a port. Displays are spread throughout the 1826 warehouse and many have a sociological bent.

Delfshaven is easily reached from the metro stop of the same name by walking 1km west from De Heuvel Park or by taking tram No 4, 6 or 9.

OTHER SIGHTS

The city's history is preserved at one of the few surviving 17th-century buildings in the centre at the **Historisch Museum Het Schielandhuis** (☎ 217 67 67; Korte Hoogstraat 31; adult/child €3/ 1.50; ✆ 10am-5pm Tue-Sat, 11am-5pm Sun & holidays). Exhibits focus on items from everyday life through the ages, such as the (purportedly) oldest surviving wooden shoe.

The **Nederlands Fotomuseum** (☎ 213 2011; www.nederlandsfotomuseum.nl; Witte de Withstraat 63; adult/child €2.30/1.60; ✆ Tue-Sun 11am-5pm) is a fabulous little photo museum which has a small exhibition space, but is really an archive, resource and information centre for photographers. The museum will stay in the Witte de Withstraat in 2004 but is moving to the Las Palmas building in 2005. Its activities were recently bolstered by a bequest from one H Weertheim, who wanted to 'further the interests of photography in the Netherlands'. His posthumous generosity is your gain.

Nearby, the **Wereldmuseum** (World Museum; ☎ 270 71 72; www.wereldmuseum.rotterdam.nl; Willemskade 25; adult/child €6/3; ✆ 10am-5pm Tue-Sat) is dedicated to providing a user-friendly repository of multiculturalism for people of all ages to use to better understand each other. Wonderfully apt that it's in a polyglot port like Rotterdam. The building is dominated by a huge sculpture of a stylised woman by artist Nikki de Saint Phalle. Enter through the statue's legs.

On the south side of the Koningshaven, in the middle of an old dock district being reborn as a trendy neighbourhood, there is a solemn reminder of the recent past. A fragment of a **wall** that once surrounded a warehouse on the spot has been preserved. The site was the departure point for Jews being sent first to Westerbork and then on to concentration camps during WWII (see p259 for more detail).

Tours

There are harbour tours offered daily, year-round, by **Spido** (☎ 275 99 88; Leuvehoofd; adult/child €7/4.50; ✆ 9.30am-5pm Jun-Sep; 11am-3.30pm Oct; 11am-2pm Thu-Sun Nov-Mar; 75 min every 45min). Departures are from the pier at Leuvehoofd near the Erasmusbrug and the Leuvehaven metro stop. Longer trips are possible in the high season.

A special tour departs at 10.30am on Tuesdays (€20/15) for a nearly seven-hour trip to the final bit of the Delta Project which protects the Nieuwe Waterweg.

Festivals & Events

Rotterdam has countless multicultural, arts and seasonal festivals. Some of the cooler ones include:

JUNE

De Parade A nationwide inverse-circus tour, where the audiences are in the ring and all manner of music, theatre, film and variety performances go on around them. It hits all the big cities and has an incredibly lively atmosphere. Entry's usually free, performances are on a pay per view basis.

JULY

Zomer Carnaval (Summer Carnival; ☎ 414 17 72) Usually held the last weekend of July. It is a carnival-like bash with music, parades, dancing and parties.

Zomerpodium (Summer Stage) Starting toward the end of July and running into August, Zomerpodium has become an entity unto itself, featuring all manner of outlandish excuses to Get Your Freak On in the hot streets of Rotterdam. There's been a Bollywood Ball, brass band contests, stand-up comedy and more. Pleinbioscoop (see Cinema, p218) is part of the Zomerpodium programme too.

AUGUST

FFWD Dance Parade (☎ 433 13 00) Turns the centre into one big open-air club with areas for techno, hip-hop, big beat etc. Floats on the back of trucks drive through town, and everyone waves their set in the air like they just don't care. By big, we mean 350,000 people turned up in 2003, despite the 35°C heat.

Wereld Havendagen (World Harbour Festival; ☎ 403 40 65) Celebrates the role of the harbour, which directly or indirectly employs over 300,000 people. There are lots of open houses, ship tours and fireworks.

Sleeping

The tourist office will make room reservations for €3. **Use-It** (see Information, p211) will do the same and they have negotiated several cheap deals with hotels during slow periods, so it's worth checking with them in the low season.

BUDGET

City Camping of Rotterdam (☎ 415 34 40; Kanaalweg 84; person/tent €4.70/3.70, 2-person cabins €27.70) Open all year and has a laundry. It's a 20-minute walk northwest from CS or take bus No 33 in the direction 'Airport'.

Sleep-in De Mafkees (☎ 240 91 58; www.sleep -in.nl; Schaatsbaan 41-45; dm €10) A friendly, cheap winner just two minutes from Rotterdam CS. The area's not the greatest, but it has an atmospheric bar, a free movie every night and a 'honeymoon suite' you can claim if you can prove that you are very much in love! There's a short lock-out for cleaning.

Short Stay Accommodations (☎ 295 35 62; ssa hostel@yahoo.com; Willem Buytewechstraat 206c; dm/d €13/15; ☾ 6am-11pm; ✗) This fantastic budget apartment set-up spans three floors with a couple of different sharing options. The owners are great and the place clean, with laundry facilities and linen included. Breakfast is €4. It's one of the places Use-It books fee-free. It's also in a quieter area (Delfshaven) and close to the best sights either by foot or metro. Offering one of the best-value doubles around, it's highly recommended.

Stayokay Rotterdam (☎ 436 57 63; www.stayokay .com/rotterdam; Rochussenstraat 107-109; dm from €20; ☾ reception until 1am) Stayokay Rotterdam is well located for the museums, spotlessly clean, offers bike hire, has wonderful gals running reception, a friendly cat, and a low-key bar that can get quickly and amusingly out of hand, depending on which young loudmouth pours the drinks... It's a 10-minute walk from CS and close to the Dijkzigt metro stop.

Hotel Boat De Clipper (☎ 331 42 44; Scheepmakers- haven; bed €22.50) In a city whose hub has been the harbour for centuries, it's no surprise there's waterborne accommodation. This

cool little 'botel' is, naturally, a little cramped, but hey – it's a fair trade-off for getting into the whole Rotterdam spirit of things – ie closer to the waterline. An interesting alternative.

MID-RANGE

Hotel Amar (☎ 425 57 95; fax 477 73 21; Mathenes- serlaan 316; s/d €30/45) This is a friendly, small place in a leafy neighbourhood close to the Museumplein and to good shopping and nightlife. The rooms are simple but comfy, and you can get a discount on the already competitive prices if you book through Use-It (see Information, p211). Guests can use bikes for free and all rooms have TV.

Maritime Hotel Rotterdam (☎ 411 92 60; www .maritimehotel.nl; Willemskade 13; s/d/t €69/76/89; ⌨) This hotel caters to seamen ashore from their boats, but all are welcome. The modern facility boasts free Internet access, a big breakfast buffet and cheap bar.

Hotel Central (☎ 414 07 44; Kruiskade 12; s €80) Kitsch aficionados will *love* Hotel Central. For one thing, the décor looks like it hasn't been updated in 40 years, yet it's addictively comfy and invitingly atmospheric. You'll feel like kicking back with a Martini while wearing something bright orange and flammable. The rooms are great, service ditto, and fabulous deals can be had if you book through Use-It.

Bazar (☎ 206 51 51; www.hotelbazar.nl; Witte de Withstraat 16; s/d/t €60/75/120) A popular place, possibly due to its excellent themed rooms, but more likely due to its polyethnic vibe, air of tolerance and fantastic ground-floor bar and restaurant. This is what Rotterdam's all about – the intermingling of cultures to create something new, multifaceted and inclusive. Rarely do all the elements come together seamlessly, but it works here. Rooms have a bathroom and all have TV. Take tram No 5 (direction Willemsplein) from CS two stops, or walk 15 minutes.

TOP END

Hotel Eden Savoy (☎ 413 92 80; fax 404 57 12; Hoogstraat 81; s/d €105/118; ☒ ⌨ ✗) A well-equipped, if slightly generic, place near Oude Haven. Popular with tour groups, it's a four-star beast with all the expected trimmings: in-house movies, modem ports in the rooms, minibar, room service, a fitness centre – the Full Monty. It's a five-minute walk from the Blaak train, metro and tram station. If it sounds interesting, check Use-It's specials and it might sound even more so.

Bilderberg Parkhotel Rotterdam (☎ 436 36 11; www.parkhotelrotterdam.nl; Westersingel 70; s/d €105/ 155; 🍴 🖵 ⊠ P) Smack bang amidst Rotterdam's most notable sights and attractions, the Parkhotel may be part of a large corporate hotel chain, but that can have advantages. Its primary activity is catering to short stays (for business-people) year-round, which can often mean bargains and last-minute deals for leisure travellers when summer occupancy is well down. Rooms are comfy, clean and have all the mod cons.

Hotel New York (☎ 439 05 00; www.hotelnewyork.nl; Koninginnenhoofd 1; r €91-208; 🍴 🖵 ⊠ P) The city's favourite hotel achieved that status through a deadly combination of community nostalgia – it's housed in the former headquarters of the Holland-America passenger ship line – and excellent service and facilities. Often booked far in advance, it's noted for its views, café and boat shuttle taking guests across the Nieuwe Maas to the centre (Veerhaven or Leuvehaven). The posh Art Nouveau rooms – with many original and painstakingly restored décor items and fittings – are divine, and worth it if you can afford it. Rotterdam's best.

Eating

Rotterdam has many great places to eat. The city's (always growing) population of immigrants and a steady stream of corporate clientele floating through town on business means that choices (and prices) are widely varied.

CAFÉS

Café Gallery Abrikoos (☎ 477 41 40; Aelbrechtskolk 51; tapas from €4.50; 🕑 lunch & dinner Tue-Sun) This is a bright and cheery tapas bar filled with art. It has a variety of soups, salads and mains and wicked mediterranean mini-meals. Addictively cool and a great way to start a long evening.

De Twijfelaar (☎ 413 26 71; Mauritsstraat 173; mains €7-8; 🕑 lunch & dinner) A dark café whose name means 'the doubter'. Its vegetarian menu is popular with students who like the prices almost as much as the food. Great salads, sandwiches and flesh-free feasts. A DJ provides music until 11pm weeknights and 2am weekends.

Jazz Café Dizzy's (☎ 477 30 14; 's-Gravendijkwal 129; mains €10-15; 🕑 dinner) One of the city's best music bars is also one of its most popular restaurants, with a gorgeous garden terrace. It's in a sleazy part of town, but the menu and service at Dizzy's are all class. Try the meat stew with parsley *stamppot*, so authentically Dutch it's apparently made to a *recept van grootmoeder* ('grandmother's recipe'). Soul food. There's live music every Tuesday and jam nights Mondays. The standard is high, as the majority of blow-ins are local conservatorium students.

Café Restaurant De Unie (☎ 411 73 93; Mauritsweg 34; mains €12-15) This charming place preserves the 1924 facade of Mondriaan-esque red, yellow and blue. The 1986 interior is less successful, although the huge windows open onto the ponds. The menu has many tasty items for under €15. It also has a small theatre where there are occasional political debates. To enjoy these, you'll need to understand some Dutch.

Café 't Bolwerk (☎ 414 73 03; Geldersekade 1C; mains €15; 🕑 lunch & dinner) 't Bolwerk is on the ground floor of the historic White House tower on Oude Haven. It has free bowls of peanuts (toss the shells on the floor like everyone else does) and tangerines – to chase away scurvy. The kitchen does steaks and the like for good prices. It's popular with the after-work crowd and after midnight on weekends it can get pretty noisy when dancing starts.

QUICK EATS

Gheestige Willem (☎ 477 20 20; Willem Buytewechstraat 160a; mains €7-8) This lovely combined space has fab takeaway vegie food and is also an art gallery, so you can gaze at the walls while you wait. Delfshaven is nearby, and has some good spots where you can picnic.

RESTAURANTS

Tampopo Noodle Bar (☎ 225 15 22; 's-Gravendijkwal 128; mains €10-12; 🕑 dinner) A Wagamamas for a city too cool to need a Wagamamas, this trendy and stylish Asian restaurant is actually superior. Film nerds will notice it's named after a Japanese indie movie in which food was a prominent theme. Big bowls of noodle soups, loaded with vegies, meats and seafood are a steal at the price, and it's accordingly popular.

Baden Ajoe (☎ 290 01 56; Vijf Werelddelen; rijsttafel around €20; 🕑 dinner) This great restaurant is part of the huge Vrij Entrepot complex of shops and restaurants in a restored warehouse south of the Nieuwe Maas. The up-market Indonesian fare is served in lovely surroundings and – in nice weather – it has tables outside along the water.

Kip (Chicken; ☎ 436 99 23; Van Vollenhovenstraat 25; mains €25; ☻ dinner Tue-Sun) This lovely place is more elegant than its fast-foody moniker might imply. It's actually a very classy dining establishment and its menu broad. It's won a slew of 'Lekkers' (the Dutch restaurant-rating big-ups) and has crisp, white tablecloths, a delicate dining room and delicious and immaculately prepared meat, poultry and vegetable concoctions with a haute cuisine feel.

Bonne Bouche (☎ 270 99 33; Van Vollenhovenstraat 60; mains €25; ☻ dinner Tue-Sat) This enchanting French brasserie couldn't seem more out of place by the Rotterdam docks. An epicure's delight, with gorgeous examples of regional specialties and twists on the classics to delight Francophile diners. The 'contra-filet of Limousine beef in a parsley cream

---

DE PARKHEUVEL – STARRY STARRY BITE

Parkheuvel (☎ 436 05 30; Heuvelaan 21; 3-course menu from €41.70; ☻ lunch & dinner Mon-Sat) lays claim to the enviable title of the Netherlands' 'Best Restaurant'. It made Dutch news headlines by being awarded a third Michelin star. For those out of the culinary-star loop, this is a BIG deal, because to hang onto these elite (French, naturally) Super-Restaurant ratings, you have to maintain the stratospheric standard – you can actually lose stars.

Chef Cees Helder produces exquisite dishes to the highest standards and, recently and more voluminously, to rapturous reviews and accolades. Lowly travel writers have neither the wardrobe or pennies to eat in the beautifully styled dining room overlooking the park, but locals who have done so sing its praises in something approaching reverential whispers – no mean feat in Dutch, even for the Dutch.

A three-course meal including wine will require more than just a healthy wallet; you will also need discretion and social poise.

The pinnacle of Randstad fine dining.

---

sauce' or 'grilled breast of duckling with mushroom puree' are exquisite.

SELF-CATERING
Konmar Superstore (☎ 290 99 88; Vijf Werelddelen 33) This supermarket has a selection of foods from around the world and lots of deli items good for picnics.

Close to CS, there are loads of markets on West Kruiskade.

Drinking
Stalles & Parket (☎ 436 16 55; Nieuwe Binnenweg 9-11a) Worth visiting, this old place (and Consul/Volcano below) is on a great stretch of road near tons of good shops and other cafés and bars. We're talking classic Dutch brown café, but with a hip twist. Stalles & Parket pulls people of all ages and dispositions. Food is simple but good, the beer range fine. It's a place genuinely loved by employees and visitors alike and has that un-nameable something that makes a bar inviting – you'll pop in for one drink and stay for four.

De Consul/Volcano (☎ 436 33 23, Westersingel 28) This is also run by the same people as Stalles & Parket and is a combined film/music café around the corner; offering a similar vibe and trade but with a more artsy bent.

Locus Publicus (☎ 433 17 61; Oostzeedijk 364) Beer heaven, and the perfect place to take friends who think they know a thing or two about the malty stuff. For the picky, LP has more than 200 beers on its menu. One of the best specialist beer cafés in the whole country, atmospheric and addictive.

Entertainment
CLUBS
Off-Corso (☎ 411 38 97; Kruiskade 22) There's cool, and then there's Off-Corso, the city's proving ground for nascent trance, house and hip-hop uber-DJs pumps, with a come-as-you-wanna-be-remembered club vibe reflected in its varied roster of entertainment and late action. A winner.

De Regenboog (The Rainbow; ☎ 413 91 25; Van Oldenbarneveldtstraat 148a) OK, so it's considered a bit of a meat market, but then is that really *always* a bad thing? You gotta respect all colours of the *regenboog*, honey. Queers, dykes, particularly fabulous straights – all are welcome. Security are pleasantly light-hearted yet diligent. The sounds are house, house and more house. Need we mention the karaoke potential? Admission prices vary with programme.

Gay Palace (☎ 414 14 86; Schiedamsesingel 139; admission €5) Described by scenesters as 'back from the dead', the Palace still has a huge dance floor and is popular with gays, lesbians and straights who dig any kind of music that sounds like it wears a too-short skirt.

MUSIC

Rotown (☎ 436 26 69; www.rotown.nl; Nieuwe Binnenweg 19) This music legend is many things at once: a great bar, a cool, smoky brown café, a dependable live rock venue and one of the hottest meeting places in Rotterdam. Its programme features everything from new local talent to established international acts to crossover experiments, pulling artsy types and the independent minded. If it's musical and risky, yet lacking in ostentation, it's probably on at Rotown. Bimonthly programme available everywhere. Admission prices and opening hours vary with programme.

De Doelen (☎ 217 17 17; Schouwburgplein 50) This is the concert centre for the Rotterdam Philharmonic Orchestra. Tickets are understandably pricey, but then the orchestra is world class.

COFFEESHOPS

There's a huge number of coffeeshops in Rotterdam, probably the highest concentration outside the capital.

Desire (Nieuwe Binnenweg 148; ☽ 7am-4am) One of several joints, so to speak, on this street; this one has the best ventilation, rarely a priority. The friendly staff will explain the hoops you have to go through to buy something to smoke. As with any coffeeshop, the clientele can be chilled or spine-chilling, so use your judgement *before* you light up.

THEATRE

Schouwburg (☎ 411 81 10; Schouwburgplein 25) The main cultural centre with a rotating calendar of dance, theatre and drama. Note the cool light fixtures with red necks out the front.

Luxor Theater (☎ 413 83 26; www.luxortheater.nl; Posthumalaan 1) A major new performance venue (2001), the Luxor features every kind of entertainment you can possibly imagine. Check out its excellent website or pick up one of its abundant programmes around town for more details.

CINEMA

Pick up every well-designed club and bar flyer you see in eateries, nightspots, clothes retailers or music stores, as plenty of the better establishments have their own film nights and independent screenings. For a more regular schedule try the following.

Pathé Cinemas (☎ 0900-1458; www.pathe.nl; in Dutch; Schouwburgplein 101; screening €5-7) A large and dramatic-looking multiplex with the usual array of Hollywood output and some more interesting lesser-known films.

Lantaren/Venster (☎ cashier 277 22 77; Gouvernestraat 133; screening €5) A great central art-house alternative. For your fix of existential angst on celluloid, look no further. It publishs a great quarterly/seasonal fold-out agenda, which details the entire programme, from one-off screenings to week-long auteur retrospectives.

De Pleinbioscoop (Museumplein; screening free; ☽ mid-Aug–Sep) An annual open-air screening season in the Museumpark. It's free and the insufficient seating provided usually results in throngs of locals toting their own, plus wine, snacks and good vibes. There are classics, arthouse stuff and blockbusters, but the real star attraction is the *gezellig* feeling in the air. Experience the untranslatable.

International Film Festival Rotterdam (☽ Jan) This annual film festival is world renowned and, while lacking the glamour of the Cannes or Venice festivals, still pulls some huge names, particularly from the arty end of the spectrum (Buscemi, Von Trier). It's in January, when it's cold and wet, and indoors is certainly the place to be.

Shopping

Rotterdam has gone for Sunday shopping in a big way and most stores in the centre are open noon to 5pm. The **Lijnbaan**, lined with mainstream shops, was a trendsetter when it began opening over the period 1951 to 1966. The idea of car-free and pedestrianised shopping arcades was copied with more or less success worldwide. Rotterdam's latest shopping strip is **Beurstraverse** – or Koopgoot (Shopping Ditch), as it is known by the locals. It runs from Lijnbaan to Hoogstraat and passes under Coolsingel.

Nieuwe Binnenweg is a vivacious mix of stylish restaurants, dive-y coffee shops, old boozers and stores selling used CDs, vintage clothing, and plastic/fluorescent clubbing baubles fit only for the wildest nightspots.

There are also cool second-hand and retro clothing shops on the **Meent**.

West Kruiskade, five minutes south of CS, has a welter of ethnic groceries and stores.

There's a cluster of great cafés, restaurants and shops on and near the **Witte de Withstraat**, about a five- to 10-minute walk from the centre.

Getting There & Away
AIR
Rotterdam Airport (☎ 446 34 44) is 4km northwest of the centre, off the E19/A13. It's a sleepy place with basic services, ATMs etc. Various **KLM subsidiaries** (☎ 020-474 77 47) have flights to/from Paris, London and Manchester. Some are operated by **VLM** (☎ 415 77 77), a Belgian commuter airline. **British Airways** (☎ 437 89 11) has flights to/from London, Manchester and Birmingham. On weekends, there are often cheap fares available, so it's worth checking if you don't want to go through Amsterdam's Schiphol.

TRAIN
Rotterdam CS is an ageing station that is due to get a glitzy replacement in a huge project (building should begin in 2005). It's on the main line from Amsterdam south, and Thalys services between Brussels and Paris stop here. See the Transport chapter for details (p313).

Services are frequent to all points on the railway network. They include:

Destination	Price (€)	Duration (min)	Frequency (per hr)
Amsterdam	11.20	62	4
Den Haag	3.50	15	4
Middelburg	7.50	90	1
Utrecht	8.10	40	2

BUS
Rotterdam is a hub for Eurolines bus services to the rest of Europe. See the Transport chapter for details (p312). The long-distance bus stops are immediately west of CS. The **Eurolines office** (☎ 412 44 44; Conradstraat 20; ✆ 9.30am-5.30pm Mon-Fri, 9.30am-3pm Sat) is there as well.

Virgin Express Airlines (☎ 0800-0227773; www .virgin-express.com) operates a frequent bus to

and from Brussels Airport that connects with its discount flights around Europe. The price of the bus is included in the ticket.

CAR & MOTORCYCLE
Rotterdam is well linked by motorways to the rest of the Netherlands and Belgium.

Car rental firms at the airport include:

Avis	(☎ 298 24 24)
Budget	(☎ 437 86 22)
Europcar	(☎ 437 18 26)
Hertz	(☎ 415 82 39)

In addition, **Avis** (☎ 433 22 33; Kruisplein 21; ✆ 8am-6pm Mon-Fri, 8am-1pm Sat) has another convenient location across from CS.

BOAT
The new **Fast Ferry** (☎ 0900-2666399; one-way/ return €1.50/2.50, bike €1/2) links Rotterdam with Dordrecht and is a good option for day trips, or in place of the train. The boat leaves from Willemskade at least once an hour during the day, and takes 35 minutes.

Getting Around
TO/FROM THE AIRPORT
Bus No 33 makes the 15-minute run from the airport to CS every 12 minutes throughout the day. A taxi takes 10 minutes to the centre and costs around €20.

PUBLIC TRANSPORT
Rotterdam's trams, buses and metro are provided by **RET** (☎ 0900-9292; www.ret.rotterdam.nl). Most converge in front of CS, where there is an **information office** (✆ 6am-11pm Mon-Fri, 8am-11pm Sat & Sun) that also sells tickets. There are other information booths in the major metro stations.

Public transport in Rotterdam is easy. For destinations in the centre you won't need to use it, but for Delfshaven and even Oude Haven you might want a lift.

The metro operates two lines, one of which terminates at CS. Beurs/Churchillplein is the interchange station between the lines. Machines to validate tickets are at the station entrances.

Fast and frequent trams cover much of the city. Validate your strip ticket on board. On buses, have the driver validate your strips.

RET sells one-/two-/three-day tickets (dag-kaart) for €6/9/12. These are only good value if you plan to use public transport a lot.

ZUID HOLLAND & ZEELAND

CAR & MOTORCYCLE

Rotterdam has numerous places to park, including along the streets. Look for the blue P signs for large and enclosed garages.

TAXI

For a taxi, call ☎ 462 60 60.

BICYCLE

The **bicycle shop** (☎ 412 62 20) at CS is underground off the metro station.

AROUND ROTTERDAM

The popular ferries to/from Harwich in the UK dock in **Hoek van Holland**, 28km west of Rotterdam (see Transport p314). The town itself is really just a ferry port that has been gussied up with the addition of an artificial beach, just north of the centre on the road to **Monster**. The beaches here are fairly inaccessible, so if you can get to them, you should be free from crowds. Trains to/from Rotterdam run every 15 minutes (€4.30, 31 minutes) and are timed to provide good connections for the ferries.

Across the busy Nieuwe Waterweg from Hoek van Holland is **Europoort**, the huge shipping port right near the entrance to the North Sea. Ferries to/from Hull in the UK dock here. For those not driving, there are buses to/from Rotterdam CS and Amsterdam CS that are timed to connect with the ferries. Reserve these when you buy your ferry ticket.

BLOWING IN THE WIND

Windmills are an icon of the Netherlands. However, long before they starred on a zillion postcards, they played a vital role in the Dutch people's efforts to reclaim land from the sea and in the economic development of the nation.

The earliest known windmills appeared in the 13th century. Simply built around a tree trunk, these were called post mills. The entire top of the mill could be turned to face the wind. Inside, the shaft of the sails was directly linked to a grinding stone which was used to make flour.

The major innovation came about 100 years later. The hollow post mill looked the same from the outside, but inside there was a huge difference. By having the rotating top of the mill mounted on a hollow central core, a drive shaft could be connected to the sails. Through a series of gears, this could then in turn be used for all manner of activities, the most important of which was pumping water. Hundreds of these windmills were soon built on dykes throughout Holland and the mass drainage of land began.

The next major advancement in Dutch windmill technology came in the 16th century with the invention of the rotating cap mill. Rather than having to turn the huge body of the mill top to face the wind, the operators could rotate just the tip which contained the hub of the sails. This made it possible for mills to be operated by just one person.

Besides pumping water, mills were used for many other industrial purposes, such as sawing wood, making clay for pottery and, most importantly for art lovers, crushing the pigments used by painters.

By the mid-19th century, there were over 10,000 windmills operating in all parts of the Netherlands. But the invention of the steam engine soon made them obsolete. By the end of the 20th century there were only 950 operable windmills left, but this number seems to have stabilised and there is great interest in preserving the survivors. The Dutch government runs a three-year school for prospective windmill operators, who must be licensed.

Running one of the mills on a windy day is as complex as being the skipper of a large sailing ship, and anyone who's been inside a mill and listened to the massive timbers creaking will be aware of the similarities. The greatest hazard is a runaway, when the sails begin turning so fast that they can't be slowed. This often ends in catastrophe as the mill tears itself apart.

Little can be sadder than the sight of an abandoned mill, stripped of its sails and standing forlorn and denuded. But opportunities to see working windmills abound. **Kinderdijk** (p221) in Zuid Holland and **Zaanse Schans** (p147) in Noord Holland both have large collections of working mills. See the relative sections for details.

Just about every operable windmill in the nation is open to visitors on National Mill Day, usually on the second Saturday of May. Look for windmills flying blue flags.

LEANNE LOGAN

Sculpture at the entrance to the French embassy, Den Haag (p193)

ZAW MIN YU

Binnenhof, Den Haag (p195)

Police station, Den Haag (p193)

ZAW MIN YU

Binnenhof, Den Haag (p195)

ZAW MIN YU

Former cheese-weighing house,
Gouda (p202)

CHRIS MELLOR

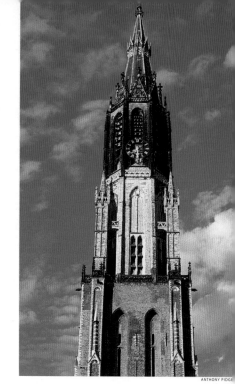

ANTHONY PIDGE

Oude Kerk, Delft (p206)

A stained-glass window in St Janskerk, Gouda (p202)

LEE FOS

KINDERDIJK

This is the best spot in the Netherlands to see windmills. Named a Unesco World Heritage Site in 1997, it has 19 windmills strung out on both sides of canals dug behind the tall dykes at the confluence of the Lek river and several tributaries and channels.

This spot has been a focus of Dutch efforts to reclaim land from the water for centuries. It's a starkly beautiful area, with the windmills rising above the empty marshes and waterways like so many sentinels.

Exacerbating the feeling of having stepped through a ripple in the space-time continuum is the endless creaking and structural groaning of the ship-like mills. Only once you hear these ghostly sounds can you really appreciate what a delicate skill it must have been to operate a mill, particularly in inclement weather.

Several of the most important types of windmills are here, including hollow post mills and rotating cap mills (see the boxed text, p220). The latter are among the highest in the country as they were built to better catch the wind. The mills are kept in operating condition and date from the 18th century.

A visit to Kinderdijk can occupy at least half a day. From the bus stop and parking area, there are more than 4km of paths along the dykes that run past the windmills. On any Saturday in July and August from 2pm to 5pm, all 19 windmills are in operation, an unforgettable sight that was once common but now impossible to find anywhere else. At other times, one of the mills functions as a **visitors centre** (☎ 078-613 28 00; admission €2; ☻ 9.30am-5.30pm Mon-Sat Apr-Sep).

To reach Kinderdijk, take any of the many local trains from Rotterdam CS to Rotterdam Lombardijen station three stops southwest. From there catch the hourly bus No 154 to Kinderdijk. By car, take the N210 12km east from Rotterdam. Watch for the signs for Kinderdijk. There is a car ferry (€2) across the Lek to the parking area.

DORDRECHT

☎ 078 / pop 118,000

Sitting at the confluence of the Oude Maas river and several tributaries and channels, Dordrecht has also been at the confluence of Dutch history. The first free assembly of Holland and Zeeland was held here in

Het Hof in 1572. It was also the scene of meetings between Protestant theologians from 1618 to 1619 which resulted in the triumph of the strict Calvinists over more moderate sects.

With its lovely canals and busy port, Dordrecht enjoyed much affluence, especially from the wine trade during the 17th century, evidenced in the town's charmingly pretty architecture. Much of this legacy remains and you can spend a delightful day wandering the oval-shaped old town.

Dordrecht is worth an overnight stop and there are numerous cafés and restaurants, some with fine views of the busy waterway along two sides of the city. The town is also the gateway to the lovely Biesbosch National Park.

Orientation

The train station is a good 700m walk from the centre, a journey that passes through some less interesting, newer areas. In the old town, most of the sights are on or near the three old canals, the Nieuwehaven, the Wolwevershaven and the Wijnhaven.

Information

The **tourist information office** (☎ 613 28 00; www.vvvzhz.nl; Stationsweg 1; ☻ noon-5.30pm Mon, 9am-5.30pm Tue-Fri, 11am-4pm Sat, 11am-3pm 1st Sun of month) is near the train station. It sells a good walking-tour booklet (€2.50) and also rents 'Talking Walls' audio (CD) walking tours of the city for €5. It also markets a number of multiday bicycle tours of the region that include accommodation.

The **GWK money exchange** (☎ 8am-8pm Mon-Sat, 10am-5pm Sun) is in the train station. There are ATMs outside the station and in town.

The **post office** (☎ 613 21 11; Johan de Wittstraat 120; ☻ 9am-6pm Mon-Fri, 9am-1pm Sat) is near the station.

The **library** (☎ 613 00 77; Groenmarkt 53; web access per hr €2; ☻ noon-8pm Tue-Fri, 10am-1pm Sat) is in a large, modernised building.

Sights & Activities
WALKING TOUR

Begin the tour on the **Visbrug**, the bridge over Wijnhaven which gives fine views of the dignified **town hall**. At the north end of Visbrug turn right onto Groenmarkt. As you walk northeast you pass many of the oldest houses in town, many from the early 1600s.

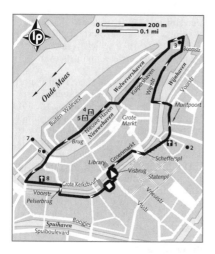

€2.50/1.50; 🕙 10am-5pm Tue-Sat, noon-5pm Sun) at No 26. It has a collection of materials from WWII and shows the privations of the region during the war. Look for the propeller prised from a Lancaster bomber in front.

Almost next door is the **Museum Simon van Gijn (5)** (☎ 613 37 93; adult/child €5/3; 🕙 11am-5pm Tue-Sun) at No 29. It shows the life of an 18th-century patrician.

While adults will be busy with the museums, kids will be drawn to the Brug ('bridge'), the simply named structure arching over the canal that is great fun for running up and down. Continue southwest to the Engelenburgerbrug over the Nieuwehaven's access to the Oude Maas. Take an immediate right onto narrow Engelenburgerkade. At No 18 is **Beverschaep (Beaver & Sheep House) (6)**, a structure from 1658 that gets its name from the animals supporting a coat of arms over the door. At the end of the street is **Blauwpoort (7)**, another old trading gate.

Retrace your steps and continue southwest to the base of the **Grote Kerk (8)** (☎ 614 46 60; tower adult/child €2/1; 10.30am-4.30pm Apr-Oct). Finished 40 years after it was begun in 1460, the church's massive tower was never completed, as it started leaning during construction. You can climb to the top – a mere 279 steps – from where there are excellent views of the town. Inside, the choir stalls are finely carved and there are several lovely stained-glass windows.

Walk behind the church on curving Kerkstraat to Grote Kerksbuurt. Cross the first bridge, Pelserbrug, stopping halfway to admire the view over the tiny canal that runs behind the houses on either side. At the south end of the bridge, turn left onto Voorstraat and follow it back to Visbrug, the starting point.

At the next square, Scheffersplein, cross diagonally to Voorstraat. The canal runs under this area, which is home to numerous markets. Voorstraat is the main retail street.

Just a bit further along on the right is the **Augustinerkerk (1)**, an old church with a facade dating from 1773. Just past it watch carefully for a passage leading to **Het Hof (2)**. The setting alone – especially at night – is moody and evocative. It's here that the states of Holland and Zeeland met in 1572.

Back out on Voorstraat continue north to the next bridge over the canal (Nieuwbrug). Cross over to Wijnstraat and turn right, continuing north. Many of the lopsided houses along here date from the peak of the wine trade, when the nearby canals were filled with boats bearing the fermented stuff.

The street ends at an attractive bridge. Pass along the west or left side of the canal to the river where you will be standing at the **Groothoofdspoort (3)**, once the main gate into town. Walk west along the pavement and view the traffic on the waterways and Oude Maas river.

Circling to the south, you see the Kuipershaven, the street along the Wolwevershaven, another old canal lined with beautifully restored old wine warehouses and filled with many pleasure boats. As you walk along here, you'll see artists at work in their studios in the old buildings. At the tiny bridge, cross over to the north side of the Nieuwehaven. On the right, watch for the **Museum 1940–1945 (4)** (☎ 613 01 72; adult/child

DORDRECHTS MUSEUM

Away from the old town, the **Dordrechts Museum** (☎ 648 21 48; Museumstraat 40; adult/child €3.50/2; 🕙 11am-5pm, closed Mon) has works by local artists. It's the oldies that are the most noteworthy, especially pieces by Jan van Goyen and Albert Cuyp. The former (1596–1656) was one of the first Dutch painters to capture the interplay of light on landscapes. Look for his *View of Dordrecht*. Cuyp lived in Dordrecht his entire life (1620–91) and is known for his many works painted in and around his hometown.

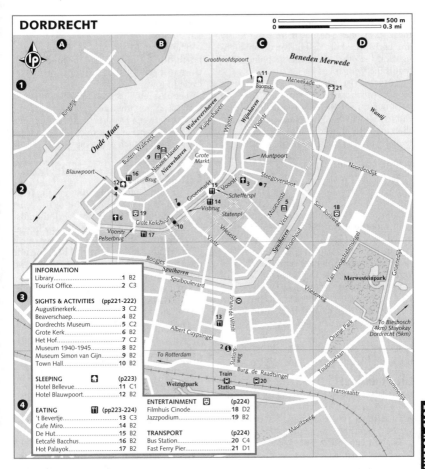

DORDRECHT

INFORMATION	
Library................................1	B2
Tourist Office.........................2	C3

SIGHTS & ACTIVITIES (pp221-222)	
Augustinerkerk.......................3	C2
Beaverschaep.........................4	B2
Dordrechts Museum..................5	C2
Grote Kerk............................6	B2
Het Hof...............................7	C2
Museum 1940-1945..................8	B2
Museum Simon van Gijn............9	B2
Town Hall...........................10	B2

SLEEPING (p223)	
Hotel Bellevue......................11	C1
Hotel Blauwpoort...................12	B2

EATING (pp223-224)	
't Bevertje..........................13	C3
Cafe Miro...........................14	B2
De Hut..............................15	B2
Eetcafé Bacchus....................16	B2
Hot Palayok.........................17	B2

ENTERTAINMENT (p224)	
Filmhuis Cinode.....................18	D2
Jazzpodium..........................19	B2

TRANSPORT (p224)	
Bus Station..........................20	C4
Fast Ferry Pier......................21	D1

To Biesbosch
(4km) Stayokay
Dordrecht (5km)

To Rotterdam

ZUID HOLLAND & ZEELAND

Sleeping

Stayokay Dordrecht is an excellent combined youth hostel, campground and hotel, 7km east of the train station on the edge of Biesbosch National Park. See p224 for details. Hotel choices in Dordrecht are very limited.

The **Hotel Bellevue** (☎ 613 79 00; www.bellevue dordrecht.nl; Boomstraat 37; s/d €80/105) By far the best choice – and often the only choice – in the old centre of Dordrecht, this is a classic old place with brilliant views of the converging waterways and ceaseless shipping. The rooms have been tastefully updated and have bathroom and TV.

Hotel Blauwpoort (☎ 613 60 28; Blauwpoortsplein 9/12; per person €20) Oddly, for an establishment

in the hospitality trade, this place doesn't always accept guests. Call before you go. When open, it offers simple, clean rooms without bathroom.

Eating

De Hut (☎ 635 20 01; Voorstraat 293; daily special €9; ⏰ lunch & dinner) An innovative fast-food option fusing Dutch and Indonesian styles, meaning hearty ingredients livened up by spicier sauces. Cheap *broodjes* (€2.50 to €4) are fresh, tasty and best accompanied by one of the excellent juices.

Café Miro (☎ 620 00 17; fax 684 98 50; Voorstraat 256b; tapas from €4) A bright, bold yellow tapas bar that's visually unmissable and named after one of Spain's greatest 20th-century painters. The

Latina vibe carries through from the décor to the tapas on offer. The food is great; fresh, tasty and fairly priced. It's definitely a design high-light on the otherwise bland shopping street that is the Voorstraat.

't Bevertje (The Little Beaver; ☎ 614 30 43; Johan de Wittstraat 49; daily menu €7.95; ⏰ dinner) A cosy and petit bar/café, 't Bevertje is a delight, from the toy clowns hanging from the roof and the cute little flower-shaded terrace to the friendly prices. The specials are substantial, hearty meat, bread and potatoes type stuff, and the bar well stocked.

Hot Palayok (☎ 614 93 96; Voorstraat 397; daily menu €12; ⏰ lunch & dinner Tue-Sun) A great place offer-ing a unique blend of Filipino recipes with a Latin twist. It's as interesting as it sounds, with mouthwatering Southeast-Asian influ-enced tapas (€4 to €6) plus more substantial rice mains with meats in spicy sauces, vege-tarian options like piquant vegetable stir-fries and not-quite-satays. Deliciously different.

Eetcafé Bacchus (☎ 614 97 22; Blauwpoortsplein 13; mains €12-17; ⏰ noon-10pm) Bacchus is a warmly lit brown café with great steak and fish dishes under €14. This is typical casual dining out in the Netherlands, though its best dessert hails from a little further afield; the great tiramisu is €4.50. Go on.

Entertainment

Jazzpodium (☎ 614 08 15; Grotekerksplein 1; ⏰ 9pm-3am Wed & Fri-Sun) This has modern and im-provisational jazz and blues. Cover charge varies depending on the programme.

Filmhuis Cinode (☎ 639 79 69; St Jorisweg 76) A serious cinema devoted to off-beat and artistic films.

Getting There & Away

The train station has all the usual services and is right on the main line from Rotter-dam south to Belgium. There are also direct trains east to Breda and beyond. Some fares and schedules include:

Destination	Price (€)	Duration (min)	Frequency (per hr)
Amsterdam	13.50	80	4
Breda	4.80	17	3
Rotterdam	3.50	15	6

Buses leave from the area to your right as you exit the train station. You'll find bus

No 388 serves Utrecht every hour (€6.20, 1hr 20min).

The busy E19 south to Belgium and north to Rotterdam and beyond passes close to town for those with car or motor-cycle in tow.

The **Fast Ferry** (☎ 0900-2666399; one-way/return €1.50/2.50; 35 min) runs a convenient and scenic service between Dordrecht and Rotterdam. The boats leave at least once an hour from Merwekade, which is at stop No 12 on the bus No 20 route.

Getting Around

If you don't fancy the 700m walk from the train station to the centre of town, let alone another 500m to the Groothoofds-poort, local bus No 20 makes a circular journey from the train station past most of the major sights in town. These include the Dordrechts Museum (stop No 7) and Kuipershaven (stop No 14).

For those arriving by car or motorcycle, plan on parking just outside the old town at one of the many carparks near Statenplein.

The **bicycle shop** (☎ 614 66 42) is in the train station.

BIESBOSCH NATIONAL PARK

Covering 7100 hectares, Biesbosch Na-tional Park encompasses an area along both banks of the Nieuwe Merwede River east and south of Dordrecht. It's so big it sprawls across a provincial border; there's a part known as the Brabantse Biesbosch, further east, while the part in this province is the Hollandse Biesbosch. Before 1421 the area was reclaimed polder land and had a population of over 100,000 living in over 70 villages.

A huge storm on St Elizabeth's Day that year (18 November) breached the dykes and floodwaters, destroyed all the villages and killed pretty much everyone.

However, out of this calamity grew both new life and a new lifestyle. The floods created several channels in their wake, including what is today called the Nieuwe Merwede river. Linked to the sea, these areas were subject to twice-daily high tides. This led to the growth of tide-loving reed plants, which the descendants of the flood's survivors took to cultivating.

Fast forward to 1970 when one of the first parts of the Delta Project shut off the tides to the area. The reeds, which had been growing wild during the decades since the collapse of the reed markets, began to die, focusing attention on what is one of the largest expanses of natural space left in the Netherlands.

The park is home to beavers (reintroduced to the Brabant part of the park in 1988) and voles as well as scores of birds. There's an observation point right near the visitors centre where you can observe some that have been fenced off in their own little pond. Or you could patiently seek them out in the park…

The best way to visit the park is to start at the **visitors centre** (☎ 630 53 53; www .biesbosch.org; Baanhoekweg 53; ☺ 9am-5pm Tue-Sun year-round; 1-5pm Mon May & Jun, 9am-5pm Mon Jul & Aug), some 7km east of the Dordrecht train station. There are all the usual displays about the park's ecology and you can rent kayaks and canoes (from €5 per 2½ hr) to explore the park and its many channels and streams. There are also numerous trails through the marshlands and along the river.

The centre is also the boarding place for a variety of **boat tours** (adult/child from €4.50/3; 1hr) of the Biesbosch. The longer cruises are better, though, because they go to more places, including the **Biesboschmuseum** on the southern shore of the Nieuwe Merwede.

Eating & Sleeping
Stayokay Dordrecht (☎ 621 21 67; www.stayokay.com /dordrecht; Baanhoekweg 25; dm from €20; tent/camper €3/5) has many kinds of accommodation. It's a good idea to reserve in advance. The hotel, which has a bar and restaurant, is in a modern building right next to the park and is 1km west of the visitors centre. The staff are lovely.

Getting There & Away
The hotel and park are easy bike rides from the train station (7km). Otherwise, bus No 5 (every 30 minutes) travels to within 2km of Stayokay and 3km of the park. But if you tell the driver you're going to either, a taxi will be called to take you the rest of the way for only €1.

The easiest option is to get a **taxi** (☎ 613 58 22; €3.80) from Dordrecht station direct to the Stayokay site, then rent a bike there and get about the park/area or into town that way.

ZEELAND

Zeeland's three fingers of land are really just islands set in the middle of a vast delta through which many of Europe's rivers drain, including the Rijn (Rhine), Schelde and Maas. The name, which means Sea Land, could not be more appropriate as the boundary between the two is thin indeed.

For centuries the plucky Zeelanders have been battling the North Sea waters, and not always with success. The St Elizabeth's Day flood of 1421 killed over 100,000 and forever altered the landscape – and some would argue the disposition – of the Netherlands and its people. More recently, the huge flood of 31 January 1953 killed almost 2000, left 500,000 homeless and destroyed 800km of dykes.

The result of this last calamity is the Delta Project, an enormous multidecade construction programme that aims to finally ensure the security of these lands. It's easily the largest construction project in modern history and has greatly altered the entire region. See the boxed text on p226 for details.

This is one of the last places in the Netherlands where you find people wearing traditional dress in everyday life. For women this means lots of layers of white lace, and for men, black suits.

Middelburg is the somnolent historic capital, while the coast along the North Sea is lined with beaches beyond the ever-present dykes. Many people venture to this place of tenuous land and omnipresent water just to see the sheer size of the Delta Project dykes and barriers.

Getting There & Away
In Zeeland, Middelburg is easily reached by train, but for most other towns you'll need to rely on the many buses. The most important include bus No 104, which makes a marathon 2½-hour journey between Rotterdam's Centraal Station and Vlissingen that follows the western edge of the province along the Delta Project. It runs every 30 minutes in both directions.

MIDDELBURG
☎ 0118 / pop 45,000
A pleasant and prosperous town, Middelburg is the capital of Zeeland and makes a

THE DELTA PROJECT

Begun in 1958, the Delta Project consumed billions of guilders, millions of labour hours and untold volumes of concrete and rock before it was completed in 1996.

The goal was to avoid a repeat of the catastrophic floods of 1953, when a huge storm surge rushed up the Delta estuaries of Zeeland and broke through dykes inland. This caused a serial failure of dykes throughout the region and much of the province was flooded.

The original idea was to block up the estuaries and create one vast freshwater network. But by the 1960s this kind of sweeping transformation was unacceptable to the Dutch public, now more environmentally aware.

So the Oosterschelde was left open to the sea tides, and 3km of movable barriers were constructed that could be lowered ahead of a possible storm surge. This barrier, between Noord Beveland and Schouwen Duiveland, is the most dramatic part of the Delta Project and the focus of the Delta Expo, which details the enormous efforts to complete the barrier.

The project raised and strengthened the region's dykes and added a movable barrier at Rotterdam harbour, the last part completed. Public opinion later shifted, but large areas of water had already been dammed and made into freshwater lakes. At Veerse Meer the fishing industry has vanished and been replaced by holiday-makers and sailboats.

The impact of the Delta Project is still being felt. At Biesbosch National Park (see p224), the reduction of tides is killing reeds which have grown for centuries. But those who recall the 1953 floods will trade some reeds for their farms any day.

good place for a pause before exploring the countryside.

Although the Germans destroyed the town's historic centre in 1940, much has been rebuilt and you can still get a solid feel for what life must have been like hundreds of years ago. The fortifications built by the Sea Beggars in 1595 can still be traced in the pattern of the main canals encircling the old town.

As the main town of Walcheren peninsula, Middelburg is fairly removed from the rest of the Netherlands – crowds are seldom a problem. Note that many of the town's sights are closed in winter.

Orientation

The train station for Middelburg is a five-minute walk across two canals from the centre. The Markt is the focus of commercial life but Middelburg's history is concentrated around the medieval Abdij (Abbey).

Information
BOOKSHOPS

De Drvkkery (☎ 88 68 86; www.de-drvkkery.nl; Markt 51) Zeeland's finest bookshop is one of the best in the country, drawing customers from as far as Belgium and Germany. It has an excellent magazine selection, simple café, sporadically-functional free internet access (15 minutes) and art/photography displays on the walls besides the oodles of books.

LAUNDRY
Laverie Souris (☎ 62 34 99; Brakstraat 14; 🕑 8.30am-6pm Mon-Fri, 8.30am-noon Sat)

LIBRARY
Zeeland Regional Library (☎ 64 40 00; Kousteensedijk 7; web access per hr €3; 🕑 5-9pm Mon, 10am-9pm Tue-Fri, 10am-1pm Sat) In a large and modern building on a canal.

MONEY
ATMs abound including at **ABN/AMRO Bank** (☎ 67 25 00; Kousteensedijk 3) and **ING Bank** (☎ 68 44 00; Markt 43).

POST
Post office (☎ 64 22 88; Lange Noordstraat 48; 🕑 8am-5.30pm Mon-Fri, 9am-1pm Sat) On a central street, two minutes' walk from the Abdij.

TOURIST INFORMATION
Tourist Shop (☎ 67 43 00; middelburg@touristshop.nl; Markt 65c; 🕑 9.30am-5.30pm Mon-Fri, 10.30am-5pm Sat) There is no longer an offical tourist office in Middelburg, but staff at this new, privately operated information centre are very helpful and engaging and offer a lot of the same services that the city-funded organisation did.
ANWB (☎ 65 99 44; Nieuwe Brug 40; walk map €3; 🕑 9.30am-5.30pm Mon-Wed &Fri-Sat, 9.30am-9pm Thu year-round, 9.30am-4pm Sun Apr-Oct) The resident cycling/touring gurus here can offer a wealth of knowledge. It publishes a free 'Tourist Pass Middelburg' that

gives discounts at most sights in town. There are also over 20 different maps of Zeeland bike-touring routes for sale.

Sights & Activities

Most of Middelburg's sights are centred around the Abdij, though the town is pretty just to stroll through, too.

ABDIJ

This huge abbey complex dates from the 12th century. It houses the regional government as well as three churches and two museums. You can start with the **Historama** (☎ 62 66 55; adult/child €2.50/1; ☒ 11am-5pm Mon-Sat year-round, noon-5pm Sun Apr-Oct), which is in the heart of the complex. Displays portray the

bleaker aspects of cloistered life and cover the history of the abbey.

The three churches are all in a cluster. The **Wandelkerk** dates from the 1600s and holds the tombs of Jan and Cornelis Evertsen, admirals and brothers killed fighting the English in 1666. It encompasses Lange Jan ('Long John' – it has its own locally brewed beer named after it), the 91m tower dating from the 14th century. Just east is the **Koorkerk**, parts of which date from the 1300s. Just west is **Nieuwe Kerk**, which has a famous organ and dates from the 16th century.

Call ☎ 61 35 96 to check the opening hours and accessibility of the churches. These are subject to more variation than usual while the Zeeuws Museum undergoes

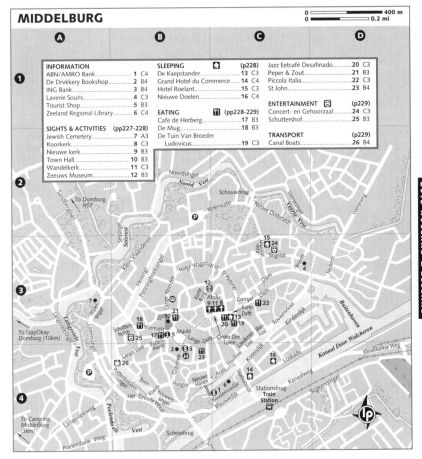

MIDDELBURG

INFORMATION			SLEEPING ☐ (p228)		Jazz Eetcafé Desafinado..........20 C3
ABN/AMRO Bank...............1 C4			De Kaepstander...................13 C3		Peper & Zout......................21 B3
De Drvkkery Bookshop.....2 B4			Grand Hotel du Commerce...14 C4		Piccola Italia.......................22 C3
ING Bank...........................3 B4			Hotel Roelant.....................15 C3		St John..............................23 B4
Laverie Souris.....................4 C3			Nieuwe Doelen...................16 C4		
Tourist Shop......................5 B3					ENTERTAINMENT ☐ (p229)
Zeeland Regional Library....6 C4			EATING ☐ (pp228-229)		Concert- en Gehoorzaal......24 C3
			Cafe de Herberg.................17 B3		Schuttershof.....................25 B3
SIGHTS & ACTIVITIES (pp227-228)			De Mug.............................18 B3		
Jewish Cemetery................7 A3			De Tuin Van Broeder		TRANSPORT (p229)
Koorkerk...........................8 C3			Ludovicus......................19 C3		Canal Boats.......................26 B4
Nieuwe kerk......................9 B3					
Town Hall.........................10 B3					
Wandelkerk.......................11 C3					
Zeeuws Museum................12 B3					

its big facelift. You should still be able to scale the heights of Lange Jan (€1.50) though.

The main reason for visiting the Abdij complex is the **Zeeuws Museum** (☎ 62 66 55; (www.zeeuwsmuseum.nl), housed in the former monks' dormitories. It has some of the best first-hand accounts and archival information on the 1953 disaster. It's closed until 2005 for refurbishment.

Before leaving the Abdij, check out the ancient **herb garden** growing in the centre courtyard.

TOWN HALL
Dominating the Markt is the **town hall** (☎ 67 54 52; admission €2; ☼ 11am-5pm Mon-Sat year-round, noon-5pm Sun Apr-Oct), a pastiche of styles. The Gothic side facing the Markt is from the 1400s while the portion on Noordstraat is more classical and dates from the 1600s.

Inside there are several sumptuous ceremonial rooms that boast treasures such as the ubiquitous Belgian tapestries. Visits to the building are by one-hour guided tours only.

OTHER SIGHTS
The area around **Damplein** (east of the Abdij) preserves many 18th-century houses, some of which have recently been turned into interesting shops and cafés.

There is a fairly large old **Jewish Cemetery** on the Walensingel. It has the all-too-common stark memorial to the many Middelburg Jews taken away to their deaths by the Nazis.

MARKET
Like every other Dutch town, Middelburg has a weekly market. However, this one, which takes place on the Markt on Thursday, is notable as it attracts many of Zeeland's conservative residents, many of whom still wear traditional dress regardless of whether or not any tourists are around.

Tours
There are **tours** (☎ 67 43 00; adult/child €5/3; ☼ 11am-4pm Apr-Oct) of the local canals that depart from the Lange Viele bridge. During the warmest months the hours are extended.

Festivals and Events
Ringrijdendagen (Ring riding days) Held on two separate days (the first in July around the Abbey square, the second in August at the Molenwater). 'Ring riders' charge about with big sticks and in silly dress on horses toward a target, trying to tilt it.

Sleeping
CAMPING
Camping Middelburg (☎ 62 53 95; Koninginnelaan 55; 2 people & tent €14) This is 3km from the train station. Take bus No 56 or 58 (every 30 minutes) and tell the driver where you want to get off.

HOSTELS
There is a **Stayokay** hostel 10km west near Domburg; see Sleeping & Eating (p230).

HOTELS
De Kaepstander (☎ 64 28 48; www.kaepstander.nl; Koorkerkhof 10; s/d with shared bathroom €35/60) This simple but pleasant place is right next door to (and run by the same people as) the Jazz Eetcafé Desafinado (see Eating p229) and has four rooms with B&B-style accommodation. The owners are lovely people.

Hotel Roelant (☎ 62 76 59; www.familiehotelroelant .nl; Koepoortstraat 10; d €75) This building dating from 1530 has basic, comfortable rooms with bathroom. It's a small, family-run establishment, a pleasant walk away from the centre on a beautiful old cobbled street. There is a nice garden and an excellent restaurant. Roelant offers many combination offers for multiday stays or bike hire.

Nieuwe Doelen (☎ 61 21 21; Loskade 3-7; low/high season €71/91) One of the Nieuwe Doelen's 26 lovely rooms makes a perfect base for exploring Middelburg. All rooms are simply, yet pleasantly, decorated. There's also an enclosed garden, perfect for a long, lingering lazy breakfast in fine weather.

Grand Hotel du Commerce (☎ 63 60 51; www .fletcher.nl, Loskade 1; s/d from €61/71) This great hotel is in a building that would look at home on the Cannes beachfront, with its gaudy red awnings overhanging every window starkly juxtaposed against the white-washed, sun-bleached walls. The rooms are fine, the staff attentive and the place has all the conveniences.

Eating
St John (☎ 62 89 95; St Janstraat 40; ☼ 8.30am-6pm Mon-Sat) A simple, cosy coffee-and-

light-meals place run by softly-spoken owners.

De Tuin Van Broeder Ludovicus (☎ 62 60 11; Lange Delft 2a) A health-food store with an organic bakery, cheese case and more. It's an excellent stop for picnickers, with pre-made dishes, cooked meats and salads sold by weight. Stock up, jump on your bike saddle and cruise Middelburg's pretty streets for a sweet canalside spot.

Jazz Eetcafé Desafinado (☎ 64 07 67; www .desafinado.nl; Koorkerkstraat 1; mains around €15; ☼ lunch & dinner) Desafinado has a lovely wood-y dining room, laid-back staff and a huge collection of jazz CDs. The piano keys glued to the underside of the bar are a nice touch. The menu incorporates local and French flavours and there's a refreshing variety of good value, delicious meals. There's also live jazz and blues Wednesday nights.

Peper & Zout (Pepper & Salt; ☎ 62 70 58; peperenzout@zeelandnet.nl; Lange Noordstaat 8; ☼ lunch & dinner) Peper & Zout has a casual yet elegant interior. The menu concentrates on fresh seafood such as mussels (€14) and various kinds of locally netted gilled beings. It's a popular place with a great wine list, and the 3-course menu option (€19.50) is fabulous value.

De Mug (The Mosquito; ☎ 61 48 51; Vlasmarkt 54; mains €17; ☼ dinner Tue-Sat) De Mug is famous beyond Middelburg for its menu of dishes prepared with unusual beers. The choices change often, and its atmosphere is that of a justifiably popular brown café, so book ahead. It shouldn't be a surprise that the beer list is long (72 brews) and boasts many rare Trappist drops.

Entertainment

Concert- en Gehoorzaal (☎ 61 27 00; Singelstraat 13) This is an old concert hall with a plush interior. There are frequent performances of chamber and other classical music at the hall.

Schuttershof (☎ 61 34 82; www.schuttershoftheater.nl, in Dutch; Schuttershofstraat 1; film adult/child €6/4) This is down a little alley but has a big interior. There's a cinema showing unusual flicks and a large, cool bar area. On some nights it has live music.

Getting There & Around

Middelburg is near the end of the train line in Zeeland and the attractive but austere station has that end-of-line feel. Services are limited: there's a very small newsstand and the lockers are hidden away in the bicycle shop. Some fares and schedules are:

Destination	Price (€)	Duration (min)	Frequency (per hr)
Amsterdam	11	150	1
Roosendaal	4.60	45	2
Rotterdam	7.50	90	1

Regional buses, including No 104, stop along Kanaalweg in front of the train station.

The **bicycle shop** (☎ 61 21 78) is to the left as you leave the station. A charming cycle route runs along the coastal dykes (see the Mantelingen Route, p73).

AROUND MIDDELBURG

The Walcheren peninsula is a very enjoyable place for biking as you can combine journeys to old towns with time at the beach.

Veere

☎ 0118 / pop 5000

Veere is a former fishing village that found a new line of work in tourism when its access to the sea on the Veerse Meer ('Veere Lake') was closed as part of the Delta Project. Happily, tourists and pleasure-seekers have obliged and the town now boasts a busy yacht harbour. Much of the town dates from the early 16th century and it is an atmospheric place to stroll around. Veere is an easy 6km trip north of Middelburg.

INFORMATION

The **tourist office** (☎ 0900-2020280; Oudestraat 28; ☼ 10am-4.30pm Mon-Sat Jul & Aug, 1.30-4.30pm Sep-Jun) is in a small building near the Grote Kerk. Staff can advise on boat rentals and bike routes.

SIGHTS & ACTIVITIES

The best thing to do in Veere is stroll. You'll feel like you've found yourself inside a Vermeer painting. Rich Gothic houses abound, a testament to the wealth brought in by the wool trade with the Scots. At the waterfront, the **Campveerse Toren** was part of the old fortifications. Look for the indications on the side showing the levels of various floods.

The **town hall** on the Markt dates from 1474 but was mostly completed in 1599. Its

ZUID HOLLAND & ZEELAND

tower is still literally stuffed with bells, 48 at last count.

At the south end of town is the 16th-century **Grote Kerk**, another edifice that never matched its designer's intentions. Its stump of a steeple (42m) looms ominously.

There are **boat trips** (☎ 41 93 67; ⏰ 11am-5pm May-Sep) on the Veerse Meer. Prices vary per boat trip.

SLEEPING & EATING

Hotel de Campveerse Toren (☎ 50 12 91; www .campveersetoren.nl; Kade 2; r from €79) A smart place in a historic building right on the waterfront. It offers comfortable rooms and fabulous views. Occupancy rises with the thermometer, as do prices.

Hotel 't Waepen van Veere (☎ 50 12 31; Markt 23-27; www.waepenvanveere.nl; d/tr/q €67.50/95/107) This hotel is on the central square. It is a small place, with just 11 rooms – and all of them are excellent. It also has an elegant restaurant.

Both of the hotels have cafés and there are a few more cafés as well as a bakery and a grocery on the Markt.

GETTING THERE & AWAY

Veere is an easy bike ride from Middelburg. Otherwise, bus No 53 makes the 12-minute run every hour (every two hours Sunday).

Domburg

☎ 0118 / pop 900

A fairly low-key beach town by Dutch standards, Domburg still gets jam-packed during summer. It's pretty tourism-oriented and best considered an extension of the beach you're on your way to if you happen to find yourself here.

INFORMATION

The **tourist office** (☎ 58 13 42; fax 58 35 46; Schuit-vlotstraat 32; ⏰ 9am-4.30pm Mon-Sat Sep-Jun, 9am-6pm Jul & Aug) is near the entrance to town on Roosjesweg. The staff are experts at ferreting out accommodation.

SIGHTS & ACTIVITIES

The **beach** is the main event here. To escape the urban crowds, head south along the tall dunes. Keep going past the golf course, a good 4km.

For information on a 35km bicycle route, the Mantelingen Route, which begins and ends at Domburg, see p73.

SLEEPING & EATING

Camping Hof Domburg (☎ 58 82 00; info@roompot.nl; Schelpweg 7; sites from €20; ⏰ year-round) Just west of the centre. Sites can accommodate up to five people.

Stayokay Domburg (☎ 58 12 54; www.stayokay .com/domburg; Duinvlietweg 8; dm from €20; ⏰ Apr-Oct) A hostel notable for its location in a real castle complete with moat, Stakokay Domburg is 2km east of Domburg and 1km from the beach. One of the best Stayokays, this is a good one to reserve in advance, as the beach is very popular. Bus No 53 from Middelburg stops along the N287 near the entrance.

Hotel Duinlust (☎ /fax 58 29 70; Badhuisweg 28; s/d €20/30) Central and with simple rooms.

The tourist office has a myriad of additional accommodation options.

Fast-food stands and restaurants line the beach roads.

GETTING THERE & AWAY

Bus Nos 52 and 53 both link Domburg to Middelburg every hour (every two hours on Sunday). Bus No 53 continues south along the beaches.

DELTA EXPO

Travelling the N57, you can't help but notice the many massive projects of the Delta Project. You will see a succession of huge dykes and dams, designed to avoid a repeat of the many floods.

Possibly the most impressive stretch is between Noord Beveland and Schouwen Duiveland, to the north. The long causeway built atop the massive movable inlets is designed to allow the sea tides in and out of the Oosterschelde. This storm surge barrier is over 3km long, spanning three inlets and two artificial islands. It took 10 years to build, beginning in 1976.

At about the midway point (Harings-vliet), the **Delta Expo** (☎ 0187-49 99 13; www .expoharingvliet.nl; adult/child under 12 €4.30/3.30; ⏰ 9am-5pm Mon-Sat, 10am-5pm Sun Apr-Sep, 9am-5pm Wed-Sat, 10am-5pm Sun Oct-Mar) is an excellent museum and visitors centre for the Delta Project (see boxed text, p226). It also provides a free information leaflet available in English, Dutch or German.

Several floors deal with the effects of the floods as well as showing how the entire massive project was built. You can also visit one of the nearby complex pylons of

ZUID HOLLAND & ZEELAND

the storm surge barrier and see how the huge movable gate works.

The level of tidal control is truly astounding. Operators are able to balance the mix of fresh water draining out into the sea against the influx of sea water with tidal flow to such an extent that they can affect the rate of corrosion on the hulls of container-ships moored in Rotterdam, this seemingly innocuous feat saving shipping firms millions of dollars in maintenance and repair costs since the sluice operations started.

On the other side of the N57 is **WaterLand Neeltje Jans** (☎ 0111-65 27 02; www.neeltjejans.nl; adult/child under 12 €12.50/9.50; ☾ 10am-5.30pm Apr-Oct, 10am-5pm Wed-Sun Nov-Mar), a park that operates in conjunction with the Expo. There's a dolphin rescue station here for treating the beached mammals, all sorts of water slides and pools, exhibits on the flora and fauna of the Delta and more.

There are combo tickets available for both attractions during the relevant months (€10).

Bus No 104 stops at the Expo on its run between Rotterdam's Spijkenisse metro station (25 min from Rotterdam CS) and Vlissingen. The buses take about an hour from Rotterdam and 30 minutes from Middelburg and run every 30 minutes.

SCHOUWEN-DUIVELAND
The middle 'finger' of the Delta, Schouwen-Duiveland, is a compact island of dunes.

Zierikzee
☎ 0111 / pop 13,300
The town grew wealthy in the 14th century from trade with the Hanseatic League. Things took a turn for the worse in 1576 when a bunch of Spaniards waded over from the mainland at low tide and captured Zierikzee, precipitating a long economic decline.

INFORMATION
The **tourist office** (☎ 41 24 50; www.vvvschouwen duiveland.nl; Meelstraat 4; ☾ 10am-5pm Mon-Fri year-round, 10am-1pm Sat Oct-Apr, 10am-3pm Sat May-Sep) is in the town hall. Its town booklet (€1) is filled with facts and a decent little map.

There are **banks** and ATMs on Havenpark.

The **post office** (☎ 41 55 55; Poststraat 39; ☾ 9am-5.30pm Mon-Fri, 10am-1pm Sat) offers the usual services.

The **library** (☎ 41 45 48; Haringvlietplein 2; web access per hr €2; ☾ 2-5pm Mon & Wed-Fri, 9.30am-noon Wed & Sat) has Internet access.

SIGHTS & ACTIVITIES
The **Maritiem Museum** (☎ 45 44 64; Mol 25; combo ticket with town hall adult/child €3/1.50; ☾ 10am-5pm Mon-Sat, noon-5pm Sun) is just off Havenpark. It is in the 's-Gravensteen, a sturdy 16th-century prison that still has its bars. Besides the displays on local seafaring, there's a fine garden out the back.

The **town hall** (☎ 45 44 64; Meelstraat 6-8; combo ticket with Maritiem Museum adult/child €3/1.50; ☾ 10am-5pm daily, noon-5pm Sun) has a unique 16th-century wooden tower topped with a statue of Neptune.

At Oude Haven, at the east end of town, the **Noordhavenpoort** and the **Zuidhavenpoort** are old city gates from the 16th and 14th centuries respectively.

SLEEPING & EATING
The tourist office has a list of local rooms for overnight stays.

Pension Beddegoed (☎ 41 59 35; Meelstraat 53; €22.50) Very centrally located and has basic but decent rooms.

Stadsbakkerij (☎ 45 04 65; Applemarkt 8; ☾ closed Sun) Cheap snacks and sandwiches.

Pannekoekenhuis 't Zeeuwse (☎ 41 61 79; Appelmarkt 6; pancakes €4-5; ☾ 10am-6pm Mon-Sat) You gotta love any place that has crayons on the tables, ostensibly for kids, though it's fun watching some of the big kids in action while they wait for their doughy delectables to arrive.

Concordia (☎ 41 51 22; Havenpark; daily special €8-10; ☾ dinner) Dominating the end of Havenpark with its terrace, this café has a broad menu with numerous tasty and filling dinners.

GETTING THERE & AWAY
The bus stop is north of the centre, a five-minute walk across the canal along Grachtweg. Bus No 132 makes the 30-minute run to Goes at least every 30 minutes. Bus No 133 runs to Rotterdam's Zuidplein metro station. The 75-minute ride leaves at least every hour.

Westerschouwen
☎ 0111 / pop 17,900
Sheltered by tall dunes, this small town at the west end of Schouwen-Duiveland

ZUID HOLLAND & ZEELAND

adjoins a vast park set among the sands and woods.

There are hiking and biking trails for outdoor enthusiasts. Although predictably busy in summer, you can easily find solitude in some of the more remote parts of the park.

The **tourist office** (☎ 65 15 13; fax 65 28 33; Noordstraat 45A; ☉ 9am-5pm Mon-Fri, 9am-2pm Sat), in the neighbouring town of Burgh-Haamstede, can help with camping, private rooms and hotel accommodation.

Hotel De Zilvermeeuw (☎ 65 22 72; Lageweg 21; r from €25; P) This hotel has nine decent rooms with bathroom. It's one of very few options.

Lageweg is lined with casual food places, including one at the bus stop.

Bus No 133 from Rotterdam via Zierikzee and Bus No 134 from Zierikzee both stop right at the sand dunes. Both run every 30 minutes. Bus No 104, the Vlissingen–Rotterdam bus, stops about 2km from Westerschouwen in Burgh-Haamstede.

ZEEUWS-VLAANDEREN

Running along the Belgian border south of the Westerschelde, Zeeuws-Vlaanderen is an unremarkable place with numerous farms and a few chemical plants.

The many small villages, such as IJzendijk, all have their 'holy trinity' of the Dutch country skyline: a church steeple, a town hall tower and a windmill.

No part of Zeeuws-Vlaanderen is joined to the rest of the Netherlands by land. Instead, there are two ferry connections. The Vlissingen–Breskens ferry is a link for the Belgian channel ferry ports.

Foot passengers can travel from Brugge in Belgium by bus No 2 to Breskens (75 minutes, hourly). From the port in Vlissingen, catch a bus or ferry to points beyond.

The other ferry route, Perkpolder to Kruiningen on Zuid Beveland, is primarily useful to local motorists. The ferry (€6 per car) runs every 30 minutes in both directions.

Friesland (Fryslân)

CONTENTS

Friesland (Fryslân in Frisian) looks as though it should feature on a milk carton – a picture of Dutch bucolic splendour. It's flat, green and there're plenty of happy cows (the namesake Friesian black and white lassies). But explore a bit and you'll find differences, some small (see Language, p235) and some more glaringly obvious.

Even by Dutch standards, the Frisians are an independent, slightly taciturn bunch. They didn't just have to build dykes to protect their land, they had to build the land itself… North Friesland segues into the Waddenzee so subtly that, aeons ago, you couldn't tell whether you were paddling through watery mud or walking on muddy water. To provide a place to live about a millennium back, the Frisians laboriously built *terpen*, essentially huge mounds of mud. You can still see some of these piles, most notably in Hogebeintum.

The Frisians became integrated further into Dutch society – not entirely willingly – in 1932 when the Afsluitdijk (Barrier Dyke) opened, closing the Zuiderzee. This provided better links to Amsterdam and the south but was devastating for small fishing villages who suddenly found themselves sitting beside a lake.

The four Frisian Islands can be a delight, whether you prefer the summery mobs of the more developed Terschelling and Ameland or exploring the unpopulated tracts of Vlieland and Schiermonnikoog.

FRIESLAND

HIGHLIGHTS

- Get your skates on for the **Elfstedentocht** (p242) in super-cold winters.
- Discover the glistening lakes around **Sneek** (p239).
- Check out the bizarre sport of **fierljeppen** (p240)
- Cycle in solitude on **Schiermonnikoog, Ameland** or **Vlieland** (p243)
- Find outdoor art all over Terschelling at the annual **Oerol** festival (p245).

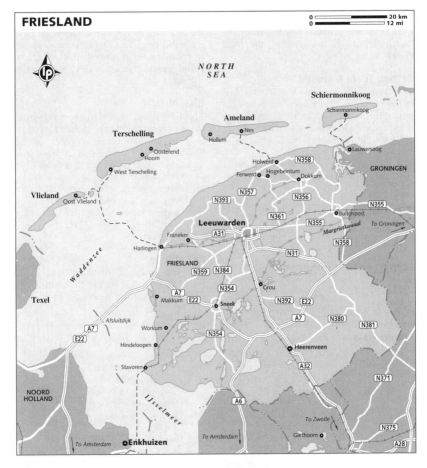

FRIESLAND

History

Having dredged their home out of the Waddenzee armload by armload, the Frisians are no strangers to struggling with their environment.

Farming, fishing and nautical know-how (the building, repair and maintenance of ships) have been the area's principal activities for centuries, and in the pre-republic era made Friesland one of the wealthiest regions in the Netherlands. Though unsubtly forced into union with the rest of the Netherlands and suffering economically after the opening of the Afsluitdijk (see boxed text, p160), it has recently enjoyed a revival as a domestic holiday destination.

Language

Frisians speak Frisian, which is actually closer (in some ways) to German and Old English than Dutch. Most people who have lived in the region for a significant time will speak some Frisian, though the majority are perfectly conversant in mainstream Dutch.

You're more likely to hear Frisian being spoken by older residents of smaller and more remote towns than by younger people. Don't worry if you can't make head nor tail of it – even the Dutch have difficulty deciphering Frisian. You'll usually see written examples, such as street signs. You might, for example, see the word 'Snits', which is the Frisian version of Sneek, the region's second city.

A ruling in 2002 officially altered the spelling of the province's name from the Dutch 'Friesland' to 'Fryslân', the local version of the name.

Getting There & Around

The capital, Leeuwarden, is easily reached by train and the entire province is accessible by car; the quickest route from Amsterdam is over the Afsluitdijk. Alternatively, you can take the car ferry from Enkhuizen to Stavoren (see p159 for details).

By bus, Interliner No 350 runs between Alkmaar in Noord Holland and Leeuwarden via Harlingen (two hours, hourly).

Getting around the province requires more patience. Netherlands Railways has privatised most local lines and standards have dropped. Nevertheless, you can reach all of Friesland by bus, train or bike.

LEEUWARDEN (LJOUWERT)

☎ 058 / pop 90,500

Leeuwarden is a pleasant, sleepy place reflecting the serenity of the surrounding farmland. Not as vivacious as Groningen to the east, the city's quiet old streets are good for wandering. There's just enough action to provide interest, though in the thick of island-jaunting season it can seem a bit of a ghost town.

History

The first Frisians formed the town from three *terpen*, the huge mounds of mud used as home sites to stay dry during floods. There is a tradition of trade and agriculture in Leeuwarden that dates from the 15th century, when it was a centre of power struggles between Friesland's wealthy dukes and those of Holland. The town's most famous daughter was saucy WWI spy/*femme fatale* Mata Hari (see boxed text below)

Orientation

The old town is compact and easily traversed on foot. Much of the commercial life is on or near the network of canals that wind through the centre.

MATA HARI

Had she been born a few decades later, Leeuwarden's own Margaretha Geertruida Zelle probably would have been given a TV chat show. Instead, the irrepressible Margaretha changed her name to Mata Hari, moved to Paris and ended up a martyr to salacious legend.

Born in 1876, Margaretha was a bright child whose friends said 'had an active imagination'; always a recipe for trouble. Her wealthy family fell apart in her teens and she married a stodgy military man 20 years her senior. While they were living in what is now Indonesia, one of their two children died in a bizarre poisoning incident.

Back in Leeuwarden in 1902, the marriage collapsed. Margaretha left her other child with the ex-husband and moved to Paris, where she began a career as a dancer and achieved wide fame, no doubt helped by the fact that she danced naked. She also changed her name to Mata Hari, which she said was Malaysian for sun.

Mata Hari's love affairs and dalliances were legendary in her own time. She favoured rich men in uniform and when WWI broke out in 1914, she had lovers in the high ranks of the military on both sides. This soon got her in trouble, as her numerous partners asked her to spy on her other partners. This web of intrigue was not helped by her keen imagination, and soon she was mistrusted by all sides.

In 1917, at age 40, she was arrested by the French for spying. There was a dubious trial, during which none of her former 'pals' offered any assistance – probably out of embarrassment – and later that year she was sentenced to death and shot.

In Leeuwarden today you can trace a good part of Mata Hari's early life as Margaretha. Her birthplace is at Kelders 33. On the nearby bridge over the canal, there is a statue of Mata Hari as a (clothed) dancer.

Much of Margaretha's childhood was spent at Grote Kerkstraat 212, which now houses the **Frysk Letterkundich Museum** (☎ 789 07 89), a small institution devoted to Frisian literature.

The Fries Museum has a large and detailed exhibit on the life of both Margaretha and Mata Hari.

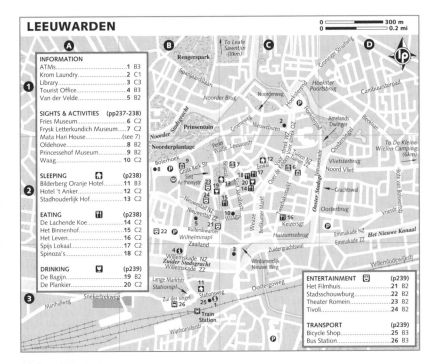

LEEUWARDEN

0 — 300 m
0 — 0.2 mi

INFORMATION	
ATMs	1 B3
Krom Laundry	2 C1
Library	3 C3
Tourist Office	4 B3
Van der Velde	5 B2
SIGHTS & ACTIVITIES (pp237–238)	
Fries Museum	6 C2
Frysk Letterkundich Museum	7 C2
Mata Hari House	(see 7)
Oldehove	8 B2
Princessehof Museum	9 B2
Waag	10 C2
SLEEPING	(p238)
Bilderberg Oranje Hotel	11 B3
Hotel 't Anker	12 C2
Stadhouderlijk Hof	13 C2
EATING	(p238)
De Lachende Koe	14 C2
Het Binnenhof	15 C2
Het Leven	16 C2
Spijs Lokaal	17 C2
Spinoza's	18 C2
DRINKING	(p239)
De Bagijn	19 B2
De Plankier	20 C2

ENTERTAINMENT	(p239)
Het Filmhuis	21 B2
Stadsschouwburg	22 B2
Theater Romein	23 B2
Tivoli	24 B2
TRANSPORT	(p239)
Bicycle Shop	25 B3
Bus Station	26 B3

Information

Van der Velde (☎ 213 23 60; Nieuwstad 90) This bookshop has a smallish but decent selection of English-language and travel books.

Library (☎ 234 77 77; Wirdumerdijk 34; web access €2 per hr; ☽ 12.30-5.30pm Mon & Thu, 10am-1pm & 7-9pm Tue & Fri, 10am-1pm Wed & Sat) Easy to find and has all the usual facilities.

Krom (☎ 213 08 45; Voorstreek WZ 102 ; ☽ 9am-5pm Mon-Fri) Will do your laundry for you.

ATMs To the right as you exit the station, and across the road on the opposite side of Stationsweg.

Post office (☎ 213 09 98; Oldehoofster Kerkhof 4; ☽ 7.30am-6pm Mon-Fri, 7.30am-1.30pm Sat)

Tourist office (☎ 0900-2024060; vvvleeuwarden@chello.nl; Sophialaan 4; ☽ 9am-5.30pm Mon-Fri, 10am-2pm Sat) The tourist office is only a short walk from the train station and has an Internet kiosk.

Sights

Most of Leeuwarden's sights are concentrated within a leisurely 10-minute walk of Nieuwestad, predominantly on the northern side (Nieuwestad NZ) of the water.

FRIES MUSEUM

The **Fries Museum** (☎ 255 55 00; www.friesmuseum.nl; Turfmarkt 11; adult/child under 18 €5/2.50; ☽ 11am-5pm, closed Mon) is spread over two historic buildings, the Kanselarij, a 16th-century courthouse, and the Eysinghaus, a mansion from the late 1700s.

The museum traces Frisian culture from the mud-stacking era onwards. The huge collection of silver items – long a local speciality – is spectacular. There is also a section on the efforts by locals to resist the Nazis, and a sombre examination of the life of Mata Hari (p236)

PRINCESSEHOF MUSEUM

Pottery lovers will adore the 17th-century palace housing the **Princessehof Museum** (☎ 294 89 58; www.princessehof.nl in Dutch; Grote Kerkstraat 11; adult/child €3.50/2; ☽ 11am-5pm Tue-Sun). It is the official museum for ceramics in the Netherlands and holds the largest collection of tiles on the planet. There's an unparalleled selection of Delftware and works from around the globe – and its Japanese, Chinese and Vietnamese sections are world class.

FRIESLAND

OTHER ATTRACTIONS

Just past the west end of Bagijnestraat, the **Oldehove** (adult/child €1/0.50; 2-5pm Tue-Sat May-Sep) dominates its unfortunate spot on the Oldehoofsterkerkhof parking lot. Things went wrong shortly after the tower was started in 1529 and it started to lean severely when it was only 40m high.

The relatively petite **Waag** dominates Waagplein, and is now surrounded by stores. It was the weigh house for butter and other goods from 1598 to 1884.

Sleeping

For B&B or pension-style accommodation – and there's tons of it – try the tourist office. Book at least one to two weeks ahead in the summer months, and don't even think about chancing it on a weekend or public holiday, especially in good weather. Snowballs have fared better in hell.

De Kleine Wielen (☎ 0511-43 16 60; fax 43 25 84; De Groene Ster 14; camp site for 2 people €16) This camp site is 6km east of the city off the N355. Bus Nos 10, 13, 50, 51 and 62 all pass close by. Tell the driver you want to get off at De Skieppepoel; it's a five-minute walk south from here.

Hotel ,t Anker (☎ 212 52 16; www.hotelhetanker.nl; Eewal 73; s/d €43/60) The Anchor is in a fun and pretty part of town, close to the nightlife district.

Bilderberg Oranje Hotel (☎ 212 62 41; oranjehotel@bilderberg.nl; Stationsweg 4; s/d from €106.50/137.50; P ⋈) This huge place looks drab on the outside, but is much nicer once you're through the doors. The rooms are well appointed, with most featuring stereo systems, pay TV and minibar. It's also conveniently located directly across from the station.

Stadhouderlijk Hof (☎ 216 21 80; info@stadhouderlijkhof.nl; Hofplein 29; r €90-275; P ⋈) A monument in itself. Once the residence of local royalty, Stadhouderlijk Hof is luxuriously appointed. The genuinely elegant rooms start fairly basic, eventually hitting some sumptuous heights (the Imperial de Luxe Suite). Breakfast and an endless array of other extravagant add-ons are available.

Eating

Het Leven (☎ 212 12 33; Druifstreek 57A; mains €10; lunch & dinner) This classic *eetcafé* (a café serving meals) has a diverse menu of dishes from the Netherlands and the rest of Europe. A great place to try sticks-to-your-ribs Dutch staples like *stamppot* (mashed pot) or *erwtensoep* (peasoup).

Spijs Lokaal (☎ 216 22 14; Eewal 54; mains €7-15; lunch & dinner) The chefs here are kept busy preparing modern European fare, blending tastes from all over for devoted locals. It's pretty popular, but if you haven't booked ahead, Spinoza's is right next door.

Spinoza's (☎ 212 93 93; Eewal 50-52; mains €12-15; dinner). A great place. Go to this simple, homey, laidback diner to eat delicious, typically European food (meat+potatoes+vegetables) at good prices. A meal for two with drinks should come to about €30.

Het Binnenhof (☎ 213 15 14; Weerd 18; mains €15-20; lunch & dinner) Formerly the Grand Café Lichtenstein, grand it still is. It has a large garden and is in a sumptuous building. The menu is at the upper end of café standard. This is a great place to linger over a couple of courses.

De Lachende Koe (The Laughing Cow, ☎ 215 82 45; Groote Hoogstraat 16; mains €10-14; dinner Tue-Sun) A great restaurant. Huge serves, delicious daily specials (meaty and vegetarian) at less than €11, and friendly service. All this in a comfy, unpretentious low-lit, country-style dining room where the menus drop down via a funky overhead pulley system. Cowabunga.

SPLURGE

If you're up for a splurge, the region's best restaurant, **Leafe Sawntjin** (Goodness Gracious!; ☎ 43 23 74; www.leafesawntjin.nl in Dutch; Lege Herewei 14; mains €20; lunch & dinner Thu-Sun), is in nearby Hijum (10km north of Leeuwarden). A fabulous place in an out of the way location, it offers a lovely view of a quaint church that sits atop a nearby *terp* (mound made from mud). The exquisite dishes, made with the finest regional produce (in autumn there's game and rare poultry) follow seasonal themes.

Figure on spending €30 to €50 per person, though the sky's the limit if you want to stretch it out into a languid, indulgent evening. Take district bus No 54 from Leeuwarden station and let the driver know you're heading for the restaurant. You'll have booked ahead, naturally.

Drinking

De Bagijn (☎ 212 77 38; Bagijnestraat 63) A cool place with good beer. Start your evening here with casual beers and finish it with a few more raucous ones.

Entertainment

There's a concentration of places around Doelesteeg, Kleine Hoogstraat and Grote Hoogstraat. Just wander from place to place and gravitate towards what looks or sounds good at the time. Thursday night is 'students night' in Leeuwarden and a few places may have happy hours as a result. You don't usually have to prove your student status.

De Plankier (☎ 213 91 18; www.cafeplankier.nl; Grote Hoogstraat 32; ☽ Tue-Sat) It's like a house party here, with different 'zones' – a small bar up front, dancing in the middle room and folks chilling out in the back room. It also serves cheap meals and filling bar snacks five nights a week.

Theater Romein (☎ 215 57 83; Bagijnestraat 59) A performance venue built in 1846, with a distinctly Spanish look. It's the scene of all manner of musical and theatrical performances. Admission and show times vary. There's also the **Stadsschouwburg Leeuwarden De Harmonie** (☎ 233 02 33; Ruiterskwartier 4) for similarly highbrow stuff.

Tivoli (☎ 212 38 87; Nieuwestad NZ 85) un-spools an interesting line-up of arthouse and festival films, as does **Het Filmhuis** (☎ 212 50 60; Ruiterskwatier 6; film €5-7).

Getting There & Around

Leeuwarden is at the end of the main train line from the south. It's also the hub for local services in Friesland. The large station has numerous services including a barber and a big newsstand. You'll find the lockers by track No 8. Fares and schedules include:

Destination	Price (€)	Duration (min)	Frequency (per hr)
Amsterdam	23.50	140	2
Groningen	7.30	55	2
Utrecht	21.30	120	2

The buses are to the left as you exit the train station.

The **bicycle shop** (☎ 213 98 00) is to the right as you exit the station. It's open until as late as 2am in the peak months.

AROUND LEEUWARDEN

The N357, which connects Leeuwarden with the Ameland ferry port at Holwerd, 23km north, passes some of the oldest settled parts of Friesland – an excellent route for driving or riding.

At Ferwerd, 6km southwest of Holwerd, watch for a road northeast to **Hogebeintum**, which is 3km off the N357. You'll soon see the highest *terp* in Friesland with a lovely old church perched on top. There are some good displays explaining the ongoing archaeological digs.

SNEEK (SNITS)

☎ 0515 / pop 32,900

'All Frisians know how to sail, and all Frisians know how to fish.' Or so some locals say. You'll likely feel a bit like a fish out of water yourself in Friesland if you're not nautically inclined. It's particularly evident in Sneek (pronounced like the English 'snake') – the gateway to the water activity hotspots of the surrounding Frisian Lakes, the IJsselmeer and the many nearby canals and rivers. If you're seriously interested in improving your sailing technique, there are generations of expertise concentrated around here.

Information

Tourist office (☎ 41 40 96; www.vvvsneek.nl; Marktstraat 18; ☽ 9am-5pm Mon-Fri, 9am-2pm Sat) Has long lists of boat rental and charter firms, sailing schools and more.

SNS Bank (☎ 41 27 96; Marktstraat1) Near the tourist office. There are ATMs throughout town.

Main post office (☎ 43 02 80; Martiniplein 15A; ☽ 9am-6pm Mon-Fri, 9am-1.30pm Sat)

Post office (Westersingel 28; ☽ 7.30am-6.30pm Mon-Fri, 7.30am-noon Sat)

Library (☎ 42 30 23; Wijde Noorderhorne 1; web access €2 per hr ; ☽ 1.30-7.30pm Mon-Fri,10.30am-1.30pm Sat) Has Internet access.

The train station has recently been stripped of many services, including lockers. The remaining employees will watch your bags, however, during office hours (7am to 7pm).

Sights & Activities

You won't find many conventional sights here in Sneek, given its overwhelming bias towards the water. The **Waterpoort** dates from 1613 and is the former gateway to the old port. Its twin towers are local landmarks. Across from the tourist office, the **town hall** (Marktstraat 15) is an excellent example of the breed.

The **Fries Scheepvaart Museum** (☎ 41 40 57; Kleinzand 14; adult/child €2/1; 🕙 10am-5pm, noon-5pm Sun) has interesting exhibits on the local seafaring life.

Anything you can do on the water is big in Sneek, which is flat and has tons of wind and no shortage of the wet stuff. For a list of some local boat rental companies, see p296.

During the summer months there are **boat cruises** on the local waters. The schedules change by whim, weather and number of operators each season. Most leave from the Oosterkade, at the end of Kleinzand. Either wander over there or inquire at the tourist office.

There are several sailing and windsurfing schools where you can learn from scratch or top up existing skills. One of the largest is **Zeilschool de Friese Meren** (☎ 41 21 41; www.zfm.nl in Dutch; Eeltjebaasweg 7), which has a range of courses.

In fact, water sports are such a big drawcard for Sneek that the local and regional tourist offices publish a separate guide solely featuring the various operators and services available.

Sleeping

The tourist office has lists of local rooms from around €18.50 to €25 per person.

De Domp Camping (☎ 41 25 59; Domp 4; camp site €12) A 20-minute walk from town. Follow the signs for the *zwembad* (public swimming pool). There are some sites for hikers that are well away from the vehicles.

Stayokay Sneek (☎ 41 21 32; www.stayokay.com /sneek; Oude Oppenhuizerweg 20; dm from €20) This is a relaxed hostel with a nice garden. From the train station, take a taxi, or walk 30 minutes through town and then southwest via Oppenhuizerweg and Kamerling Onne-straat.

De Wijnberg (☎ 41 24 21; fax 41 33 69; Marktstraat 23; s/d €60/67.50) A comfortable place with an excellent restaurant. Basic singles have toilets and are spartan but clean and tidy. Double rooms all include TV and bathroom.

Eating

There aren't many outstanding places to eat in Sneek and, in all likelihood, you'll be itching to get out on the water anyway.

Cafe De Draai (☎ 42 28 66; Wijde Noorderhorne 13; mains €10; 🕙 lunch & dinner) Located behind the library, the biggest café in Sneek is a cheery place that attracts all sorts. It has cheap *dagschotels* (daily specials) for €8,

---

FIERLJEPPEN

If you took pole-vaulting, long-jump, military-style hand-over-hand climbing and decided to combine them into a single sport, then add the thrill of doing it across a canal, you'd get *fierljeppen* (in Frisian), or *polsstokspringen* (in Dutch). The point is ostensibly distance, though avoiding serious injury – either mid-flight or against the lip of the canal during landing – is the thrilling sub-plot. Historically, jumping further than the length of the pole was the primary goal.

The skills required by competitiors are balance, endurance, agility, strength and a complete and utter disregard for personal safety. The discrete stages of a jump are to sprint full-tilt at the pole; jump on; scramble to the top, all the while gracefully controlling the pole's forward and lateral motion (and hoping your rivals haven't greased the bugger…); pray/fall; and land gracefully on a sand-bed on the other side of the canal with (hopefully) all bones and dignity intact.

The first official matches started in the 1960s, and clubs sprung up everywhere. The national championships are held annually and alternate location between Friesland and the rest of the Netherlands. In 1991, Aart de With made many competitors' poles droop with jealousy, propelling himself a staggering 19.40m, still the Dutch record. Henk Schievink holds the Frisian record with 18.89m.

The main afficionados are, naturally, the Frisians. But the sport itself has traversed one huge cultural boundary: Japan, of all places, has it's own national *fierljeppen* association.

Should you be in Friesland – and bonkers enough – you can try it yourself. **Polsstokbond Holland** (☎ 0348-552450; www.pbholland.com) do demonstrations, corporate functions, bachelor parties (oh smart, let's throw alcohol into *this* mix…) and at the end, you can have a bash, safe in the knowledge that expert maniacs will be guiding your every move.

10 beers on tap and over 80 varieties of bottled beer.

Getting There & Around
From the train station, the centre of town is a five-minute walk along Stationstraat. Trains to/from Leeuwarden cost €3.80 (20 minutes, two per hour).

Buses leave from the area to the right of the station.

The friendly staff at **Rijwielhandel Twa Tsjillen** (☎ 41 38 78; Wijde Noorderhorne 8; €5 per day) will rent you a bike.

HARLINGEN (HARNS)
☎ 0517 / pop 15,600
Of all the old Frisian ports, only Harlingen has kept its link to the sea. It's an important port and the base for ferries to Terschelling and Vlieland.

As ferry ports go, it's an attractive one, well worth a stop even if you're not heading out to the islands. Much of the centre near the port is a preserved zone of pretty 16th- and 18th-century buildings.

Information
Tourist office (☎ 0900-5400001; www.vvv -harlingen.nl in Dutch; Voorstraat 34; 1-5pm Mon, 10am-12pm & 1-5pm Tue-Fri, 10am-4pm Sat Apr-Sep; 10am-12pm & 1-5pm Tue-Fri, 10am-2pm Sat Oct-Mar) Offers the usual excellent service.

Post office (☎ 41 99 21; Grote Bredeplaats 6; 9am-6pm Mon-Fri, 10am-1.30pm Sat) Two hundred metres from the ferry terminal.

Several **banks** with ATMs can be found on Voorstraat.

Sights & Activities
Harlingen is best enjoyed on foot. Stroll along the canals, especially Noorderhaven, with its many yachts, and Zuiderhaven.

The **Gemeentemuseum Het Hannemahuis** (☎ 41 36 58; Voorstraat 56; adult/child €2.50/1; 1.30-5pm Tue-Sat Apr-Jun & Oct-Nov; 10am-5pm Tue-Sat, 1.30-5pm Sun Jul-Sep) is housed in an 18th-century building and includes material on Harlingen's past as a whaling town. Along with farming, whaling was one of the industries that made Friesland in the 1700s one of the most prosperous regions in the Netherlands. Hence the celebration of 'flensing' and 'flensers' – the process of stripping blubber from a whale's carcass and the lucky chaps who got to do it.

Sleeping
De Zeehoeve Camping (☎ 41 34 65; www.zeehoeve.nl in Dutch; Westerzeedijk 45; camp site for 2 people & tent €11) About a 1km walk south from the ferry terminal along the dyke. It has a variety of sites and facilities, including cabins.

Zeezicht Harlingen (☎ 41 25 36; www.hollandhotels .nl; Zuiderhaven 1; s/d €55/83). It's part of a chain, but don't let that mislead you. The service is better than generic, the downstairs café/bar comfortable and atmospheric, and the rooms a bargain, considering all have bathroom and include TV, phone and minibar. It's fabulously located for the ferry port (five minutes' walk) or wherever takes your fancy.

Eating
Restaurant Noorderpoort (☎ 41 50 43; Noorder-haven 17; mains €17-25; lunch & dinner) Has a casual menu of Dutch food with French flourishes. The dining room has views of the canal and ferry port. The adjoining café has sandwiches and a good selection of beers.

SOMETHING SPECIAL

The Shining
Vuurtoren van Harlingen (www.vuurtoren -harlingen.nl; Havenweg 1; r €249; see tourist information). Winter or summer, you might need to bring your sunglasses – the one stunning room available is in Harlingen's lighthouse. The suite comes with all manner of luxuries and nonpareil views. There's a slight availability catch – it's a wallet-thumper and has a two-year waiting list. Book through the tourist office.

A Tale of a Faithful Ship
In the meantime, you could stay at the **Reddingsboot Harlingen** (www.vuurtoren -harlingen.nl; Noorderhaven; r €199) operated by the same people and also bookable only through the tourist office. A little less tricky to swing, with only a few-months-long waiting list, but almost as heady an indulgence, with DVD player, minibar and a classic wooden bathtub in the room. You can also arrange to push the boat out, literally – the owners can organise trips, romantic or otherwise.

Getting There & Around

See p245 and p246 for details on the ferry service to the ports at Vlieland and Terschelling.

The ferry terminal is large and bland. Nearby there is a modern train station, Harlingen Haven. However, NoordNed runs only a few trains to here, and those don't operate every day. All the rest of the services from Leeuwarden terminate at Harlingen station, which is 1km from the centre.

FRANEKER (FRJENTSJER)

☎ 0517 / pop 21,000

You'll forgive any resident of Franeker, 6km east of Harlingen, for saying, 'We could have been Groningen!' And they could have been if Napoleon hadn't closed the university in 1810. Though it's a pleasant enough place for a visit, Franeker has spent 200 years licking its intellectual wounds. Of course, this means that it's quite well preserved and makes for a fine hour of strolling.

The highlight of the town is the **Eise Eisinga Planetarium** (☎ 39 30 70; www.planetarium-friesland.nl; Eise Eisingastraat 3; adult/child €3/2.25; ♥ 10am-5pm Tue-Sat, 1-5pm Sun Oct-Apr, 10am-5pm Tue-Sat, 1-5pm Sun & Mon May-Sep), the world's oldest working planetarium. The namesake owner was a tradesman with a serious sideline in cosmic mathematics and astrology, who clearly could have been a 'somebody' in the astronomical world. Beginning in 1774 – the year of an 'astrologically significant' planetary conjunction that many feared

indicated the end of the world – he built the planetarium himself to show how the heavens actually worked.

The planetarium room is very cool, with its model orbs and intersecting movements. It's startling to contemplate how Eisinga could have devised a mechanical timing system built to a viewable working scale that could encompass and illustrate so many different variables of time and motion.

Conducted at regular intervals is a 20-minute bilingual discussion (in Dutch and German) on Eisinga's life and how his fabulous clockworks tick.

The Harlingen–Leeuwarden train stops in Franeker 500m from the centre.

COASTAL TOWNS

Friesland has a string of coastal towns that made their living from the sea until the Zuiderzee (South Sea) was dammed and became the freshwater IJsselmeer (IJssel Lake). After a few decades in limbo, the villagers are now attracting tourists to the towns' old streets and many charms. Each town has a permanent population of under 1000 that swells in summer.

The route south from Makkum to Hindeloopen passes many traditional Frisian dairy farms.

Hindeloopen (Hylpen)

☎ 0514 / pop 1100

Huddled up against the banks of the IJsselmeer, Hindeloopen has been set apart from Friesland for centuries. Until recently,

---

A DAY AT THE RACES

Skating and the Dutch culture are interwoven and no event better symbolises this than the Elfstedentocht (Eleven Cities Race, www.elfstedentocht.nl). Begun officially in 1909, although it had been held for hundreds of years before that, the race is 200km long, starts and finishes in Leeuwarden and passes through 10 Frisian towns (11 including Leeuwarden): Sneek, IJlst, Sloten, Stavoren, Hindeloopen, Workum, Bolsward, Harlingen, Franeker and Dokkum. The record time for completing the race is six hours and 47 minutes, set in 1985.

While it is a marathon, what makes the race a truly special event is that it can only be held in years when it's cold enough for all the canals to freeze totally; this has only happened 15 times since 1909. The last time was in 1997. So how do you schedule such an event? You don't.

Instead, there is a huge Elfstedentocht committee that waits for the mercury to plummet. When it looks as though the canals will be properly frozen, 48 hours' notice is given. All work effectively ends throughout the province as armies of volunteers make preparations for the race and the thousands of competitors get ready.

On the third day, the race begins at 5.30am. The next few hours are a holiday for the rest of the Netherlands as well, as the population gathers around TVs to watch the live coverage.

the local women still wore characteristic green and red costumes that were similar to the also characteristic hand-carved furniture.

With its narrow streets, tiny canals, little bridges and long waterfront, Hindeloopen is very beautiful. In extraordinarily cold winters it is one of the key towns on the route of the *Elfstedentocht* (Eleven Cities Race, see A Day at the Races, p242) and has a quaint yet reverent museum devoted to the race.

INFORMATION

The staff at the **tourist office** (☎ 52 25 50; Nieuwstad 26; ⏰ 1-5pm Apr-Jun, 10am-5pm Jul & Aug, 1-5pm Sep & Oct) can help with accommodation and other services. For most things, you'll have to go 4km north to Workum. Unless noted, almost everything in Hindeloopen is closed from November to March.

SIGHTS & ACTIVITIES

Hindeloopen is definitely a place to just hang out and take in the scene. However, **Het Eerste Friese Schaatsmuseum** (☎ 52 16 83; www.schaatsmuseum.nl in Dutch; Kleine Weide 1-3; adult/child €2.50/1; ⏰ 10am-6pm Mon-Sat, 1-5pm Sun) is a fascinating diversion with many displays on the *Elfstedentocht* and ice-skating in general. There are detailed descriptions, pictures and displays of manufacturing techniques and developments in skating technology through the centuries, and then there are the mind-boggling logistics of the race itself, and a biographical summary on each winner of the event.

Two-time champ Evert van Benthem (in 1985 and '86) is a modern-day legend, having set the standing record for the race, and in such a dominant fashion. It was such a big deal that he's had both a cheese and wine named after him.

SLEEPING & EATING

Camping Hindeloopen (☎ 52 14 52; fax 52 32 21; Westerdijk 9; camp site €12) Cheap sites.

Skips Maritiem (☎ 52 45 50; fax 52 45 51; Oosterstrand 22; r €30) A bit of an empire on the marina. Besides servicing boats, it rents out simple rooms for two without bathrooms. Fully equipped rooms with a kitchenette are also available, for €65. There are hire bikes, too.

De Stadsboerderij (☎ 52 12 78; fax 52 30 16; Nieuwe Weide 9; r €45) This place is away from the main crowds and has comfortable rooms.

There is also a casual restaurant. But then, everything in Hindeloopen is casual.

There are more than 20 places to eat ranging from cheap fried-fish wagons to fine restaurants.

GETTING THERE & AWAY

The train stop is a pleasant 2.5km walk from town. There is an hourly service to Sneek (€2.80, 15 mins) and Leeuwarden (€4.80, 40 mins).

FRISIAN ISLANDS

The four Frisian islands are basically raised banks of sand and mud, yet have played a crucial role in protecting the Netherlands' north coast. In the 1800s the government began aggressively planting vegetation to help stabilise them. The resulting pine forests, while attractive, are definitely not native.

The islands' primary appeal is to city-bound Dutch people looking to escape to the beach, and to Germans whose half-dozen or so islands off their own northern coast are smaller and less interesting. The Dutch ones, by contrast, have all been developed for tourism, and the number of pensions, hotels and rooms and cottages for rent is enormous. Even so, in summer the islands are very crowded so don't just show up and expect to find a room. Populations routinely multiply by 10 on warm weekends.

Despite the development, all have large open spaces where you can get close to the sea grasses or the water itself. Any of the islands makes an interesting trip on its own and there are copious bicycle rentals near the ferry ports. Paths suitable for hiking and biking circle each of the islands and, away from the built-up areas, you're rewarded with long sandy beaches on the seaward sides.

That said, if you only have time for one Dutch island, it should be Texel (p161). in Noord Holland

If you want some windblown solitude, try going in the off season, though be aware it can get *very* cold and snowy this far north in winter.

Getting There & Away

Island hopping isn't really a possibility. The ferry group (Rederij Doeksen) that operates the services from the mainland to the islands has ensured the timetable

FRISIAN ISLANDS

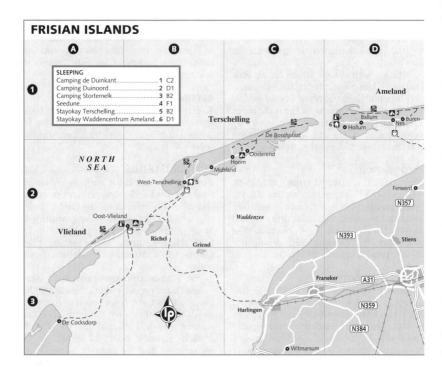

SLEEPING
Camping de Duinkant....................1 C2
Camping Duinoord.........................2 D1
Camping Stortemelk......................3 B2
Seedune..4 F1
Stayokay Terschelling...................5 B2
Stayokay Waddencentrum Ameland..6 D1

is frustratingly inflexible. There's only a certain number of transits a day, and surcharges for everything.

It's also not feasible to do day trips due to the two-hour ferry ride (unless you can make the first ferry from Harlingen at 8.45am) and the cost of the hydrofoil, which is faster but doesn't allow bikes.

All islands have banks, grocery stores and other services in their main towns, but don't expect extras like Internet access. As for the ferries, if you're bringing a car – but really, don't – be sure to reserve a spot in advance.

Vlieland
☎ 0562 / pop 1200

Historically the most isolated of the islands, Vlieland had one of its two towns washed away by a storm in the 18th century. Even today it is one of the least-visited islands. Nonresidents aren't allowed to bring cars onto its 72 sq km, meaning that away from the sole town of Oost Vlieland, it's a wild, natural place. Its 18km of beaches aren't as much fun to cycle as the untamed interior.

INFORMATION
The **tourist office** (☎ 45 11 11; www.vlieland.net in Dutch; Havenweg 10; 9am-5pm Mon-Fri, 1hr after each ferry arrival Sat & Sun) is as helpful as ever. Meaning very.

SIGHTS & ACTIVITIES
There's not much in the way of man-made attractions on Vlieland and that's exactly the point: nature is the attraction. There are a few roads around Oost Vlieland, and that's it. The rest of the island lies waiting to be explored by bike or on foot. Depending on how fit you consider yourself, cycling around Vlieland can be gentle or moderately gruelling; there are many unsealed tracks that confident 'off-roaders' can opt to tackle, opening great new sightseeing possibilities. Bike hire is around €6 per day.

The tourist office organises nature hikes and bird-watching walks. There's also a small boat running from the southern tip to Texel in summer. It's linked to town by a tractor pulling a cart (ask at the tourist office for details).

FRIESLAND

even in the high season, so it's worth checking in advance.

You can cycle around the island and there is also a little bus that wanders the few roads of Oost Vlieland.

Terschelling
☎ 0562 / pop 4800

This 110-sq-km island has a rich nautical past. The islanders once earned a living repairing ships, as many were wrecked on the uncertain waters around the island.

Terschelling is the largest, most visited and commercial Frisian island. The main town is West Terschelling, where the ferry from Harlingen docks. You can find just about any service and amusement you'd want here, many along the island's 30km of beaches.

The smaller towns of Hoorn and Oosterend are east of West Terschelling and much less commercial, but closer to the very pretty natural parts of the island.

INFORMATION
The **tourist office** (☎ 44 30 00; www.vvv-terschelling
.nl; Willem Barentszkade 19A; ⊙ 9.30am-5.30pm Mon-Sat)
is incredibly helpful, with a great range of maps for cycling or walking.

SIGHTS & ACTIVITIES
The **Terschelling Museum 't Behouden Huys** (☎ 44
23 89; www.behouden-huys.nl in Dutch; Commandeurstraat
30-32; adult/child €3/2; ⊙ 10am-5pm Mon-Fri Apr-May &
Oct, 10am-5pm Mon-Sat Jun-Sep) is a good museum covering the island's maritime past.

De Boschplaat at the eastern end of the island is a huge car-free natural reserve. It is the only EU-designated European Natural Monument in the Netherlands.

FESTIVALS & EVENTS
The annual **Oerol** outdoor performance festival on Terschelling is revered nationwide as a perfect excuse for going offshore. It started years ago with farmers letting their cows run loose one day each year (hence the name 'oerol', which means 'everywhere' or 'all over') – these days, *everybody* gets into the spirit of things. It's a wild, arty party, piercing the otherwise unflappable northern façade for 10 days each June.

SLEEPING & EATING
Camping de Duinkant (☎ 44 89 17; site for 2 people
€10) Of the many places to camp, this is

EATING & SLEEPING
Bring a packed lunch, especially if you have anything beyond even the most basic dietary restrictions – there are very few places to eat on Vlieland.

Camping Stortemelk (☎ 45 12 25; www.stortemelk
.nl in Dutch; Kampweg 1; camp site for 2 people & tent €13)
This is an enormous place set back from the beach west of town.

Pension Hotelletje de Veerman (☎ 45 13 78;
www.pensiondeveerman.nl in Dutch; Dorpsstraat 173;
s/d from €34/54) A homey place with simple rooms. Comfort's probably not your top priority if you're on Vlieland, but if it is, look no further. Basic, but sufficient.

GETTING THERE & AROUND
Many of the details for the ferries from Harlingen to Vlieland are the same as for Terschelling (p246). The cost is slightly lower (return adult/child €18.75/9.40), though, and so is the journey time at 105 minutes. The fast ferry goes via Terschelling and takes around 80 minutes. The schedule is also much less frequent; sometimes there is only one ferry a day

the most remote, at the end of the road in Oosterend.

Stayokay Terschelling (☎ 44 23 38; www.stayokay .com/terschelling; Burg van Heusdenweg 39; dm from €20) Typically efficient, the Stayokay is a simple and sandy hostel with room for 148. Reserve well in advance in summer.

Hotel-Restaurant Lutine (☎ 44 21 94; fax 44 34 46; Boomstraat 1; s/d from €25/45) The Lutine is a basic place in West Terschelling. If you're after something a little more cushy than B&B or camping digs – yet won't break the bank – here's your place. The café is casual and typical of the scores that dot the island's towns.

GETTING THERE & AROUND
Ferries leave from Harlingen for Terschelling and are operated by **Rederij Doeksen** (☎ 44 21 41; www.rederij-doeksen.nl in Dutch; adult/child return from €22.95/13) The large car ferries take two hours in either direction and depart once a day in winter and six times or more in summer. Surcharges apply for bicycles (€9.85), dogs and surfboards. Call ☎ 0517-49 15 00, or check the website for the latest schedule information. Cars are best left ashore.

There is also the passenger-only **hydrofoil** (adult/child return from €30.45/20.50; ☼ mid-Apr–Sep) that operates several times a day (50 mins). Regardless of whether or not you pay the surcharge, it may be necessary to book your return spot on the last hydrofoil back, which leaves at 4.30pm.

There are frequent buses running the length of the main road.

Ameland
☎ 0519 / pop 3600
Second only to Terschelling in popularity, Ameland has two distinct centres within its 85 sq km: Nes, near the ferry dock, and Hollum, at the west end. It's as easy to cycle around as you care to make it, and is a pleasant balance to the garishness of Terschelling or Texel, yet more lively than serene Schiermonnikoog or verdant Vlieland. The 27km of beachside paths is lovely enough, but, as with the other islands, things get more interesting as you head inland.

Of the villages, the 18th-century former whaling port of Nes is the prettiest and most carefully preserved, its streets lined with tidy little brick houses.

INFORMATION
The **tourist office** (☎ 54 65 46; www.ameland.nl in Dutch; Rixt van Doniastraat; ☼ 9am-12.30pm & 1.30-6pm Mon-Fri, 10am-3pm Sat) is useful. Buy its excellent map (€2.50).

SIGHTS & ACTIVITIES
All four towns on Ameland are interesting for a brief stroll or ride. The Ballum cemetery has some eerie tombstones of dead sailors. Hollum has a famous red and white lighthouse worth seeing, or head to the eastern end of the island to lose sight of humans.

SLEEPING & EATING
Camping Duinoord (☎ 54 20 70; www.duinoord.nl in Dutch; Jan van Eijckweg 4; camp site for 2 people & tent €13) This camp site is 2km from Nes, by the beach. It's a lovely but windy place to camp.

Stayokay Waddencentrum Ameland (☎ 55 53 53; www.stayokay.com/ameland; Oranjeweg 59; dm from €20) This Stayokay is right near the lighthouse outside Hollum. It's simple, with mostly four-bed rooms, and a perfect place to hose yourself down after a pleasant afternoon's shlepping through the Wadden mud.

Hotel Restaurant de Jong (☎ 54 20 16; fax 54 20 24; Reeweg 29; s/d from €45/60) A comfortable lodge in Nes, the Hotel de Jong has decent rooms a comfort level above other places on the island, with an almost swanky café-dining room and luxurious air that might make you forget the remoteness of the place.

Herberg De Zwaan (☎ 55 40 02; www.ameland.net /dezwaan in Dutch; Zwaneplein 6) This lovely restaurant in Hollum is popular with locals in the off season. Its building dates from 1772.

GETTING THERE & AROUND
Wagenborg (☎ 54 61 11; www.wpd.nl; adult/child return €10.60/5.60) operates ferries between Nes and the large ferry port at Holwerd on the mainland. The latter has a large parking area, for people who sensibly forego taking cars to the island. The ferries run about every two hours (45 minutes) all year. Schedules fluctuate with demand (when busy, the ferries can run hourly) – call to confirm, or check the website. There are surcharges for bicycles, dogs and cars.

To reach the Holwerd ferry terminal from Leeuwarden, take bus Nos 60 or 66 (40 minutes, hourly). From Groningen, take bus No 34 (80 minutes, four or five daily).

Taxis and a small network of public buses that serve the island's four towns meet the ferries. Nes is a 2km walk from the ferry port, or a short bus ride.

Schiermonnikoog
☎ 0519 / pop 1000

The smallest of the Frisian islands, Schiermonnikoog's name means 'grey monk island', a reference to the 15th-century clerics who once lived here. All traces of these folk are gone and the island is mostly wild. The Dutch government made Schiermonnikoog a national park in 1989 so the wilderness should remain unfettered.

The most serene of all the islands, this is the place to go if getting away from it all is your goal. The feeling of sheer isolation as you move through Schiermonnikoog's 40 sq km, or along the 18km of beaches, can be quite moving. If you come to any of Friesland's islands immediately after one of the sardine-tin-packed metropolises in the Randstad (say, Amsterdam or Rotterdam), the feeling can be quite shocking.

The island's sole town, Schiermonnikoog, is quiet, even when crowded. Nonresidents are not allowed to bring cars on to the island.

INFORMATION
The **tourist office** (☎ 53 12 33; fax 53 13 25; 🕑 9am-1pm & 2-5.30pm Mon-Fri, to 4.30pm Sat) is in the middle of town.

SIGHTS & ACTIVITIES
Here you'll find the big gal herself, Mother Nature. That's about it, but if you are looking for a such an experience then what more do you want? Get a map from the tourist office and start exploring.

The national park has a **visitors centre** (☎ 53 16 41; 🕑 10.30am-5.30pm Mon-Sat Apr-Oct, 1.30-5.30pm Sat Nov-Mar) in an old power station in town. It reveals the natural features of the island.

The island is the most popular destination for *wadlopers*, or mud-walkers from the mainland (see Pounding Mud, p256).

SLEEPING & EATING
There are many cafés lining the few streets of downtown Schiermonnikoog.

Seedune (☎ 53 13 98; www.schiermonnikoog.net /seedune in Dutch; Seeduneweg 1; camp site per person/ tent €4.30/2.50) Just north of town, with room for 800 tents.

Pension Lulu (☎ 53 13 06; www.pensionlulu.nl in Dutch; Langestreek 70; r €25) Simple rooms that are comfortable and good value. Considering you're probably out here for the wilderness vibe, this is, in fact, sheer luxury.

GETTING THERE & AWAY
Wagenborg (☎ 54 61 1; www.wpd.nl; adult/child return €11/6) runs ferries between Schiermonnikoog and the port of Lauwersoog in Groningen province at the border with Friesland. Three to five ferries make the 45-minute voyage daily depending on the season. Surcharges apply for bicycles and dogs.

Bus No 63 makes the one-hour run between Lauwersoog and Groningen five times daily. Bus No 50 makes the one-hour run between Lauwersoog and Leeuwarden five times daily.

A bus meets all incoming ferries, which arrive at the island's port, for the 3km run into the town of Schiermonnikoog.

Groningen & Drenthe

The two northeastern provinces of Groningen and Drenthe are primarily agricultural, with an emphasis on breeding pigs. One whiff of the air in the countryside will certainly erase any doubt. However, amidst the swine is one true pearl; the city of Groningen is one of the most delightful in the Netherlands, and a highly recommended stop. It has a rich history, good museums and vibrant nightlife.

In fact, the student-riddled city of Groningen is reason enough to venture to this part of the Netherlands. Its laid-back inhabitants sink the stodgy stereotype of northerners as being cold and distant. The many cafés and bars offer diversions ranging from pleasant to pounding, and the university-fuelled creativity is everywhere and visible at street level in forms as diverse as fashion- and poster- design, and the many excellent bands and musicians the town nurtures. A few day trips and the chance to engage in the unusual activity of *wadlopen* (mud-walking, see Pounding Mud, p256) are other attractions.

Though Drenthe can seem a little bland or quiet, it's a beautiful, green province, intriguing for its Stonehenge-like monuments, the eerie *hunebedden* – enormous, ancient dolmens believed to be burial mounds, most abundant around the town of Emmen.

HIGHLIGHTS

- Bouncing from café, to museum to shop to bar and back again in the lively student town of Groningen (p250)
- Trying *wadlopen* (p256) off the northern coast
- Rescuing seals at the Zeehondencreche at Pieterburen (p256)
- Walking along the walls at Bourtange (p257)
- Getting 'stoned' checking out Drenthe's *hunebedden* (p259)

GRONINGEN

Like Utrecht, Groningen is a small province named after its primary city. Beyond the buzzing town itself, the province has few notable attributes. Much of the land is used for farming, while the north coast is mostly muddy. The scenery is best near the German border where the restored town of Bourtange is worth a trip.

Getting There & Around

Groningen, the city, is well served by frequent trains. For the other sights in this region plan on car, bus or bike, or a combination thereof.

GRONINGEN CITY

☎ 050 / pop 177,300

Groningen was founded around 1000. It was an early member of the Hanseatic League and from 1251 it had a regional monopoly on the grain trade that brought it prosperity for six centuries. The university opened in 1614 and has been among Europe's most highly esteemed for studies such as theology ever since.

At any given time, up to 20,000 of Groningen's population are students at the university or other tertiary education institutions such as the medical or architecture schools. This ensures that there's plenty to do at night, and you can enjoy the latest trends and prices that are within the budget of scholars.

GRONINGEN & DRENTHE

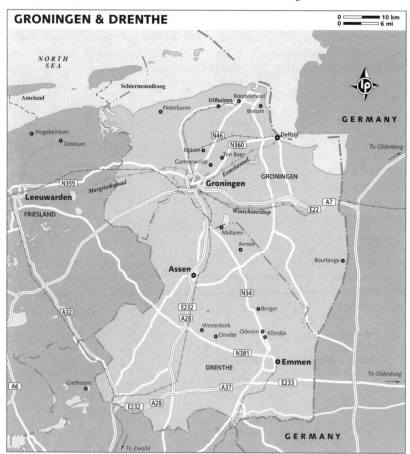

Orientation

The old centre is nicely compact and entirely ringed by canals. You can walk from one end to the other in 15 minutes. The train station is just across from the controversial Groninger Museum, a less than 10-minute walk from slightly bland but expansive Grote Markt, the main town square. Virulent anti-car policies dating from the 1970s mean that the centre is pleasantly free of traffic, although drivers will find plenty of parking around the periphery.

Information

BOOKSHOPS

Scholtens Wristers (☎ 313 97 88; www.scholtens -wristers.nl, in Dutch; Guldenstraat 20) A huge shop that includes a strong selection of academic titles amongst its enormous range.

INTERNET ACCESS

Library (☎ 368 36 83; Oude Boteringestraat 18; internet access per hr €2; ☻ 1-9pm Mon, 10am-6pm Tue-Fri, 10am-9pm Thu, 11am-4pm Sat, 1-4pm Sun) The main city library has loads of computers with Internet access.

LAUNDRY

Handy Wash (☎ 318 75 87; Schuitendiep 58; wash & dry around €6; ☻ 7.30am-8pm) Will wash your clothes – which is handy.

LEFT LUGGAGE

Lockers are in the station, between platforms 2a and 1b.

MEDICAL SERVICES

Academisch Ziekenhuis Groningen (☎ 361 61 61; Hanzeplein 1) A huge teaching hospital. Try not to end up as an exhibit in its in-house anatomy museum.

MONEY

ATMs can be found throughout town.
GWK money exchange (☻ 8am-7pm) In the train station.

POST

Post office (☎ 313 63 75; Munnekeholm 1) There is another branch closer to the train station (☎ 318 96 42; Gedempte Zuiderdiep 19)

TOURIST INFORMATION

Tourist office (☎ 0900-2023050; www.vvvgroningen.nl; Gedempte Kattendiep 6) The local tourist office offers advice on a wide range of topics and sells tickets, tours and more. Its map (€2) is excellent.

Sights & Activities

Groningen is reasonably small, and conveniently pedestrianised with most major sights lying within a 1km radius of the Grote Markt.

GRONINGER MUSEUM

Arriving by train it's impossible to miss the **Groninger Museum** (☎ 366 65 55; www.groninger -museum.nl, in Dutch; adult/child €7/3.5; ☻ 10am-5pm Tue-Sun year-round, 1-5pm Mon Jul-Aug). Built on islands in the middle of the canal in front of the station, it looks a little like what might eventuate if you left a child some colourful blocks, remnants from a few different rolls of 1980s wallpaper and random industrial bits, and told it to design a futuristic dollhouse.

If it seems designed by a committee, that's because it was. Chief architect Alessandro Mendini invited three 'guest architects' to each tackle a section. The polychromatic tile work surrounding the entrance and continuing on the inside is the work of Mendini, who re-invoked a pattern he first used on a Swatch watch he designed in 1991.

The museum was intended to combine a permanent exhibit about Groningen's rich history with an area for modern applied arts and other regional artworks. Much of the permanent collection was initially placed in galleries below the water line, with the areas above for temporary exhibitions. Locals hypothesised about the wisdom of having so much space below water level but were ignored by the architects who proclaimed the museum would stay dry 'for 200 years'. In 1998, the entire lower museum flooded. Some precious works were rushed out, literally, on the heads of swimming curators. The architects were unlocatable. Today, the permanent collection remains in the bronze tower.

The museum's schizophrenic external appearance is mirrored in the wonderfully eclectic curatorial direction (backed by a huge budget); it's quite something to see contemporary design and photography exhibitions alongside classic Golden Age Dutch paintings.

NOORDELIJK SCHEEPVAARTMUSEUM

Well worth a hour or two, the **Noordelijk Scheepvaartmuseum** (Northern Shipping Museum; ☎ 312 22 02, Brugstraat 24-26; adult/child €2.75/1.40;

GRONINGEN & DRENTHE

GRONINGEN CITY

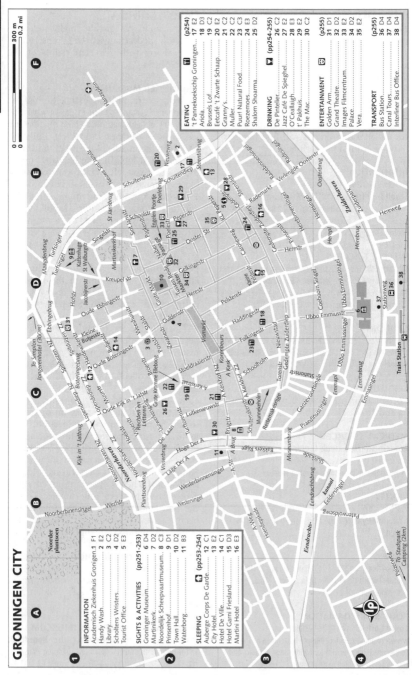

Noorder plantsoen

INFORMATION
Academisch Ziekenhuis Groningen.1 F1
Handy Wash........................... 2 E2
Library................................... 3 C2
Scholtens Wristers................. 4 D2
Tourist Office........................ 5 E3

SIGHTS & ACTIVITIES (pp251-253)
Groninger Museum................. 6 D4
Martinikerk........................... 7 D2
Noordelijk Scheepvaartmuseum.. 8 C3
Prinsenhof............................ 9 D1
Town Hall............................. 10 D2
Waterborg............................ 11 B3

SLEEPING (pp253-254)
Auberge Corps De Garde....... 12 C1
City Hotel............................. 13 E2
Hotel De Ville....................... 14 C1
Hotel Garni Friesland............ 15 D3
Martini Hotel........................ 16 E3

EATING (p254)
't Pannekoekschip Groningen... 17 E2
Ariola.................................. 18 D3
Brussels Lof......................... 19 C2
Eetcafé 't Zwarte Schaap....... 20 E2
Granny's.............................. 21 C2
Muller.................................. 22 C2
Puurt Natural Food............... 23 C3
Roezemoes........................... 24 E3
Shalom Shoarma................... 25 D2

DRINKING (pp254-255)
De Pintelier......................... 26 C2
Jazz Café De Spieghel........... 27 E2
O'Ceallaigh.......................... 28 E3
t' Pakhuis............................. 29 C2
The Mac............................... 30 C2

ENTERTAINMENT (p255)
Golden Arm......................... 31 D1
Grand Theatre...................... 32 D2
Images Filmcentrum.............. 33 E2
Palace................................. 34 D2
Vera.................................... 35 E2

TRANSPORT (p255)
Bus Station.......................... 36 D4
Canal Tours......................... 37 D4
Interliner Bus Office.............. 38 D4

GLENN VAN DER KNIJFF

Witte Huis and Mariniers Museum alongside
Oude Haven, Rotterdam (p213)

CHRIS MELLOR

The town hall in Middelburg (p228)

Rooftops and house façades in Zierikzee (p231)

JEFFREY N. BECOM

Groninger Museum, Groningen (p251)

Daffodil

A painted train in Friesland (p233)

Wad

(Y) 10am-5pm Tue-Sat, 1-5pm Sun) is well funded and well organised. The museum is laid-out over several floors of buildings that once comprised a 16th-century distillery. Just getting through the labyrinth of 18 rooms is an adventure in itself and guarantees an excellent workout.

Highlights of the museum include an intricately carved replica of the church at Paramaribo – the capital of former Dutch colony Surinam – in a bottle (Room 3), showing just how much time sailors had to kill on long voyages; and cool models demonstrating just how the many local shipyards operated throughout the centuries (Room 8). After Room 8, there are three rooms devoted to the **Niemeyer Tabaksmuseum** (Niemeyer Tobacco Museum), which is dedicated to how Dutch people have smoked through the ages. The expressions on the faces of the dummies in the first room will make you wonder what's in their pipes.

CANALS
On the western side of town, the canalside streets of **Hoge Der A** and **Lage Der A** are lined with old buildings that were once used as breweries. Water was drawn from the canals, and the yeast and resulting alcohol were counted on to take care of any 'impurities'. The façades of the houses display a variety that's best appreciated at night when they are starkly lit. A barrel hanging on the building at the corner of Visserstraat is a reminder of the neighbourhood's past.

CHURCHES & SQUARES
The **Grote Markt** is big, café-ringed and fairly charmless because of its size. It also suffered bomb damage during WWII and the rebuilding was less than sensitive. The **town hall** dates from 1810.

At the northern corner of the Grote Markt, the **Martinikerk** (☎ 311 12 77; Grote Markt; (Y) noon-5pm Tue-Sat Jun-Sep, noon-5pm Sat Oct-May) was built in the 16th century. Its tower, the Martinitoren, is 96m tall and is considered to have one of the most finely balanced profiles in the country. A climb (€2) to the top yields stellar views.

Just southwest of the Grote Markt, **Vismarkt** is a more intimate and attractive square.

Tours
Canal tours (☎ 312 83 79; (Y) depart 1.45pm) Leave from in front of the train station. The trips take 75 minutes and don't operate if the canals freeze (duh!). Book at the tourist office.

City walks (☎ 0900-2023050; adult €4; (Y) Mon Jul-Aug) The tourist office operates guided 90-minute walks conducted in English and Dutch.

Festivals & Events
Noorderslag January. A series of concerts by up-and-coming (they hope) bands, also an excuse for record company types from all over the Netherlands to get hammered, and for you to see some great live music.

Bommen Berend 28 August. A city celebration of the day the invading troops of the Bishop of Munster were repelled.

Studenten Cabaret Festival October. Draws performers from around Europe.

Sint Maarten 11 November. Locally grown sugar beets are carved into lanterns by kids, not unlike what their US counterparts do to pumpkins two weeks earlier for Halloween.

Sleeping
Check out the tourist office that publishes a list of B&Bs and pensions run by local families, starting from €20.

CAMPING
Stadspark Camping (☎ 525 16 24; www.stadscampings .nl; Campinglaan 4; 2 people & tent €10; (Y) mid-Mar–mid-Oct) Has a shop, restaurant, laundry, playground and more. From the train station, take bus No 4 (direction: Hoogkerk) about 3km west to the Stadspark stop. From there follow the signs for about 1km.

HOSTELS
Simplon Jongerenhotel (☎ 313 52 21; www.simplon jongerenhotel.nl; Boterdiep 73-2; dm from €10.60) Three hundred metres north of Noorderhaven, it's the best hostel in Groningen – clean, affordable and with decent breakfast (€4). Linen costs €2.80. There is an entertainment complex next door with a club, cinema and live bands. Take bus No 1 or 11 from the station to the Boteringestraat stop.

HOTELS
Hotel Garni Friesland (☎ 312 13 07; Kleine Pelster-straat; s/d €25/35) The Garni is bare bones but it's in a good location on a street with several cafés and the prices are unbeatable. The proprietors are also very helpful, and

will assist you with finding somewhere else if they happen to be full.

Martini Hotel (☎ 312 99 19; fax 312 79 04; Gedempte Zuiderdiep 8; r €66; 🖳 P) The Martini chain bought up a popular local hotel, but it's still a decent and unaffected place. It's also the biggest hotel in central Groningen (and has been in various guises since 1871) so it's a good bet if there's something big on in town that weekend.

Auberge Corps De Garde (☎ 314 54 37; fax 313 63 20; Oude Boteringestraat 72-74; r with/without €105/83) Simple yet comfortable. All rooms have TV. The elegant foyer is an excellent pointer to the comfortable standard maintained throughout, and it's well located for some of Groningen's best shopping and eating options.

City Hotel (☎ 588 65 65; fax 311 51 00; Gedempte Kattendiep 25; s/tw €109/124; ✖ P) Distinctive, except for the fact that the architect thought that the teensy windows were cool. But it scores everywhere else; there's a rooftop deck with good views and free coffee and tea on every floor around the clock. Rooms all have baths and TV, including in-house movies.

Eating

Gedempte Zuiderdiep is lined with cheap fast-food places and cafés of all stripes, but don't let that fool you – student town it may be, but there are some very fine dining options for the fatter-walleted traveller. There's also an organic food market on Tuesday at Vismarkt. Unless otherwise noted, the following are open daily.

De 7e Hemel (7th Heaven; ☎ 314 51 41; www .zevendehemel.nl; Zuiderkerkstraat 7; 2-course meal €14-17; 🏵 dinner Tue-Sat) A great vegetarian and organic eatery serving fantastic food. The restaurant also serves meat dishes, but only using organically farmed meats. The delicious mains and set-menu combinations are served in a comfortable, uncluttered dining room.

Brussels Lof (☎ 312 76 03; A-Kerkstraat 24; 3-course menu €29; 🏵 dinner Thu-Mon) This upmarket 'vegetarian' place has fish and vegetarian creations on a creative dinner menu. The 'loftier' side of veggie and quasi-vegetarian eating in Groningen, but for a good reason; the food is excellent, ditto the atmosphere, and the staff are really attentive and friendly.

Roezemoes (Hubbub; ☎ 314 03 82; Gedempte Zuiderdiep 15; light meal around €7; 🏵 lunch & dinner) It has been around some time. So long in fact that this typical brown café still has bullet holes from the 1672 invasion attempt. Sandwiches start at €3 and pasta dishes are also available. It's open until well after midnight and on many nights there's live blues.

Eetcafé 't Zwarte Schaap (The Black Sheep; ☎ 311 06 91; Schuitendiep 52; meals around €14; 🏵 dinner) One of a string of casual eetcafés on this side of the canal. Look for a black sheep, as per the café's name, over the door to find this one for hearty dinners.

Puur! Natural Food (☎ 311 61 75; Folkingestraat 13; meals €2-6; 🏵 lunch & dinner Tue-Sun) A fantastic coffee and health-food bar serving really tasty bagels, salads and other bread-y delights. They also have a great range of exotic teas and freshly squeezed juices and smoothies at cheap prices.

Ariola (☎ 318 19 48; Folkingestraat 54; meals from €3.50) Ariola is an outstanding little Italian deli. Its incredible smells and the crowd milling around the doorway eating should tell you something. *Broodjes* (filled bread-rolls) are made to order with Italian fillings (pestos, cheeses, char-grilled vegetables and olives). There are also huge serves for 'one' of home-made pastas and lasagne.

Drinking

At night Poelestraat and the adjoining streets hum with energy from people cruising, scoping, canoodling, drinking etc.

O'Ceallaigh (☎ 314 76 94; Gedempte Kattendiep 13) Respected newspaper *Volkskrant* called O'Ceallaigh 'the best Irish pub in the Netherlands'. They were right. This family-run business is the real deal; small, smoky, with super-friendly staff and frequent live music, it's a delight.

't Pakhuis (☎ 318 06 96) Just off Peperstraat (to the left if you're heading away from Poelstraat) in a tiny alley. Don't worry though, you can't miss it. It's musty, dark, a little bit groovy, a lot noisy and a little bit odd. Fab-shabby décor, with threadbare velvet throwing out a quasi-trashy vibe of a classy joint gone endearingly downmarket. A few hours here could be many things; 'boring' isn't one of them.

De Pintelier (☎ 318 51 00; Kleine Kromme Elleboog 9) Buzzing with gossip from noon until late.

Relatively unchanged since 1920, it has a long wooden bar and thicket of tables. It's also got an impressive selection of *jenevers* (gin-like liqueur) – more than 30 from 4 different countries – as well as 10 great beers on tap. A great watering hole, and a Groningen landmark.

Jazz Café De Spieghel (☎ 312 63 00; Peperstraat 11) A perennial favourite with the locals – this lively brown café with regular live jazz music, a smooth sultry atmosphere and a great bar stocked with whatever you need to accompany all those blue notes.

Entertainment

To find out what's going on around town, check out some of the posters that appear everywhere. The free and widely available *Uit-Loper* is a simple listing of each week's music and films. It's in Dutch, but not difficult to nut out using contextual clues.

CLUBS

Clubs open and close regularly in Groningen. As well as trying the ones we've listed, keep an eye out for flyers and ask around for the latest hot spots. Or follow your ears toward the obvious banging of soon-to-be damaged subwoofers in the general direction of Poelstraat.

Vera (☎ 313 46 81; www.vera-groningen.nl; Oosterstraat 44) The place to be to get the drop on the next big things in rock. Its cluey crew have had their fingers on the global musical pulse for decades, showcasing U2 to 30-odd people in the early 1980s. Nirvana played here to a crowd of about 60 people years before anyone knew Kurt Cobain.

Palace (☎ 313 91 00; www.thepalace.nl, in Dutch; Gelkingestraat 1) A huge club on a street with numerous coffeeshops and cafés. It's a venue for all types of music, including house, techno, rock, blues and more.

Golden Arm (☎ 313 16 76; www.goldenarm.nl, in Dutch; Hardewikerstraat 7; 🕑 from 11.30pm Thu-Sat) A gay club and bar in a huge old storehouse. It's pretty laid-back and inclusive.

THEATRE & CINEMA

Grand Theatre (☎ 314 46 44; Grote Markt 35) Has a constantly changing bill of live theatre.

Images Filmcentrum (☎ 312 04 33; Poelestraat 30; film ticket €7) Shows a good mix of offbeat films, festival titles and classics. It's got a great café/bar area looking out onto the Poelstraat where you can pontificate on all things cine while watching the crowds flow by.

Shopping

Folkingestraat has a funky strip of offbeat shops, as does Oude Bouteringestraat. Zwanestraat has more typical high-street fare. Regular markets are held most days on either Grote Markt, Vismarkt or both.

Getting There & Away

Ryanair (www.ryanair.com) now operates a service between Groningen Eelde and London Stansted – see the Transport chapter, p311. There's a shuttle bus between Eelde and Groningen CS (adult €5; matched to flight times).

The 1896 train station is a sight in itself now that a restoration finished in 2001 has returned it to its original glory. Look upwards in the main entrance hall as the ceiling alone is stunning.

Some train fares and schedules include:

Destination	Price (€)	Duration (min)	Frequency (per hr)
Amsterdam	24.50	140	2
Leeuwarden	7.30	50	2
Rotterdam	27.30	160	2
Utrecht	22.30	120	2

The bus station is to the right as you exit the train station. An **Interliner Bus Office** (🕑 7.15am-6.30pm Mon-Fri, 8am-5pm Sat) sells tickets and gives useful information on regional buses.

Getting Around

You won't need public transport to get around Groningen unless you're going to the hostel or the campsite. The buses leave from in front of the train station and bus Nos 1 to 6 pass near Grote Markt.

As mentioned earlier, cars are discouraged from entering the centre of Groningen, but there are many parking areas nearby.

The **bicycle shop** (☎ 312 41 74) is to the left of the train station entrance as you exit. For information on a 40km bicycle route, the Paterwoldsemeer Route, which begins and ends at Groningen, see Cycling in the Netherlands (p77).

ZEEHONDENCRECHE PIETERBUREN

The north Groningen coastal town of Pieterburen houses the **Zeehondencreche** (seal creche; ☎ 52 65 26; www.zeehondencreche.nl; Hoofdstraat 94a; tour €1; ✆ creche always open, shop 9am-6pm).

Lenie 't Hart loves seals. And, in 1971, deciding local water-based activities and excessive pollution were directly affecting the health, well-being and ecology of the local seals off Groningen's north coast, decided to do something about it.

'Doing something about it' meant rallying members of the scientific community, pro-active members of the maritime industries and animal-huggers to unite in support of a specialised rehabilitation and rescue centre devoted entirely to the Waddenzee mammals.

The Zeehondencreche has attracted the respect of international marine biologists, environmental activists and animal protection agencies around the world. The facility 'exports' knowledge to communities elsewhere with interests in preserving the ecology of seals, and 'imports' goodwill, donations, and volunteer workers and research interns to further the sanctuary's ongoing lobbying and rehabilitation activities.

Find out how you can be involved (you can even 'adopt' a seal) by visiting the website.

To get to the Zeehondencreche, take the train from Groningen to Warffum, and then bus 68 to Pieterburen.

UITHUIZEN

☎ 0595 / pop 8750

This small farm town would not be worth a visit except for **Menkemaborg** (☎ 43 19 70; Menkemaweg 2; €4; ✆ 10am-5pm Apr-Sep, 10am-4pm Tue-Sun Oct-Mar, closed Jan), the moated estate just east of town. Originally a fortified castle, it received its present gentrified appearance in the 17th century. Since then it has barely been altered, making it one of

---

POUNDING MUD

The north coast of Groningen is a sloppy mess. But for the locals, it is a land of golden – er, brown – opportunity. When the tide is out they enjoy a good few hours of *wadlopen* (mud-walking). The mud stretches all the way to the Frisian islands offshore and treks of up to 12km are possible, although the 7km walk to Schiermonnikoog is the most popular. Once on the island, you can watch the brown waters of the Waddenzee return with the rising tide and then take a ferry back to the mainland. The important point to remember when considering a stint on the mud is not to head out without a skilled guide. It's all too easy to get lost on the mud flats and without a good knowledge of the tides, you can end up under water, permanently.

Those who enjoy *wadlopen* say that it is strenuous, even exhilarating, given that if you lag too much the rising tide washes you away. A major Dutch TV ad campaign for muesli bars recently featured a feet-dragging guy – obviously listless from a lack of muesli bars – being swallowed by the gloop.

They also say that there is a certain intoxicating quality to being out in an absolutely flat place where the wet, brown mud reflects the often grey skies above and frames of reference evaporate.

The centre for *wadlopen* is the tiny village of Pieterburen, 22km north of Groningen (giving you a great excuse to visit the Zeehondencreche, above).

There are several groups of trained guides based here. They include:

Wadloopcentrum (☎ 0595-52 83 00; www.waarnaartoe.nl, in Dutch; Hoofdstraat 105)

Dijkstra's Wadlooptochten (☎ 0595-52 83 45; www.wadloop-dijkstra.nl, in Dutch; Hoofdstraat 118)

Costs are from €8 (for the 2.5-hour, 8km walks) to €20 (for the 4.5 hour, 20km trek to Schiermonnikoog), with additional costs such as the ferry ride back and possible pick-up in Groningen. It's essential to book in advance. You will be told what clothes to bring depending on the time of year.

If you're taking public transport to Pieterburen, you can use bus No 168 from Groningen (one hour, four daily), or catch a train to Warffum (25 minutes, hourly) and then connect with one of several buses to Pieterburen. Work out in advance which routing is best by calling (☎ 0900-9292, €0.30/min).

the most authentic manor houses in the Netherlands.

Across from Menkemaborg, the **Museum 1939–1945 Cold War Historical Center** (☎ 43 41 00; Dingeweg 1; adult/child €4/2; ☻ 9am-6pm Apr-Oct) manages to cover a fair amount of history with its eclectic collection of military gear. There are planes, tanks, weapons and just about any other type of military item – once financed by hard-pressed taxpayers the world over.

Hourly trains run between Uithuizen and Groningen (€4.80, 34 minutes). The train station (it's really more of a stop) is a 1km walk west of Menkemaborg. There's no bike rental.

BOURTANGE
☎ 0599 / pop 1200

Huddled near the German border, Bourtange was built in the late 1500s and represented the pinnacle of the arms and fortification at the time. Behind its walls and moats it could withstand months of siege by an invading army.

It's common to find evidence of the fortress building that was all the rage 500 years ago throughout the Netherlands. But in most towns the walls are long gone. By the early 1960s Bourtange's walls had been mostly breached or levelled and the moats were largely filled in. A road even ran through the present town centre.

In 1964, however, the regional government decided to restore the battlements and the town itself to its 1742 appearance, when the fortifications around the citadel had reached their maximum size. It took three decades, during which time roads were moved, buildings demolished, others reconstructed and archaeologists generally had a party.

The results are impressive and Bourtange is stunningly pretty. The star-shaped rings of walls and canals have been completely rebuilt and the village has been returned to a glossier version of its 18th-century self. It's a cliché, but a visit to Bourtange is truly a step into the past, a time when rogue armies wandered the lands and villagers hid behind defenses designed to keep them at bay.

The region around Bourtange is off the beaten path and consists of pretty countryside and tree-shaded canals that are ideal for exploring by bike.

Orientation
From the parking area and tourist office, you pass through two gates and across three drawbridges over the moats, before you reach the old town proper. The entire course is over 500m long and was intended to be as circuitous as possible so that if you were an unwelcome visitor the townsfolk could take plenty of pot-shots at you. Though once designed to frustrate invaders, the course now delights all but the laziest visitors.

Information
Tourist office (☎ 35 46 00; William Lodewijkstraat 33; ☻ 10am-5pm Mon-Fri, 12.30-5pm Sat & Sun) Just outside the main entrance to the old town. This is a good place for a brief visit as there are detailed displays showing the reconstruction and restoration. Aerial photographs show the remarkable changes between 1965 and the late 1990s. The English-language booklet (€1.50) is a good guide to the town.

Sights & Activities
Inside the walls at the core, Bourtange's old town consists of a few dozen restored buildings along little streets radiating off a tree-shaded central square, the **Marktplein**. Among the old buildings are several that were used by the militia, including **officers' quarters** and large **stone barracks**. A **synagogue** built in 1842 has a plaque on the side listing the 42 local people taken away to their deaths by the Nazis, a huge number given the town's small size.

There are tons of photo opportunities, from the cobbled beauty of the streets and the neat hedgerows and home decorations themselves, to the vantage points of the watchtowers, to the slightly tackier, brightly repainted artillery and machinery that are strewn strategically within the city walls.

The best way to explore Bourtange is by walking along said walls, which afford views over the town and countryside. You can almost imagine what it must have been like when a lookout would spot some motley crew of invaders heading towards the town. On one corner there is a little hut built high over the inner moat. Closer inspection reveals that it not only provided relief for the militia, but ensured that the waters below were not potable for unwanted visitors.

Sleeping & Eating

Albertha Hof (☎ 35 47 37; Vlagtwedderstraat 57; campsites/d €10/35) Just outside the walls (there is no place to stay inside the walls), this is one of several small family-run places that has rooms and fields for camping.

In the old town, there are two places to eat on the Marktplein. Both places have tables outside in fine weather.

Hotel/Restaurant De Staakenborgh (☎ 35 42 16; Vlagtwedderstraat 33; s/d without bath €25/45) A little more upmarket than Albertha Hof, the Staakenborgh is a pleasant place to stay. The restaurant serves the usual Dutch standards in heaping portions.

't Oal Kroegie (☎ 35 45 80; Markt; ☺ 10am-10pm) More geared towards providing light meals; its menu has mostly snacks, sandwiches and pancakes. It has a few good beers on tap as well.

Getting There & Away

By public transport from Groningen, take the train east to Winschoten (€5, 33 minutes, two every hour). Then take bus No 14 south to Vlagtwedde (25min, at least one every hour) and transfer to (mini)bus No 72 for Bourtange (10 minutes, at least one per hour). With waiting time and transfers, count on the trip taking about two hours – the No 72 bus only runs after 1pm, at half-hour intervals. The return service from Bourtange leaves from the Marktplein at 15 and 45 minutes after the hour, starting at 1.45pm.

By car, you'll need a good road map as there are several minor roads involved in the journey.

If touring by bike, combine Bourtange with visits over a few days to the **hunebedden** (p259) in Drenthe, some 30km to the west.

DRENTHE

The agricultural province of Drenthe is the least densely populated in the Netherlands. There aren't many people here, or, for that matter, sights of much interest to visitors, despite its inherent green beauty. It is a very quiet place; Vincent van Gogh wrote of Drenthe in 1833: 'Here is peace'. He later went mad.

People were enjoying the quiet in Drenthe as early as 3000 BC, when prehistoric tribes lived here amid the bogs and peat. In fact, it's these early residents who are responsible for what is possibly the most interesting aspect of Drenthe today, the *hunebedden*. These large grey stones were used as burial chambers and many survive today in a line of towns between Emmen and Groningen. There are also some interesting open-air museums that highlight the province's history of hard work as well as one that covers a much darker chapter in Dutch history.

Though it's certainly pretty in a rural-charm kind of way, there's certainly no other reason to spend the night in Drenthe. While travelling through the region, you'll notice many traditional farmhouses with thatched roofs. These are huge affairs because they accommodate not just the family but also the barnyard animals.

Groningen and Zwolle (p267) are much more attractive and convenient places to use as bases for exploration.

EMMEN

☎ 0591 / pop 108,200

A modern city of industry, Emmen is a useful transportation centre for Drenthe and the *hunebedden*. The **tourist office** (☎ 61 30 00; www.vvvemmen.nl; Marktplein 9; ☺ 10am-5pm Mon-Fri, 10am-1pm Sat, until 4pm Sat Jun-Aug) has a good range of bike maps for exploring the *hunebedden* and the pleasant staff can help with finding accommodation.

The town's zoo, **Noorder Dierenpark** (☎ 85 08 50; Hoofdstraat 18; www.zoo-emmen.nl; adult/child €16/14; ☺ 9am-5pm) is a short walk from the train station and is actually a stronger reason to consider the area for use as your travel base, if only for a day or two. It is noted for its apes and African animals displayed in a 'natural' setting. Of course, few areas of the savannahs have weather like this.

If you end up with a little time to kill in Emmen, do so at **Brasserie** (☎ 61 66 75; Hoofdstraat 53) between the station and Marktplein. It's large and lively and has a fine selection of beers and cheap sandwiches.

Emmen is at the end of the train line from Zwolle (around €10, 51 minutes, 2 per hour). The station has lockers and is 600m from the tourist office. Buses leave from in front of the station. The station has a **bicycle shop** (☎ 61 37 31).

HUNEBEDDEN

Borger, a little town 17km northwest of Emmen, is the centre for the prehistoric *hunebedden*, though there is an example that is only 15 to 20 minutes' walk from Emmen's centre (ask at the tourist office). Here and along the N34 road are most of the 53 known examples of these impressive groupings of sombre grey stones in the Netherlands.

Little is known about the builders of the *hunebedden*, except that they took burying their dead very seriously. The arrangements of the huge stones – some weighing 20,000 kg – were each used to bury many people, along with their personal items and tools.

The **Nationaal Hunebedden Informatiecentrum** (☎ 0591-23 63 74; hunebed.info@tref.nl; Bronnegerstraat 12; adult/child €3/2; ☻ 10am-5pm Mon-Fri, 11am-5pm Sat & Sun) in Borger is the logical place to start a tour. Here there are many displays relating to the stones as well as excavated artefacts. There are also good maps for finding the many nearby sites.

Away from Borger running north from Emmen to Groningen along the N34 (a quite picturesque route) are the villages of Klijndijk, Odoorn, Annen and Midlaren that have *hunebedden*.

Getting There & Around

Bus No 59 operates hourly between Emmen and Groningen, stopping at Borger and the other four *hunebedden* towns. You may want to limit your visit to Borger and one other town. Getting on and off buses to view piles of big grey rocks can get tiresome after a bit.

Watch for the large brown signs showing a pile of rocks while driving or biking (the best ways to quickly view a smattering of *hunebedden*).

ASSEN

☎ 0592 / pop 60,700

This farming centre is not worth the stop except as a means of getting to the sights nearby. The **tourist office** (☎ 31 43 24; vvvassen@wxs.nl, in Dutch; Marktstraat 8; ☻ 9am-6pm Tue-Fri, noon-6pm Mon, 9am-5pm Sat) has the usual maps and information.

The town's one attraction, the **Drents Museum** (☎ 31 27 41; www.drentsmuseum.nl; Brink 1; adult/child €5/3; ☻ 11am-5pm Tue-Sat) has *hunebedden* artefacts and various artworks and furnishings from Drenthe's history.

The tourist office and museum are 500m from the station by way of Stationsstraat. The station itself is on the main train line between Zwolle (€10, 41 minutes, three every hour) and Groningen (€4.20, 17 minutes, three every hour).

Buses depart from the area to the left as you exit the train station. The **bicycle shop** (☎ 31 04 24) is right next door.

AROUND ASSEN

A foundation (☎ 0593-32 23 35) governs the tiny village of **Orvelte**, 17km south of Assen. Its goal is to preserve the feel of a 19th-century Drenthe community. No cars are permitted and owners can't alter the old buildings in uncharacteristic ways. The residents mainly engage in traditional activities; there's the butcher, the baker…you get the idea. During summer, there are lovely vegetable gardens growing near every house.

Orvelte's not an 'attraction' as such, but you're welcome to visit and wander around. Orvelte is on the No 22 bus route from Assen and is more authentic than the hyper-Dutchness of Volendam (p150), and more secular and familiar than the strict Calvinist religious community at **Staphorst** (www.staphorst.nl, in Dutch), which is just over the provincial border in Overijssel. Quasi-Amish and techno-reticent as Staphorst's purported to be, the *gemeente* or 'municipality' has its own website – cyber-Luddites; now that's a postmodern phenomenon.

KAMP WESTERBORK

About 10km north of the nice little farming community of Westerbork is a site that has given that name a place in the annals of the Holocaust.

Kamp Westerbork (☎ 59 26 00; www.kampwesterbork.nl; Oosthalen 8, Hooghalen; adult/child €3.85/2; ☻ 10am-5pm Mon-Fri year-round, 1pm-5pm Sat & Sun Sep-Jun, 11am-5pm Sat & Sun Jul & Aug), ironically, was built by the Dutch government in 1939 to house German Jews *fleeing* the Nazis. When the Germans invaded in May 1940, they found Westerbork ideal for their own ends. At first the camp remained relatively benign, but beginning in 1942 it became a transit point for those being sent to the death camps. Over 107,000 Dutch Jews and over 250 Roma were shipped

GRONINGEN & DRENTHE

through Westerbork. The vast majority never returned.

Today the camp, 6km south of Assen, is a memorial to the murdered and holocaust museum. Most of the buildings are gone, but the remaining monuments are moving. Consisting mainly of documents and personal effects, the displays are intimate and evocative. Anne Frank was interred here before meeting her own fate at Bergen-Belsen, though undue attention on Westerbork's most famous detainee is thankfully defrayed.

Bus No 22 (12min, every 30 minutes Monday to Friday, much less often Saturday and Sunday) from Assen stops in Hooghalen, 2km west of the camp. You'd be better off getting a taxi from Assen.

Overijssel & Gelderland

Overijssel and Gelderland don't have a blockbuster attraction like an Amsterdam or a Maastricht – although Hoge Veluwe National Park comes close. On the other hand, the two have lots of small pleasures that together add up to a compelling draw.

Zwolle is a great little town, while the quieter Deventer and Kampen are similarly delightful; all three were key member towns of the Hanseatic League (p267). You might be tempted to jump in a low boat in Weerribben National Park, a strange and beautiful area of wetlands, overflowing with life and atmosphere that almost feels alien.

Nijmegen has fun cafés, an energetic student population, and hosts an annual march that has ballooned in the modern era into a week-long party. For history buffs or descendants of WWII service-people, there are many memorials and locations to explore here and near Arnhem, where attempts to liberate the occupied Netherlands went horribly awry for the Allies in 1944. And there's possibly the world's finest Van Gogh collection at the Kröller-Müller Museum.

The two provinces are interesting to explore and make a welcome slowdown from the Randstad.

HIGHLIGHTS

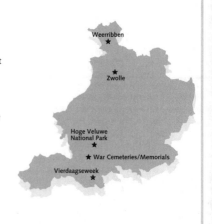

- Exploring the stunning **Hoge Veluwe National Park** (p276) , and the Kröller-Müller Museum buried deep within – some of the world's best art within one of nature's finest efforts.

- Losing yourself in the **Weerribben** (p263) , Overijssel's strange wetlands

- Paying your respects to the liberators of the Dutch in Gelderland's **war cemeteries and memorials** (p275)

- Immersing yourself in Hanseatic **Zwolle** (p267) , Overijssel's charming capital

- Walking your feet off in Nijmegen's **Internationale Wandelvierdaagse** (p272), then taking the load off at one of its many great bars and cafés

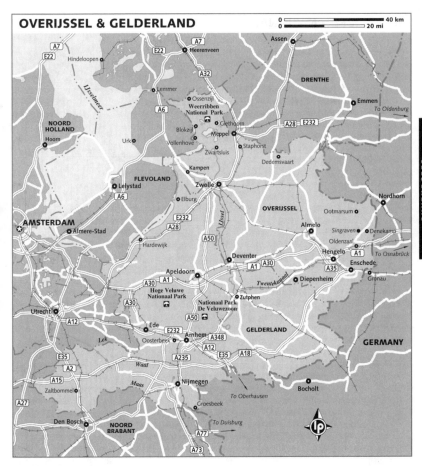

OVERIJSSEL

Overijssel means 'beyond the IJssel', after the river forming much of the province's western border. The province is hilly in the east near Germany and flat and soggy in the west along the former coastline, now land-locked by Flevoland's Noordoostpolder.

Deventer makes a good base for exploration of Overijssel, though Zwolle is the capital. Giethoorn in the north is pretty as well, but be aware of swollen summer crowds.

WEERRIBBEN NATIONAL PARK

A bizarre, serene and occasionally eerie landscape of watery striations, **Weerribben**
National Park is 3500 hectares of marshy land. This entire area was worked by peat and reed harvesters; jobs among the hardest imaginable. The long water-filled lines across the landscape are the result of peat removal. The stripes occurred because, as one line of peat was dug, it was laid on the adjoining land to dry.

Reed harvesting was no easier, and still goes on; you can see huge piles at many points in the park. Generations of harvesters lived out here with scant outside contact. Even now, their descendants live on some of the farms in the surrounding countryside in Ossenzijl and Blokzijl.

Weerribben is also an amazing natural landscape and an important stop for

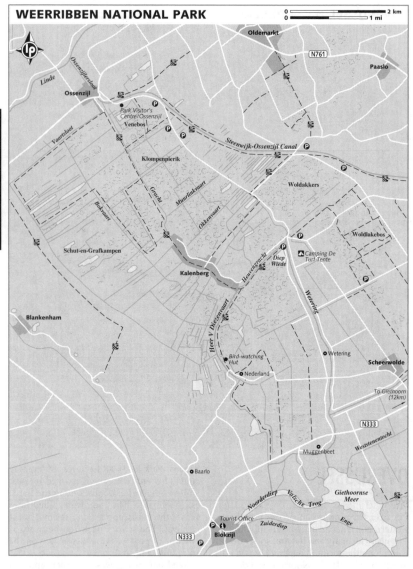

WEERRIBBEN NATIONAL PARK

migratory birds in Europe. Riding along one of the isolated bike paths or rowing the channels is an other-worldly experience. It's not how Weeribben looks, but how it sounds that's unsettling; as you move through the sea of reeds, you'll hear the calls, clucks, coos and splashes of numerous birds, fish, frogs, otters and eels – this still, huge environment actually seems alive. It's very easy to let your mind play tricks on you. Maximise the X-Files factor by setting off as close to sunset as you dare.

The park **visitors centre** (☎ 0561-47 72 72; 🕙 10am-5pm Tue-Fri, 12pm-5pm Sat & Sun) is in Ossenzijl, a tiny village on the northern edge of the park. You can't miss it, as all roads and signs point to it and the entire village is essentially a support resource for the park. It has tons of information including dozens of maps of different cycling and walking routes and advice on boat and canoe rental.

To reach Ossenzijl, take bus No 81 from Steenwijk, a stop on the train line from Leeuwarden to Zwolle. The bus takes 25 minutes and runs every two hours on weekdays and just a few times on weekends. You can rent bikes at the **bicycle shop** (☎ 0521-51 39 91; ☺ 7am-8pm) in Steenwijk. Ossenzijl is about 18km from Steenwijk.

DEVENTER
☎ 0570 / pop 87,600

This old Hanseatic League town is an undiscovered gem. Within its circle of canals there's not one gift shop. Nowhere to buy wooden shoes? Whatever will you do? Perhaps find somewhere quiet and beautiful to read? Not such a bad idea actually; curiously (for such an apparently quiet and out-of-the-way town) Deventer plays host to Europe's largest book fair in early August. Bibliophiles

and book vendors from all over the Netherlands, Belgium and Germany flock here for a concentrated burst of trading.

Deventer was already a busy mercantile port as far back as AD 800. It maintained its prosperous trading ties for centuries, evidence of which you'll see in its richly detailed old buildings.

Information
Library (☎ 67 57 00; Brink 70; internet access per hr €2.40; ☺ 10am-6 pm Mon-Wed & Fri, 10am-8pm Thu, 10am-2pm Sat) Has a digital lab on the second floor.
Post office (☎ 67 63 58; Diepenveenseweg 1; ☺ 9am-6pm Mon-Fri, 9am-12.30pm Sat) Behind the train station.
Tourist office (☎ 0900-3535355, €0.30/min; www.vvvdeventer.nl; Keizerstraat 22; ☺ 9am-6pm Mon-Fri, 9am-5pm Sat) Shares a large space with the ANWB. There are many guides and maps for sale as well as all manner of travel gear.

Sights
Brink is the main square and Deventer's commercial heart. The town's famous **Waag**, the 1528 weigh house in the middle of the square, was restored in 2003. Look

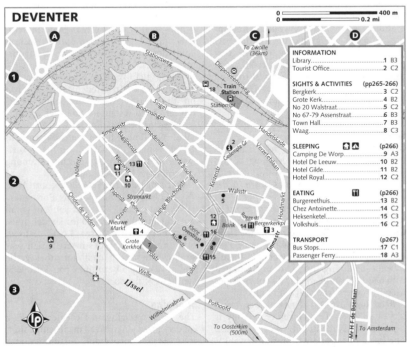

DEVENTER

| 0 | 400 m |
| 0 | 0.2 mi |

INFORMATION	
Library	1 B3
Tourist Office	2 C2

SIGHTS & ACTIVITIES	(pp265-266)
Bergkerk	3 C2
Grote Kerk	4 B2
No 20 Walstraat	5 C2
No 67-79 Assenstraat	6 B3
Town Hall	7 B3
Waag	8 C3

SLEEPING	(p266)
Camping De Worp	9 A3
Hotel De Leeuw	10 B2
Hotel Gilde	11 B2
Hotel Royal	12 C2

EATING	(p266)
Burgereethuis	13 B2
Chez Antoinette	14 C2
Heksenketel	15 C3
Volkshuis	16 C2

TRANSPORT	(p267)
Bus Stops	17 C1
Passenger Ferry	18 A3

for the cauldron on the north side; a gruesome and well-supported legend tells of a 16th-century clerk boiled alive in it, after being discovered substituting cheap metals for precious ones in the local money supply. Who says you can't rile the Dutch?

The **Grote Kerk** (☎ 61 25 48; Grote Kerkhof; ⏰ 10am-5pm Mon-Sat) is the city's main church. It stands on a site where other churches were razed by flames and other catastrophes time and again, before the present Gothic number was built between 1450 and 1530.

The best activity in Deventer is simply strolling its pretty streets admiring the buildings. The town is so well preserved that few streets have nothing to see. Highlights include Walstraat, where No 20 shows a woman climbing down the wall while hanging by a sheet. On Assenstraat and Polstraat there are wall-carvings and window decorations created over several centuries. Assenstraat 67–79 is more contemporary and recalls the French sabotage of the *Rainbow Warrior*.

Activities

The banks of the IJssel river are a scenic place for biking.

Riding 36km north to Zwolle is a fine option. You can either make the trip one-way and stay there, or return by train. A good 32km round trip follows the river north to Olst, where you take a ferry across and return along the other side to Deventer. You can do the same thing going south to Zutphen, a 47km trip.

Sleeping

Camping De Worp (☎ 61 36 01; Worp 12; sites from €10; ⏰ May-Sep) Deventer's camping option is right across the IJssel from the centre of town and about two minutes north of the passenger ferry.

Oosterkim (☎ 61 36 48; Pothoofd 500; per person €20-30) Something different is this 1929 freight ship that's now a B&B. Moored by the IJssel 1km east of the Wilhelminabrug along Pothoofd, its quarters are cramped, but there's a beautiful dining/sitting room decorated with nautical paraphernalia. It's run by super friendly owners who also offer tours.

Hotel Royal (☎ 61 18 80; royal@royal-deventer.nl; Brink 94; s/d €55/65) This Deventer standby is right on Brink, making it a worthy choice. The basic but spotless rooms all have TV

and bathroom. It's also home to a good Mexican restaurant on the ground floor.

Hotel de Leeuw (☎ 61 02 90; deleeuw@home.nl; Nieuwstraat 25; r €71-107) This lovely building with well-designed, yet simple rooms, dates back to 1645. It's on a popular shopping street no more than 10 minutes from all Deventer has to offer. The hotel has reduced rates for longer stays.

Hotel Gilde (☎ 64 18 46; info@gildehotel.nl; Nieuwstraat 41; s/d from €75/100) This charming building is a restored 17th-century convent. It's the swishest place in Deventer, despite the austerity of its former tenants.

Eating

Burgereethuis (☎ 61 91 98; info@burgerweeshuis.nl; Bagijnenstraat 9). A mellow café with friendly staff, cheap tap beer (€1 to €2), the Burgereethuis sports a cool courtyard and live music five nights a week, in the neighbouring multi-purpose venue, Burgerweeshuis. Basic sandwiches, toasties and bar snacks cost around €3. Great laid-back ambience.

Volkshuis (☎ 60 02 54; Kleine Overstraat 97a; lunch €3-6; dinner €10-15; ⏰ lunch & dinner) Run by and supporting people with disabilities, Volkshuis uses its own produce to create simple food with quality organic ingredients, including vegetarian options such as chilli 'non' carne. Friendly service, flavoursome dishes.

Heksenketel (☎ 61 34 12; Brink 62; mains €10; ⏰ lunch & dinner) Inspired by the cauldron on the nearby Waag. Its menu offers typical Dutch restaurant fare such as satay (chicken or beef), schnitzel with fries and salad. You'll need to eat *something* solid to go with one of the beers from their excellent selection, seriously placing it among the country's best beer cafés.

Chez Antoinette (☎ 61 66 30; Roggestraat 10-12; ⏰ dinner Tue-Sun) It has popular Portuguese meals that average €15, but you can go all out and spend €25 to €30 for six delicious, Latin-influenced courses. Local seafood, beef and poultry stocks meet Iberian seasonings like saffron, chilli, tomatoes, garlic and olive oil in a beautifully pan-European synthesis of flavours.

Shopping

The local speciality is Deventer Koek, a mildly-spiced gingerbread made with honey. It is widely available and, for once with a

THE HANSEATIC LEAGUE

Although primarily composed of northern German cities such as Lübeck and Hamburg, the Hanseatic League also included several Dutch towns. The powerful trading community was organised in the mid-13th century, its member towns quickly growing rich off importing and exporting goods including grain, ore, honey, textiles, timbers and flax. The league was not a government as such, but would defend its ships from attack and entered into monopolistic trading agreements with other groups, such as the Swedes. That it achieved its powerful trading position through bribery, boycotts and general fiscal ruthlessness shouldn't sound unusual to business students today. League members did work hard to prevent war among their partners for the simple reason that conflict was bad for business. Seven Dutch cities along the IJssel were prosperous members of the league: Hasselt, Zwolle, Kampen, Hattem, Deventer, Zutphen and Doesburg.

It's ironic that the League's demise in the 15th century was mostly attributable to the Dutch. Amsterdam's traders recognised a good thing and essentially beat the league at its own game, out-muscling it in market after market.

'local speciality', it is made by local people for local people who actually enjoy it.

Getting There & Around

Deventer sits at the junction of two train lines; service is good in all directions, making it a good hub. There's more accomodation around here than in Zwolle. Services at the train station are not great. However, there are lockers in the main concourse. Some fares and schedules are:

Destination	Price (€)	Duration (min)	Frequency (per hr)
Amsterdam	12.50	75	1
Apeldoorn	2.80	12	2
Arnhem	6.40	36	2
Enschede	8.50	43	2
Nijmegen	8	51	2
Zwolle	4.60	24	2

The bus area is located to the right as you leave the train station.

The **bicycle shop** (☎ 61 38 32) is in the train station.

There is parking around the town's periphery, but the best place to park is the free lot on the west bank of the IJssel. To get there, take the free passenger ferry. The voyage takes less than five minutes and operates most of the day and night. The pier on the town side is near Vispoort.

ZWOLLE

☎ 038 / 110,000

Zwolle gained wealth as the main trading port for the Hanseatic League cities of the

IJssel and those in Germany. It's a compact town that can occupy an afternoon or a night, or longer in summer, when a seemingly endless schedule of small festivals and the weekend market keep this jewel in the Overijssel crown twinkling.

Information

GWK exchange office (☒ 8am-8pm Mon-Sat, 10am-8pm Sun) In the train station.
Post office (☎ 421 78 21; Nieuwe Markt 1A; ☒ 9am-6pm Mon-Fri, 9am-2pm Sat)
Tourist office (☎ 0900-1122375; info@vvvzwolle.nl; Grote Kerkplein 14; ☒ 9am-5pm Mon-Fri, 9am-4pm Sat) Helpful and central.

Sights & Activities

The **Stedelijk Museum Zwolle** (☎ 421 46 50; secr@museumzwolle.nl; Melkmarkt 41; adult/child €4/2; ☒ 10am-5pm Tue-Sat, 1-5pm Sun) has a fine collection of items, including much Hanseatic material. It also hosts about 25 special exhibitions a year, ranging from high-art painting retrospectives to contemporary photography and multimedia.

Standing on the Oude Vismarkt, you have a good view of the other main sights. The **Grote Kerk** is grand but was grander before the usual series of disasters knocked down the tower etc. Next door, the **town hall** has a similarly old part (15th century) and an incongruous newer part. The 15th-century **Sassenpoort** is one of the remaining town gates. It's at the corner of Sassenstraat and Wilhelminasingel.

Ecodrome (☎ 421 50 50; Willemsvaart 19; adult/child under 12 €9.95/8.35; ☒ 10am-5pm Apr-Oct, 10am-5pm Wed, Sat & Sun Nov-Apr) is a science-based,

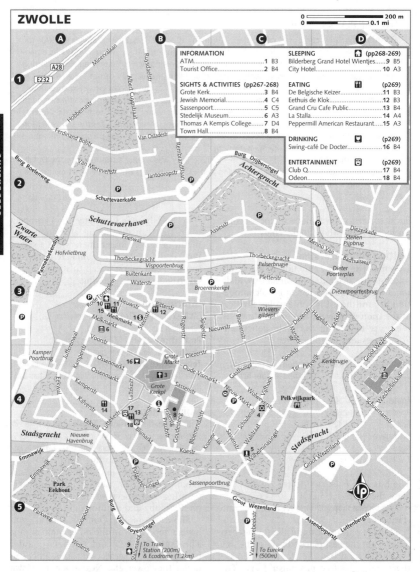

ZWOLLE

INFORMATION	
ATM.................................1 B3	
Tourist Office....................2 B4	
SIGHTS & ACTIVITIES (pp267-268)	
Grote Kerk.......................3 B4	
Jewish Memorial................4 C4	
Sassenpoort......................5 C5	
Stedelijk Museum...............6 A3	
Thomas A Kempis College......7 D4	
Town Hall.........................8 B4	

SLEEPING (pp268-269)	
Bilderberg Grand Hotel Wientjes......9 B5	
City Hotel........................10 A3	
EATING (p269)	
De Belgische Keizer.............11 B3	
Eethuis de Klok..................12 B3	
Grand Cru Cafe Public..........13 B4	
La Stalla..........................14 A4	
Peppermill American Restaurant.....15 A3	
DRINKING (p269)	
Swing-café De Docter............16 B4	
ENTERTAINMENT (p269)	
Club Q............................17 B4	
Odeon.............................18 B4	

interactive multimedia education centre housed in futuristic-looking buildings. Best suited to travellers with kids in tow, it's a 1km walk turning right from the station.

The best way to appreciate the canals is on a **boat tour** (☎ 444 54 28; €4; ☻ 2pm Mon-Sat Jun-Sep). Boats depart from near the Nieuwe Havenbrug.

People from Zwolle say they know they're home when they see the **Peperbus** (peppermill), the huge former church unmissable as you approach town.

Sleeping

Accommodation is tight here. Try the tourist office's booking service; there are some excellent B&Bs run by friendly locals, starting at around €20 to €25.

City Hotel (☎ 421 81 82; fax 422 08 29; Rode Torenplein 10-11; s/d €50/65) An unaffected place as down-to-earth as people from Zwolle themselves. Well located with good, basic rooms, it's one of few central options. It's worth phoning ahead.

Bilderberg Grand Hotel Wientjes (☎ 425 42 54; fax 425 42 60; Stationsweg 7; s from €75) This truly is a grand place, with the usual facilities. Big on comfort.

Eating

La Stalla (☎ 421 25 83; Kamperstraat 7-9; mains €17; 🍴 lunch & dinner Tue-Sat, dinner Sun) This fantastic restaurant offers a Dutch take on Italian cuisine. The food sure tastes good and the portions are generous.

Eethuis de Klok (☎ 423 02 67; dishes €2-10, set menu €10-12) A fab little *eetcafé* (pub serving meals) on the corner of Steenstraat and Nieuwstraat. It's superb, with a delightful atmosphere and wide-ranging menu of superior versions of Dutch meat-and-potato themed combinations.

Grand Cru, Café Public (☎ 422 66 00; Blijmarkt 23; mains from €10; 🍴 dinner Tue-Sun) Very popular with locals. That may also be because it's right next to Odeon (see this page). It has a good menu of items similar to De Klok.

Peppermill American Restaurant (☎ 423 08 06; info@thepeppermill.nl; Melkmarkt 56; mains €15-20; 🍴 dinner Tue-Sun) Named after Zwolle's landmark the Peperbus, but its culinary roots lie further afield. Chef Ronald Kok prepares classy North American cuisine, including 'soul food', Mexican and Cajun.

Drinking

Swing-café De Docter (☎ 421 52 35; info@dedocter.nl; Voorstraat 3) A great place, peopled by a music-centric crowd. It's dark, musty, features live rock bands a few nights per week, has inviting open frontage, and ample supplies of Hertog Jan, a great Brabant pilsener.

De Belgische Keizer (☎ 421 10 11; Melkmarkt 58) De Keizer is a cosmopolitan beer café, with an impressive list of brews, many from the southern neighbours. There's also a good range of French and Belgian influenced *broodjes* (filled breadrolls) and typically Dutch bar snacks from €5 to €10. A great way to round off an afternoon at the nearby Stedelijk. Museum.

Entertainment

eureka (☎ 422 29 03; Assendorperplein 9) If you're feeling Bohemian, don't miss this magical place; a community arts space-cum-venue-cum-café. There's no particular clientele; that's eureka's charm. People of every age, disposition or species (dogs are a common sight) roam its creaky floors. The mood is warm and inclusive. Vegan and vegetarian snacks from €2, bottles of Grolsch also €2.

Odeon (☎ 428 82 80; info@schouwburg-odeon.nl; Blijmarkt 25) A multi-purpose entertainment venue hosting everything from theatre and dance to live rock and electronica nights, this grand building is a nightlife hub in Zwolle.

Club Q (Blijmarkt 15) is a huge, loud club – the biggest in Zwolle – that should enable you to keep it goin' awn, 'til the break o' dawn. Should that be your wish.

Shopping

The market occupies most of the former Melkmarkt, Oude Vismarkt and the star-shaped centre in general on Friday and Saturday. Fish, fresh fruit and vegetables, clothes – anything goes. There's also cheap cheese and bread, a great way to stock up for a picnic. Pelkwijkpark or the area just south of Kerkbrugje are great areas for this.

In summer, market day is often augmented by alfresco music – anything from blues to Germanic 'oom-pah' sonic terrorism.

Getting There & Around

Zwolle is a transfer point for trains and has good connections. The lockers are below the tracks. Some fares and schedules are:

Destination	Price (€)	Duration (min)	Frequency (per hr)
Deventer	4.60	24	2
Groningen	15	60	2
Leeuwarden	12	60	2

Local buses leave from the right as you exit the station. Intercity services are 100m further over in the same direction.

The **bicycle shop** (☎ 421 45 98) is to the left of the station.

KAMPEN

☎ 038 / pop 48,900

Another lovely Hanseatic city 15km west of Zwolle, Kampen is a perfect day-trip. The compact centre will probably not hold you for more than a few hours, though its surrounding parklands are pretty. Kampen is picturesque and easy cycling (20 minutes) from Zwolle.

Information

The **tourist office** (☎ 331 35 00; info@vvvkampen.nl; Oudestraat 151; ⏰ 9.30am-5.30pm Mon-Fri, 9.30am-4pm Sat). Staff can help organise a private room (about €25 to €30). Be sure to get its walking tour booklet (€1). It's impossible to get lost in Kampen; it's small and layed out in a linear fashion, parallel to the IJssel.

Sights & Activities

The major sights lie along Oudestraat. The **Nieuwe Toren** is immediately obvious: it's the 17th-century tower with the incredible lean.

There's a little statue of a cow here, linked to an old story: a local farmer mistook moss growing atop the tower for grass and wondered aloud how the cows would get up there to graze. Kampen's residents became the butt of Dutch jokes for years. This classic piece of folklore is still commemorated by the annual hoisting of a stuffed cow up the tower. They *were* smart enough to stop using a real cow.

Two 15th-century **city gates** survive along the gorgeous park on Kampen's west side.

Sleeping & Eating

Camping Seveningen (☎ 331 48 91; Frieseweg 7; sites €10; ⏰ Apr-Oct) Campin' in Kampen is enjoyable, as Camping Seveningen is on a pretty spot on the water. From the train station walk northwest along the river for 20 minutes.

Hotel Van Dijk (☎ 331 49 25; fax 331 65 08; IJsselkade 30-3; r from €56). This IJssel-side standby is a great place to stay, should Kampen's laconic charms win you over.

There are several cafés along Oudestraat.

Getting There & Around

Trains make the run between Kampen and Zwolle (€2.50, 10 minutes, two per hour). There's a small phalanx of bus stands behind the train station.

NORTHERN OVERIJSSEL

Before the Noordoostpolder (see Flevoland, p168) was created, this part of Overijssel was

on the Zuiderzee. Today, the former coastal villages are landlocked, but maintain their links to the water through the spiderweb of canals that crisscross this marshy area. It's a difficult place to get around without a bike and energetic legs or a car; buses are infrequent and often involve inconvenient connections. It's certainly worth the effort to explore as you'll take in great scenery and feel a bit detached from the rest of the Netherlands.

Giethoorn

☎ 0521 / pop 4400

Giethoorn calls itself the Dutch Venice. Despite this delusional self-aggrandisement, the town *is* a sentimental place for the Dutch. It was the setting for a popular film *(Fanfare)* about the local folk, which – although funny – also spoke a fair amount of truth. Giethoorn, opposite to most Dutch geography, is built on water crossed by a few bits of land. Farmers even used to move their cows around in rowboats filled with hay.

Recently, Giethoorn has been 'discovered' in a big way, appearing in summer to be peopled entirely by sun-burnt holidaymakers, parked cheek-by-jowl in miles of identical camper-vans along the ample canalside space.

The entire area is a joy to pedal through. At any time there are countless opportunities for boat rides, although joining a cow will be tougher these days.

INFORMATION

The **tourist office** (☎ 36 12 48; vvv.giethoorn@wxs.nl; Beulakerweg 114A; ⏰ 9am-6pm Mon-Sat, 9am-5pm Sun May-Sept; 9am-5pm Mon-Fri Oct-Apr) is on the main road, and is the best place to get your accommodation options sorted as there are scores of camping grounds, rooms and cabins for rent. The town itself, five minutes away from the tourist office, has banks and other services.

SLEEPING

Camping Brederwiede (☎ 36 15 05; Binnenpad 1; campsite from €12) is typical of the scores of camping grounds. It is 10 minutes from the main bus stop.

Huize Beulaekewyck (☎ 06-22 82 36 33; Beulakerweg 128; per person €20). This little place has splendid views of a nature preserve. It's one of hundreds of options.

GETTING THERE & AROUND

Bus No 70 serves Giethoorn on its route between Steenwijk (18 minutes) and Zwolle (1 hour). Service is hourly on weekdays and shocking on weekends.

It's difficult to get around Giethoorn without a boat, a bike or a combination thereof. A few of the canalside service stations run bike-hire services (€6 per day) – if you arrive bike-less, best make one your first stop.

GELDERLAND

Geldvince's real beauty, others will instantly recognize the shapes and features of some critical moments in history that have moulded the character of Dutch society recognizable as typical today.

But it's Hoge Veluwe National Park's call that rings loudest here, and its screamer of a modern art museum. With its beautiful forestry and superb cultural repository, it's the shining star of this lush province.

NIJMEGEN

☎ 024 / pop 156,300

There's a rivalry between Nijmegen and Maastricht for the title of 'oldest city in the Netherlands'. These days, it's archaeologically accepted that Nijmegen is older. The Roman Empire conquered Nijmegen in AD 70, promptly burning it down. A sad taste of things to come.

Primarily a trading and manufacturing town, it survived many invasions right up until WWII. A marshalling point for German forces, it was bombed heavily by the Americans in February 1944. Later that year, the town was devastated by the 'Operation Market Garden' fiasco (see boxed text p274).

The postwar years have seen many rebuilding schemes, of varying success. Nijmegen gives great nightlife, helped along by its 13,000 students, and is a good base for exploring Gelderland.

Information

Karreman Wasserettes (☎ 355 10 76; St Jacobslaan 430) Laundry, not too inconvenient at 15 minutes from the centre by bus Nos 5 and 8 (direction: Hatert).

Library (☎ 327 49 11; Mariënburg 29; www.bibliotheek nijmegen.nl; web access per hr €5; ✆ 2-6pm Mon-Wed, 2-8pm Fri, 10am-2pm Sat) In the Mariënburg shopping complex, diagonally oppositeLux Filmcentrum.

GWK exchange office (✆ 8am-9pm) In the train station.

ATMs are scattered throughout the centre of town.

Post office (☎ 323 90 92; Van Schevichavenstraat 1; ✆ 8am-6pm Mon-Fri, 8am-1pm Sat)

Tourist office (☎ 0900-1122344; www.vvvnijmegen.nl; Keizer Karelplein 2; ✆ 9.30am-5.30pm Mon-Fri, 9.30am-5pm Sat) Typically helpful and offers the usual array of accommodation booking services and good maps.

Sights & Activities

Museum Het Valkhof (☎ 360 88 05; Kelfkensbos 59; www.museumhetvalkhof.nl; adult/child €4.50/3; ✆ 10am-5pm Tue-Fri; 2-5pm Sat, Sun & public holidays) is housed in a striking building, the heaving, 16-sided St Nicolaaskapel – originally a replica of Charlemagne's palace at Aachen – that has been remodeled and reworked in a multitude of styles (depending on who held power in Nijmegen) during its 950-year

---

ANIMAL ATTRACTIONS

There is a surfeit of zoological parks in Gelderland and near the borders of neighbouring provinces; Gelderland's cities make great bases for exploring all three.

Flipper's family holds the spotlight in Harderwijk's aquatic megapark, **Dolfinarium** (☎ 0900-3653456; www.dolfinarium.nl; Strandboulevard Oost 1 Hardewijk; €20; ✆ 10am-6pm mid-Dec–Oct, 10am-5pm Sat & Sun Nov–mid-Dec). There are also sharks, stingrays, seals and other aquatic life.

You'll go bananas for Apeldoorn's primate-centric zoo, **Apenheul** (☎ 055-357 57 57; www.apen heul.nl; JC Wilslaan 21-31; adult/child under 9 €13/11; ✆ 9.30am-5pm Apr, May, Sep & Oct; 9.30am-6pm Jun-Aug). The little kleptos that come and sit on your shoulder aren't just being friendly – if you haven't got any food, they'll try to make off with something small and shiny. Pierced guys and gals, consider yourself warned.

Arnhem's **Burgers' Zoo** (☎ 442 45 34; www.burgerszoo.nl; Schelmseweg 85; adult/child 4-9 €14.50/12.50; ✆ 9am-7pm or sunset) tries to recreate the natural environments of its many animals. The critters mostly don't buy this ruse, given the climate.

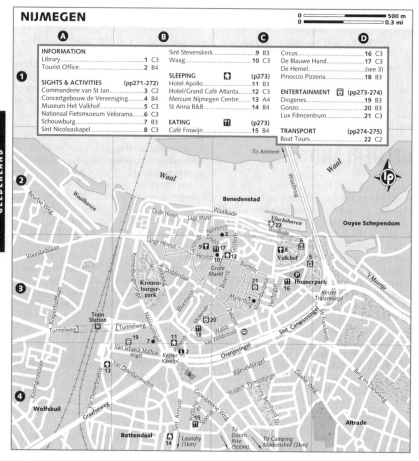

NIJMEGEN

INFORMATION	Sint Stevenskerk........................9 B3	Circus..............................16 C3
Library..............................1 C3	Waag.................................10 C3	De Blauwe Hand.............17 C3
Tourist Office.....................2 B4		De Hemel......................(see 3)
	SLEEPING (p273)	Pinoccio Pizzeria.............18 B3
SIGHTS & ACTIVITIES (pp271-272)	Hotel Apollo.........................11 B3	
Commanderie van St Jan..........3 C2	Hotel/Grand Café Atlanta......12 B3	**ENTERTAINMENT** (pp273-274)
Concertgebouw de Vereeniging...4 B4	Mercure Nijmegen Centre....13 A4	Diogenes.........................19 B3
Museum Het Valkhof................5 C3	St Anna B&B.........................14 B4	Gonzo.............................20 B3
Nationaal Fietsmuseum Velorama....6 C3		Lux Filmcentrum.............21 C3
Schouwburg...........................7 B3	**EATING** (p273)	
Sint Nicolaaskapel...............8 C3	Café Frowijn........................15 B4	**TRANSPORT** (pp274-275)
		Boat Tours.....................22 C2

---

life-span. The collections in the museum cover regional history and art and there is a first-rate section of Roman artefacts.

The **Nationaal Fietsmuseum Velorama** (National Cycling Museum; ☎ 322 58 51; www.velorama.nl; Waalkade 107; adult/child €4.60/2.80; ☿ 10am-5pm Mon-Fri, 11am-5pm Sun & public holidays) is a small but interesting museum with over 250 bikes. It is a must-see for anyone who's marvelled at the unnerving Dutch affinity with two-wheelers.

Cruises (☎ 323 32 85; from €5; ☿ Apr-Oct) on the Waal depart from the waterfront along Waalkade. Some go all the way to Rotterdam (€22.50).

A few important bits of the old town either survived the war or have been reconstructed.

The **Waag** (weigh house) on Grote Markt was built in 1612.

Sint Stevenskerk (☎ 360 47 10; tower climb €1; ☿ 1-4pm Sat & Sun) is the large 14th-century church.

Commanderie van St Jan, near Grote Markt on Franseplaats, was a 12th-century hospital for the knights of St John. It has a healthier use today: it's a brewery (see De Hemel, p273).

Festivals & Events

Nijmegen's big event is the **Internationale Wandelvierdaagse** (www.4daagse.nl), a four-day, 120km- to 200km-long march held in mid-July every year. It has a long history: the first one was held in 1909. Thousands walk it, getting debilitating blisters, while thousands more get debilitating hangovers, as the Wandelvierdaagse is the city's excuse for a week-long party.

Competitors set off in a different direction (north, south, east, west) each day, and there are varying route classifications according to gender and age.

Fitness types be warned: even the shortest or easiest route is a minimum of 30km a day. It ain't just a lark, either – the registration fee is at least €25 to €40 depending on which category you fall into. See the website for details.

Sleeping

Camping Maikenshof (☎ 684 16 51; fax 684 28 83; Oude Kleefsbaan 134; campsites from €10) To get to the campsite take bus No 6 (from the train station) east for 6km (direction: Beek) to the last stop in Berg en Dal.

Hotel Apollo (☎ 322 35 94; www.apollo-hotel -nijmegen.nl; Hamerstraat 14; s/d €66/89) is a basic, friendly place. Most rooms have TV, bathroom and are spartan but comfy.

Hotel Atlanta (☎ 360 30 00; www.atlanta-hotel.nl; Grote Markt 38-40; s/d €55/80) This place is a short stroll from Hotel Apollo and pretty similar to it. It's another great value option, surprising for accommodation that's also home to a popular café on the Grote Markt.

St Anna Bed & Breakfast (☎ 350 18 08; www.sintanna.nl; St Annastraat 208; s with/without bathroom €70/55, d €82) One of the most charming accommodations in Nijmegen. St Anna's owners also run a travel agency specialising in New Zealand, which explains the sheep motif. There are numerous comforts and a wonderfully warm welcome. It's a 10-minute walk south of Keizer Karelplein.

Mercure Nijmegen Centre (☎ 323 88 88; fax 324 20 90; Stationsplein 29; r €83-148; 🖳 ✂ Ⓟ) A large hotel aimed at business travellers. Super comfortable, well-appointed, aesthetically on the bland side, but spotlessly clean. That's hotel chains for you.

Eating & Drinking

Pinoccio Pizzeria (☎ 32 36 98; Molenstraat 99; meals €10-12) Pinoccio straddles a rare line between fine-dining and budget haven. Monday to Wednesday there is a half-price pizza and pasta special. The entire roof is

obscured by thousands of used chianti bottles hanging there.

Café Frowijn (☎ 324 16 13; info@nijmegen -totaal.nl; Pontanusstraat 51; tapas €4-5, mains €10-15; 🕑 lunch & dinner) This brown café has a Mediterranean spin on things and great music. An unaffected place, with a menu of Dutch favourites, augmented by some fish-out-of-water (literally and figuratively) tapas. It's also got one of the prettiest terraces in Nijmegen.

Circus (☎ 360 66 56; www.restauranthetcircus.nl; Kelfkensbos 21; mains €12-25; 🕑 dinner) A more stylish restaurant than its free-wheeling moniker implies, with exotic animals – such as kangaroo – on the menu. For vegetarians, there are steaming pots of filling fondue.

De Blauwe Hand (The Blue Hand; ☎ 360 61 67; Achter de Hoofdwacht 3; snacks €3-5) The best bar in Nijmegen. An ancient survivor whose name derives from its 17th-century customers, workers at a nearby dye shop. It's friendly and atmospheric, and the banner over the ancient bar reads: 'A frosty mug of rich beer gives you warmth, joy and sweet pleasure'. The perfect little Dutch bar.

De Hemel (☎ 360 61 67; Franseplaats 1; 🕑 12-8pm Tue-Sun) The brewery in the ancient Commanderie van St Jan (p272) is worth a visit of its own. The beer is excellent and the snacks are salty and oily enough to make you want to drink more of it. Just like they're supposed to.

Entertainment

The free monthly Quo Vadis is available all over the place and will definitely help you make the most of however much time you have in Nijmegen. It has listings for cinemas, museums, club nights and themes, restaurants and cafés and almost makes our efforts redundant. Bastards.

Nijmegen boasts two large, formal performance venues, the **Schouwburg** (Keizer Karelplein 32) and the **Concertgebouw de Vereeniging** (Oranjesingel 11A; ☎ 322 11 00 schedule & ticket info, both venues).

LIVE MUSIC

Diogenes (☎ 360 48 42, ☎ 360 67 38; www.diogenes .nu; Van Schaeck Mathonsingel 10; cover €1.80-5; 🕑 Tue-Sat) Anything goes at Nijmegen's alternative stalwart, from grinding Death Metal to pop-culture quiz-nights, theatre-sports, teen-oriented pop-parties, films and art displays. Check their monthly program (in Dutch, but with many pictures) for details.

Doornroosje (☎ 355 98 87; www.doornroosje.nl; Groenewoudseweg 322) A super-eclectic multi-purpose venue that's been serving up 1001 flavours of Nijmegen's nightlife since 1970, with live comedy and music from electronica and house to indie-rock and world music. It's got its own gym, with a 10% discount on membership just for flashing their monthly guide.

Gonzo (www.gonzonijmegen.nl; Molenstraat 99) A student-oriented dungeon providing cold beer, hot music and smokey ambience. There are film screenings Wednesday nights, live music on Thursday and Saturday and late hijinks other evenings. It's a good option when other places have shut, often pounding til 4am. There's a giant red starfish out the front.

CINEMA

Lux Filmcentrum (☎ 381 68 55; www.lux-nijmegen.nl; Mariënbrug 38-39; €6-7, 5-film card €25) will delight movie buffs, with a packed program that covers a wide spectrum. Its weekly guide is available from nearly every retailer in Nijmegen. The ground floor houses a fantastic café.

Getting There & Around

The train station is large and modern with many services. Lockers are near the ticket windows. Fares and schedules from Nijmegen include:

Destination	Price (€)	Duration (min)	Frequency (per hr)
Amsterdam	15	90	2
Arnhem	3.10	12	5
Den Bosch	6.50	30	4

OPERATION MARKET GARDEN

Before leaving on an enormous military invasion of the Netherlands in September 1944, a British general told his troops, 'This is a tale you will tell your grandchildren and mightily bored they'll be'. Sadly, thousands didn't survive the mission to bore their grandchildren.

The battle was called Operation Market Garden, a scheme by British General Bernard Montgomery to end WWII in Europe by Christmas. Despite advisers warning that the entire operation was likely to fail, Montgomery pushed on. He had often groused that the Americans under General George Patton were getting all the headlines in their charge across France. The plan was for British forces in Belgium to make a huge push along a narrow corridor to Arnhem in the Netherlands where they would cut off large numbers of German troops from being able to return to Germany, thereby allowing the British to dash east to Berlin and end the war.

The entire plan was dubious from the start. About 10,000 British troops were to be parachuted into Arnhem where they would hold a key bridge for two days while another force of Allied troops fought their way north from Belgium to relieve them. The odds were long from the start. The British paratroops were only given two days rations and the forces from the south had to cross 14 bridges, all of which had to remain traversable and lightly defended for the plan to work.

Everything went wrong. The southern forces encountered some of the German army's most hardened troops and the bridges weren't all completely intact. This, in effect, stranded the Arnhem paratroops. They held out there and in neighbouring Oosterbeek for eight days without food or reinforcements. The survivors, a mere 2163, retreated under darkness. Over 17,000 other British troops were killed.

The results of the debacle were devastating for the Dutch. Arnhem and other towns were levelled and hundreds of civilians killed. The Dutch resistance, thinking that liberation was at hand, came out of hiding to fight the Germans. But without the anticipated Allied forces supporting them, hundreds were captured and killed.

Finally Montgomery abandoned the Netherlands. The winter of 1944–45 came to be known as the 'winter of hunger' with starvation rife as no food could be imported from Allied-held Belgium and the Germans had enough problems without feeding the Dutch. Most of the country was still occupied when the war ended in Europe in May 1945.

OVERIJSSEL & GELDERLAND

Regional and local buses depart from the area in front of the station.

The **bicycle shop** (☎ 322 96 18) is underground in front of the station.

ARNHEM
☎ 026 / pop 141,500

All but levelled during WWII, Arnhem's centre is a nondescript prosperous township that's not really a compelling place to stay. However, there are several museums and attractions around its northern outskirts and the city is a good base for Hoge Veluwe National Park.

Information

Tourist office (☎ 370 02 26; info@vvvarnhem.nl; Willemsplein 8; ☻ 9am-6pm Mon-Fri, 9am-1pm Sat) A 5 to 10 minute walk east of the train station. It's a good place to get maps for cycling in the region.

GWK exchange office (☻ 7.30am-9pm Mon-Sat, 9am-9pm Sun) In the train station. There are several ATMs nearby.

Sights & Activities

Near the Markt, close to the station, the **Grote Kerk** originally dated from the 15th century but has been heavily reconstructed.

Twenty minutes' walk west, the **Museum voor Moderne Kunst** (☎ 351 24 31; www.mmkarnhem .nl; Utrechtseweg 87; €6; ☻ 10am-5pm Tue-Fri, 11am-5pm Sat & Sun) has a commanding spot overlooking the Rijn (Rhine). Its modern art collection represents Arnhem's determination to look forward. Most of the collection is by Dutch artists and the progressive curatorial policy is that at least half of the works on display at any time must be by women.

The **Nederlands Openluchtmuseum** (☎ 357 61 11; Schelmseweg 89; adult/child €11.20/7.50; ☻ 10am-5pm Apr-Oct) is an open-air museum of Dutch heritage with a collection of buildings and artefacts from every province. There's everything here from farmhouses and old trams to working windmills. Volunteers in authentic costume demonstrate traditional skills such as weaving, smithing and farming.

On the same site, **HollandRama** conveys similar information in a 'spectacular multimedia show' targeted squarely at the Playstation generation. Open the same hours as the Openluchtmuseum, but all year.

Sleeping & Eating

For camping information see Hoge Veluwe National Park, p278.

Stayokay Arnhem (☎ 442 01 14; www.stayokay .com /arnhem; Diepenbrocklaan 27; d €20) Inconvenient for the town centre, at 2km north of town, but perfectly situated for seeing a lot of the sights on Arnhem's outskirts, especially by bike. It has quads, doubles and family rooms. Take bus No 3 (direction: Alteveer) and get off at Rijnstate Ziekenhuis (hospital). If they're full, there's another **Stayokay** (☎ 333 43 00; Kerklaan 50) in nearby Doorwerth.

Pension Parkzicht (☎ 442 06 98; fax 443 62 02, Apeldoornsestraat 16; s without bathroom €35, tw with/without bathroom €70/60; ℗) This convenient place is 10 minutes – downhill – from the station and has basic, decent rooms including triples and quads. It's okay to bring your pets to this laid-back place, too (dogs are welcome in the Hoge Veluwe, but not necessarily at every hotel).

Hotel Old Dutch (☎ 442 07 92; info@old-dutch.nl; Stationsplein 8-10; s/d from €72.50/95). Conveniently located for transport connections, it's across the road from the main train station with comfortable, pretty rooms and a homey, friendly feel. The best all-round option within walking distance of Arnhem's commercial centre.

Cafés rim the Korenmarkt, a pretty generic nightlife area with many variations on similar themes. Further east, **Café Verheyden** (☎ 443 70 35; Wezenstraat 6; lunch €5-15) has sandwiches, soups, salads and fresh seafood at moderate prices in a stylish 19th-century building.

Getting There & Around

Arnhem's train station was being renovated at the time of writing. The lockers are by platform No 4. Fares and schedules include:

Destination	Price (€)	Duration (min)	Frequency (per hr)
Amsterdam	11	70	2
Deventer	6.40	36	2
Nijmegen	3.10	12	5

Buses and public transport leave from in front of the station, although the renovation sporadically affects this.

The **bicycle shop** (☎ 442 17 82) is to the right as you exit the station.

WWII CEMETERIES
Groesbeek

Just inside Gelderland's southern border, 10km south of Nijmegen in the small town of Groesbeek, are a WWII museum and two cemeteries.

The **National Liberation Museum 1944–45** (☎ 397 44 04; www.bevrijdingsmuseum.nl; Wylerbaan 4; adult/child aged 7-15/veteran €5.50/3/free; ✆ 10am-5pm Mon-Sat, noon-5pm Sun & public holidays) aims to show the causes, events and outcomes of the Allied efforts leading to the liberation of the Netherlands. Using interactive displays and historical artefacts, visitors can 'relive' the strategic decisions and tactical actions of the various campaigns and battle locations. The ambitious museum also attempts to define for younger visitors what the ideals of democracy, freedom and human rights mean, and why people continue to die fighting to protect them.

Groesbeek Canadian War Cemetery, nearby, is a mausoleum dedicated to the soldiers who fell here during 'Operation Market Garden' (p274). Of the 2,610 Commonwealth soldiers commemorated here, the overwhelming majority – 2,331 – are Canadian.

There is a memorial listing by name 1,000 soldiers whose graves' whereabouts are unknown.

Jonkerbos War Cemetery in the tiny township of Jonkerbos (a short distance from Nijmegen) is the final resting place of predominantly British servicemen.

Oosterbeek

An old suburb 5km west of Arnhem, Oosterbeek was the scene of heavy combat during Operation Market Garden (p274).

The **Airborne Museum Hartenstein** (Map p277; ☎ 333 77 10; www.airbornemuseum.org; Utrechtseweg 232; adult/child/veteran €4.50/3.50/3.50; ✆ 11am-5pm Mon-Sat, 12-5pm Sun) is located in a mansion the British used as HQ during the battle. The museum is 800m south of the Oosterbeek train stop (to/from Arnhem €1.60, five minutes, hourly). It is, however, best reached by the No 1 trolleybus which serves both Oosterbeek and Arnhem train stations.

The **Oosterbeek War Cemetery** (Map p277) is 200m northeast of Oosterbeek train station (follow the signs). Over 1700 Allied (mostly British and Free Polish) troops are buried here.

The tourist offices in either Nijmegen or Arnhem can provide more specific information on how to visit any or all of these monuments to the Allied war fallen.

HOGE VELUWE NATIONAL PARK

The Netherlands' largest national park, the **Hoge Veluwe** (☎ 0318-59 16 27; www.hogeveluwe.nl; adult/child €5/2.50, park & museum €10/5, car €5; ✆ 9am-5.30pm Nov-Mar, 8am-8pm Apr, 8am-9pm May & Aug, 8am-10pm Jun & Jul, 9am-8pm Sep, 9am-7pm Oct), would be a fantastic place to visit for its marshlands, forests and sand dunes alone, but its brilliant museum makes it unmissable. Cars are not admitted after 8pm.

The park was purchased by Anton and Helene Kröller-Müller, a wealthy German-Dutch couple, in 1914. He wanted hunting grounds, she wanted a museum site. They got both.

It was given to the state in 1930; in 1938 a museum opened for Helene's remarkable art collection. A visit to the park can fill an entire day, and even if you don't have a bike, you can borrow one of the park's hundreds of famous free 'white bicycles'.

Information

The ticket booths at each of the three entrances at Hoenderloo, Otterlo and Schaarsbergen have basic information and highly useful park maps (€2.50). In the heart of the park, the main visitors centre is an attraction itself. It has displays on the flora and fauna, including one showing the gruesome results when a deer has a bad day and a crow has a good day.

The Park

Roads through the park are limited. There are many bike paths and hiking trails, 42km in fact, with three routes signposted. The most interesting area is the **Wildbaan** south of the Kröller-Müller Museum. At the north edge, **Jachthuis St Hubert** is the baronial hunting lodge Anton had built. Named after the patron saint of hunting (but not the hunted), you can tour its woodsy interior.

Kröller-Müller Museum

One of the best museums in the Netherlands, the **Kröller-Müller** (☎ 0318-59 12 41; www.kmm.nl; Houtkampweg 6; adult/child under 12 €5/2.50; ✆ 10am-5pm Tue-Sun & public holidays) has works by Picasso, Gris, Renoir, Sisley and Manet, but it's the Van Gogh (1853–90) collection that makes it world-class.

It's about 10km into the park, but well worth the hour's cycling to witness a stun-

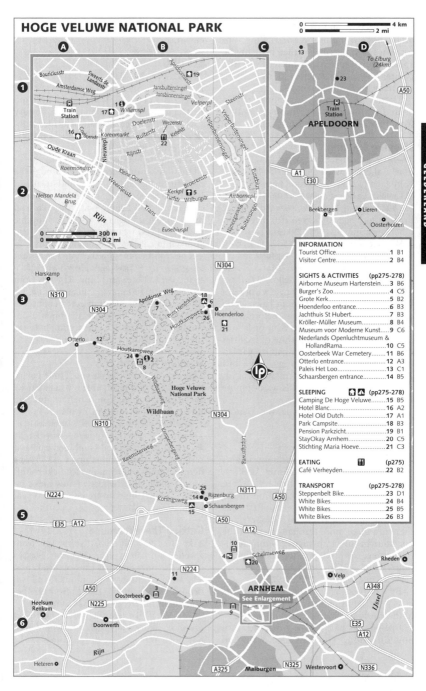

HOGE VELUWE NATIONAL PARK

0 — 4 km
0 — 2 mi

OVERIJSSEL & GELDERLAND

INFORMATION
Tourist Office..............................**1** B1
Visitor Centre............................**2** B4

SIGHTS & ACTIVITIES   (pp275-278)
Airborne Museum Hartenstein.....**3** B6
Burger's Zoo..............................**4** C5
Grote Kerk.................................**5** B2
Hoenderloo entrance..................**6** B3
Jachthuis St Hubert.....................**7** B3
Kröller-Müller Museum................**8** B4
Museum voor Moderne Kunst.....**9** C6
Nederlands Openluchtmuseum &
   HollandRama..........................**10** C5
Oosterbeek War Cemetery.........**11** B6
Otterlo entrance........................**12** A3
Paleis Het Loo...........................**13** C1
Schaarsbergen entrance.............**14** B5

SLEEPING   (pp275-278)
Camping De Hoge Veluwe.........**15** B5
Hotel Blanc................................**16** A2
Hotel Old Dutch........................**17** A1
Park Campsite............................**18** B3
Pension Parkzicht.......................**19** B1
StayOkay Arnhem......................**20** C5
Stichting Maria Hoeve...............**21** C3

EATING   (p275)
Café Verheyden.........................**22** B2

TRANSPORT   (pp275-278)
Steppenbelt Bike.......................**23** D1
White Bikes...............................**24** B4
White Bikes...............................**25** B5
White Bikes...............................**26** B3

ning collection of Van Gogh's work (and other modern masterpieces) rivalling – in some ways surpassing – that held in the eponymous Amsterdam museum of the painter's work. In a series of rooms you can trace his development as an artist.

There's an evocative sculpture garden behind the museum. The museum is 1km from the Hoge Veluwe visitors centre.

Sleeping & Eating

There is a hostel in Arnhem (p275). For hotels, the towns of Deventer (p266) and Nijmegen (p273) make good bases.

Camping De Hooge Veluwe (☎ 026-443 22 72; fax 443 68 09; Koningsweg 14; site €13; ♥ Apr-Oct) Right by the southern Schaarsbergen entrance is another campsite. Bus No 12 passes close by.

Stichting Maria Hoeve (☎ 055-378 10 35; maria hve@euronet.nl; Deelenseweg 25; € negotiable, tent site from €4) Bartering is not dead. Maria Hoeve – a listed WWOOF site (Willing Workers On Organic Farms, see www.wwoof.org for details) – is an old farm in Hoenderloo operating on an 'honesty basis.' Before arriving, guests negotiate the services or labour they'll provide in return for use of facilities including a cottage, perma-culture garden and grounds for horse-riding. Take bus 110 or 108 from Apeldoorn, stopping in Hoenderloo. From there, it's a 10-minute walk.

There are decent cafés at the visitors centre and at the museum.

Getting There & Around

There is a bus service from the train stations in Arnhem and Apeldoorn. From Arnhem, take bus No 2 (direction: Deelevy OC) to the Schaarsbergen entrance and on to the Kröller-Müller Museum. The first bus leaves at 10.10am (April to October) and there are three more through the day (one per hour in July and August). From Apeldoorn, bus No 110 leaves the station every hour from 8.42am to 4.42pm. Confirm services in advance (☎ 0900-9292).

By car there is parking at the visitors centre, museum and lodge. Or you can park at the entrances and use a 'white bicycle'.

By bike, the park is easily reached from any direction. You can also wait and use a free white bicycle, available at the entrance.

ELBURG

☎ 0525 / pop 21,700

Elburg is gorgeous. But if Zwolle is a picture, Elburg is a postcard. It's almost a little too perfect in its sculpted, cobbled 16th-century splendour, very much aware of its own cuteness. Compact and gridlike, the centre is easily explorable on foot.

One highlight is the old harbour. Continue all the way down Jufferenstraat, through the old gate at the end of Vischpoortstraat and into the harbour itself, where a small flotilla of pleasure and fishing boats can take you on a boat tour. There's also an enjoyable market in good weather, where you can help yourself to cheap snacks or local crafts.

The **tourist office** (☎ 68 15 20; www.vvvelburg.nl; Ledige Stede 31; ♥ 9am-5pm Mon-Fri year-round, 10am-4pm Sat May-Aug) is easily found. The bus from Zwolle stops 100m away. Take the first left off Jufferenstraat. It's transected about 100 metres down by the Oude Vischmarkt defining the only sizeable intersection in town, the hub of Elburg's tiny shopping area.

Sleeping & Eating

There's slim to no chance you'll find a place to stay in Elburg itself, unless you get lucky at the tourist office. You're better off seeing Elburg as a day trip from Zwolle.

De Haas (☎ 68 17 37; www.restaurantdehaas.nl; Jufferenstraat 21; mains €14; ♥ lunch & dinner Tue-Sat; dinner Sun & Mon) is a great combined café and restaurant. There's something for everyone here. It stands out from the schlockier stuff on the main drag, whose menus make no bones about their awareness that repeat business is unlikely.

Getting There & Around

Take Bus No 100, 200, 184 or 144 from Zwolle train station on any weekday. Bus No 100 is the only one that runs on weekends. The service runs every 30 minutes, and will deposit you about 100 metres from the beginning of Jufferenstraat, the main drag.

Feet or a bike, are the only ways to get around. Elburg's so small you won't need any other way.

Noord Brabant
& Limburg

CONTENTS

The bottom of the Netherlands belies most clichés about the country. Tulips, windmills and dykes are scarce. What you do find are some rare hills, and, even rarer, Catholics.

Neither Noord Brabant (North Brabant) nor Limburg has its roots in the asceticism of the north, a fact glaringly reinforced during *carnaval* – the streets fill with fireworks, bands and impromptu parties. In fact, both provinces' proximity to Belgium and all those indulgent Catholic monasteries – most of which doubled as excellent micro-breweries – means there's an astounding array of excellent edibles in the south.

You can sample fantastic beers, cheeses and desserts everywhere, reflected in the Dutch labeling of the Brabant/Limburg lifestyle as *bourgondisch*; like the epicurean inhabitants of Burgundy, France, they love to eat and drink heartily.

Big provinces packed with big hearted people means big diversions: Noord Brabant is home to the Netherlands' most popular tourist attraction (über theme-park De Efteling), the biggest street fair in Benelux (the Tilburgse Kermis) and Limburg hosts Europe's biggest art sale, The European Fine Art Foundation show.

The real outstanding 'attraction' down here, though, is the city of Maastricht, as diametrically different from Amsterdam as its geographic position, except in one key area: its people are just as irreverent and just as interested in having a blast.

HIGHLIGHTS

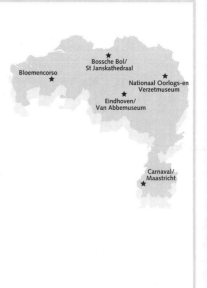

- Celebrating the 'truth in flesh' *(carne vale)* at **carnaval** in Maastricht (p290).

- Indulging in Den Bosch of Dutch desserts – a **Bossche bol** (p283) – in Noord Brabant's capital.

- Admiring the beautifully lit exterior of gorgeous **St Janskathedraal** (p282) at dusk in Den Bosch.

- Saying it with flowers in a *big* way at **Bloemencorso** in Zundert (p285).

- Losing yourself among some of the best European modern art in Eindhoven's **Van Abbemuseum** (p283).

- Contemplating the tragic failure of the Allied forces in 1944s Operation Market Garden at the **National Oorlogs- en Verzetmusueum** (p293) in Overloon.

- Hanging out in **Maastricht** (p287).

  Yes, we meant to say it twice. Just go.

NOORD BRABANT

The Netherlands' largest province spans the bottom of the country, from the waterlogged west to the elevated east. Den Bosch is its main city and an interesting place to spend the day, though Breda is even nicer. The towns here have mostly transformed from wealthy medieval fiefdoms to laid-back shopping, studying and tourism towns.

Despite its size, Noord Brabant won't hold you up. It's primarily a land of agriculture and industry, nicely peppered with a few towns pleasant and engaging enough to use as way stations on your pilgrimage to Limburg or beyond.

'S-HERTOGENBOSCH (DEN BOSCH)

☎ 073 / pop 132,500

You'll hear the Dutch using both the full name, 's-Hertogenbosch, and the shortened Den Bosch ('den-*boss*') when talking about this town. Unless you have some kind of cultural or genetic advantage giving you full control of those harsh Dutch consonants, it's fine to use the simpler version.

The longer version means 'the duke's forest' which was apt in the 12th century when there was a castle and forest here. Both are long gone.

The capital of Noord Brabant has a remarkable church, a good museum, some fine cafés, a local delicacy (the *Bossche*

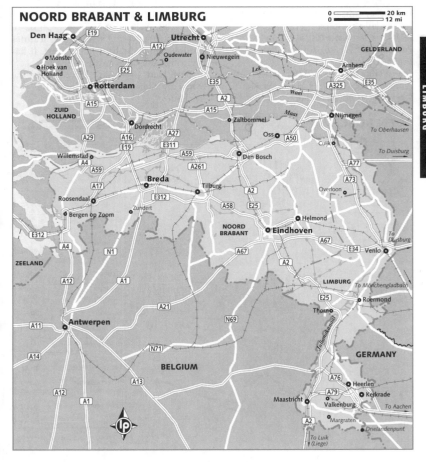

NOORD BRABANT & LIMBURG

NOORD BRABANT & LIMBURG

bol) and makes a good place to spend a day. The old streets around Kruisstraat and Snellestraat make for enjoyably aimless strolling.

Orientation

The town's pedestrianised centre is based around the Markt, a 10-minute walk east of the train station.

Information

Adr Heinen (☎ 613 00 12; Kerkstraat 27) A decent selection of books.

Library (☎ 612 30 33; Hinthamerstraat 72; web access per hr €2.40; 🕑 11am-8pm Mon-Fri, 11am-4pm Sat & Sun) Many computers for your surfing pleasure.

Bosch Medicentrum (☎ 616 20 00; Nieuwstraat 34) The regional hospital.

GWK money exchange (🕑 8am-8pm Mon-Sat, 8am-5pm Sun) In the train station.

ATMs There are several on the Markt.

Post office (☎ 613 43 63; Kerkstraat 67; 🕑 9am-6pm Mon-Fri, 9am-2pm Sat)

Tourist office (☎ 0900-1122334; www.vvvs-hertogenbosch.nl; Markt 77; 🕑 11am-5.30pm Mon, 9am-5.30pm Tue-Fri, 9am-4pm Sat)

Sights & Activities

The main attraction is **St Janskathedraal** (🕑 10am-4.30pm), one of the finest Gothic churches in the Netherlands. It took from 1336 to 1550 to complete its construction. There's an interesting contrast between the red brick tower and the ornate stone buttresses. The interior is fairly barren because the Protestants, who controlled the church from 1629 to 1810, stripped its decor away.

The **town hall** was given its classical baroque appearance in 1670. There's a statue of local artist Hieronymus Bosch in front. De Raadskelder is a 16th-century Gothic cellar kitchen/restaurant right under the town hall. The ambience is nothing short of inspirational.

The **Noordbrabants Museum** (☎ 687 78 77; www.noordbrabantsmuseum.nl; Verwersstraat 41; adult/child €5.70/3; 🕑 10am-5pm Tue-Fri, noon-5pm Sat) in the former governor's residence, features exhibits about Brabant life and art. It has drawings and other work by Bosch.

Boat tours (🕑 Apr-Oct) leave from the canal by Sint Janssingel. Check the pier for times.

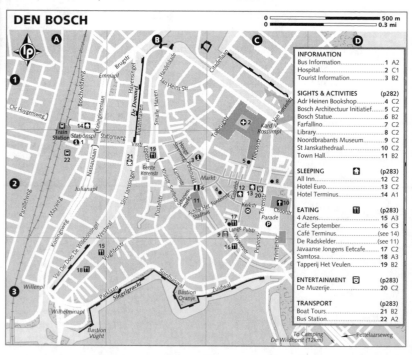

DEN BOSCH

0 _____ 500 m
0 _____ 0.3 mi

INFORMATION	
Bus Information	1 A2
Hospital	2 C1
Tourist Information	3 B2

SIGHTS & ACTIVITIES	(p282)
Adr Heinen Bookshop	4 C2
Bosch Architectuur Initiatief	5 C2
Bosch Statue	6 B2
Farfallino	7 C2
Library	8 C2
Noordbrabants Museum	9 C2
St Janskathedraal	10 C2
Town Hall	11 B2

SLEEPING	(p283)
All Inn	12 C2
Hotel Euro	13 C2
Hotel Terminus	14 A1

EATING	(p283)
4 Azens	15 A3
Cafe September	16 C3
Café Terminus	(see 14)
De Raadskelder	(see 11)
Javaanse Jongens Eetcafe	17 C2
Samtosa	18 A3
Tapperij Het Veulen	19 B2

ENTERTAINMENT	(p283)
De Muzerije	20 C2

TRANSPORT	(p283)
Boat Tours	21 B2
Bus Station	22 A2

Sleeping

Camping De Wildhorst (☎ 0413-29 14 66; Meerstraat 30; site €10) This camping ground is in Heeswijk-Dinther about 12km to the southeast. Take bus No 158 to the church at Heeswijk and then it's 2km.

Hotel Terminus (☎ 613 06 66; fax 613 07 26; Boschveldweg 15; r from €27) Terminus, as its name suggests, is close to the station and actually has decent rooms for this price. It also has a great bar with a good beer selection and regular live folk music.

All Inn (☎ /fax 613 40 57; Gasselstraat 1; s/d €30/45; ☯ closed Aug & carnaval) All Inn is on the lovably shabby but clean side.

Hotel Euro (☎ 613 77 77; www.eurohotel-denbosch .com; Hinthamerstraat 63; s/d from €65/85; ✗ P) Standard rooms that will suit business travellers or leisure travellers who like comfort. Great central location.

Eating

You do have to try the local speciality, a heart-failure-inducing calorie fest known as a *Bossche bol* (den Bosch ball). It's a chocolate-coated cake-y thing the size of a softball, filled with sweetened cream. Absolutely delicious, especially with coffee.

Café September (☎ 613 03 08; Verwersstraat 55-57; meals €4-8; lunch & dinner) September is in a little white building. Inside there are eight beers on tap and 80 more in bottles. It's more of a drinking/people watching place, but simple meals are served as well.

Tapperij Het Veulen (☎ 612 30 38; Korenbrugstraat 9A; meals €5-9; lunch & dinner) It's great when a place is down-to-earth enough to let you throw the peanut shells on the floor, from the comfortable vantage of simple wooden tables. It has unusual cheeses to go with the many beers.

Javaanse Jongens Eetcafé (☎ 613 41 07; Korte Putstraat 27; meals €10-20; lunch & dinner) This place has truly inspired decor; there are carved wooden tigers everywhere. The Indonesian food is excellent.

Samtosa (☎ 612 51 22; Vughterstraat 161; meals €28; ☯ dinner) A fantastic vegetarian restaurant on a lovely street. The menu is inventive, extensive and delicious, featuring influences from the Mediterranean to Southeast Asia to India.

4 Azen (☎ 614 15 74; www.4azen.nl; Vughterstraat 100-106; meals €19.50; ☯ dinner Tue-Sun) This elegant bistro is a treat, the three-course special a substantial winner. The menu changes every six weeks, but an example of the excellent fare is veal escalopes with aubergine mousse and morel sauce.

Entertainment

De Muzerije (☎ 614 10 84; Hinthamerstraat 74) One of those big multicultural places with ongoing programs of all different kinds of theatre, dance, film and the like.

Getting There & Around

The train station is new and brimming with services, including a good grocery store aimed at travellers. Lockers are on the concourse over the tracks. Some fares and schedules are:

Destination	Price (€)	Duration (min)	Frequency (per hr)
Amsterdam	11.00	60	2
Maastricht	16.00	90	1
Nijmegen	6.50	30	4
Utrecht	6.50	30	4

Buses leave from the area to the right as you exit the station. There is a very helpful **bus information office** (☯ 8am-7pm Mon-Fri, 10am-5.30pm Sat).

The **bicycle shop** (☎ 613 47 37) is below the station.

EINDHOVEN

☎ 040 / pop 206,000

A mere village in 1900, Eindhoven grew exponentially thanks to Philips (founded here in 1891). During the 1990s, the electronics giant found it was having trouble recruiting employees to work in its hometown, but its research and engineering arms remain. It solved the problem by moving to Amsterdam. Which sums up the woes of this huge industrial town; not an amazingly pleasant place, though not without merits.

Eindhoven is best known for its football team, PSV who routinely dominate the national league. Matches always sell out, mostly to fanatically devoted locals.

If you visit Eindhoven, the charming blue and white **tourist office** (☎ 246-3005; www.vvveindhoven.nl; Stationsplein 1; ☯ 7.30am-7pm Mon-Fri, 7.30am-noon Sat), in front of the train station, can provide information.

The main attraction here is the excellent **Stedelijk Van Abbemuseum** (☎ 275 52 75;

www.vanabbemuseum.nl; Bilderdijklaan 10; adult/child over 12/child under 12 €8.50/4/free; ☺ 11am-5pm Tue-Sun). It's wonderful, with a first-rate collection of 20th-century paintings (including works by Picasso, Chagall, and Kandinsky) almost but not quite matching the greatness of the Stedelijk Museum in Amsterdam (p109) or the Boijmans van Beuningen in Rotterdam (p212).

There's a uniquely dense nightlife district, **Het Stratumseind**, where more than 30 cafés, bars and restaurants within a single stretch of street make it one of the most concentrated areas in the country. There are many options, and obviously bar-hopping is made easier by the proximity.

Eindhoven Airport (www.eindhovenairport.nl) is 6km west of the centre, and aimed at business travellers.

The train station is at a junction of lines to Amsterdam, Maastricht, Rotterdam and Venlo.

TILBURG
☎ 013 / pop 198,000
With one of the highest ratios of students in the Netherlands (almost 15% of the population) you'd expect a more progressive vibe. Its centre bears the scars of unfortunate 1960s urban renewal schemes; think East Berlin. Tilburgers are quick to defend their home, though.

A former textile town, Tilburg is today in flux, now that the mills have closed due to foreign competition.

To catch the most famous reason for visiting Tilburg, time your visit for the middle of July, when the **Tilburgse Kermis** (Tilburg Fair; www.vvvtilburg.nl) takes place for around two weeks. Basically an enormous street-party, but far from having a socio-cultural basis like *carnaval*, it's simply a massive influx of street-fair and -fare. Rides, beer, bad chart music, sugary treats, stalls offering stuffed prizes for games of 'skill,' all clog Tilburg's centre like cholesterol in an artery. It's the biggest fair in Benelux, and for that reason alone remarkable.

DE EFTELING
Near Tilburg, in the unassuming town of Kaatsheuvel is **De Efteling** (☎ 0900-33835464, www.efteling.nl; Europalaan 1, Kaatsheuvel; admission €21), the biggest domestic 'tourist' attraction in the Netherlands. The 'Dutch Disneyland'

pulls over 3 million visitors annually, its 40-year history as a family favourite undiminished by the emergence of newer competitors such as Six Flags (p171).

All the usual suspects are here: huge scary rides (ditto prices), walk-through entertainment with animatronic robot models, scenes from popular stories and fairy tales, live shows performed by talent who couldn't make the cut for Cirque Du Soleil, sticky hands, crying…

There's accommodation on site – for full details see the website. To get to De Efteling, take bus No 136 or 137 from Tilburg or Den Bosch train station.

BREDA
☎ 076 / pop 164,500
Breda is a lovely town. The streets are lined with interesting shops and cafés, it has some flower-filled parks and its main church is a stunner.

Breda's present peace belies its turbulent past. Its proximity to the Belgian border means it has been overrun by invading armies many times. The town centre is a 10-minute walk south from the station through large, leafy park, the Valkenberg.

Information
GWK money exchange (☺ 8am-8pm) In the train station.
Post office (☎ 522 55 20; Willemstraat 30; ☺ 9am-6pm Mon-Fri, 10am-1.30pm Sat)
Tourist office (☎ 0900-5222444; www.vvvbreda.nl; Willemstraat 17; ☺ 10.30am-5.30pm Tue-Fri, 10.30am-5pm Sat) Near the train station. There is another branch on Grote Markt 38.

Sights & Activities
The **Valkenberg** (Falcon Mountain) is the huge park between the station and the centre. Hunting falcons were trained here for the royalty. On the south side is the 12th-century **Begijnhof**. Breda is a wonderfully preserved example of these homes, which sheltered unmarried women and were found throughout the Netherlands.

The **castle** is worth a quick look; approach from the south and you'll also see the **Spanjaardsgat** (Spanish gate) a reminder of just one of the various incursions the town has endured.

The **Grote Kerk** (☺ 10am-5pm Mon-Sat, 1-5pm Sun) recently emerged from years of restoration,

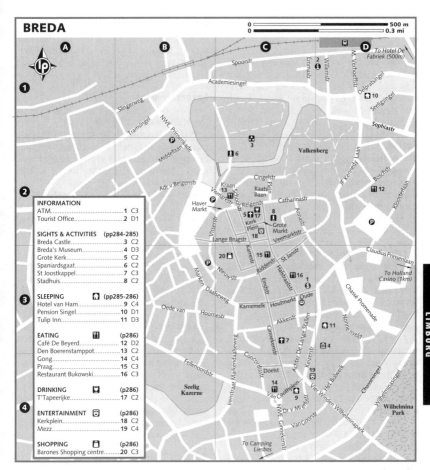

BREDA

0 — 500 m
0 — 0.3 mi

INFORMATION
ATM..1 C3
Tourist Office............................2 D1

SIGHTS & ACTIVITIES (pp284-285)
Breda Castle..............................3 C2
Breda's Museum........................4 D3
Grote Kerk................................5 C2
Spaniardsgaat...........................6 C2
St Joostkappel...........................7 C3
Stadhuis....................................8 C2

SLEEPING (pp285-286)
Hotel van Ham...........................9 C4
Pension Singel.........................10 D1
Tulip Inn.................................11 D3

EATING (p286)
Café De Beyerd........................12 D2
Den Boerenstamppot................13 C2
Gong......................................14 C4
Praag.....................................15 C3
Restaurant Bukowski...............16 C3

DRINKING (p286)
T'Tapeerijke............................17 C2

ENTERTAINMENT (p286)
Kerkplein................................18 C2
Mezz......................................19 C4

SHOPPING (p286)
Barones Shopping centre..........20 C3

removing the grime from its now-gleaming white stones. It was built from the 15th century to the 17th century and is the Netherlands' most beautiful Gothic church.

Festivals & Events

The **Bloemencorso** (www.bloemencorsozundert.nl) is a huge annual parade of gorgeously decorated, multi-coloured floats – constructed entirely from flowers – through the streets of Zundert, 20km southwest of Breda. Early September.

Sleeping

Camping Liesbos (☎ 514 35 14; fax 514 65 55; Liesdreef 40; sites €13; ☼ Apr-Oct) To get to the campsite, take bus No 10 or 111 (direction: Etten-Leur) to the Boswachterij Liesbos stop.

Hotel van Ham (☎ 521 52 29; hotel.van.ham@hetnet.nl; Van Coothplein 23; s/d/tr €40/60/85) John and Sylvia van Hooydonk are the proud proprietors of this charming hotel, which is also home to a delightful café-restaurant. It's fabulously located, in a building that's been a prominent meeting point for more than 100 years. The rooms are lovely.

Pension Singel (☎ 521 62 71; pensionsingel@planet .nl; Delpratsingel 14; per person €20.40) Simple though charming singles and doubles. It's a five-minute walk from the station.

Hotel De Fabriek (☎ 581 00 08; Speelhuislaan 150; s/d €55/70). This laid-back, quiet place has comfortable rooms and is in a quieter area; breakfast is €9 extra. It's a five- to 10-minute walk off to your left from behind the station.

Tulip Inn (☎ 520 51 73; www.hotel-keyser.nl; Keizerstraat 5; s/d €73/93) It's part of a chain, but sets itself apart by its attentive staff – its strongest asset. Its restaurant serves lunch and dinner Monday to Friday and dinner on Saturday.

Eating

Den Boerenstamppot (☎ 514 01 62; Schoolstraat 3; meals €4-6.80; ☺ lunch & dinner Mon-Sat). This homey diner has delicious and authentic food at old-time prices. Their delicious *stamppot* (a thick mash of potatoes and green vegetables) is served drowning in home-style butter-based gravy and served with sausages, Brabant's specialty.

Café De Beyerd (☎ 521 42 65; www.beyerd.nl; Boschstraat 26; lunch €8; ☺ lunch & dinner Thu-Tue) The Beyerd is a highly regarded beer café, with more than 122 brews. The perfect place to try some *bitterballen* (small crumbed, deep-fried balls of meaty delight) or other typical beer-accompanying snacks.

Praag (☎ 514 00 74; www.praag.nl; Grote Markt 13; mains under €10; ☺ lunch & dinner) Praag is a cosmopolitan bar/eatery with funky décor and great food, ultra-modern and in stark contrast to a lot of the more traditional terrace cafés on the Markt. Meal items range from sandwiches to tapas and there's a cool bar.

Gong (☎ 521 66 96; www.restaurantgong.nl; Van Coothplein 24; mains €15-17; ☺ dinner) Great Asian and Pacific Rim fusion cuisine. It's cool, mostly healthy, and – better yet – tasty and affordable.

Restaurant Bukowski (☎ 529 75 55; info@restaurantbukowski.nl; Halstraat 21a; mains €18-28; ☺ lunch & dinner) This place wouldn't have let the writer and 'dirty old man' it's named after through the doors! Bukowski's slick *haute cuisine* (tomato risotto and pan-fried lamb with runner beans in a herb and goat cheese sauce) may mean blowing your budget. Do so, heeding the great barfly himself: 'Some people never go crazy; how horrible their lives must be!'

Drinking

Bruxelles Belgian Beer-café (☎ 521 52 11; fax 521 55 15; Havermarkt 7) A cavernous (yet somehow cosy) wooden beer hall/eatery with a very popular terrace on the Havermarkt,

the Bruxelles has an excellent selection of Belgian beers. Think monasteries and strong, infinite varieties of brewed bubbly stuff. Hang around here for a while and become a Trappist artist.

Entertainment

There's a concentration of places around the Havermarkt, of varying quality.

Pick up **UitLoper** (info line ☎ 514 39 15) Breda's free weekly entertainment guide, covering cinema, theatre, clubs art exhibitions and more. Anything that looks like it sells a good time will be in UitLoper.

Mezz (☎ 515 66 77; www.mezz.nl; Keizerstraat 101; café ☺ 12-3pm for lunch) If Swiss artist HR Giger designed a nightclub, it might look like Mezz (is it a headless mechanical armadillo or a giant metal dolmade?). Either way, it's new, super-hip, with a great bar and cool staff to match its eclectic program – everything from drum'n'bass nights to latin swing and rock. It publishes its own guide, widely available around Breda. Prices and hours vary by programs.

Kerkplein (www.kerkpleinbreda.nl) A bangin' club, located right behind the Grote Kerk on Kerkplein, that goes well into the morning offering punters the chance to get up to the kind of ructions they can later confess to across the road.

Breda is also home to the biggest **Holland Casino** (www.hollandcasino.nl) in Europe, comfortably ensconced in a beautiful building that was once a military barracks.

Getting There & Around

The train station has all the usual services. Some fares and schedules are:

Destination	Price (€)	Duration (min)	Frequency (per hr)
Amsterdam	16.40	110	4
Den Bosch	6.30	33	2
Roosendaal	3.70	17	2
Rotterdam	7.10	32	3

Buses leave from the area to the right as you exit the station.

The bicycle shop is right next to the station. For information on a 52km bicycle route, the Baronie Route, which begins and ends at Breda, see the special section Cycling in the Netherlands.

SLOT LOEVESTEIN

☎ 0183

Near the tiny, beautiful little walled town of Woudrichem you'll find the 14th-century castle **Slot Loevestein** (☎ 0183-44 71 71; www.slotloevestein.nl; adult/child €4.60/2.65; ⊙ 10am-5pm Mon-Fri, 1-5pm Sat & Sun May-Sep; 1-5pm Sat, Sun & Wed Oct-Apr). The ancient keep is wonderfully evocative, perhaps more so for the difficulty of getting there. It's been a prison, residence and toll castle, though more recently it's hosted a varied calendar of cultural events (check the website). It's best accessed by the ferry from Woudrichem, which stops right out front.

WEST NOORD BRABANT

Near the border with Zeeland, Noord Brabant more closely resembles its soggy neighbour. Canals and rivers crisscross the land and everything is absolutely flat. There's not much reason to spend a lot of time trying to make sense of the region, but you might want to check out two of its towns.

Roosendaal is a major rail junction for lines north to Rotterdam, south to Belgium, east to Breda and west to Zeeland.

Except for one week a year, **Bergen op Zoom** is unremarkable. It was plundered at various times by the Spanish, French and even, in 1814, the British. The results look like the aftermath of a big party – a hodge-podge of buildings and styles. But if you want to see the aftermath of a real party, show up on the Wednesday after Shrove Tuesday. Its *carnaval* is the most raucous west of Maastricht, drawing revellers from throughout Europe who basically go on a four-day bender.

LIMBURG

This long and narrow province at times barely seems part of the Netherlands, especially in the south where it's hilly. There are all sorts of amusingly dire notices on the A2 motorway into Maastricht warning drivers of impending 'steep grades' that would be considered minor humps in other countries.

Maastricht is the star – actually, the blazing supernova – of Limburg. Little else warrants a fraction of the time Maastricht demands.

MAASTRICHT

☎ 043 / pop 122,000

Hanging down from the rest of the Netherlands, hemmed in between Belgium and Germany, Maastricht was saved from war damage in the 20th century; the Dutch government simply didn't bother defending it.

In centuries past, however, Maastricht was captured at various times by most of Europe's powers. This legacy as a crossroads for invaders gave Maastricht its existing pan-European flavour. The average citizen bounces easily between Dutch, English, French, German, Flemish and more. Appropriately, the city hosted two seminal moments in the history of the European Union: on 10 December 1991, the 12 members of the then European Community met to sign the treaty for economic, monetary and political union, reconvening the following February to sign the treaty creating the EU.

Maastricht has an energy belying its size. The people are irreverent, there's hordes of university students and the streets are steeped in history. No Netherlands itinerary is really complete without visiting Maastricht. If you're heading this way by rail or road to Belgium, you'd be doing yourself a disservice to bypass it: Maastricht's more interesting than even some of the biggest cities of the Netherlands' southern neighbour.

Orientation

The centre of Maastricht is quite compact, bisected by the Maas river. The area on the east side is known as Wyck, and to the south of here is the new area of Céramique. The walk from the train station to the Vrijthof, the cultural heart, takes 15 minutes.

The other major square, the Markt, underwent a massive reconstruction beginning in 2001 that was meant to undo the damage caused by previous massive reconstructions. Most of the Markt is now carparkt. Whether or not this constitutes progress is, of course, debatable.

Information
BOOKSHOPS

Plantage Boekhandel (☎ 321 08 25; Nieuwstraat 9) A good selection of travel and English-language books.

Hermione (☎ 321 60 91; Rechtstraat 72). This fantastic second-hand bookshop has a great range and the perfect 'there's method in our madness' display vibe.

MAASTRICHT

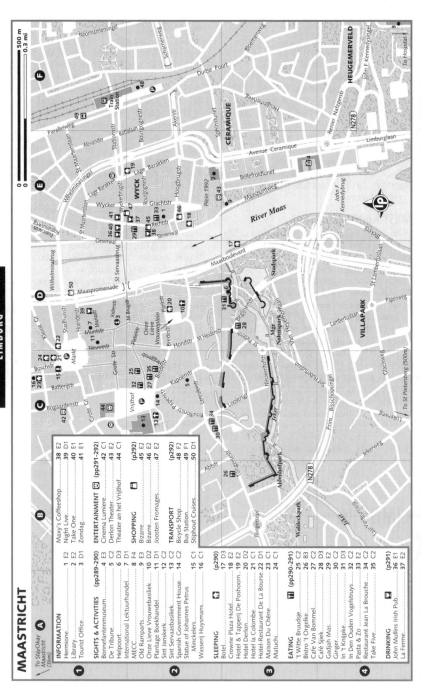

To StarOkay Maastricht (3km)

INFORMATION
Hermione	1	E2
Library	2	E2
Tourist Office	3	D1

SIGHTS & ACTIVITIES (pp289–290)
Bonnefantenmuseum	4	E3
De Tribune	5	C2
Helpoort	6	D3
International Lektuurhandel	7	D1
MECC	8	F4
Old Ramparts	9	E3
Onze Lieve Vrouwebasiliek	10	D1
Plantage Boekhandel	11	D1
Sint Janskerk	12	C2
Sint Servaasbasiliek	13	C2
Spanish Government House	14	C2
Statue of Johannes Petrus Minckelers	15	C1
Wasserij Huysmans	16	C1

SLEEPING (p290)
Botel	17	D3
Crowne Plaza Hotel	18	E2
Hotel & Tapperij De Poshoom	19	E2
Hotel Derlon	20	D2
Hotel la Colombe	21	C1
Hotel-Restaurant De La Bourse	22	C1
Matuchi	23	C1

EATING (pp290–291)
't Witte Bruudsje	24	C1
Bistro 't Orgelke	25	C2
Cafe Van Bommel	26	B3
Café Sjiek	27	C2
Gadjah Mas	28	D2
Ginger	29	E2
In 't Knipke	30	C3
In Den Ouden Vogelstruys	31	D3
Pasta & Zo	32	E2
Restaurant Jean La Brouche	33	C2
Take Five	34	C2
	35	C2

DRINKING (p291)
John Mullins Irish Pub	36	E1
La Ferme	37	E2

Maxy's Coffeeshop	38	E2
Night Live	39	D1
Take One	40	E1
Zondag	41	E1

ENTERTAINMENT (pp291–292)
Cinema Lumiere	42	C1
Derlon Theater	43	E2
Theater an het Vrijthof	44	C1

SHOPPING
Bizarre	45	E2
Bizarre	46	E2
Joosten Fromages	47	E2

TRANSPORT (p292)
Bicycle Shop	48	F1
Bus Station	49	F1
Stiphout Cruises	50	D1

INTERNET ACCESS

Library (☎ 350 56 00; Ave Céramique 50; web access per hr €4; ⌚ 10am-5pm Mon, Wed, Fri & Sat; 10am-8pm Tue & Thu) Bright and inviting with Internet access.

LAUNDRY

Wasserij Huysmans (☎ 325 09 59; Boschstraat 82) Seems to have erratic hours, but it's the most conveniently located.

MEDICAL SERVICES

Academisch Ziekenhuis Maastricht (☎ 387 65 43; P Debyelaan 25) A huge academic hospital just east of the MECC exposition centre.

MONEY

GWK money exchange office (⌚ 8am-9pmMon-Sat, 8am-6pm Sun) In the train station.

POST

Post office (☎ 329 91 99; Statenstraat 4; ⌚ 9am-6pm Mon-Fri, 9am-1.30pm Sat) There's another post office (☎ 321 45 11; Stationstraat 60) nearer the train station open similar hours.

TOURIST INFORMATION

Tourist office (☎ 325 21 21; www.vvvmaastricht.nl; Kleine Staat 1; ⌚ 9am-6pm Mon-Fri, 9am-5pm Sat, 11am-3pm Sun) Has reams of English-language information on the city and surroundings.

Sights & Activities

Maastricht's many delights are scattered along both banks of the Maas, but it's always a pleasant stroll from one side to the other. There's tons of historical info to chew over around the Vrijthof, and beautiful streets winding through and around it, while there are some great museums and remnants of the medieval city in the Wyck district.

BONNEFANTENMUSEUM

The **Bonnefantenmuseum** (☎ 3290190; www.bonne fantenmuseum.nl; Ave Céramique 250; adult/child under 12 €6.50/free; ⌚ 11am-5pm Tue-Sun) features a 28m tower that's now a local landmark. Designed by Aldo Rossi, the museum opened in 1995, and is well laid-out with collections divided into departments, each on its own floor – Old Masters and medieval sculpture on one floor, contemporary art by Limburg artists on the next. A dramatic sweep of stairs beckons visitors to both floors.

Space is devoted to special exhibitions and shows, of which there are usually four

annually, two following classical/historical themes, two on more contemporary material. It also espouses an ongoing commitment to solo exhibitions by young and emerging artists, and is the patron of the major bi-annual Vincent Van Gogh Award for Contemporary Art in Europe.

VRIJTHOF

A large square dominated by **Sint Servaas-basiliek** (adult/child €2/1; ⌚ 10am-5pm Apr-Oct, Sun Nov-Mar), Vrijthof is surrounded by lively cafés and cultural institutions.

A pastiche of architecture dating from AD 1000, Sint Servaasbasiliek is a huge barn of a place that makes for a good wander.

Sint Janskerk is a small 17th-century Gothic church, one of the most beautiful in the Netherlands. A remarkable red colour, it photographs beautifully. Climb to the top (€1.15) for gorgeous views.

The 16th-century **Spanish Government House** (☎ 321 13 27; €2.50; ⌚ 1-5pm Wed-Sun) is so named because this is where Philip II outlawed his former lieutenant Willem the Silent at the start of the Eighty Years' War. There's a small museum with items from the building's later years.

STREETS, SQUARES & BRIDGES

The best way to see Maastricht is to just stroll. Streets not to miss include those south and east of Vrijthof; you'll be rewarded with a medieval labyrinth punctuated by interesting shops and cafés.

Onze Lieve Vrouweplein is an intimate café-filled square named after its church, the **Onze Lieve Vrouwebasiliek** (⌚ 10am-5pm; treasury adult/child €2/1) which has parts dating from before AD 1000 and may well be built on the foundations of a Roman cathedral. There is a separate treasury area that houses gaudy jewels and riches you can see for a small and worhtwhile fee.

The statue at the north end of the **Markt** is of **Johannes Petrus Minckelers**, who holds a flaming rod; he invented gas light.

The busy pedestrian **Sint Servaasbrug** dates from the 13th-century and links Maastricht's centre with the Wyck district.

FORTIFICATIONS

At the end of Sint Bernardusstraat, the **Helpoort** is the oldest surviving town gate in the Netherlands (1229). Across the Maas in the new Céramique district, you can see the remains of the 13th-century ramparts and fortifications.

Much of Maastricht is riddled with defensive tunnels dug into the soft sandstone over the centuries. The best place to see the tunnels is **Sint Pietersberg**, 2km south of Helpoort. The large fort has tunnels throughout the hill. The tourist office leads **cave tours** (☎ 321 78 78; adult/child €3/1.75; ☻ 3.30pm daily Jul-Aug & school holidays). Bus No 29 goes past the fort from Vrijthof. Thirteen species of bats have been found living below the surface.

Tours

Stiphout Cruises (☎ 351 53 00; Maaspromenade 27; adult/child €5/3; ☻ daily Apr-Oct, Sat & Sun Nov-Dec) runs boat cruises on the Maas. On certain days there are day-long round-trip cruises to Liege in Belgium (adult/child €15/6) although you can get a single ticket.

The tourist office runs 90-minute English-language **walking tours** (adult/child €3/1.80; ☻ 12.30 Jul & Aug).

Festivals & Events

Two events stand out from the busy Maastricht calendar:

Carnaval Celebrated with greater vigour in Maastricht than anywhere else in Europe, save Venice (Italy) and Sitges (Spain), the orgy of partying and carousing begins the Friday before Shrove Tuesday and lasts until the last person collapses sometime on Wednesday. *Everything* stops for Carnaval.

TEFAF Europe's largest annual art show is held in late March at the cavernous MECC exposition hall just south of Céramique. Over 200 exhibitors converge on Maastricht offering masterpieces to those with a few million euros spare. The event is open to the public, so go browse.

Sleeping

Maastricht is a popular weekend destination throughout the year, so reservations are a must. The tourist office has a list of private rooms it can book.

HOSTELS

Stayokay Maastricht (☎ 346 67 77; www.stayokay .com/maastricht; Dousbergweg 4; d from €20; ☻) The hostel is fine, but sadly quite inconvenient to the town centre, as you're beholden to bus schedules which are sketchy at best, and it's a good 40 minute walk. The hostel's got tennis courts.

Matuchi (☎ 354 06 92; Kleine Gracht 34; r from €60) Initially, Matuchi looks like an Asiatic/Eastern-influenced take on the Korova milk-bar from Stanley Kubrick's *A Clockwork Orange*, with severely hip lighting offsetting post-modern furniture and décor. This stylish place calls itself a hostel, but it's really an ambitious, excellently designed bar with many accommodation options and a great eatery. New, flashy and very cool.

HOTELS

Maison Du Chêne (☎ 321 35 23; www.maastrichthotel .com; Boschstraat 104; s/d €40/60) This is a fine budget option in an elegant 1855 building. The rooms have baths and are very clean. There is a good brasserie on the ground floor, where you can have breakfast in the mornings.

Hotel la Colombe (☎ 321 57 74, www.hotel lacolombe.nl; Markt 30; s/d €59/75) In a simple, white building on the Markt. The rooms are equally unadorned but all have TV and bath. This unassuming but quite lovely hotel has a decent café.

Hotel & Tapperij De Poshoorn (☎ 321 73 34; www.poshoorn.nl; Stationsstraat 47; s/d €57.50/70) A good place with a great café. The rooms are simple but all have bathroom and TV. They also have triples and quads; breakfast is €6.50 extra but well worth it.

Hotel Derlon (☎ 321 67 70; www.hotelderlonmaas tricht.activehotels.com; Onze Lieve Vrouweplein 6; r from €155; ☒ ☐ ☒) This is easily the best place to stay in town with lovely rooms and enthusiastic staff. The breakfast room in the basement is built around Roman ruins.

Eating

Maastricht's streets are lined with restaurants and cafés. A brilliant website (www .eureview.com/web/maastricht) compiled by students, lists many places, from cheap *eetcafés* to highbrow dining.

CAFÉS

Take Five (☎ 321 09 71; Bredestraat 14; lunch €6; ☻ lunch & dinner) One of the best bars or eateries in Maastricht on a quieter street parallel to the cramped terraces of heaving Platielstraat. It combines fusion cooking with a stark interior, chill-out music and engaging staff who have the skinny on *every* cool happening in Maastricht. On many nights there's live jazz.

In Den Ouden Vogelstruys (☎ 321 48 88; Vrijthof 15; ☿ lunch & dinner) If you must eat or drink on the main pedestrian ogling drag, this is the one to be at. Try some local *Limburgse kaas* (Limburg cheese) with a heavy Trappist beer (€4 to €5 for both).

In 't Knijpke (☎ 321 65 25; Bernardusstraat 13; ☿ lunch & dinner) This wonderful cellar café is a combination cheese-seller, mini-cinema and restaurant, with delicious French standards like frog's legs, onion soup and other Gallic delights. Go there for the priceless atmosphere, though – one of the best in a town chock-full of great cafés.

Tapperij De Poshoorn (☎ 321 73 34; Stationsstraat 47; ☿ lunch & dinner) A brilliant beer café in the hotel of the same name is a classic bar with a small but sensational beer list (52 brews) and great daily specials for under €10. Meat, bread, potatoes, cheese, beer – all five of the Dutch food groups are represented. Vegetables make their typical cameo appearance.

Café Sjiek (☎ 321 01 58; Sint Pieterstraat 13; meals €10-14; ☿ lunch & dinner) Always packed with locals. Give your name to the wise-cracking bartenders and settle back with some of the fine beers and wines while you wait for a spot to open up.

QUICK EATS

't Witte Bruudsje (☎ 321 00 57; Platielstraat 12; ☿ 10am-2am) Fresh salads and various gourmet hot snacks. Good for cheap and cheerful eating on the run

RESTAURANTS

Gadjah Mas (☎ 321 15 68; www.gadjahmas.nl; Rechtstraat 42; mains from €15; ☿ lunch & dinner) This fabulous restaurant has many vegetarian options among its menu of authentic Indonesian food that is as carefully presented as the artistic interior. Worth a splurge, the eponymous (and enormous) Gadjah Mas rijsttafel is almost a bargain at €32.50 per person.

Restaurant Jean La Brouche (☎ 321 46 09; Tongersestraat 9; 3-course menu €28; ☿ dinner Mon-Sat) Classic cuisine. Think pressed white table cloths and cutlery with a bit of heft to it. If you're a fan of old-style, 'no tricks' French cooking, eat here.

Bistro 't Orgelke (☎ 321 69 82; www.orgelke.nl; Tongersestraat 42; mains/set menus €17/21; ☿ lunch & dinner) *Stoofpot* – thick, hearty stew – is a Dutch staple. And you can try whatever kind you like here; chicken, lamb, beef or a vegetarian option, all served with potatoes as part of a set menu.

Ginger (☎ 326 50 22; Tongersestraat 7; mains €9-12; ☿ lunch & dinner) Super-cool and healthy Asian noodle soups come to Maastricht. And Ginger's the place to get them. Fabulous fresh ingredients. Serene and wonderful contemporary dining.

Pasta & Zo (☎ 325 41 54; Rechtstraat 38; mains from €7; ☿ lunch Mon-Sat, dinner all week) A superior pasta joint, offering at least 10 types of home-made sauces on a variety of pasta. The take-away serves are a filling bargain, and absolutely delicious.

SELF-CATERING

Joosten Fromages (☎ 321 44 64; Wyckerbrugstraat 43) A superb selection of local cheeses and other produce that can make for a great picnic.

Drinking

Take One (☎ 321 64 23; Rechtstraat 28) A long, narrow tavern little changed since the 1930s. It has an incredible (and endearingly hand-written) beer list – well over 100 – and is usually peopled by in-the-know locals, casually shelling their peanuts onto the floor. Join in.

La Ferme (☎ 321 89 28; Rechtstraat 29) is a mellow gay bar.

Entertainment

Pick up a copy of **Week In, Week Uit**, a free weekly magazine (available in many places) to get the low-down on Maastricht's fab night-life. The town punches well above its weight in party potential; Maastricht has the best nightlife outside the Randstad.

Zondag (Sunday; ☎ 321 93 00; www.cafézondag.nl; Wyckerbrugstraat 42) Maastricht's coolest bar/café pulls the stylish, well-heeled 20- to 30-something crowd, drawn by the cosy bar, entertainment from live Latin music to break-beat DJs, and friendly staff. Light lunches (paninis, soups, salads) and tapas/bar snacks are available daily.

Night Live (☎ 0900-2020158; Kesselskade 43) A disco in an old church that opens after midnight at weekends; the cover charge is around €4. Everything from mad gabber idiocy to 1980s-throwback retro nights take place here, so check the abundant posters plastered all over town before you come.

Maxy's Coffeeshop (Rechtstraat 49; ☉ 10am-midnight) Go here for all your spliff-related requirements.

Derlon Theater (☎ 350 71 71; Plein 1992) Near the new library and has drama and music. The café has fine river views from the terrace.

Cinema Lumiere (☎ 321 40 80; Bogaardenstraat 40B) Off-beat and classic films.

Shopping

Wyck has a fun variety of stores, including **Bizarre** (☎ 627 68 44; Rechtstraat 90 & 44) which has a selection that speaks for itself. Kapoenstraat off Vrijthof is another good street for interesting shops.

Getting There & Away

Maastricht Airport is a small facility served by KLM subsidiaries (☎ 020-474 77 47) which have flights to London and connecting flights to Schiphol. It is 10km north of the centre. Bus Nos 51 and 61 go there every two hours (25 minutes).

Maastricht has a grand old train station with numerous services. Some fares and schedules are:

Destination	Price (€)	Duration (min)	Frequency (per hr)
Amsterdam	24.50	155	1
Rotterdam	23.50	140	2
Utrecht	21	120	1

There is an hourly international service to Liege (€6.80, 30 minutes), from where you can catch trains to Brussels, Paris and Cologne.

The bus station is to the right as you exit the train station. Eurolines has one bus a day to/from Brussels (€14, two hours). Interliner has hourly buses to/from Aachen (€2.80, one hour).

Getting Around

You may not ever need the local buses.

There is car & motorcycle parking in massive underground lots by the river.

The **bicycle shop** (☎ 321 11 00) is in a separate building to the left as you exit the station.

There's an excellent cycle route in the hills around Maastricht (see the Plateau Route, p76).

AROUND MAASTRICHT

The hills and forests of southern Limburg make for excellent hiking and biking. The **Drielandenpunt** (the convergence of the Netherlands, Belgium and Germany) is on the highest hill in the country (323m). It is an excellent driving or biking destination. It's in Vaals, 26km southeast of Maastricht.

Valkenburg

☎ 043 / pop 17,900

This small town in the hills east of Maastricht has possibly the most overcommercialised centre in the Netherlands. The town attracts gobs of tour buses filled with folks who appreciate such a scene. But away from the town are excellent trails and cycle paths through the nearby forests.

The **tourist office** (☎ 0900-9798; www.vvvzuid limburg.nl; Dorrenplein 5) has a huge selection of maps of the area and is good at making recommendations. You might start at the over-restored **castle** (€4; ☉ 10am-4pm) above town from where trails radiate out through the countryside.

Cycle Center (☎ 601 53 38; De Valkenburg 8b; ☉ 9am-6pm Tue-Fri, 9am-5pm Sat Oct-Mar) rents everything from simple bikes to mopeds. Prices start at €8 per day for simple models, while mountain bikes cost €20. It's five minutes north of the station.

ASP Adventure (☎ 601 15 08; www.aspadventure.nl) gives 90-minute guided tours (€20, call ahead) of the networks of caves that riddle the soft sandstone of the hills. There are many options, including riding bikes underground.

Valkenburg is easily reached from Maastricht by train (€2.10, 12 minutes, two per hour).

Ten kilometres east of Maastricht, in Margraten is the **Netherlands American Cemetery and Memorial** (www.abmc.gov/ne.htm; ☉ 9am-5pm). Dedicated to US soldiers who died in the 'Operation Market Garden' offensive (see boxed text, p274) and the general Allied push to liberate the Dutch, it's a sombre memorial with row after row of silent white crosses the stark but necessary testament to the futility of war.

Bus service to the cemetery runs from Maastricht's train station. The site is easily reached by taxi.

NORTH LIMBURG

Clinging to the Maas river and barely 30km across at its widest point, the northern half of Limburg is a no-nonsense place of industry and agriculture. **Venlo**, the major town, has a small historic quarter near the train station. It's worth a quick look if you are changing trains for the hourly service to Cologne (90 minutes), as are **Thorn** and **Roermond**.

Nationaal Oorlogs- en Verzetmuseum

Overloon, a tiny and otherwise unremarkable town on the border with Noord Brabant, was the scene of fierce battles between the Americans, British and the Germans as part of Operation Market Garden in 1944. The heart of the battlefield is now the site of the **National War & Resistance Museum** (☎ 0478-64 18 20; Museumpark 1; adult/child €6/4; ☖ 10am-5pm), a sober and thoughtful place that examines the role of the Netherlands in WWII.

To reach the museum take the hourly train to Venray from either Roermond (€6.80, 40 minutes) or Nijmegen (€5.80, 25 minutes). Then call a treintaxi (0478-51 10 00, see p320) and buy your ticket (€3.80) from the ticket machine. The museum is 7km from the station. Make arrangements with the driver for your return.

Directory

CONTENTS

ACCOMMODATION

Hitting the hay in Holland is an easy task. You'll be spoilt for choice, from cheerful youth hostels and budget guesthouses to fancy luxury and boutique hotels with every imaginable extra. Note that a good part of the country suffers from the 'Amsterdam effect': because transport is so efficient and the city is so popular, many visitors stay in the capital even if they're travelling further afield.

B&Bs

While scarce in the cities, in the country bed-and-breakfast places offer a great opportunity to mix with friendly locals (not to mention breakfasts big enough to last most of the day). Local tourist offices keep a list of B&Bs on file.

Camping & Caravan Parks

The Dutch are avid campers, even in their own country. Campgrounds tend to be self-contained communities with shops, cafés, playgrounds and swimming pools. Lists of sites with ratings (one to five stars) are available from the ANWB and tourist offices. Addresses listed in this book open April to October, unless indicated otherwise.

Expect to pay roughly €8 to €20 for two people and a tent overnight, plus €3 to €6 for a car. Caravans are popular – every one in 15 residents owns one – so there are oodles of hook-ups.

Simple bungalows or *trekkershutten* (hiker huts, from €23) are an option. A typical hiker hut has four bunks, cooking facilities and electricity, but you'll need to bring your own sleeping bags, dishes and utensils.

Rough camping is illegal. To get away from it all, seek out *natuurkampeerterreinen* (nature campgrounds) attached to farms. You'll enjoy a simpler and less crowded existence than at the major campgrounds. Reserve through tourist offices.

Hotels

The Dutch rating system goes up to five stars; accommodation with less than one star can call itself a pension or guesthouse but not a hotel. The stars aren't very helpful

---

PRACTICALITIES

- Use the metric system for weights and measures.

- Buy or watch videos on the PAL system.

- Keep abreast of things back home in the *International Herald Tribune*, the *Guardian*, or the *Times* or weeklies the *Economist*, *Newsweek* or *Time* on newsstands.

- Watch or listen to the BBC, CNN and a welter of Euro-stations.

- Plug your hairdryer into a Continental two-pin adapter before you tap the electricity network (220V to 240V AC, 50 Hz).

because they measure the amenities and the number of rooms but not the quality of the rooms themselves. Hotels tend to be small, with less than 20 rooms.

Many establishments have steep stairs but no lifts, which can pose problems for the mobility-impaired. Most top-end and a few mid-range hotels do have lifts.

Tourist offices can book hotel rooms virtually anywhere in the country for a small fee (usually a few euros). GWK offices take hotel reservations, charging a small fee and 10% of the room charge in advance. The **Netherlands Reservation Centre** (☎ 0299-68 91 44; www.hotelres.nl; Nieuwe Gouw 1, 1442 LE Purmerend) accepts bookings from abroad. You can generally save money by booking directly with the hotel, but many won't take credit cards and may insist on a down payment.

Prices vary, but in cities you should expect to pay under €50 for a double room in a budget hotel, up to €125 in a mid-range hotel and from €125 for the top end. Prices in Amsterdam tend to be higher.

Last but not least, when booking for two people, make clear whether you want two single (twin) beds or a double bed.

Hostels

The **Netherlands Youth Hostel Association** (NJHC; ☎ 020-501 31 33; www.stayokay.com; Postbus 9191, 1006 AD Amsterdam) still uses the Hostelling International (HI) logo but confusingly, the hostels themselves now go under the name Stayokay. The organisation is edging upmarket with a greater variety of rooms, prices and hotel-style facilities designed to lure groups and families.

A youth hostel card costs €14.50 at the hostels, or non-members can pay an extra €2.50 per night and after six nights you're a member. HI members can get discounts on international travel and pay less commission on money exchange at GWK offices. Members and non-members have the same privileges and there are no age limits.

Apart from the usual dormitories there are rooms for one to eight people depending on the hostel. Nightly rates range from €17 to €26 per person for dorm beds. Be sure to book ahead, especially in high season.

Rental Accommodation

Special rules apply to rental accommodation to combat a perpetual housing shortage.

Rents under €564 per month require a housing permit, but you aren't likely to get one swiftly, so expect to pay substantially more – say, €900 for a smallish two-bedroom flat in a not-grotty area of Amsterdam. Rents vary quite a bit in the big cities, with Amsterdam and Den Haag at the top and Rotterdam somewhere near the bottom of the scale. Most Dutch residents usually find a place through the so-called housing corporations after waiting a couple of years.

Some lucky folks find places in the classifieds of the daily *Telegraaf* (Wednesday), *Volkskrant* or *Parool* (Saturday), or through the twice-weekly *ViaVia*. See Media (p39). All the papers have websites with rental ads in Dutch, and scan under 'Te huur' or 'Huurwoningen'. The Expatica (www.expatica.com/holland) website also has small ads. If a flat sounds good, pick up the phone right then and there because it may be gone in a matter of hours. Beware that some people try to let out their rent-subsidised flats to foreigners at inflated prices, which is illegal.

If speed is of the essence, try the following agents:

Amsterdam Apartments (☎ 020-626 59 40; www.amsterdamapartments.nl; Kromme Waal 32, Amsterdam) Furnished apartments from €550 per week – lots with central locations.

Intercity Room Service (☎ /fax 020-675 00 64; Van Ostadestraat 348, Amsterdam) Flat-shares per month from €300, furnished apartments per month from €1150. Good only if you need a room absolutely right now. Commission is two weeks' rent (higher for longer than six months).

University Accommodation

There's a crazy shortage of student housing in the Netherlands, with some waiting lists stretching years into the future. In other words, forget it.

ACTIVITIES

The most popular outdoor activities are linked to the defining characteristics of the Dutch landscape: flat land and water. There is no shortage of sports clubs and special-interest groups for your favourite pastime as the Dutch have a penchant for organisation.

Boating

It seems like all Dutchies own a boat; stroll by the canals and lakes a you'll see all manner of water craft, some impossibly whacky, often decades old, lovingly maintained and enjoyed in weather fair or nasty. Small canoes and sailboats can be hired on lakes like Loosdrechtse Plassen or Nieuwkoopse Plassen in Utrecht province. In Friesland, the region around Sneek is an ideal base for an inland boating holiday, glistening with hundreds of lakes linked by canals.

Sailing on a traditional boat is an unforgettable experience. Named for its ruddy sails, the 'brown fleet' of restored flat-bottomed vessels is a familiar sight on the vast IJsselmeer at weekends. The cheapest rental option are *botters*, old fishing boats with long, narrow leeboards and sleeping berths for up to eight passengers. Larger groups can go for converted freight barges known as *tjalks* (smacks), ancient pilot boats or massive clippers. You'll also find motorboats for gliding through the country canals.

The **Netherlands Board of Tourism** (www
.visitholland.com) will match you up with boat rental firms depending on your location, budget and what type of boat you want. On the website, follow the 'boat rental' link under 'Search'. Local tourist offices will also have a list of boat rentals. The **Royal Dutch Watersports Association** (☎ 030-656 65 50; www.knwv.nl, in Dutch; Daltonlaan 400, 3584 BK Utrecht) provides advice on boating rules and hundreds of links to relevant websites.

The following companies have typical rates, bearing in mind that everything is negotiable (after all, bargaining is a Dutch tradition):

Boat Charter Holland (☎ 0515-42 46 17; Eeltjebaasweg 3, Sneek) Represents rental firms all over the Netherlands and Friesland in particular.

Enkhuizen Yachtcharter (☎ 0228-32 32 00; www.enkhuizenyachtcharter.nl; Oosterhavenstraat 13, Enkhuizen) Charges from €875 per week for its luxury ocean-going yachts.

Flevo Sailing (☎ 0320-26 03 24; www.flevosailing.nl, in Dutch; Oostvaardersdijk 59c, Lelystad) Rents out four-passenger sailing yachts from €205 per day.

Hollands Glorie (☎ 0294-27 15 61; www.hollandsglorie.nl; Ossenmarkt 6, Muiden) Has *tjalks* per day/weekend/week from €440/1240/2340 for groups of 12. Departs from harbours around the country including Amsterdam, Edam, Hoorn, Medemblik and Muiden.

Holland Zeilcharters (☎ 0299-65 23 51; www.sailing.nl; Het Prooyen 4a, Monnickendam) Has *botters* from €385 per day (12 to 14 people) and loads of other options.

Top of Holland Yacht Charter (☎ 0512-58 50 82; www.topofholland.com; Postbus 330, Drachten) Represents companies in Friesland, the IJsselmeer region and Zuidholland, renting out everything from small sailboats to large cabin cruisers.

Cycling

Cycling is a way of life in the Netherlands. The country offers easy cycling terrain with many designated paths including loads of off-road routes through pastures and woodland. The infrastructure gives priority to bikes over other forms of transportation, and car drivers often yield to cyclists even when the latter is pushing his/her luck. For more on traffic rules and specific bike routes see Cycling in the Netherlands (p70).

Skating

The Netherlands is practically tailor-made for inline skating. City parks are breeding grounds for the latest flashy manoeuvres on half-pipes, but the popularity of skating is such that day trips have been mapped throughout the country. The Achterhoek region (the eastern part of Gelderland) combines quiet conditions with a nice variety of landscapes; the Graafschap area in the northwest has seven signposted skating routes with a total length of 200km. The list of places to skate is endless – any dyketop can be perfect for a spin. See the **iSkate** (www.iskate.nl) website for details of events, hot skating spots and night skates, though the **Skatebond Nederland** (Dutch Skating Club; www.skatebond.nl, in Dutch) is more authoritative.

Ice skating was part of the Dutch psyche long before scarved figures appeared in Golden Age winterscapes. The first skates were made from cow shanks and ribs, with hand-drilled holes and tied to the feet. When canals and ponds freeze over, everyone takes to the ice, and you can join them with a pair of hockey skates (the best thing for beginners) bought either second-hand or from a department store. The famous **Elfstedentocht** (Eleven Cities' Race, p242) takes place in Friesland every seven years on average, and even Crown Prince Willem-Alexander took part in 1986, to be greeted by Queen Beatrix at the finish line. Not surprisingly, the Dutch have had more than their fair share of ice-skating champions.

Walking

The Dutch are avid walkers and hikers, in almost any weather and surroundings. The International Nijmegen Four Days March (*Internationale Wandelvierdaagse*; p272) is the world's largest walking event that attracts more than 40,000 strident enthusiasts every July.

For salt breezes you might head for the coasts of Friesland, Zeeland or the coastal towns along the IJsselmeer. National parks like Hoge Veluwe, Weerribben or Biesbosch offer a varied backdrop ranging from bogs to dunes to forest. The pretty, undulating knolls of Limburg can be a welcome change after the flatlands in the rest of the country. Thinly populated provinces like Drenthe are ideal for untroubled treks through quiet farmland.

Nederlandse Wandelsportbond (Netherlands Hiking Club; ☎ 030-231 94 58; www.nwb-wandelen.nl, in Dutch; Pieterskerkhof 22, Utrecht) is a goldmine of information about the nicest paths and events. Branches of the ANWB motoring club, tourist offices and bookshops have more brochures than you can shake a walking stick at.

Windsurfing

Abundant water and near-constant breezes make a perfect combination for windsurfing. Most developed beaches along the coast of the North Sea, the IJsselmeer and the Wadden Islands have places that rent windsurf boards (look for *'surfplanken'* in Dutch) as well as equipment for the zanier kitesurfing, which requires greater skills to master. In winter, the frozen lakes become racecourses for ice surfing with breakneck speeds of 100km per hour or more.

Websites like **Windlords** (www.windlords.com/nl) list the most popular locations to windsurf around the country. You can also inquire at any tourist office.

BUSINESS HOURS

As a general rule, banks open 9am to 4pm and offices 8.30am to 5pm on weekdays, while shops open 9am to 6pm Monday to Saturday. Post offices are generally open 9am to 6pm weekdays.

And now for the exceptions:

On Monday many shops don't open till noon, but on Thursday or Friday evenings they stay open until 8pm or 9pm, the so-called *koopavond* (evening shopping). Department stores and supermarkets close around 6pm weekdays and 5pm on Saturday, but big supermarkets in the city stay open until 8pm.

Most regular shops outside the city centres close at 5pm or 6pm weekdays and at midday Saturday, depending on their line of trade; almost all are closed on Sunday. In the city centres, however, an increasing number of shops are open Sundays from noon to 5pm, especially on the first weekend of the month. Shops in Rotterdam and Den Haag are open every Sunday afternoon.

Most museums are closed on Monday. Government offices, private institutions and monuments keep limited opening hours; these hours are mentioned in this book where possible.

Hours vary, but restaurants are usually open from 11am to 2.30pm or 3pm for lunch and 5.30pm to 10pm or 11pm for dinner. Most bars open by 11am and close between midnight and 2am. Nightclubs tend to open at 9pm or 10pm and close at 3am or 4am, although some places keep buzzing till dawn.

CHILDREN

Lonely Planet's *Travel with Children* by Maureen Wheeler is worth reading if you're unsure about travelling with kids. Much of her advice is valid in the Netherlands, where there is a lot to keep them occupied. Attitudes to children are very positive, and Dutch children tend to be spontaneous and confident thanks to a relaxed approach to parenting.

Practicalities

Some hotels have a no-children policy – check when you book. Most restaurants have high chairs and children's menus. Facilities for changing nappies, however, are limited to the big department stores, major museums and train stations and you'll pay to use them. Breast-feeding is generally OK in public if done discreetly. Kids are allowed in pubs but aren't supposed to drink until they're 16.

When you take the train, children aged under four travel free if they don't take up a seat. Ages four to 11 pay a so-called Railrunner fare of €1 so long as an adult comes along.

Sights & Activities

De Zaanse Schans (p147) near Amsterdam is a great afternoon out with its re-created windmill village, traditional Dutch houses, cheese farm and craft centre. Further north the island of Texel has the Ecomare (p161), with oodles of birds and seals and stroke-able fish.

A child's fantasies can run wild at De Efteling amusement park (p284), especially in the maze or Fairy Tale Forest. Six Flags Holland (p171) has kiddie rides, shows and a kind roller coaster.

Animal parks abound and the the good-natured frolics at the Dolfinarium will keep smiles on little faces all day long (p271). The Apenheul will show the little ones what it means to really monkey about (p271).

CLIMATE CHART

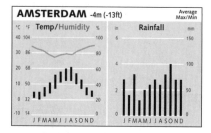

COURSES

Language

Dutch is a close relative of English but that doesn't make it easy to learn. Standard courses take months and intensive courses last several weeks. Make inquiries well in advance.

The **Volksuniversiteit Amsterdam** (☎ 020-626 16 26; www.volksuniversiteitamsterdam.nl, in Dutch; Rapenburgerstraat 73, 1011 VK Amsterdam) offers a range of well-regarded day and evening courses costing €152 to €403. The **Tropen-instituut** (Royal Institute for the Tropics; ☎ 020-568 85 59; www.kit.nl; Postbus 95001, 1090 HA Amsterdam) has intensive language courses with a large component of 'cultural training', aimed specifically at foreigners moving to the Netherlands. It's fairly expensive but very effective.

The **British Language Training Centre** (☎ 020-622 36 34; www.bltc.nl; Nieuwezijds Voorburgwal 328E, 1012 RW Amsterdam) offers Dutch and English courses and has a good reputation.

The **Amsterdam Summer University** (☎ 020-620 02 25; www.amsu.edu; Keizersgracht 324, 1016 EZ Amsterdam) conducts all of its courses and workshops in English (apart from its Dutch language training). Subjects focus on arts and sciences, as befits the traditions of the Felix Meritis building that houses it.

CUSTOMS

EU nationals can bring virtually anything they like, provided it's for personal use and they paid local tax in an EU country. Visitors from a European country outside the EU and not resident in the EU can import goods and gifts s valued up to €167 (bought tax-free) as well as 200 cigarettes or 50 cigars or 250g of tobacco; 1L of liquor more than 22% alcohol or 2L under 22% alcohol; and 60g of perfume.

Visitors from outside Europe and residents outside Europe can bring in 400 cigarettes (or 100 cigars or 500g of tobacco) plus other goods, spirits, wines and perfumes as for non-EU Europeans. Bringing meat or meat products, flowers, fruit, plants and protected species to the Netherlands is illegal. Tobacco and alcohol may only be imported by people aged 17 and over.

DANGERS & ANNOYANCES

Much of the Netherlands is utterly safe but caution is advised in the larger cities. Amsterdam and Rotterdam require a modicum of big-city street sense, though it'll seem positively tame after New York or Johannesburg. Don't carry more money than you need – use a second wallet or purse and keep your main one safe. Walking around with conspicuous valuables or tourist gear will only invite trouble.

A car with foreign registration is a popular target for smash-and-grab theft. Don't leave things in the car: remove registration and ID papers and the radio/stereo if possible.

If something is stolen, get a police report for insurance purposes but don't expect the police to retrieve your property or to apprehend the thief – put the matter down to experience. It's not a police state and usually there's very little they can do.

Mosquitoes can be a pain in summer. They breed in stagnant parts of the canals and in water under houses, and in parts of the country near lakes or canals, people sleep under netting.

While great for the environment, bicycles can be quite a menace to pedestrians. When crossing the street look for speeding bikes as well as cars; straying into a bike lane without looking both ways is a no-no. During city rush hours you may actually find yourself waiting to cross in the flow of bikes.

Intensive urban development means there's often little grass for dog dirt, and you may spend more time watching the pavement than the sights.

Smokers still have the most rights here and pub visits can be fumigating, although the situation is slowly improving.

Scams

Big cities breed scams. Take special care in the train stations: someone might want to help you put your bags into a luggage locker, lock the door and hand you the key. When you return you find the key fits a different locker and your stuff is gone. If something feels wrong about a stranger who approaches you, chances are your instincts are right. Thieves sometimes masquerade as police (see the Amsterdam chapter for details, p87).

DISABLED TRAVELLERS

Travellers with mobility problems will find the Netherlands fairly well equipped despite the limitations of some older buildings. A large number of government offices and museums have lifts or ramps; many hotels, however, are in old buildings where steep, narrow stairs are the only option. Restaurants tend to be on ground floors, though sometimes include a few steps up or down.

Train and public transport stations have lifts, and most train stations and public buildings have toilets for the disabled. The trains themselves have wheelchair access in most instances, and people with a disability get discounts on public transport. For those with impaired vision, train timetables are published in Braille and banknotes have raised shapes on the corners for identification. **Netherlands Railways** (☎ 030-235 55 55) has an information line with details of all their services for travellers with disabilities.

DISCOUNT CARDS

Museum-goers should invest in a *Museum-kaart* that gives access to 400 museums

across the country. It costs €30 (€17 for under 26s), and usually pays for itself after three visits.

A Hostelling International card is useful at the official youth hostels (called Stay-okay in the Netherlands) – nonmembers are welcome but pay €2.50 more per night. Other hostels may give small discounts. If you don't pick up a HI card before leaving home you can buy one at youth hostels in the Netherlands.

Teachers, professional artists, museum conservators and certain categories of students may get discounts at a few museums or even be admitted free – it can depend on the person behind the counter. Bring proof of affiliation like an International Teacher Identity Card (ITIC).

The tourist offices and some large hotels in Amsterdam sell the Amsterdam Pass. This contains 32 vouchers that give free public transport anywhere in the city, free entry to most museums and 25% discount on some attractions and restaurants. It's a wise investment and costs €26/36/46 for one/two/three days.

The **Cultureel Jongeren Paspoort** (Cultural Youth Passport, CJP; €11) gives people aged under 27 big discounts to museums and cultural events around the country. Anyone with even a passing interest in the arts is well advised to pick one up from a tourist office.

Senior Cards

The minimum age for senior discounts is 65 (60 for the partner) for public transport, museum entry fees, concerts and more. You could try flashing your home-country senior card but you might have to show your passport too.

Senior travellers concerned about personal safety, take heart: people up to 24 years of age are six times more likely to become a victim of crime here than those aged over 65.

Student & Youth Cards

An **International Student Identity Card** (ISIC; www.isic.org) will get some admission discounts and might pay for itself through discounted air and ferry tickets. The same applies to hostel cards. They're available through student unions or student travel agencies.

EMBASSIES & CONSULATES
Dutch Embassies & Consulates

Diplomatic representation abroad includes:
Australia (☎ 06-273 3111; www.netherlands.org.au/
index.html; 120 Empire Circuit, Yarralumla, Canberra, ACT
2600)
Belgium (☎ 02-679 17 11; www.nederlandseambassade
.be; ave Herrmann-Debroux 48, 1160 Brussels)
Canada (☎ 613-237 50 30; www.netherlandsembassy.ca;
Suite 2020, 350 Albert St, Ottawa, Ont K1R 1A4)
France (☎ 01-40 62 33 00; www.amb-pays-bas.fr;
7-9 Rue Eblé, 75007 Paris)
Germany (☎ 030-20 95 60; www.dutchembassy.de;
Friedrichstrasse 95, 10117 Berlin)
Ireland (☎ 01-269 34 44; www.netherlandsembassy.ie;
160 Merrion Road, Dublin 4)
Italy (☎ 06-321 5827; www.olanda.it; Via Michele
Mercati 8, 00197 Rome)
Japan (☎ 03-5401 0411; www.oranda.or.jp; Shiba-koen,
3-6-3 Minato-ku, 105 0011 Tokyo)
New Zealand (☎ 04-471 6390; www.netherlandsem
bassy.co.nz; Investment House, cnr Ballance & Featherston
Sts, Wellington)
United Kingdom (☎ 020-7590 3200;
www.netherlands-embassy.org.uk; 38 Hyde Park Gate,
London SW7 5DP)
USA (☎ 202-244 5300; www.netherlands-embassy.org;
4200 Linnean Ave NW, Washington, DC 20008)

Embassies & Consulates in the Netherlands

Amsterdam is the country's capital but
confusingly, Den Haag is the seat of govern-
ment – so that's where all the embassies are.
They include:
Australia (☎ 070-310 82 00; www.australian-embassy
.nl; Carnegielaan 4)
Belgium (Map p196; ☎ 070-312 34 56;
www.diplomatie.be/thehague; Alexanderveld 97)
Canada (☎ 070-311 16 00; www.dfait-maeci.gc.ca
/canadaeuropa/netherlands; Sophialaan 7)
Finland (☎ 070-363 8575; www.finlande.nl; Groot
Hertoginnelaan 16)
France (Map p196; ☎ 070-312 58 00; www.amba
france.nl; Smidsplein 1)
Germany (☎ 070-346 9754; www.duitse-ambassade.nl;
Groot Hertoginnelaan 18-20)
Ireland (☎ 070-363 09 93; www.irishembassy.nl; Dr
Kuijperstraat 9)
Italy (☎ 070-302 10 30; www.italy.nl; Alexanderstraat
12)
Japan (☎ 070-346 95 44; www.nl.emb-japan.go.jp;
Tobias Asserlaan 2)
New Zealand (☎ 070-346 93 24; www.nzembassy.com;
Carnegielaan10-IV)

South Africa (☎ 070-392 45 01; www.zuidafrika.nl;
Wassenaarseweg 40)
Sweden (☎ 070-412 02 00; www.swedenabroad.com
/thehague; Van Karnebeeklaan 6A)
United Kingdom (Map p196; ☎ 070-427 04 27;
www.britain.nl; Lange Voorhout 10)
USA (Map p196; ☎ 070-310 92 09; www.usemb.nl;
Lange Voorhout 102)

Consulates in Amsterdam include:
Denmark (Map p82-83; ☎ 020-682 9991; Radarweg 503)
France (Map p96-97; ☎ 020-530 69 69; Vijzelgracht 2)
Germany (Map p95; ☎ 020-673 62 45;
Honthorststraat 36-38)
Italy (Map p96-97; ☎ 020-550 20 50; Vijzelstraat 79)
Norway (Map p95; ☎ 020-624 23 31; Keizersgracht 534-I)
Spain (Map p96-97; ☎ 020-620 38 11; Frederiksplein 34)
United Kingdom (Map p82-83; ☎ 020-676 43 43;
Koningslaan 44) Near Vondelpark.
USA (Map p95; ☎ 020-575 53 09; Museumplein 19) Near
the Concertgebouw.

FESTIVALS & EVENTS

Following are the cream of the crop of the
largest and most important events in the
country, which may well be reason for a
special trip. More goings-on are listed in
the destination chapters.

February/March
Carnaval Weekend before Shrove Tuesday. Celebrations
with gusto that would do Rio or New Orleans proud,
mostly in Catholic provinces of Noord Brabant, Gelderland
and Limburg. Maastricht's party means days of unihibited
drinking, dancing and street music.

March
Maastricht Art Show (☎ 041-164 50 90,
www.tefaf.com) For 10 days in the first half of March.
Europe's largest art show is your chance to pick up a
Monet, or at least do some serious browsing.

April
Koninginnedag (Queen's Day) 30 April. Celebrations
throughout the country feature much wearing of orange,
drinking and flea-market activity. Processions, dances and
live music.

May
Herdenkingsdag & Bevrijdingsdag (Remembrance
Day & Liberation Day) 4 & 5 May. The fallen from WWII
are honoured in an Amsterdam ceremony, followed by live
music, debate and a market the next day.
Nationale Molendag (National Mill Day) Second
Saturday. Nearly every working windmill in the country

(more than 600 in total) throws open its doors to visitors. Look for the sweet blue pennants.

June
Holland Festival Virtually all month. The country's biggest extravaganza for theatre, dance, film and pop music, with a justified claim to cutting-edge innovation (www.hollandfestival.nl).

July
North Sea Jazz Festival (www.northseajazz.nl, in Dutch) Mid-July, held in Den Haag. Top-flight jazz festival, Europe's biggest, attracts big names from around the world and the crowds to match.
Dance Valley (www.dancevalley.nl) Last weekend of July or first weekend of August. This outdoor dance technothon draws over 100 DJs and bands performing to fields of 40,000 or more.

August
Gay Pride Canal Parade First Saturday. The only water-borne gay parade in the world, with lots of pride showing on the outlandish floats.
FFWD Dance Parade (☎ 010-433 13 00; www.ffwdheinekendanceparade.nl) Downtown Rotterdam turns into one big open-air techno club in early August complete with dozens of trucked-in floats. Attendance hit a massive 350,000 in 2003.
Uitmarkt Three days in late August. The re-opening of Amsterdam's cultural season with free concerts and information booths around the big museums and Leidseplein (www.uitmarkt.nl).
Lowlands (www.lowlands.nl) Last weekend in August. Biddinghuizen (Flevoland), last weekend. Alternative music and cultural mega-bash at Six Flags (p171), with campgrounds for the masses.

November
Sinterklaas Intocht Mid-November. Every year the Dutch Santa Claus arrives 'from Spain' with his staff and Black Pete helpers at a different port.

December
Sinterklaas 5 December. Families exchange small gifts ahead of religious celebrations for Christmas.

FOOD
The restaurant reviews in the destination chapters cater to all tastes and budgets with an emphasis on the most typical cuisines (although good atypical places are included too). See the Food & Drink chapter (p62) for more details.

Prices tend to be high by European standards. As a general rule, snacks and light takeaway items cost about €3 to €8, while a three-course sit-down meal at a mid-priced restaurant will run from €18 to €30 including a beer or glass of wine; the bill rises to €40 to €60 at the swish top-end places with Michelin stars. Tourist centres like Amsterdam tend to be expensive and you may get much better value for money out in the provinces. Ethnic eateries, particularly with Surinamese and Chinese-Indonesian menus, are a reliable stand-by for cheap and tasty food.

GAY & LESBIAN TRAVELLERS
The best national source of gay and lesbian information is **COC** (☎ 020-626 30 87; www.coc.nl, in Dutch; Postbus 3836, 1001 AP Amsterdam). It has branches throughout the country that are happy to offer advice to newcomers.

Partisan estimates put the proportion of gay and lesbian people in Amsterdam at 20% to 30%. This is probably an exaggeration, but Amsterdam is certainly one of the gay capitals of Europe. Mainstream attitudes have always been reasonably tolerant, but it wasn't until the early 1970s that the age of consent for gay sex was lowered to 16. The last decade has seen considerable progress: it's now illegal to discriminate against job-seekers on the basis of sexual orientation. A landmark move came in 2001, when the Netherlands became the first country to legalise same-sex marriage.

The government has long subsidised the national gay and lesbian organisation COC, one of the world's largest organisations for gay and lesbian rights. Now trade unions research the lot of homosexual employees, the police advertise in the gay media for applicants, and homesexuals are admitted to the armed forces on an equal footing.

Amsterdam's well-developed scene isn't typical of the country as a whole. The further one gets from the capital, the more often gay and lesbian bars and clubs operate behind dark windows. Rotterdam is an exception, as are the university towns with large, albeit transient gay and lesbian populations.

HOLIDAYS
Public Holidays
People take public holidays seriously and you won't get much done. Most museums adopt Sunday hours on the days below (except Christmas and New Year) even if

they fall on a day when the place would otherwise be closed.

Many people treat Remembrance Day (4 May) as a day off.

Carnaval is celebrated with vigour in the Catholic south. Huge lager-fed parties are thrown in the run-up to Shrove Tuesday and little work gets done.

The holidays are:

Nieuwjaarsdag New Year's Day. Parties and fireworks galore.

Goede Vrijdag Good Friday.

Eerste Paasdag Easter Sunday.

Tweede Paasdag Easter Monday.

Koninginnedag 30 April. Queen's Day.

Bevrijdingsdag 5 May. Liberation Day. This isn't a universal holiday: government workers have the day off but almost everyone else has to work.

Hemelvaartsdag Ascension Day.

Eerste Pinksterdag Whit Sunday (Pentecost).

Tweede Pinksterdag Whit Monday.

Eerste Kerstdag 25 December. Christmas Day.

Tweede Kerstdag 26 December. Boxing Day.

School Holidays

School holidays are staggered across three regions (north, central and south) to relieve congestion on the roads. Generally the holidays are scheduled as follows:

Spring Holiday Two weeks in mid-February, also known as 'crocus' holiday.

May Holiday The first week of the month.

Summer Holiday July, August and sometimes the first few days of September.

Autumn Holiday Second half of October.

Christmas Holiday Two weeks through the first full week of January.

INSURANCE

Seriously consider taking out travel insurance. Medical or dental costs might already be covered through reciprocal health-care arrangements, but you'll still need cover for theft or loss, and for unexpected changes to travel arrangements (ticket cancellation etc). Check what's already covered by your local insurance policies or credit card issue.

See also the Insurance sections of the Health chapter (p321) and the Transport chapter (p317).

INTERNET ACCESS

If you pack a laptop, note that Dutch phones have a cord with a four-prong plug.

Adapters are available at the airport and retail outlets. Most phones also have a modular RJ-11 plug on the other end, so you can always plug right into your modem.

Major Internet service providers such as AOL, AT&T and Earthlink have access numbers in the Netherlands. Once here you can rely on Internet cafés and other access points like libraries or hotels to collect your mail. You'll need to keep three pieces of information handy: your incoming (POP or IMAP) mail server name, your account name and your password. You can always set up an email account with free providers like Hotmail or Yahoo, and have your 'home' email forwarded to that account.

LEGAL MATTERS

The Dutch police *(politie)* are a pretty relaxed lot and helpful to travellers. You're unlikely to incite their ire unless you do something instinctively wrong – like chucking litter or smoking a joint under their noses.

Officers can hold you up to six hours for questioning and another six if they can't establish your identity. If the matter's serious, you can be detained for 24 hours. You won't have the right to a phone call but they'll notify your embassy or consulate. Relax – you're presumed innocent until proven guilty.

In principle there's a 'limited' requirement for anyone over 12 years of age to carry ID. Roughly speaking this means on public transport, at soccer games, in the workplace or when opening a bank account. Foreigners should carry their passport or a photocopy of the relevant data pages; a driving licence isn't sufficient.

LEGALITIES

Legal age for voting & driving: 18

Age of consent: 12 (but 16 if the parents object)

Homosexual marriage: yes, from age 18

Drugs

Contrary to what you may have heard, marijuana is illegal. The confusion arises because the authorities distinguish between 'soft' drugs (eg, cannabis) and addictive 'hard' drugs like heroin, crack or cocaine. Possession of soft drugs up to 5g is tolerated but larger amounts make you a 'dealer' and subject to prosecution.

The key phrase is *gedogen*. This wonderful word means officials condemn the action but look the other way if common sense dictates. Hard drugs are treated as a serious crime, but under the unique Dutch drug policy, the authorities tend to treat genuine, registered addicts as medical cases rather than hardened criminals.

These tolerant policies attract many drug tourists; drugs are cheaper and more readily available, and generally of better quality, in the Netherlands than elsewhere. The country has become a major exporter of high-grade marijuana (grown locally) and is the European centre for the production of ecstasy. Much of Europe's cocaine passes through Rotterdam harbour.

For more about soft drugs, see the boxed text 'Coffeeshops' (p128).

WARNING

Never, ever buy drugs on the street: you'll get ripped off or mugged.

Don't light up in view of the police, or in an establishment without checking that it's OK to do so. The Dutch detest tourists who think they can just smoke dope anywhere.

Prostitution
Prostitution is legal in the Netherlands – based on the view that its practitioners are victims rather than criminals. The industry is protected by law, and prostitutes pay tax and even have their own lobby. Health checks are performed regularly to check for disease, and some prostitutes qualify for pensions and insurance. Much of this open policy stems from a desire to undermine the role of pimps and the underworld in the sex industry.

That hasn't always helped the plight of prostitutes, many of them immigrants from the Third World and Eastern Europe. In Amsterdam's Red Light district you have little to fear as the streets are well-policed but the back alleys are more dubious. This also goes for other Dutch cities such as Rotterdam and Den Haag. Even towns such as Leiden and Groningen have their red-light areas plopped down amid otherwise quiet streets.

Road Laws
Drink driving is considered a major crime in the Netherlands. See the Car & Motorcycle section of the Transport chapter (p316) for details on the rules of the road.

MAPS
The maps in this book will probably suffice. Lonely Planet's handy *Amsterdam City Map* is plastic-coated for the elements, and has a street index that covers the most popular parts of the city.

Otherwise the best road maps of the Netherlands are those produced by Michelin and the Dutch automobile association ANWB. The ANWB also puts out provincial maps detailing cycling paths and picturesque road routes. You'll find a wide variety of maps for sale at any tourist office, as well as at bookstores and newsstands.

MONEY
ATMs
Automatic teller machines can be found outside most banks, at airports and most train stations. Credit cards like Visa and MasterCard/Eurocard are widely accepted, as well as cash cards that access the Cirrus network. Logos on ATMs show which cards they accept. Beware that if you're limited to a maximum withdrawal per day, the 'day' will coincide with that in your home country. Also note that using an ATM can be the cheapest way to exchange your money from home – but check with your home bank for service charges before leaving.

Cash
Cash is still common and nothing beats it for convenience – or risk of theft/loss. Plan to pay cash for most daily expenses. However, staff at upmarket hotels might cast a furtive glance if you pay a huge bill with small-denomination notes rather than a credit card, and car-rental agencies will probably refuse to do business if you only have cash. Keep the equivalent of about US$50 separate from the rest of your money as an emergency stash.

Credit Cards
All major international cards are recognised and you will find that most hotels, restaurants and major stores accept them. But always check first to avoid, as they say, disappointment. Shops often levy a 5% surcharge

(or more) on credit cards to offset the commissions charged by card providers.

To withdraw money at a bank counter instead of from an ATM, go to a GWK branch (see Moneychangers below). You'll need to show your passport.

Report lost or stolen cards to the following 24-hour numbers:

American Express (☎ 020-504 80 00, 9am-6pm Mon-Fri; ☎ 020-504 86 66 other times)
Diners Club (☎ 020-654 5511)
Eurocard and MasterCard (☎ 030-283 55 55)
Foreigners are advised to ring the emergency number in their home country to speed things up.
Visa (☎ 020-660 06 11)

International Transfers

Transferring money from your home bank will be easier if you've authorised somebody back home to access your account. In the Netherlands, find a large bank and ask for the international division. A commission is charged on telegraphic transfers, which can take up to a week but usually less if you're well prepared; by mail, allow two weeks.

The GWK (see Moneychangers below) is an agent for Western Union and money is transferred within 15 minutes of lodgment at the other end. The person lodging the transfer pays a commission that varies from country to country. Money can also be transferred via American Express and Thomas Cook at their Amsterdam offices.

Moneychangers

Avoid the private exchange booths dotted around tourist areas. They're convenient and open late hours but rates or commissions are lousy, though competition is fierce and you may do OK if you hunt around. Banks and the Postbank (at post offices) stick to official exchange rates and charge a sensible commission, as does the **GWK** (Grenswisselkantoor; ☎ 0900-0566; www.gwk.nl).

Generally your best bet for exchanging money is to use GWK. Offices are in almost every medium-sized and larger train station as well as at the borders on major highways. Many locations, such as those at Amsterdam's Centraal Station and at Schiphol airport, are open 24 hours.

Travellers Cheques

Banks charge a commission to cash travellers cheques (with ID such as a passport).

American Express and Thomas Cook don't charge commission on their own cheques but their rates might be less favourable. Shops, restaurants and hotels always prefer cash; a few might accept travellers cheques but their rates will be anybody's guess.

The use of eurocheques is on the decline, although you can still cash them at banks and GWKs with a guarantee card. Few shops accept them.

POST

Post offices are generally open 9am to 6pm weekdays and 10am to 1pm Saturday. Poste restante is best handled in Amsterdam.

Mail is delivered locally Monday to Saturday. Unless you're sending mail within the post office's local region, the slot to use in the rectangular, red letter boxes is *Overige Postcodes* (Other Postal Codes).

For queries about postal services ring ☎ 058-233 33 33.

Postal Rates

Letters up to 20g within Europe cost €0.59 (air mail, known as 'priority') or €0.55 (standard); beyond Europe they are €0.75 (priority) or €0.70 (standard). Postcards cost €0.59 to anywhere outside the country. A *priorityblad* (aerogramme) is €0.50. Within the country, letters up to 20g or postcards cost €0.39.

Standard mail (also available within Europe for parcels and printed matter) is not much cheaper than priority and takes about twice as long to reach the destination. For instance, a priority parcel to the UK takes two to three days, whereas standard takes four to five; to the USA, it's four to six days as opposed to eight to 12.

Addresses

The postal code – four numbers followed by two letters – comes in front of the city or town name, eg 1017 LS Amsterdam. The codes are complicated and there's little apparent logic to them, but they pinpoint an address to within 100m. The telephone book provides the appropriate postal code for each address. Most post offices stock a complete set of the country's phone books.

There are a few peculiarities with street numbers. Sometimes they're followed by a letter or number (often in Roman numerals). Letters (eg No 34A or 34a) usually indicate the appropriate front door when two or more share the same number, whereas numbers (34-2, 34r2 or 34-II) indicate the appropriate floor. In modern dwellings, letters often indicate the appropriate apartment irrespective of the floor. The suffix 'hs' (34hs) stands for *huis* (house) and means the dwelling is on the ground floor, which may be half a floor above street level (in which case it's sometimes called *beletage*, the floor behind the door bell). The suffix 'bg' stands for *begane grond* (ground floor). The suffix *sous* stands for *souterrain* and means the dwelling is in the basement.

SOLO TRAVELLERS

Dutch café society provides a great environment for meeting people. The Dutch are uninhibited when it comes to striking up conversations with complete strangers, whether at the next table in a restaurant or in a supermarket queue, and the openness tends to be contagious. People from abroad may find themselves thawing more quickly than at home, with conversations stretching into the wee hours with complete strangers.

Booking into a group activity such as a walking tour or boat trip is a good recipe for making contacts that could last a lifetime. Young travellers also hook up with likeminded people at youth hostels or budget hotels. Nightclubs in cities like Amsterdam and Rotterdam draw a large, fun-loving contingent of foreigners, and many also make their way to beach parties in places like Bloemendaal or Scheveningen. Single females should try to join forces before hitting the clubs – that's what the Dutch do.

TELEPHONE

The Dutch phone network is efficient and prices are reasonable by European standards. Most public phones accept credit cards as well as various phonecards. Phone booths are scattered around towns and you can always call from a post office.

For national directory inquiries, call the voice-activated service at ☎ 118 (€0.60 per number) or ☎ 0900-8008 for a human operator (€1.15 per number). International directory inquiries can be reached on ☎ 0900-8418 (€1.15 per number). To place a *collect gesprek* (collect call) within the Netherlands, ring ☎ 0800-0101 (free call); for international collect calls, ☎ 0800-0410

(free call). For other operator-assisted calls, ring ☎ 0800-0410 (free call, though you'll be charged a €3.50 service fee if you could have rung the country direct).

Costs

The official, KPN-Telecom public phone boxes charge €0.30 per minute for all national calls, around the clock. The minimum charge from a public phone is €0.20. Phones in cafés, supermarkets and hotel lobbies often charge more. Calling from private phones is considerably cheaper. Typically, calls within the metropolitan area cost €0.03 a minute from 8am to 7pm weekdays, €0.02 a minute in the evenings, and €0.01 a minute from midnight to 8am and from 7pm Friday to 8am Monday. There's a €0.04 connection charge. Calls outside the metropolitan area cost €0.04 a minute between 8am and 7pm weekdays, and half that at other times. At the time of writing, to call Britain and the USA cost €0.05 to €0.07 per minute, and Australia €0.19 – but these rates jump to between €0.30 and €0.40 when ringing from a KPN phone box.

Ringing a mobile number costs €0.50 per minute from a public phone and around €0.30 from a private line.

Mobile Phones

The Netherlands uses GSM 900/1800, which is compatible with the rest of Europe and Australia but not with the North American GSM 1900 (though some North Americans have dual or triple-band phones that do work here). Check with your service provider about using your phone in the Netherlands, and beware of calls being routed internationally, which becomes *very* expensive.

Prepaid mobile phones, which run on chips that store call credits, should be available at mobile shops for under €100. Packages with prepaid SIM cards have spread like wildfire – look out for KPN, Telfort, Orange, T-Mobile and Vodaphone with deals between €15 and €30.

Phone Codes

To ring abroad, dial ☎ 00 followed by the country code for your target country, the area code (you usually drop the leading 0 if there is one) and the subscriber number. Area codes for Dutch cities covered in this

DIRECTORY

book are given at the start of the cities' listings. The country code for calling the Netherlands is ☎ 31.

Many information services use phone numbers beginning with ☎ 0800 (free) or ☎ 0900 (which cost between €0.10 and €0.70 per minute depending on the number). To avoid running up big phone bills, care should be taken whenever dialling ☎ 0900.

Numbers beginning with ☎ 06 are mobile or pager numbers.

Phonecards

Most public telephones are cardphones and there's no shortage of prepaid cards to fill them. Various cards are available at post offices, train station counters, tourist and GWK offices and tobacco shops for €5, €10 and €20. KPN's Hi card is the most common but other brands are muscling in – T-Mobile, Orange, Vodaphone, Belnet and others – with rates superior to KPN's. Note that railway stations have Telfort phone booths that require a Telfort card (available at GWK offices or ticket counters), although there should be KPN booths outside.

Lonely Planet's ekno Communication Card is aimed specifically at independent travellers. It provides budget international calls from public as well as private phones, a range of messaging services, free email and travel information. Join online at www.ekno.lonelyplanet.com, or by phone from the Netherlands by dialling ☎ 0800-0233971 (free call). For local calls, however, you're better off with a KPN card.

TIME

The Netherlands is on Central European time, GMT/UTC plus one hour. Noon is 11am in London, 6am in New York, 3am in San Francisco, 6am in Toronto, 9pm in Sydney and 11pm in Auckland, and then there's daylight-saving time. Clocks are put forward one hour at 2am on the last Sunday in March and back again at 3am on the last Sunday in October.

When telling the time, beware that Dutch uses half to indicate 'half before' the hour. If you say 'half eight' (8.30 in many forms of English), a Dutch person will take this to mean 7.30. Dutch also uses constructions like *tien voor half acht* ('ten to half eight'; 7.20) and *kwart over acht* ('quarter past eight'; 8.15).

TOURIST INFORMATION

Within the Netherlands, tourist information is supplied by the **VVV** (Vereniging voor Vreemdelingenverkeer, Netherlands Tourism Board; www.vvv.nl), which has offices throughout the country. Although each tourist office is locally run, they all have a huge amount of information that covers not just their area but the rest of the country as well. However, most VVV publications cost money and there are commissions for services (eg, €3 to €15 to find a room, €2 to €3 on theatre tickets).

The **VVV information line** (☎ 0900-4004040; 🕑 9am-5pm weekdays) costs €0.55 per minute. People ringing from abroad should try ☎ 020-551 25 25 (free). See the individual city listings for details on local services as well as opening hours.

Other Information Sources

The VVV is useful for mainstream tourist information but other places might serve you better.

The Dutch automobile association **ANWB** (☎ 0800-0503; www.anwb.nl, in Dutch; 🕑 10am-6pm Mon-Sat) has free or discounted maps and brochures. It provides a wide range of useful information and assistance if you're travelling with any type of vehicle (car, bicycle, motorcycle, yacht etc). In many cities the VVV and ANWB share offices. You'll probably have to show proof of membership of your automobile club. Its offices are open until 9pm on *koopavond* (evening shopping), which is either on Thursday or Friday night.

VISAS

Tourists from nearly 60 countries – including Australia, Canada, Israel, Japan, South Korea, New Zealand, Singapore, the USA and most of Europe – need only a valid passport to visit the Netherlands for up to three months. EU nationals can enter for three months with just their national identity card.

Nationals of most other countries need a so-called Schengen visa, named after the Schengen Agreement that abolished passport controls between the EU member states (except the UK and Ireland) plus Norway and Iceland. A visa for any of these countries is valid for 90 days within a six-month period. Some countries may impose restrictions on some nationalities.

Schengen visas are issued by Dutch embassies or consulates and can take a while to process (expect up to two months). You'll need a passport valid until at least three months after your visit, and be able to prove sufficient funds for your stay. Fees vary depending on your nationality – the embassy or consulate can tell you more. Tourist visas can be extended for another three months maximum, but you'll need a good reason and the extension will only be valid for the Netherlands, not the Schengen area.

In Amsterdam, visa extensions are handled by the **Vreemdelingenpolitie** (Aliens' Police; Map p82-83; ☎ 020-559 63 00; Johan Huizingalaan 757; ⓧ 8am-5pm Mon-Fri) out in the southwestern suburbs. You can call them about visa extensions for anywhere in the country.

Study visas must be applied for via your college or university in the Netherlands. For working visas, see the Work section on p307. Also check www.lonelyplanet.com – go to destinations/europe/netherlands for up-to-date visa information.

WOMEN TRAVELLERS

There's little street harassment in Dutch cities where most women will feel safe. Amsterdam is probably as secure as it gets in the major cities of Europe. Just take care in the Red Light District, where it's best to walk with a friend to minimise unwelcome attention.

The feminist movement is less politicised than elsewhere and certainly more laid-back. Efforts focus on practical solutions such as cultural centres, bicycle repair shops run by and for women, or support systems to help women set up businesses.

All addresses below are in Amsterdam, where most women's organisations are based. Elsewhere look under *Vrouwenhuis* (Women's House) in the phone directory.
De Eerste Lijn (The First Line; ☎ 020-613 02 45) Hotline for victims of sexual violence.
Rutgershuis Amsterdam (Map p82-83; ☎ 020-616 62 22; Sarphatistraat 618) Clinic offering information and help with sexual problems and birth control, including morning-after pills.
Het Vrouwenhuis (Women's House; Map p94; ☎ 020-625 20 66; Nieuwe Herengracht 95) Centre for several women's organisations that holds workshops, exhibitions and parties. There's also a bar and a library.

WORK

All-important work permits must be applied for by your employer in the Netherlands; in general, the employer must prove that the position cannot be filled by someone from within the EU before offering it to a non-EU citizen. Nationals from many countries must apply for a Temporary Entry Permit (MVV, or *Machtiging tot Voorlopig Verblijf*). Citizens of EU countries as well as Australia, Canada, Iceland, Japan, Monaco, New Zealand, Norway, Switzerland and the USA are exempt.

You'll need to apply for temporary residence before an employer can ask for your work permit. The process should take five weeks and cost €430; contact the Dutch embassy or consulate in your home country.

In the Netherlands, residence permits are issued by the **Immigratie en Naturalisatiedienst** (☎ 070-370 35 55; www.ind.nl; Postbus 30125, 2500 GC Den Haag). For details of work permits, contact the **CWI** (Employment Services Authority; ☎ 079-371 29 03; www.cwinet.nl; Postbus 883, 2700 AW Zoetermeer). The CWI also runs a bilingual website (www.werk.nl) with up-to-date job offers.

The minimum adult wage is about €1250 a month after tax.

Transport

CONTENTS

The Netherlands is an extraordinarily simple place to reach. Amsterdam's Schiphol Airport has copious air links worldwide, including many on low-cost European airlines, and the train links on high-speed trains are especially good from France, Belgium and Germany. Other land options are user-friendly and the border crossings are nearly invisible thanks to the EU. There are also several ferry links with Britain and Scandinavia.

What's more, once you get to the Netherlands the transport stays hassle-free. Most journeys by rail, car or bus are so short that you can reach most regional destinations before your next meal.

GETTING THERE & AWAY

ENTERING THE COUNTRY
Passport
In principle all passengers with passports are allowed entry to the Netherlands, although those coming from 'suspected terrorist centres' may be detained for questioning.

AIR
Airports & Airlines
Conveniently near Amsterdam, Schiphol Airport is the Netherlands' main international

> **THINGS CHANGE...**
> The information in this chapter is particularly vulnerable to change. Prices for international travel are volatile, routes are introduced and cancelled, schedules change, special deals come and go, and rules and visa requirements are amended. Airlines and governments seem to take a perverse pleasure in making price structures and regulations as complicated as possible. You should check directly with the airline or a travel agent to make sure you understand how a fare (and ticket you may buy) works. In addition, the travel industry is highly competitive and there are many lurks and perks.
>
> The upshot is that you should get opinions, quotes and advice from as many airlines and travel agents as possible before you part with your hard-earned cash. The details given in this chapter should be regarded as pointers and are not a substitute for your own careful, up-to-date research.

airport and the third busiest in Europe. It's the seat of Dutch passenger carrier KLM, and dozens of other airlines have direct flights and connections to all continents. For flight information call ☎ 0900-0141 or go to www.schiphol.nl.

Rotterdam Airport is much smaller but has handy links to London via Belgium's VLM, which also serves Hamburg, Manchester and Milan.

Eindhoven, Groningen and Maastricht act as feeder airports to Amsterdam, catering to business travellers and holiday charters to sunny climes. From Eindhoven, KLM and Ryanair serve London while KLM also flies to/from Hamburg and Paris. The tiny Groningen Airport Eelde as well as Maastricht-Aachen Airport have cheap Ryanair flights to London Stansted.

AIRLINE OFFICES
Airline offices in Amsterdam are listed under *Luchtvaartmaatschappijen* in the pink pages of the phone book. Dial ☎ 020 before these numbers if you're calling from outside the

---

DUTCH AIRPORT WEBSITES

www.eindhovenairport.nl
www.gae.nl
www.maastrichtairport.nl, in Dutch
www.rotterdam-airport.nl
www.schiphol.nl

Amsterdam area. Some airlines don't have proper offices in the Netherlands and are best contacted using the Internet or email.

Aer Lingus (☎ 517 47 47; www.aerlingus.com; Heiligeweg 14)

Air France (☎ 654 57 20; www.airfrance.nl; Evert van de Beekstraat 7; Schiphol)

Air India (☎ 624 81 09; www.airindia.com; Papenbroeksteeg 2)

Alitalia (☎ 676 44 79; www.alitalia.com; Van Baerlestraat 70)

British Airways (☎ 346 95 59; www.britishairways.com; Neptunusstraat 33; Hoofddorp)

British Midland (☎ +44-1332 854 321; www.flybmi.com)

Cathay Pacific (☎ 653 20 10; www.cathaypacific.nl; Evert van de Beekstraat 18; Schiphol)

China Airlines (☎ 646 10 01; www.china-airlines.com; De Boelelaan 7 6hg)

Delta Air Lines (☎ 201 35 36, www.delta.com; Evert van de Beekstraat 7; Schiphol)

El Al (☎ 644 01 01; www.elal.com; Prof Bavincklaan 5; Amstelveen)

EasyJet (☎ 023-568 48 80; www.easyjet.com)

Garuda Indonesia (☎ 550 26 40, www.garuda-indonesia.nl; Singel 540)

Japan Airlines (☎ 305 00 60; www.jal-europe.com; Jozef Israelskade 48E)

KLM (☎ 474 77 47; www.klm.nl; Amsterdamseweg 55; Amstelveen)

Lufthansa (☎ 582 94 56; www.lufthansa.nl; Wibautstraat 129)

Malaysia Airlines (☎ 521 62 62; www.malaysiaairlines.com.my; Weteringschans 24A)

Northwest Airlines (☎ 474 77 47; www.nwa.com; Amsterdamseweg 55; Amstelveen)

Qantas (☎ 569 82 83; www.qantas.com.au; Neptunsstraat 33; Hoofddorp)

Ryanair (☎ 0900-2022184; www.ryanair.com)

Singapore Airlines (☎ 548 88 88; www.singaporeair.com; De Boelelaan1067)

South African Airways (☎ 554 22 88; www.flysaa.com; Polarisavenue 49; Hoofddorp)

Thai Airways (☎ 596 13 01; www.thaiairways.com; Wibautstraat 3)

Transavia (☎ 406 04 06; www.transavia.nl; Westelijke Randweg 3)

United Airlines (☎ 201 37 08; www.unitedairlines.nl; Strawinskylaan 831)

DEPARTURE TAX

There is a small departure tax (about €25) included in the cost of tickets from Dutch airports.

Tickets

Airfares can gouge anyone's budget but you can reduce the cost by finding discounts. For long-term travel there are plenty of discount tickets valid for 12 months, allowing multiple stopovers with open dates. Short-term travellers can snag cheaper fares by travelling midweek, staying away at least one Saturday night or taking advantage of quickie promotional offers.

When you're looking for bargain airfares, the Internet offers a wealth of options from on-line booking agencies, travel agents and the airlines themselves. No-frills carriers operating in Europe sell direct to travellers and regularly undercut the major airlines.

The travel industry has been battered in recent years, but leading travel agents such as STA Travel (which has offices worldwide) and Council Travel in the USA appear to have weathered the storm. And they do offer good prices to many destinations.

For details of on-line booking agencies to Amsterdam Schiphol airport, see Air Tickets on the Web, below.

AIR TICKETS ON THE WEB

Here's a shortlist of sites that sell air tickets to/from Schiphol Airport:

www.cheapflights.com (US & UK)
www.eltexpress.com (US)
www.flightcentre.ca (Canada)
www.priceline.com (US)
www.skydeals.co.uk (UK)
www.trailfinder.com (UK)
www.vliegtarieven.nl, in Dutch (the Netherlands)
www.waarheenwaarvoor.nl (the Netherlands)

TRANSPORT

COURIER FLIGHTS

Courier flights are a great bargain if you're lucky enough to find one. Air-freight companies expedite delivery of urgent items by sending them with you as your baggage allowance. You are permitted to bring along only one carry-on bag, but you get a steeply discounted ticket in return.

Booking a courier ticket takes some effort. They are not readily available and arrangements have to be made a month or more in advance. You won't find courier flights to all destinations either – just on the major air routes.

Courier flights are occasionally advertised in the newspapers, or you can contact air-freight companies listed in the phone book. Another possibility is to join the **International Association of Air Travel Couriers** (IAATC; US ☎ 308-632-3273; UK ☎ 0800-0746 481; www.courier.org). The membership fee (US$45 or UK£32) gets members access to on-line lists of courier companies and updated schedules, daily updates of last-minute specials and the bimonthly magazine, *Shoestring Traveler*. Joining this organisation, however, doesn't guarantee that you'll get a courier flight.

FREQUENT FLYERS

Most airlines offer frequent-flyer deals that can earn you a free air ticket or other goodies. To qualify, you have to accumulate sufficient mileage with the same airline or airline alliance. Many airlines have 'blackout periods', or times when you cannot fly for free on your frequent-flyer points (Christmas and Chinese New Year, for example). The worst thing about frequent-flyer programmes is that they tend to lock you into one group of airlines, and that group may not always have the cheapest fares or most convenient flight schedule.

INTERCONTINENTAL (RTW) TICKETS

RTW tickets give you a limited period (usually a year) in which to circumnavigate the globe. You can go anywhere the airlines go as long as you don't backtrack. The number of stopovers or total number of separate flights is decided before you set off and they usually cost a bit more than a basic return flight.

STUDENT & YOUTH FARES

Full-time students and people under 26 can get better deals than other travellers. This doesn't always mean cheaper fares but can include more flexibility to change flights and/or routes. You show a document proving your date of birth or a valid International Student Identity Card (ISIC) when buying your ticket and boarding the plane.

TRAVELLERS WITH SPECIAL NEEDS

Most international airlines can cater to people with special needs – travellers with disabilities, people with young children and even children travelling alone.

Travellers with special dietary preferences (vegetarian, kosher etc) can request meals on advance notice. If you are travelling in a wheelchair, most international airports can provide an escort from check-in desk to plane where needed, and ramps, lifts, toilets and phones are generally available.

Airlines usually allow infants under two years of age to fly for free or 10% of the adult fare. Reputable international airlines usually provide nappies (diapers), tissues and other items needed to keep babies bouncy. For children between the ages of two and 12, the fare on international flights is usually 50% of the regular fare or 67% of a discounted fare.

From Africa

KLM has numerous services to Africa. Kenya Airways and South African Airways also have frequent links to Amsterdam. From Johannesburg, low season return fares to Amsterdam are around R12900 (US$2199). Flights via another European city are considerably cheaper than direct flights.

Rennies Travel (www.renniestravel.com) and **STA Travel** (www.statravel.co.za) have offices throughout Southern Africa. Check their websites for branch locations.

From Asia

The major Asian airlines, such as Singapore Airlines, Cathay Pacific, Japan Airlines, Malaysia Airlines and Garuda Indonesia, have flights into Amsterdam. Although most flights are via another European capital, there are some direct links to Amsterdam. It's a good idea to shop around as there are often some good deals on offer. From Bangkok, return fares to Amsterdam are around US$1500. Return fares from Singapore start from US$850, from Hong Kong expect to pay around US$1250 and US$1100 from Tokyo for a return fare.

Bangkok has a number of travel agents including **STA Travel** (☎ 02-236 0262; www.statravel .co.th)

In Singapore, the best bet is still STA Travel (☎ 65-737 7188; www.statravel.com.sg).

In Hong Kong good agencies include **Hong Kong Student Travel** (☎ 2730 0888; www.hkst.com.hk, in Chinese) and STA Travel (☎ 2736 16180; www .statravel.com.hk).

Recommended agencies in Japan include **No 1 Travel** (☎ 3205 6073; www.no1-travel.com) and **STA Travel** (☎ 5391 3205; www.statravel.co.jp).

From Australia

Flights from Australia to Amsterdam generally go via a Southeast Asian capital such as Kuala Lumpur, Bangkok or Singapore, and occasionally another European city. Expect to pay around A$1700 for a return in low season, but shop around as there are often good deals on offer (see From Asia, p310)

Quite a few travel offices specialise in discount air tickets. Some travel agents, particularly smaller ones, advertise cheap air fares in the travel sections of weekend newspapers, such as the *Age* in Melbourne and the *Sydney Morning Herald* in Sydney.

Contact **STA Travel** (☎ 1300 360 960; www.statravel .com.au) for the location of branches. **Flight Centre** (☎ 131 600; www.flightcentre.com.au) has offices throughout Australia. For on-line bookings, try www.travel.com.au.

From Canada

Air Canada and Air France are among the airlines that serve Amsterdam from Toronto. Fares vary from C$400 in winter to C$700 in summer.

Canadian discount air ticket sellers are also known as consolidators. The *Globe & Mail*, *Toronto Star*, *Montreal Gazette* and the *Vancouver Sun* carry travel agents' ads and are good places to look for cheap fares.

Travel CUTS (☎ 866-246 9672; www.travelcuts.com) is Canada's national student travel agency and has offices in all major cities.

From Continental Europe

Amsterdam is well connected to almost all other European cities with airports. KLM and the major airlines of each country all serve each other. You should be able to find return fares from the major hub airports such as Copenhagen, Frankfurt, Paris and Madrid for €75 to €175.

Generally, there is not much variation in airfare prices for departures from the main European cities. All the major airlines are usually offering some sort of deal, and travel agents generally have a number of deals on offer, so shop around.

Across Europe dozens of travel agencies have ties with **STA Travel** (www.statravel.com), where cheap tickets can be purchased and STA-issued tickets can be altered (usually for a US$25 fee).

France has a network of student travel agencies that can supply discount tickets to travellers of all ages. **OTU Voyages** (☎ 01 44 41 38; www.otu.fr) has 27 offices around the country. General travel agencies in Paris that offer some of the best services and deals include **Nouvelles Frontiéres** (☎ 0825 000 747; www.nouvelles-frontieres.com) and **Voyageurs du Monde** (☎ 01 42 86 16 00; www.vdm.com).

In Italy, a good all-round agency is **Elsy Viaggi** (☎ 06-683 2096; www.elsyviaggi.com).

Belgium, Switzerland and Greece are also good places for buying discount air tickets. In Belgium, **Airstop** (☎ 070-233 188; www.airstop.be) offers great cut-rate deals for both students and non-students.

From New Zealand

Reaching Amsterdam from Auckland means you have a choice of transiting though Los Angeles or via a Southeast Asian city, and usually one other European city. Low season return fares start from around US$2199.

Both **Flight Centre** (☎ 0800 243 544; www .flightcentre.co.nz) and **STA Travel** (☎ 0800 874 773; www.statravel.co.nz) have branches throughout the country. For on-line bookings try www.travel.co.nz.

From the UK & Ireland

KLM, British Airways and British Midland fly to the Netherlands from the UK. Budget airlines EasyJet and Ryanair do too, and have made big inroads into business of the mainstream carriers. Watch for special fares that can be as low as UK£1 for a single, although €40 to €60 is more likely in peak periods.

Ticket discounters are known as bucket shops in the UK. Discount air travel is big business in London, and advertisements for many travel agents appear in the travel pages of the weekend broadsheets, such as the *Independent* on Saturday and the

TRANSPORT

Sunday Times. Also look out for the free magazines such as TNT.

Popular travel agencies include **STA Travel** (☎ 0870-1600 599; www.statravel.co.uk) with offices throughout the UK. It sells tickets to all travellers but caters especially to young people and students. Other recommended agencies include **Trailfinders** (☎ 020-7938 3939; www.trailfinders.co.uk) and **Bridge the World** (☎ 0870-443 23 99; www.bridgetheworld.co.uk).

From Ireland, fares run from about IR£130 in low season for return flights from Dublin to Amsterdam, but can cost twice that much in high season. Travelling via London may save money. **USIT** (☎ 0818-200020; www.usitnow.ie) has 22 branches in Ireland and Northern Ireland specialising in student and independent travel.

From the US

Continental Airlines, Delta Air Lines, Northwest Airlines and United Airlines all have nonstop services to Amsterdam from the cities in the US. Fares vary by season, from a low of US$300/500 from the east coast/west coast in winter to a high of US$700/900 in summer.

Discount travel agents in the USA are known as consolidators (although you probably won't see a sign on the door saying 'Consolidator'). The *New York Times*, the *Los Angeles Times*, the *Chicago Tribune* and the *San Francisco Chronicle* all produce Sunday travel sections in which you will find consolidators' ads.

Council Travel (☎ 800-226 8624, www.counciltravel .com; 205 E 42 St, New York), America's largest student travel organisation, has around 100 locations in the USA. **STA Travel** (☎ 800-777 0112; www.statravel.com) has offices in Boston, Chicago, Miami, New York, Philadelphia, San Francisco and other major cities.

LAND
Bicycle

The Netherlands are extremely bike-friendly; once you're in the country you can pedal almost everywhere on dedicated bicycle paths. Everything is wonderfully flat, but that also means powerful wind and it always seems to come from ahead.

Bicycles can travel by air. You can take them apart and put them in a bike bag or box, but it's much easier simply to wheel your bike to the check-in desk, where it

should be treated as a piece of baggage. You may have to remove the pedals and turn the handlebars sideways so that it takes up less space in the aircraft's hold; check all this with the airline well in advance, preferably before you pay for your ticket.

Your bike can also travel with you on the Eurostar and Thalys high-speed trains from Belgium, France and the UK provided you can disassemble the bike and fit it into a stowage bag that will fit into the normal luggage storage racks on board.

Bus

Amsterdam and Rotterdam are well connected to the rest of Europe and North Africa by long-distance bus. For details about regional buses in the Netherlands, call the **transport information service** (☎ 0900-9292; per minute €0.50).

The most extensive European bus network is maintained by **Eurolines** (☎ +44-08705 143219; www.eurolines.com) a consortium of coach operators. It offers a variety of passes with prices that vary by time of year. Returns from London to Amsterdam start from UK£38 for adults. The journeys take 10 to 12 hours and stop at Rotterdam and Den Haag or Utrecht. See the destination chapters for more fare details.

Busabout (☎ +44-20-7950 1661; www.busabout .com) is a UK-based budget alternative to Eurolines. It runs coaches on circuits in Continental Europe including one through Amsterdam; a Busabout pass costs €359 (€329 for youth and student-card holders) for two weeks, and passes are available for three weeks to three months. Services to/from Amsterdam run from April to October.

Gullivers Reisen (☎ +49-30-31 10 21 10; www .gullivers.de, in German) links Berlin to Amsterdam (€49/89 for single/returns, nine hours, once daily). Sleeper coach beds are available for another €10 – a wise investment.

Car & Motorcycle

For details about car ferries from England see Sea, p314 .

Drivers of cars and riders of motorbikes will need the vehicle's registration papers, third-party insurance and an international drivers' permit in addition to their domestic licence. It's a good idea to also have complete insurance coverage – be sure to ask for a Green Card from your insurer.

The ANWB (see Tourist Offices in the Directory, p306) provides a wide range of information and services if you can show a letter of introduction from your own automobile association.

Traffic flows freely among EU countries so border posts are largely a thing of the past. Customs officials still make spot checks, however, of vehicles that draw their attention (ie riding low with kegs of foreign beer).

Hitching

Hitching is never entirely safe anywhere in the world and we don't recommend it. Travellers who decide to hitch should understand that they are taking a small but potentially serious risk.

Many Dutch students have a government-issued pass allowing free public transport. Consequently the number of hitchhikers has dropped dramatically and car drivers are no longer used to the phenomenon. Hitchers have reported long waits.

On Channel crossings from the UK, the car fares on the Harwich–Hoek van Holland ferry as well as the shuttle through the Channel Tunnel include passengers, so you can hitch to the continent for nothing at no cost to the driver (though the driver will still be responsible if you do something illegal).

Looking for a ride out of the country? Try the notice boards at universities, public libraries and youth hostels. **Bugride** (http://europe.bugride.com) is a good meeting place for European drivers and potential passengers.

From Belgium & Germany

BICYCLE

Long-distance bicyclists can choose from a variety of safe, easy, specially designated routes to get to the Netherlands from Belgium and Germany. The bicycle paths are *Landelijke Fietsroutes* (LF) and retain that label in northern Belgium. The LF2 route runs 340km from Brussels via Gent to Amsterdam; the LF4 stretches 300km from Enschede near to the German border to Den Haag.

Beware that mopeds also use bike paths and might be travelling well above their 40km/h speed limit (30km/h in built-up areas). Only competition cyclists and posers tend to wear bicycle helmets, but that shouldn't stop you from protecting your own cranium.

If you want to bring your own bike, consider the risk of theft in Amsterdam – rental might be the wiser option. Repair shops are as common as *frites* vendors in the Netherlands – most train stations even have a bicycle shop with a resident mechanic.

For select cycle routes see the special section Cycling in the Netherlands (p70) .

CAR & MOTORCYCLE

The main entry points from Belgium are the E22 (Antwerp–Breda) and the E25 (Liege–Maastricht). From Germany there are loads of border crossings but the chief arteries are the E40 (Cologne–Maastricht), the E35 (Düsseldorf–Arnhem) and the A1 (Hanover–Amsterdam).

TRAIN

The Netherlands has good train links to Germany, Belgium and France. All Eurail, Inter-Rail, Europass and Flexipass tickets are valid on the Dutch national train service, **Nederlandse Spoorwegen** (NS; www.ns.nl). See the Getting Around section (p318) for more about trains within the country.

Major Dutch train stations have international ticket offices, and in peak periods it's wise to reserve seats in advance. You can buy tickets on local trains to Belgium and Germany at the normal ticket counters.

For international train information ring the **Teleservice NS Internationaal** (☎ 0900-9296, per minute €0.25). For national trains, simply turn up at the station: you'll rarely have to wait more than an hour for a train to anywhere. If you book ahead, NS charges a €3 reservation fee per ticket.

There are two main lines south from Amsterdam. One Intercity/Eurocity train passes through Den Haag and Rotterdam and on to Antwerp (€26.40, 2¼ hours, hourly trains) and Brussels (€31.40, three hours, hourly trains). The other line south goes via Utrecht and Maastricht to Luxembourg City (€55.20, 6¼ hours, every one to two hours), and on to France and Switzerland. You can go via Arnhem to Cologne (€47, three hours, once daily) and east towards Berlin (€82, six hours, three times daily).

Most IC/EC trains require a €2 surcharge in the Netherlands; German surcharges depend on which type of train you take and exactly when, but the system's in flux

TRANSPORT

– check ahead. Travellers under 26 get a 25% discount.

Weekend returns are much cheaper than during the week. A weekend return Amsterdam–Brussels (departure Friday to Sunday, return by Monday) is 40% cheaper than a regular ticket.

The high-speed train, the Thalys, runs six times a day between Amsterdam and Antwerp (€33.50, 2¼ hours), Brussels (€39.50, 2½ hours) and Paris (€87, 4¼ hours). Under 26s get a 45% discount and seniors with a Rail Europe Senior (RES) card are entitled to 30% off travel outside the Netherlands.

The German ICE high-speed service runs six times a day between Amsterdam and Cologne (€45, 2½ hours) and on to Frankfurt (€68.80, 4 hours). 'Super Day Returns' are available to Cologne for half-price. There's also a night train between Amsterdam and Munich (€103.20) – expect fat surcharges for the sleeper berths.

From The UK
BICYCLE
Most cross-Channel ferries don't charge foot passengers extra to take a bicycle. You can also bring your two-wheeler on the Eurostar – see p314.

BUS
Eurolines runs a regular coach service to Amsterdam from London's Victoria coach station. The journey takes about 10 hours, and the coaches have onboard toilets, reclining seats and air-conditioning. Prices for a return trip are UK£47/44 for adults/under-26s.

CAR & MOTORCYCLE
Ferries take cars and motorcycles to the Netherlands from several ports in the UK. Le Shuttle express trains will take vehicles from the UK to France from where you can drive to the Netherlands (see Train, p314, and Sea, p314) for details.

TRAIN
Rail Europe (☎ 0990-848 848; www.raileurope.com) will get you from London to Amsterdam on the highly civilised Eurostar passenger train service from Waterloo Station through the Channel Tunnel to Brussels, with an onward Thalys connection from there. This takes about 5¼ hours in total

and starts from UK£90 return in 2nd class with special deals. A bicycle costs UK£20 one-way.

Eurotunnel (☎ 08705-850850; www.eurotunnel.com) runs a 'drive-on, drive off' shuttle linking Folkstone, UK to Calais, France, on a 35-minute journey via the Channel Tunnel. Cars/motorcycles cost from UK£143/68.50 with advance reservations.

SEA
From the UK
FERRY
Several companies operate car/passenger ferries between the Netherlands and the UK. Most travel agents have details of the following services but might not always know the finer points. For information on train-ferry-train services, see the earlier Train section. Reservations are essential for motorists in high season, although motorcycles can often be squeezed in.

Stenaline (☎ 08705-70 70 70; www.stenaline.com) sails between Harwich and Hoek van Holland, west of Rotterdam. The fast HSS ferries take only 3¾ hours and depart in each direction twice a day. Foot passengers pay upwards of UK£26 return. Fares for a car with up to five people range from UK£250 to UK£303 return depending on the season and day of week. A motorcycle and driver cost UK£98 to UK£154 in low/high season. Options such as reclining chairs and cabins cost extra and are compulsory on night crossings.

Train-boat-train combos are cheaper but take two to three hours longer. Stenaline has return fares from London to Amsterdam starting at UK£64 (for those aged under 26) or UK£79 for everyone else. Special return deals cost £50. The train links go via Harwich in the UK and Hoek van Holland in the Netherlands and take a total of about 8½ hours.

P&O North Sea Ferries (☎ 08705-20 20 20; www.ponsf.com) operates an overnight ferry every evening (11 hours) between Hull and Europoort (near Rotterdam). Return fares start at UK£62 for a foot passenger, UK£341 for a car with up to four people and UK£76 for a motorcycle and driver. Prices here include berths in an inside cabin, and luxury cabins are available.

DFDS Scandinavian Seaways (☎ 08705-33 30 00; www.dfdsseaways.co.uk) sails between Newcastle and IJmuiden, which is close to Amsterdam. The 15-hour sailings depart every other day. The earlier you book, the lower your fare: single fares start at UK£29 for a foot passenger in an economy berth with private facilities, plus UK£46 for a car. Motorcycle and driver pay a total UK£49 one-way. Bear in mind prices can go up more than 50% in high season.

Most ferries don't charge for a bike and have no shortage of storage space.

TOURS

There are scads of package tours to the Netherlands that combine transport and accommodation. Apart from your travel agent, many airlines, ferry operators and national train companies offer some good deals with valuable extras, such as museum passes.

GETTING AROUND

The Netherlands is a very easy place to get around. If you are sticking to the major cities and sights, you won't need a car as the train and bus system blankets the country. Or you can do as the Dutch do and provide your power on a bike.

AIR

The only domestic commercial flights link Amsterdam Schiphol to Eindhoven and Maastricht airports. They're chiefly used by business passengers transferring to international flights at Schiphol and flights are relatively expensive.

BICYCLE

With 20,000km of cycling paths, a *fiets* (bicycle) is the way to go. The **ANWB** (p317) publishes cycling maps for each province and tourists offices always have numerous routes and suggestions. Major roads have separate bike lanes, and, except for motorways, there's virtually nowhere bicycles can't go. That said, in places such as the Delta region and along the coast you'll often need muscles to combat the North Sea headwinds.

Over 100 stations throughout the country have bicycle facilities for rental, protected parking, repair and sales. Details are noted in the city listings in this book.

Bicycles are prohibited on trains during the weekday rush hours (6.30am to 9am

and 4.30pm to 6pm), except for the Hoek van Holland boat train. There are no restrictions on holidays, weekends or during July and August.

You may bring your bicycle on to any train as long as there is room. Some trains such as the single-level Intercity carriages have very limited space. However, on popular stretches there's often a special bicycle carriage that increases capacity. If your planned train has no room for your bike, you'll have to wait for the next train.

You'll need to purchase an extra ticket for your bike. A day pass for bikes (€6) is valid in the entire country regardless of the distance involved. There are no fees for collapsible bikes so long as they can be considered hand luggage.

For more information about cycling see the special section Cycling in the Netherlands (p70) and Bicycle under Local Transport (p318).

Hire

Although about 85% of the population owns bikes, and there are more bikes than people, bikes are also abundantly available for hire. In most cases you'll need to show your passport, and leave an imprint of your credit card or a deposit (€25 or €100). Private operators charge €4 to €6 per day, and €25 to €30 per week. Train station hire shops (called *Rijwiel* shops) may be slightly cheaper, at €5.40/22 per day/week. You must return the bike to the same station.

Purchase

Your basic used bicycle (no gears, with coaster brakes, maybe a bit rickety) can be bought for around €50 to €75 from bicycle shops or the classified ads. Count on paying €100 or more for a reliable two-wheeler with gears. Stolen bikes are available on the street for as little as €15, but it's highly illegal and the cash usually goes straight into a junkie's arm. Good new models will start around €200 on sale, but top-of-the-line brands can cost €1000 or more.

BOAT
Ferry

Ferries connect the mainland with the five Frisian Islands. See the relevant sections in the Friesland chapter (p243) for details. Other ferries span the Westerschelde in the south of Zeeland, providing road links to the bit of the Netherlands south of here and Belgium. These are popular with people using the Zeebrugge ferry terminal and run frequently year-round. There is also a frequent ferry service on the IJsselmeer linking Enkhuizen with Stavoren and Urk. You'll also find a few small river ferries providing crossings for remote stretches of the IJssel and other rivers.

Hire

Renting a boat is a popular way to tour the many rivers, lakes and inland seas. Boats come in all shapes and sizes from canoes to motor boats to small sailing boats to large and historic former cargo sloops. Prices span the gamut and there are hundreds of rental firms throughout the country. See the Boating section of the Directory, p295.

BUS

Buses are used for regional transport rather than for long distances, which are better travelled by train. They provide a vital service, especially in parts of the north and east, where trains are less frequent or nonexistent. The national strippenkaart (see Local Transport, p317) is used on most regional buses. The fares are zone-based, but figure on roughly one strip for every five minutes of riding.

There are no special passes and only one class of travel. Reservations aren't possible on either regional or municipal lines, most of which run quite frequently.

CAR & MOTORCYCLE

Dutch freeways are extensive but are prone to congestion. Those around Amsterdam and the A4 south to Belgium and the A2 southeast to Maastricht are especially likely to be jammed at rush hours and during busy travel periods; a total length of 350km or more isn't unheard of during the holiday season.

Smaller roads are usually well maintained, but the campaign to discourage car use throws up obstacles – you may find the road narrows to a single lane in sections, or an assortment of speed-bumps and other 'traffic-calming schemes'.

ROAD DISTANCES (KM)

	Amsterdam	Apeldoorn	Arnhem	Breda	Den Bosch	Den Haag	Dordrecht	Eindhoven	Enschede	Groningen	Haarlem	Leeuwarden	Leiden	Maastricht	Nijmegen	Rotterdam	Tilburg	Utrecht
Amsterdam	---																	
Apeldoorn	86	---																
Arnhem	99	27	---															
Breda	101	141	111	---														
Den Bosch	88	91	64	48	---													
Den Haag	55	133	118	72	102	---												
Dordrecht	98	133	102	30	65	45	---											
Eindhoven	121	109	82	57	32	134	92	---										
Enschede	161	75	98	212	162	224	200	180	---									
Groningen	203	147	172	260	236	252	248	254	148	---								
Haarlem	19	117	114	121	103	51	94	136	184	204	---							
Leeuwarden	139	133	158	248	222	188	234	240	163	62	148	---						
Leiden	45	125	110	87	99	17	60	132	192	242	42	178	---					
Maastricht	213	201	167	146	124	223	181	86	274	348	228	334	239	---				
Nijmegen	122	63	18	101	44	135	98	62	134	208	135	194	131	148	---			
Rotterdam	73	128	118	51	81	21	24	113	195	251	70	206	36	202	114	---		
Tilburg	114	115	88	25	25	102	60	34	186	260	129	246	117	123	68	81	---	
Utrecht	37	72	64	73	55	62	61	88	139	195	54	181	54	180	85	57	81	---

Automobile Associations

For motoring information, contact the **ANWB** (Royal Dutch Touring Association; ☎ 070-314 71 47; www.anwb.nl, in Dutch; Wassenaarseweg 220, Den Haag).

Driving Licence

You'll need to show a valid driving licence when hiring a car in the Netherlands. Visitors from outside the EU should also consider an international driving permit (IDP). Car rental firms will rarely ask for one but the police might do so if they pull you up. An IDP can be obtained for a small fee from your local automobile association – bring along a valid licence and a passport photo - and is valid for one year together with your original licence.

Fuel

Like much of Western Europe, petrol is very expensive. At the time of research it was about €1.15 per litre (about US$4 per gallon). Gasoline (petrol) is *benzine* in Dutch, while unleaded fuel is *loodvrij*. Leaded fuel is no longer sold in the Netherlands. Liquid petroleum gas can be purchased at petrol stations displaying LPG.

Petrol isn't noticeably more or less expensive outside of towns. Cheaper fuel is generally available from cut-rate chains such as Tango or TinQ – just ask the locals.

Hire

The Netherlands is well covered here. However, outside Amsterdam, the car hire companies can be in inconvenient locations if you're arriving by train. You can look for local car rental firms in telephone directories under the heading *Autoverhuur*. You must be at least 23 years of age to hire a car in the Netherlands. Some car-hire firms levy a small surcharge (eg €10) for drivers under 25. Most will ask either for a deposit or a credit card imprint as a guarantee of payment. See the Amsterdam chapter for contact details of international rental firms (p135).

Insurance

When hiring a car we strongly recommend you take out collision damage waiver (CDW), an insurance policy which limits your financial liability for damage – otherwise you'll be liable for damages up to the full value of the vehicle.

> **DID YOU KNOW?**
>
> More than 800 unmanned radar cameras (known as *flitspalen*) watch over Dutch motorways.

If you rely on your credit card for cover, take time to review the terms and conditions. In the event of an accident you may be required to pay for repairs out of your own pocket and reclaim the sum from the credit card company later, a procedure that can be fraught with problems.

Note that at most car rental firms, CDW does not cover the first €500 to €1000 of damages incurred, so you're liable for this amount.

Road Rules

Like the rest of Continental Europe, traffic travels on the right. The minimum driving age is 18 for vehicles and 16 for motorcycles. Seat belts are required for everyone in a vehicle, and children under 12 must ride in the back if there's room.

The standard European road rules and traffic signs apply. Trams always have the right of way. If you are trying to turn right, bikes have priority. One grey area is at roundabouts: in principle, approaching vehicles have right of way, but in practice they yield to vehicles already travelling on the circle.

Speed limits are 50km/h in built-up areas, 80km/h in the country, 100km/h on major through-roads and 120km/h on freeways (sometimes 100km/h, clearly indicated). The blood-alcohol limit when driving is 0.05%.

HITCHING

Hitching is never entirely safe in any country in the world, and we don't recommend it. Travellers who decide to hitch should understand that they are taking a small but potentially serious risk. People who do choose to hitch will be safer if they travel in pairs and let someone know where they are planning to go.

LOCAL TRANSPORT
Bus, Tram & Metro

Buses and trams operate in most cities, and Amsterdam and Rotterdam also have metro networks.

There is a national fare system. You buy a *strippenkaart* (strip card) which is valid throughout the country, and stamp off a number of strips depending on how many zones you plan to cross. The ticket is then valid on all buses, trams, metro systems and city trains for an hour, or longer depending on the number of strips you've stamped. In most towns you punch two strips (one for the journey and one for the zone), with an additional strip for each additional zone.

In the central areas of cities and towns, you usually will only need to stamp two strips – the minimum fee (see boxed text 'Stripp Tease'). When riding on trams and metros it's up to you to stamp your card as fare dodgers can be fined on the spot. On trams the machines are usually on-board although for the metros they are at the entrance to the platforms.

A 15-strip card costs €6.20 and is available all over the place – tobacco shops, post offices, train-station counters, many bookshops and newsagencies.

The buses are more conventional, with drivers stamping the strips as you get on. Bus and tram drivers sell two-/three-strip cards for €1.60/2.40. More economical are 15-strip cards for €6.20 or 45-strip ones for €18.30 – these are available at train and bus stations, post offices, many tourist offices or tobacconists. More than one person can use a *strippenkaart* (see Stripp Tease, below), and children and pensioners get reductions. Note that if you get

---

STRIPP TEASE

Some well-meaning travellers are tempted to punch every single field on a *strippenkaart*. But remember, passengers on Dutch public transport need to validate their tickets only once per trip regardless of how many people travel on the same ticket. You're travelling alone within one zone – say, central Amsterdam? The canal belt and surrounding districts are one zone but require *two* strips; fold the ticket and punch the second available strip. You're with a friend? Punch the fourth strip (but *not* the second strip as well – this would invalidate the journey of one traveller). And so on. Journeys to another zone take three strips per person; when in doubt consult the transport maps at bus/tram stops, or ask the driver.

---

caught without a properly stamped strip, playing the ignorant foreigner (the 'doofus' strategy) will guarantee that you get fined €30.

Bicycle

Any Dutch town you visit is liable to be blanketed with bicycle paths, either on the streets or as smooth off-road routes. In many cases the fastest way to get around is by bike.

Taxi

Usually booked by phone – officially you're not supposed to wave them down on the street – taxis also hover outside train stations and hotels and cost roughly €12 for 5km. Even short trips in town can get expensive quickly. There are also *treintaxis* (p320).

TOURS

Several companies offer tours of Holland aboard luxury riverboats. Aimed at older and well-heeled travellers, these tours are more like cruises than actual sightseeing tours.

Anglo Dutch Tours (☎ 020-85 11 15 51; www.anglodu tchsports.co.uk; Imperial House, Edgware Rd, London NW9 5AL, UK) Cyclists are well catered for with programmes such as cycling with sailing, castles, woodland and parks.

Cycletours Holland (☎ 020-627 40 98; www.cycle tours.com; Buiksloterweg 7A, Amsterdam) Conducts short tours of up to a week by bicycle and canal barge. A one-week tour starts at €500 (cabin with shared shower and toilet).

Hat Tours (☎ 0299-69 07 71; www.hat-tours.com; Venediën 26-I, 1441 AK Purmerend) Does much the same thing and appeals to cyclists and nature lovers.

Holland River Line (☎ 026-353 17 30; www.holland riverline.nl; Rijnkade 12, 68 11 HA Arnhem) Cruise in style with one of the biggest operators, with lazy trips along Dutch rivers into Belgium and Germany.

Lowlands Travel (☎ 06-23 34 20 46; www.lowlands travel.nl; Korvelplein 176, 5025 JX Tilburg) For down-to-earth nature and culture-oriented holidays, try the tours which run from three days to a week for groups of two to eight people, mostly outdoorsy types aged 20 to 40. Readers have recommended this operator in glowing terms.

TRAIN

Dutch trains are efficient, fast and comfortable – most of the time. Trains are frequent and serve domestic destinations at regular intervals, sometimes five or six times an hour. Short-term visitors may be fortunate, but overall the network has been plagued by poor punctuality in recent years. Rush-hour periods around the Randstad seem to notch up the most delays. The situation may be improving if only because the **Nederlandse Spoorwegen** (Netherlands Railways, NS; national inquiries ☎ 0900-9292, international inquiries ☎ 0900-9296; www.ns.nl) has little choice: its profitability is linked to its on-time rates. Some rural lines have been hived off to combination train-and-bus operators who coordinate schedules across the region.

Classes

The longest train journey in the Netherlands takes about 4½ hours (eg Maastricht–Groningen), but most trips are shorter. Trains have 1st-class sections but these are often little different from the 2nd-class areas and, given the short journeys, not worth the extra cost.

Trains can be an all-stops *stoptrein*, a faster *sneltrein* (Fast Train, indicated with an 'S'), or an even faster Intercity (IC). Intercity Express (ICE) trains travel between Amsterdam and Cologne and only stop in Utrecht and Arnhem; they're quite fast (a 10-minute saving to Arnhem) but you pay a €2 supplement at the counter or ticket machine, or €4 on board the train.

The high-speed Thalys only stops at Amsterdam, Schiphol, Den Haag and Rotterdam before going on to Antwerp, Brussels and Paris (or Luxembourg). It requires a special ticket, available at the international ticket counters.

Costs

Tickets cost the same during the day as in the evening, and can be bought at the window or ticketing machines. Buying a ticket on board means you'll pay almost double the normal fare.

Many stations now rely on ticketing machines to cut personnel costs and queues at the counters. The machines are fairly complicated with instructions in Dutch only. Check your destination on the alphabetical list of place names, enter the relevant code into the machine; then choose 1st/2nd class; *zonder/met korting* (without/with discount, eg, if you have a discount card; see Train Passes, p320); *vandaag geldig/zonder datum* (valid today/without date). The machine will then indicate how much it wants to be fed – coins only, though change is

given. With the tickets without date, you can travel on another day but you'll have to stamp the ticket in a yellow punch gadget near the platforms.

With a valid ticket you can break your journey along the direct route. Day return tickets are 10% to 15% cheaper than two one-ways, apart from the *weekendretour* (weekend return); which costs the same as a normal return and is valid from 7pm Friday to 4am Monday.

A *dagkaart* (Day Pass) for unlimited train travel throughout the country costs €38 (2nd class) or €60 (1st class), which is the same as you'll pay for a return ticket to any destination more than 233km away. Add €4.50 for an *OV-dagkaart* (Public Transport Day Pass) and you'll have use of trams, buses and metros as well.

If you plan to do a lot of travelling, consider investing €49 in a *Voordeel-Urenkaart* valid for one year, which gives 40% discount on train travel weekdays after 9am, as well as weekends, public holidays and the whole months of July and August. The discount also applies to up to three people travelling with you on the same trip. As well, the card gives access to evening returns valid from 6pm (but not on Fridays) that are up to 65% cheaper than normal returns. A similar version for those aged 60 and over gives an additional seven days' free travel a year. The card is available at train station counters (passport photo required, plus driving licence or passport for the 60-plus version).

Reservations

Services along the major routes stop around midnight (often much earlier on minor routes), but there are night trains once an hour in both directions along the Utrecht–Amsterdam–Schiphol–Leiden–Den Haag–Delft–Rotterdam route. *Intercityboekje* (€2) is a handy small booklet listing the schedules of all IC trains, with an excellent map of the entire system.

In stations, schedules are posted by route. Figure out where you're going and look up

---

DID YOU KNOW?

Dog owners can travel with Fido all day long on Dutch trains using a *Dagkaart Hond* (Doggie Day Pass; €3)

the schedule and track numbers. One annoyance: trip duration and arrival time information aren't included on the station schedules, so you'll have to ask staff.

For train and ticketing information and to make reservations, ring the national **public transport number** (☎ 0900-9292; per minute €0.50; ☷ 6am-midnight Mon-Fri, 7am-midnight Sat & Sun). The NS website (www.ns.nl) has complete schedules – click on '*Reisinfo*' then 'English'.

Train Passes

There are several train passes for people living outside the Netherlands. These can all be purchased in Europe or in the Netherlands, with the exception of the Holland Rail Pass. You'll need to show your passport.

Eurodomino passes are good for three to eight days' unlimited travel during a one-month period in one of 20 European countries. For the Netherlands, the three-day pass costs UK£37/27 in 2nd class for adults/under 26s, and about 50% more in 1st class. The five-day version runs UK£53/44 for adults/under 26s, and roughly two-thirds more for 1st class.

The Holland Pass allows you unlimited travel for any three or five days within one month, at a cost of UK£64/96 for adults in 2nd class. There are no reductions for youths or seniors, and the deal generally isn't as good a value as the Eurodomino pass.

If your trip will encompass all three Low Countries, the Benelux Pass is useful as it covers Belgium and Luxembourg in addition to the Netherlands. The pass is good for any five days in one month and includes a substantial Eurostar discount if you are travelling from the UK. In 2nd class it costs UK£114/86 for adults/under 26s. A 1st-class version costs 50% more for adults and there's no age discount.

Inter-Rail passes are good for people who can show they have lived in Europe

for at least six months. A 2nd-class pass covering the Netherlands, Belgium, Luxembourg and France costs UK£219/149 for adult/under 26 for unlimited travel during 22 days.

All of the above passes can be bought from the UK's **International Rail** (☎ 0196-2773646; www.international-rail.com).

Outside Europe the Eurailpass is heavily marketed. Good for 17 countries, it's more than overkill if you're just visiting the Netherlands or even Benelux. A 15-day pass costs US$414 for youths in 2nd class. Adults pay US$498, but only 1st-class travel with at least one other adult (who pays the same price). You can buy these at travel agents or **Europe Rail** (www.europerail.com), an international sales arm of the French railways.

Treintaxi

More than 100 train stations offer an excellent *treintaxi* (train taxi) service that takes you to/from the station within a limited area. This costs €3.80 per person per ride at a train-station counter or ticketing machine, or €4.80 direct from the driver. The service operates daily from 7am (from 8am Sunday and public holidays) till the last train. There's usually a special call box outside near the normal taxi rank.

These are special taxis and it's a shared service – the driver determines the route and the ride might take a bit longer than with a normal taxi, but it's usually much cheaper. Ask the counter operator or taxi driver for a pamphlet listing all participating stations and the relevant phone numbers for bookings. There's also a central **information number** (☎ 0900-8734682).

The *treintaxi* service is handy for reaching places far from stations that don't have frequent bus services. Unfortunately some major stations (Amsterdam CS, Den Haag CS or HS, Rotterdam CS) are excluded.

Health

Travel health depends on your predeparture preparations, your daily healthcare while travelling and how you handle any medical problem that does develop. For the Netherlands, peace of mind is the first thing to pack as healthcare and medical facilities are generally excellent.

BEFORE YOU GO

Prevention is the key to staying healthy while abroad. A little planning before departure, particularly for pre-existing illnesses will save trouble later: see your dentist before a long trip; carry a spare pair of contact lenses and glasses; and take your optical prescription with you. Bring medications in their original, clearly labelled, containers. A signed and dated letter from your physician describing your medical conditions and medications, including generic names, is also a good idea. If carrying syringes or needles, be sure to have a physician's letter documenting their medical necessity.

INSURANCE

If you're an EU citizen, an E111 form, available from health centres or, in the UK, post offices, covers you for most medical care. The E111 will not cover you for non-emergencies or emergency repatriation home. Citizens from other countries should find out if there is a reciprocal arrangement for free medical care between their country and the country visited. If you do need health insurance, make sure you get a policy that covers you for the worst possible scenario, such as an accident requiring an emergency flight home. Find out in advance if your insurance plan will make payments directly to providers or reimburse you later for overseas health expenditures.

RECOMMENDED VACCINATIONS

No jabs are required to travel to the Netherlands. The World Health Organization (WHO) recommends that all travellers should be covered for diphtheria, tetanus, measles, mumps, rubella and polio, as well as Hepatitis B, regardless of their destination. Since most vaccines don't produce immunity until at least two weeks after they're given, visit a physician at least 6 weeks before departure.

ON-LINE RESOURCES

The WHO's publication *International Travel and Health* is revised annually and is available on line at www.who.int/ith/. Other useful websites include www.mdtravelhealth.com (travelhealth recommendations for every country; updated daily), www.fitfortravel .nhs.uk (general travel advice for the layman), www.ageconcern.org.uk (advice on travel for the elderly) and www.mariestopes.org.uk (information on women's health and contraception).

NATIONAL HEALTH WEBSITES

It's usually a good idea to consult your government's travel health website before departure, if one is available:

Australia: www.dfat.gov.au/travel/
Canada: www.travelhealth.gc.ca
United Kingdom: www.doh.gov.uk/travel advice/
United States: www.cdc.gov/travel/

FURTHER READING

Health Advice for Travellers (currently called the 'T6' leaflet) is an annually updated leaflet by the Department of Health in the UK available free in post offices. It contains some general information, legally required and recommended vaccines for different countries, reciprocal health agreements and an E111 application form. Lonely Planet's *Travel with Children* includes advice on travel health for younger children. Other recommended references include *Traveller's Health* by Dr Richard Dawood (published by Oxford University Press) and *The Traveller's Good Health Guide* by Ted Lankester (published by Sheldon Press).

IN TRANSIT

DEEP VEIN THROMBOSIS

Blood clots may form in the legs during plane flights, chiefly because of prolonged immobility. The longer the flight, the greater the risk. The chief symptom of deep vein thrombosis (DVT) is swelling or pain of the foot, ankle or calf, usually – but not always – on just one side. When a blood clot travels to the lungs, it may cause chest pain and breathing difficulties. Travellers with any of these symptoms should immediately seek medical attention.

To prevent the development of DVT on long flights you should walk about the cabin, contract the leg muscles while sitting, drink plenty of fluids and avoid alcohol and tobacco.

JET LAG & MOTION SICKNESS

To avoid jet lag (which is common when crossing more than five time zones), try drinking plenty of non-alchoholic fluids and eating light meals. Upon arrival, get exposure to natural sunlight and readjust your schedule (for meals, sleep and so on) to the time zone you're in as soon as possible.

Antihistamines such as dimenhydrinate (Dramamine) and meclizine (Antivert, Bonine) are usually the first choice for treating motion sickness. A herbal alternative is ginger.

IN THE NETHERLANDS

AVAILABILITY & COST OF HEALTHCARE

Good healthcare is readily available and for minor self-limiting illnesses pharmacists can give valuable advice and sell over-the-counter medication. They can also advise when more specialised help is required and point you in the right direction. The standard of dental care is usually good, however it is sensible to have a dental checkup before a long trip.

TRAVELLER'S DIARRHOEA

If you develop diarrhoea, be sure to drink plenty of fluids, preferably an oral rehydration solution, eg dioralyte. A few loose stools don't require treatment but, if you start passing more than four or five stools a day, you should start taking an antibiotic (usually a quinolone drug) and an antidiarrhoeal agent (such as loperamide). If diarrhoea is bloody, persists for more than 72 hours or is accompanied by fever, shaking, chills or severe abdominal pain you should seek medical attention.

ENVIRONMENTAL HAZARDS
Heatstroke

Heat exhaustion (yes, it can happen!) occurs following excessive fluid loss with inadequate replacement of fluids and salt. Symptoms include headache, dizziness and tiredness. Dehydration is already happening by the time you feel thirsty – aim to drink sufficient water to produce pale, diluted urine. To treat heat exhaustion, replace fluids with water and/or fruit juice, and cool the body with cold water and fans. Treat salt loss with salty fluids such as soup or bouillon, or add a little more table salt to foods than usual.

Heat stroke is much more serious, resulting in irrational and hyperactive behaviour and eventually loss of consciousness and death. Rapid cooling by spraying the body with water and fanning is ideal. Emergency fluid and electrolyte replacement by intravenous drip is recommended.

Insect Bites & Stings

Mosquitoes are found in most parts of Europe and are well represented in the Netherlands. They may not carry malaria but can cause irritation and infected bites. Use a DEET-based insect repellant.

Bees and wasps only cause real problems to those with a severe allergy (anaphylaxis.) If you have a severe allergy to bee or wasp stings carry an 'epipen' or similar adrenaline injection.

Bed bugs lead to very itchy lumpy bites. Spraying the mattress with crawling insect killer after changing bedding will get rid of them.

Scabies are tiny mites which live in the skin, particularly between the fingers. They cause an intensely itchy rash. Scabies is easily treated with lotion from a pharmacy; other members of the household also need treating to avoid spreading scabies between asymptomatic carriers.

LYME DISEASE

Ticks can carry a serious bacterial infection called Lyme Disease. A bite from an infected tick may produce a red welt and a 'bull's eye' around the spot within a day or two. Mild flu-like symptoms (headache, nausea etc) may follow or may not, but antibiotics are needed to avoid the next stage of of the illness – pain in the joints, fatigue, and fever. If left untreated, Lyme disease can cause mental and muscular deterioration.

The most risky areas in the Netherlands are in the wooded areas of Friesland, Groningen and Drenthe, Hoge Veluwe National Park, parts of Zeeland and on the Wadden Islands. The best prevention is to wear clothing that covers your arms and legs when walking in grassy or wooded areas, apply insect repellent containing DEET and check your body for ticks after outdoor activities.

If a tick has attached itself to you, use tweezers to pull it straight out – do not twist it. Do not touch the tick with a hot object like a cigarette because this can cause the tick to regurgitate noxious saliva into the wound. And do not rub oil or petroleum jelly on it.

TRAVELLING WITH CHILDREN

All travellers with children should know how to treat minor ailments and when to seek medical treatment. Make sure the children are up-to-date with routine vaccinations, and discuss possible travel vaccines well before departure as some vaccines are not suitable for children under a year.

In hot, moist conditions, any wound or break in the skin is likely to let in infection. The area should be cleaned and kept dry.

Remember to avoid contaminated food and water. If your child has vomiting or diarrhoea, lost fluid and salts must be replaced. It may be helpful to take rehydration powders for reconstituting with boiled water.

Children should be encouraged to avoid and mistrust any dogs or other mammals because of the risk of rabies and other diseases. Any bite, scratch or lick from a warm blooded, furry animal should immediately be thoroughly cleaned. If there is any possibility that the animal is infected with rabies, immediate medical assistance should be sought.

WOMEN'S HEALTH

Emotional stress, exhaustion and travelling through different time zones can all contribute to an upset in the menstrual pattern. If using oral contraceptives, remember some antibiotics, diarrhoea and vomiting can stop the pill from working and lead to the risk of pregnancy – remember to take condoms with you just in case. Time zones, gastrointestinal upsets and antibiotics do not affect injectable contraception.

Travelling during pregnancy is usually possible but there are important things to consider. Always seek a medical check-up before planning your trip. The most risky times for travel are during the first 12 weeks of pregnancy and after 30 weeks. Illness during pregnancy can be more severe so take special care to avoid contaminated food and water and insect and animal bites. A general rule is to only use vaccines, like other medications, if the risk of infection is substantial. Remember that the baby could be in serious danger if you were to contract infections such as typhoid or hepatitis. Some vaccines are best avoided; for example, those that contain live organisms. However, there is very little evidence that damage has been caused to an unborn child when vaccines have been given to a woman very early in pregnancy before the pregnancy was suspected. Take written records of the pregnancy with you. Ensure your insurance policy covers pregnancy delivery and postnatal care, but remember insurance policies are only as good as the facilities available. Always consult your doctor before you travel.

SEXUAL HEALTH

Emergency contraception is most effective if taken within 24 hours after unprotected sex. The International Planned Parent Federation (www.ippf.org) can advise about the availability of contraception in different countries.

When buying condoms, look for a European CE mark, which means they have been rigorously tested, and then keep them in a cool dry place or they may crack and perish. Condoms are widely available from pharmacies and vending machines in many restaurants and nightclubs.

The Rutgers Foundation manages seven regional centres in the Netherlands that provide a range of sexual and reproductive health care services. Emergency contraception can be obtained at short notice. Contact the telephone helpline at ☎ 0900-9398 (€0.50 per minute) or ☎ 030-231 34 31. The Amsterdam centre, the **Rutgershuis** (Map p82-83; ☎ 020-616 6222; Sarphatistraat 618), is open for walk-in visitors.

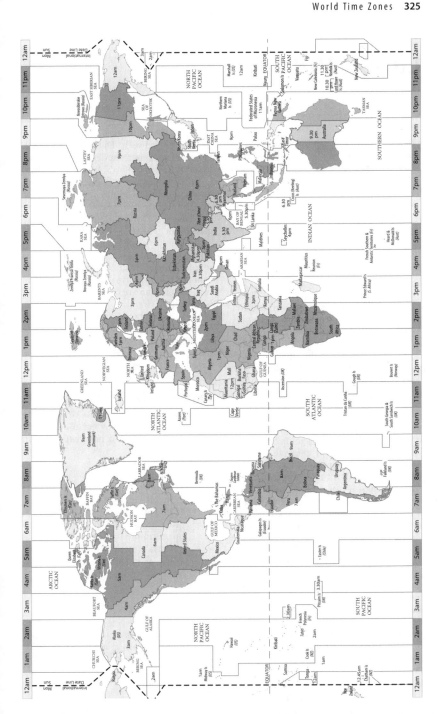

Language

Almost every Dutch person from age five onwards seems to speak English, often very well and better than you'll ever learn Dutch, so why bother? That's a good question because you'll rarely get the opportunity to practise: your Dutch acquaintances will launch into English, probably because they relish the opportunity to practise their language skills. Nevertheless, a few words in Dutch show goodwill, which is always appreciated, and you might even get to understand a bit more of what's going on around you. The phrase *Spreekt u Engels?* (Do you speak English?) before launching into English is best used with older people. The young, thanks to years of English in school, as well as exposure to vast amounts of English language media (movies are usually subtitled rather than dubbed), will likely look at you like you've gone around the bend if you ask about their English skills.

The people of the northern Friesland province speak their own language. Although Frisian is actually the nearest relative of the English language, you won't be able to make much sense of it, and you'll have to go to a small-town shop or a farm to really hear it anyway. It's not the dominant language in the province, but most of the locals know some as a sign of cultural pride.

Most English speakers use the term 'Dutch' to describe the language spoken in the Netherlands and 'Flemish' for that spoken in the northern half of Belgium. Both are in fact the same language, called Netherlandic *(Nederlands)* or simply, Dutch. The differences between Dutch and Flemish *(Vlaams)* are similar in degree to those between British and North American English.

Dutch nouns come in one of three genders: masculine, feminine (both with *de* for 'the') and neuter (with *het* for 'the'). Where English uses 'a' or 'an', Dutch uses *een*, regardless of gender.

There's also a polite and an informal version of the English 'you'. The polite form is *u* (pronounced with the lips pursed and rounded), the informal is *je*. As a general rule, people who are older than you should be addressed as *u*.

For useful information on food and dining out, including Dutch words and phrases, see the Food & Drink chapter on p62. For more extensive coverage of Dutch than we have space for here, get a copy of Lonely Planet's *Europe phrasebook*.

PRONUNCIATION

Note that the following lists describe the pronunciation of the letters used in our guides to pronunciation, not written Dutch.

Vowels

a	as the 'u' in 'run'
e	as in 'bet'
i	as in 'hit'
o	as in 'pot'
u	pronounced with pursed, rounded lips, as in the French *tu*
ə	a neutral vowel, as the 'a' in 'ago'
aa	as the 'a' in 'father'
ee	as in 'eel'
oa	as in 'boat'
oo	as in 'zoo'
ow	as in 'cow'
ay	as in 'say'
əy	similar to the sound of 'er-y' in 'her year' (with no 'r' sound) or, if you're familiar with it, as the 'eui' in the French *fauteuil*
eu	similar the 'er' in 'her', but with no 'r' sound

WHAT'S IN A NAME?

Dutch, like German, strings words together, which can baffle a foreigner trying to decipher (let alone remember) street names. *Eerste Goudsbloemdwarsstraat* (First Marigold Cross Street) is a good example! Chopping a seemingly endless name into its separate components might help a bit. The following terms appear frequently in street names and on signs:

baan – path, way
binnen – inside, inner
bloem – flower
brug – bridge
buiten – outside, outer
dijk – dyke
dwars – transverse
eiland – island
gracht – canal
groot – great, large, big
haven – harbour
hoek – corner
huis – house
kade – quay
kapel – chapel
kerk – church
klein – minor, small
laan – avenue
markt – market

molen – (wind)mill
nieuw – new
noord – north
oost – east
oud – old
plein – square
poort – city gate, gate
sloot – ditch
sluis – sluice, lock
steeg – alley
straat – street
toren – tower
veld – field
(burg)wal – (fortified) embankment
weg – road
west – west
wijk – district
zuid – south

Consonants

Most consonants in the pronunciation guides are similar to their English counterparts (**b**, **d**, **f**, **g**, **h**, **k**, **l**, **m**, **n**, **p**, **s**, **t**, **v**, **w**, **z**). A few trickier sounds are listed below:

ch	as in 'chip'
g	as in 'go'
kh	as the 'ch' in the Scottish *loch*; it's like a hiss produced by tightening the tongue against top ot the throat
ng	as in 'ring'
r	trilled, either with the tongue forward or held back restricting the flow of air in the throat
y	as in 'yes'
zh	as the 's' in 'pleasure'

ACCOMMODATION

I'm looking for a ...	*Ik ben op zoek naar een ...*	ik ben op zook naar ən ...
camping ground	*camping*	kem·ping
guesthouse	*pension*	pen·syon
hotel	*hotel*	ho·tel
youth hostel	*jeugdherberg*	yeukht·her·berkh

Where is a cheap hotel?
Waar is een goedkoop hotel?
waar is ən khoot·koap ho·tel

What is the address?
Wat is het adres?
wat is hət a·dres

Could you write the address, please?
Kunt u het adres opschrijven alstublieft?
kunt u hət a·dres op·skhray·van als·tu·bleeft

Do you have any rooms available?
Heeft u een kamer vrij?
hayft u ən kaa·mər vray

I'd like (a) ...	*Ik wil graag een ...*	ik wil khraakh ən ...
bed	*bed*	bet
single room	*eenpersoons-kamer*	ayn·pər·soans·kaa·mər
double room	*tweepersoons-kamer*	tway·pər·soans·kaa·mər
room with two beds	*kamer met twee bedden*	kaa·mər met tway be·dən
room with a bathroom	*kamer met badkamer*	kaa·mər met bat·kaa·mər
to share a dorm	*bed op een slaapzaal*	bet op ən slaap·zaal

How much is it ...?	*Hoeveel is het ...?*	hoo·vayl is hət ...?
per night	*per nacht*	pər nakht
per person	*per persoon*	pər per·soan

Is breakfast included?
Is ontbijt inbegrepen?
is ont·bayt in·bə·khray·pən

LANGUAGE

MAKING A RESERVATION
(for phone or written requests)

To ...	*Tot ...*
From ...	*Van ...*
Date	*Datum*
I'd like to book ...	*Ik wil ... reserveren.* (see the list under 'Accommodation' for bed and room options)
in the name of ...	*op naam van ...*
for the night/s of ...	*voor de nacht(en) van ...*
credit card	*kredietkaart*
number	*nummer*
expiry date	*vervaldag*
Please confirm availability and price.	*Gelieve de prijs en beschikbaarheid te bevestigen.*

May I see the room?
Mag ik de kamer zien?   makh ik də *kaa·*mər zeen
Where is the bathroom?
Waar is de badkamer?   waar is də *bat·*kaa·mər
I'm leaving today.
Ik vertrek vandaag.   ik vər·*trek* van·*daakh*
We're leaving today.
Wij vertrekken vandaag.   way vər·*tre·*kən van·*daakh*

CONVERSATION & ESSENTIALS

Hello.
Dag/Hallo.   dakh/ha·*loa*
Goodbye.
Dag.   dakh
Yes.
Ja.   yaa
No.
Nee.   nay
Please.
Alstublieft. (pol)   als·tu·*bleeft*
Alsjeblieft. (inf)   a·shə·*bleeft*
Thank you (very much).
Dank u (wel). (pol)   *dangk* u (wel)
Dank je (wel). (inf)   *dangk* yə (wel)
Thanks.
Bedankt. (pol or inf)   bə·*dangt*
That's fine/You're welcome.
Graag gedaan.   khraakh khə·*daan*
Excuse me.
Pardon.   par·*don*
or *Excuseer mij.*   eks·ku·*zayr* may
I'm sorry.
Sorry/Excuses.   so·ree/eks·ku·zəs

How are you?
Hoe gaat het met u/jou? (pol/inf)   hoo khaat hət met u/yow
I'm fine, thanks.
Goed, bedankt.   khoot, bə·*dangt*
See you soon.
Tot ziens.   tot zeens
What's your name?
Hoe heet u? (pol)   hoo hayt u
Hoe heet je? (inf)   hoo hayt yə
My name is ...
Ik heet ...   ik hayt ...
Where are you from?
Waar komt u vandaan? (pol)   waar komt u van·*daan*
Waar kom je vandaan? (inf)   waar kom yə van·*daan*
I'm from ...
Ik kom uit ...   ik kom əyt ...
I (don't) like.
Ik hou (niet) van ...   ik how (neet) van ...
Just a minute.
Een moment.   ən mo·*ment*

DIRECTIONS

Where is ...?
Waar is ...?   waar is ...
How do I get to ...?
Hoe kom ik bij ...?   hoo kom ik bay ...
(Go) straight ahead.
(Ga) rechtdoor.   (khaa) rekht·*doar*
(Turn) left.
(Ga) naar links.   (khaa) naar lings
(Turn) right.
(Ga) naar rechts.   (khaa) naar rekhs
at the corner
op de hoek   op də hook
at the traffic lights
bij de verkeerslichten   bay də vər·*kayrs·*likh·tən

SIGNS

Ingang	Entrance
Uitgang	Exit
Informatie/Inlichtingen	Information
Open	Open
Gesloten	Closed
Verboden/Niet Toegelaten	Prohibited
Kamers Vrij	Rooms Available
Vol	Full/No Vacancies
Politiebureau	Police Station
WC's/Toiletten	Toilets
Heren	Men
Dames	Women

What street/road is this?
Welke straat/weg is dit?   wel·kə straat/wekh is dit?

behind	*achter*	akh·tər
in front of	*voor*	vor
far (from)	*ver (van)*	ver (van)
near (to)	*dichtbij*	dikht·bay
opposite	*tegenover*	tay·khən·oa·vər

beach	*strand*	strant
bridge	*brug*	brukh
castle	*kasteel*	kas·tayl
cathedral	*kathedraal*	ka·tay·draal
island	*eiland*	ay·lant
main square	*stadsplein*	stats·playn
market	*markt*	markt
old city	*oude stad*	ow·də stat
palace	*paleis*	pa·lays
ruins	*ruines*	rwee·nəs
sea	*zee*	zay
square	*plein*	playn
tower	*toren*	toa·rən

EMERGENCIES

Help!
Help!   help

There's been an accident.
Er is een ongeluk   ər is ən on·khə·luk
gebeurd.   khə·beurt

I'm lost.
Ik ben de weg kwijt.   ik ben də wekh kwayt

Go away!
Ga weg!   kha wekh

Call ...!	*Haal ...*	haal ...
a doctor	*een doktor*	ən dok·tər
the police	*de politie*	də po·leet·see

HEALTH

I need a doctor.	*Ik heb een dokter*	ik hep ən dok·tər
	nodig.	noa·dikh
Where is the	*Waar is het*	waar is hət
hospital?	*ziekenhuis?*	zee·kən·həys
I'm ill.	*Ik ben ziek.*	ik ben zeek
It hurts here.	*Het doet hier pijn.*	hət doot heer payn

I'm ...	*Ik ben ...*	ik ben ...
asthmatic	*asthmatisch*	ast·maa·tis
diabetic	*suikerziek*	səy·kər·zeek

I have epilepsy.
Ik heb epilepsie.   ik hep ay·pee·lep·see

I'm allergic	*Ik ben allergisch*	ik ben a·ler·khis
to ...	*voor...*	voar ...
antibiotics	*antibiotica*	an·tee·bee·o·tee·ka
aspirin	*aspirine*	as·pee·ree·nə
penicillin	*penicilline*	pay·nee·see·lee·nə
bees	*bijen*	bay·ən
nuts	*noten*	noa·tən

antiseptic	*ontsmettings-*	ont·sme·tings·
	middel	mi·dəl
aspirin	*aspirine*	as·pee·ree·nə
condoms	*condooms*	kon·doams
constipation	*verstopping*	vər·sto·ping
contraceptive	*anticonceptie-*	an·tee·kon·sep·see·
	middel	mi·dəl
diarrhoea	*diarree*	dee·a·ray
medicine	*geneesmiddel/*	khə·nays·mi·dəl/
	medicijn	may·dee·sayn
sunscreen	*zonnebrandolie*	zo·nə·brant·oa·lee
tampons	*tampons*	tam·pons
nausea	*misselijkheid*	mi·sə·lək·hayt

LANGUAGE DIFFICULTIES

Do you speak English?
Spreekt u Engels?   spraykt u eng·əls

Does anyone here speak English?
Spreekt er hier   spraykt ər heer
iemand Engels?   ee·mant eng·əls

How do you say ... in Dutch?
Hoe zeg je ...   hoo zekh yə ...
in het Nederlands?   in hət nay·dər·lants

What does ... mean?
Wat betekent ...?   wat bə·tay·kənt ...

I (don't) understand.
Ik begrijp het (niet).   ik bə·khrayp hət (neet)

Please write it down.
Schrijf het alstublieft op.   skhrayf hət als·tu·bleeft op

Can you show me (on the map)?
Kunt u het mij tonen   kunt u hət may toa·nən
(op de kaart)?   (op də kaart)

NUMBERS

0	*nul*	nul
1	*één*	ayn
2	*twee*	tway
3	*drie*	dree
4	*vier*	veer
5	*vijf*	vayf
6	*zes*	zes
7	*zeven*	zay·vən
8	*acht*	akht
9	*negen*	nay·khən
10	*tien*	teen
11	*elf*	elf

LANGUAGE

12	*twaalf*	*twaalf*
13	*dertien*	*der·teen*
14	*veertien*	*vayr·teen*
15	*vijftien*	*vayf·teen*
16	*zestien*	*zes·teen*
17	*zeventien*	*zay·vən·teen*
18	*achttien*	*akh·teen*
19	*negentien*	*nay·khən·teen*
20	*twintig*	*twin·təkh*
21	*eenentwintig*	*ayn·en·twin·təkh*
22	*tweeëntwintig*	*tway·en·twin·təkh*
30	*dertig*	*der·təkh*
40	*veertig*	*vayr·təkh*
50	*vijftig*	*vayf·təkh*
60	*zestig*	*zes·təkh*
70	*zeventig*	*zay·vən·təkh*
80	*tachtig*	*takh·təkh*
90	*negentig*	*nay·khən·təkh*
100	*honderd*	*hon·dərt*
1000	*duizend*	*dəy·zənt*
2000	*tweeduizend*	*twee·dəy·zənt*

PAPERWORK

name	*naam*	naam
nationality	*nationaliteit*	na·syo·na·lee·*tayt*
date of birth	*geboortedatum*	kha·*boar*·tə·daa·təm
place of birth	*geboorteplaats*	kha·*boar*·tə·plaats
sex (gender)	*geslacht*	khə·*slakht*
passport	*paspoort*	*pas*·poart
visa	*visum*	*vee*·zum

SHOPPING & SERVICES

I'd like to buy ...
Ik wil graag ... kopen. ik wil khraakh ... *koa*·pən
How much is it?
Hoeveel is het? hoo·vayl is hət?
I don't like it.
Ik vind het niet leuk. ik vint hət neet leuk
May I look at it?
Mag ik het zien? makh ik hət zeen
Can I try it (on)?
Kan ik het eens proberen? kan ik hət ayns pro·*bay*·rən
I'm just looking.
Ik kijk alleen maar. ik kayk a·*layn* maar
It's cheap.
Het is goedkoop. hət is khoot·*koap*
It's too expensive (for me).
Het is (mij) te duur. hət is (may) tə dur
I'll take it.
Ik neem het. ik naym hət

Do you accept ...? *Accepteert u ...* ak·sep·*tayrt* u ...
  credit cards *kredietkaarten* kray·*deet*·kaar·tən
  travellers cheques *reischeques* *rays*·sheks

more	*meer*	mayr
less	*minder*	*min*·dər
smaller	*kleiner*	*klay*·nər
bigger	*groter*	*khroa*·tər

I'm looking for ... *Ik ben op zoek naar ...* ik ben op zook naar ...
  the bank *de bank* də bangk
  a bookshop *een boekenwinkel* ən *boo*·kən·win·kəl
  the chemist/ pharmacy *de drogist/ apotheek* də dro·*khist* a·po·*tayk*
  the city centre *het stadscentrum* hət *stat*·sen·trum
  a clothing store *een kledingzaak* ən *klay*·ding·zaak
  the church *de kerk* də kerk
  the ... embassy *de ... ambassade* də ... am·ba·*saa*·də
  the exchange office *het wisselkantoor* hət *wi*·səl·kan·toar
  a laundry *een wasserette* ən wa·sə·*re*·tə
  the market *de markt* də markt
  the museum *het museum* hət mu·*say*·əm
  the newsagency *de krantenwinkel* də *kran*·tən·wing·kəl
  the post office *het postkantoor* hət *post*·kan·toar
  a public toilet *een openbaar toilet* ən *oa*·pən·baar twa·*let*
  the stationers *de kantoorboekhandel* də kan·*toar*·book·han·dəl
  a supermarket *een supermarkt* ən *su*·pər·mart
  the tourist office *de VVV* də vay·vay·*vay*

What time does it open/close?
Hoe laat opent/ sluit het? hoo laat *oa*·pənt/ sləyt hət

I want to change ... *Ik wil ... wisselen.* ik wil ... *wi*·sə·lən
  money *geld* khelt
  travellers cheques *reischeques* *rays*·sheks

TIME & DATES

What time is it?
Hoe laat is het? hoo laat is hət
It's (8 o'clock).
Het is (acht uur). hət is (akht ur)

in the morning	*'s morgens*	*smor*·ghəns
in the afternoon	*'s middags*	*smi*·dakhs
in the evening	*'s avonds*	*saa*·vonts
When?	*Wanneer?*	wa·*nayr*
today	*vandaag*	van·*daakh*
tomorrow	*morgen*	*mor*·khən
yesterday	*gisteren*	*khis*·tə·rən

Monday	*maandag*	*maan*-dakh
Tuesday	*dinsdag*	*dins*-dakh
Wednesday	*woensdag*	*woons*-dakh
Thursday	*donderdag*	*don-dər*-dakh
Friday	*vrijdag*	*vray*-dakh
Saturday	*zaterdag*	*zaa*-tər-dakh
Sunday	*zondag*	*zon*-dakh

January	*januari*	*ya*-nu-aa-ree
February	*februari*	*fay*-bru-aa-ree
March	*maart*	maart
April	*april*	a-*pril*
May	*mei*	may
June	*juni*	*yu*-nee
July	*juli*	*yu*-lee
August	*augustus*	ow-*gus*-tus
September	*september*	sep-*tem*-bər
October	*oktober*	ok-*to*-bər
November	*november*	no-*vem*-bər
December	*december*	day-*sem*-bər

TRANSPORT
Public Transport
What time does the ... leave?
Hoe laat vertrekt ...? hoo laat vər-*trekt* ...
What time does the ... arrive?
Hoe laat komt ... aan? hoo laat komt ... aan

boat	*de boot*	də boat
bus	*de bus*	də bus
plane	*het vliegtuig*	hət *fleekh*-təykh
train	*de trein*	də trayn
tram	*de tram*	də trem

Where is ...?	*Waar is ...?*	waar is ...
the airport	*de luchthaven*	də *lukht*-haa-vən
the bus stop	*de bushalte*	də *bus*-hal-tə
the metro station	*het metro-station*	hət *may*-tro-sta-syon
the train station	*het (trein)-station*	hət (trayn) sta-*syon*
the tram stop	*de tramhalte*	də *trem*-hal-tə

I'd like ... ticket.	*Ik wil graag ...*	ik wil khraakh ...
a one-way	*een enkele reis*	ən *eng*-kə-lə rays
a return	*een retourticket*	ən rə-*toor*-ti-ket
a 1st-class	*eerste klas*	*ayr*-stə klas
a 2nd-class	*tweede klas*	*tway*-də klas

I want to go to ...
Ik wil naar ... gaan. ik wil naar ... khaan
The train has been cancelled/delayed.
De trein is afgelast/vertraagd. də trayn is af-*khə*-last/vər-*traakht*

| **the first** | *de eerste* | də *ayr*-stə |
| **the last** | *de laatste* | də *laat*-stə |

platform	*spoor/perron*	spoar/pe-*ron*
number	*nummer*	*nu*-mər
ticket office	*loket*	*loa*-ket
timetable	*dienstregeling*	*deenst*-ray-khə-ling

Private Transport

I'd like to hire a/an ...	*Ik wil graag een ... huren.*	ik wil khraakh ən ... *hu*-rən
bicycle	*fiets*	feets
car	*auto*	*ow*-to
motorbike	*motorfiets*	*mo*-tər-feets

ROAD SIGNS

Afrit/Uitrit	Exit (from freeway)
Eenrichtingsverkeer	One Way
Gevaar	Danger
Ingang	Entrance
Omleiding	Detour
Oprit	Entrance (to freeway)
Tol	Toll
Uitgang	Exit
Veboden Toegang	No Entry
Verboden in te Halen/ Inhaalverbod	No Overtaking
Verboden te Parkeren/ Parkeerverbod	No Parking
Vertragen	Slow Down
Voorrang Verlenen	Give Way
Vrij Houden	Keep Clear

Is this the road to ...?
Is dit de weg naar ...? is dit də wekh naar ...
Where's a service station?
Waar is er een benzinestation? waar is ər ən ben-*zee*-nə-sta-syon
Please fill it up.
Vol alstublieft. vol als-tu-*bleeft*
I'd like (30) litres.
Ik wil graag (dertig) liter. ik wil khraakh (*der*-tikh) *lee*-tər
diesel
diesel *dee*-zəl
leaded petrol
gelode benzine khə-*lo*-də ben-*zee*-nə
unleaded petrol
loodvrije benzine loat-*vray*-ə ben-*zee*-nə
(How long) Can I park here?
(Hoe lang) Kan ik hier parkeren? (hoo lang) kan ik heer par-*kay*-rən
Where do I pay?
Waar kan ik betalen? waar kan ik be-*taa*-lən
I need a mechanic.
Ik heb een mecanicien nodig. ik hep een may-ka-nee-*sye* *noa*-dikh

The car/motorbike has broken down (at ...).
Ik heb auto/motorfiets — ik heb *ow*·to/*moa*·tər·feets
pech (in ...) — pekh (in ...)
The car/motorbike won't start.
De auto/motorfiets — də *ow*·to/*moa*·tər·feets
wil niet starten. — wil neet *star*·tən
I have a flat tyre.
Ik heb een lekke band. — ik heb ən *le*·kə bant
I've run out of petrol.
Ik zit zonder benzine. — ik zit *zon*·dər ben·*zee*·nə
I've had an accident.
Ik heb een ongeluk gehad. — ik hep ən *on*·khə·luk khə·*hat*

TRAVEL WITH CHILDREN
I need (a/an) ... *Ik heb ... nodig.* ik hep ... *noa*·dikh
Do you have *Heeft u ...?* hayft u ...
(a/an) ...?
  car baby seat *een autozitje* ən *ow*·to·zi·chə
    voor de baby voar də *bay*·bee
  child-minding *een oppasdienst* ən op·pas·*deenst*
  service

children's menu *een kindermenu* ən *kin*·dər·mə·nu
(disposable) *(wegwerp-)* (wekh·werp·)
  nappies/diapers *luiers* *lə*y·ərs
formula (milk) *melkpoeder (voor* *melk*·poo·dər (voar
  zuigflessen) *zə*ykh·fle·sən)
(English- *een babysit (die* ən *bay*·bee·sit (dee
  speaking) *Engels spreekt)* eng·əls spraykt)
  babysitter
highchair *een kinderstoel* ən *kin*·der·stool
potty *een potje* ən *po*·chə
stroller *een wandel-* ən *wan*·dəl·
  wagen waa·khən

Is there a baby change room?
Kan ik hier ergens — kan ik heer er·khəns
de baby verschonen? — də *bay*·bee vər·*skhoa*·nən
Do you mind if I breastfeed here?
Stoort het u als ik — stoart hət u als ik
hier de borst geef? — heer də *borst* gayf
Are children allowed?
Zijn kinderen toegelaten? zayn *kin*·də·rən *too*·khə·la·tən

Also available from Lonely Planet:
Europe phrasebook

Glossary

(See also the Language chapter for a list of terms commonly encountered in street names and sights.)

abdij – abbey
amsterdammertje – phallic-shaped posts, about knee-high, lining streets of inner Amsterdam
ansichtkaart – postcard
apotheek – chemist/pharmacy

bad– bath, pool
beiaard – carillon (set of tuned church bells that chime automatically)
benzine – petrol/gasoline
bevrijding – liberation
bezet – occupied
bezoeker – visitor
bibliotheek – library
borrel(tje) – general term for a strong alcoholic drink , spirit
bos – woods, forest
boterham – sandwich
botter – type of 19th-century fishing boat
brandweer – fire brigade/department
broodje – breadroll (with filling)
bruin café – brown café; traditional Dutch pub
buurt – neighbourhood

café – pub, bar; also known as *kroeg*
coffeeshop – café authorised to sell cannabis
CS – Centraal Station

dagschotel – daily special in restaurants
douche – shower
drop – salted or sweet liquorice

eetcafé – cafés serving meals

fierljeppen – see *polsstokspringen*
fiets – bicycle
fietsenstalling – secure bicycle storage
fietspad – bicycle path

gasthuis – hospice, hospital (old)
gemeente – municipal, municipality
gevel – gable, façade
gezellig – convivial, cosy

GG&GD – Municipal Medical & Health Service
GVB – Gemeentevervoerbedrijf (Amsterdam municipal transport authority)
GWK – Grenswisselkantoor; official money exchange offices

hal – hall, entrance hall
haven – port
herberg – hostel
hervormd – reformed (as in church)
hof – courtyard
hofje – almshouse or series of buildings around a small courtyard, also known as Begijnhof
hoofd – main

jacht – yacht
jenever – Dutch gin; also spelled g*enever*

kaas – cheese
kantoor – office
kassa – cashier, check-out
koffiehuis – espresso bar (as distinct from a *coffeeshop*)
klompen – clogs
klooster – cloister, religious house
koningin – queen
koninklijk – royal
korfbal – a cross between netball, volleyball and basketball
krakers – squatters
kunst – art
kwartier – quarter

loodvrij – unleaded petrol/gasoline
luchthaven – airport

markt – town square
meer – lake
molen – windmill

NS – Nederlandse Spoorwegen; national railway company

paleis – palace
polder – area of drained land
polsstokspringen – pole-jumping over canals (Frisian: *fierljeppen*)
postbus – post office box
postzegel – postage stamp

raam – window
Randstad – literally 'rim-city'; the urban agglomeration including Amsterdam, Utrecht, Rotterdam and Den Haag
regen – rain
Rijk, het – State, the
rondleiding – guided tour

schaap – sheep
scheepvaart – shipping
schilder – artist, painter
schouwburg – theatre
schuilkerk – clandestine church
sluis – lock (for boats/ships)
spionnetje – outside mirror allowing a house occupant to see who's at the door downstairs
spoor – platform (in train station)
stadhouder – stadholder, or chief magistrate
stadhuis – town hall
stedelijk – civic, municipal
steeg– alley, lane
stichting – foundation, institute
straat– street, road
strand – beach
strippenkaart – punchable multi-ticket used on public transport

terp – mounds of packed mud in Friesland that served as a refuge during floods
treintaxi – taxi especially for train passengers
tuin – garden
tulp – tulip
turf – peat

veer/veerboot – ferry
verzet – resistance
Vlaams – Flemish
voorlichting – information
VVV – tourist office

waag – old weigh house
wadlopen – mud-walking
wasserette/wassalon – laundrette
weeshuis – orphanage
weg– road, street
werf – wharf, shipyard
wielklem – wheel clamp attached to illegally parked vehicles
windmolen – windmill
winkel – shop

zaal – hall
zee – sea
ziekenhuis – hospital

Behind the Scenes

THIS BOOK
This is the 2nd edition of *The Netherlands*, written by Jeremy Gray and Reuben Acciano. The 1st edition was written by Ryan Ver Berkmoes and Jeremy Gray.

THANKS from the authors
Jeremy Gray Those deserving a warm thank you include: Mirjam Schuiling of Tourisme Recreatie Nederland; friendly staff at VVV offices on my beats; the nice drawbridge operator at Oudewater, who was full of tales; colleague Reuben Acciano for Italo-Dutch flair and being a good sport with my queries; Andy Bender for joining me on the Amsterdam club circuit; and a multitude of helpful travellers. Last but not least, I send Petra a heartfelt hug for her love and support.

Reuben Acciano Without the knowledge, honesty, faith and love of the following people, my contribution would've been impossible. To my co-author Jeremy Gray (and Petra) for your hospitality and guidance. To Ryan Ver Berkmoes, for your brilliant foundation. Had it not been for your fine work on *Netherlands 1*, I might still be crying under a *hunebed* (or a tractor) in Drenthe now.

To my family – Tony, Vickie, Gabrielle and Chiara Acciano; thanks for this life. To my extended family in the Netherlands, whose indulgence brought me humility, comfort, joy and calories. In Breda: Fotis and Marielle Varetidis (my saviours!), Anke and Edward, Lilian and Johan, Tante Sel and Oom Vent, Harry and Louisa and anyone I've forgotten.

In Amsterdam: Thea and Aart, Ton Selling, the divine Simone, the charming Bruno and *het duiveltje* Tobias; to Jurriaan for space to be me and my first live Ajax experience! In Heemstede: Keesje, Eva and Ivy – you do *not* suck! Thanks also to Kees and Berty Klomp and all the Haarlemmers and IJmuidenaars; to Oom Cor and Tante Mien – you are inspirational. In Groningen: the wonderful Vincent Zwiggelar and Eloise Dumaurie – three nights in Groningen, forever in my heart; the sweet Jordy Renes in Zwolle, staff at Stayokays everywhere (but particularly Rottterdam) who put me up, and put up with me.

Thanks to friends old and new: Kate (daisies in her footsteps) Aitken and dangerous Dan Herriott, Terry Hill, all the Kelly/Hill/Holiday clan, Matt Lezowski, wee Suzy Q and Nick, the Fairfield Mansion gang for overwhelming kindness and good times.

To my sparkling twin, Clancy Jones – *ik hou van jou, zus.*

And *grazie mille* to impossible, incomparable Clarabella (MK) – 'the reasons for the seasons, and the madness of the moon'.

CREDITS
Series Publishing Manager Virginia Maxwell oversaw the redevelopment of the country guides series with help from Maria Donohoe. Regional Publishing Manager Katrina Browning steered the development of this title. The series was designed by James Hardy, with mapping development by Paul Piaia. The series development

THE LONELY PLANET STORY
The story begins with a classic travel adventure: Tony and Maureen Wheeler's 1972 journey across Europe and Asia to Australia. There was no useful information about the overland trail then, so Tony and Maureen published the first Lonely Planet guidebook to meet a growing need.

From a kitchen table, Lonely Planet has grown to become the largest independent travel publisher in the world, with offices in Melbourne (Australia), Oakland (USA), London (UK) and Paris (France).

Today Lonely Planet guidebooks cover the globe. There is an ever-growing list of books and information in a variety of media. Some things haven't changed. The main aim is still to make it possible for adventurous travellers to get out there – to explore and better understand the world.

At Lonely Planet we believe travellers can make a positive contribution to the countries they visit – if they respect their host communities and spend their money wisely.

SEND US YOUR FEEDBACK

We love to hear from travellers – your comments keep us on our toes and help make our books better. Our well-travelled team reads every word on what you loved or loathed about this book. Although we cannot reply individually to postal submissions, we always guarantee that your feedback goes straight to the appropriate authors, in time for the next edition. Each person who sends us information is thanked in the next edition – and the most useful submissions are rewarded with a free book.

To send us your updates – and find out about LP events, newsletters and travel news – visit our award-winning website: **www.lonelyplanet.com**.

Note: We may edit, reproduce and incorporate your comments in Lonely Planet products such as guidebooks, websites and digital products, so let us know if you don't want your comments reproduced or your name acknowledged. For a copy of our privacy policy visit www.lonelyplanet.com/privacy.

team included Shahara Ahmed, Susie Ashworth, Gerilyn Attebery, Jenny Blake, Anna Bolger, Verity Campbell, Erin Corrigan, Nadine Fogale, Dave McClymont, Leonie Mugavin, Rachel Peart, Lynne Preston and Howard Ralley.

This title was commissioned and developed in Lonely Planet's London office by Tim Ryder and Judith Bamber. Cartography for this guide was developed by Mark Griffiths. Editing was coordinated by Barbara Delissen, with assistance from Paul Harding, Victoria Harrison, Margedd Heliosz, John Hinman, Joanne Newell, Nina Rousseau and Katrina Webb. Coordinating cartographer Csanád Csutoros was assisted by Tony Fankhauser, Jack Gavran, Valentina Kremenchutskaya, Chris Lee-Ack, Kim McDonald, Jacqui Saunders, Andrew Smith and Natasha Velleley. The book was laid out by Margaret Jung, and Sally Darmody and Laura Jane assisted with indexing. The cover was designed by Brendan Dempsey. Project manager Glenn van der Knijff oversaw the production of the book. Thanks to Quentin Frayne and Annelies Mertens for the language chapter. *Bedankt allemaal!*

THANKS from Lonely Planet

Many thanks to the travellers who used the last edition and wrote to us with helpful hints, useful advice and interesting anecdotes:

A Marlies Aanhaanen, Nick Adlam, Amie Albrecht, Cynthia Ang, Elizabeth Arnstein **B** Renee Banky, Heidi Bardsley, Kate Barfield, Ivan Bartal, Wes Beard, Rogier Beekman, Tony Bellette, Barb Bellinger, Walt Bilofsky, Andy Blackett, Trinka Brine, George Aaron Broadwell, Carol Brown, Hanna Bruin, Craig Bryant, Jeroen Buter **C** Natasha Cabrera, Robert Caden, Maurice Carboeux, Carolyn Castiglia, Yau-Man Cheng, Penelope Collins, Paul Conway, Brenda Cooke, Erwin Coombs, Nathan Coombs, Anne M Core, Nicole Coulom, Martin Croker, Ricardo Cuan **D** Frans & Mei-lan de Lange-Wang, Shane de Malmanche, Dan de Voogd, Steve Dougherty, Sam Durkin **E** Jutta Eberlin, Bronwyn Edwards **F** Johnathan Farley, Amanda Feeney, Tyler Flood, Fayette Fox, Agnes Frank, Peter Franzese **G** Angel Gambrel, Eveline Gebhardt, John & Betty Geddes, Periklis Georgiadis, Bart Giepmans, John Goss, John Graven, Beth Gray, Joe Green, Dan Greenberg **H** Marilena Hadjilogiou, Mariska Hansen, Donald Hatch, Edward Haughney, Linda Hendry, Lisa Herb, Henk Hiddinga, Helen Hols, Peter Hopcroft, Amy & Birger Horst **J** R Jackson, Marco Jacobs, Milla Jansen, Tushar Jiwarajka, Eric Johnson, Steven Johnson, Miles Johnston, Oliver Johnston, Martin Jonsson **K** Sandra Kastermans, Kim King, Dorothy Koenig, Mark Kohler, Minette Korterink, Kurt Kron, Nicole Kroon **L** Klaas & Lysette Lebbing, Ankie Lenders, Michael Lin, Barbara Lopes-Cardozo, Stephanie Ludmer, Nick Lux **M** Marsha Maarschalkerweerd, Antti Maattanen, Diana Maestre, Paul McKnight, Lucas Meijknecht, Kees Meijll, Constance Messer, Bartlett Miller, Ming Ming Teh, Heather Monell, Rebekah Moore, Jim Moss, Marcus Muhlethaler **N** Samantha Nelson, Henrik Skov Nielsen, William Noble **O** Ricardo Olaeta, Min Tzy Ong, Aaron Osterby **P** Jill Pearson, Valentina M Pennazio, Peter J Perkins, Brian Perrett, Gemma Phillips, John Pilgrim, Tony & Jill Porco, Adrian Pritchard, Jan Propper **R** Francesco Randisi, Neil Rawlings, Jonathan Rebholz, Kurt Rebry, Maurits Renes, Mary Richards, Paul Roos, Jeffrey Ian Ross, Theo Ruigrok **S** Niels Sadler, Monique Samsen, Christopher Schrader, Brett Shackelford, Mary Sheargold, Kim Shrosbree, Susan Shweisky, Don Simpson, Anneke Sips, Hazel Smith, K Smith-Jones, Don & Phyllis Snyder, Jaime Stein, Annie Stolk, Christina Strauch, Chris Sturdy, Brigitte Sucre, Victoria Svahn **T** Terence Tam, Anouchka-Virginie Thouvenot, Janneke T Tinga, Robert Tissing, Jens Tobiska **V** Erwin van Dam, Marlies van den Nieuwendijk, Arthur van der Mast, Chris van der Starre, Erwin van Engelen, Sofie van Hapert, Han van Kasteren, Jacqueline van Klaveren, Irene van Seggelen, Nathalie van Spaendonck, Frank van Wagtendonk, Ron Vermeulen, Thomas von Hahn, R Vos, Fons Vrouenraths **W** Vera Wellner, Astrid Wevers, Rob Wheaton, Vincent Wiers, Jan Williamson, Steve & Judith Willis, Fiona Wilson, Andrew Woolf **Y** Maryam Yahyavi

Index

000 Map pages
000 Location of colour photographs

INDEX

000 Map pages
000 Location of colour photographs

348

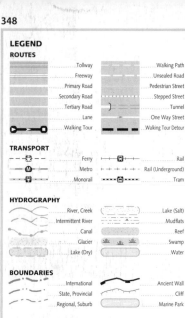

LEGEND

ROUTES

	Tollway		Walking Path
	Freeway		Unsealed Road
	Primary Road		Pedestrian Street
	Secondary Road		Stepped Street
	Tertiary Road		Tunnel
	Lane		One Way Street
	Walking Tour		Walking Tour Detour

TRANSPORT

	Ferry		Rail
	Metro		Rail (Underground)
	Monorail		Tram

HYDROGRAPHY

	River, Creek		Lake (Salt)
	Intermittent River		Mudflats
	Canal		Reef
	Glacier		Swamp
	Lake (Dry)		Water

BOUNDARIES

	International		Ancient Wall
	State, Provincial		Cliff
	Regional, Suburb		Marine Park

POPULATION

◎	CAPITAL (NATIONAL)	⊚	CAPITAL (STATE)
●	**Large City**	○	**Medium City**
●	Small City	○	Town, Village

AREA FEATURES

	Area of Interest		Land
	Beach, Desert		Mall
	Building		Market
+ + +	Cemetery, Christian		Park
× × ×	Cemetery, Other		Sports
	Forest		Urban

SYMBOLS

SIGHTS/ACTIVITIES	INFORMATION	SHOPPING
Beach	Bank, ATM	Shopping
Buddhist	Embassy/Consulate	**TRANSPORT**
Castle, Fortress	Hospital, Medical	Airport, Airfield
Christian	Information	Border Crossing
Confucian	Internet Facilities	Bus Station
Diving, Snorkeling	Parking Area	Cycling, Bicycle Path
Hindu	Petrol Station	General Transport
Islamic	Police Station	Taxi Rank
Jain	Post Office, GPO	Trail Head
Jewish	Telephone	**GEOGRAPHIC**
Monument	Toilets	Hazard
Museum, Gallery	**SLEEPING**	Lighthouse
Picnic Area	Sleeping	Lookout
Point of Interest	Camping	Mountain, Volcano
Ruin	**EATING**	National Park
Shinto	Eating	Oasis
Sikh	**DRINKING**	Pass, Canyon
Skiing	Drinking	River Flow
Taoist	Café	Shelter, Hut
Winery, Vineyard	**ENTERTAINMENT**	Spot Height
Zoo, Bird Sanctuary	Entertainment	Waterfall

NOTE: Not all symbols displayed above appear in this guide.

LONELY PLANET OFFICES

Australia
Head Office
Locked Bag 1, Footscray, Victoria 3011
☎ 03 8379 8000, fax 03 8379 8111
talk2us@lonelyplanet.com.au

USA
150 Linden St, Oakland, CA 94607
☎ 510 893 8555, toll free 800 275 8555
fax 510 893 8572, info@lonelyplanet.com

UK
72–82 Rosebery Ave,
Clerkenwell, London EC1R 4RW
☎ 020 7841 9000, fax 020 7841 9001
go@lonelyplanet.co.uk

France
1 rue du Dahomey, 75011 Paris
☎ 01 55 25 33 00, fax 01 55 25 33 01
bip@lonelyplanet.fr, www.lonelyplanet.fr

Published by Lonely Planet Publications Pty Ltd
ABN 36 005 607 983

© Lonely Planet 2004

© photographers as indicated 2004

Cover photographs: Yellow tulips, Van der Leeden/Zefa Images (front); Souvenir clogs, Amerens Hedwich/Lonely Planet Images (back). Many of the images in this guide are available for licensing from Lonely Planet Images: www.lonelyplanetimages.com.